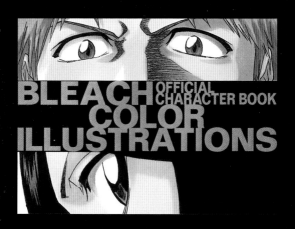

BLEACH COLOR ILLUSTRATIONS

OFFICIAL CHARACTER BOOK

In color!
Beautiful illustrations
omitted from
the graphic novel!

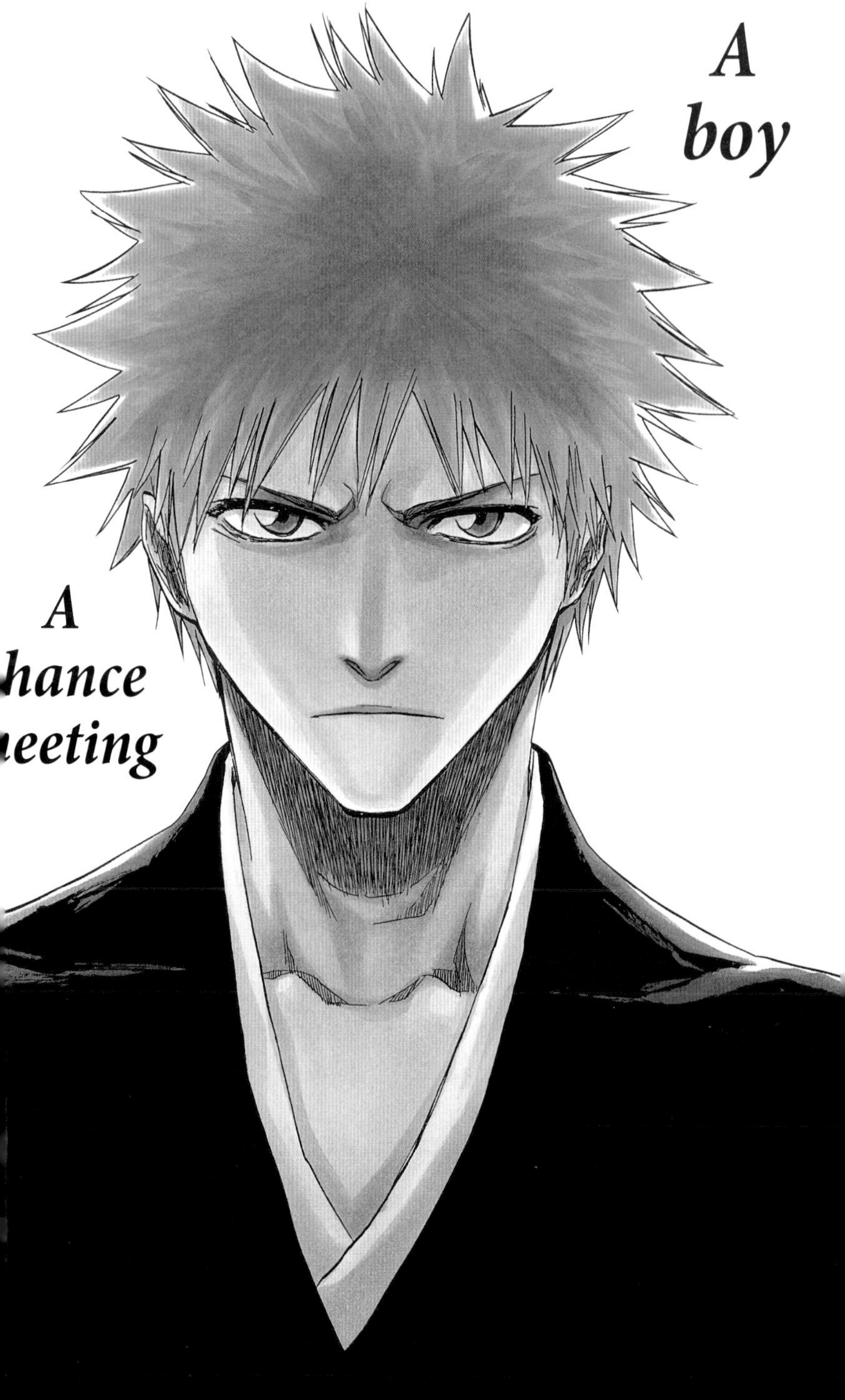
A
boy
A
hance
eeting

Cover of 2004 *Weekly Jump* Volume 52

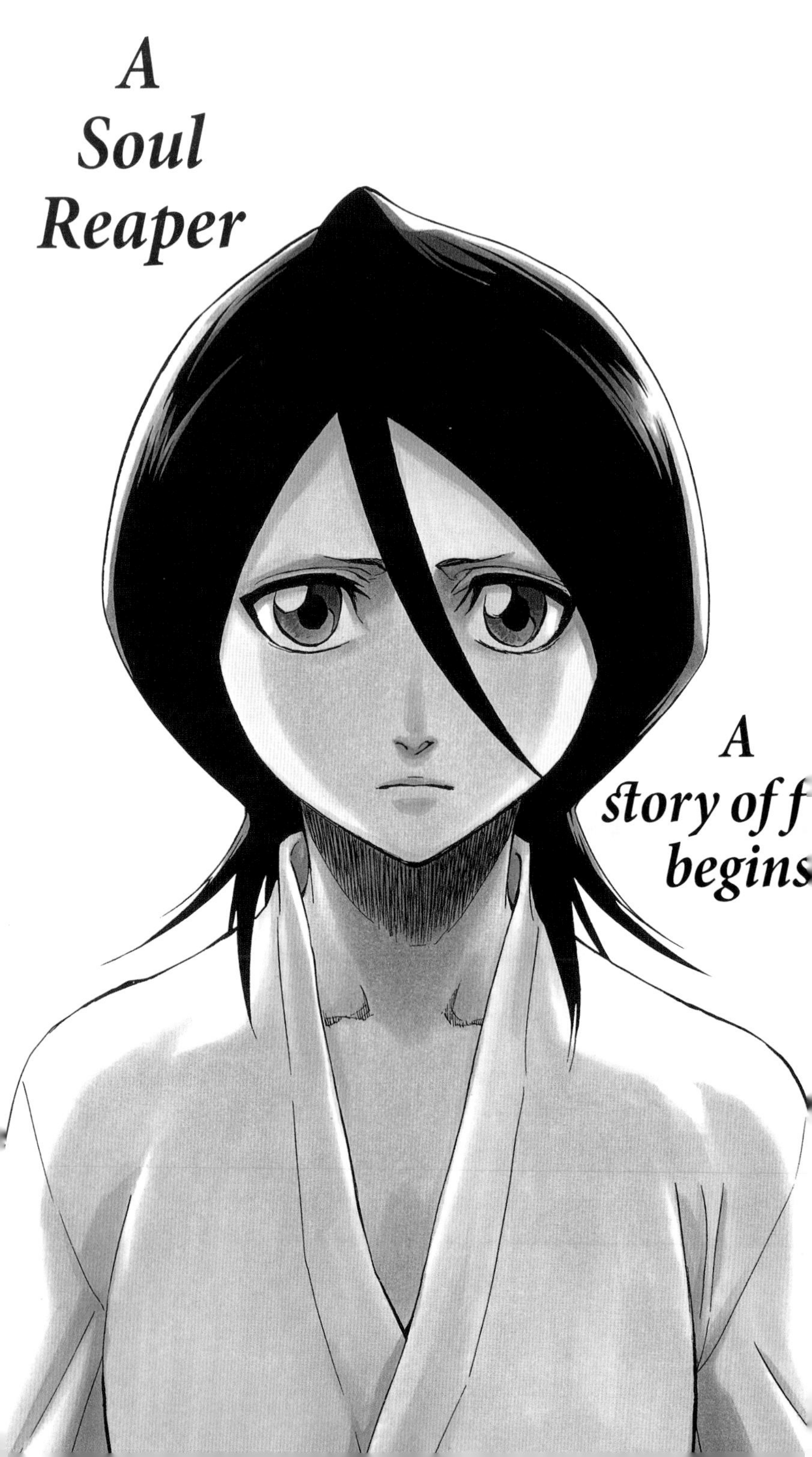
A Soul Reaper
A story of f
begins

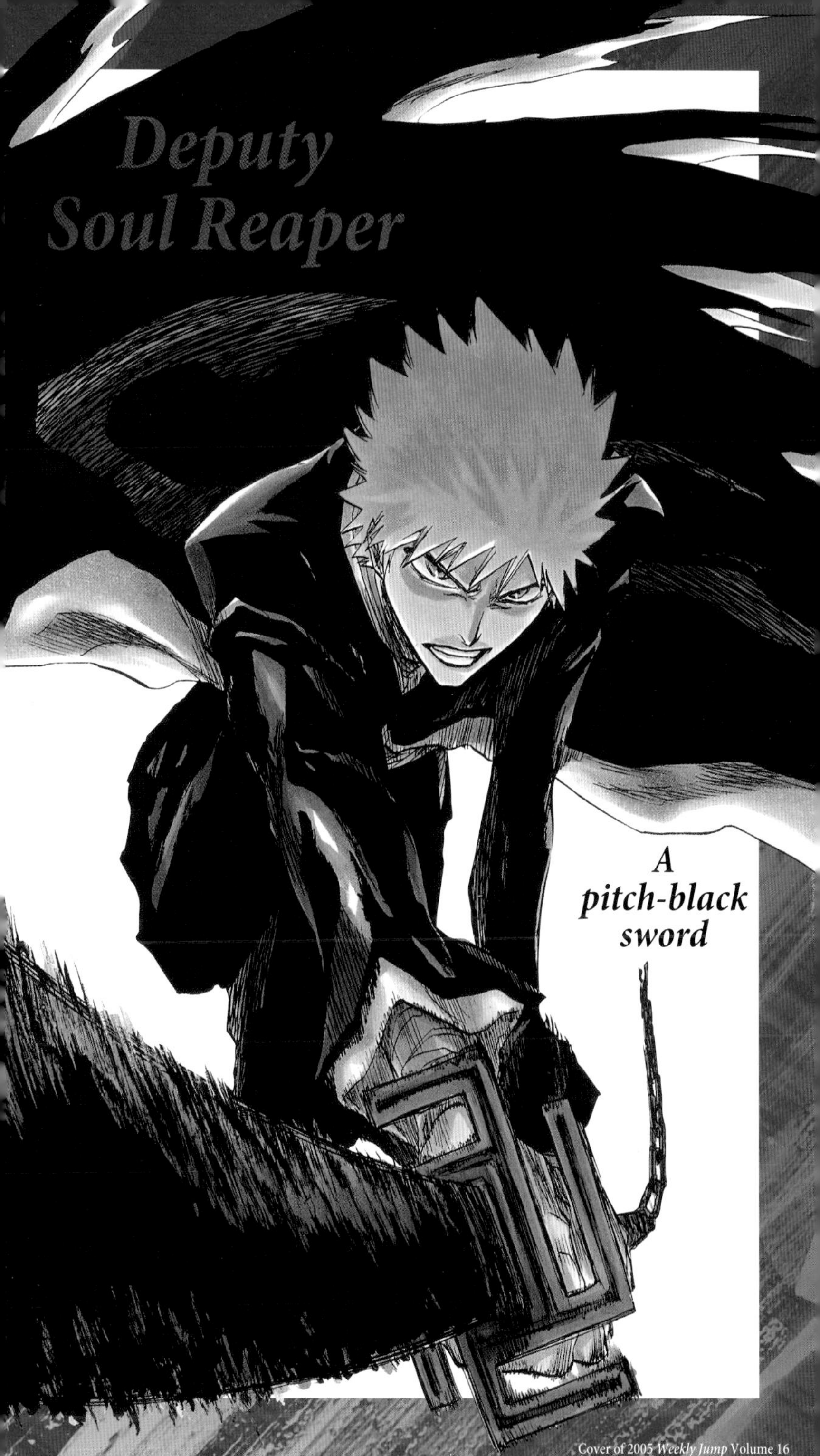
Deputy
Soul Reaper
A
pitch-black
sword

Cover of 2005 *Weekly Jump* Volume 16

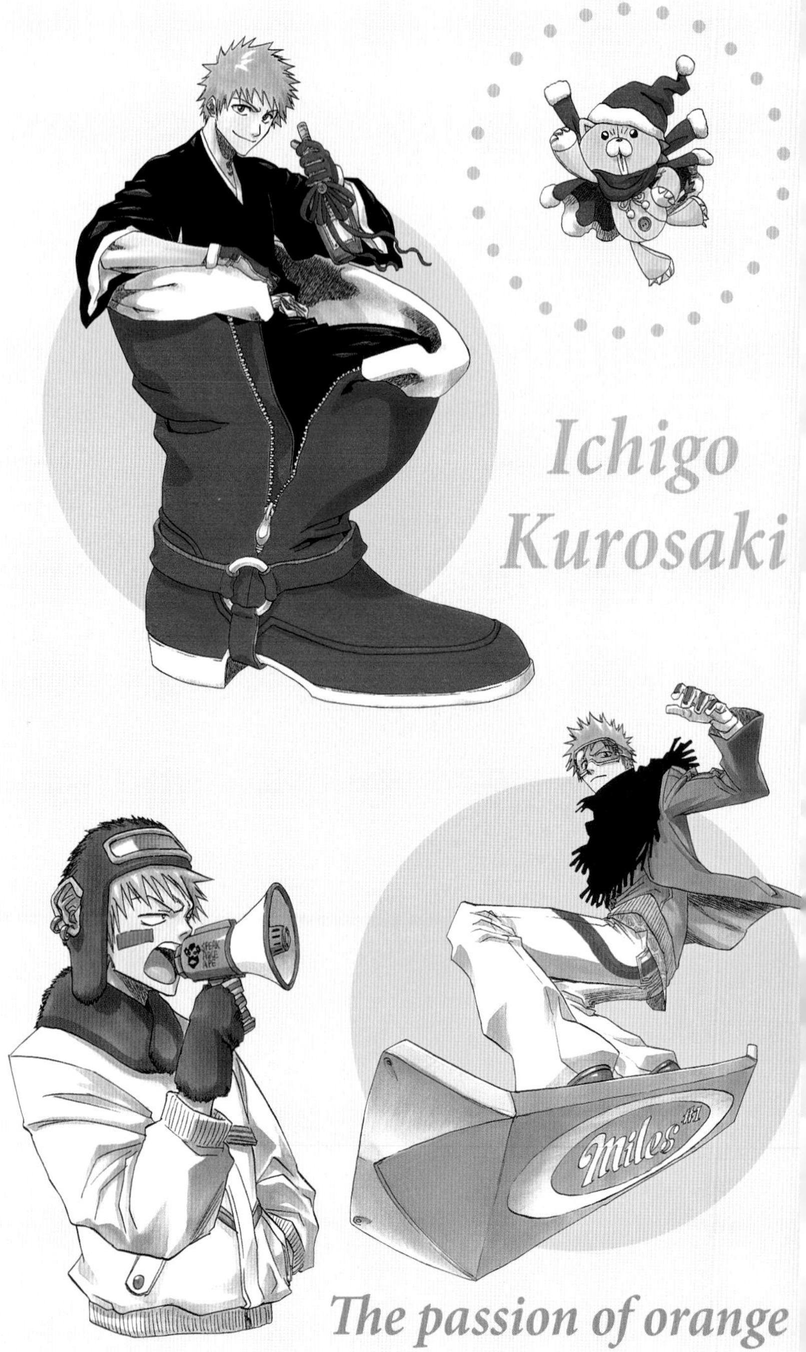
Ichigo Kurosaki
The passion of orange

Top: Cover of 2004 *Weekly Jump* Combined Volumes 3 & 4
Bottom Right: Cover of 2004 *Weekly Jump* Combined Volumes 4 & 5
Bottom Left: Cover of 2004 *Weekly Jump* Combined Volumes 6 & 7

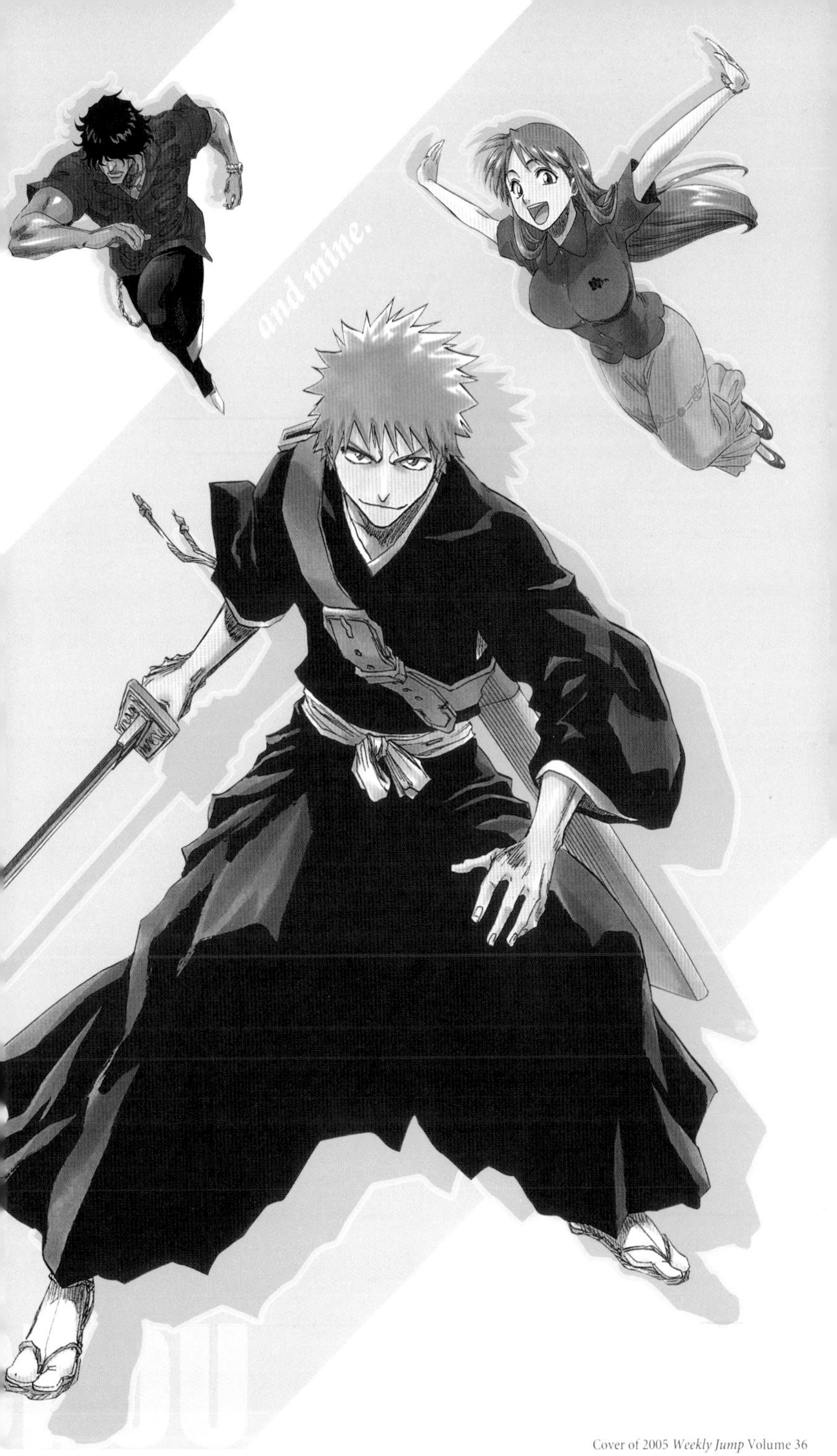
and mine.
Cover of 2005 *Weekly Jump* Volume 36

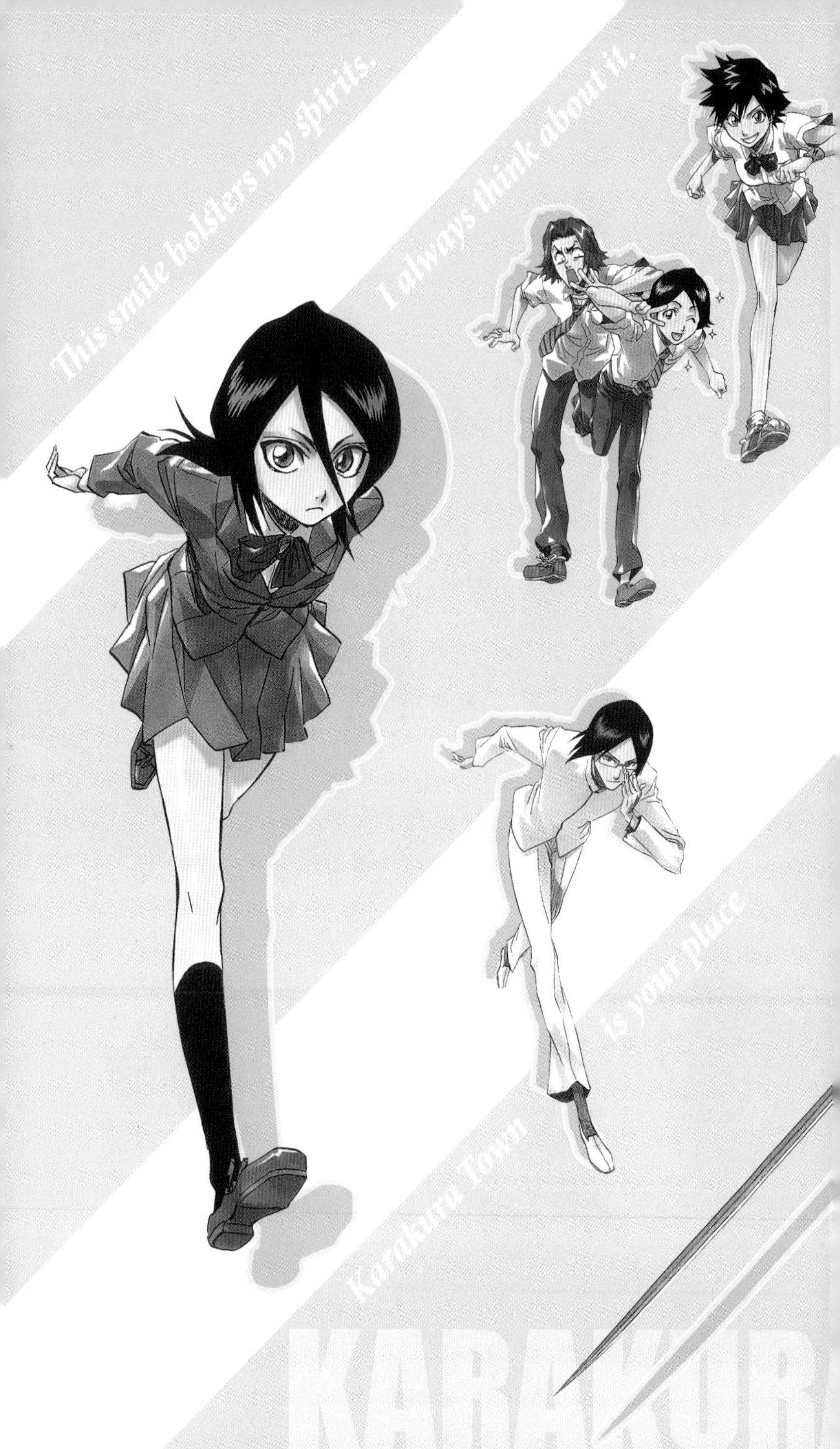
This smile bolsters my spirits.
I always think about it.
Karakura Town
is your place
KARAKURA

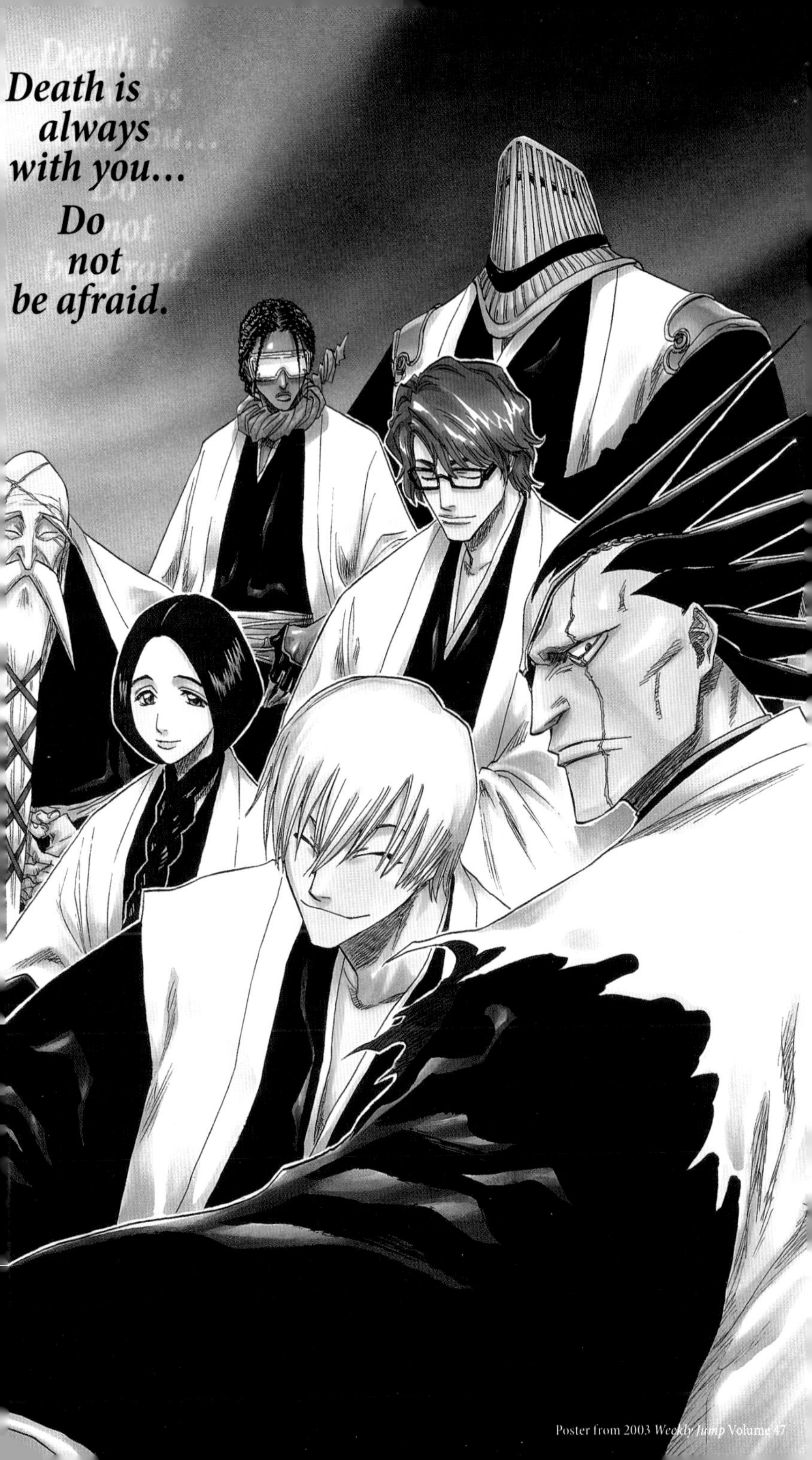
Death is always with you... Do not be afraid.
Poster from 2003 *Weekly Jump* Volume 47

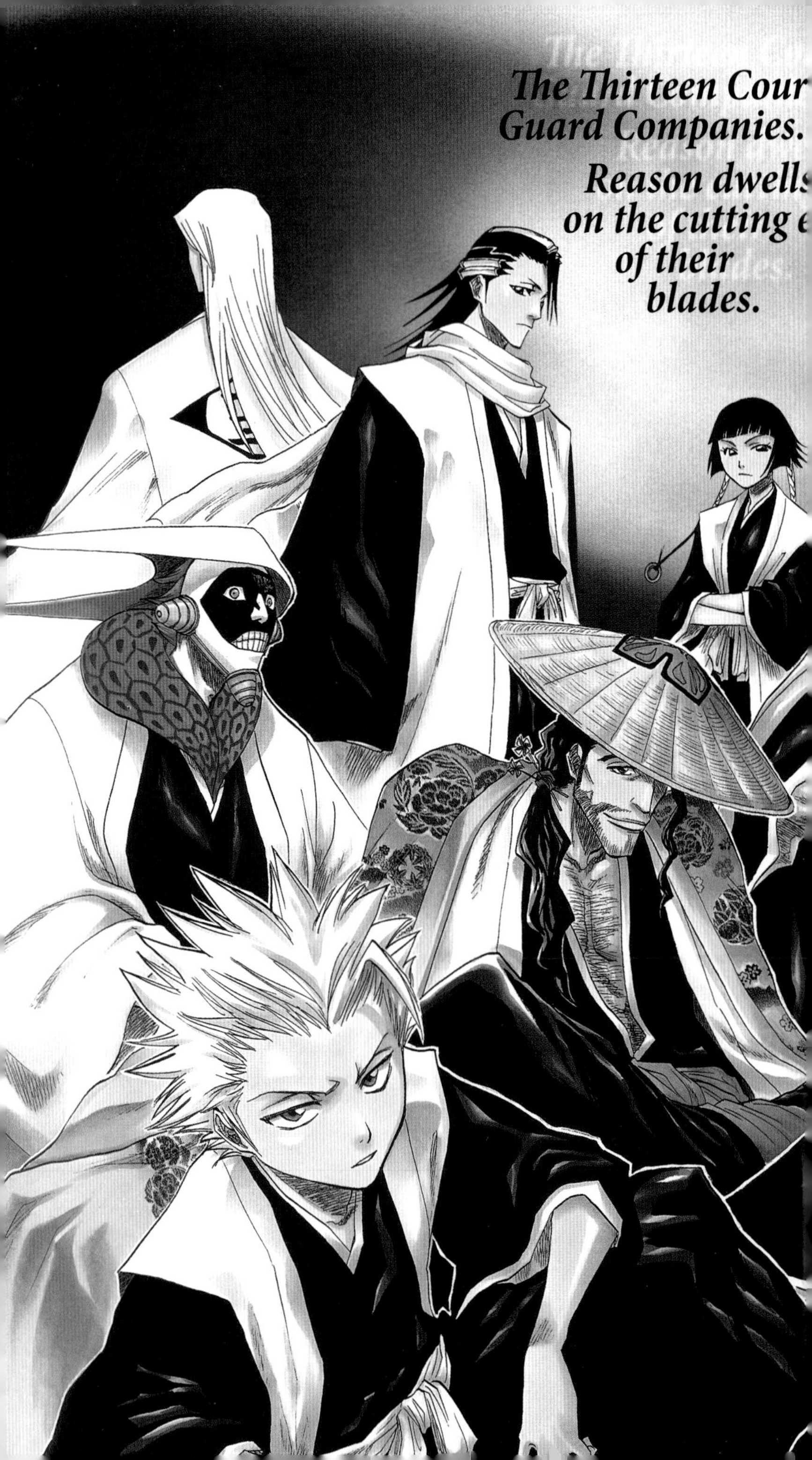
The Thirteen Cour
Guard Companies.
Reason dwell
on the cutting
of their
blades.

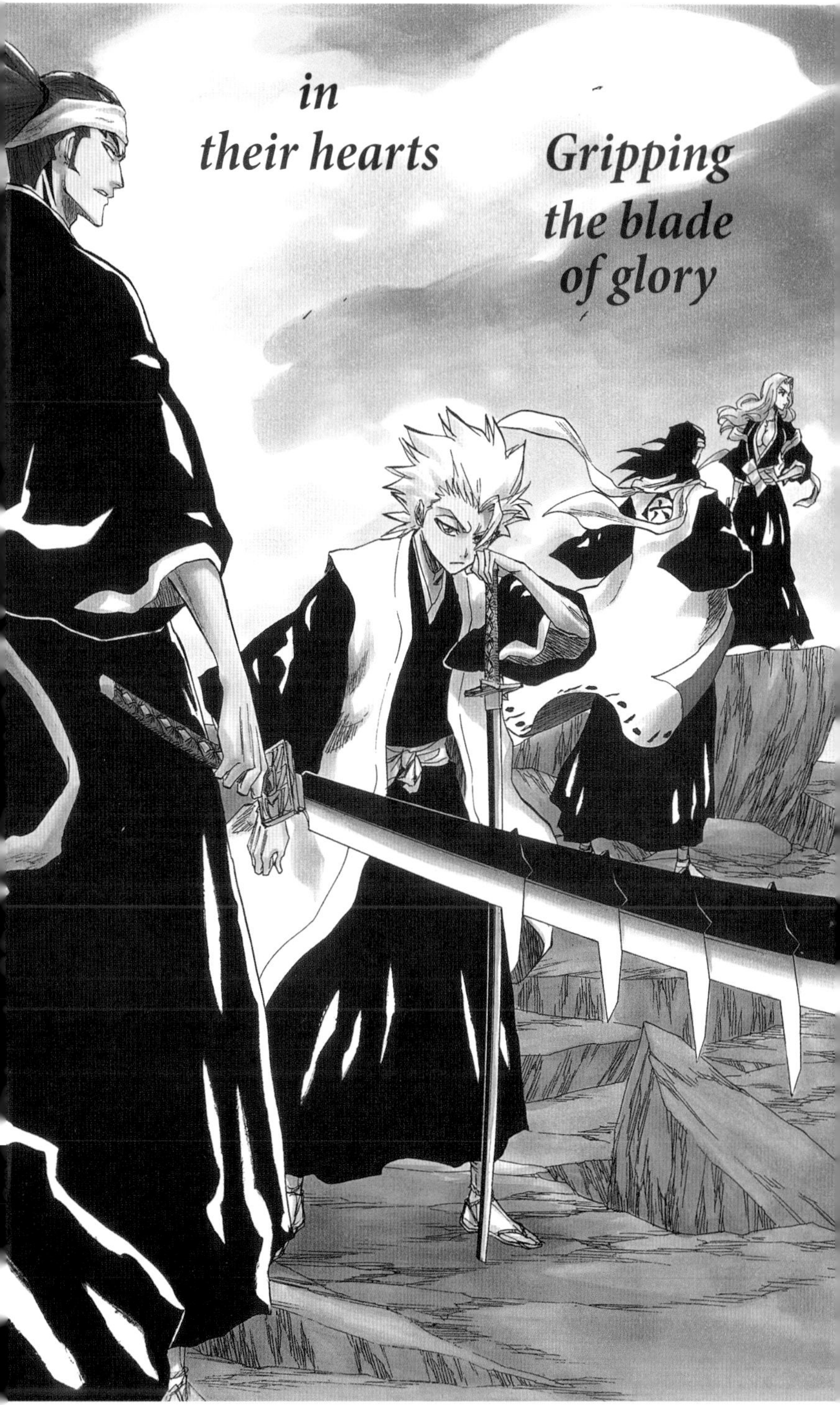
Gripping
the blade
of glory
in
their hearts

Special poster from Special Edition *Jump* Heroes

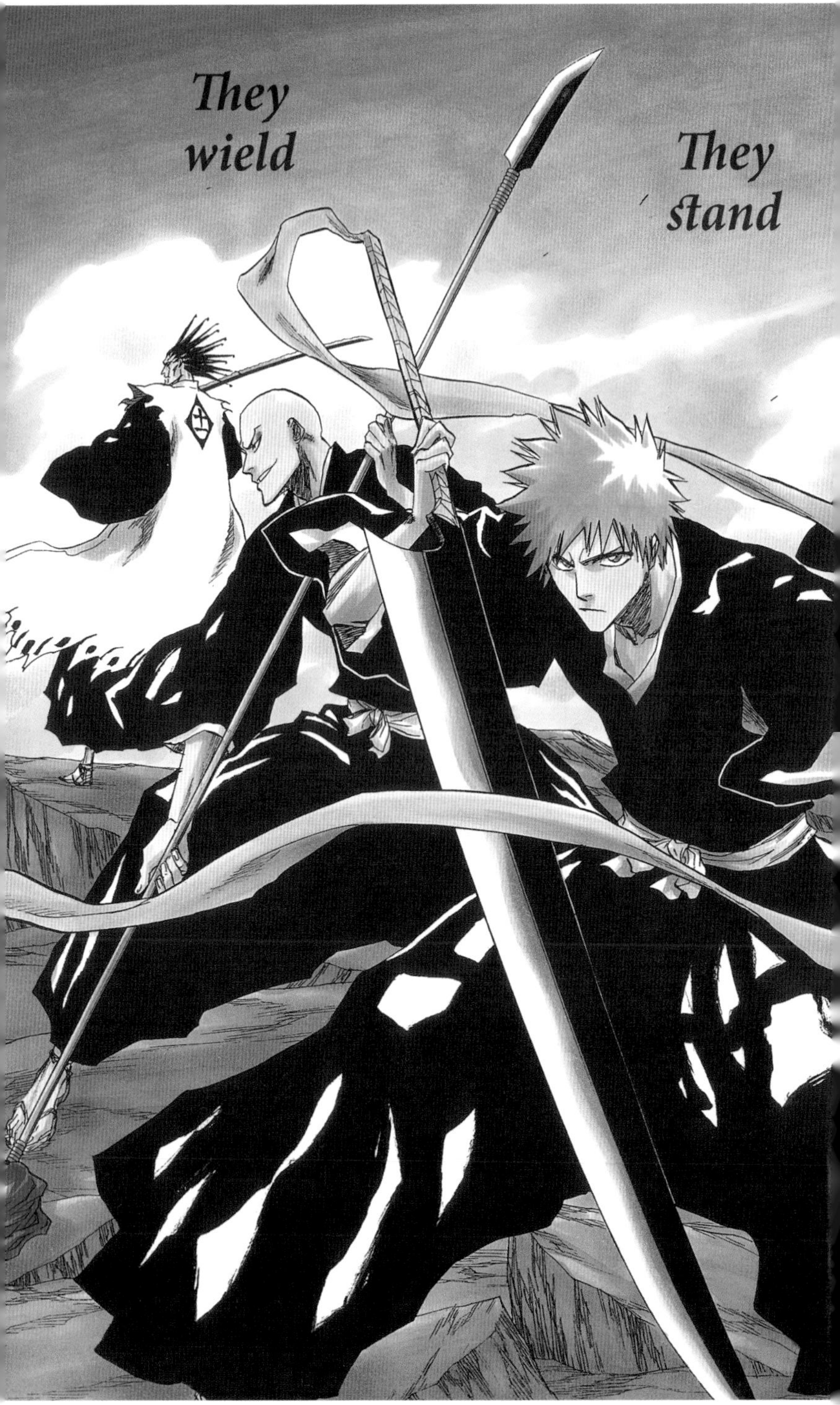
They stand
They wield

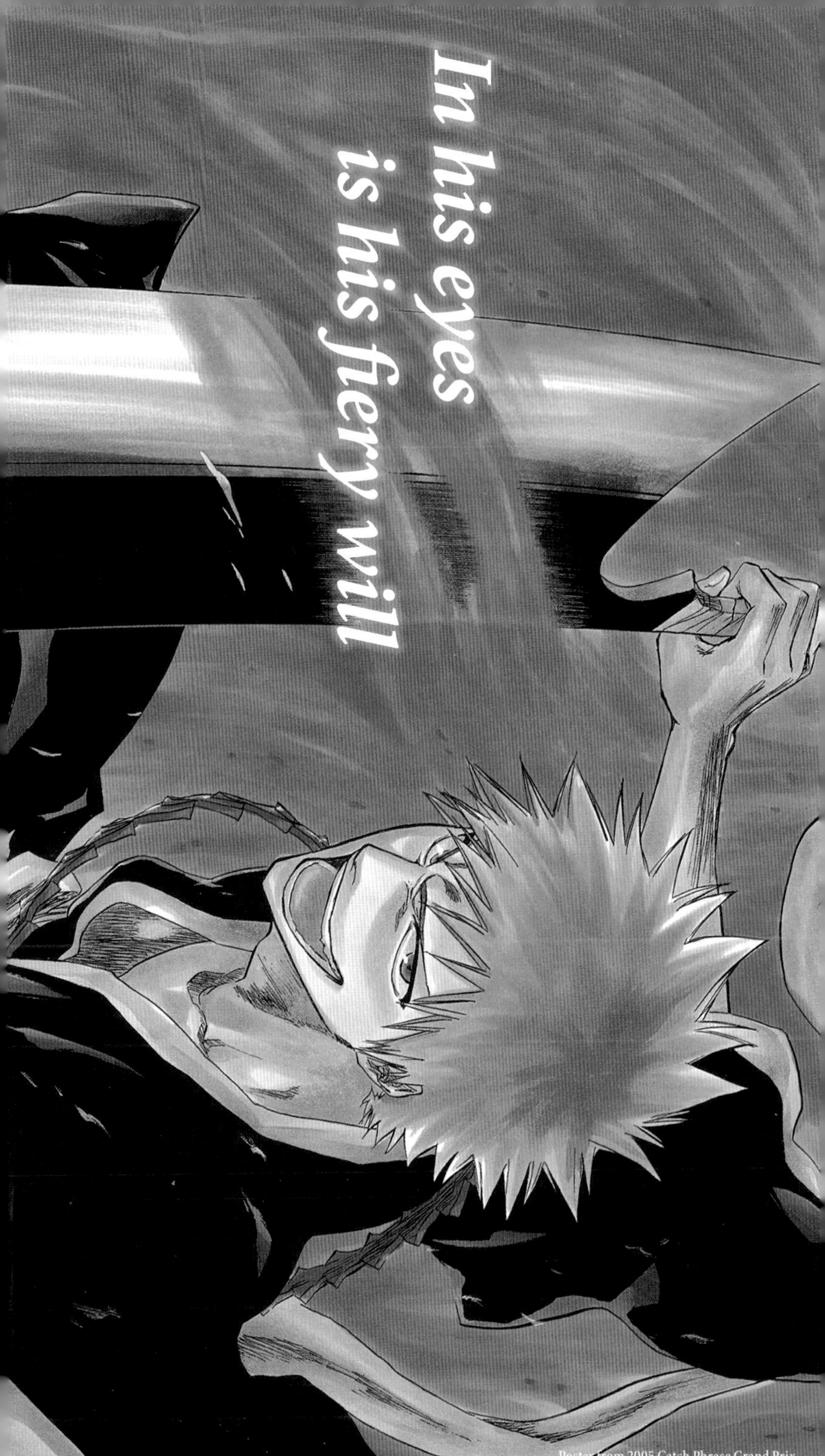
In his eyes
is his fiery will

Poster from 2005 Catch Phrase Grand Prix

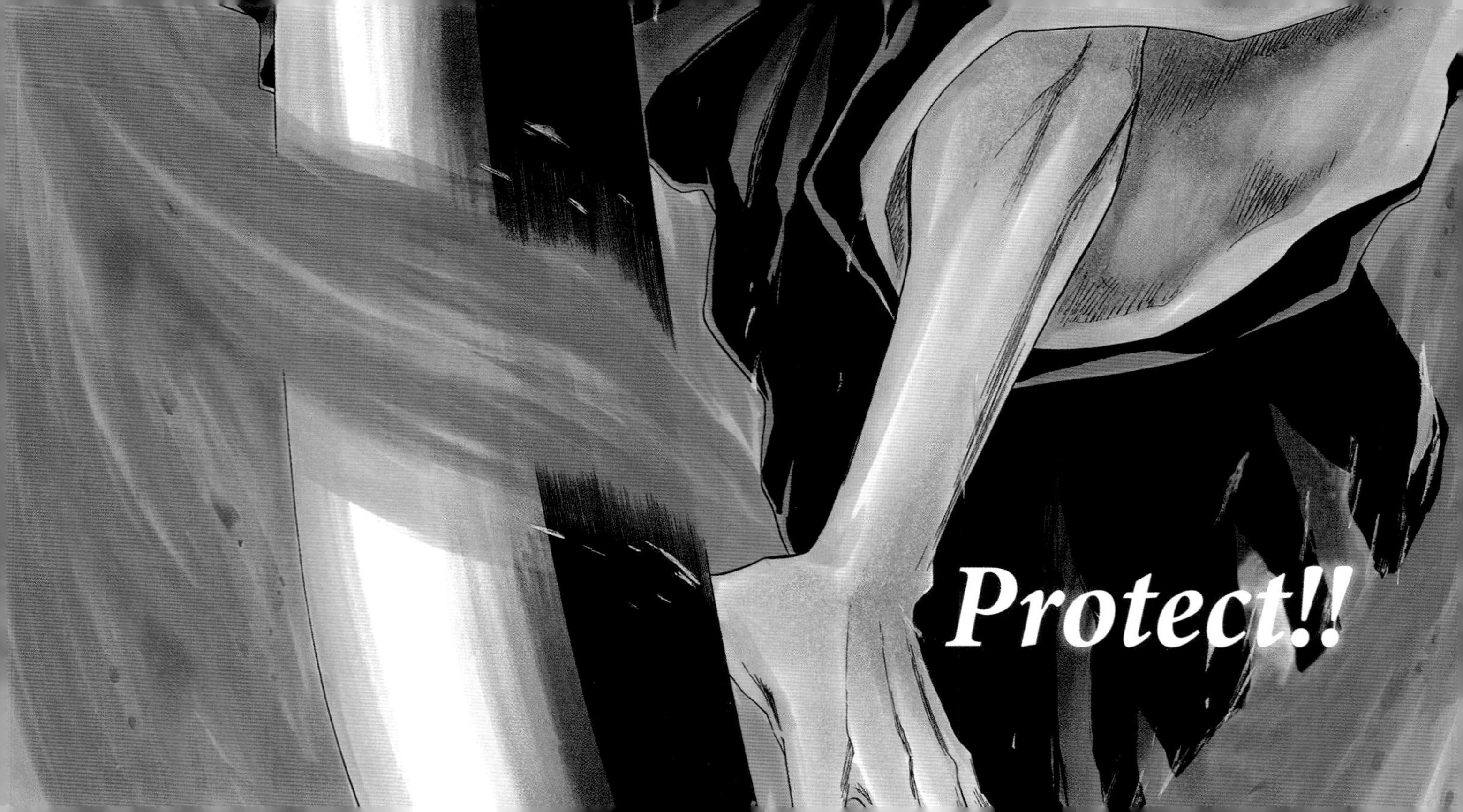
Protect!!

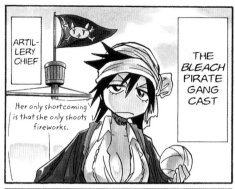

Special 4-panel Manga

Formed! The Bleach Pirate Gang?!

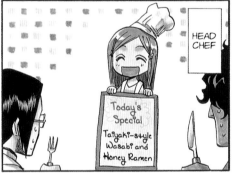

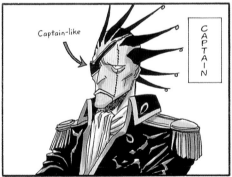

THE BLEACH PIRATE GANG CAST
ARTIL-LERY CHIEF
Her only shortcoming is that she only shoots fireworks.
HEAD CHEF
Today's Special
Taiyaki-style Wasabi and Honey Ramen
CAPTAIN
Captain-like
SAY.
DO I HAVE TO WEAR THIS PIRATE HAT?
WHO THE HELL ARE YOU?!
QUARTER-MASTER (NO SUITABLE CHARAC-TERS)

THE REST OF THE CAST ARE URURU (LOOKOUT), KEIGO (LUGGAGE CARRIER), KISUKE (SAFE KEEPER), RUKIA (TREASURE), KON (TREASURE BOX), KANONJI (ART PIECE ON THE BOW OF THE SHIP), ETC.

A special project from 2003 *Weekly Jump* Combined Volumes 22 & 23

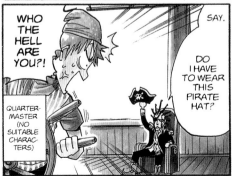

Kubo's personally signed art boards Revealed!!

Introducing rare art boards! All are illustrated and signed, and were drawn for the Jump Festa Anime Tour or given as gifts to readers! The drawings, including the one of Tatsuki wearing a Soul Reaper uniform, can only be seen here!

bleach

BLEACH
weeklyjump.
35th anniversary

bleach
kubotite

買えコラー!!!
こづかいとかバイト代とか
なんかもうそんなん使い果たして
徒歩で帰る勢いで買え!!!
オレと姐サンと井上サンのグッズだ!!

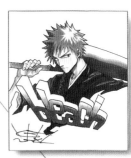

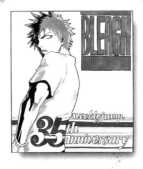

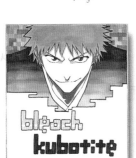

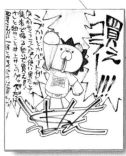

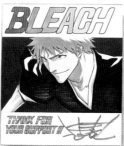

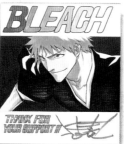

HEY, BUY THIS!
Walk straight home after you buy it, because up your allowance and your pay check! Buy S goods, or Inoue's, or mine! Don't buy any of I

BLEACH
THANK FOR YOUR SUPPORT!!

BLEACH
HEAT
The Soul
15

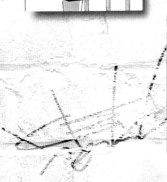

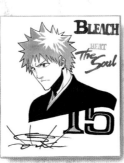

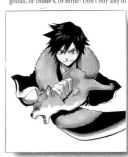

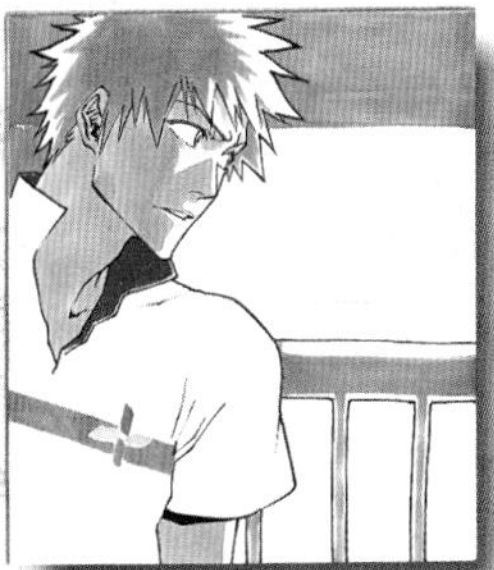

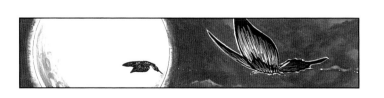

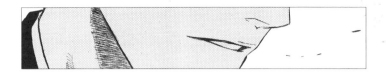

The sun that locks the Heavens

BLEACH
OFFICIAL CHARACTER BOOK SOULs.

SHONEN JUMP PROFILES

TITE KUBO

SOULS.

ENTS

BLEACH
OFFICIAL CHARACTER BOOK

EXTRA TRACK

BONUS TRACK

SPECIAL INSERT Extra Chapter

CONT

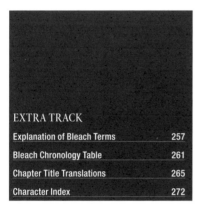

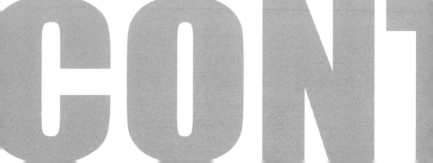

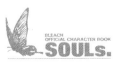

BLEACH
OFFICIAL CHARACTER BOOK
SOULs.

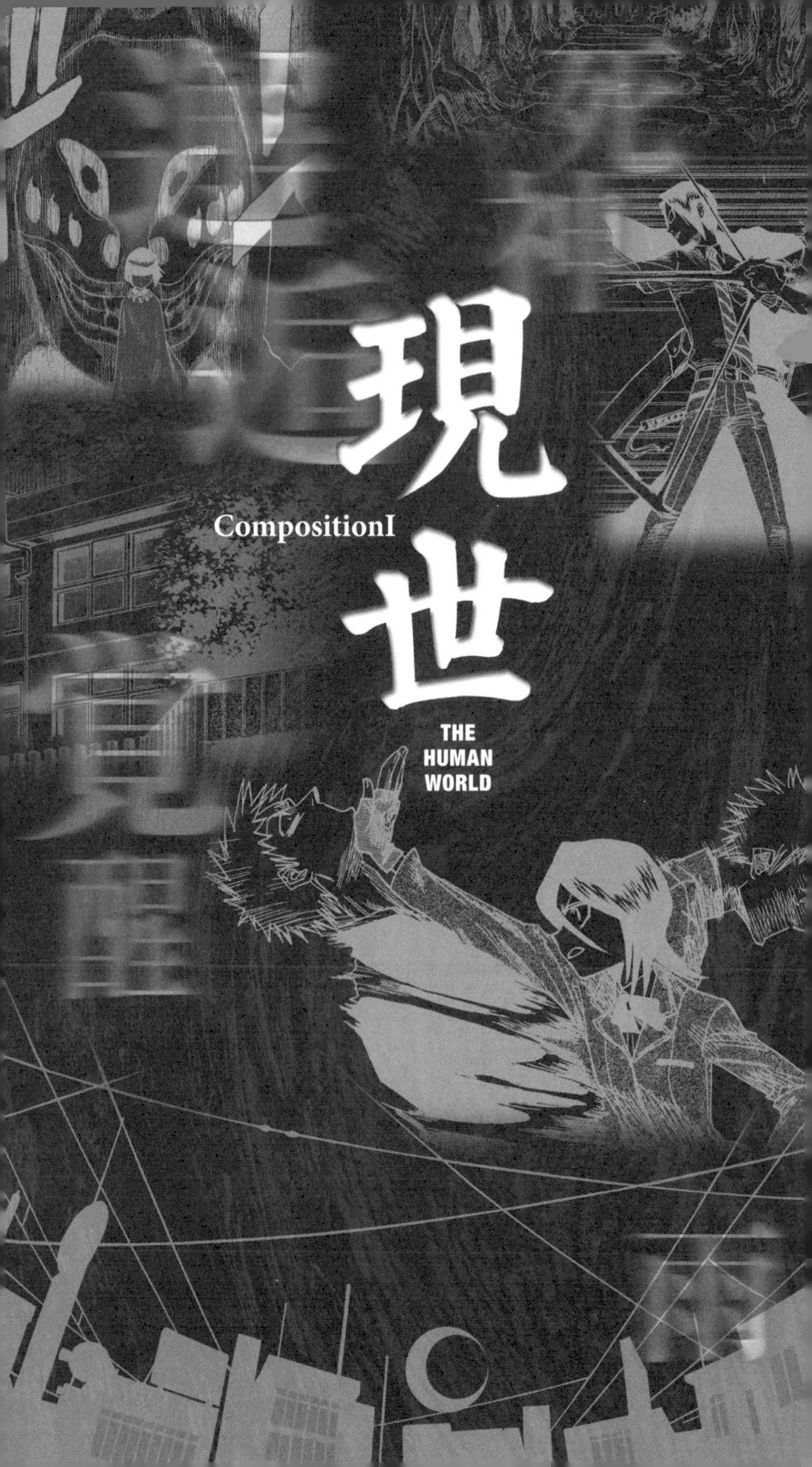

現世
CompositionI
THE
HUMAN
WORLD

EXPLANATION OF THE HUMAN WORLD

INTRODUCTION

Some people believe in evil spirits, and some don't. But people's individual beliefs have little to do with reality. Behind buildings on dimly lit nights and within lonely, abandoned structures hidden from the moonlight…strange beings lurk in the shadows. People with strong spirit energy can see them, but most people live peacefully without ever noticing them. Focus your eyes on the darkness. You should be able to see them—the strange beings that live in the darkness…

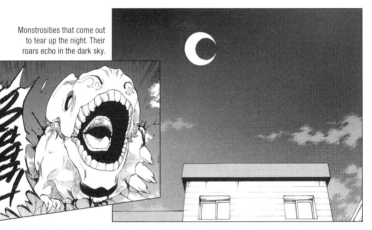

Monstrosities that come out to tear up the night. Their roars echo in the dark sky.

THE SPIRITUAL GUARDIANS OF THE HUMAN WORLD

SOUL REAPERS

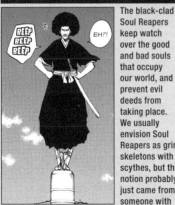

BEEP BEEP BEEP

EH?!

The black-clad Soul Reapers keep watch over the good and bad souls that occupy our world, and prevent evil deeds from taking place. We usually envision Soul Reapers as grim skeletons with scythes, but this notion probably just came from someone with a good imagination. This is what Soul Reapers really are.

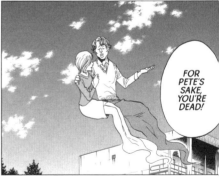

FOR PETE'S SAKE, YOU'RE DEAD!

CONGREGATED SOULS

Those who continue to have an attachment to the human world even after they have died, commonly known as ghosts, exist all around the world. Those with strong spirit energy see the souls as regular people (but might be happier not being able to see them…).

Visitors from another world who wear black uniforms called shihakushô and carry swords known as zanpaku-tô. Their missions vary greatly. Aside from performing konsô to lead the souls of the dead to the Soul Society (the afterworld), they sublimate and destroy evil spirits, or Hollows, to protect people. They shoulder all the soul-related jobs.

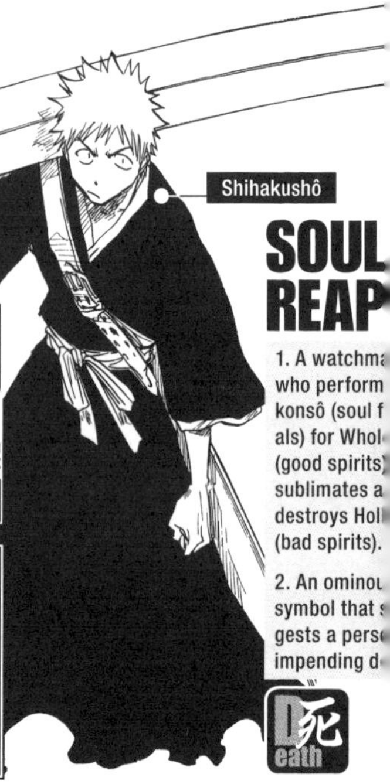
Zanpaku-tô
Shihakushô

THE BALANCER OF SOULS

Soul Reapers also balance the total number of souls by moving and managing the souls of the human world.

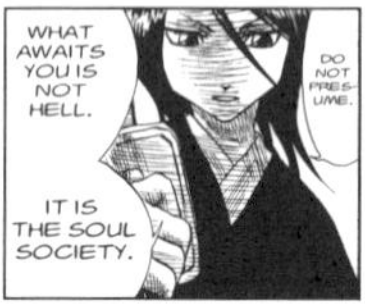
DO NOT PRESUME.
WHAT AWAITS YOU IS NOT HELL.
IT IS THE SOUL SOCIETY.

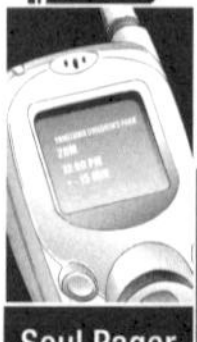

Soul Pager

SOUL REAP

1. A watchma who perform konsô (soul f als) for Whol (good spirits) sublimates a destroys Holl (bad spirits).

2. An ominou symbol that s gests a pers impending d

D 死 eath

WHOLE

1. The soul of a person who has died. 2. The generic term for ghosts.

Soul Reapers also balance the total number of souls by moving and managing the souls of the human world.

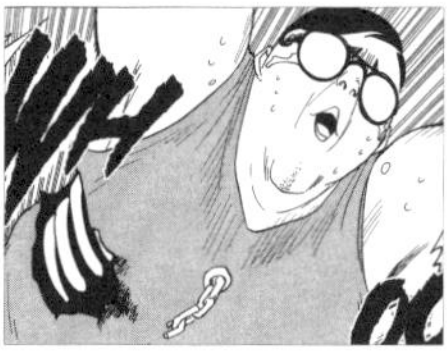

Evil souls that vary widely in looks and abilities. Hollows are feared as evil spirits or monsters. Their faces are hidden by strangely shaped masks. They are very savage and dangerous. Never approach if you see one.

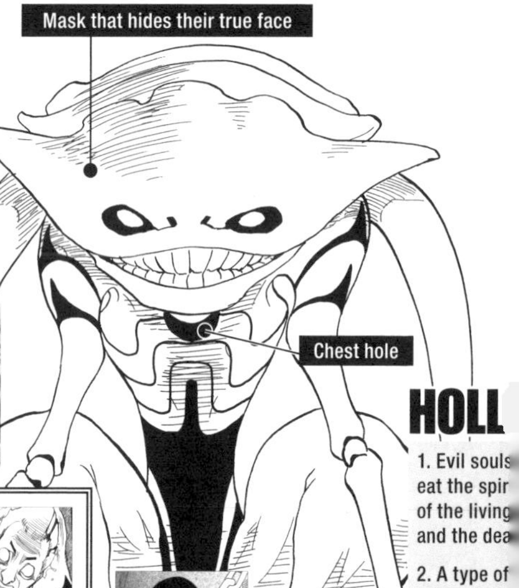
Mask that hides their true face
Chest hole

THOSE WHO EAT SOULS

The hole on their chest is the heart they have lost. Hollows eat other souls in order to bury that loss.

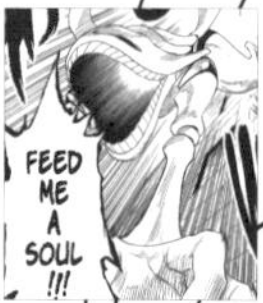
FEED ME A SOUL !!!

HOLL

1. Evil souls eat the spir of the living and the dea

2. A type of evil spirit.

H 虚 ollow

HOLLOW TRANSFORMATION

1. When a Whole turns into a Hollow. 2. The process of that transformation.

Souls that were once Wholes can also turn into Hollows after a long time has passed. Everything is impermanent.

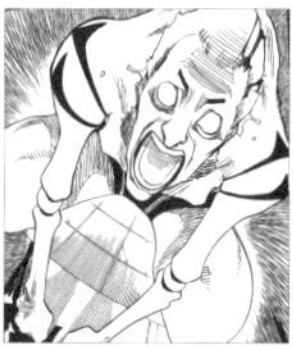

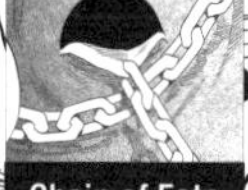

Chain of Fate

Let's explain in detail the town that is the setting of this story

KARAKURA TOWN MAP

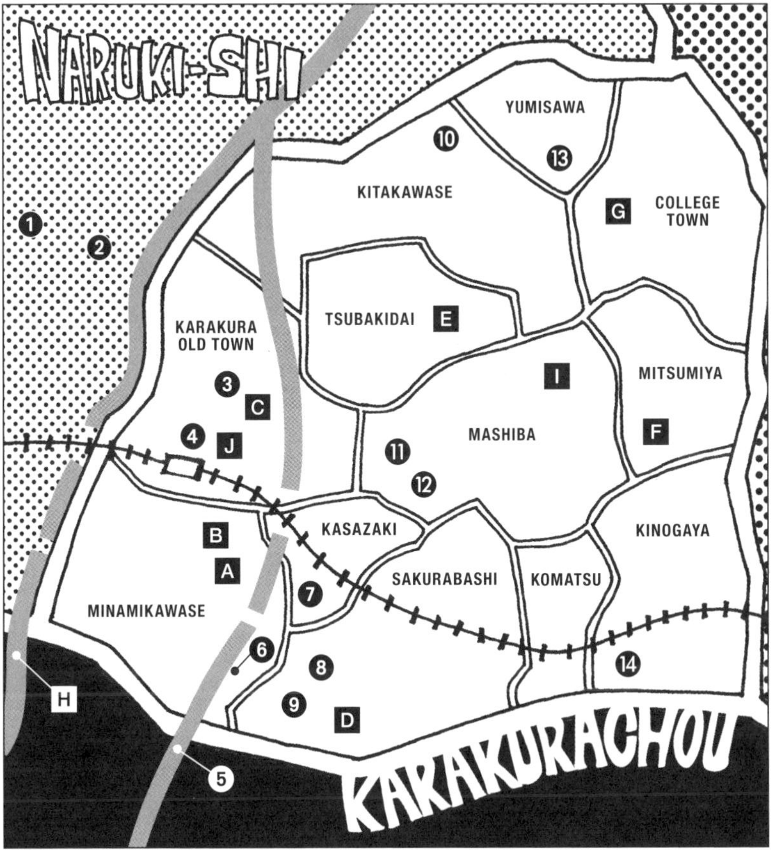
NARUKI-SHI
YUMISAWA
KITAKAWASE
COLLEGE TOWN
TSUBAKIDAI
KARAKURA OLD TOWN
MITSUMIYA
MASHIBA
KASAZAKI
KINOGAYA
SAKURABASHI
KOMATSU
MINAMIKAWASE
KARAKURACHOU

❶ Kojima Family (3 Chome 1-11)	❽ (New) Orihime's House (3 Chome 12-3-403)
❷ Asano Family (4 Chome 3-9-707)	❾ Tsubakidai Park
❸ Karakura Shopping District	❿ Uryû's House (7 Chome 16-1-103)
❹ Karakura Old Town Station	⓫ Karakura Community Park
❺ Karasu River	⓬ Mashiba Middle School
❻ Chad's House (4 Chome 11-8-201)	⓭ Yumisawa Children's Park
❼ Hirohyaku Supermarket	⓮ Remains of the Sukari Building

A AN EVER-CHEERFUL AND FUN FAMILY! THE KUROSAKI FAMILY

DO OR DIE
OUTTA THE WAY!!

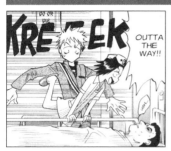

The Kurosaki family consists of Ichigo, his father Isshin (a practicing physician) and Ichigo's younger twin sisters, Karin and Yuzu. Their household, which is connected to the Kurosaki Clinic, goes into an uproar whenever there's an emergency patient! They're a close-knit family that never stops smiling.

MASAKI FOREVER

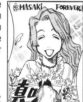

MASAKI'S PHOTOGRAPH
Ichigo lost his mother, Masaki, when he was young. A giant photograph of her watches over the family.

C FURIN HALL

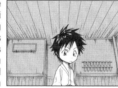

The town's karate dojo, where Tatsuki has been going to since she was little. The Women's Karate Inter-High Tournament Second Place Champion trained here. Ichigo and Tatsuki met at this dojo.

E MATSUKURA HOSPITAL

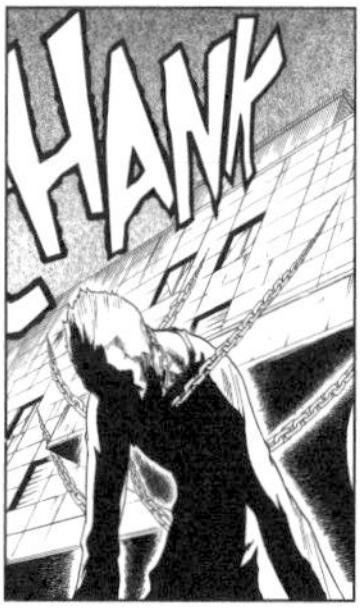

The abandoned hospital that the charismatic spirit medium, Don Kanonji, used as a filming location for his hit occult show, *Spontaneous Trips to Spiritual Hot Spots*. It's a Karakura Town tourist spot.

KARAKURA TOWN

Karakura is a suburb near the center of Tokyo, far away from the noise of the city. It's a pretty average town. Its residents live peacefully and lead quiet lives. The town's center lies between the Onose River, which flows to the west of town, and its tributary the Karasu River. Karakura Old Town Station is in the center of town.

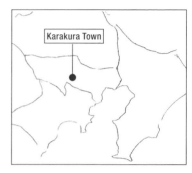

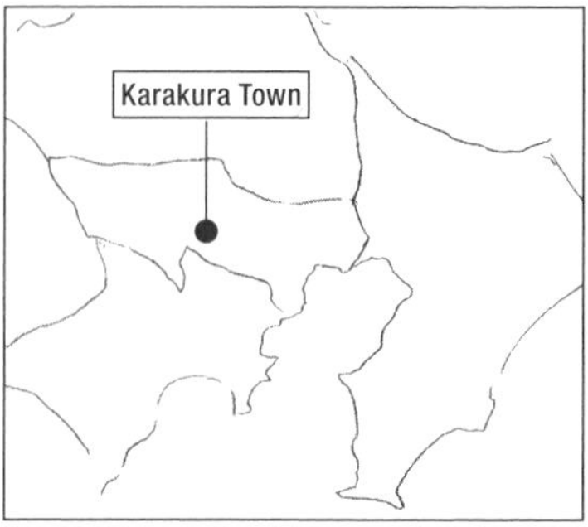

Karakura Town

B THE ARISAWA FAMILY

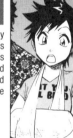

Just a few minutes away from the Kurosaki Family is the home of Tatsuki, Ichigo's childhood friend. Ichigo and Tatsuki have often worked together because they live close to each other.

D (OLD) INOUE FAMILY

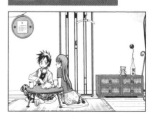

Orihime moved away from her parents older brother because of family problems. alone in her apartment even after her bro in a sudden car accident. Her best friend often sleeps over.

F THEIR RARE AND UNUSUAL ITEMS WILL SHOCK YOU! URAHARA SHÔTEN

A SPIRITUAL STATION IN TOWN WITH THINGS YOU WISH YOU HAD

Urahara, with his trademark clogs and hat that covers his eyes, runs the general store. He's lazy, so he keeps his hours short, but his wide selection of goods draws quite a few customers.

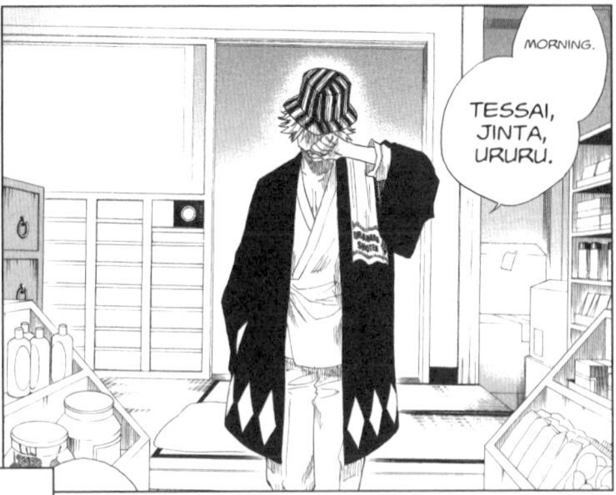
MORNING.
TESSAI, JINTA, URURU.

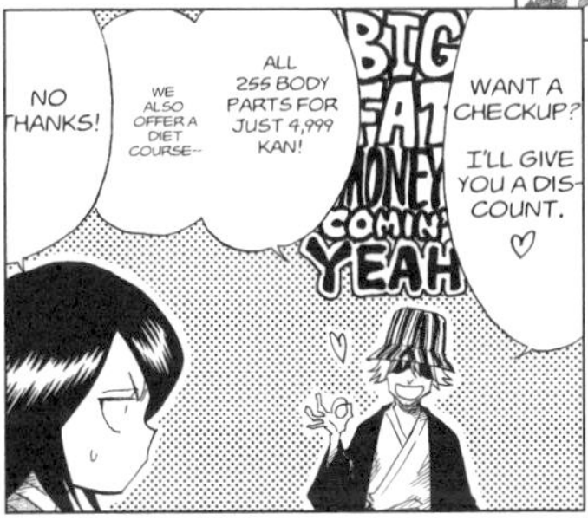
WANT A CHECKUP? I'LL GIVE YOU A DISCOUNT. ♡
ALL 255 BODY PARTS FOR JUST 4,999 KAN!
WE ALSO OFFER A DIET COURSE--
NO THANKS!

A general store on the eastern outskirts of Karakura Town. It has a wide selection of merchandise to choose from. It even has what every child yearns for—cheap sweets! It also secretly sells spirit items from the Soul Society. Rukia frequently went to the store when she was dispatched to the human world. Its prices are honest and very cheap.

G KARAKURA 1ST HIGH SCHOOL

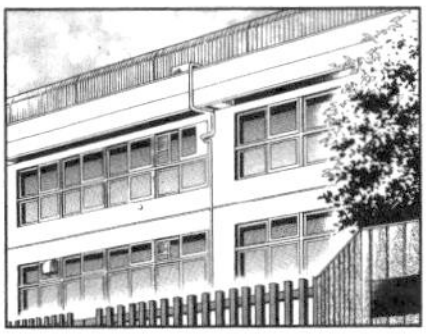

The public high school that Ichigo and his friends attend. It's a pretty normal high school, but for some reason, it is known to receive a lot of applications from delinquents. It's also famous for its strong karate team.

H ONOSE RIVER

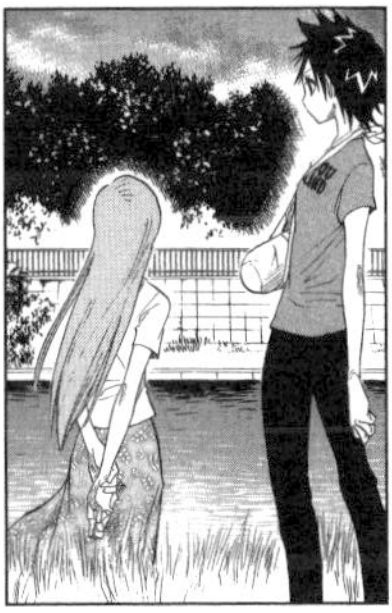

A fireworks display is held here every summer. It is always bustling with people. Tatsuki and Orihime come here every autumn to see the red fireflies.

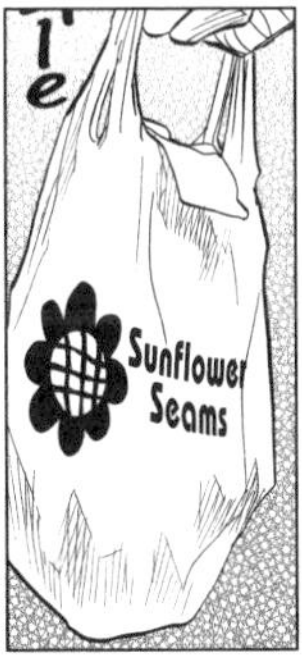
Sunflower Seams

I SUNFLOWER SEWING

The 24-hour dressmaking store that Uryû, the president of the craft club, patronizes. It is highly valued by craft lovers for its tendency to disregard profit.

J KARAKURA GENERAL HOSPITAL

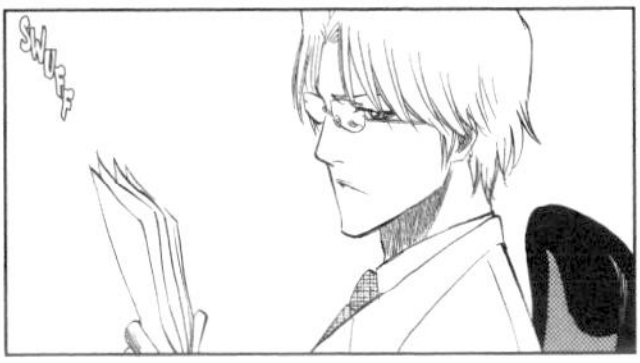

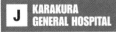

The general hospital near the Karakura Old Town Station. Many patients from outside of Karakura Town visit it because it's easy to get to and has well-regulated medical facilities. Uryû's father, Ryûgen Ishida, is the director of this large hospital.

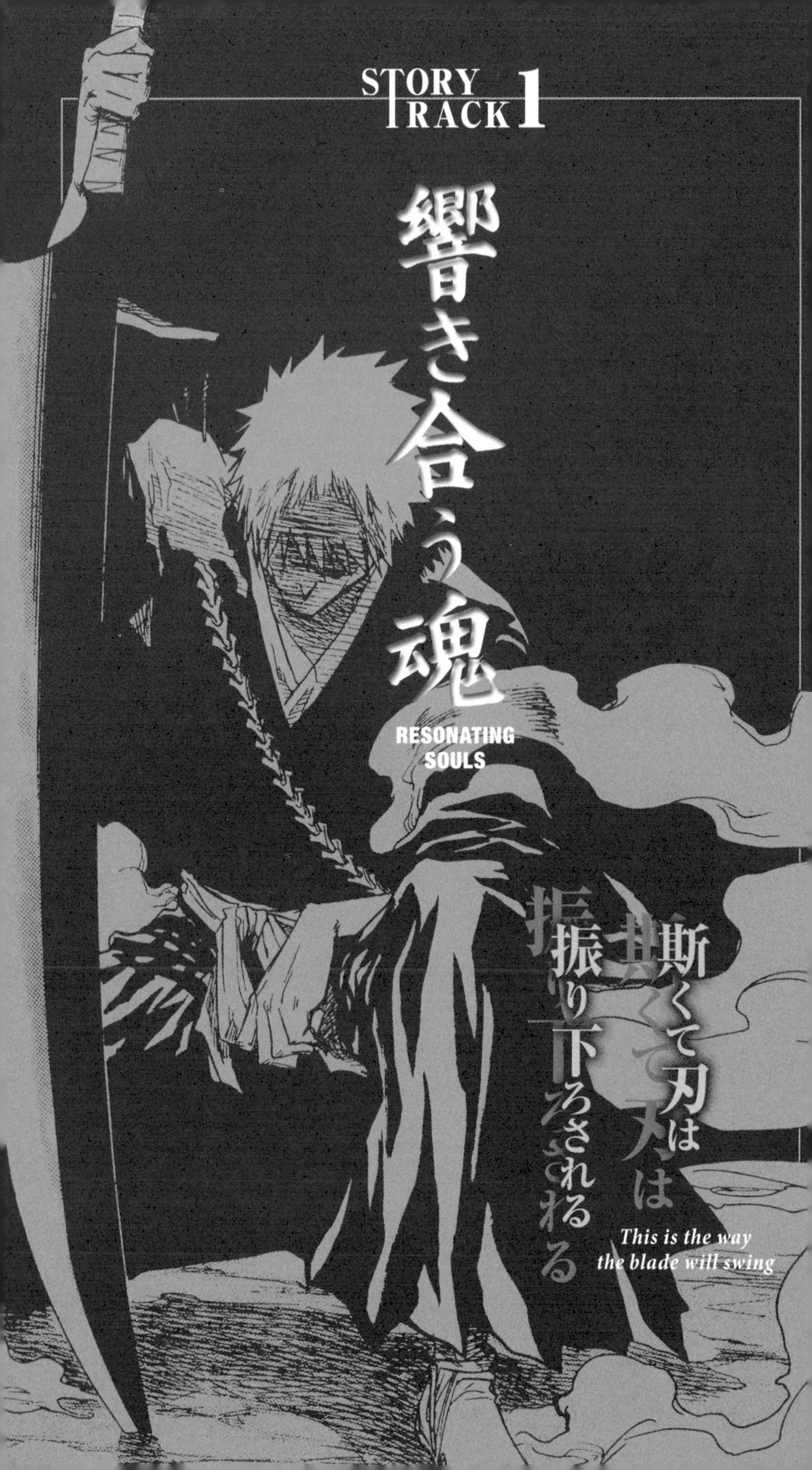
STORY TRACK 1
響き合う魂
RESONATING SOULS
斯くて刃は
振り下ろされる
This is the way
the blade will swing

NORMAL BOY WITH MANY PROBLEMS

ICHIGO KUROSAKI — CHARACTER FILE 1-a

黒崎一護

ORANGE-HAIRED HIGH SCHOOL STUDENT WITH STRONG SPIRITUAL POWER

A pretty normal(?!) high school student whose brows are always knitted, as if he's in a bad mood. Despite his scary exterior, he has a kind personality. He cannot ignore people in trouble. He was born with strong spiritual energy.

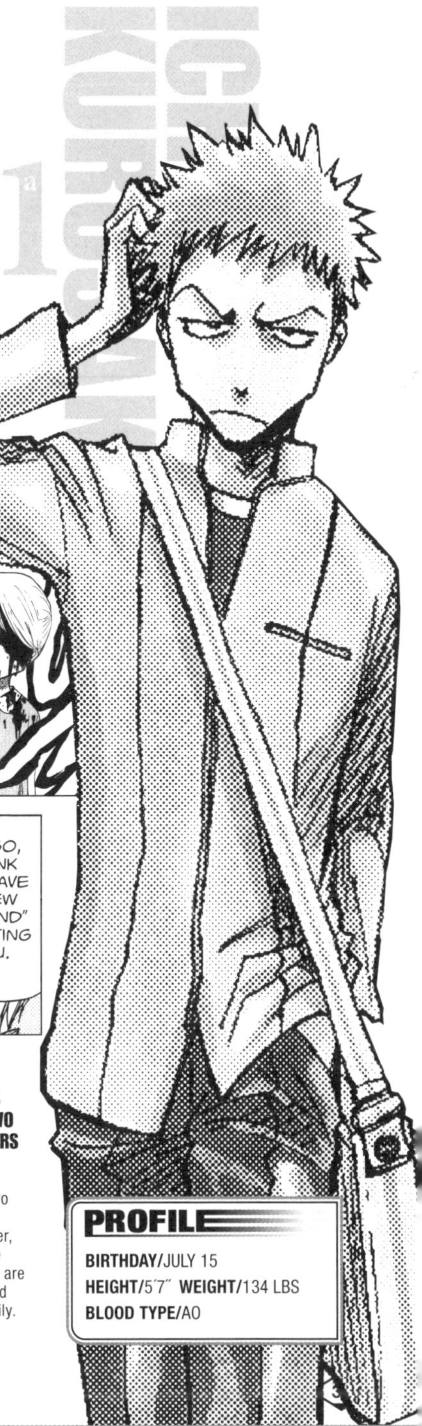

ICHIGO
KUROSAKI
1-a

SPECIAL TALENT: HE CAN SEE GHOSTS

Ichigo has been able to see ghosts ever since he can remember. He even helps the ghosts out of his innate sense of justice.

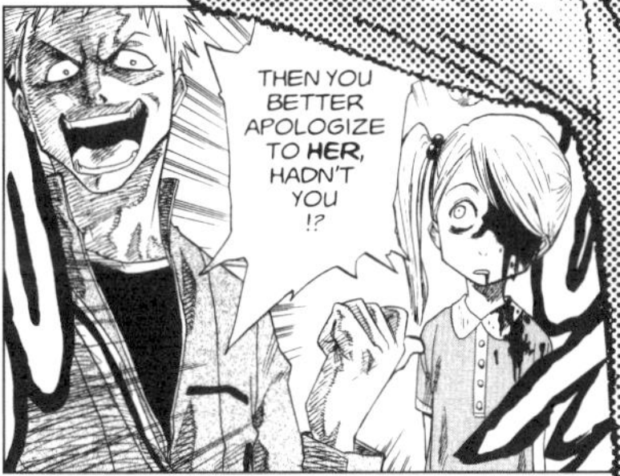

THEN YOU BETTER APOLOGIZE TO **HER**, HADN'T YOU !?

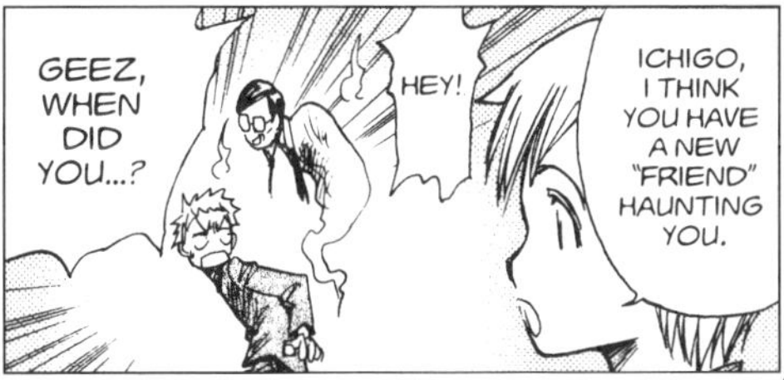

ICHIGO, I THINK YOU HAVE A NEW "FRIEND" HAUNTING YOU.
HEY!
GEEZ, WHEN DID YOU...?

He's often haunted by wandering spirits because of that.

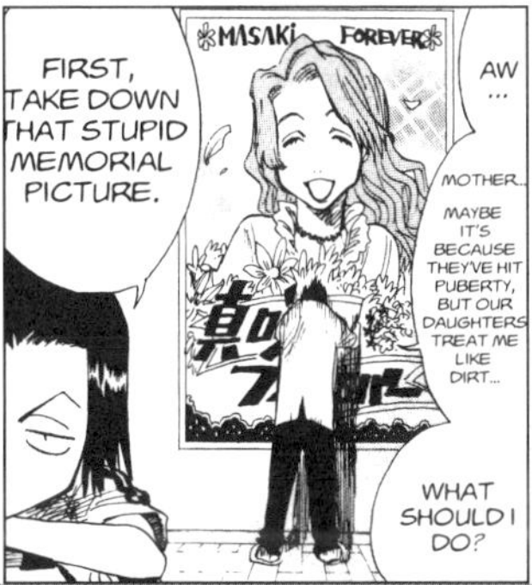

AW ...
MASAKI FOREVER
MOTHER... MAYBE IT'S BECAUSE THEY'VE HIT PUBERTY, BUT OUR DAUGHTERS TREAT ME LIKE DIRT...
FIRST, TAKE DOWN THAT STUPID MEMORIAL PICTURE.
WHAT SHOULD I DO?

LIVES WITH HIS FATHER AND TWO YOUNGER SISTERS

Ichigo's family consists of his father and his two younger sisters. He lost his mother, Masaki, when he was young. They are a harmonious and affectionate family.

PROFILE

BIRTHDAY/JULY 15

HEIGHT/5′7″ **WEIGHT**/134 LBS

BLOOD TYPE/AO

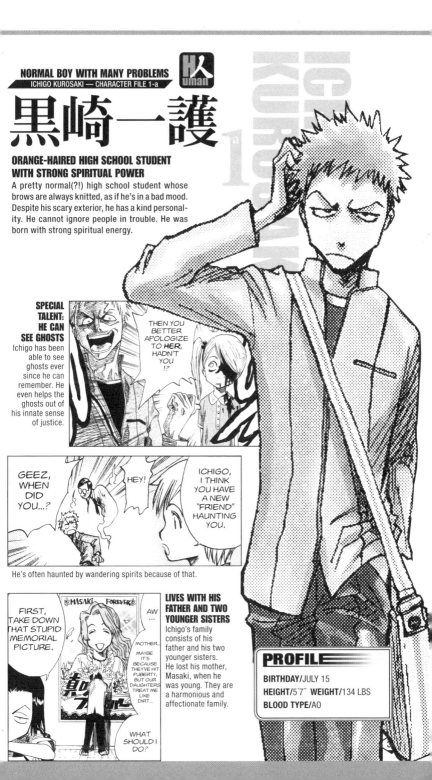

邂逅

A CHANCE MEETING

An Encounter with a Soul Reaper
VOL. 1-1

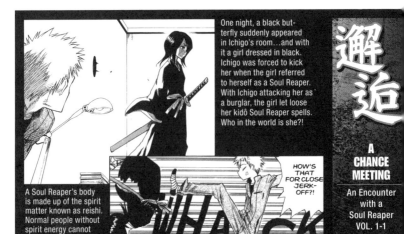

One night, a black butterfly suddenly appeared in Ichigo's room…and with it a girl dressed in black. Ichigo was forced to kick her when the girl referred to herself as a Soul Reaper. With Ichigo attacking her as a burglar, the girl let loose her kidô Soul Reaper spells. Who in the world is she?!

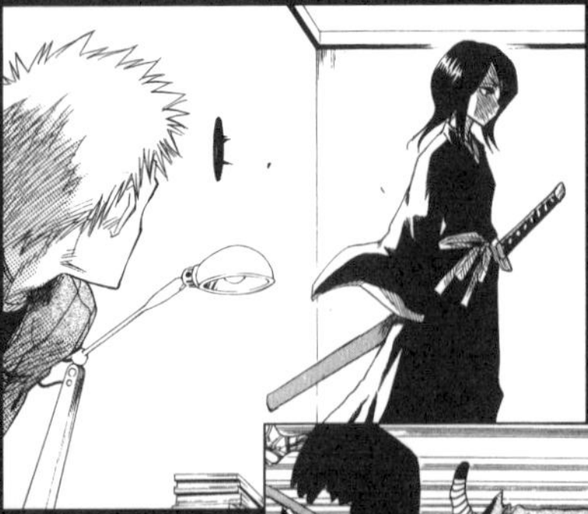

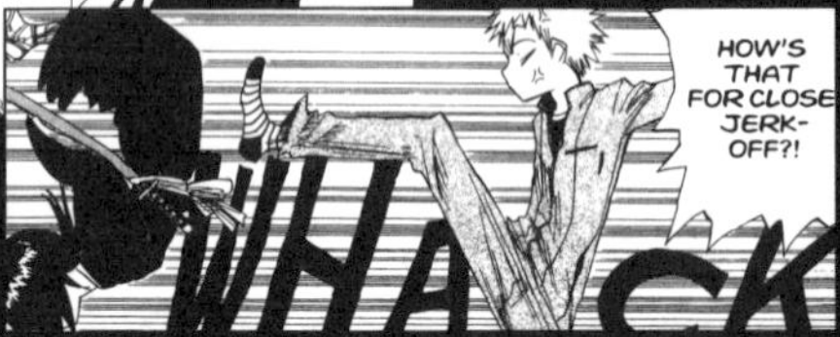
HOW'S THAT FOR CLOSE JERK-OFF?!
WHACK

A Soul Reaper's body is made up of the spirit matter known as reishi. Normal people without spirit energy cannot even see Soul Reapers.

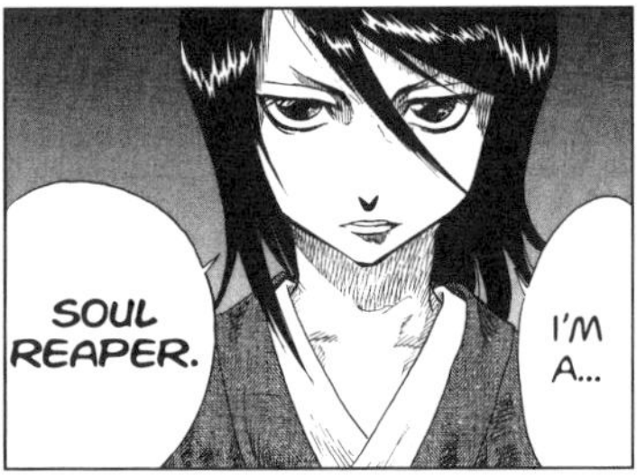
I'M A…
SOUL REAPER.

She wears a shihakushô and wears a zanpaku-tô at her waist like a samurai… A Soul Reaper?

THE VISITOR FROM THE SOUL SOCIETY

The mysterious girl who calls herself a Soul Reaper came to the human world from the Soul Society. She speaks in an old-fashioned manner and has a high-handed attitude. She calls Ichigo a snotty brat.

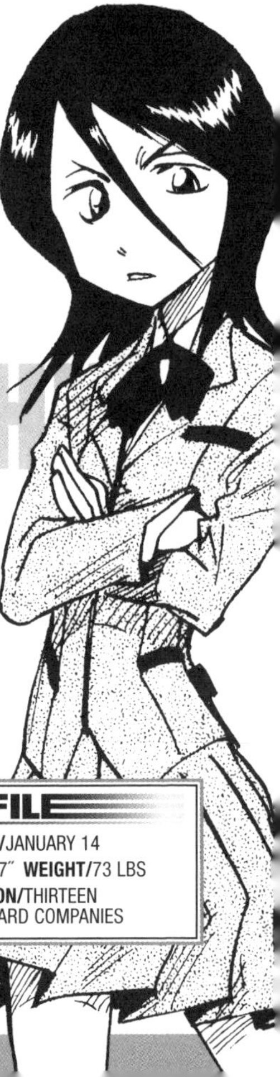

RUKIA KUCHIKI

THE GIRL WHO SUDDENLY APPEARED

RUKIA KUCHIKI — CHARACTER FILE 2-a

Death 死

朽木ルキア

2a

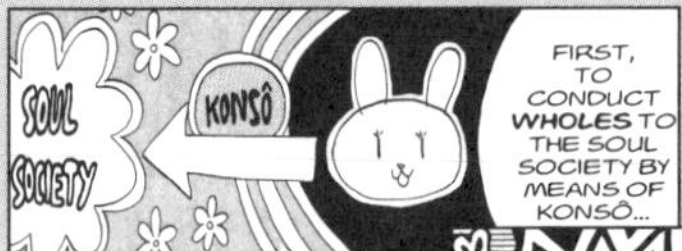
FIRST, TO CONDUCT WHOLES TO THE SOUL SOCIETY BY MEANS OF KONSÔ…
KONSÔ
SOUL SOCIETY

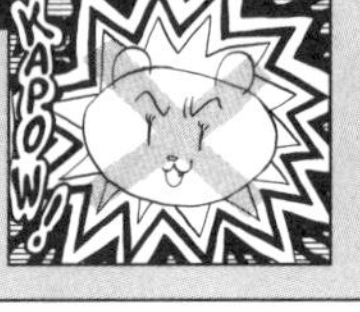
KAPOW!

EXTREMELY BAD DRAWINGS
Rukia's illustrations are kitschy and chic. She's good and bad?!

PROFILE

BIRTHDAY/JANUARY 14
HEIGHT/4′7″ **WEIGHT/**73 LBS
AFFILIATION/THIRTEEN COURT GUARD COMPANIES

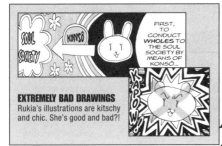

NORMAL BOY WITH MANY PROBLEMS

ICHIGO KUROSAKI — CHARACTER FILE 1-b

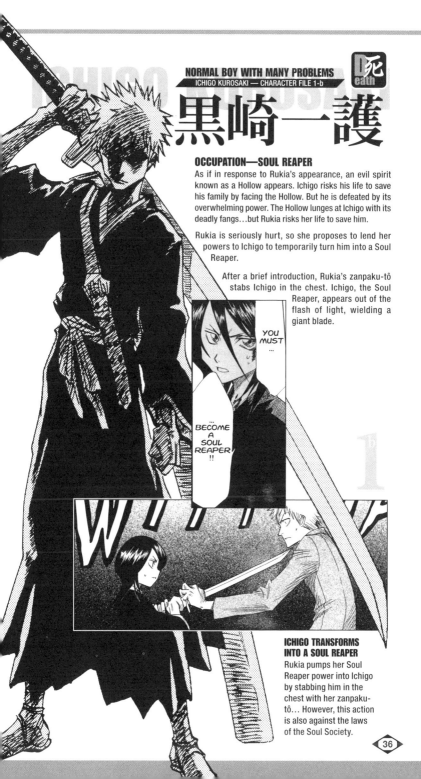

黒崎一護

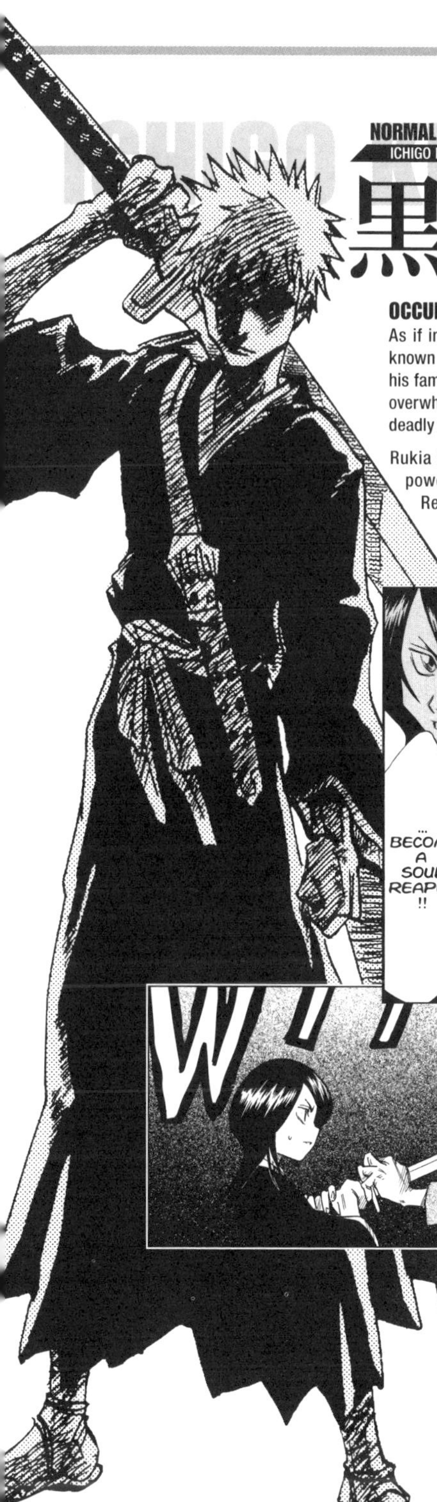

OCCUPATION—SOUL REAPER

As if in response to Rukia's appearance, an evil spirit known as a Hollow appears. Ichigo risks his life to save his family by facing the Hollow. But he is defeated by its overwhelming power. The Hollow lunges at Ichigo with its deadly fangs…but Rukia risks her life to save him.

Rukia is seriously hurt, so she proposes to lend her powers to Ichigo to temporarily turn him into a Soul Reaper.

After a brief introduction, Rukia's zanpaku-tô stabs Ichigo in the chest. Ichigo, the Soul Reaper, appears out of the flash of light, wielding a giant blade.

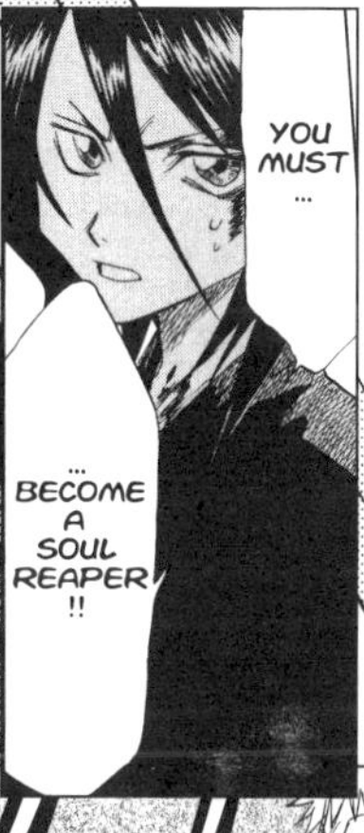

YOU MUST …
… BECOME A SOUL REAPER !!

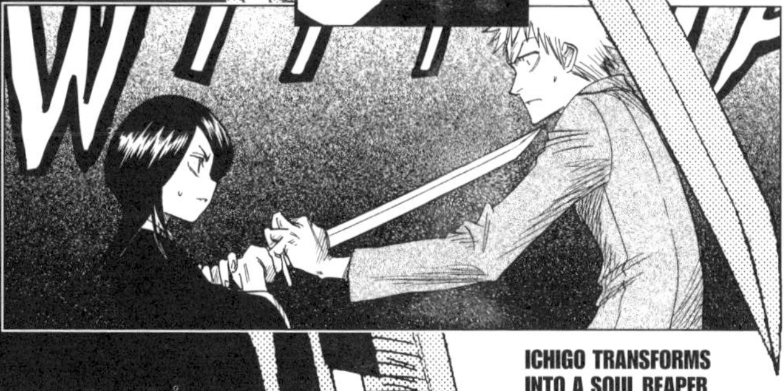

ICHIGO TRANSFORMS INTO A SOUL REAPER

Rukia pumps her Soul Reaper power into Ichigo by stabbing him in the chest with her zanpaku-tô… However, this action is also against the laws of the Soul Society.

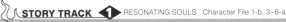

Hollow 虚

THE WANDERING DENIZEN OF THE DARK

FISHBONE D — CHARACTER FILE 3

フィッシュボーンD

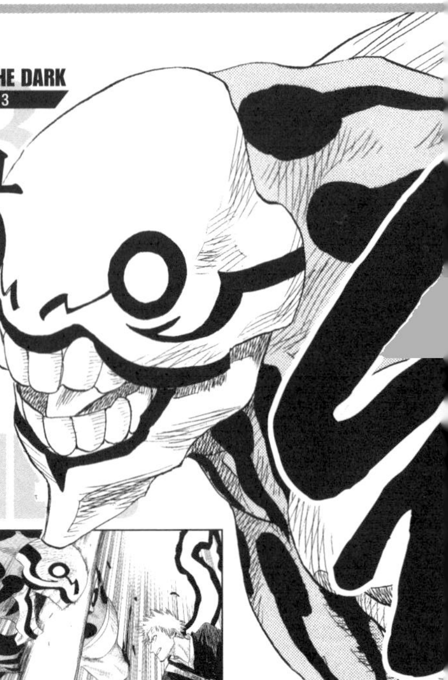

MONSTROSITIES

The Hollow that attacked the Kurosaki Family was lured to their home by Ichigo's strong spiritual energy. It is called Fishbone D because of its fish-like mask. It belongs to the lowest level of Hollows. Its fighting ability is very low.

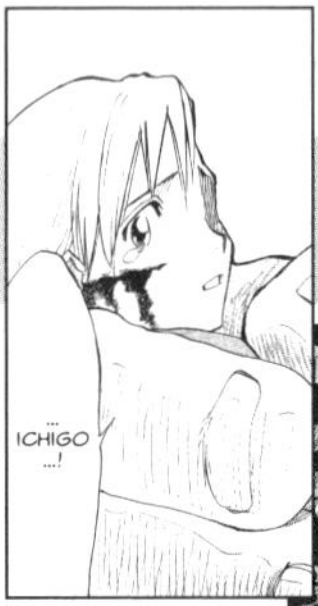
...ICHIGO ...!

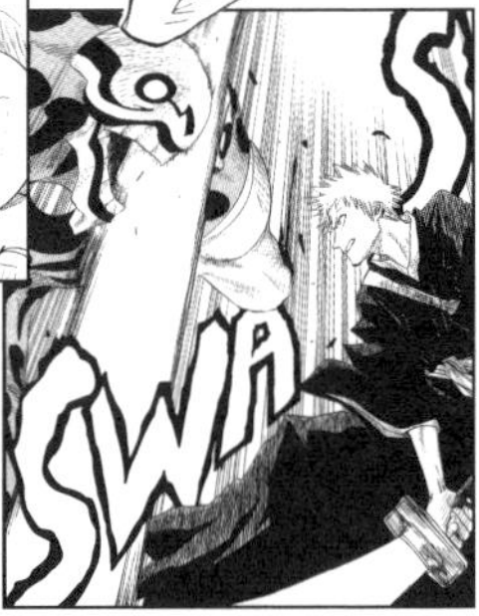
SWA

Ichigo slices Fishbone D in two. But Ichigo ends up having to help Rukia with her Soul Reaper work in exchange.

DATA

TYPE/LOW LEVEL HOLLOW

DISPOSITION/LOW INTELLIGENCE AND VERY AGGRESSIVE

NOTEWORTHY MENTION/NOTHING IN PARTICULAR

KUROSAKI FAMILY

LIVELY ALL YEAR ROUND!!

黒崎夏梨

KARIN KUROSAKI — 6-a

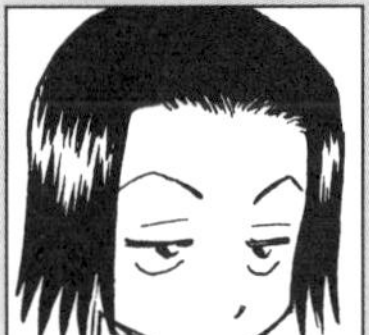

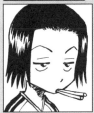

Yuzu's twin sister. She's a coolheaded realist, but has strong spiritual energy like her older brother.

PROFILE

BIRTHDAY/MAY 6
HEIGHT/4′4″
WEIGHT/68 LBS

黒崎遊子

YUZU KUROSAKI — 5

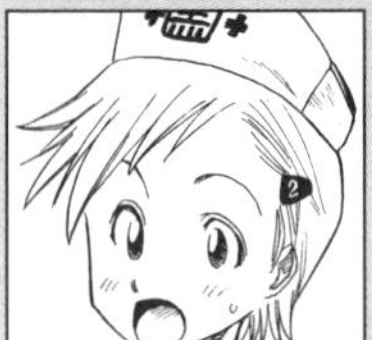

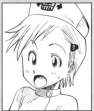

Even though she's only in the fifth grade, she's a reliable person who's in charge of all the house chores. She has low spiritual energy.

PROFILE

BIRTHDAY/MAY 6
HEIGHT/4′6″
WEIGHT/68 LBS

黒崎一心

ISSHIN KUROSAKI — 4

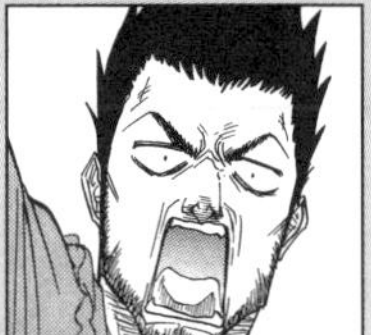

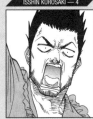

The breadwinner of the Kurosaki family and a practicing physician. He's so energetic it's annoying.

PROFILE

BIRTHDAY/DECEMBER 10
HEIGHT/6′1″
WEIGHT/176 LBS
BLOOD TYPE/AB

The book e's holding is *The Guide to Performers volume 21*, a book bout all the comedians that ever existed.

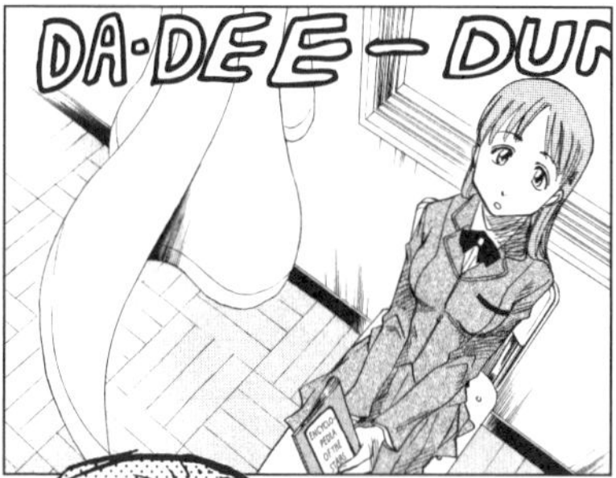
DA-DEE-DUN
ENCYCLOPEDIA OF THE STARS

A MYSTERIOUS, EXTREMELY INNOCENT GIRL

The innocent, big-breasted girl in Ichigo's class. She's secretly in love with him. She always has a carefree smile and a sunny disposition. But she has no parents and her older brother is dead, so she's currently living by herself. Her hobbies include telling jokes and doing the karate moves that she learned from Tatsuki.

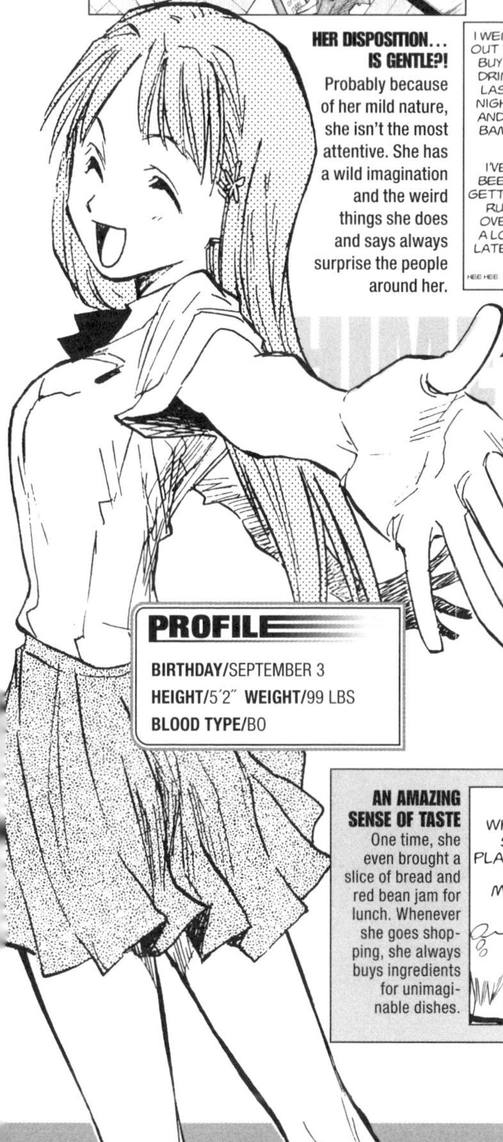

HER DISPOSITION... IS GENTLE?!

Probably because of her mild nature, she isn't the most attentive. She has a wild imagination and the weird things she does and says always surprise the people around her.

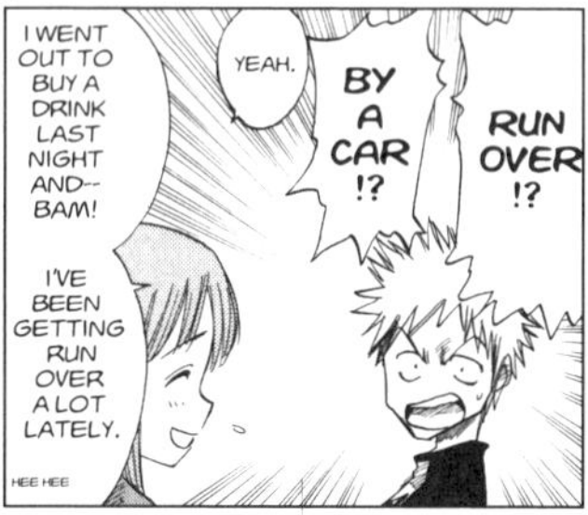
RUN OVER !?
BY A CAR !?
YEAH.
I WENT OUT TO BUY A DRINK LAST NIGHT AND-- BAM!
I'VE BEEN GETTING RUN OVER A LOT LATELY.
HEE HEE

A SPOTLESS, PURE HEART

ORIHIIME INOUE — CHARACTER FILE 7-a

井上織姫

PROFILE

BIRTHDAY/SEPTEMBER 3

HEIGHT/5′2″ **WEIGHT/**99 LBS

BLOOD TYPE/BO

AN AMAZING SENSE OF TASTE

One time, she even brought a slice of bread and red bean jam for lunch. Whenever she goes shopping, she always buys ingredients for unimaginable dishes.

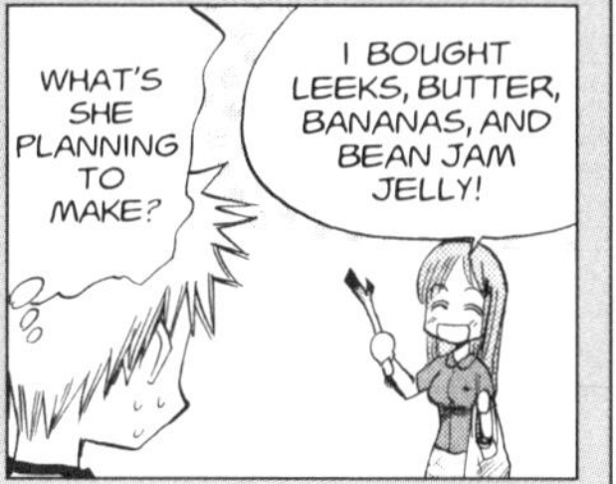
I BOUGHT LEEKS, BUTTER, BANANAS, AND BEAN JAM JELLY!
WHAT'S SHE PLANNING TO MAKE?

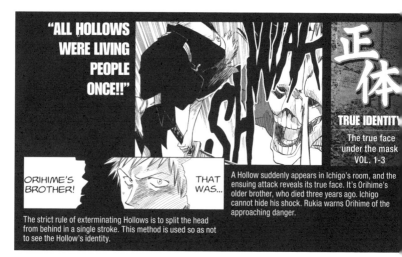

"ALL HOLLOWS WERE LIVING PEOPLE ONCE!!"

正体

TRUE IDENTITY

The true face under the mask
VOL. 1-3

THAT WAS...
ORIHIME'S BROTHER!

A Hollow suddenly appears in Ichigo's room, and the ensuing attack reveals its true face. It's Orihime's older brother, who died three years ago. Ichigo cannot hide his shock. Rukia warns Orihime of the approaching danger.

The strict rule of exterminating Hollows is to split the head from behind in a single stroke. This method is used so as not to see the Hollow's identity.

THE SECOND STRONGEST HIGH SCHOOL GIRL IN JAPAN

Orihime's best friend. She protected Orihime from bullies and opened up Orihime's heart, which had been closed off until then. Her given name should actually be in kanji rather than hiragana. She has been friends with Ichigo ever since they were 4 years old. She has been going to a karate dojo since childhood and is a second-degree black belt. She placed second at the Karate Inter-High Tournament. She is caring, hates dishonesty, and understands Ichigo well. She's a C-cup.

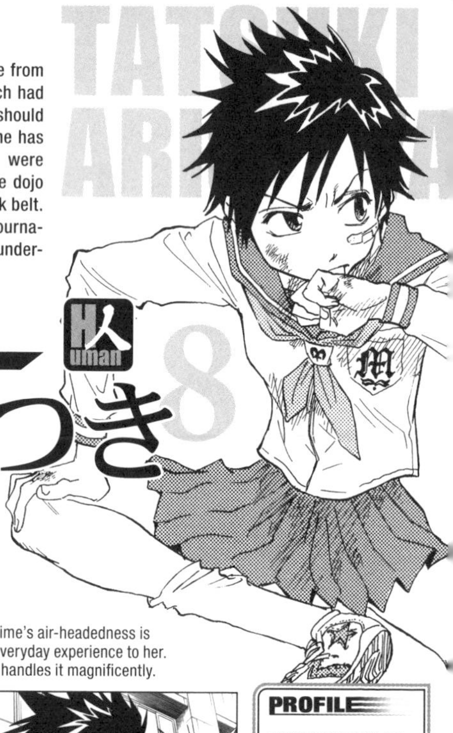

A STRONG WILL IN HER STARE

TATSUKI ARISAWA — CHARACTER FILE 8

H人 uman 8

有沢たつき

WHAT DO YOU HAVE TODAY, TATSUKI ?!
LUCKY YOU. UNFORTUNATELY MINE'S STANDARD ISSUE SLOP.
I'VE GOT SWEET BEAN PASTE AND BREAD!

Orihime's air-headedness is an everyday experience to her. She handles it magnificently.

PROFILE

BIRTHDAY/JULY 17
HEIGHT/5′0″
WEIGHT/90 LBS
BLOOD TYPE/AO

WHAT'S THE MATTER !!
I'M JUST ONE LITTLE GIRL !!

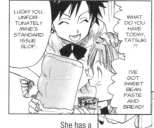

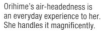

She has a tomboyish personality and is more hot-blooded than Ichigo. She mercilessly swings her fists at anyone she sees as an enemy.

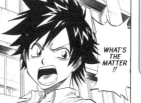

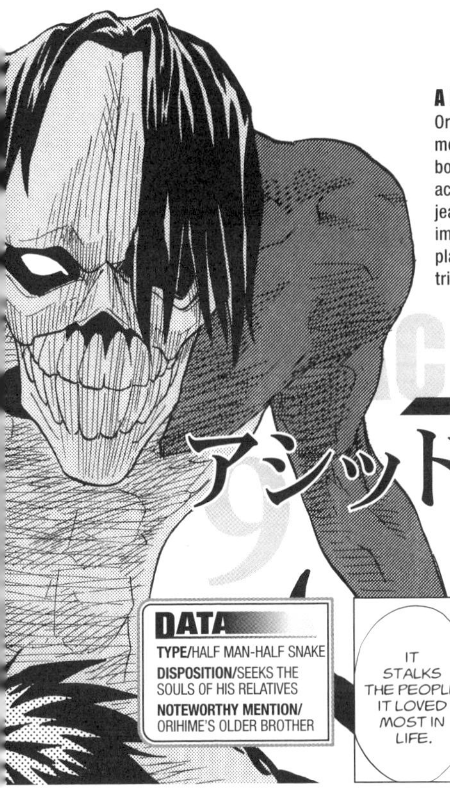

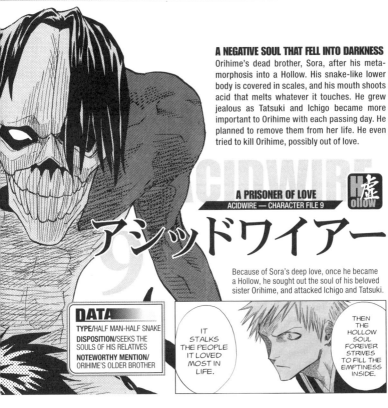

A NEGATIVE SOUL THAT FELL INTO DARKNESS

Orihime's dead brother, Sora, after his metamorphosis into a Hollow. His snake-like lower body is covered in scales, and his mouth shoots acid that melts whatever it touches. He grew jealous as Tatsuki and Ichigo became more important to Orihime with each passing day. He planned to remove them from her life. He even tried to kill Orihime, possibly out of love.

ACIDWIRE

H 虚 ollow

A PRISONER OF LOVE

ACIDWIRE — CHARACTER FILE 9

アシッドワイアー

9

Because of Sora's deep love, once he became a Hollow, he sought out the soul of his beloved sister Orihime, and attacked Ichigo and Tatsuki.

DATA

TYPE/HALF MAN-HALF SNAKE

DISPOSITION/SEEKS THE SOULS OF HIS RELATIVES

NOTEWORTHY MENTION/ ORIHIME'S OLDER BROTHER

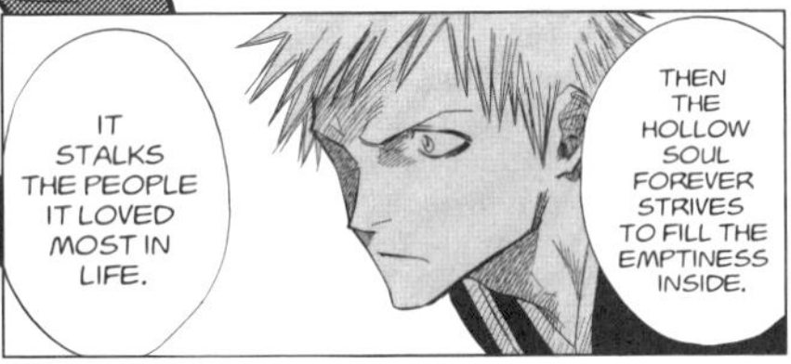
THEN THE HOLLOW SOUL FOREVER STRIVES TO FILL THE EMPTINESS INSIDE.
IT STALKS THE PEOPLE IT LOVED MOST IN LIFE.

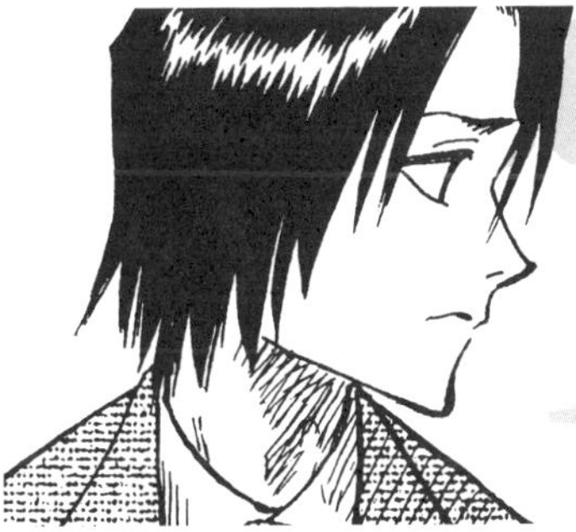

SORA INOUE

H 人 uman

ORIHIME'S DEAD OLDER BROTHER

SORA INOUE — CHARACTER FILE 10

井上昊

10

Orihime's older brother by 15 years. He protected Orihime from their parents' abuse and tenderly raised her. He left his parents at 18, taking 3-year-old Orihime with him. The two then lived together. On the morning of his first argument with Orihime, he was killed in a traffic accident.

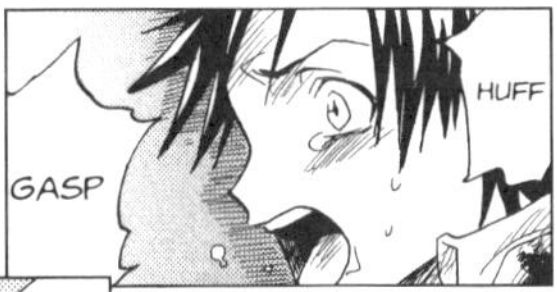
HUFF
GASP

His pride in having lovingly raised Orihime evolved into a twisted love when he became a Hollow. He tried to regain Orihime's love from Ichigo by killing her.

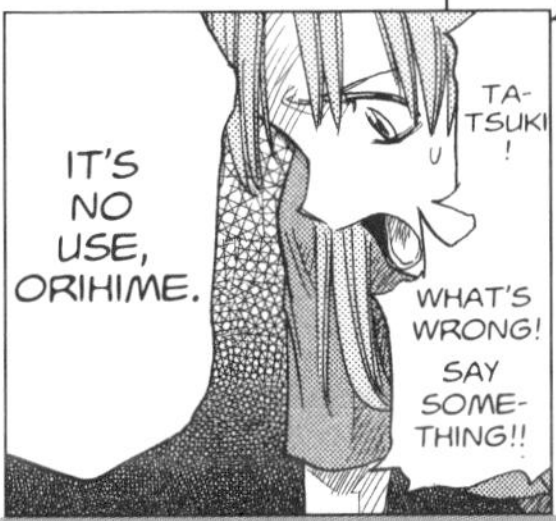
TA-TSUKI!
WHAT'S WRONG! SAY SOME-THING!!
IT'S NO USE, ORIHIME.

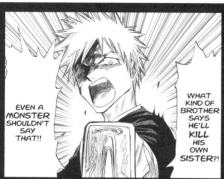

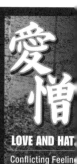

愛憎

LOVE AND HAT

Conflicting Feelin

VOL. 1-4~6

WHAT KIND OF BROTHER SAYS HE'LL KILL HIS OWN SISTER?!
EVEN A MONSTER SHOULDN'T SAY THAT!!

Orihime begins crying when she sees her brother hurting Tatsuki and Ichigo. But Sora, who's gone mad from the Hollow transformation, becomes infuriated. He grabs Orihime, screaming, "Then she will die for me," and tries to crush her.

"I'M SORRY... SORA."

THE ROLE OF AN OLDER BROTHER

Ichigo explodes in anger over Sora's horrible deeds. He says, "It's the job of a big brother to protect his younger siblings." It is a principle that Ichigo himself practices.

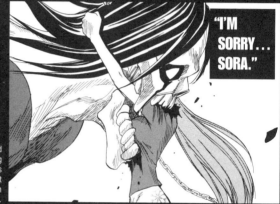

Orihime hugs her transformed brother rather than escaping his fangs. Sora regains consciousness from that action and decides to return to the sky of his own volition.

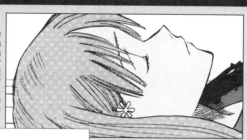

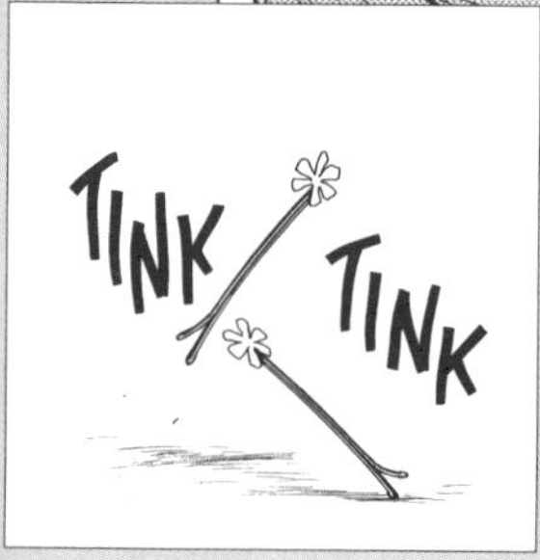

A GIFT FROM BIG BROTHER SORA

ORIHIME'S HAIRPINS

Every day Orihime wears the hairpins that were her first and last gift from her brother Sora. It's as if she's spending time with him.

TINK
TINK

Orihime's two hairpins are Sora's first gift to her. But Orihime didn't like them, and they got into their first argument with each other. It was the first time she didn't say good-bye to him when he went out... Then Sora got into a traffic accident and never returned. Now Orihime always has those hairpins with her and continues to wear them.

A BURNING HEART HIDDEN WITHIN HIS FEW WORDS

The large man of few words who has been friends with Ichigo since middle school. Despite his rough exterior, he is kind and has good grades. He loves cute things, and there was even a time he chased after Kon, the stuffed animal. Ichigo and his friends call him by his nickname, "Chad." He was born in Okinawa and grew up in Mexico.

A steel beam hits Chad! But he isn't hurt.

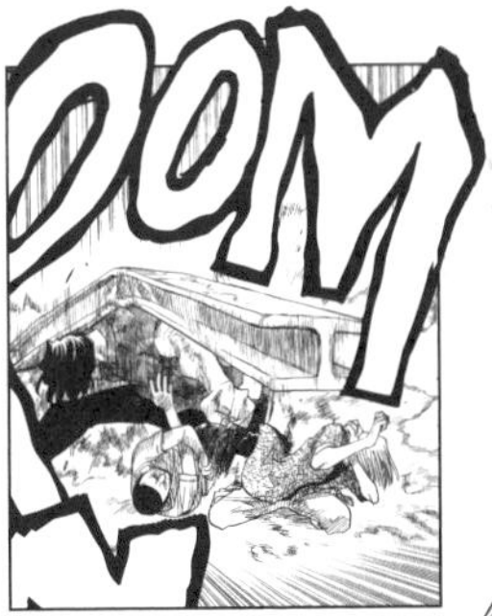
DOM

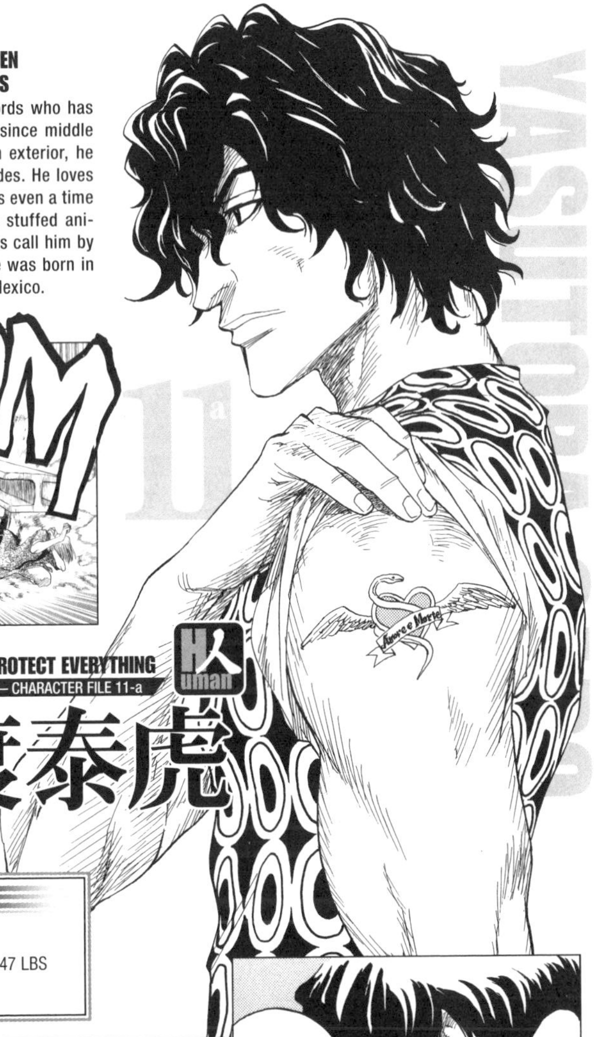

A STRONG FIST TO PROTECT EVERYTHING

YASUTORA "CHAD" SADO — CHARACTER FILE 11-a

茶渡泰虎

PROFILE

BIRTHDAY/APRIL 7

HEIGHT/6′5″ **WEIGHT**/247 LBS

BLOOD TYPE/AO

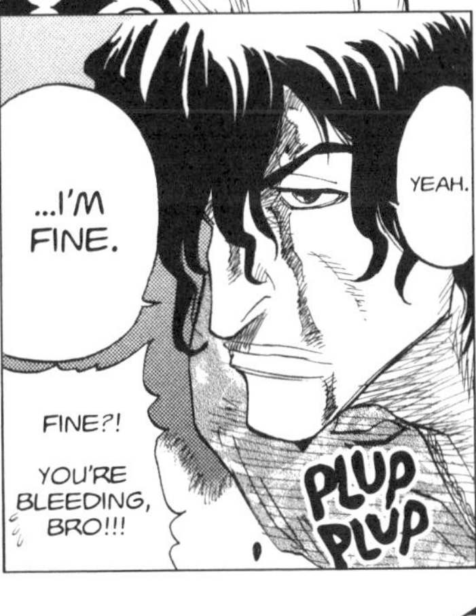
YEAH.
...I'M FINE.
FINE?!
YOU'RE BLEEDING, BRO!!!
PLUP PLUP

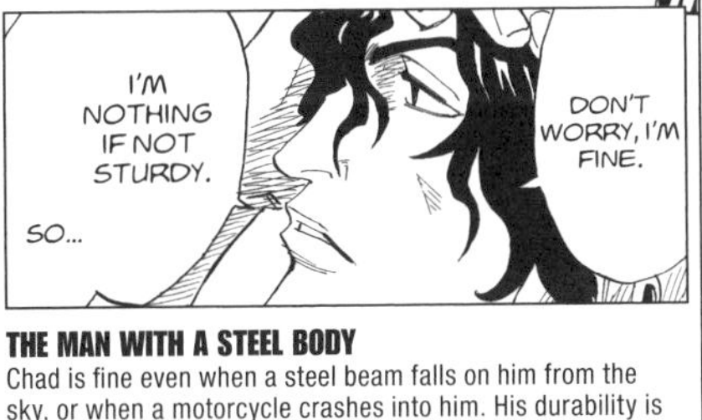
DON'T WORRY, I'M FINE.
I'M NOTHING IF NOT STURDY.
SO...

THE MAN WITH A STEEL BODY

Chad is fine even when a steel beam falls on him from the sky, or when a motorcycle crashes into him. His durability is well beyond that of humans and on par with monsters. But he almost never uses his giant fists for himself.

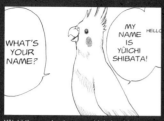

鸚哥

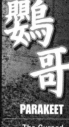

PARAKEET

The Cursed Parakeet
VOL. 1-7

A cursed parakeet that continues to bring misfortune to its owners. Chad loves cute things, so a friend forces the parakeet on him. Chad finds himself being chased by a mysterious Hollow and living on the run with Yûichi the parakeet.

MY NAME IS YÛICHI SHIBATA!
WHAT'S YOUR NAME?

Yûichi the parakeet can use high-level human speech. It doesn't seem like it's haunted by evil spirits, but…

Chad is severely wounded and hauled to the Kurosaki Clinic. It looks like his wounds are from a Hollow…

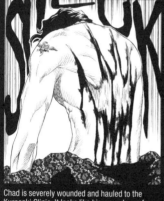

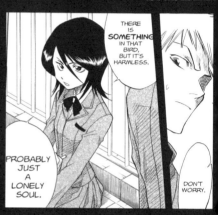

THERE IS SOMETHING IN THAT BIRD, BUT IT'S HARMLESS.
DON'T WORRY.
PROBABLY JUST A LONELY SOUL.

石田竜弦

RYÛGEN ISHIDA — 12

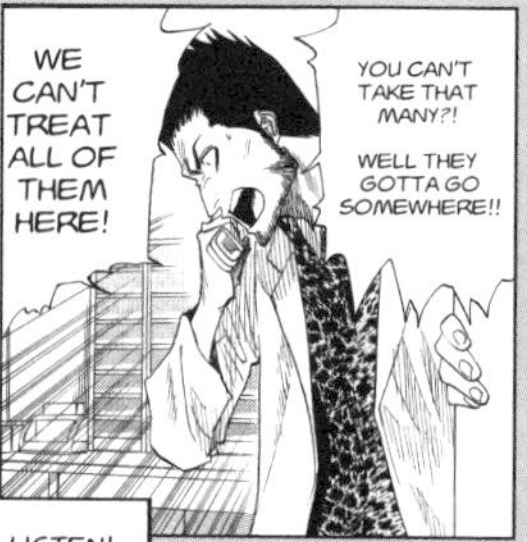

Ryûgen looks a lot like Uryû. There's another side to the director of the Karakura General hospital…?!

PROFILE

BIRTHDAY/MAY 14
HEIGHT/5′8″
WEIGHT/150 LBS

A RELATIONSHIP HIDDEN IN THE PAST

ISSHIN KUROSAKI AND RYÛGEN ISHIDA

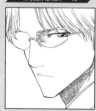

There is a traffic accident near the Kurosaki Clinic and many of the wounded are being brought in. Isshin calls the Karakura General Hospital to deal with the situation.

YOU CAN'T TAKE THAT MANY?!
WELL THEY GOTTA GO SOMEWHERE!!
WE CAN'T TREAT ALL OF THEM HERE!

LISTEN!
TELL YOUR BOSS IT'S A REQUEST FROM KUROSAKI!
HE'LL FIND ME SOME FREE BEDS REAL QUICK!
DO IT!!
TMP TMP TMP
SQUEEK

It seems that Ichigo's father Isshin and Uryû Ishida's father Ryûgen have a close relationship like the one between their sons. But wouldn't the director of a small-town clinic be completely different from the director of a large hospital?!

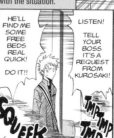

A BOY LONGING FOR HIS MOTHER

YÛICHI SHIBATA — CHARACTER FILE 13

S 魂 oul

シバタユウイチ

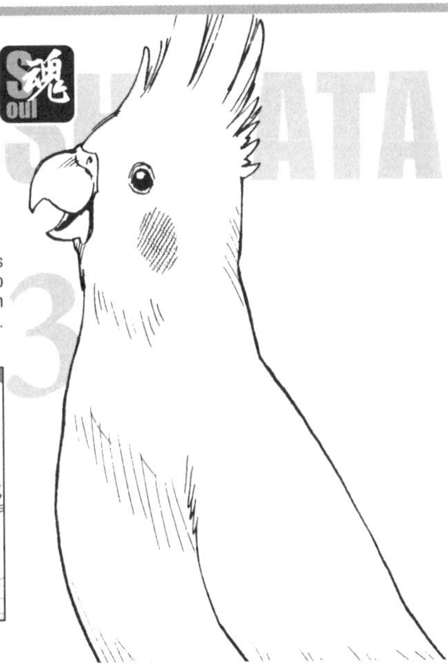

THE BOY HAUNTING A PARAKEET

A boy's soul was sealed in a parakeet after it was removed by a Hollow. Believing in the Hollow's promise to bring back his mother, he participates in a game in which he has to run away from the Hollow for three months. Everyone who gets involved with him dies.

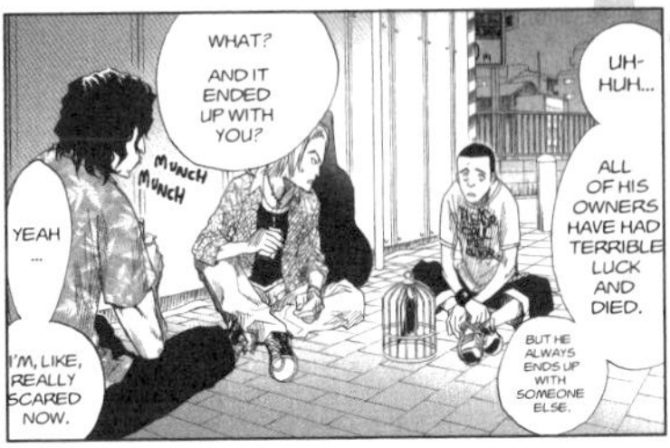
UH-HUH...
ALL OF HIS OWNERS HAVE HAD TERRIBLE LUCK AND DIED.
BUT HE ALWAYS ENDS UP WITH SOMEONE ELSE.
WHAT?
AND IT ENDED UP WITH YOU?
MUNCH MUNCH
YEAH ...
I'M, LIKE, REALLY SCARED NOW.

In reality, the Hollow was using Yûichi as bait in order to eat the souls of those associated with the boy.

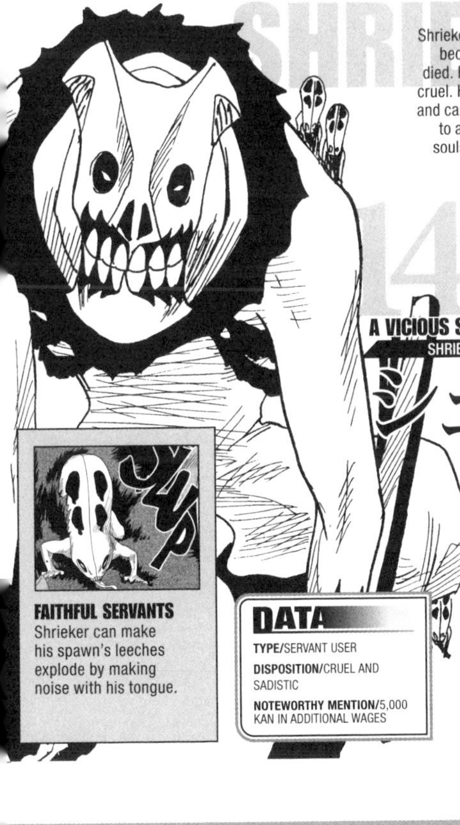

EX-SERIAL KILLER

Shrieker is a serial killer who became a Hollow after he died. He is very cunning and cruel. He has the ability to fly and can command his spawn to attack. He even ate the souls of two Soul Reapers.

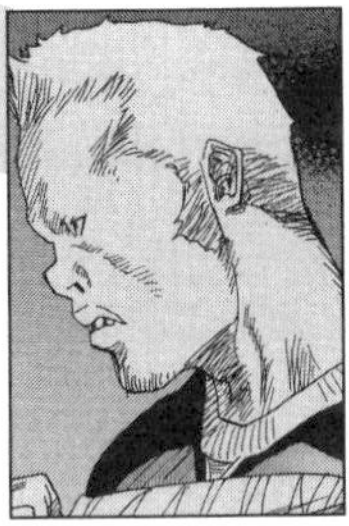

A VICIOUS SOUL THAT PLAYS WITH DEATH

SHRIEKER — CHARACTER FILE 14

H 虚 ollow

シュリーカー

FAITHFUL SERVANTS

Shrieker can make his spawn's leeches explode by making noise with his tongue.

DATA

TYPE/SERVANT USER

DISPOSITION/CRUEL AND SADISTIC

NOTEWORTHY MENTION/5,000 KAN IN ADDITIONAL WAGES

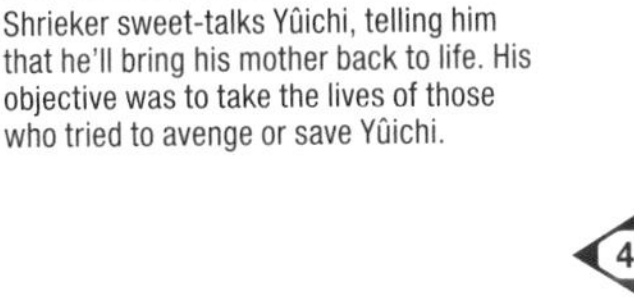
RUN FROM ME FOR THREE MONTHS!
IF HE DID IT, I'D BRING MOMMY BACK TO LIFE!

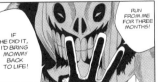

Shrieker sweet-talks Yûichi, telling him that he'll bring his mother back to life. His objective was to take the lives of those who tried to avenge or save Yûichi.

放鳥 BIRD RELEASED

The Birdcage is Opened
VOL. 2-8~12

An enraged Ichigo destroys Shrieker with a slash of his zanpaku-tô. But it has been a while since the chain of fate connected to Yûichi's soul was cut. He can no longer return to his body...

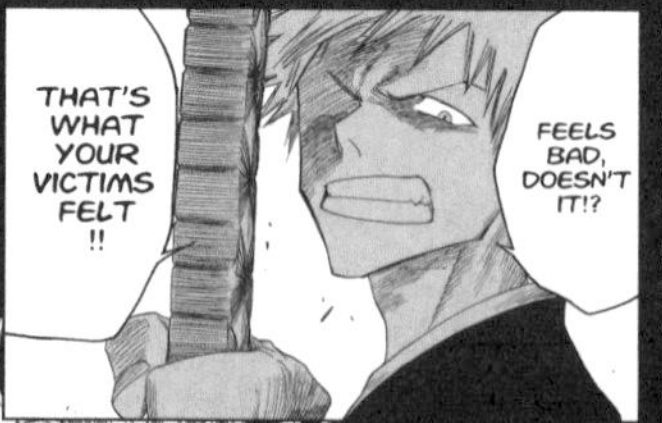
FEELS BAD, DOESN'T IT!?
THAT'S WHAT YOUR VICTIMS FELT !!

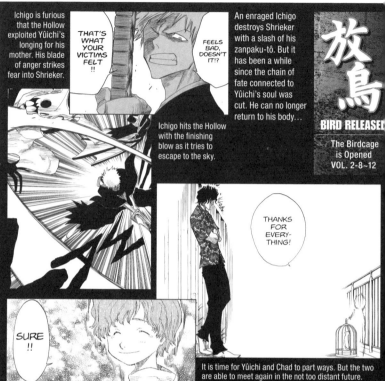

Ichigo is furious that the Hollow exploited Yûichi's longing for his mother. His blade of anger strikes fear into Shrieker.

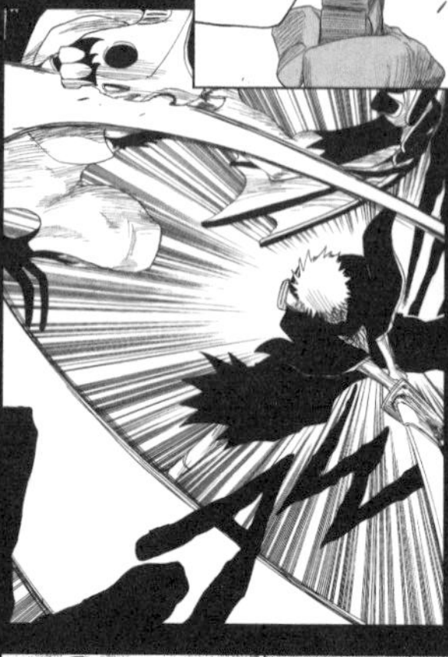

Ichigo hits the Hollow with the finishing blow as it tries to escape to the sky.

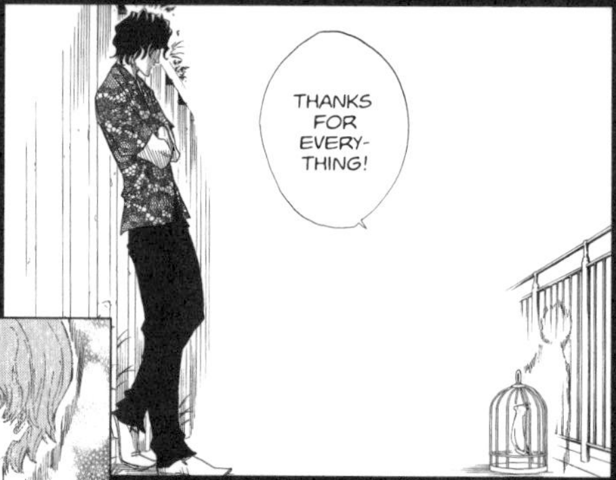
THANKS FOR EVERY-THING!

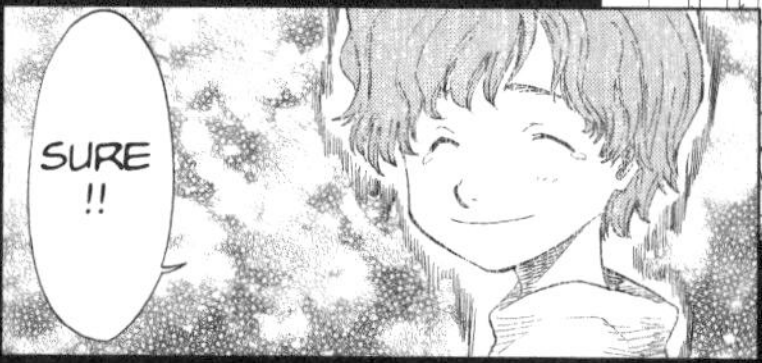
SURE !!

It is time for Yûichi and Chad to part ways. But the two are able to meet again in the not too distant future.

THE CONVICTION OF EVIL SPIRITS

THE GATES OF HELL

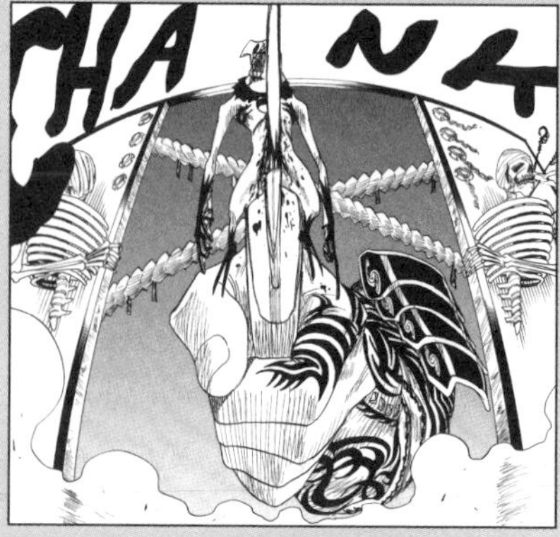

The Gates of Hell appear with a rumble the moment that Ichigo delivers the finishing blow to Shrieker. The doors open and a giant blade appears and stabs Shrieker! There is a creepy laugh as the evil spirit is led to Hell...

THE SUBLIMATION OF HOLLOWS

When a Hollow is sliced with a zanpaku-tô, it is cleansed of the sins it committed as a Hollow, and is led into the Soul Society. This is called sublimation. Souls that live in the Soul Society are reborn again into the human world.

THE DESTRUCTION OF HOLLOWS

Not all Hollows are sent to the Soul Society. Hollows that committed serious crimes when they were alive are sent to Hell. Also, if they are destroyed by a Quincy, Hollows are completely vanquished and cannot ever return to the Soul Society.

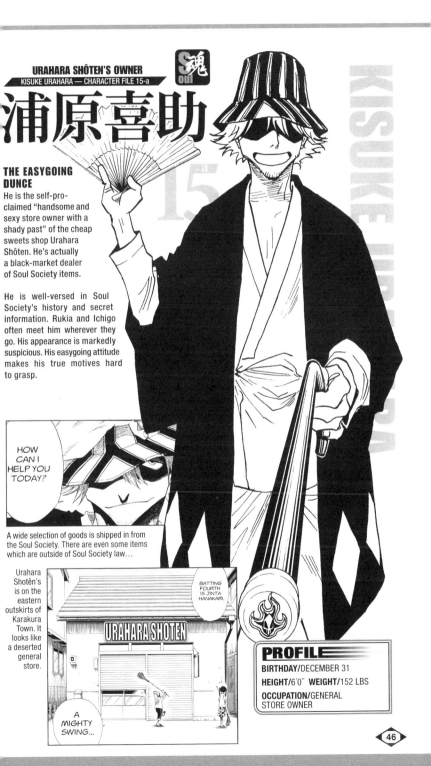

URAHARA SHÔTEN'S OWNER

KISUKE URAHARA — CHARACTER FILE 15-a

浦原喜助

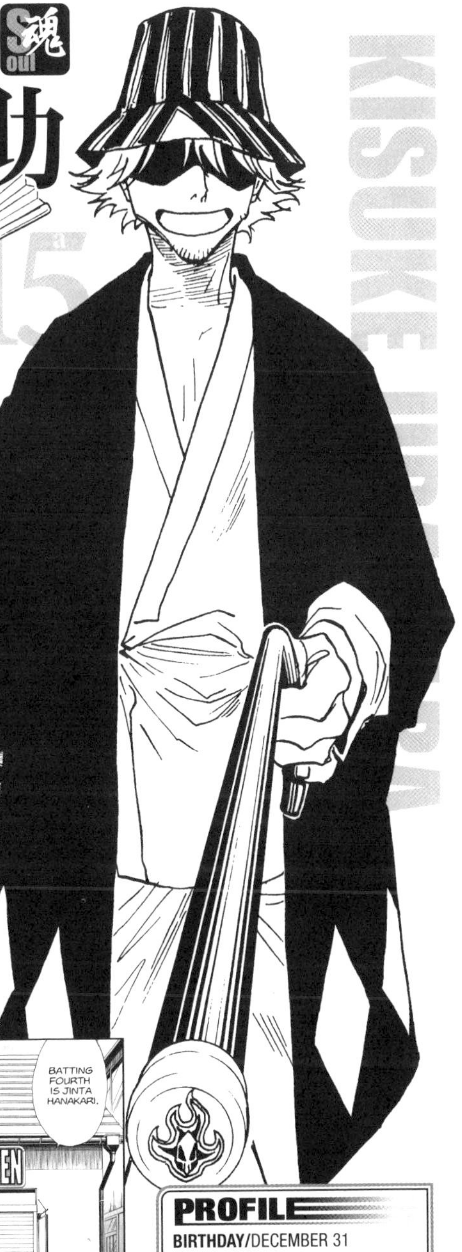

THE EASYGOING DUNCE

He is the self-proclaimed "handsome and sexy store owner with a shady past" of the cheap sweets shop Urahara Shôten. He's actually a black-market dealer of Soul Society items.

He is well-versed in Soul Society's history and secret information. Rukia and Ichigo often meet him wherever they go. His appearance is markedly suspicious. His easygoing attitude makes his true motives hard to grasp.

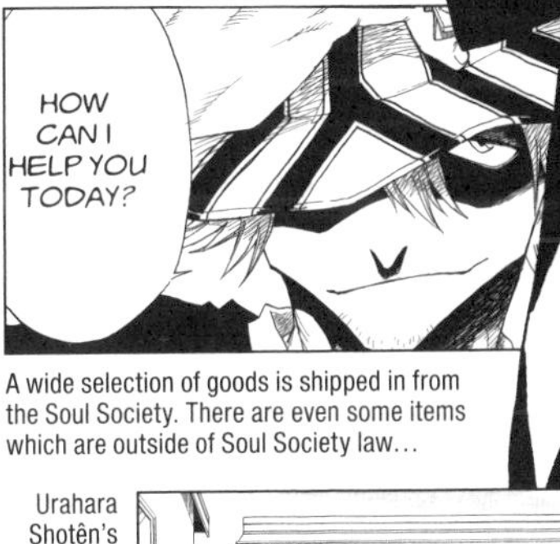
HOW CAN I HELP YOU TODAY?

A wide selection of goods is shipped in from the Soul Society. There are even some items which are outside of Soul Society law...

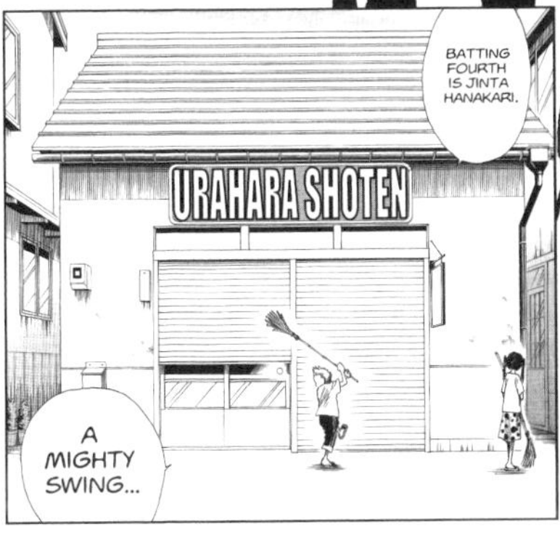
BATTING FOURTH IS JINTA HANAKARI.
URAHARA SHOTEN
A MIGHTY SWING...

Urahara Shotên's is on the eastern outskirts of Karakura Town. It looks like a deserted general store.

PROFILE

BIRTHDAY/DECEMBER 31

HEIGHT/6′0″ **WEIGHT**/152 LBS

OCCUPATION/GENERAL STORE OWNER

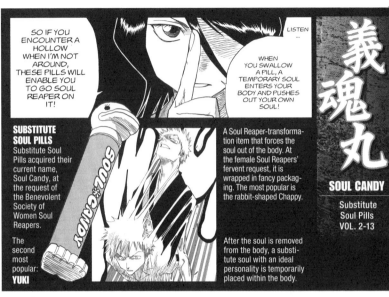

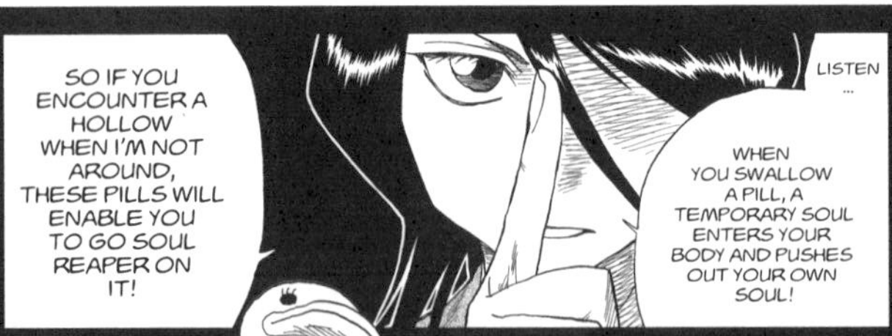
LISTEN ...
WHEN YOU SWALLOW A PILL, A TEMPORARY SOUL ENTERS YOUR BODY AND PUSHES OUT YOUR OWN SOUL!
SO IF YOU ENCOUNTER A HOLLOW WHEN I'M NOT AROUND, THESE PILLS WILL ENABLE YOU TO GO SOUL REAPER ON IT!

義魂丸

SOUL CANDY

Substitute Soul Pills VOL. 2-13

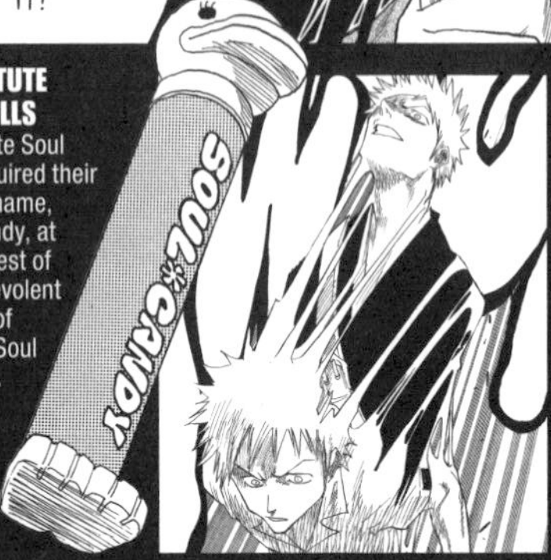
SOUL CANDY

A Soul Reaper-transformation item that forces the soul out of the body. At the female Soul Reapers' fervent request, it is wrapped in fancy packaging. The most popular is the rabbit-shaped Chappy.

After the soul is removed from the body, a substitute soul with an ideal personality is temporarily placed within the body.

SUBSTITUTE SOUL PILLS
Substitute Soul Pills acquired their current name, Soul Candy, at the request of the Benevolent Society of Women Soul Reapers.

The second most popular: **YUKI**

DOING BUSINESS IN UTTER CHAOS!!

URAHARA SHÔTEN EMPLOYEES

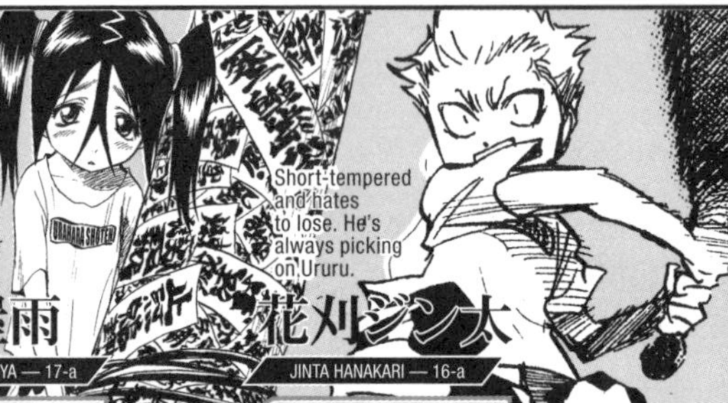
URAHARA SHOTEN

Short-tempered and hates to lose. He's always picking on Ururu.

花刈ジン太

JINTA HANAKARI — 16-a

PROFILE
BIRTHDAY/APRIL 4
HEIGHT/4′1″
WEIGHT/55 LBS

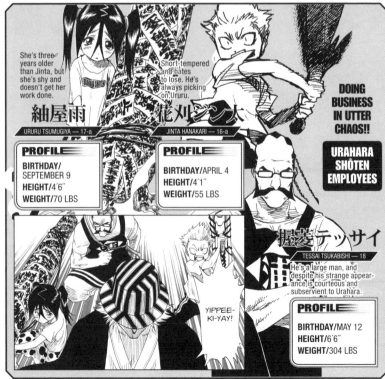

She's three years older than Jinta, but she's shy and doesn't get her work done.

紬屋雨

URURU TSUMUGIYA — 17-a

PROFILE
BIRTHDAY/ SEPTEMBER 9
HEIGHT/4′6″
WEIGHT/70 LBS

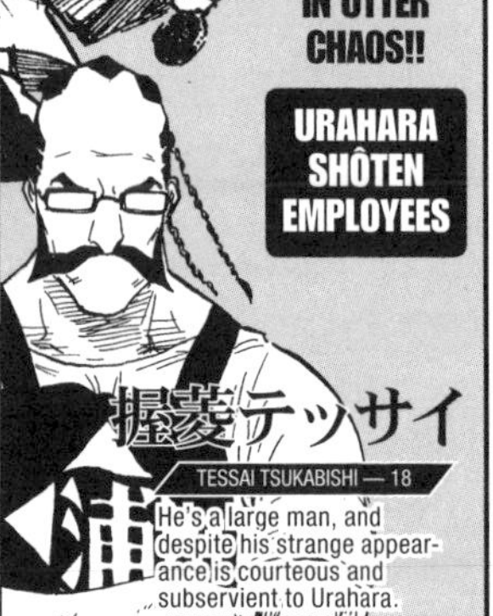

握菱テッサイ

TESSAI TSUKABISHI — 18

He's a large man, and despite his strange appearance is courteous and subservient to Urahara.

PROFILE
BIRTHDAY/MAY 12
HEIGHT/6′6″
WEIGHT/304 LBS

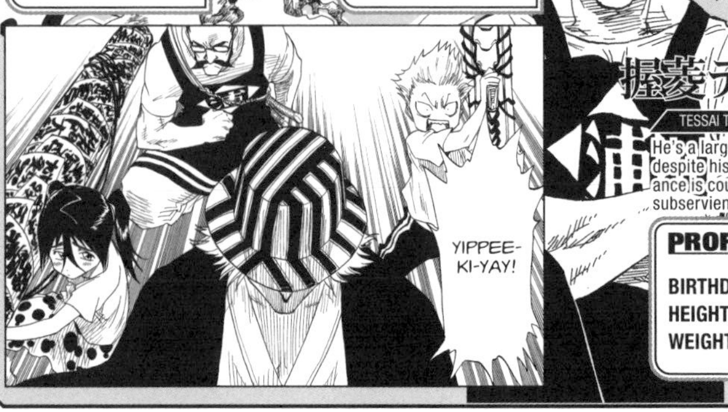
YIPPEE-KI-YAY!

UNDERPOD MOD-SOUL

An underpod mod-soul that was developed in the Soul Society. He was supposed to be disposed of when the project was cancelled. Luckily, he was mixed in with some shoddy mod-souls and was able to escape. Ururu accidentally gave him to Rukia. He planned to run away with Ichigo's body. He has incredible leg strength. He surpassed the unofficial vertical jump record by over 16 feet.

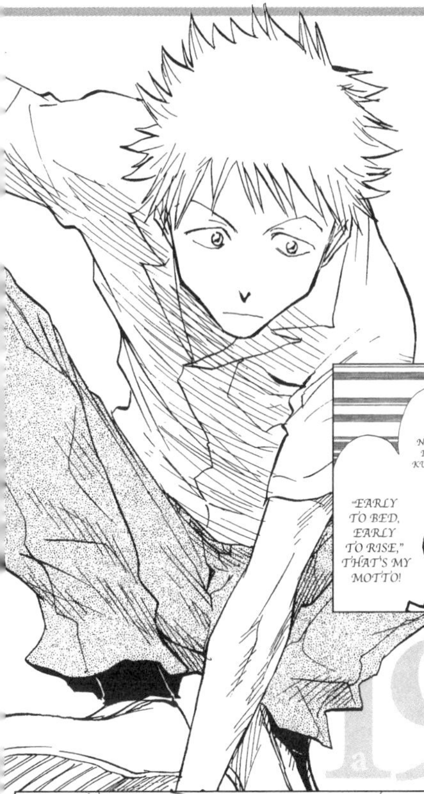

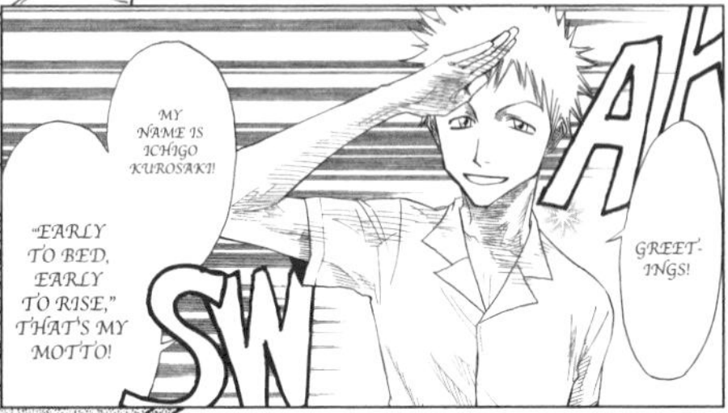
AK
GREET-INGS!
MY NAME IS ICHIGO KUROSAKI!
"EARLY TO BED, EARLY TO RISE," THAT'S MY MOTTO!
SW

ICHIGO VERSION

KON — CHARACTER FILE 19-a

19a コン KON

PROFILE

BIRTHDAY/ DECEMBER 30
HEIGHT/5′7″
WEIGHT/134 LBS

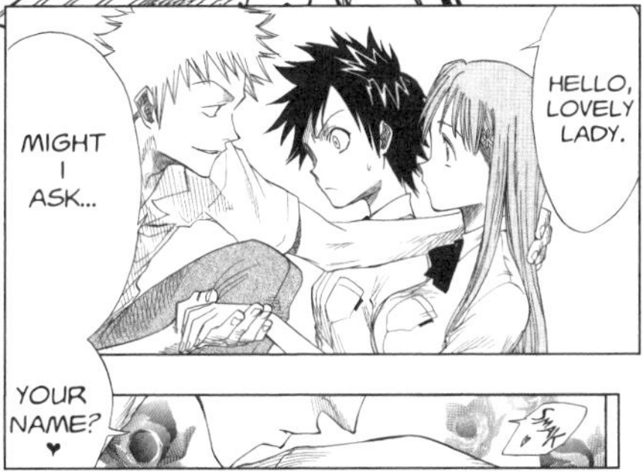
HELLO, LOVELY LADY.
MIGHT I ASK...
YOUR NAME? ♥

INDISCREET TOWARDS CUTE GIRLS?!

He's cheery, lewd, and loves big breasts. He doesn't show any interest in small-breasted women (Rukia is the exception). He's a straightforward being who lives by his instincts.

MOCK SOUL FOR ANTI-HOLLOW COMBAT

"MOD-SOUL"

Mock souls that specialize in combat. They were developed for Spearhead, a project that aimed to inject special fighting souls into human corpses. The project was abandoned for ethical concerns, and an order was given to have all the mod-souls destroyed.

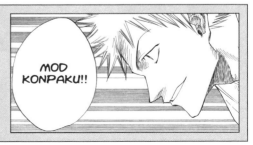

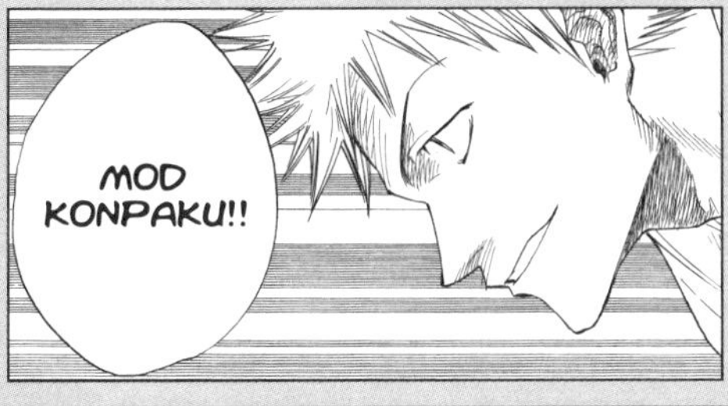
MOD KONPAKU!!

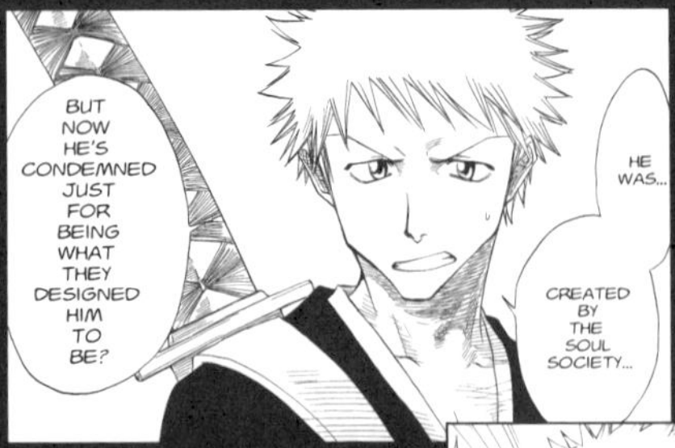
HE WAS...
CREATED BY THE SOUL SOCIETY...
BUT NOW HE'S CONDEMNED JUST FOR BEING WHAT THEY DESIGNED HIM TO BE?

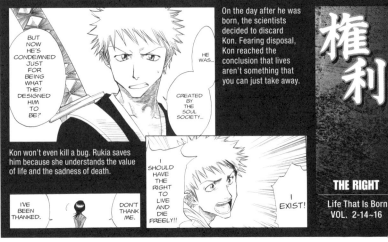

On the day after he was born, the scientists decided to discard Kon. Fearing disposal, Kon reached the conclusion that lives aren't something that you can just take away.

権利

THE RIGHT

Life That Is Born
VOL. 2-14~16

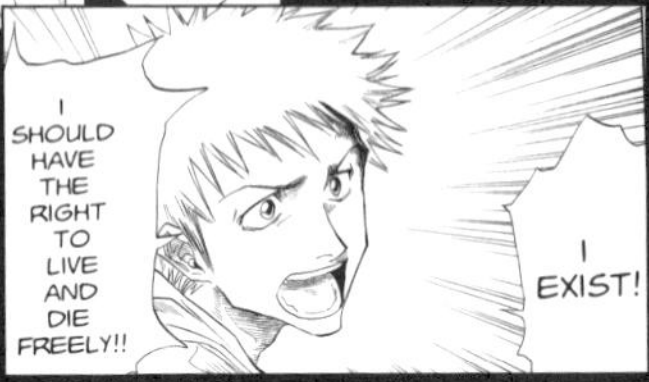
I EXIST!
I SHOULD HAVE THE RIGHT TO LIVE AND DIE FREELY!!

Kon won't even kill a bug. Rukia saves him because she understands the value of life and the sadness of death.

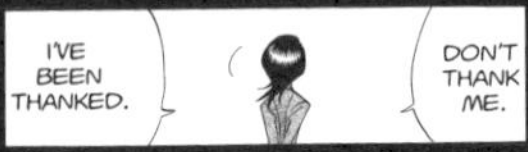
DON'T THANK ME.
I'VE BEEN THANKED.

STUFFED ANIMAL VERSION

KON — CHARACTER FILE 19-b

コン KON 19

THE KUROSAKI FAMILY'S NEW FREELOADER

The mod-soul that was taken from Urahara partly by force. He was put into a stuffed animal that was discarded by the roadside because Rukia and Ichigo couldn't find a convenient body for him. His name, Kon, comes from the word kaizo konpaku, which means mod-soul in Japanese (Ichigo says that he would have been annoyed if Kon were called "Kai" because it sounds cool). Since then, Kon has switched between the stuffed animal and Ichigo's body many times.

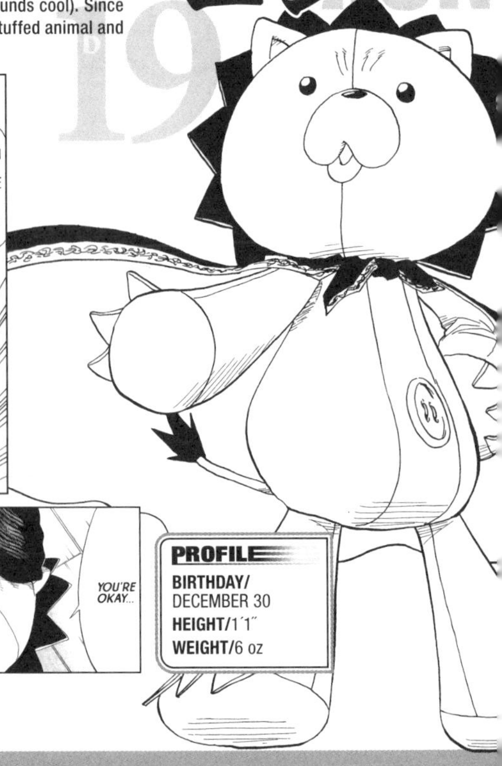

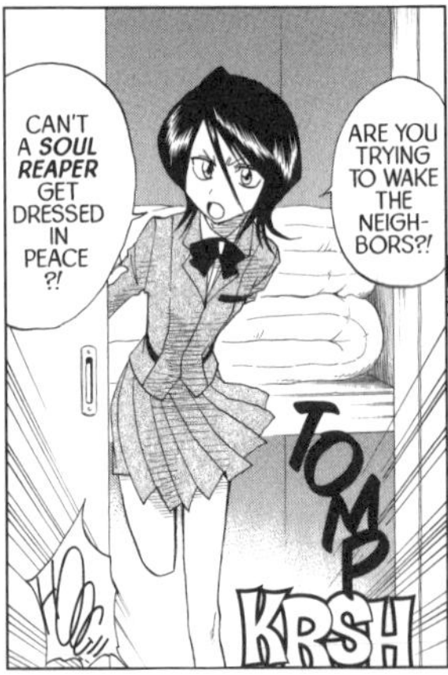
ARE YOU TRYING TO WAKE THE NEIGHBORS?!
CAN'T A SOUL REAPER GET DRESSED IN PEACE?!
TOMP
KRSH

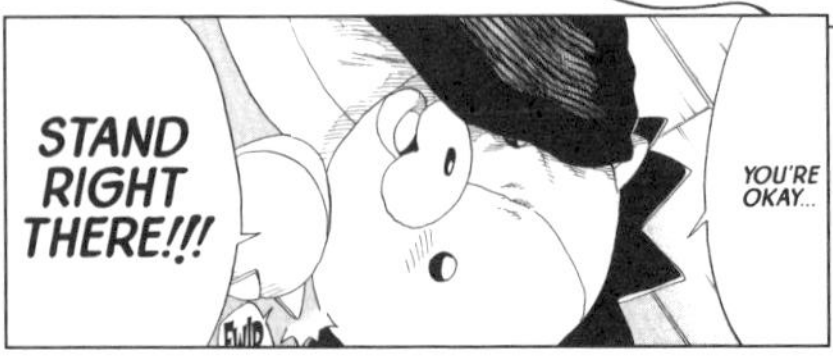
YOU'RE OKAY...
STAND RIGHT THERE!!!

PROFILE

BIRTHDAY/ DECEMBER 30

HEIGHT/ 1′1″

WEIGHT/ 6 oz

"SHE WAS THE CENTER OF OUR UNIVERSE."

Ichigo lost his mother Masaki when he was nine. Ichigo's childhood friend Tatsuki said that Masaki was "the most beautiful mother." She always smiled, and treated Ichigo and his sisters gently. She was the perfect mother. She was a cherished and beloved member of her family. She gave the Kurosakis peace and relief.

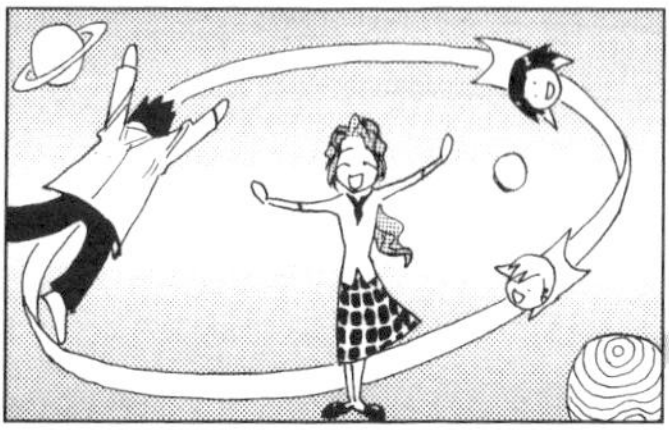

Masaki was loved by everyone and was always the center of the household.

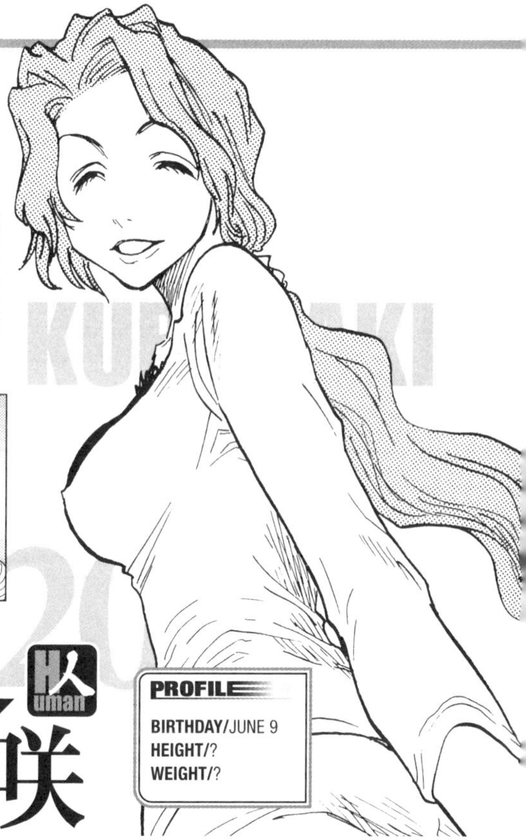

LOVE THAT TOLERATES EVERYTHING

MASAKI KUROSAKI — CHARACTER FILE 20

黒崎真咲

PROFILE

BIRTHDAY/JUNE 9
HEIGHT/?
WEIGHT/?

"...I REMEMBER THINKING I WANTED TO PROTECT MY MOTHER, WHO ALWAYS PROTECTED ME."

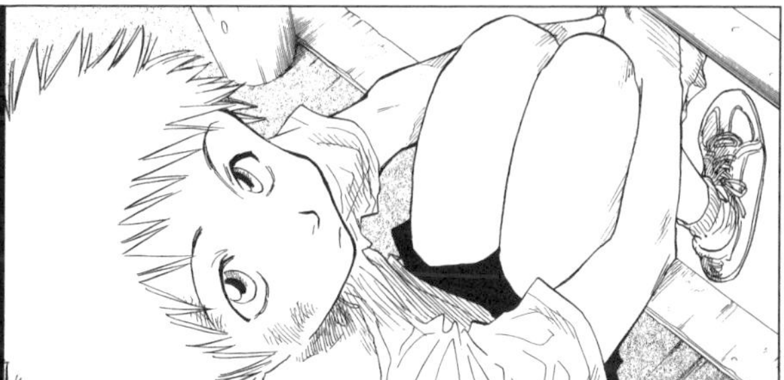

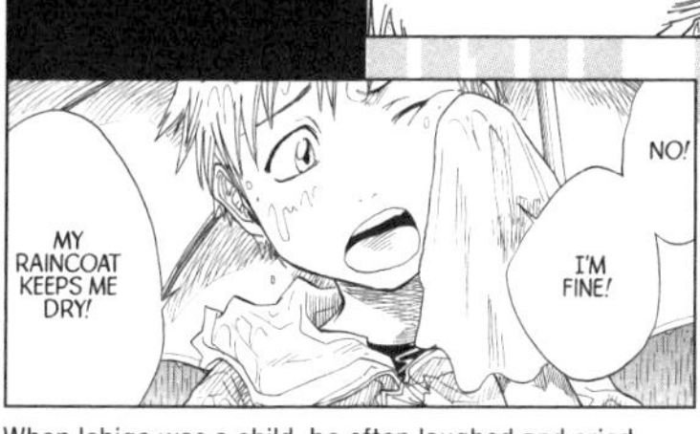
NO!
I'M FINE!
MY RAINCOAT KEEPS ME DRY!

When Ichigo was a child, he often laughed and cried.

A NINE-YEAR-OLD BOY

ICHIGO KUROSAKI — CHARACTER FILE 1-c

黒崎一護

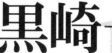

He was a mama's boy who was always by Masaki's side. His spirit energy was strong even at a young age.

6/17

JUNE 17

The Continually Falling Rain
VOL. 3-17~19

June 17, six years ago. The rain poured heavily during the early summer. Under the gloomy, gray skies, the river became dangerously flooded. Ichigo was walking along the riverside with his mother, holding her hand, when he saw a girl with short hair. The girl was standing in the rain without an umbrella, and looked as if she were planning to jump in the river. Ichigo broke free from Masaki and ran towards the girl. Why Ichigo decided to run after the girl is unknown. When he regained consciousness, the rain was pelting his body and the girl was gone. Masaki, embracing Ichigo as if to shield him from the rain, was cold. She never moved again.

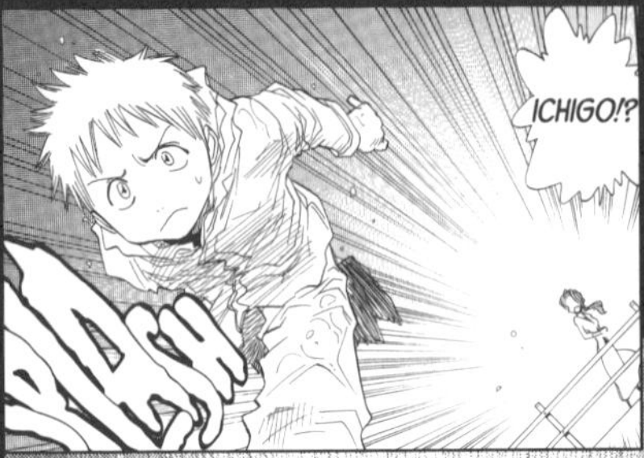
ICHIGO!?

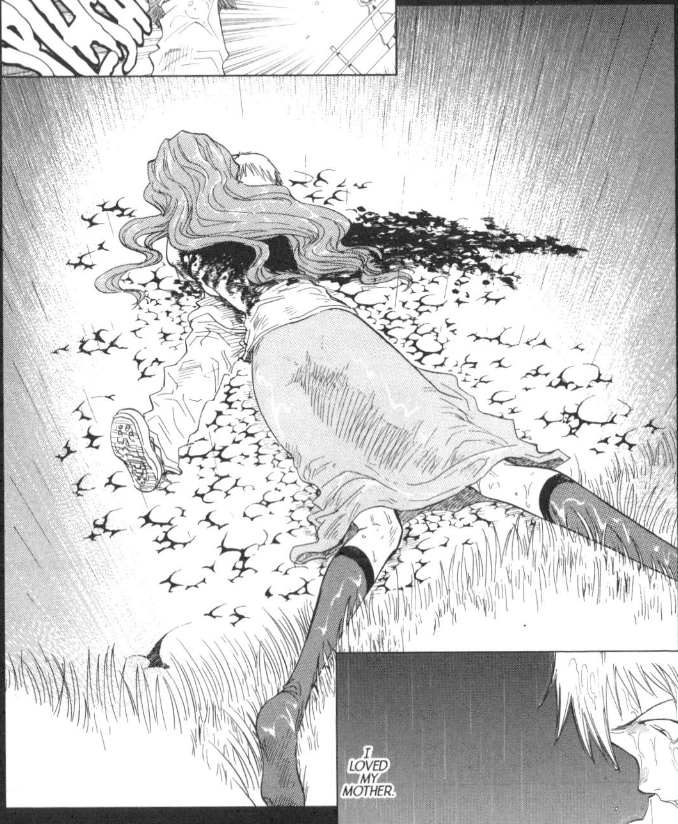

Ichigo lost his beloved mother six years ago on June 17. It never stopped raining.

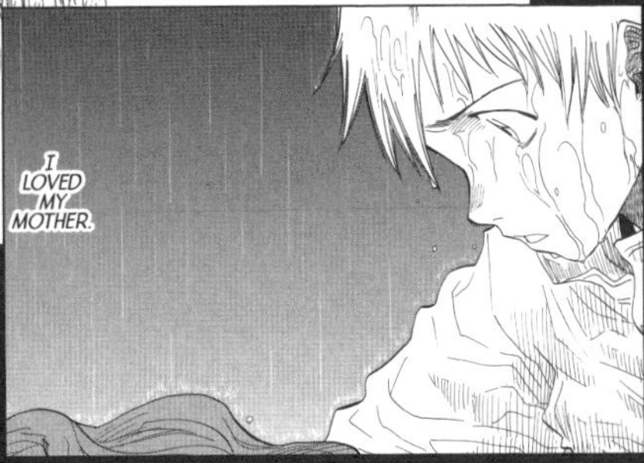
I LOVED MY MOTHER.

Masaki, whom he was supposed to protect, was dead. That scar was etched deeply into his heart.

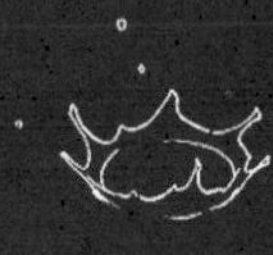

It's been six years since his mother Masaki passed away. Ichigo's sorrow has faded with time and he's returned to a normal life. But the anniversary of Masaki's death reawakens painful memories. Visiting Masaki's grave has become an annual event for the Kurosaki family. Ichigo and his family finish visiting the grave and pass the rest of the day as they please. That's when Karin notices a girl standing by the cliff. It is the same girl that Ichigo encountered six years ago. Ichigo and Rukia rush towards the area when they sense an unusual spiritual pressure. Can they get there in time to save Yuzu and Karin from the evil clutches of the Hollow that's attacking them?!

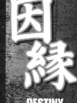

因縁

DESTINY

The Hollow From Six Years Ago
VOL. 3-20~21

AAAK
AAAAAAH!

THIS GIRL...
KRERK
KRERK
ACK
ACK
...IS TOO NOISY!

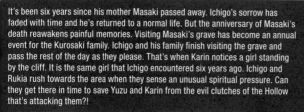

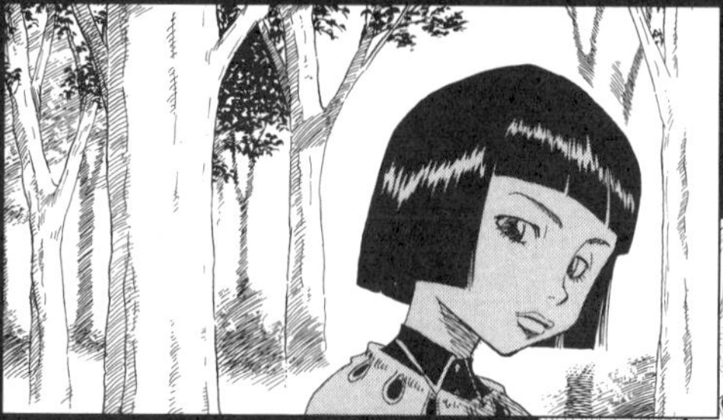

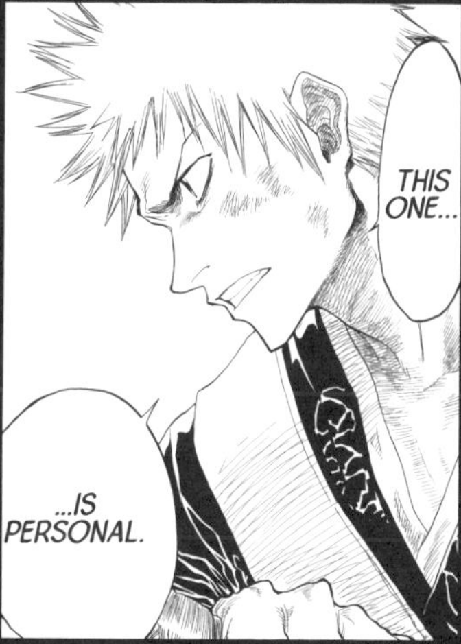

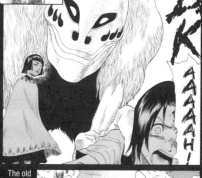

The old Hollow tries to eat Yuzu and Karin when they approach his bait.

The girl that he met six years ago. Bewildered at their sudden reunion, Ichigo fervently presses the girl for answers.

THIS ONE...
...IS PERSONAL.

RUKIA AND ICHIGO

A DEEPENING BOND

Masaki's death is a deep scar that Ichigo has yet to talk about. Ichigo begins to trust Rukia on a deeper level when she considerately avoids asking questions about Masaki. Their mutual trust shortens the distance between them.

WHEN YOU FEEL LIKE TALKING...
...WHEN YOU WANT TO TELL ME...

I'LL LISTEN.

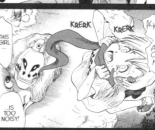

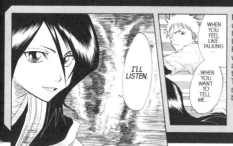

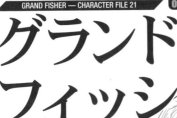

AN OLD SOUL REAPER-EATING HOLLOW

GRAND FISHER — CHARACTER FILE 21

H 虚 ollow

グランドフィッシャー

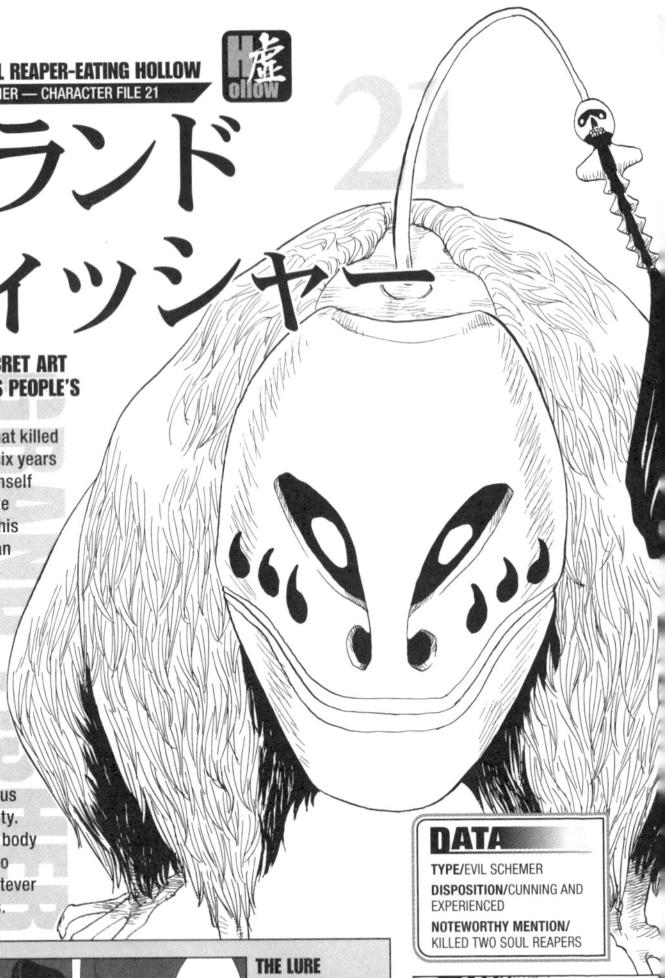

A CUNNING SECRET ART THAT CONFUSES PEOPLE'S EMOTIONS

The old Hollow that killed Ichigo's mother six years ago. He hides himself and alters the lure that grows from his head into a human shape. He feeds on humans with strong spiritual energy. He has increased his strength this way and used it to evade the Soul Reapers for 54 years. He's pretty famous in the Soul Society. He has a special body that allows him to change into whatever shape he wishes.

DATA

TYPE/EVIL SCHEMER

DISPOSITION/CUNNING AND EXPERIENCED

NOTEWORTHY MENTION/ KILLED TWO SOUL REAPERS

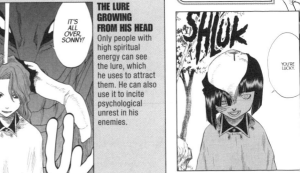

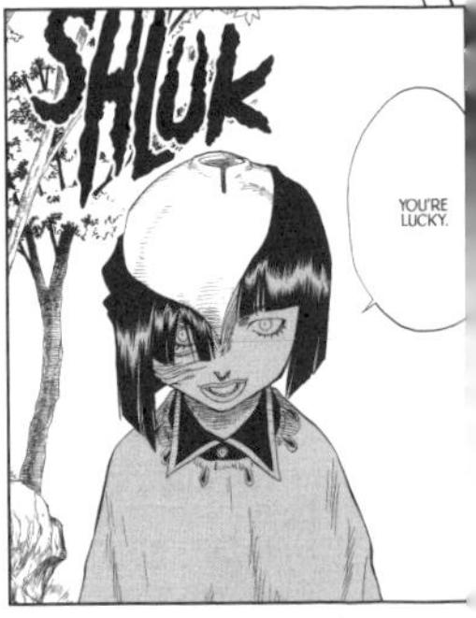
SHLUK
YOU'RE LUCKY.

The top of the girl's head splits to reveal her true form. She is actually a lure.

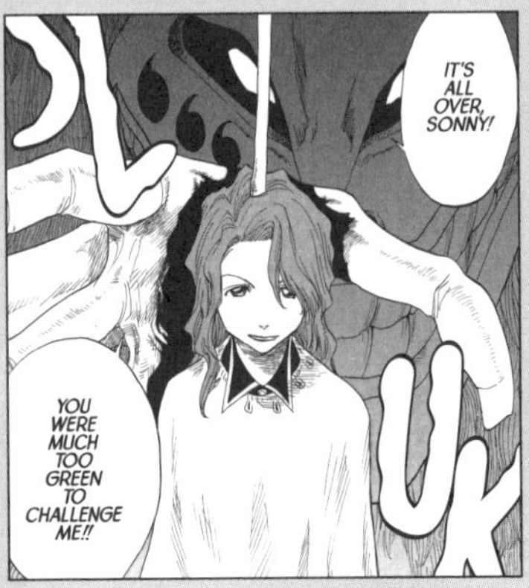
IT'S ALL OVER, SONNY!
YOU WERE MUCH TOO GREEN TO CHALLENGE ME!!

THE LURE GROWING FROM HIS HEAD

Only people with high spiritual energy can see the lure, which he uses to attract them. He can also use it to incite psychological unrest in his enemies.

仇討

VENGEANCE

A battle defending pride
VOL. 3-22~25

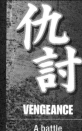

Ichigo turns down Rukia's help and swings his sword to avenge his mother! Grand Fisher uses the claws on his left hand to peer into his opponent's memories and his right hand to copy a form onto his lure. Ichigo cannot hide his shock when the lure transforms into his mother...

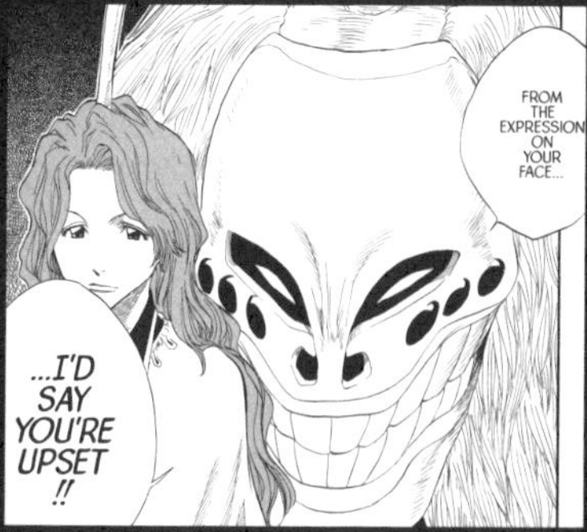
FROM THE EXPRESSION ON YOUR FACE...
...I'D SAY YOU'RE UPSET !!

HIS MOTHER'S UNFORGETTABLE FACE
The lure, posing as Masaki the way she was long ago, affectionately calls Ichigo's name. Ichigo's heart wavers.

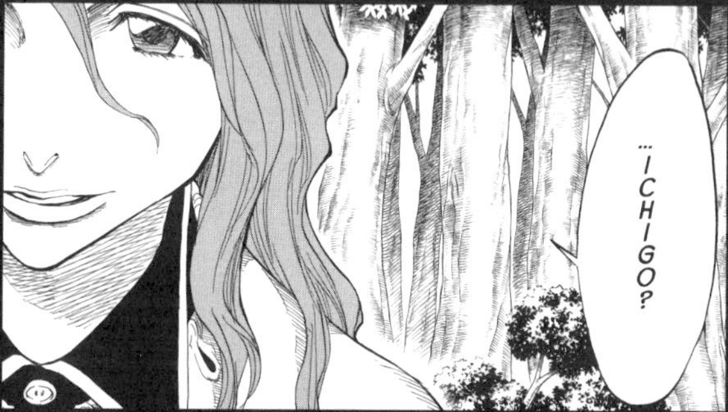
...ICHIGO?

ICHIGO'S RESOLVE
Even though Ichigo delivers a fatal blow, the fierce battle is unresolved... Ichigo vows to become even stronger in order to avenge Masaki.

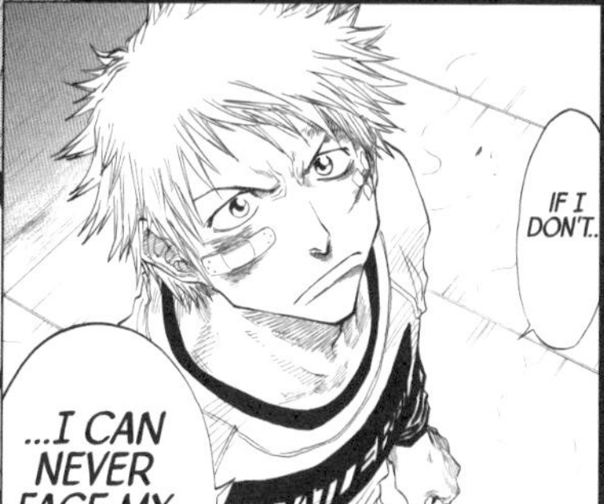
IF I DON'T..
...I CAN NEVER FACE MY MOTHER!

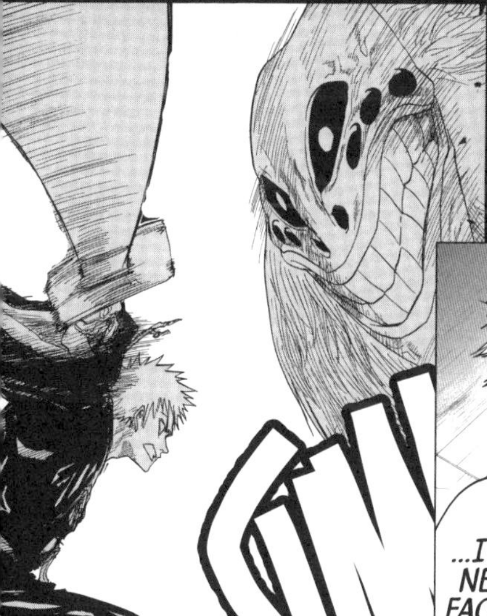

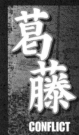

葛藤
CONFLICT

Rukia's memorie
VOL. 3-23~24

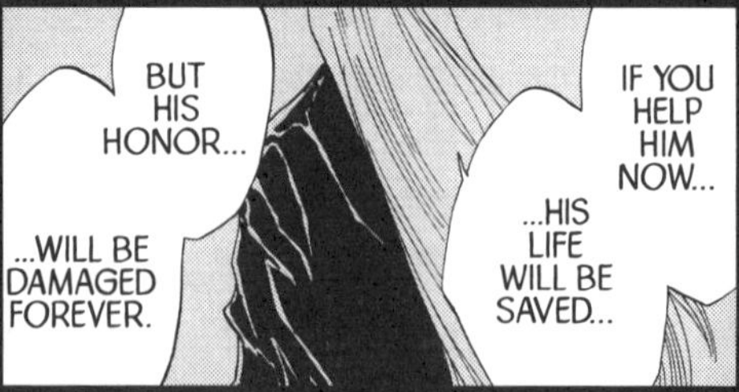
IF YOU HELP HIM NOW...
...HIS LIFE WILL BE SAVED...
BUT HIS HONOR...
...WILL BE DAMAGED FOREVER.

When going into battle, one must decide whether one is fighting a battle to protect one's life, or a battle to protect one's pride.

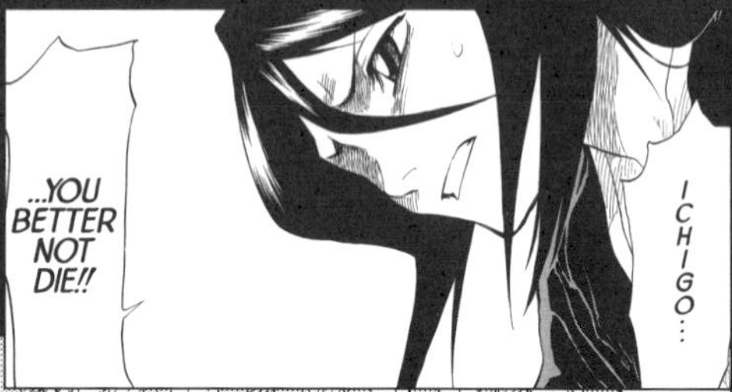
ICHIGO...
...YOU BETTER NOT DIE!!

Rukia is worried about the outcome of the battle, which is out of her hands. She is haunted by a recurring memory. Rukia tells herself that this battle is a battle to protect Ichigo's pride, and mutters several times to herself not to interfere. Ichigo barely survives, and Rukia is relieved, saying, "Thank you..."

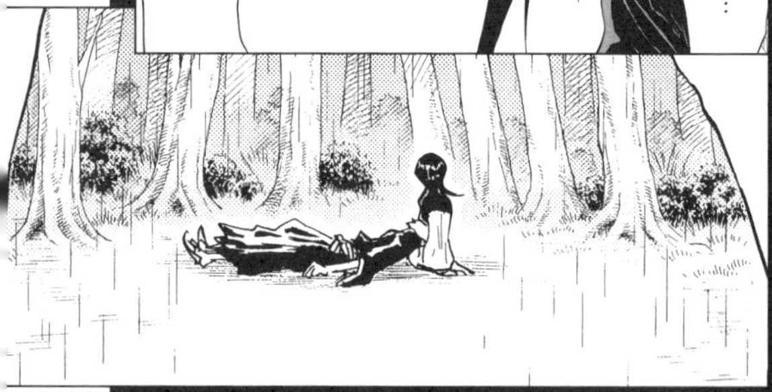

Ichigo passes out. Rukia gently places his head on her lap and keeps watch over him in the continually falling rain.

THE HOLLOW ARMY THAT SLINKS IN THE DARKNESS

THE HOLLOW ORGANIZATION

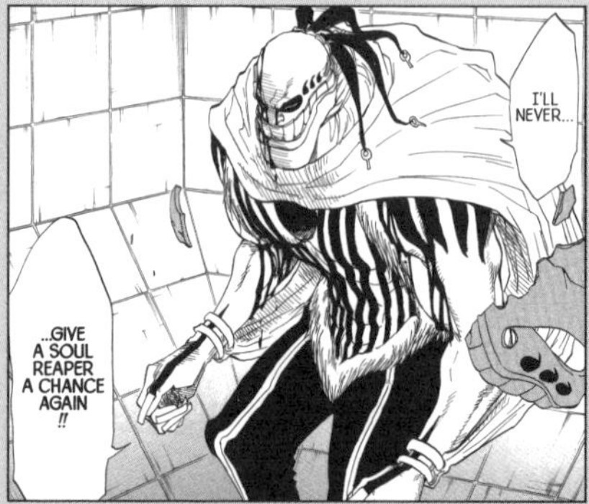
I'LL NEVER...
...GIVE A SOUL REAPER A CHANCE AGAIN!!

The Grand Fisher received fatal injuries to his main body, so he discards it and retreats into his lure. He gains even more power and vows to take his revenge on Ichigo.

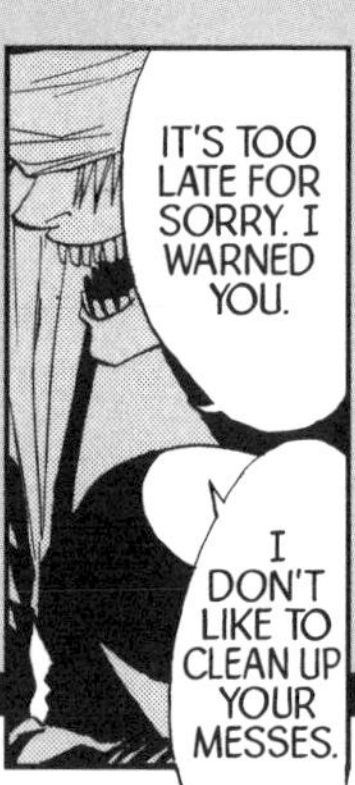
IT'S TOO LATE FOR SORRY. I WARNED YOU.
I DON'T LIKE TO CLEAN UP YOUR MESSES.

A HOLLOW'S MASK
Grand Fisher is completely healed and has his mask ripped off. He's in a completely different form from when he fought Ichigo. The Hollow army tries to gain even more powers by removing their masks. They'll be seen again in the near future, standing in Ichigo's way...

KARAKURA 1ST HIGH SCHOOL

CLASS 1-3 CLASSMATES

ICHIGO AND RUKIA'S UNIQUE CLASSMATES. STAND, ATTENTION, BOW!

浅野啓吾

KEIGO ASANO — 22

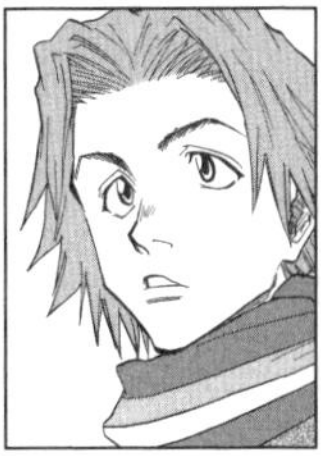

He looks like he'd be popular, with his fairly good looks and playful disposition, but he's an unfortunate stray sheep at a distance from the flock.

小川みちる

MICHIRU OGAWA — 24

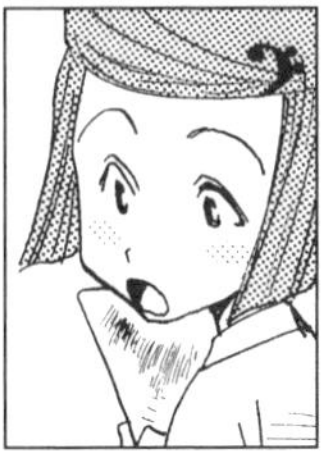

A shy girl who's in the same craft club as Uryû. She's a little scared of Ichigo.

越智美諭

Teacher

MISATO OCHI — 28

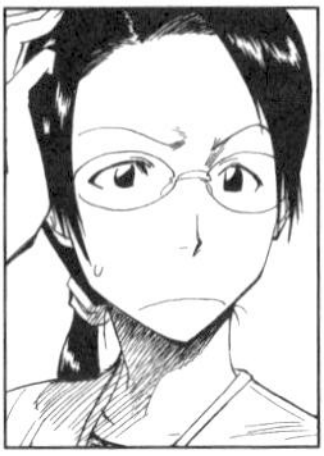

She leads the class in a carefree and haphazard style, even though she has a lot of problem students. She teaches Japanese.

小島水色

MIZUIRO KOJIMA — 23

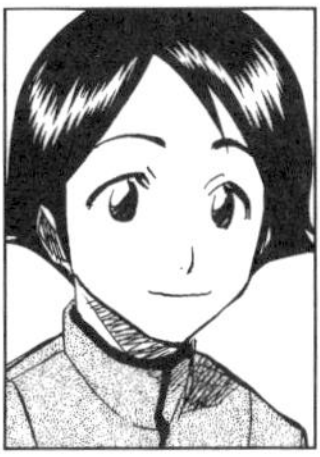

He has a cute face, but he's actually a [redacted]. He's usually with Keigo, but their relationship is closer to that of master and servant.

本匠千鶴

CHIZURU HONSHO — 25

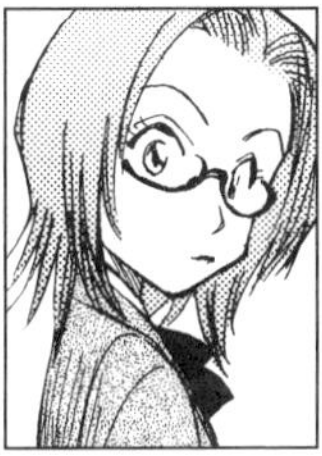

A big, beautifully blooming lily. She repeatedly tries to seduce Orihime, but is always stopped by Tatsuki.

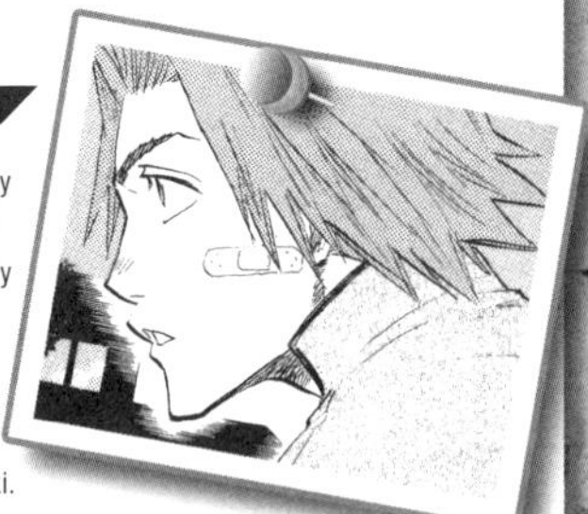

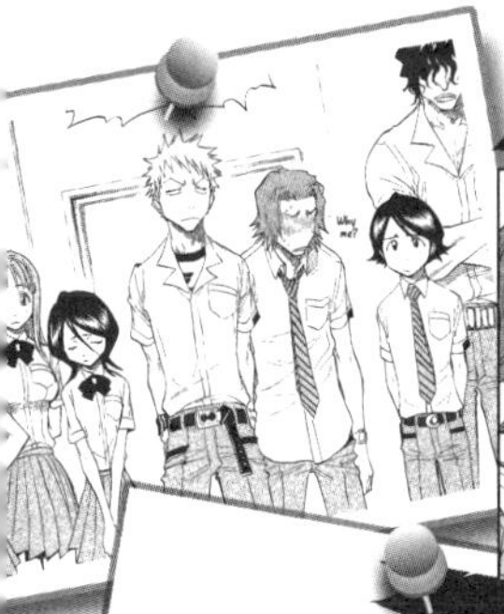

夏井真花

MAHANA NATSUI — 26

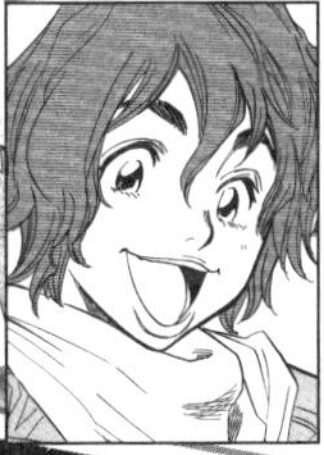

A voluptuous, big breasted girl who's second in looks only to Orihime. She always has her shirt open at the neck. She has a manly, straight-forward personality.

国枝鈴

RYÔ KUNIEDA — 27

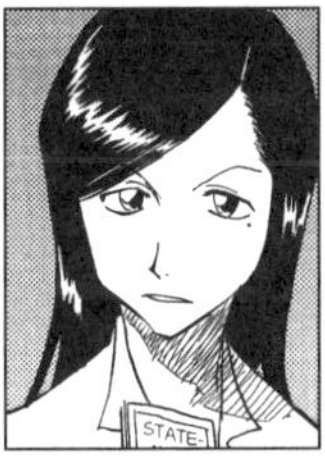
STATE-

An honor student who serves as the class president. In the track and field team, she's in charge of sprinting. She can run 100 meters in 12 seconds flat.

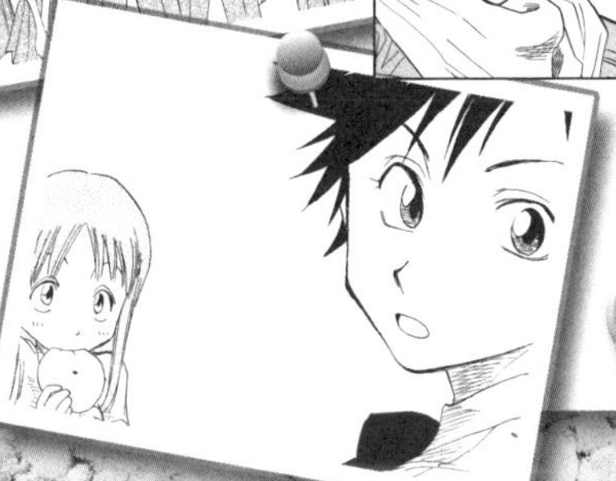

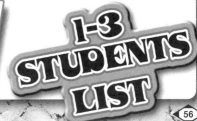

1-3 STUDENTS LIST

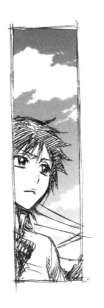

bleach   25.2

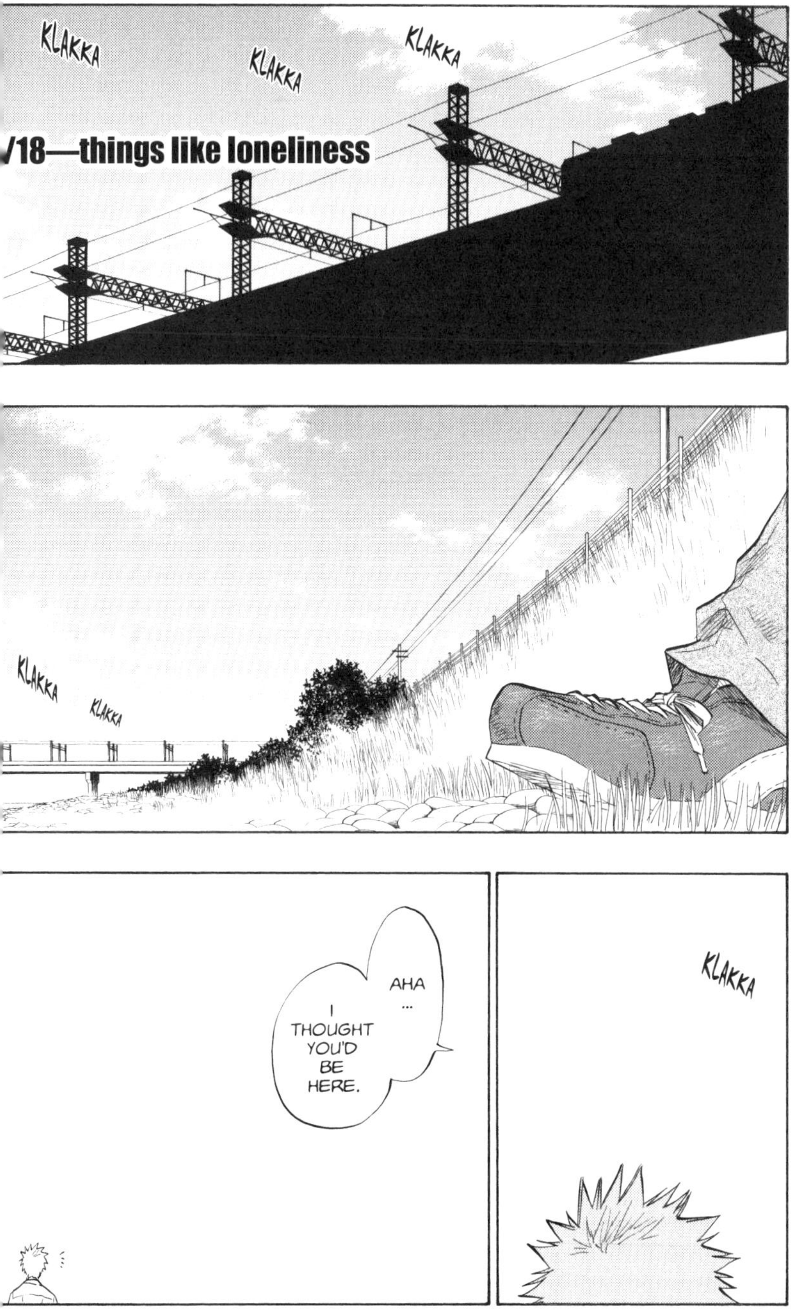
KLAKKA
KLAKKA
KLAKKA
/18—things like loneliness
KLAKKA
KLAKKA
KLAKKA
AHA...
I THOUGHT YOU'D BE HERE.

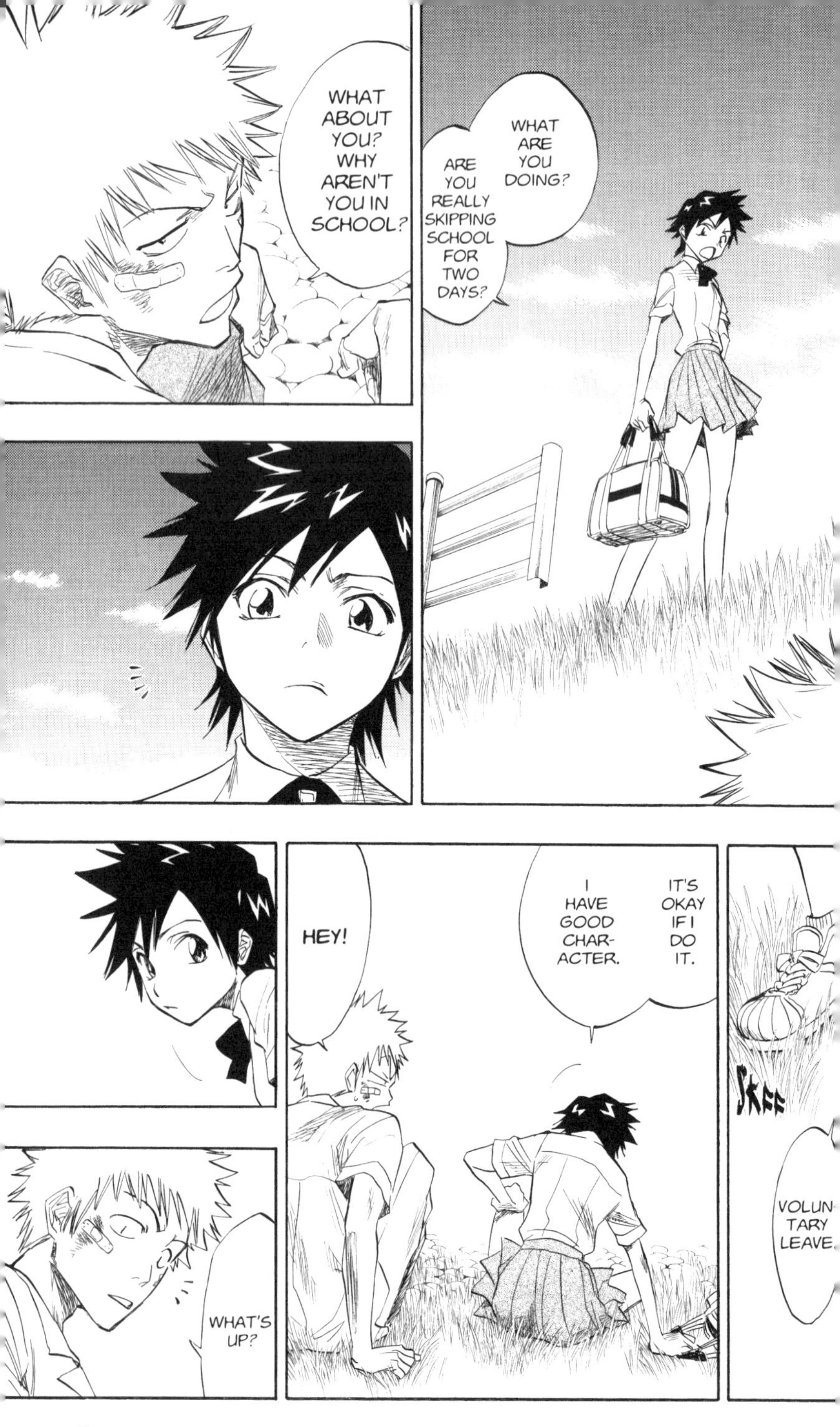
WHAT ARE YOU DOING?
ARE YOU REALLY SKIPPING SCHOOL FOR TWO DAYS?
WHAT ABOUT YOU? WHY AREN'T YOU IN SCHOOL?
SKFF
VOLUNTARY LEAVE.
IT'S OKAY IF I DO IT.
I HAVE GOOD CHARACTER.
HEY!
WHAT'S UP?

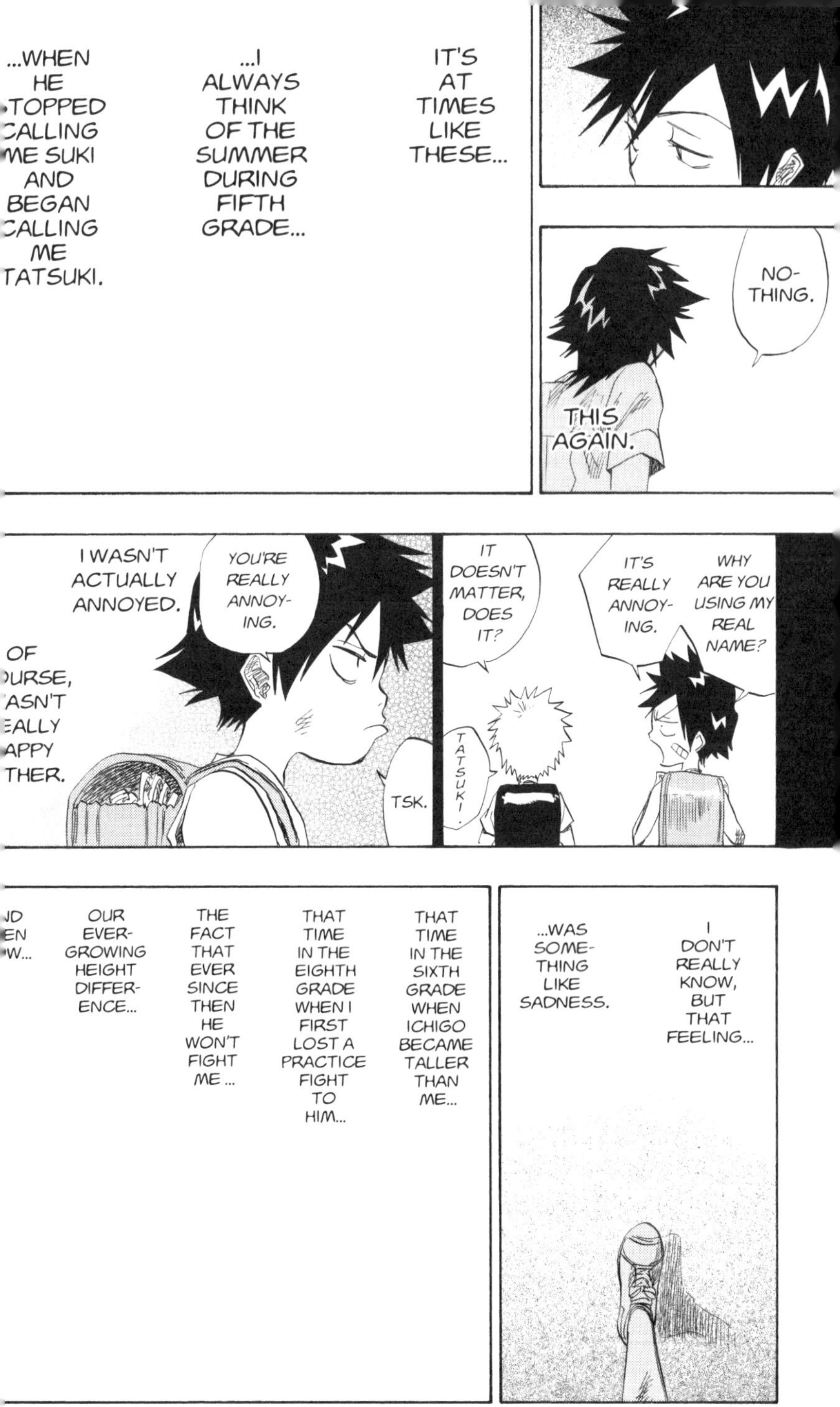
NO-THING.
THIS AGAIN.
IT'S AT TIMES LIKE THESE...
...I ALWAYS THINK OF THE SUMMER DURING FIFTH GRADE...
...WHEN HE TOPPED CALLING ME SUKI AND BEGAN CALLING ME TATSUKI.
WHY ARE YOU USING MY REAL NAME?
IT'S REALLY ANNOY-ING.
IT DOESN'T MATTER, DOES IT?
TATSUKI.
YOU'RE REALLY ANNOY-ING.
TSK.
I WASN'T ACTUALLY ANNOYED.
OF URSE, ASN'T EALLY APPY THER.
I DON'T REALLY KNOW, BUT THAT FEELING...
...WAS SOME-THING LIKE SADNESS.
THAT TIME IN THE SIXTH GRADE WHEN ICHIGO BECAME TALLER THAN ME...
THAT TIME IN THE EIGHTH GRADE WHEN I FIRST LOST A PRACTICE FIGHT TO HIM...
THE FACT THAT EVER SINCE THEN HE WON'T FIGHT ME...
OUR EVER-GROWING HEIGHT DIFFER-ENCE...

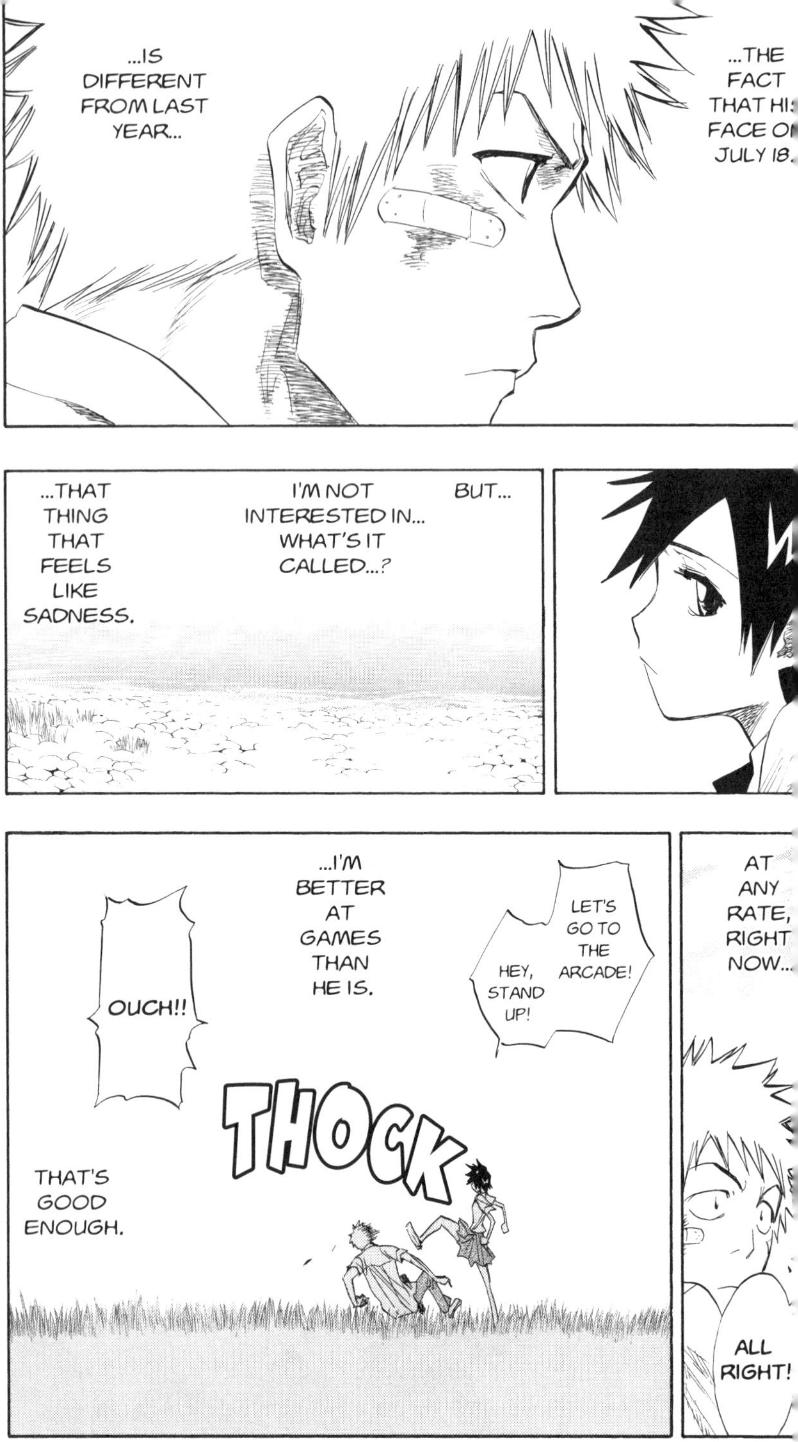
...THE FACT THAT HI FACE O JULY 18.
...IS DIFFERENT FROM LAST YEAR...
BUT...
I'M NOT INTERESTED IN... WHAT'S IT CALLED...?
...THAT THING THAT FEELS LIKE SADNESS.
AT ANY RATE, RIGHT NOW...
ALL RIGHT!
LET'S GO TO THE ARCADE!
HEY, STAND UP!
...I'M BETTER AT GAMES THAN HE IS.
OUCH!!
THOCK
THAT'S GOOD ENOUGH.

end

Kanonji talks likes he's stuck in the '70s, baby.

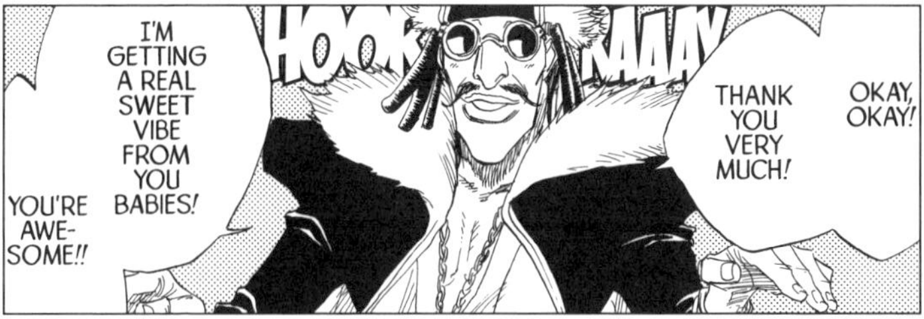
OKAY, OKAY!
THANK YOU VERY MUCH!
I'M GETTING A REAL SWEET VIBE FROM YOU BABIES!
YOU'RE AWE-SOME!!

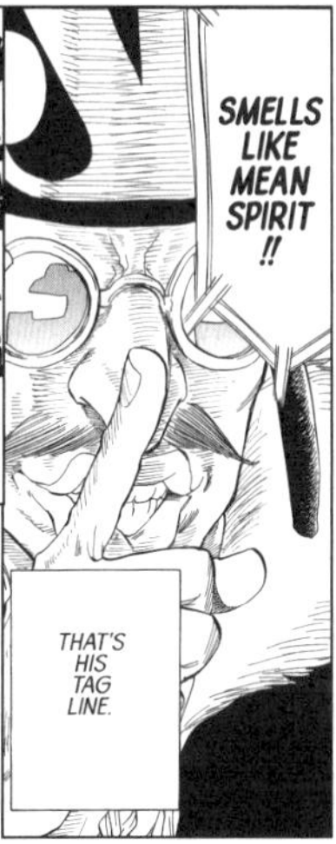
SMELLS LIKE MEAN SPIRIT!!

THAT'S HIS TAG LINE.

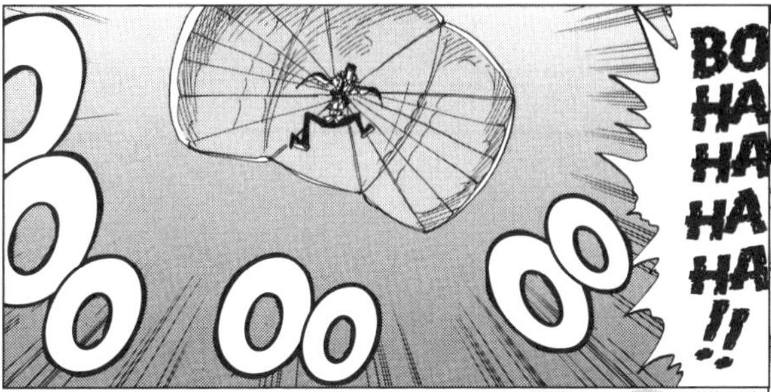
BO HA HA HA HA!!
OOOOOOOOOO

PROFILE

BIRTHDAY/MARCH 23
HEIGHT/6′1″ **WEIGHT/**156 LBS
BLOOD TYPE/B0

A TOP-NOTCH ENTERTAINER

It's Kanonji's style to use a lot of elaborate entrances and catchphrases.

THE CHARISMATIC SPIRIT MEDIUM

DON KANONJI — CHARACTER FILE 29-a

ドン・観音寺

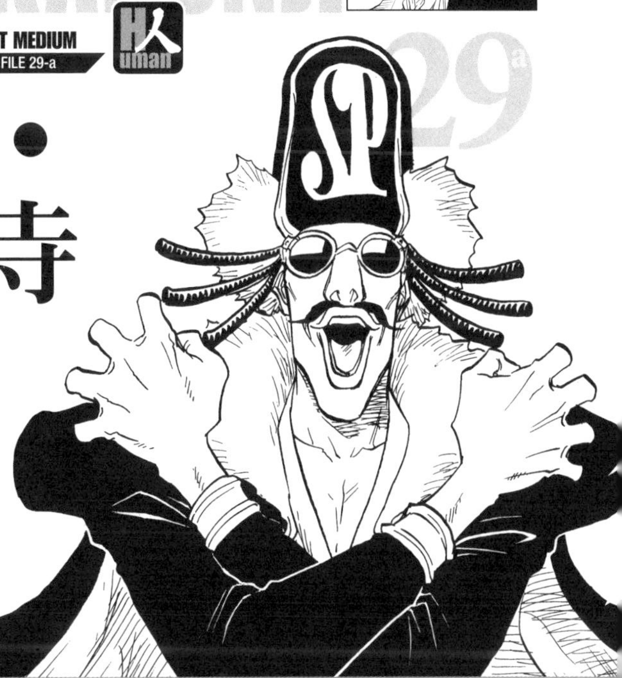

THE PSYCHIC HERO OF THE LIVING ROOM!!

The charismatic spirit medium that makes audiences across the country go wild. Kanonji is best known for his signature pose, the one where he crosses his hands across his chest and loudly laughs, "Bo ha ha ha ha!" Kanonji is so popular that people copy his pose!!

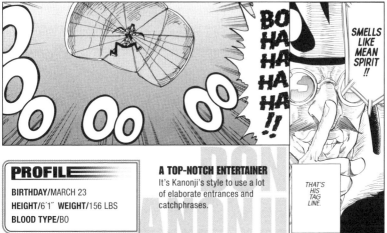

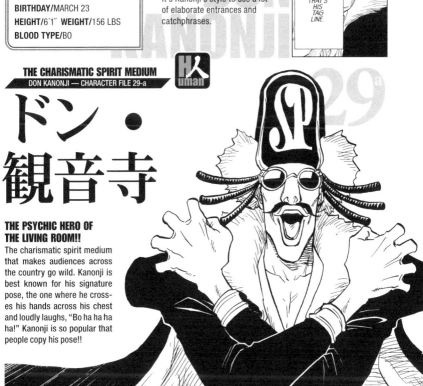

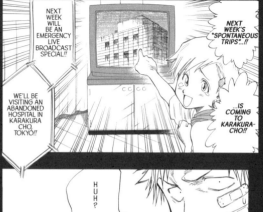

浄霊

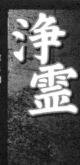

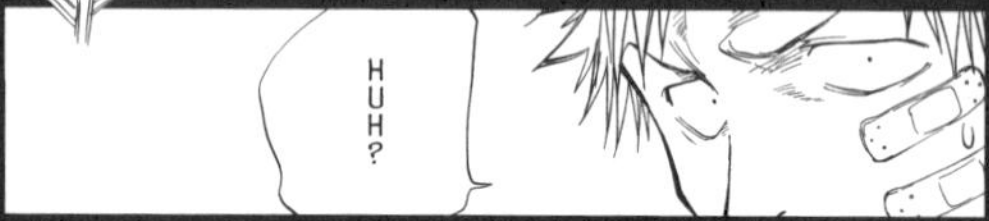

PURGE SPIRITS

An emergency live broadcast
VOL. 4-27

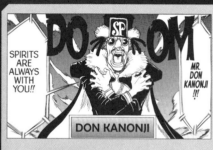

A vengeful spirit's screams echo throughout Karakura's abandoned hospital every night. *Spiritual Hot Spots* is going to have a live broadcast here next week.

NEXT WEEK'S "SPONTANEOUS TRIPS"...!!
...IS COMING TO KARAKURA-CHO!!
NEXT WEEK WILL BE AN EMERGENCY LIVE BROADCAST SPECIAL!!
WE'LL BE VISITING AN ABANDONED HOSPITAL IN KARAKURA CHO, TOKYO!!

HUH?

AN AUDIENCE RATING OF MORE THAN 25 PERCENT

SPONTANEOUS TRIPS TO SPIRITUAL HOT SPOTS

The extremely popular occult show that Don Kanonji hosts. It airs during golden time at 8 p.m. Every week it receives good viewer ratings of over 25 percent. It's incredibly popular with younger viewers.

DO OM
SP
MR. DON KANONJI!!!
SPIRITS ARE ALWAYS WITH YOU!!
DON KANONJI

EVEN POPULAR AT SCHOOL!!

Spiritual Hot Spots is even popular with high school students. They always talk about the show the day after it airs. An unbearable number of students do Kanonji impersonations.

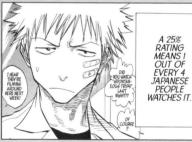

A 25% RATING MEANS 1 OUT OF EVERY 4 JAPANESE PEOPLE WATCHES IT.
DID YOU WATCH "SPONTANEOUS TRIPS" LAST NIGHT??
OF COURSE!!
I HEAR THEY'RE FILMING AROUND HERE NEXT WEEK!

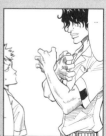

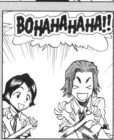

BOHAHAHAHA!!
BOHAHAHAHA!!
...

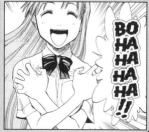

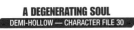

A DEGENERATING SOUL

DEMI-HOLLOW — CHARACTER FILE 30

Soul 魂 30

半虚

DEMI-HOLLOW

AN ENTRAPPED SOUL

A Whole that is degenerating into a Hollow. It happens to a soul that clings to a person or place and is attached there by a chain. They become Hollows when the hole on their chest opens up and they lose their hearts. It usually takes a year to become a Hollow.

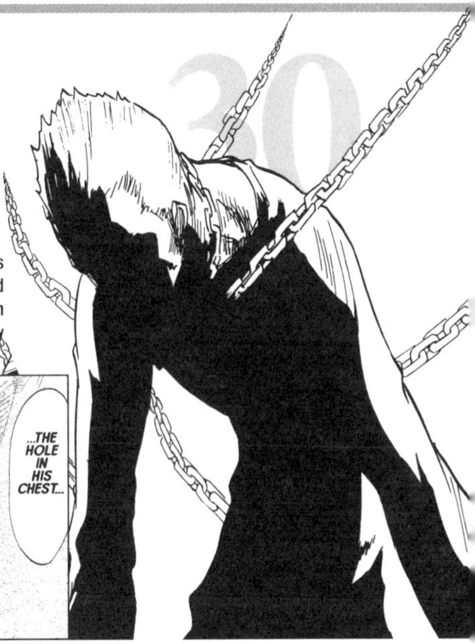

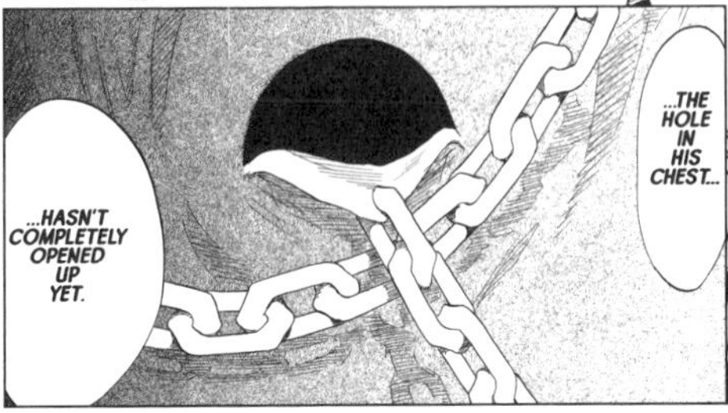
...THE HOLE IN HIS CHEST...
...HASN'T COMPLETELY OPENED UP YET.

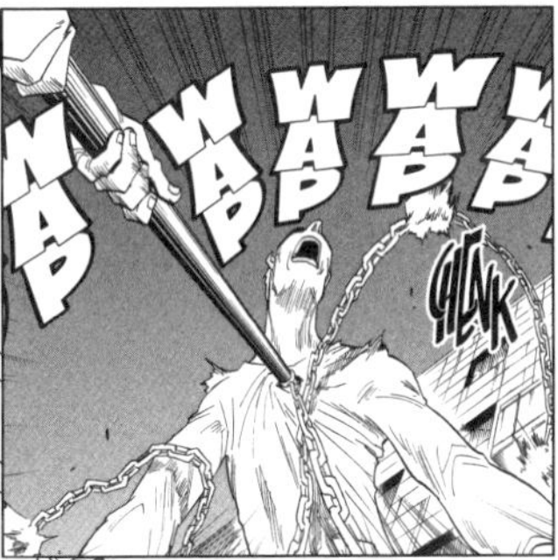
WAP
WAP
WAP
WAP
WAP

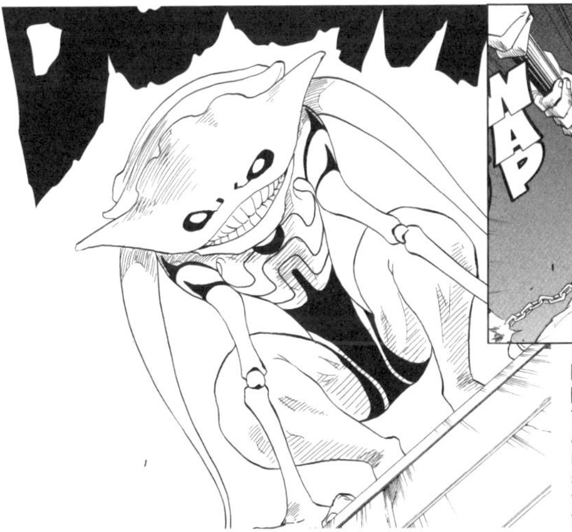

FINALLY TRANSFORMED INTO A HOLLOW?!

The Demi-Hollow transforms into a Hollow because of Kanonji's botched soul purification. Kanonji screams, "Mission Accomplished!!" when he mistakenly thinks that the purification was completed.

URYÛ...HERE?!

THE MYSTERIOUS FIGURE

When Kanonji's soul purification started to look dangerous, there was someone who tried to step up before Ichigo... Black hair, white shoes, and someone who, like Ichigo, could see the Demi-Hollow.

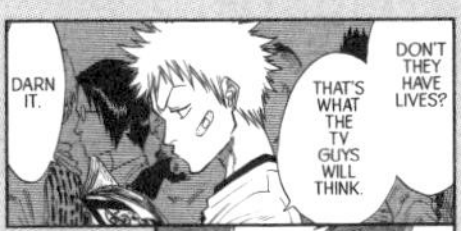
DON'T THEY HAVE LIVES?
THAT'S WHAT THE TV GUYS WILL THINK.
DARN IT.

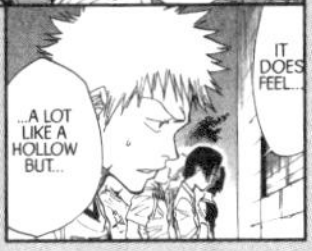
IT DOES FEEL...
...A LOT LIKE A HOLLOW BUT...

A big event in Karakura Town! The place is bustling with young people.

The mysterious person who quickly reacts and dashes over to the fence before Ichigo.

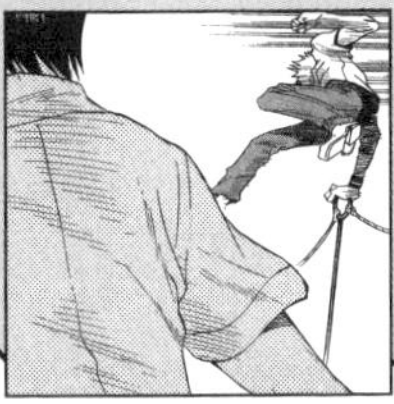

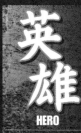

英雄

HERO

The Reason He Can't Step Aside VOL. 4-28~32

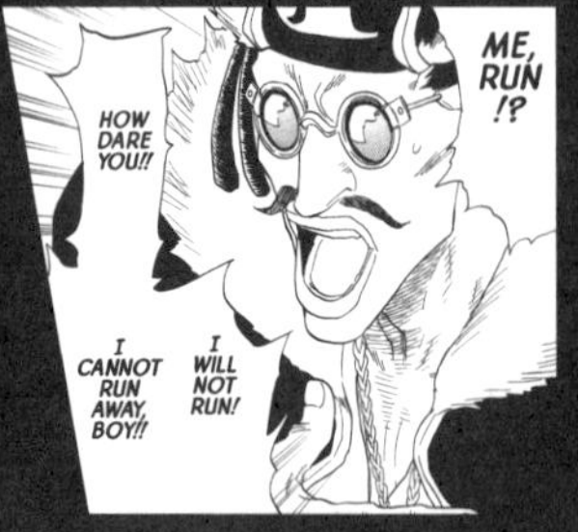
ME, RUN !?
HOW DARE YOU!!
I WILL NOT RUN!
I CANNOT RUN AWAY, BOY!!

Kanonji doesn't run away from the first Hollow. Instead, he determinedly faces it head-on. A Hero of Justice cannot turn his back on the enemy in front of the nation's children! Ichigo takes Kanonji with him and lures the Hollow into the hospital. The battle moves to the roof and the Hollow is wonderfully defeated with a strike to the back of its head!!

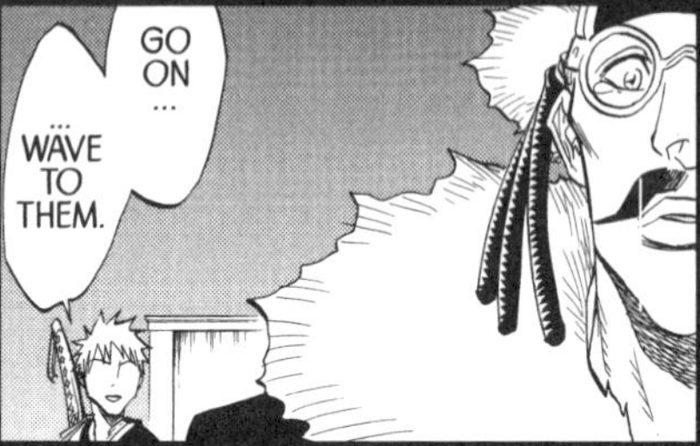
GO ON ...
... WAVE TO THEM.

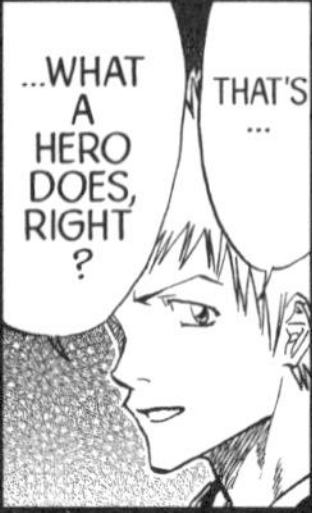
THAT'S ...
...WHAT A HERO DOES, RIGHT ?

A TRUE HERO

No matter the situation, one must live up to the expectations of the fans. Ichigo says that that is what a true hero would do. Kanonji is deeply moved by these words.

DEFEND THE PEACE!!

THE HEROES OF KARAKURA TOWN

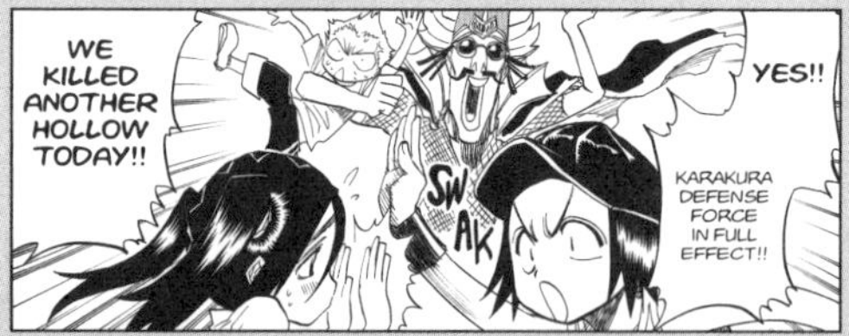
YES!!
WE KILLED ANOTHER HOLLOW TODAY!!
KARAKURA DEFENSE FORCE IN FULL EFFECT!!
SWAK

The hero unit that Don Kanonji formed by gathering children who could see spirits. Due to the active role that the Karakura Defense Unit plays, the Soul Reaper Kurumadani doesn't have anything to do!!

KARAKURA SUPERHEROES

黒崎夏梨

KARIN KUROSAKI — 6-b

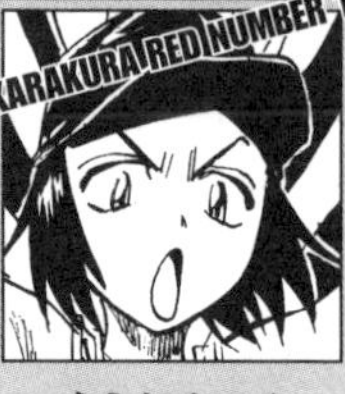
KARAKURA RED NUMBER 1

ドン•観音寺

DON KANONJI — 29-b

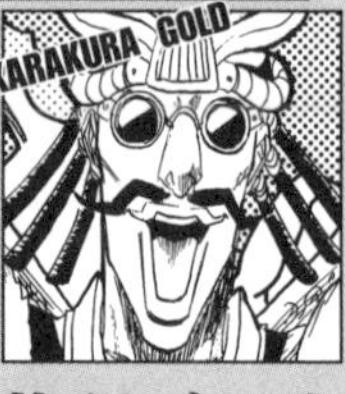
KARAKURA GOLD

紬屋雨

URURU TSUMUGIYA — 17-b

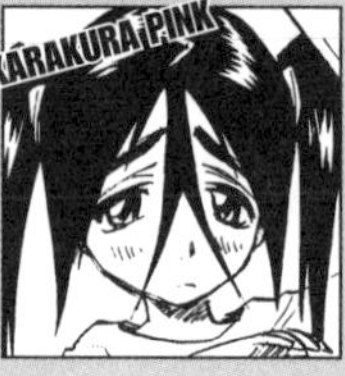
KARAKURA PINK

花刈ジン太

JINTA HANAKARI — 16-b

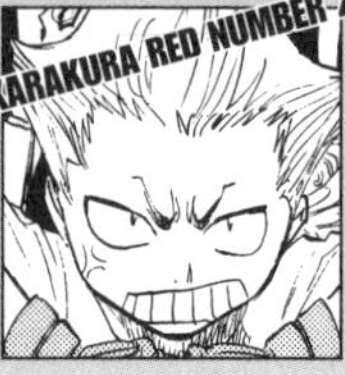
KARAKURA RED NUMBER 2

PROFILE

BIRTHDAY/JUNE 25

ZANPAKU-TÔ/ TSUCHINAMAZU

SHIKAI/GOOD MORNING! TSUCHINAMAZU

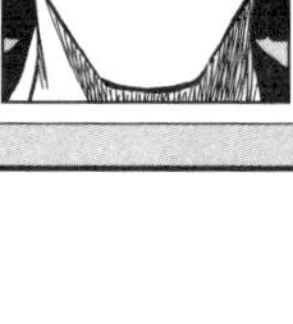

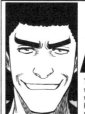

車谷善之助

ZENNOSUKE KURUMADANI — CHARACTER FILE 31

The Soul Reaper with an afro who is posted in Karakura Town to replace Rukia.

A CLASSMATE WHO HATES SOUL REAPERS

URYÛ ISHIDA — CHARACTER FILE 32-a

石田雨竜

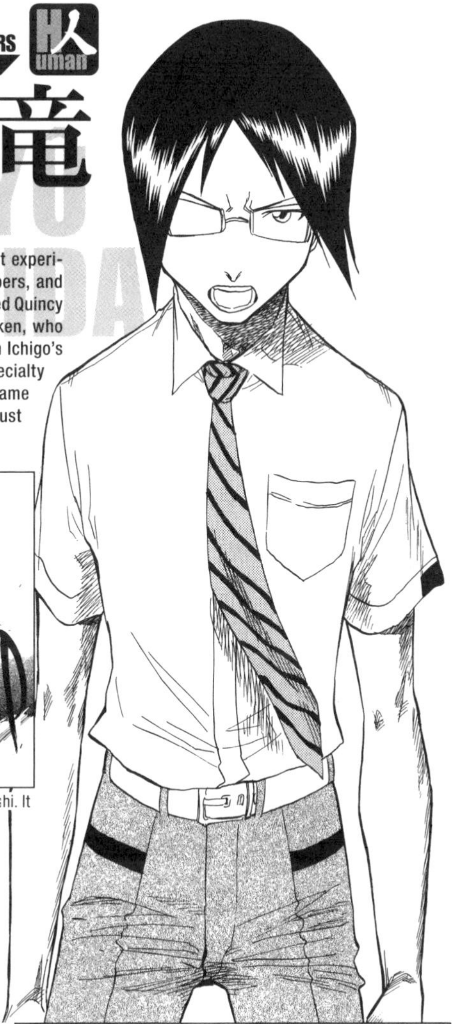

THE LONE QUINCY WHO IMPALES HOLLOWS

One of the few surviving Quincies. His past experiences have made him averse to Soul Reapers, and he is strongly repulsed by Ichigo. He inherited Quincy techniques from his dead grandfather, Sôken, who tutored him when he was young. Uryû is in Ichigo's class and is at the top of his grade. His specialty is needlework. He's so talented that he became the president of the craft club when he was just a first-year.

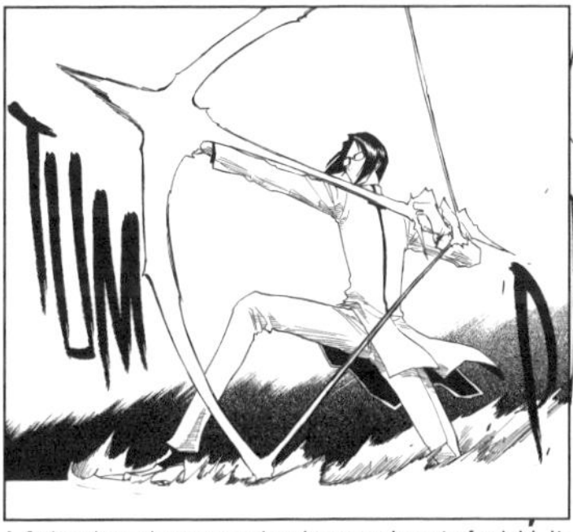

A Quincy's main weapon is a bow made out of reishi. It can destroy Hollows in long-range attacks.

PROFILE

BIRTHDAY/NOVEMBER 6

HEIGHT/5′6″ **WEIGHT/**121 LBS

BLOOD TYPE/AB

A STRONG HATRED OF SOUL REAPERS

Uryû suddenly appears before Ichigo and shows great hostility towards him. Uryû announces to the perplexed Ichigo, "I hate Soul Reapers."

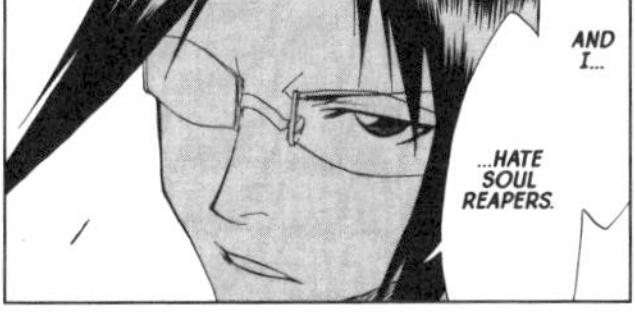
AND I...
...HATE SOUL REAPERS.

THE SPIRIT WEAPON KOJAKU

The Quincy's unique spirit weapon, Kojaku, is formed by gathering reishi in the Quincy cross on the right hand. The arrows that it releases are also made of reishi.

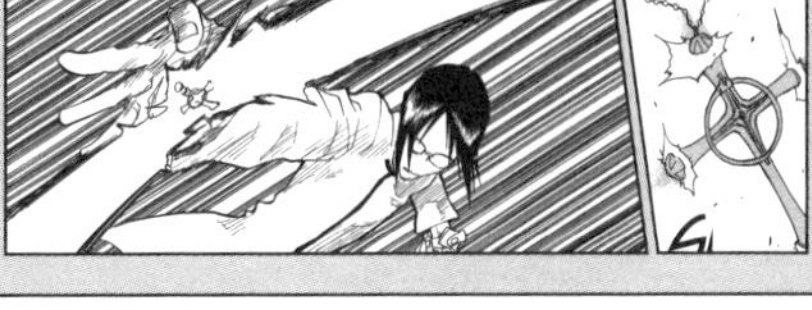

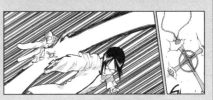

対立 OPPOSITION

Soul Reaper versus Quincy
VOL. 4-33~ VOL. 5-

Uryû, the Quincy who hates Soul Reapers, challenges Ichigo to a duel. Who is better? To decide, they take on the Hollows that have appeared throughout Karakura Town!

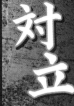

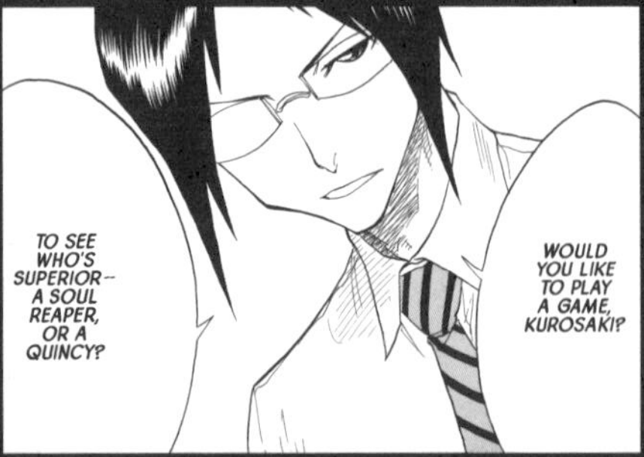
WOULD YOU LIKE TO PLAY A GAME, KUROSAKI!?
TO SEE WHO'S SUPERIOR-- A SOUL REAPER, OR A QUINCY?

A LARGE OUTBREAK OF HOLLOWS!
Uryû scatters bait to call forth Hollows. Whoever defeats the most Hollows within 24 hours is the winner, but...

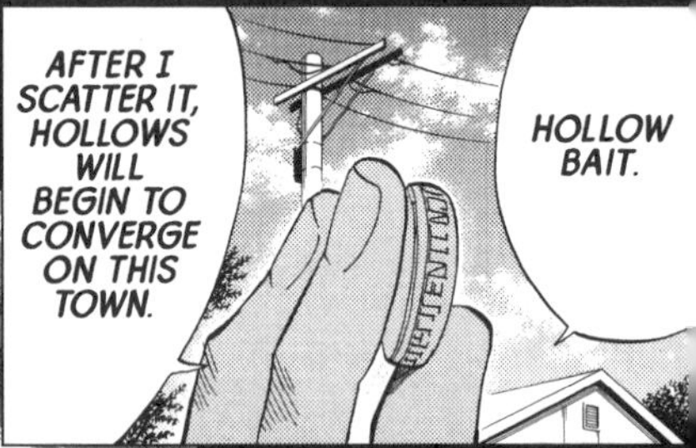
HOLLOW BAIT.
AFTER I SCATTER IT, HOLLOWS WILL BEGIN TO CONVERGE ON THIS TOWN.

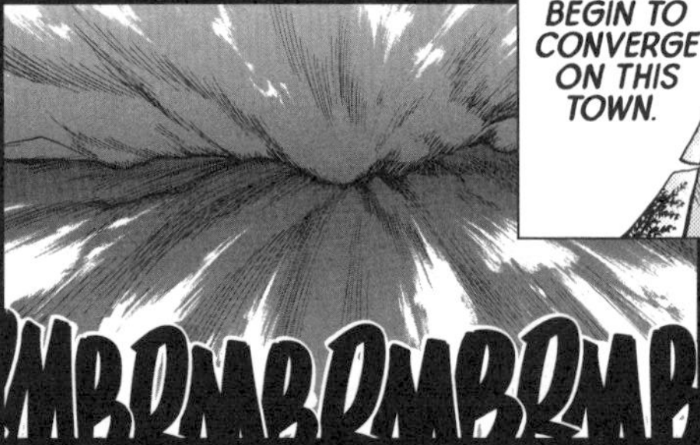

The sky cracks and is filled with heavily agitated waves. The amount of Hollows that gather exceed Uryû's expectations. They multiply to unimaginable numbers... And then—?!

A FAMILY OF EXORCISTS

QUINCY

A tribe of exorcists that has strong spiritual energy and anti-Hollow abilities. Unlike Soul Reapers, who purify Hollows and lead them to the Soul Society, Quincies completely destroy Hollows. Worried that the world will collapse, the Soul Society decided to exterminate the Quincy tribe...

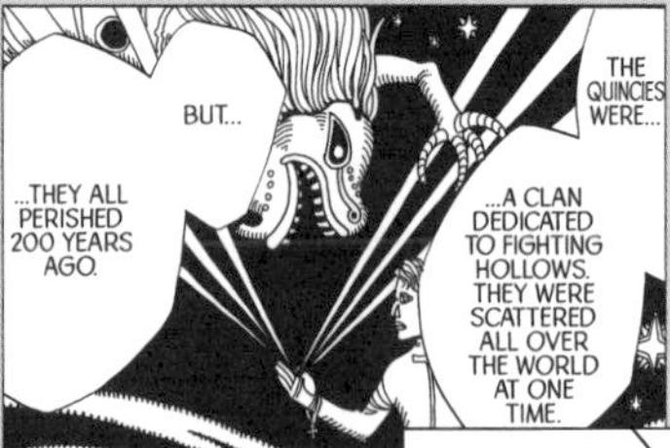
THE QUINCIES WERE...
...A CLAN DEDICATED TO FIGHTING HOLLOWS. THEY WERE SCATTERED ALL OVER THE WORLD AT ONE TIME.
BUT...
...THEY ALL PERISHED 200 YEARS AGO.

THE COLLAPSE OF THE WORLD
The Quincies have the ability to destroy Hollows. It is a dangerous ability that can upset the balance between the human world and the Soul Society. When souls don't return to the Soul Society and the number of souls that remain in the human world increases, the equilibrium is disturbed, triggering the collapse of the world.

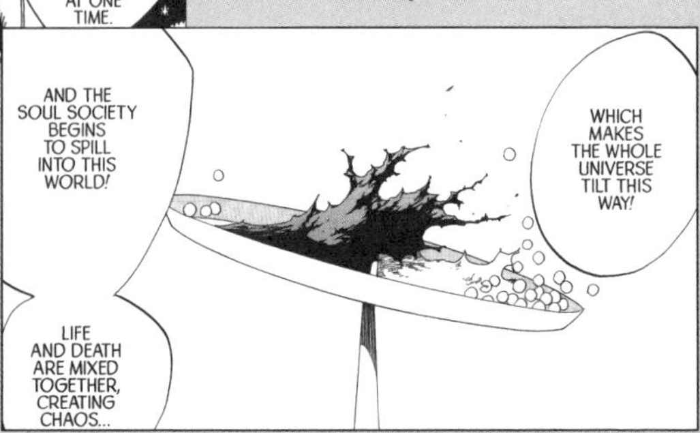
WHICH MAKES THE WHOLE UNIVERSE TILT THIS WAY!
AND THE SOUL SOCIETY BEGINS TO SPILL INTO THIS WORLD!
LIFE AND DEATH ARE MIXED TOGETHER, CREATING CHAOS...

覚醒

AWAKENING

The power to protect
VOL. 5-38~40

A group of Hollows suddenly flood the town. Chad faces the Hollows along with Ichigo's younger sister, Karin. But Chad has problems fighting since he can't see the Hollows. Then, one of Karin's friends appears…

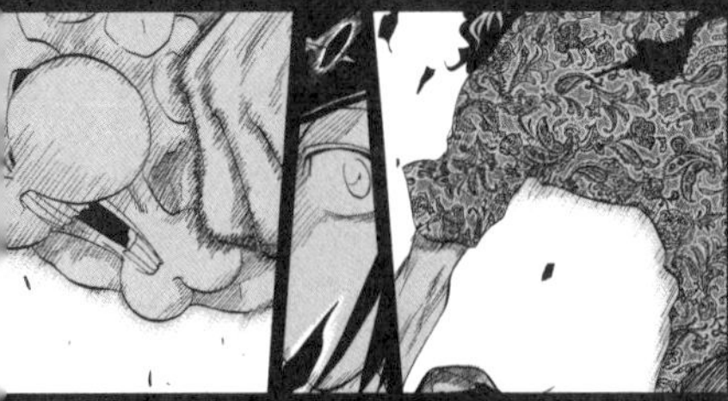

Chad hears his abuelito's voice and his own promise in his head.

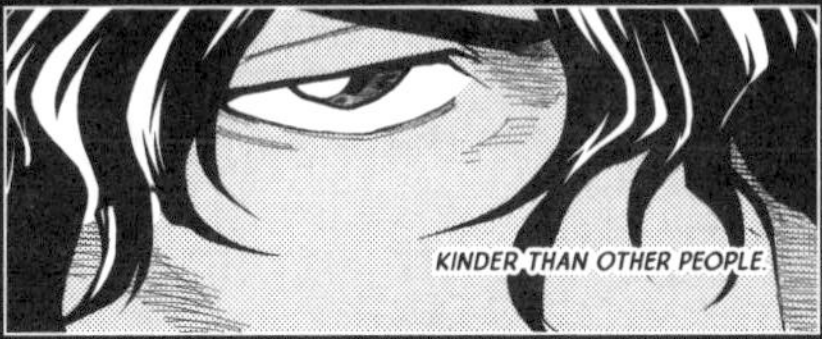
KINDER THAN OTHER PEOPLE.

The Hollow's strong arms lunge out at Karin, who has jumped out to protect a friend!

Human 人

A TRANSFORMED RIGHT ARM

YASUTORA SADO — CHARACTER FILE 11-b

茶渡泰虎

YASUTORA SADO

"GIVE ME THE POWER."

Chad is kind and doesn't like harming others. Things get desperate when the Hollow's strong arm approaches him. His abuelito's kind words and Chad's desire to protect awaken Chad's hidden power. Suddenly, Chad's right arm transforms and easily blows away the Hollow's arm in one stroke.

11b

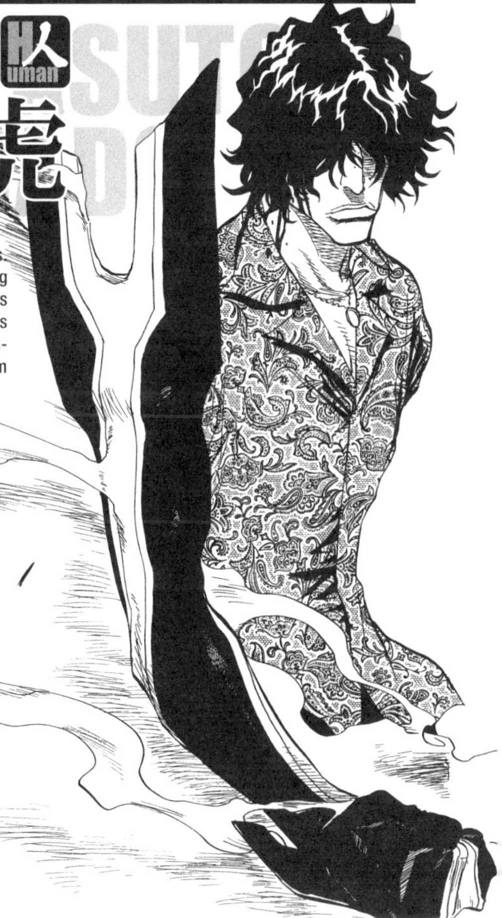

TACTICS

EMERGING POWER/
TRANSFORMED RIGHT ARM

TECHNIQUE NAME/POWER PUNCH

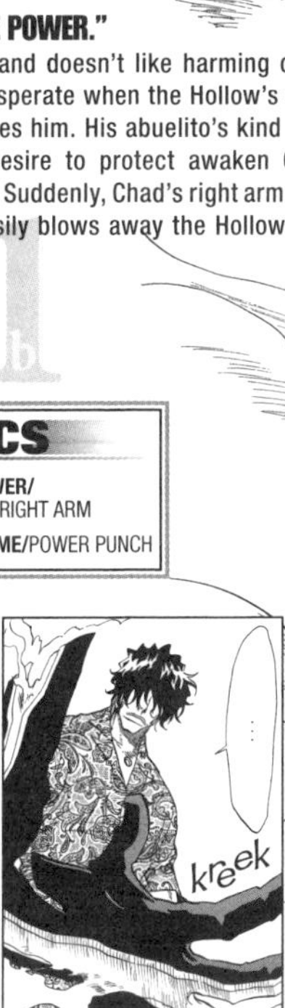
…
kreek

Chad is bewildered by his body's sudden transformation. He couldn't see Hollows before, but now he can.

BULBOUS G

A HEAVY-WEIGHT HOLLOW

BULBOUS G — CHARACTER FILE 33

Hollow 虛

バルバスG

INCREDIBLE STRENGTH

A giant Hollow that was lured to the human world by Uryû's bait. It is drawn to Chad's strong spiritual energy, and chases him persistently. The Hollow torments Chad with his incredible strength. Chad's strong desire to protect Karin awakens his powers, and he destroys the Hollow in a single blow.

33

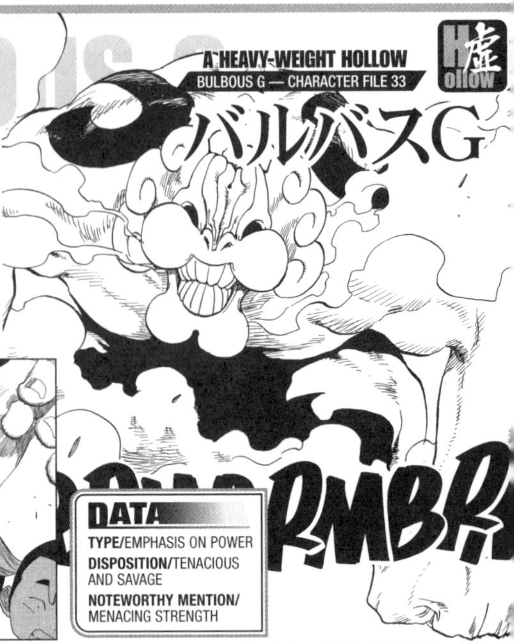
RMBR

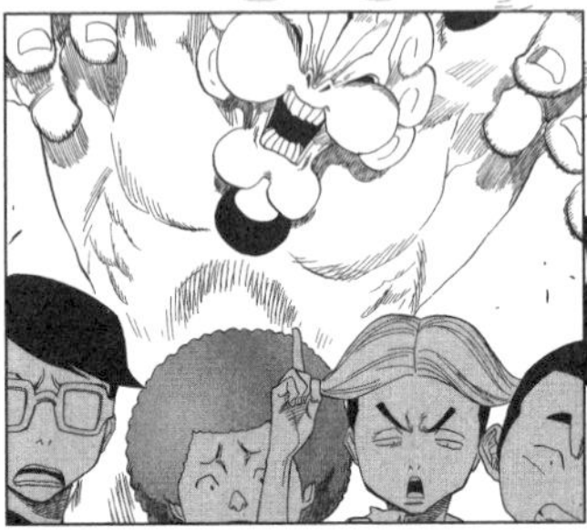

DATA

TYPE/EMPHASIS ON POWER

DISPOSITION/TENACIOUS AND SAVAGE

NOTEWORTHY MENTION/ MENACING STRENGTH

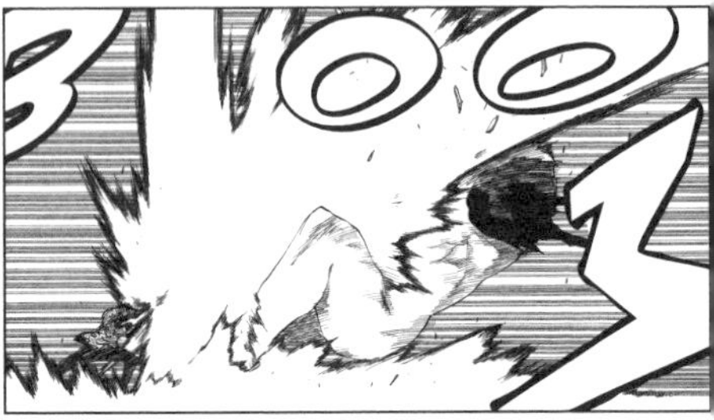

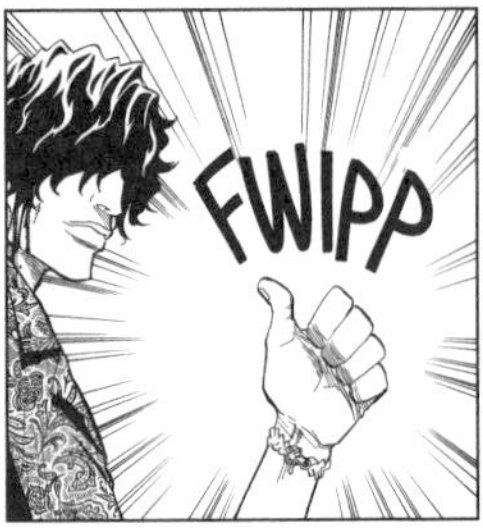
FWIPP

Chad's powers awaken during a tight situation, and he smashes Bulbous G's head!!

HIS TEACHINGS ARE STILL IN HIS HEART

オスカー・ホアキン・デ・ラ・ロサ

OSCAR JOAQUIN DE LA ROSA — CHARACTER FILE 34

ABUELITO/ GRANDFATHER

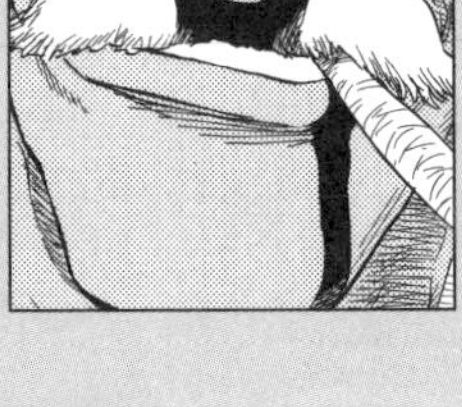

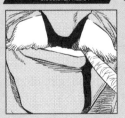

Chad's Mexican grandfather who taught and guided Chad from the boy's youth. He's Chad's benefactor.

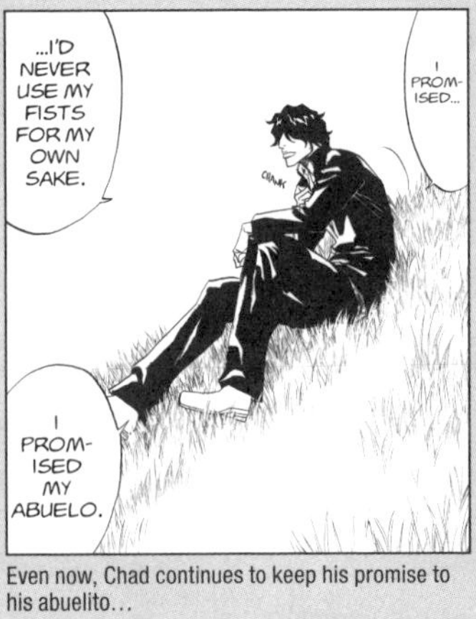
I PROM-ISED...
...I'D NEVER USE MY FISTS FOR MY OWN SAKE.
I PROM-ISED MY ABUELO.

Even now, Chad continues to keep his promise to his abuelito...

覚醒

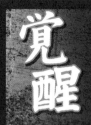

AWAKENING

The power called forth
VOL. 5-41~43

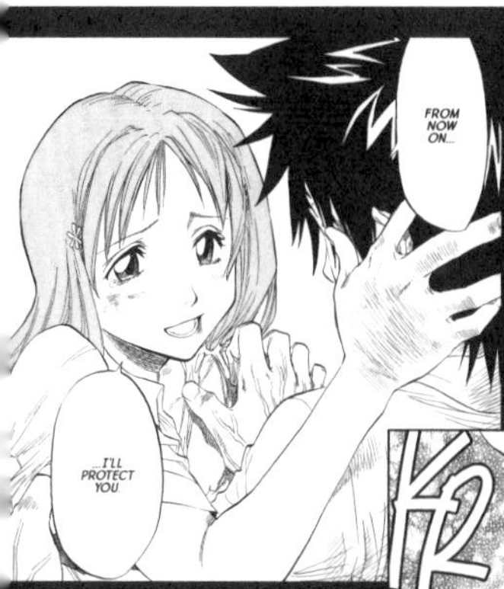
FROM NOW ON...
...I'LL PROTECT YOU.

The Hollows that appear in the human world raid Karakura 1st High School. Students who are being controlled by a Hollow attack Orihime! Tatsuki appears and helps her escape danger, but Tatsuki comes under the Hollow's control. Orihime's feelings towards Tatsuki awaken her power.

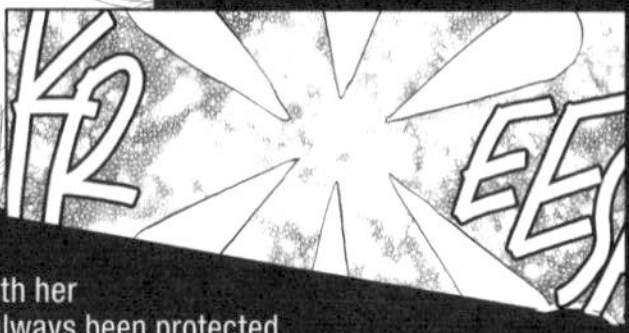

Orihime's hairpin flies off and Orihime's power is awakened along with her intense spiritual energy. Orihime has always been protected until now. This is the first time that Orihime wishes to protect another person.

SHUNSHUNRIKKA

ORIHIME INOUE — CHARACTER FILE 7-b

H人uman

井上織姫

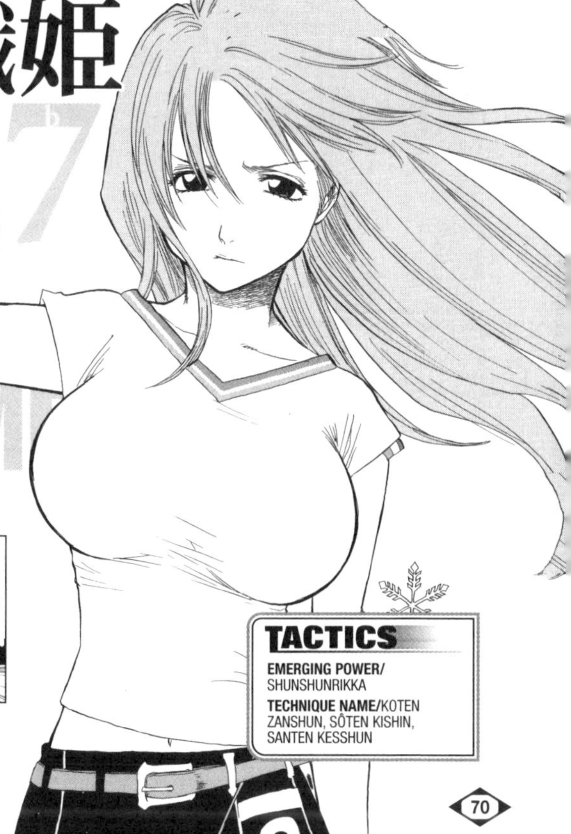

"I SHOW NO MERCY TO ANYONE WHO HURTS TATSUKI!"

Other students picked on Orihime in middle school. Orihime's best friend Tatsuki was the one who saved her from those gloomy days. Now Tatsuki is bleeding right before Orihime's eyes. Tatsuki's tears tell Orihime that Tatsuki is striking at her against her will. Orihime's desire to protect Tatsuki awakens her ability, the Shunshunrikka, and she goes into battle.

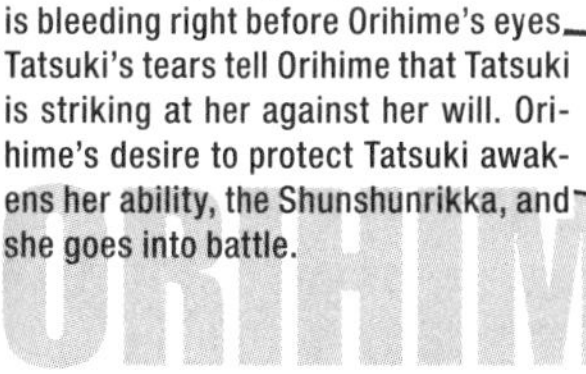
FAIRIES! FLYING FAIRIES ARE TALKING TO ME!!
Hmph.
NICE REACTION! VERY NICE!!

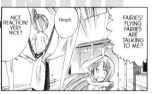

Orihime is unable to understand what has happened to her body. Shunô is pleased at her predictable reaction.

TACTICS

EMERGING POWER/ SHUNSHUNRIKKA

TECHNIQUE NAME/ KOTEN ZANSHUN, SÔTEN KISHIN, SANTEN KESSHUN

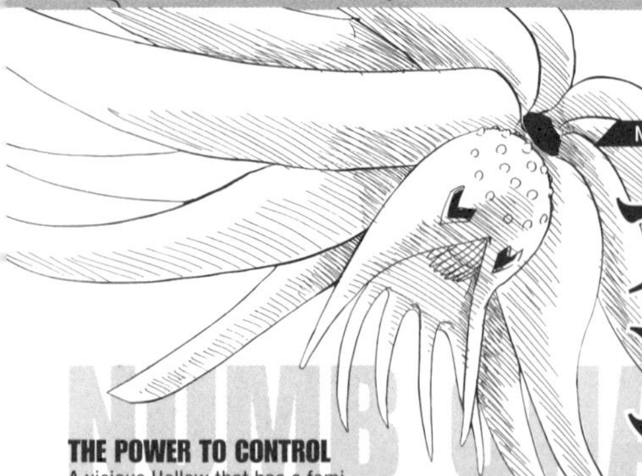

Hollow

A HYSTERICAL HOLLOW

NUMB CHANDELIER — CHARACTER FILE 35

ナムシャンデリア

NUMB CHANDELIER

THE POWER TO CONTROL

A vicious Hollow that has a feminine way of speaking. It has a vulgar and cruel disposition. Its weapons are the seeds it shoots from its head. If the seeds are shot into a victim, who can then be controlled in any way the Hollow likes. It has the ability to fly, and can even attack from the sky.

DATA

TYPE/CONTROLLING OTHERS

DISPOSITION/FEMININE TONE OF VOICE

NOTEWORTHY MENTION/HAS ABILITY TO CONTROL PEOPLE

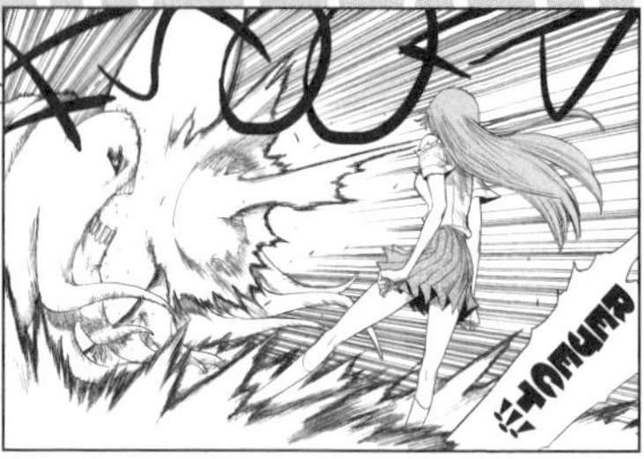

Orihime's ability, the Shunshunrikka, is awakened by Tatsuki's tears. It easily slices the Hollow in two.

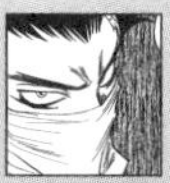

椿鬼
Tsubaki has a coarse attitude and is in charge of the Shunshunrikka's attacks. He's the only one who displays an ability by himself.

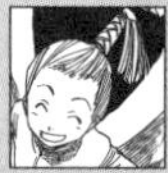

舜桜
Shunô acts as leader of the group. He teaches Orihime how to use the Shunshunrikka.

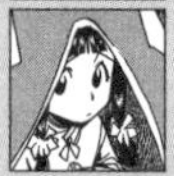

あやめ
Ayame has a quiet personality. She's in charge of the Shunshunrikka's healing ability along with Shunô.

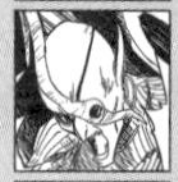

火無菊
Hinagiku is part of the Shunshunrikka's defense. He's just as excessively energetic as Tsubaki.

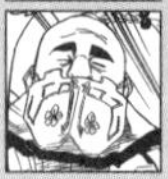

梅厳
Baigon is partly responsible for the Shunshunrikka's defense. He's brawny and has a large body.

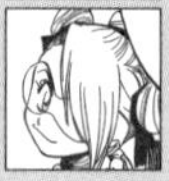

リリイ
Lily is part of the Shunshunrikka's defense. She has a futuristic style.

THREE POWERS	
	KOTEN ZANSHUN The power to reject the fusion of matter and split it.
	SÔTEN KISHUN The power to surround something and return it to the way it was before it was destroyed.
	SANTEN KESSHUN The power to repel attacks by placing a shield between the enemy and Orihime.

ORIHIME'S POWER

SHUNSHUNRIKKA

Orihime's spirit energy was harbored in the pair of hairpins that she got from her brother. The Shunshunrikka appeared in the form of six spirits. She has three techniques that use the spirits in combination with a spirit chant and the technique name. She's sometimes teased by the Shunshunrikka, probably because she's not used to her ability…

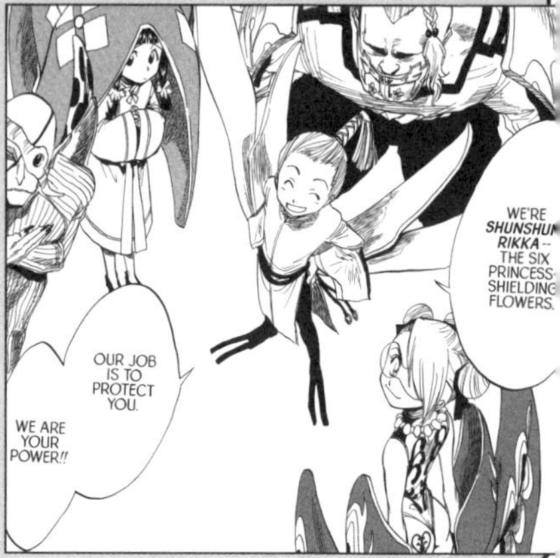
WE'RE SHUNSHU RIKKA-- THE SIX PRINCESS-SHIELDING FLOWERS.
OUR JOB IS TO PROTECT YOU.
WE ARE YOUR POWER!!

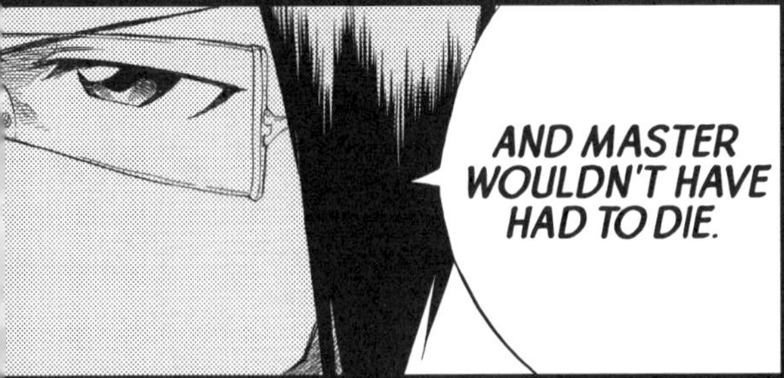
AND MASTER WOULDN'T HAVE HAD TO DIE.

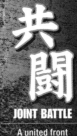

共闘

JOINT BATTLE

A united front
VOL. 6-44~47

The Hollows are greater in number than expected. Ichigo suggests to Uryû that they fight together, but Uryû refuses. He begins talking about the death of his grandfather, Sôken.

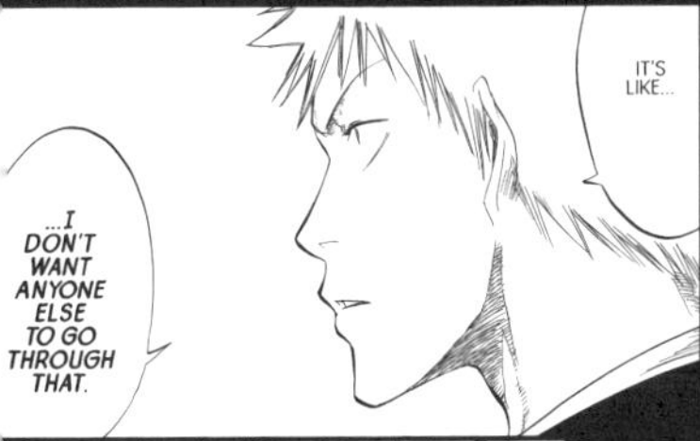
IT'S LIKE...
...I DON'T WANT ANYONE ELSE TO GO THROUGH THAT.

The two fight together despite their different feelings and points of view. They both hope not to bring grief to anyone.

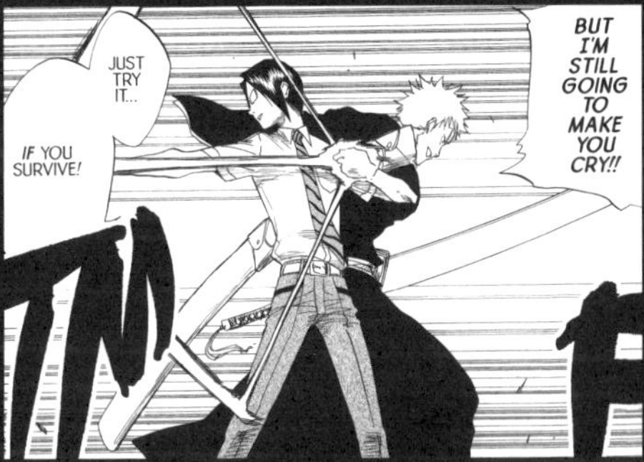
BUT I'M STILL GOING TO MAKE YOU CRY!!
JUST TRY IT...
IF YOU SURVIVE!

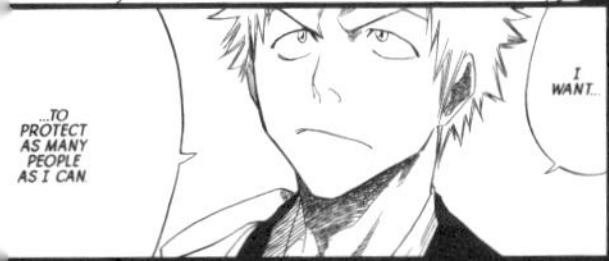
I WANT...
...TO PROTECT AS MANY PEOPLE AS I CAN.

THEIR OWN REASONS
Ichigo fights because he doesn't want anyone to experience personal tragedy like he has. Uryû fights to avenge his grandfather and to prove his Quincy powers.

A SURVIVING QUINCY

URYÛ'S MASTER

石田宗弦

SÔKEN ISHIDA — 36

He is Uryû's grandfather and his Quincy master. As one of the last surviving Quincies, he was kept under careful watch by the Soul Reapers. Sôken complained to the Soul Reapers about the need for the Quincies and tried to pave the way for a symbiotic relationship. But he died in battle when a group of giant Hollows attacked him. Uryû was a child at the time.

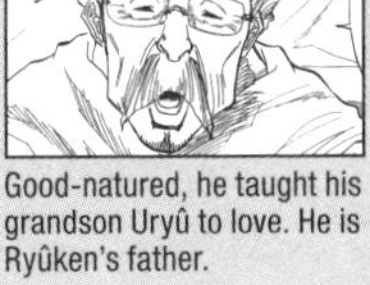

Good-natured, he taught his grandson Uryû to love. He is Ryûken's father.

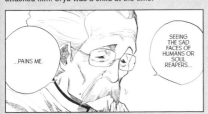

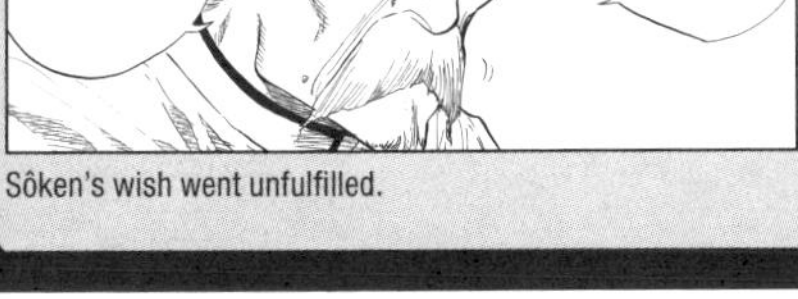
SEEING THE SAD FACES OF HUMANS OR SOUL REAPERS...
...PAINS ME.

Sôken's wish went unfulfilled.

PROFILE

BIRTHDAY/MARCH 22
HEIGHT/5′3″
WEIGHT/115 LBS

37

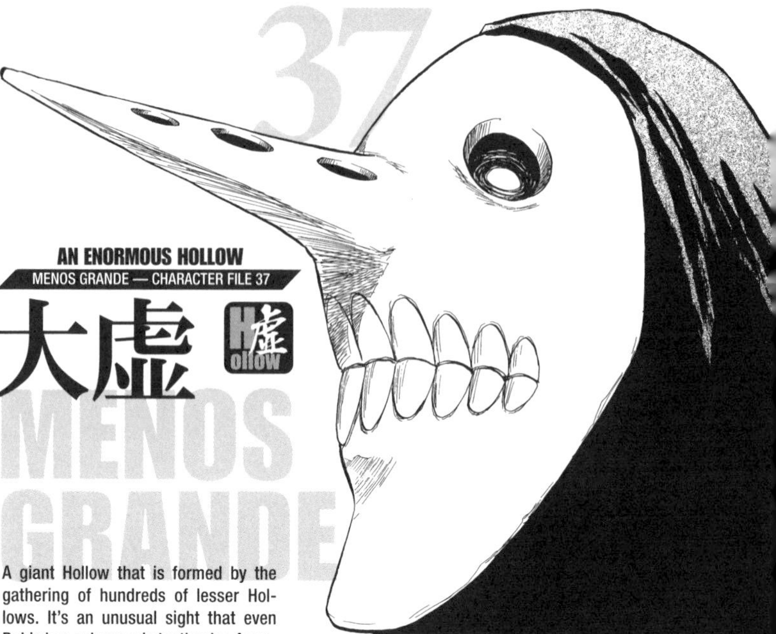

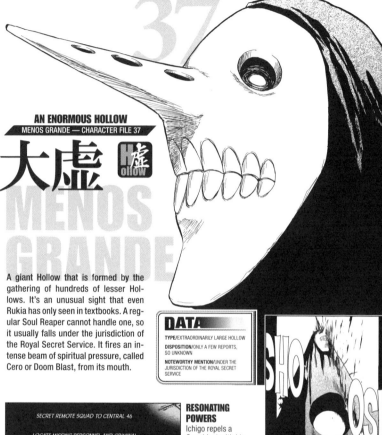

AN ENORMOUS HOLLOW

MENOS GRANDE — CHARACTER FILE 37

大虚

H 虚 ollow

MENOS GRANDE

A giant Hollow that is formed by the gathering of hundreds of lesser Hollows. It's an unusual sight that even Rukia has only seen in textbooks. A regular Soul Reaper cannot handle one, so it usually falls under the jurisdiction of the Royal Secret Service. It fires an intense beam of spiritual pressure, called Cero or Doom Blast, from its mouth.

DATA

TYPE/EXTRAORDINARILY LARGE HOLLOW

DISPOSITION/ONLY A FEW REPORTS, SO UNKNOWN

NOTEWORTHY MENTION/UNDER THE JURISDICTION OF THE ROYAL SECRET SERVICE

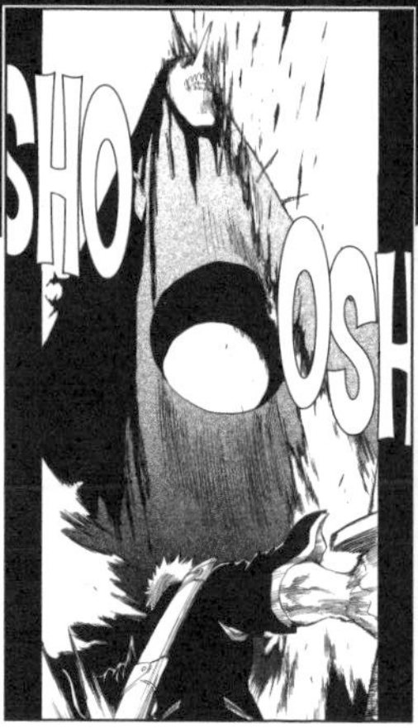
SHOOSH

RESONATING POWERS

Ichigo repels a Cero blast with his zanpaku-tô. It causes Ichigo's dormant power to explode. He slices the Menos Grande in two and sends it back to Hueco Mundo.

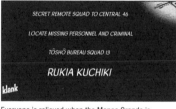

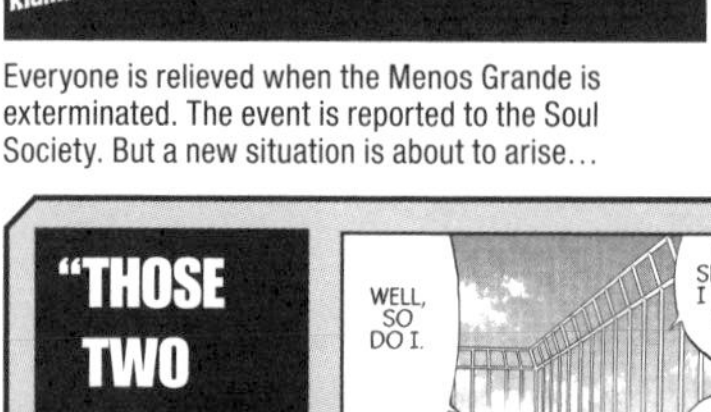
SECRET REMOTE SQUAD TO CENTRAL 46
LOCATE MISSING PERSONNEL AND CRIMINAL
TÔSHÔ BUREAU SQUAD 13
RUKIA KUCHIKI
klank

Everyone is relieved when the Menos Grande is exterminated. The event is reported to the Soul Society. But a new situation is about to arise…

"THOSE TWO ARE A LOT ALIKE."

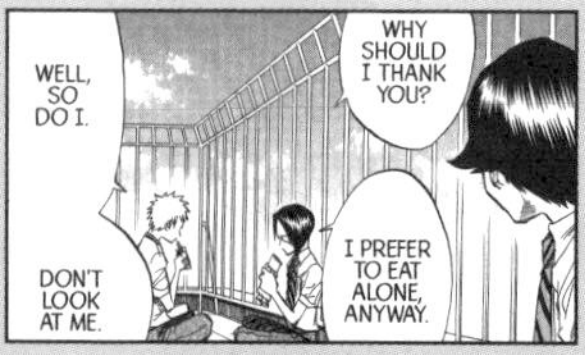
WHY SHOULD I THANK YOU?
WELL, SO DO I.
I PREFER TO EAT ALONE, ANYWAY.
DON'T LOOK AT ME.

Mizuiro understands the friendship between the two, even though at first glance they look like they're always quarreling with each other.

Ichigo and Uryû come to understand each other's feelings by fighting together. Their peaceful everyday life returns, and they begin a strange and awkward friendship(?!)…

THEY'RE SUCH GOOD FRIENDS THAT THEY QUARREL?!

ICHIGO AND URYÛ

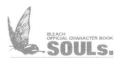

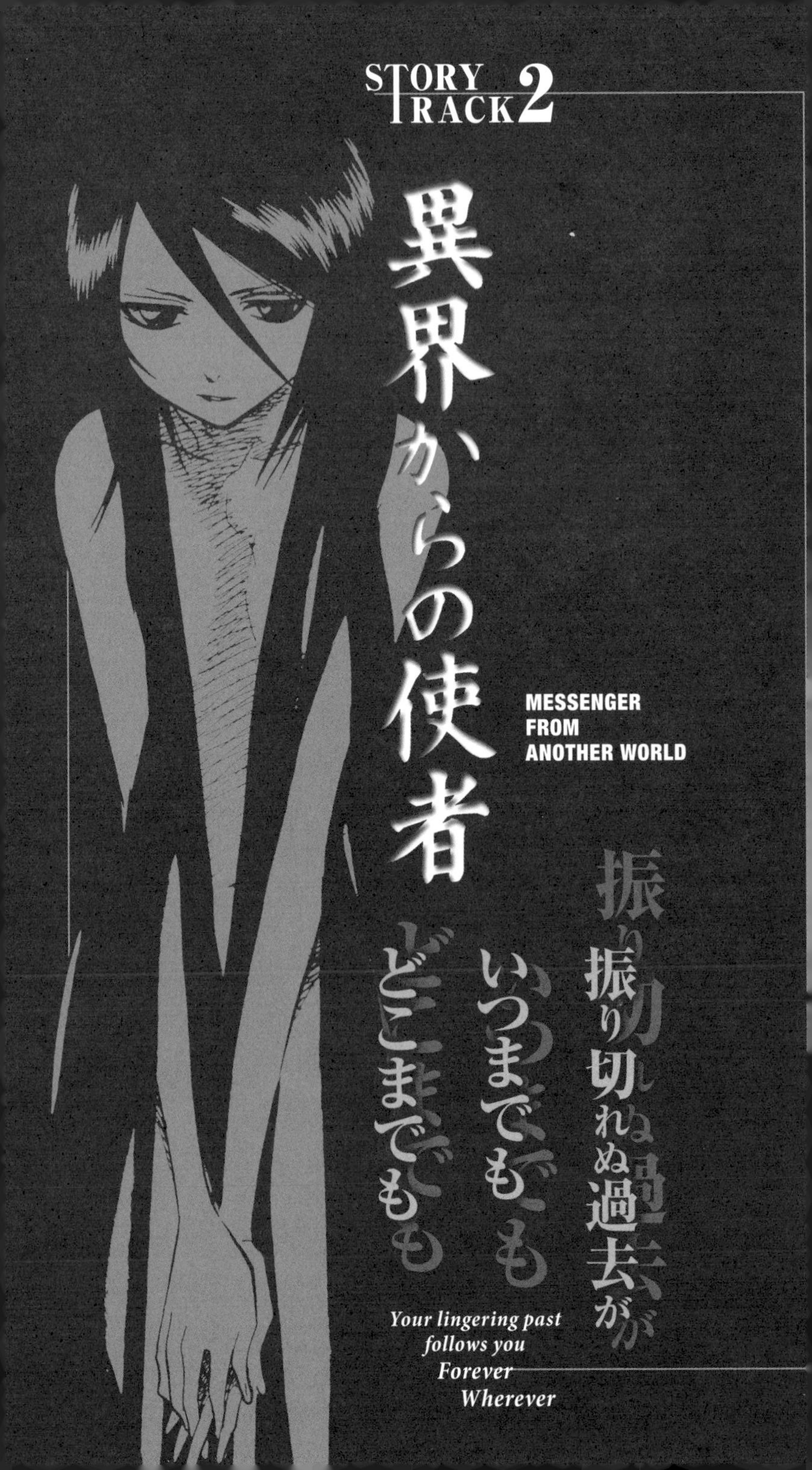
STORY TRACK 2
異界からの使者
MESSENGER FROM ANOTHER WORLD
振り切れぬ過去が
いつまでも
どこまでも
Your lingering past follows you Forever Wherever

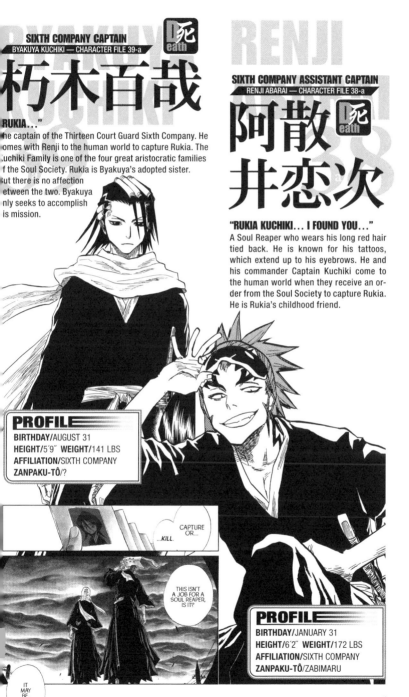

SIXTH COMPANY CAPTAIN

BYAKUYA KUCHIKI — CHARACTER FILE 39-a

朽木百哉

RUKIA..."

he captain of the Thirteen Court Guard Sixth Company. He omes with Renji to the human world to capture Rukia. The uchiki Family is one of the four great aristocratic families f the Soul Society. Rukia is Byakuya's adopted sister. ut there is no affection etween the two. Byakuya nly seeks to accomplish is mission.

SIXTH COMPANY ASSISTANT CAPTAIN

RENJI ABARAI — CHARACTER FILE 38-a

阿散井恋次

"RUKIA KUCHIKI... I FOUND YOU..."

A Soul Reaper who wears his long red hair tied back. He is known for his tattoos, which extend up to his eyebrows. He and his commander Captain Kuchiki come to the human world when they receive an order from the Soul Society to capture Rukia. He is Rukia's childhood friend.

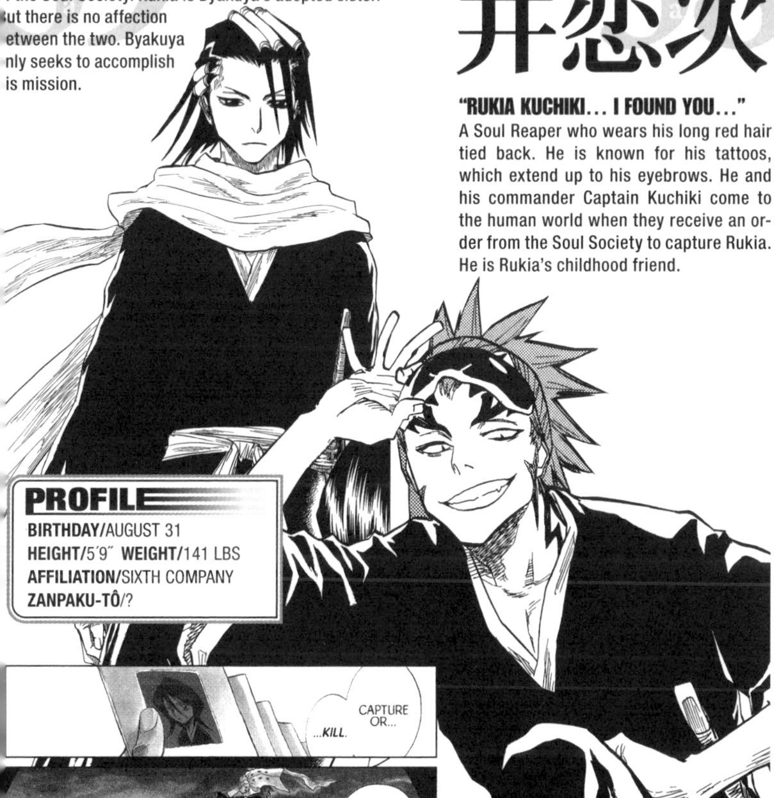

PROFILE

BIRTHDAY/AUGUST 31

HEIGHT/5′9″ **WEIGHT/**141 LBS

AFFILIATION/SIXTH COMPANY

ZANPAKU-TÔ/?

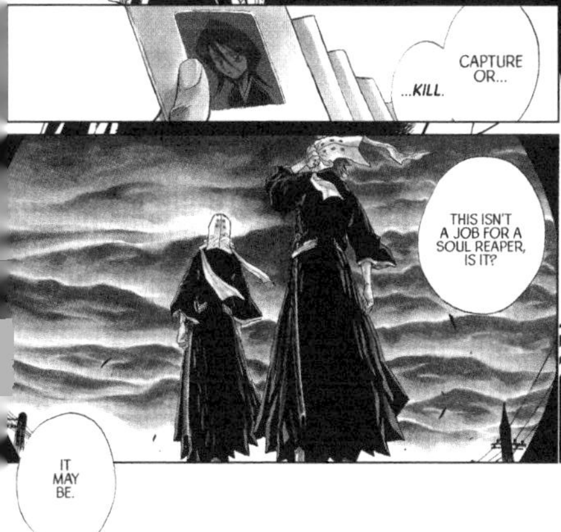

CAPTURE OR...
...KILL.
THIS ISN'T A JOB FOR A SOUL REAPER, IS IT?
IT MAY BE.

PROFILE

BIRTHDAY/JANUARY 31

HEIGHT/6′2″ **WEIGHT/**172 LBS

AFFILIATION/SIXTH COMPANY

ZANPAKU-TÔ/ZABIMARU

追跡 PURSUIT

Messengers from the Soul Society
VOL. 6-51~52

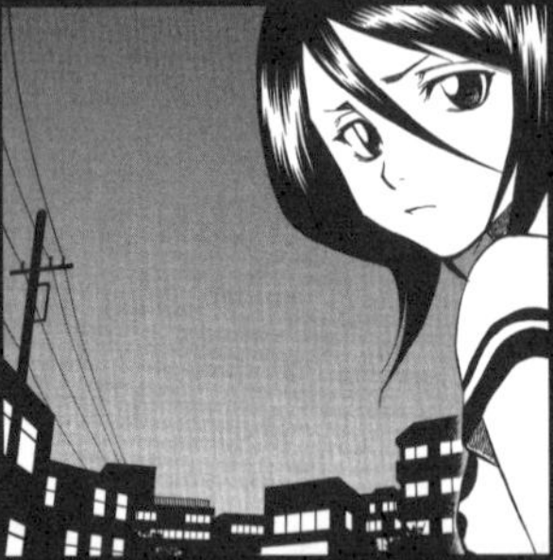

Rukia is sure that news of the event with the Menos Grande has leaked to the Soul Society. She leaves Ichigo, saying goodbye with only a note. She had hoped that her pursuers would leave Ichigo alone, but it was all in vain. The Soul Society's best trackers, Renji and Byakuya, are right behind her.

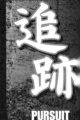

For a while, Rukia hid her identity as a Soul Reaper and became a student. Memories of her time in the human world flash through her head as she flees her pursuers in the night…

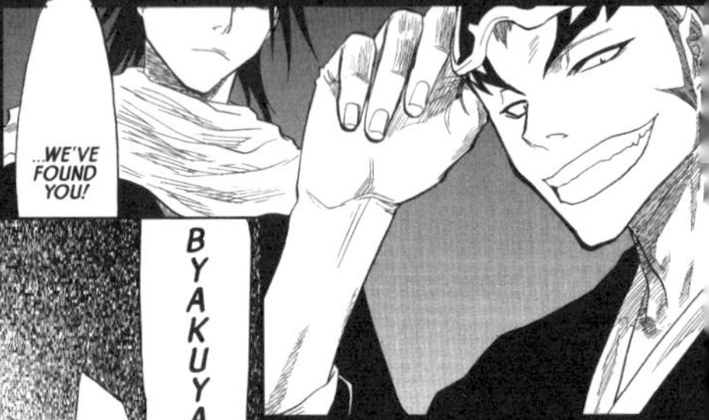

...WE'VE FOUND YOU!

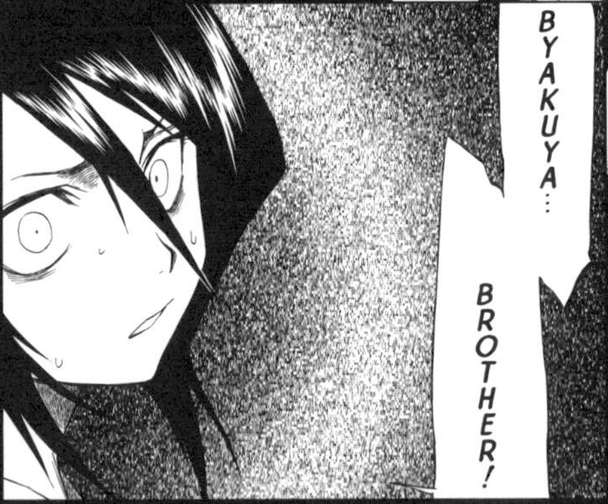

BYAKUYA...
BROTHER!

THE BEST TRACKERS

Rukia's childhood friend Renji and her older brother Byakuya were sent from the Soul Society! They point their zanpaku-tô at Rukia and demand to know the location of the human who had stolen her Soul Reaper powers. At that moment, Uryû notices the presence of Soul Reapers and rushes to the scene, but…

HAVE FUN DECIPHERING!

RUKIA'S NOTE

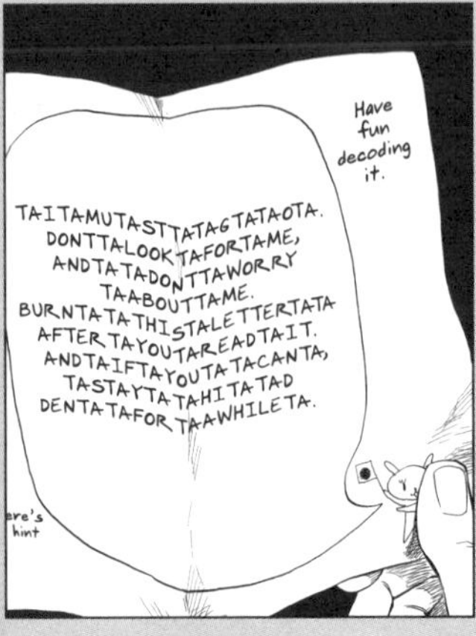

Have fun decoding it.
TAITAMUTASTTATAGTATAOTA.
DONTTALOOKTAFORTAME,
ANDTATADONTTAWORRY
TAABOUTTAME.
BURNTATATHISTALETTERTATA
AFTERTAYOUTAREADTAIT.
ANDTAIFTAYOUTATACANTA,
TASTAYTATAHITATAD
DENTATAFORTAAWHILETA.

On the envelope is a picture of a rabbit and the message, "Sorry for the trouble." Inside the envelope is a witty message written in a code that Rukia probably just learned. The code is pretty simple, and Ichigo deciphers it without the hint. To read the note, one need only remove the "ta"s throughout.

A strange illustration that can't really be called a hint. Is it a tanuki?

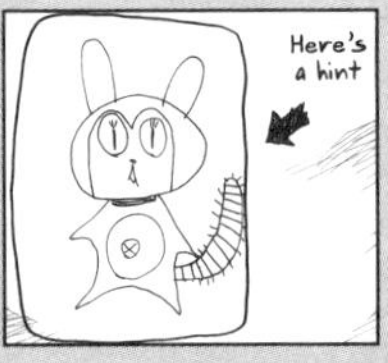

Here's a hint

接触

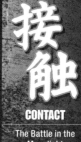

CONTACT

The Battle in the Moonlight
VOL. 7-53~56

Renji defeats Uryû in a single attack and overpowers Ichigo when he appears. He continues to dominate the battle. That's when Ichigo learns about Rukia's crime and its extremely harsh penalty.

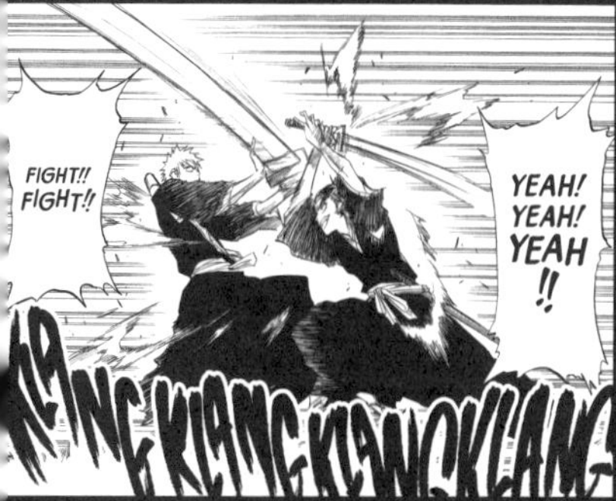
YEAH! YEAH! YEAH!!
FIGHT!! FIGHT!!

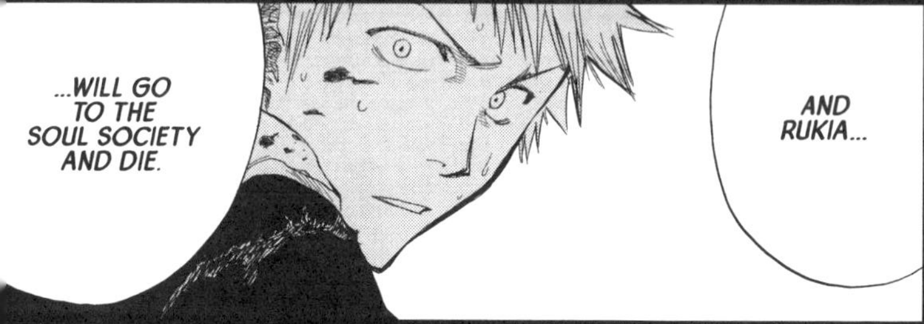
AND RUKIA...
...WILL GO TO THE SOUL SOCIETY AND DIE.

UKIA'S CRIME

ukia is guilty of the transfer of oul Reaper powers to a human. ven though it was an emergency tuation, this is a serious offense the Soul Society. Renji and yakuya were ordered to capture ukia out of consideration for her.

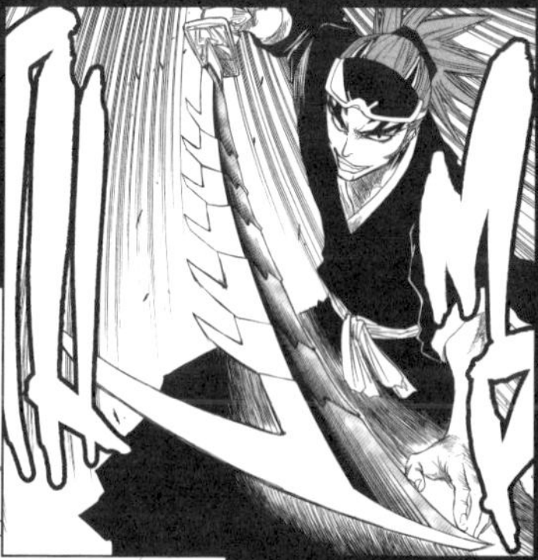

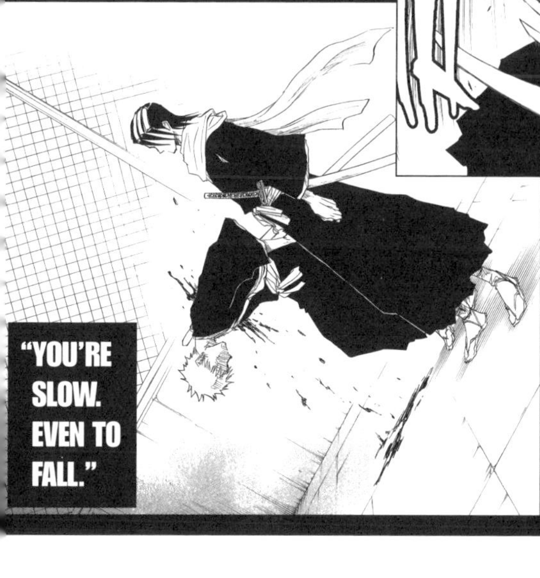

DEFEAT

Ichigo attacks Renji with overwhelming strength, but is defeated instantaneously by Byakuya. Byakuya removes Ichigo's Soul Reaper powers and declares that Ichigo only has a few minutes left to live.

"YOU'RE SLOW. EVEN TO FALL."

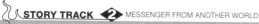

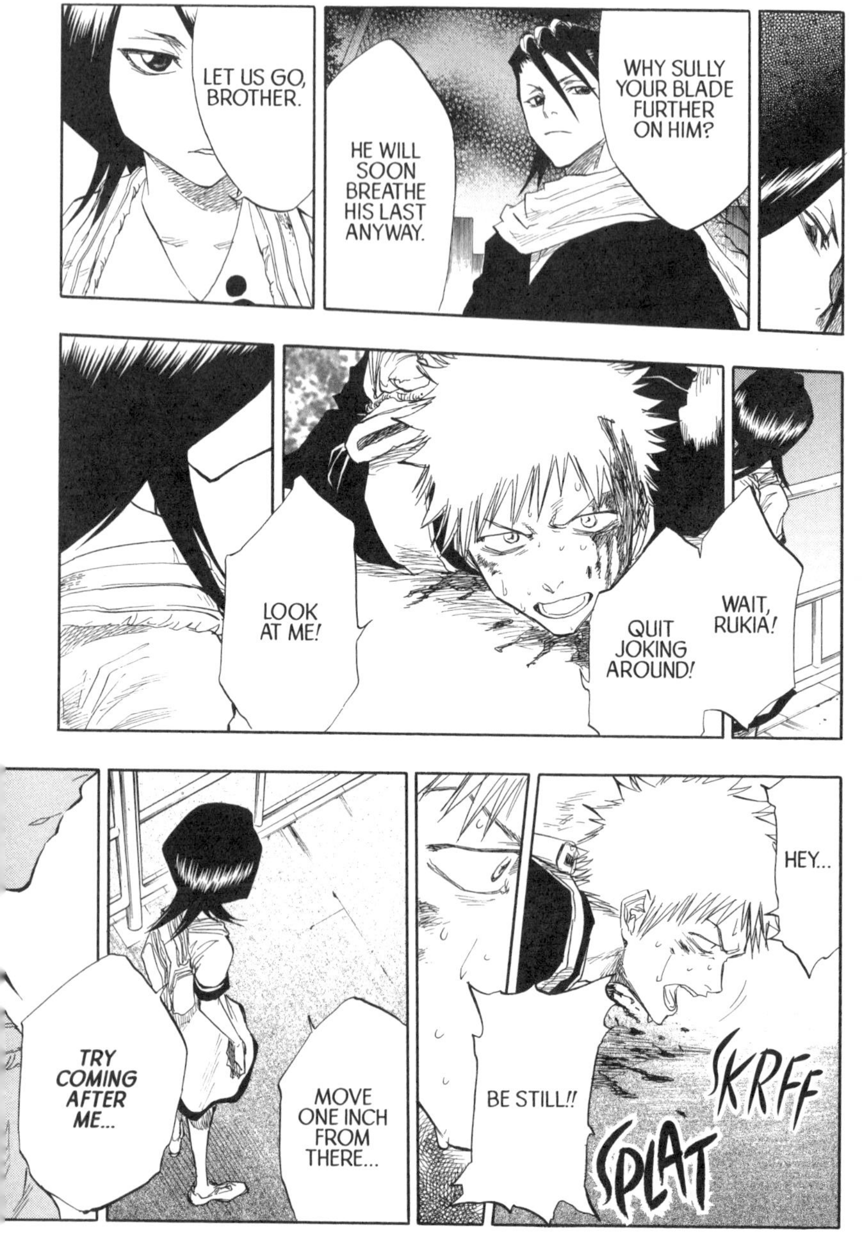
WHY SULLY YOUR BLADE FURTHER ON HIM?
HE WILL SOON BREATHE HIS LAST ANYWAY.
LET US GO, BROTHER.
WAIT, RUKIA!
QUIT JOKING AROUND!
LOOK AT ME!
HEY...
SKRFF
SPLAT
BE STILL!!
MOVE ONE INCH FROM THERE...
TRY COMING AFTER ME...

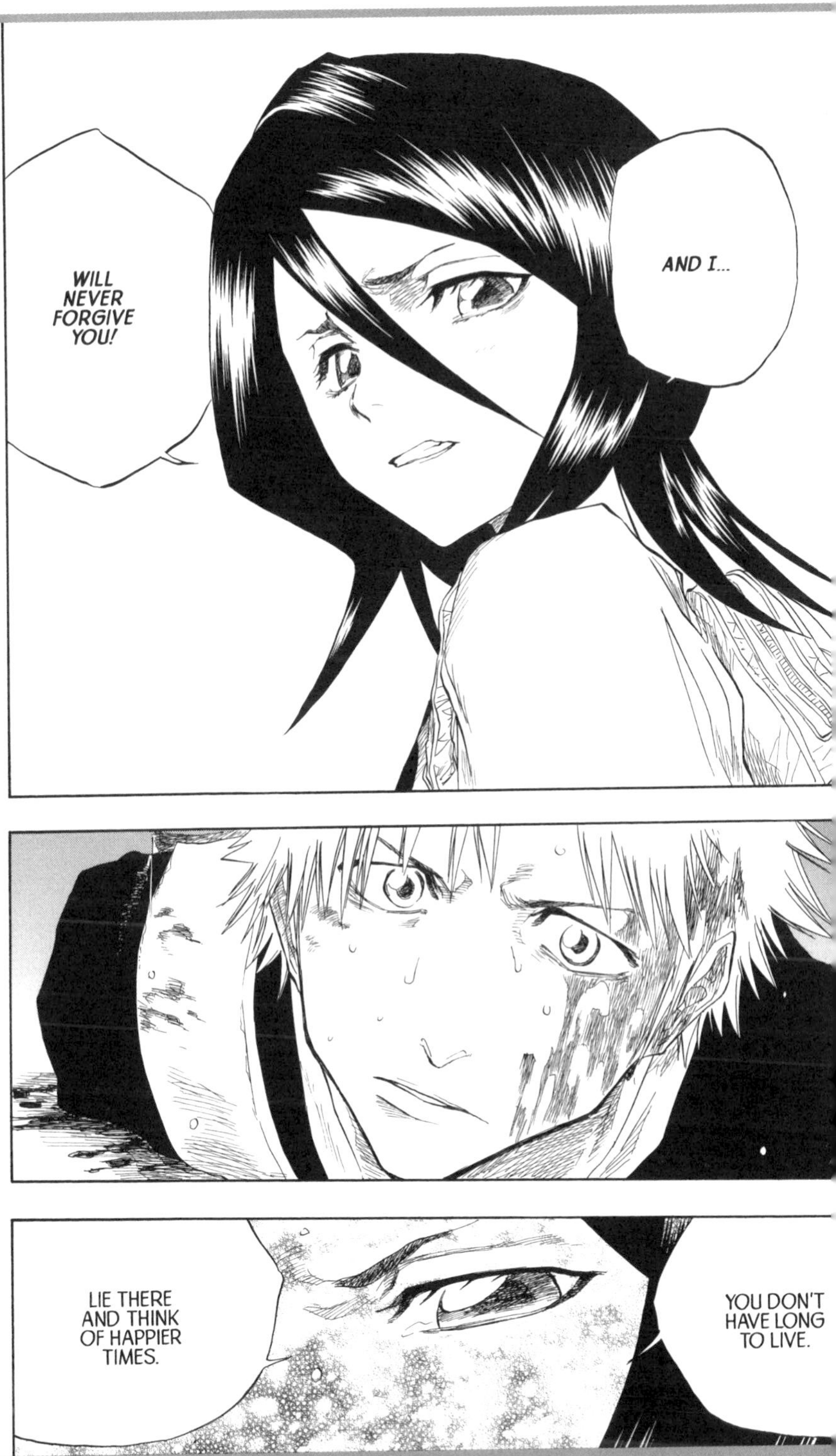
AND I...
WILL NEVER FORGIVE YOU!
YOU DON'T HAVE LONG TO LIVE.
LIE THERE AND THINK OF HAPPIER TIMES.

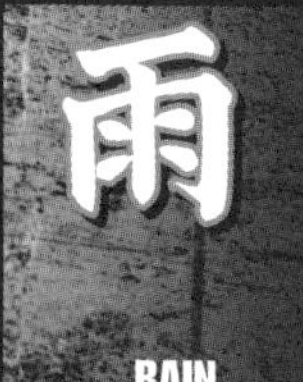
雨

RAIN

Never-ending Rain
VOL. 7-56~57

Byakuya defeats Ichigo almost instantly. Without thinking, Rukia rushes toward him, but Renji holds her back. Ichigo uses the last of his strength to grab Byakuya's sleeve, and Byakuya's eyes turn cold. Rukia kicks Ichigo's hand away and upbraids him for his rudeness toward her brother and says that she will go to the Soul Society of her own volition.

Ichigo is unable to understand what just happened, but he guesses her true feelings from the tears in her eyes as she looks back at him. Rukia leaves for the Soul Society and Ichigo is left alone as it begins to rain.

The rain brings back memories for Ichigo. His mother Masaki protected him once, and this time Rukia protected him. He is overwhelmed with regret... Ichigo screams out and curses his helplessness.

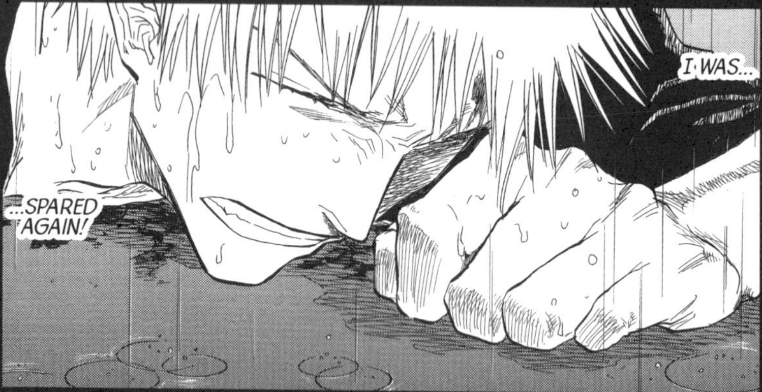
I WAS...
...SPARED AGAIN!

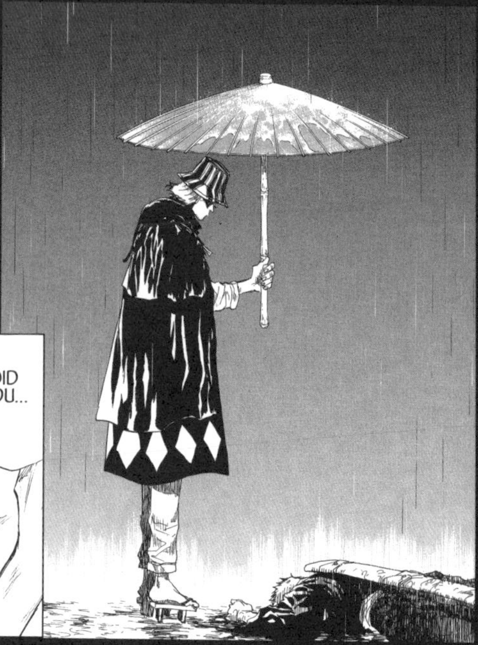

URAHARA'S HELP

Ichigo's body grows cold from the rain and loss of blood. As his vision fades, he sees a man approach. It's Urahara. Urahara tends Uryû's wounds and treats Ichigo's injuries at his shop. When Ichigo wakes up, Urahara quietly gives him an announcement.

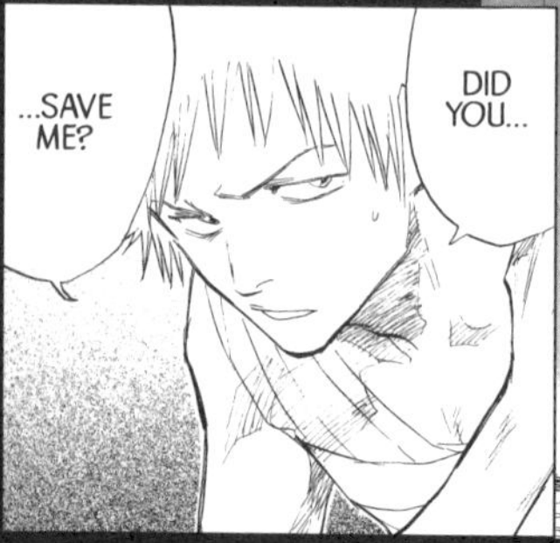
DID YOU...
...SAVE ME?

SOUL REAPER INSTRUCTOR

KISUKE URAHARA — CHARACTER FILE 15-b

Soul 魂

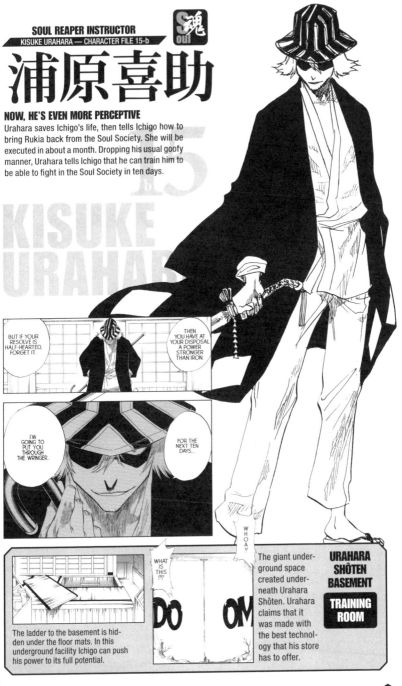

浦原喜助

NOW, HE'S EVEN MORE PERCEPTIVE

Urahara saves Ichigo's life, then tells Ichigo how to bring Rukia back from the Soul Society. She will be executed in about a month. Dropping his usual goofy manner, Urahara tells Ichigo that he can train him to be able to fight in the Soul Society in ten days.

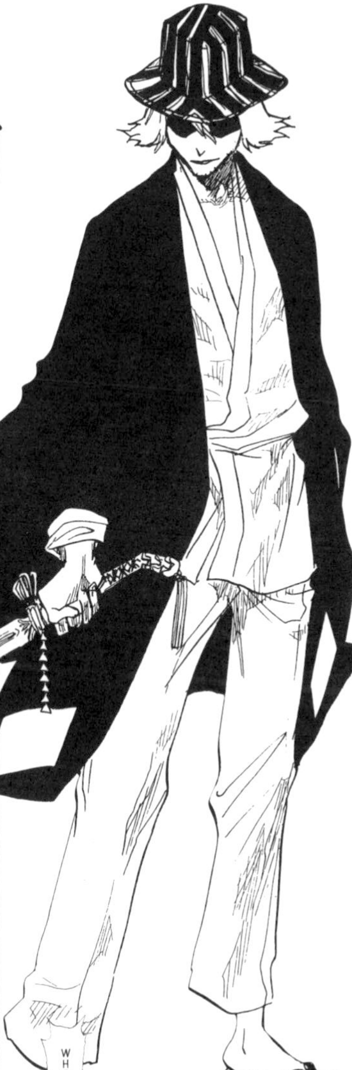

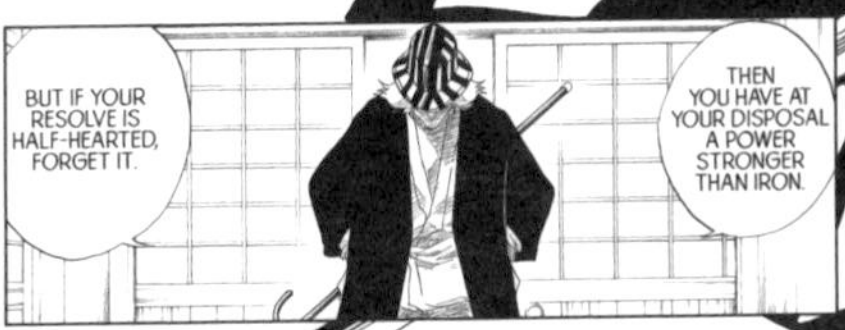
THEN YOU HAVE AT YOUR DISPOSAL A POWER STRONGER THAN IRON.
BUT IF YOUR RESOLVE IS HALF-HEARTED, FORGET IT.

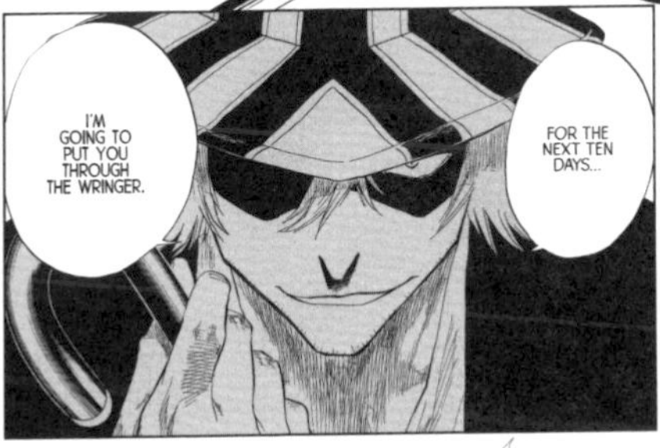
FOR THE NEXT TEN DAYS...
I'M GOING TO PUT YOU THROUGH THE WRINGER.

URAHARA SHÔTEN BASEMENT

TRAINING ROOM

The giant underground space created underneath Urahara Shôten. Urahara claims that it was made with the best technology that his store has to offer.

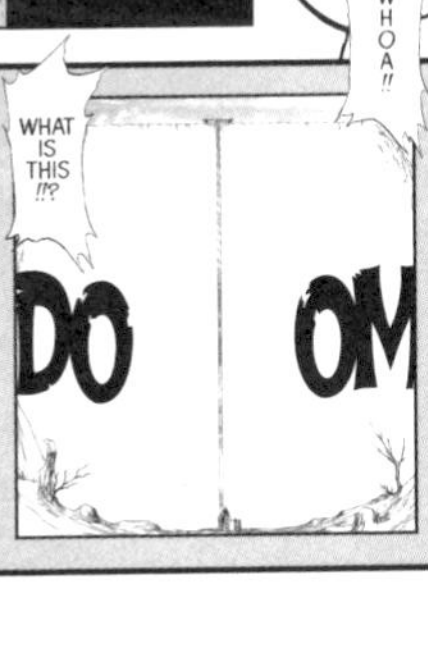
WHOA!!
WHAT IS THIS !!?
DO OM

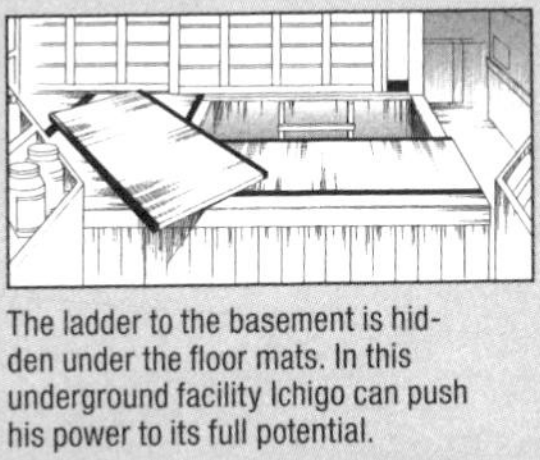

The ladder to the basement is hidden under the floor mats. In this underground facility Ichigo can push his power to its full potential.

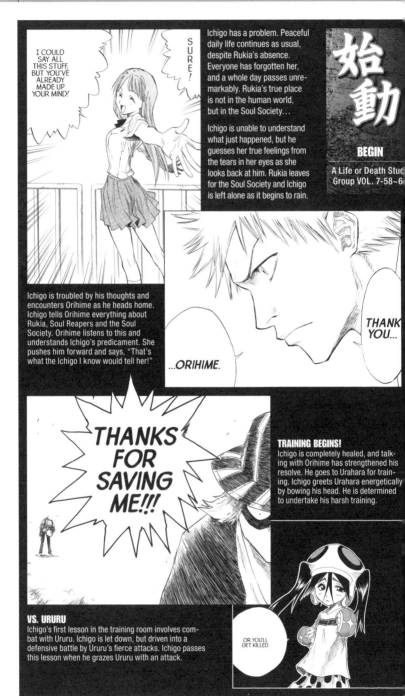

始動

BEGIN

A Life or Death Stuc
Group VOL. 7-58~6

Ichigo has a problem. Peaceful daily life continues as usual, despite Rukia's absence. Everyone has forgotten her, and a whole day passes unremarkably. Rukia's true place is not in the human world, but in the Soul Society...

Ichigo is unable to understand what just happened, but he guesses her true feelings from the tears in her eyes as she looks back at him. Rukia leaves for the Soul Society and Ichigo is left alone as it begins to rain.

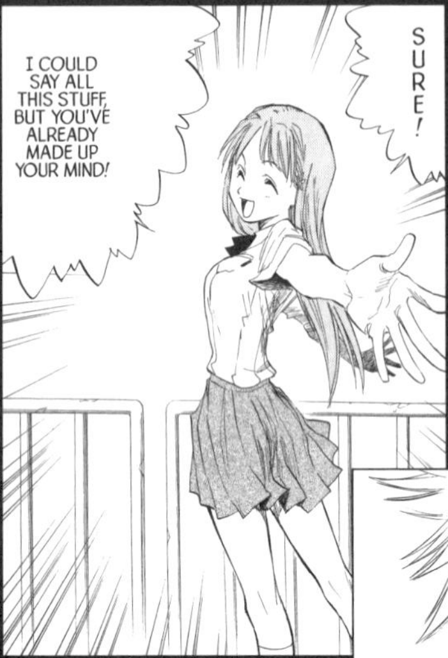
SURE!
I COULD SAY ALL THIS STUFF, BUT YOU'VE ALREADY MADE UP YOUR MIND!

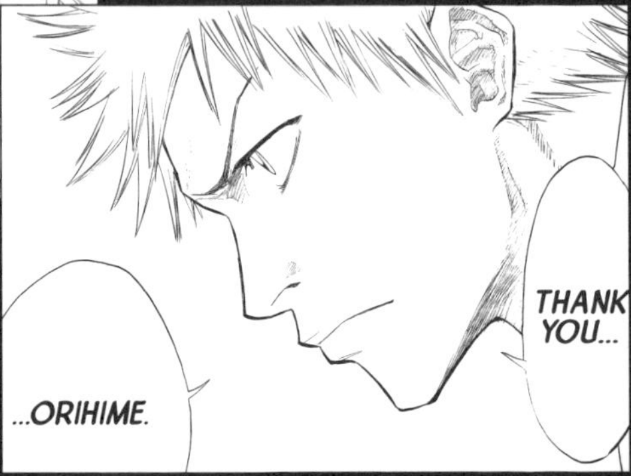
THANK YOU...
...ORIHIME.

Ichigo is troubled by his thoughts and encounters Orihime as he heads home. Ichigo tells Orihime everything about Rukia, Soul Reapers and the Soul Society. Orihime listens to this and understands Ichigo's predicament. She pushes him forward and says, "That's what the Ichigo I know would tell her!"

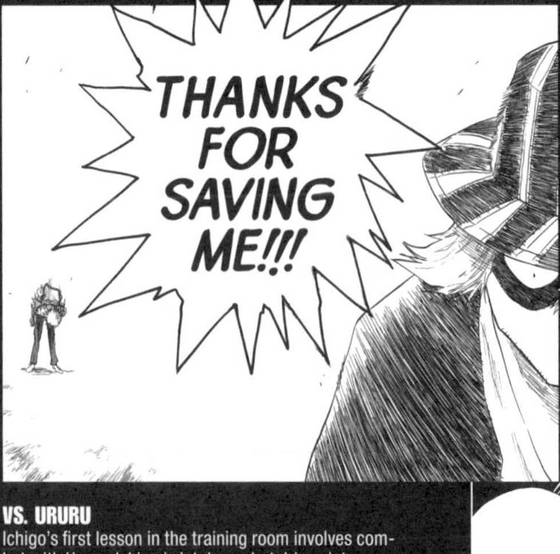
THANKS FOR SAVING ME!!!

TRAINING BEGINS!
Ichigo is completely healed, and talking with Orihime has strengthened his resolve. He goes to Urahara for training. Ichigo greets Urahara energetically by bowing his head. He is determined to undertake his harsh training.

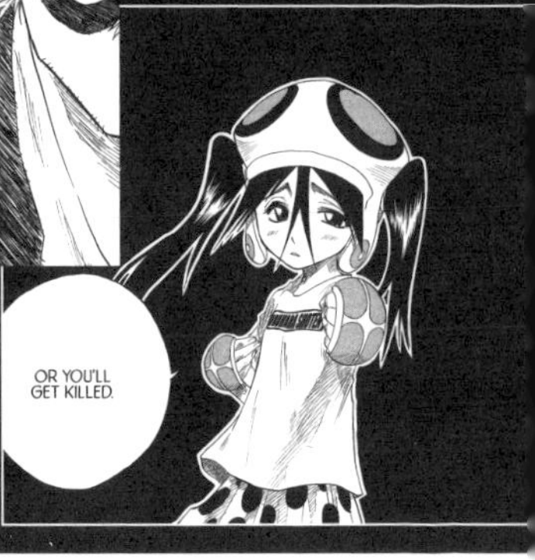
OR YOU'LL GET KILLED.

VS. URURU
Ichigo's first lesson in the training room involves combat with Ururu. Ichigo is let down, but driven into a defensive battle by Ururu's fierce attacks. Ichigo passes this lesson when he grazes Ururu with an attack.

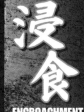

浸食
ENCROACHMENT

The Pit of Despair (Shattered Shaft)
VOL. 7-61~VOL. 8-62

Ichigo's chain of fate is cut and he is pushed into the shattered shaft. With his arms restrained, Ichigo has 72 hours to climb out of the pit. When time runs out and Ichigo's chain of fate disappears, Ichigo begins to transform into a Hollow.

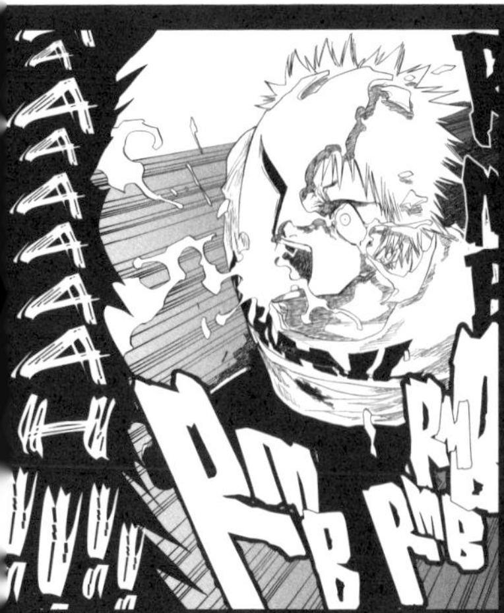
RMB RMB
RMB

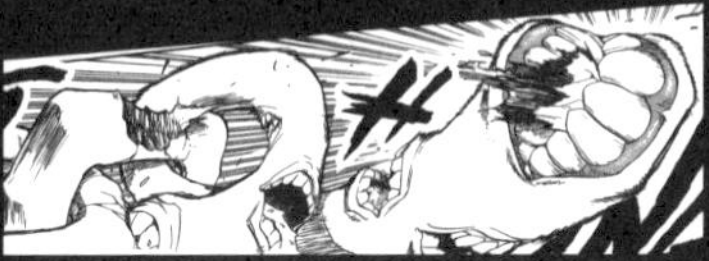

THE ONE WHO LEADS SOULS

THE MAN IN BLACK — CHARACTER FILE 40-a

Soul 魂

黒衣の男

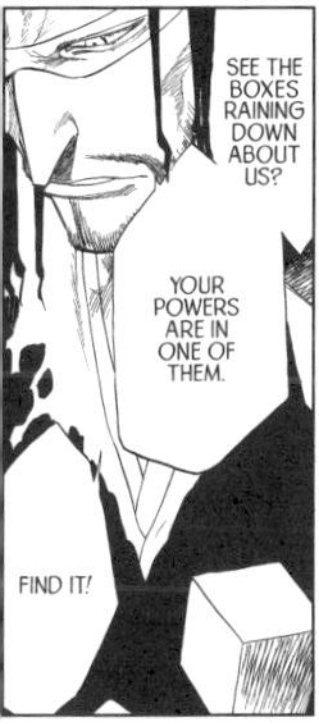
SEE THE BOXES RAINING DOWN ABOUT US?
YOUR POWERS ARE IN ONE OF THEM.
FIND IT!

ICHIGO'S OWN SOUL REAPER POWER

Byakuya only removed the power that Ichigo received from Rukia. Ichigo's *own* Soul Reaper powers dwell deep within his soul.

THE INNER EXISTENCE WITHIN THE SOUL

40

The man in black appears within Ichigo's internal world while Ichigo is becoming a Hollow. The man's name is blacked out and Ichigo cannot hear him. The man tells Ichigo to search for the Soul Reaper power that is hidden within him. Ichigo tries his best to find his power as his internal world begins to crumble...

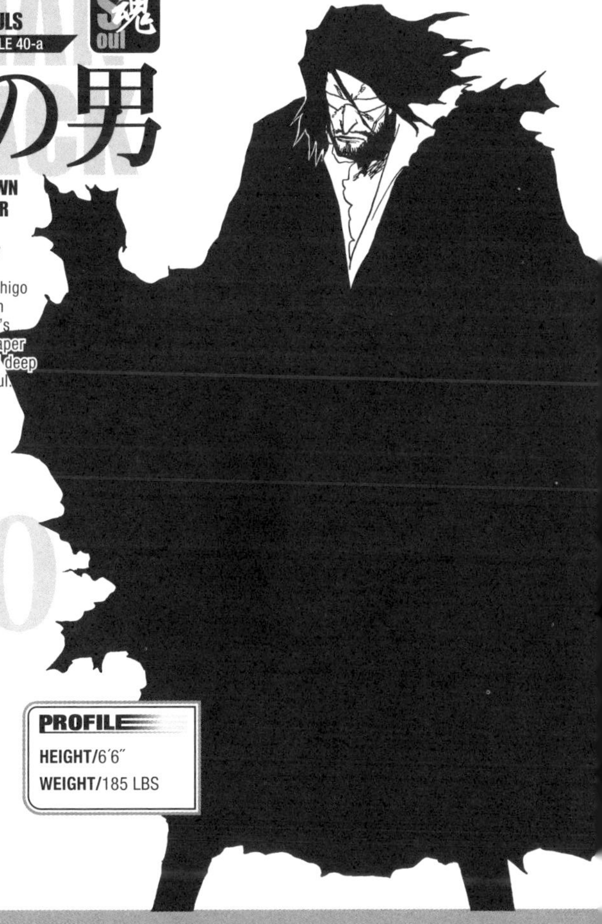

PROFILE

HEIGHT/6′6″

WEIGHT/185 LBS

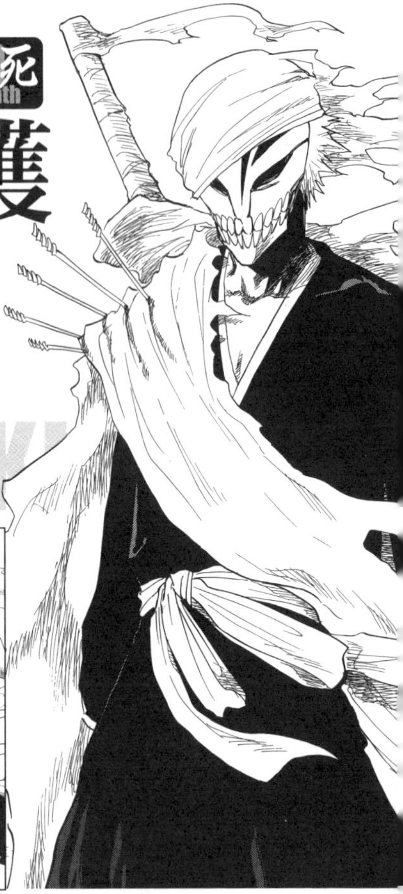

NEWLY-GAINED SOUL REAPER POWERS

D死 eath

ICHIGO KUROSAKI — CHARACTER FILE 1-d

黒崎一護

A SHIHAKUSHÔ AND A HOLLOW MASK

Ichigo barely manages to find his Soul Reaper powers in his crumbling internal world. When his Hollow transformation is at its peak, a black shadow flies out of the pit with a thundering sound. It wears a shihakushô and strange mask on his face… Is he a Soul Reaper? Or is he…

The figure breaks his mask with the hilt of his broken zanpaku-tô… Beneath it is Ichigo, who has regained his Soul Reaper powers.

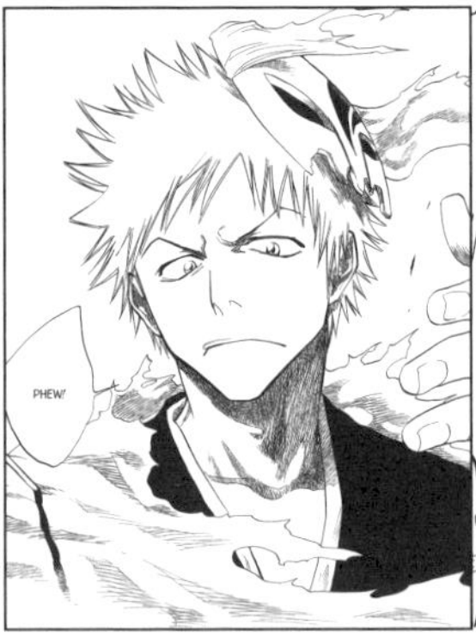
PHEW!

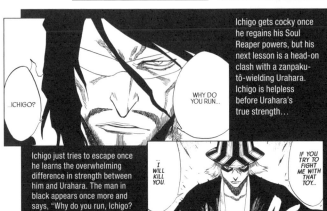

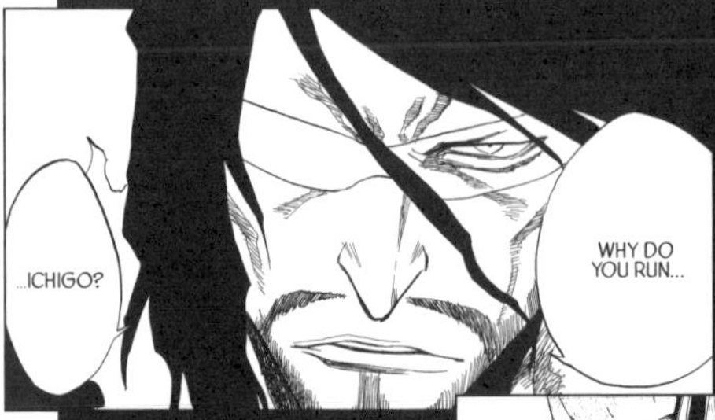
WHY DO YOU RUN...
...ICHIGO?

Ichigo gets cocky once he regains his Soul Reaper powers, but his next lesson is a head-on clash with a zanpaku-tô-wielding Urahara. Ichigo is helpless before Urahara's true strength…

恐怖

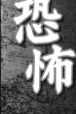

FEAR

Absolute differenc in strength
VOL. 8-64~66

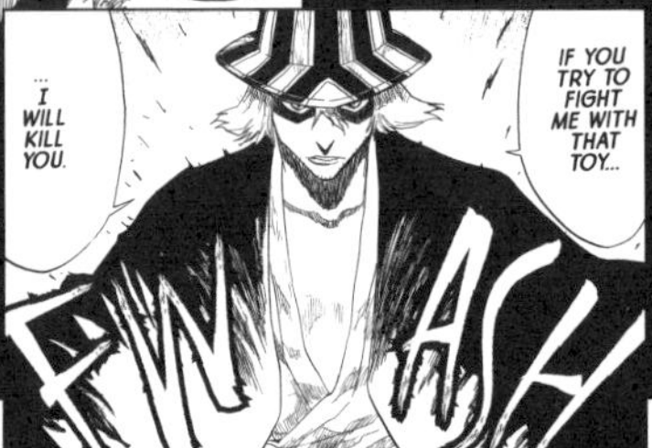
IF YOU TRY TO FIGHT ME WITH THAT TOY...
... I WILL KILL YOU.
FWASH

Ichigo just tries to escape once he learns the overwhelming difference in strength between him and Urahara. The man in black appears once more and says, "Why do you run, Ichigo? You still haven't called me."

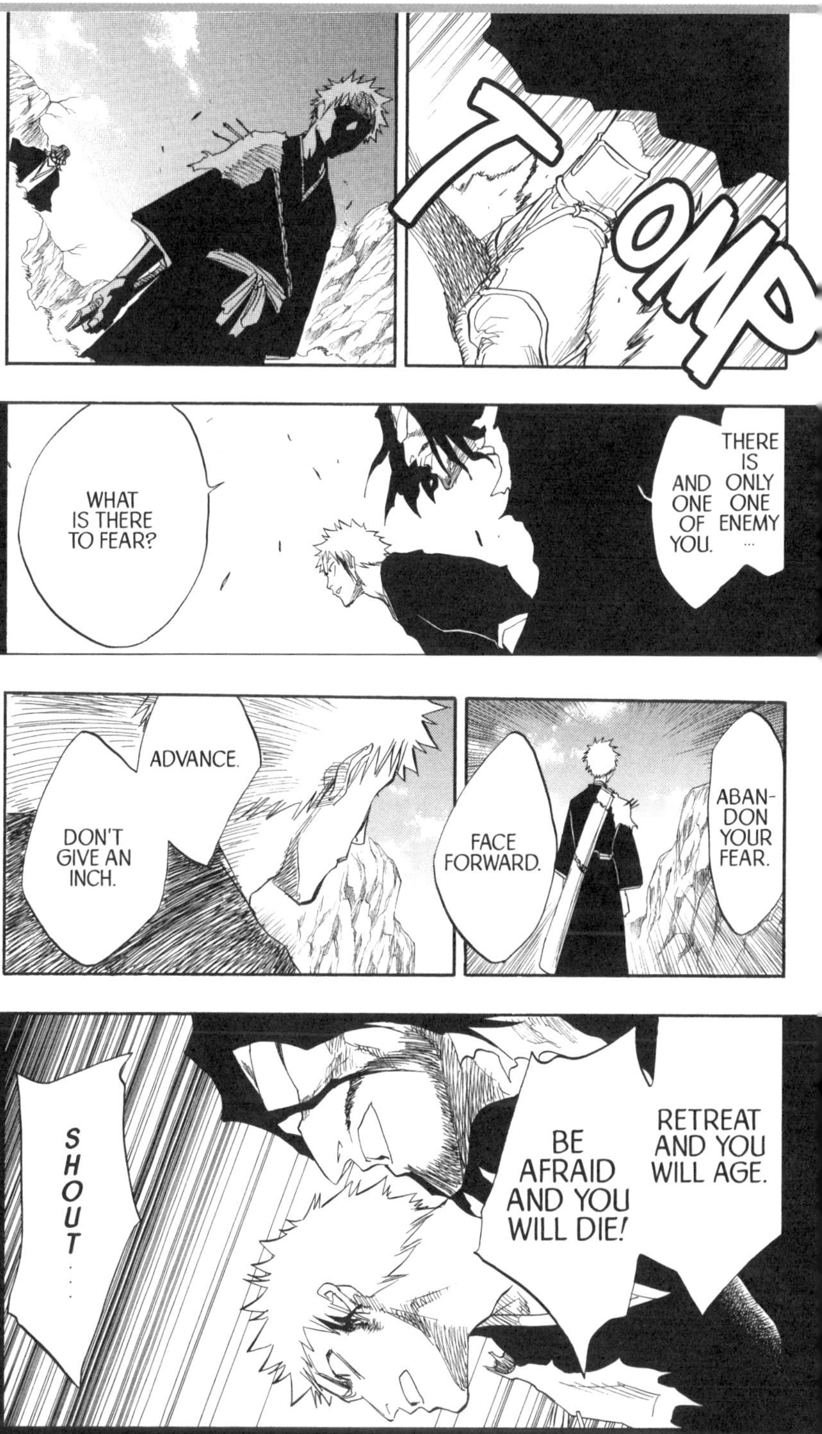
TOMP
THERE IS ONLY ONE ENEMY...
AND ONE OF YOU.
WHAT IS THERE TO FEAR?
ABANDON YOUR FEAR.
FACE FORWARD.
ADVANCE.
DON'T GIVE AN INCH.
RETREAT AND YOU WILL AGE.
BE AFRAID AND YOU WILL DIE!
SHOUT...

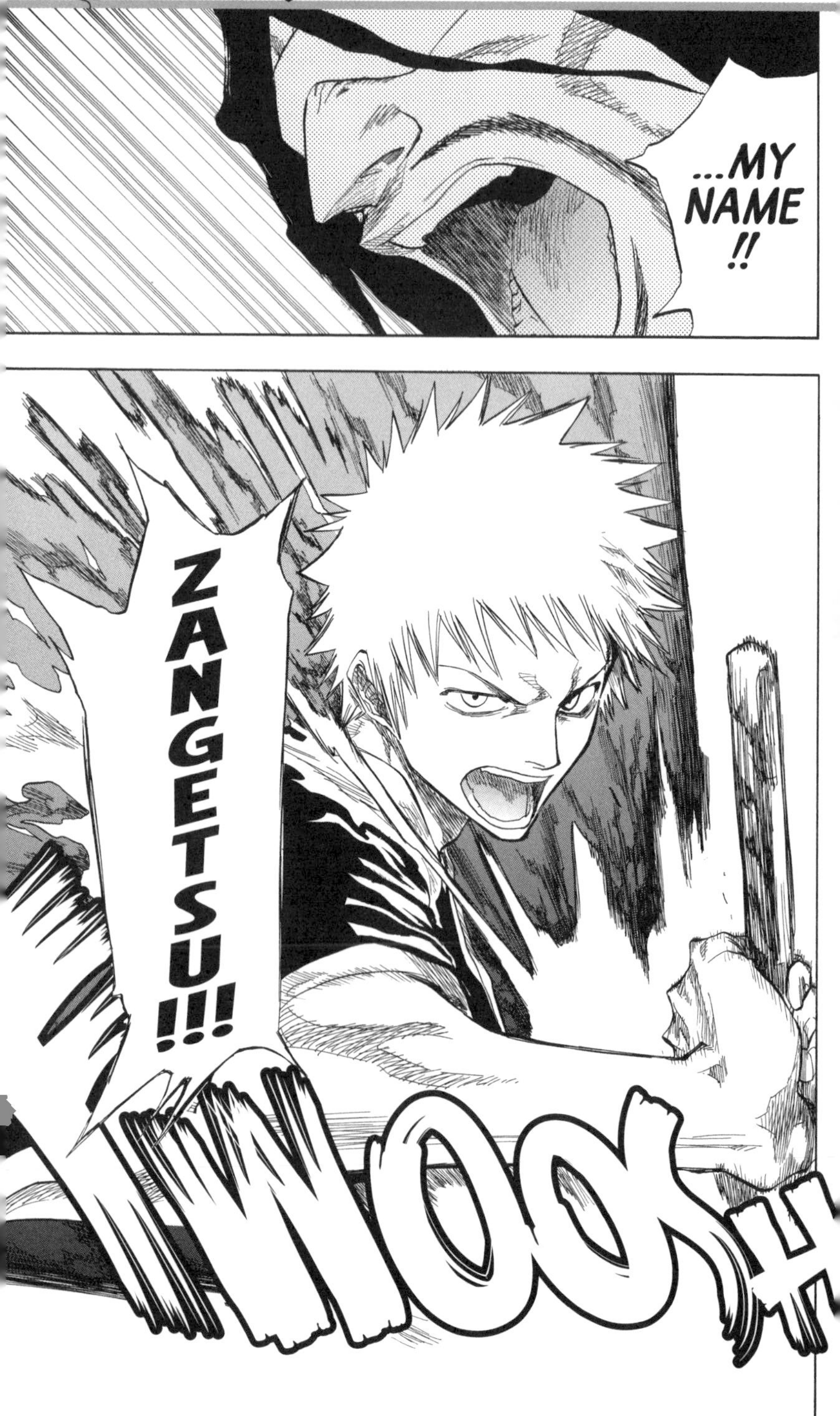
...MY NAME !!
ZANGETSU!!!
WHOOSH

顕現

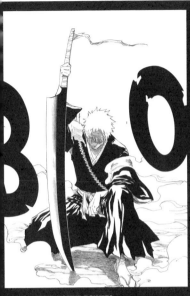

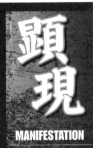

MANIFESTATION

His name is Zangetsu
VOL. 8-66~67

Spurred on by the man in black, Ichigo yells the man's name, "Zangetsu!!"

Ichigo's released spiritual pressure overwhelms his surroundings and envelops him like smoke. When he is visible again, there is something in his hands. A huge unrefined power that has neither a sword guard nor a sheath… Zangetsu.

DO OM
LESSON THREE…
YOU PASSED!

SUPERB DESTRUCTIVE POWER!
Ichigo gains Zangetsu and focuses immense spiritual power into his arm. Urahara senses danger the moment that Ichigo swings his raised arm, and defends himself with one of Benihime's techniques. He lets out a sigh of relief at the sight of Ichigo's destructive power.

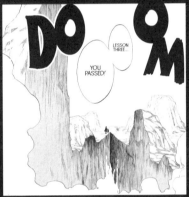

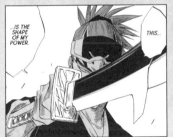

ABILITY RELEASE KEYWORD

A ZANPAKU-TÔ'S NAME

The zanpaku-tô of low-ranking Soul Reapers are called Asauchi and don't have names. But the zanpaku-tô of Soul Reapers of rank have names. In its sealed state, a zanpaku-tô has the form of a Japanese sword. But when its name is called, it goes into shikai state and its form and abilities change drastically.

THIS…
…IS THE SHAPE OF MY POWER.

RENJI ABARAI
ZABIMARU
Renji's Zabimaru has a special form that consists of aligned blade segments. It can extend and shrink at will and frequently changes its angle of attack, like a whip.

SCREAM…
RED PRINCESS!!

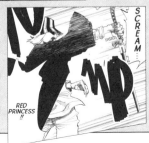

KISUKE URAHARA
BENIHIME
Benihime usually takes the form of a sword cane, but in its shikai state, it transforms into a straight sword without a sword guard. It has special abilities, such as the Shield of Blood Mist.

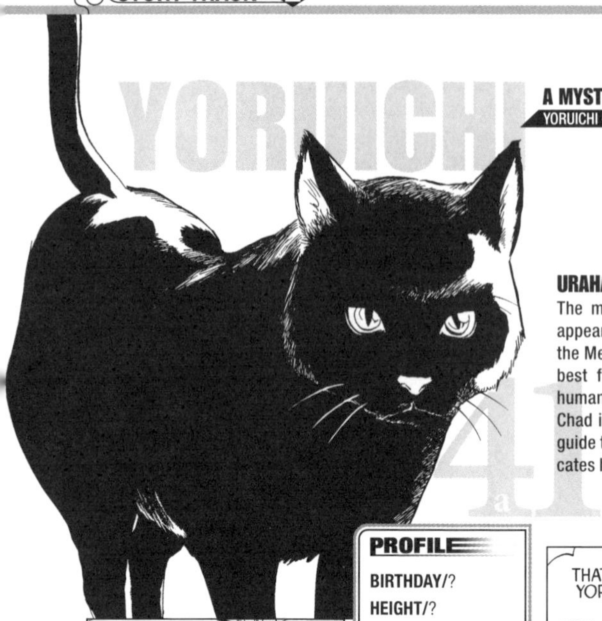

A MYSTERIOUS BLACK CAT

YORUICHI — CHARACTER FILE 41-a

夜一

URAHARA'S OLD FRIEND

The mysterious black cat that suddenly appears at Urahara's Shôten the day after the Menos Grande attack. He is Urahara's best friend and can communicate with humans. Besides helping Orihime and Chad improve their abilities, he acts as a guide to the Soul Society. His speech indicates his high rank.

PROFILE

BIRTHDAY/?

HEIGHT/?

WEIGHT/?

CHAD AND ORIHIME'S TEACHER

Mr. Yoruichi undertakes Chad and Orihime's instruction. He asks Uryû if he would like to be instructed as well, but Uryû declines.

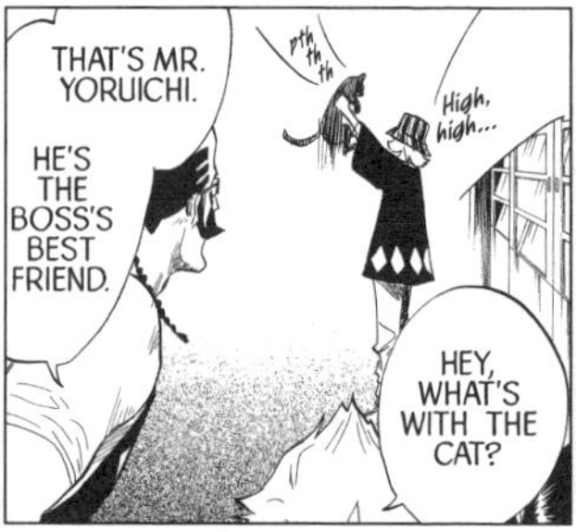
pth th th
High, high...
THAT'S MR. YORUICHI.
HE'S THE BOSS'S BEST FRIEND.
HEY, WHAT'S WITH THE CAT?

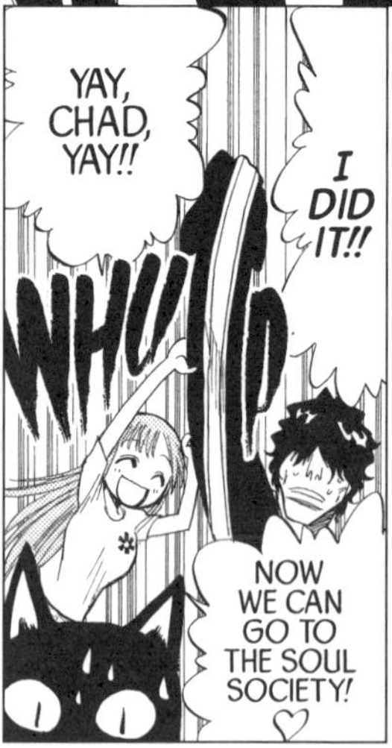
I DID IT!!
YAY, CHAD, YAY!!
WHUD
NOW WE CAN GO TO THE SOUL SOCIETY! ♡

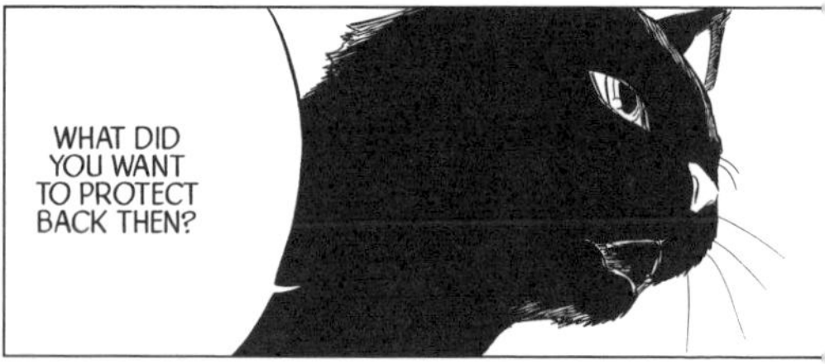
WHAT DID YOU WANT TO PROTECT BACK THEN?

Mr. Yoruichi tries to make Chad and Orihime remember what triggered the appearance of their abilities by asking them what their purpose is in going to the Soul Society.

URYÛ'S INDEPENDENT TRAINING

A SECRET QUINCY TOOL

Uryû realizes his weakness and goes to train in the mountains. He has a special tool known as the Scattered Spirits Glove which was passed down to him by his teacher, Sôken. Using the sanreishutô glove requires resourcefulness and constant training.

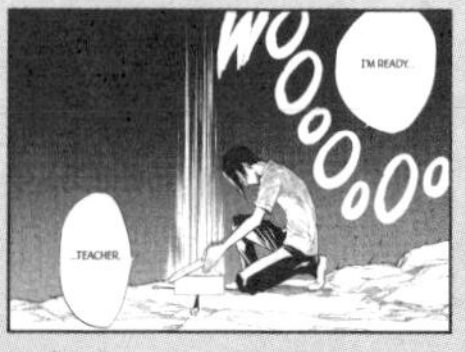
WOOOOOOOO
I'M READY.
...TEACHER.

Uryû learns a secret technique by manifesting and maintaining his Kojaku for seven solid days and nights.

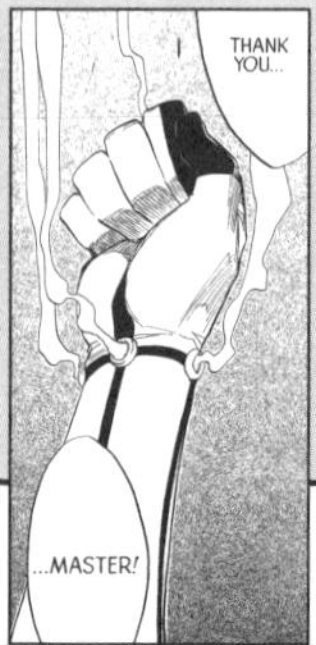
THANK YOU...
...MASTER!

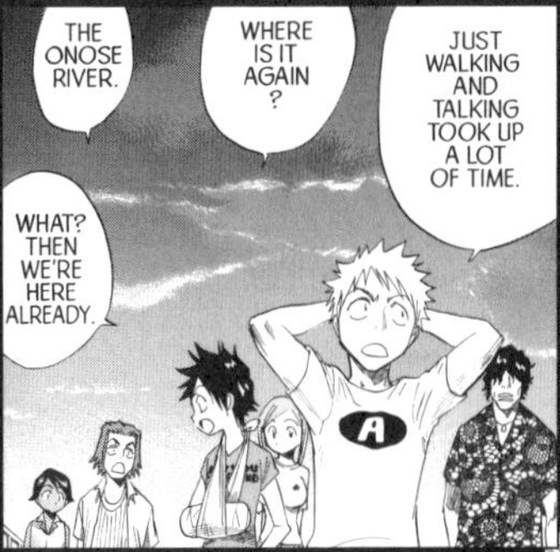
JUST WALKING AND TALKING TOOK UP A LOT OF TIME.
WHERE IS IT AGAIN ?
THE ONOSE RIVER.
WHAT? THEN WE'RE HERE ALREADY.

Ichigo and his friends' harsh training ends and they take a short moment to enjoy everyday life while Urahara is preparing to open the gate to the Soul Society. Ichigo and his friends accept an invitation from Keigo and go to a fireworks display in a neighboring town. Chad and Orihime relax with their friends during their short break.

決意

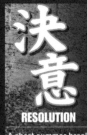

RESOLUTION

A short summer break
VOL. 8-68

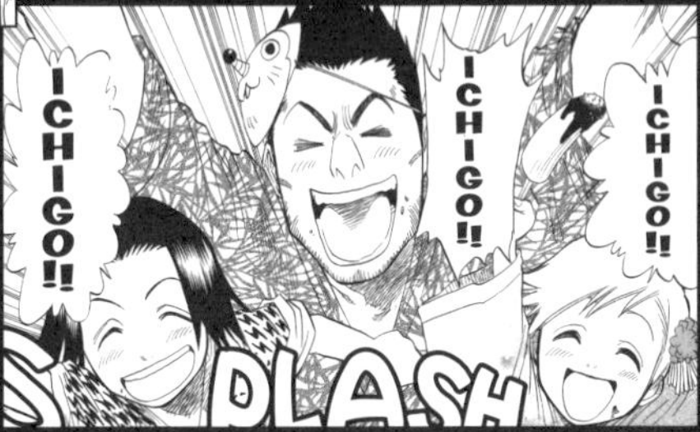
ICHIGO!!
ICHIGO!!
ICHIGO!!

BRIEF FAMILY TIME

The members of the Kurosaki family come chasing after Ichigo. They're drunk on sake and are more energetic than usual! On the way home from the fireworks display, Ichigo strengthens his resolve to leave by telling his father Isshin that he is going to go on a trip.

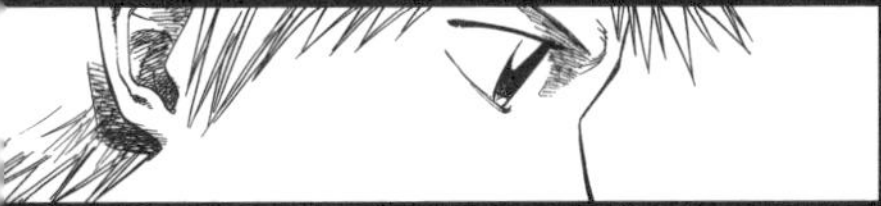

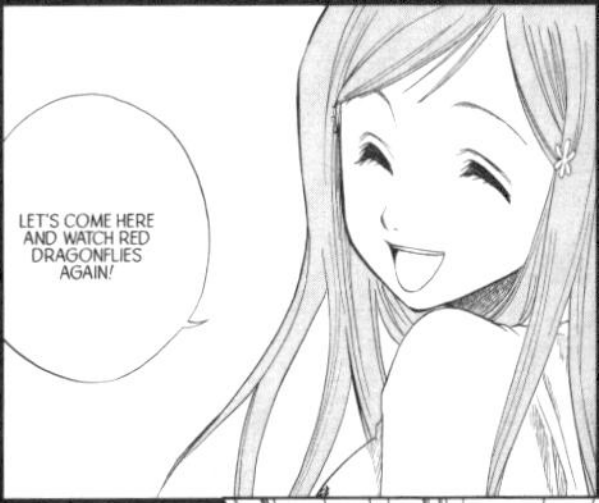
LET'S COME HERE AND WATCH RED DRAGONFLIES AGAIN!

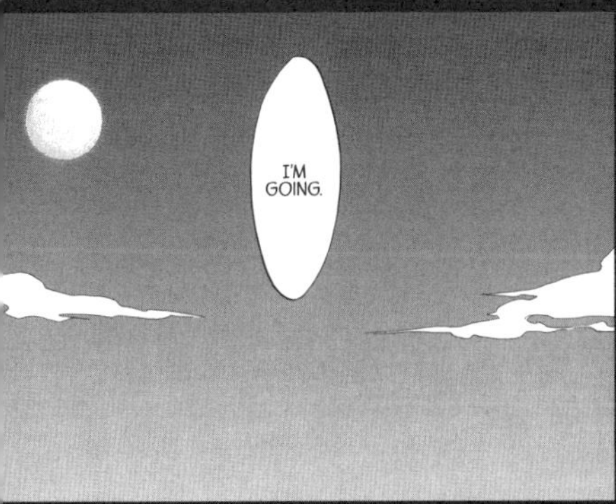
I'M GOING.

Tatsuki's sharp intuition is quick to realize the difference in Orihime. Tatsuki doesn't ask about it and promises Orihime that they will meet again.

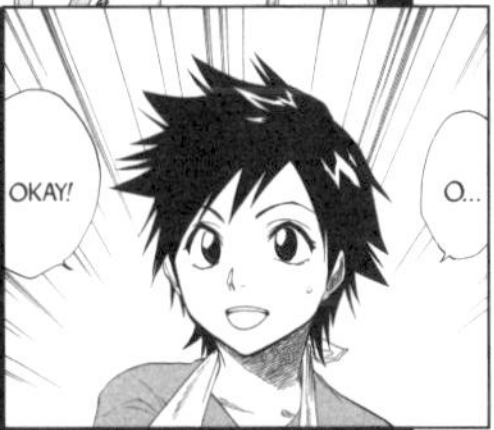
O...
OKAY!

A MASS OF LUCK AND PRAYERS

MASAKI'S LUCKY CHARM

Ichigo leaves his house late at night after receiving summons from Urahara. Isshin is waiting for this moment and unquestioningly hands Ichigo a specially made lucky charm Masaki had given him. Ichigo accepts his gift and promises Isshin that he will return safely.

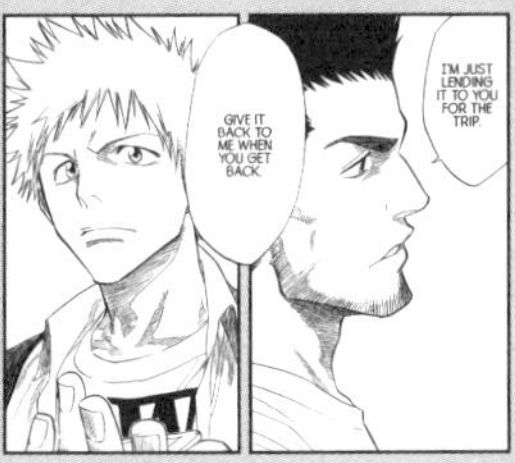
I'M JUST LENDING IT TO YOU FOR THE TRIP.
GIVE IT BACK TO ME WHEN YOU GET BACK.

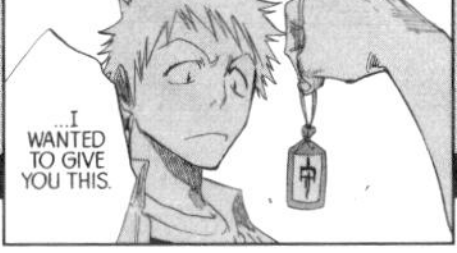
...I WANTED TO GIVE YOU THIS.

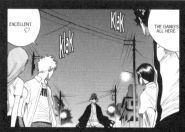

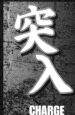

突入 CHARGE

The Time to Depar
VOL. 8-69~70

THE GANG'S ALL HERE.
Klak
Klak
EXCELLENT. ♡

The time to depart finally comes. Orihime, Chad, and Uryû, who is in formal attire, have been summoned and gather front of Urahara Shôten. Urahara is waiting there. He leads them through the underground training room to the Senkaimon that leads to the Soul Society. They stand before the gate. It's time!

THE WILL TO MOVE AHEAD

It takes four minutes for the Senkaimon to connect to the Soul Society. Everyone hesitates, but Mr. Yoruichi, who has taken up the role as a guide, tells them of the importance of moving ahead. Everyone departs without second thoughts. Ichigo tells Mr. Yoruichi, "Then I'll have to win!"

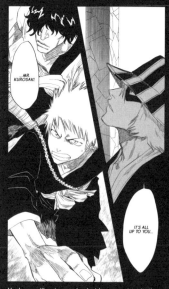

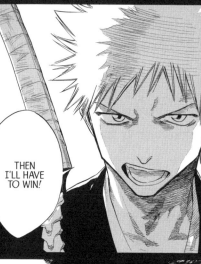

THEN I'LL HAVE TO WIN!
EXACTLY!

...MR. KUROSAKI.
IT'S ALL UP TO YOU...

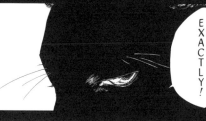

Urahara will not say why, but he cannot go to the Soul Society with them. He leaves the future to Ichigo.

THE GATE TO THE SOUL SOCIETY

SENKAIMON

Zakk

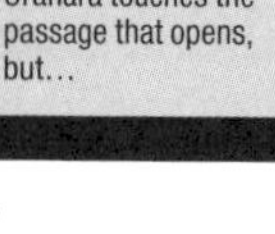

Urahara touches the passage that opens, but...

The Senkaimon connects the Soul Society to the human world. The one that Urahara made has a reishi converter, which takes humans like Uryû and the others into consideration. This modified one can be used by regular people.

Fwoom

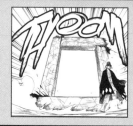

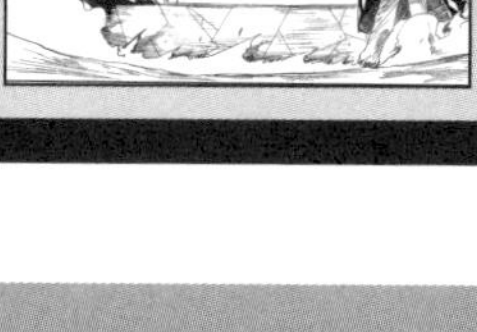

BLEACH FUN! FUN!! FUN!!!

Christmas in Carmine

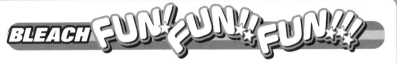

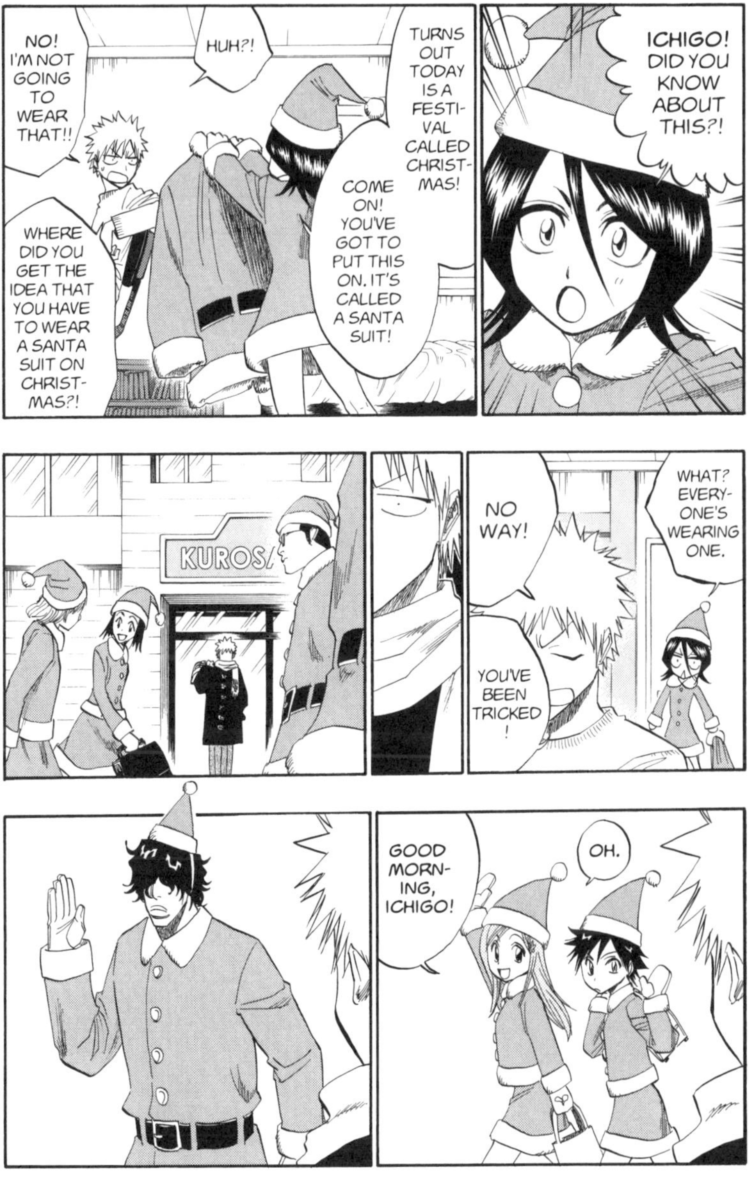
ICHIGO! DID YOU KNOW ABOUT THIS?!
TURNS OUT TODAY IS A FESTIVAL CALLED CHRISTMAS!
HUH?!
NO! I'M NOT GOING TO WEAR THAT!!
COME ON! YOU'VE GOT TO PUT THIS ON. IT'S CALLED A SANTA SUIT!
WHERE DID YOU GET THE IDEA THAT YOU HAVE TO WEAR A SANTA SUIT ON CHRISTMAS?!
WHAT? EVERYONE'S WEARING ONE.
NO WAY!
YOU'VE BEEN TRICKED!
KUROSA
OH.
GOOD MORNING, ICHIGO!

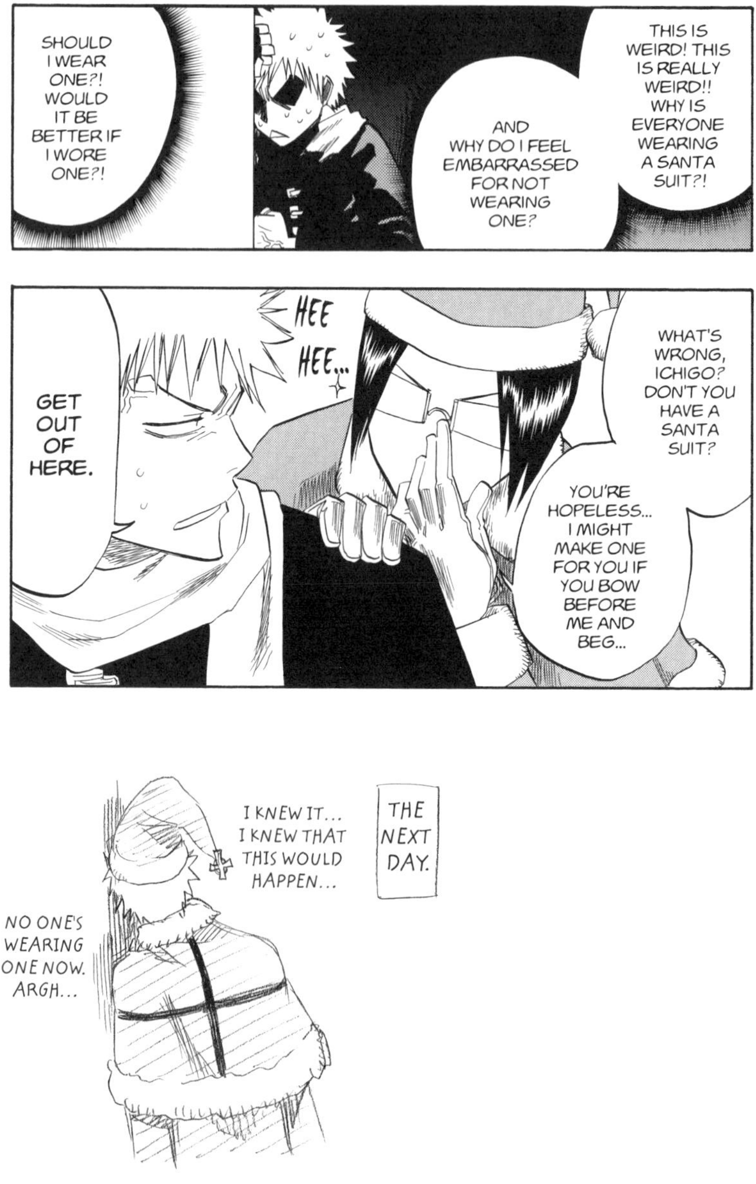
THIS IS WEIRD! THIS IS REALLY WEIRD!! WHY IS EVERYONE WEARING A SANTA SUIT?!
AND WHY DO I FEEL EMBARRASSED FOR NOT WEARING ONE?
SHOULD I WEAR ONE?! WOULD IT BE BETTER IF I WORE ONE?!
WHAT'S WRONG, ICHIGO? DON'T YOU HAVE A SANTA SUIT?
YOU'RE HOPELESS... I MIGHT MAKE ONE FOR YOU IF YOU BOW BEFORE ME AND BEG...
HEE HEE...
GET OUT OF HERE.
THE NEXT DAY.
I KNEW IT... I KNEW THAT THIS WOULD HAPPEN...
NO ONE'S WEARING ONE NOW. ARGH...

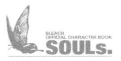

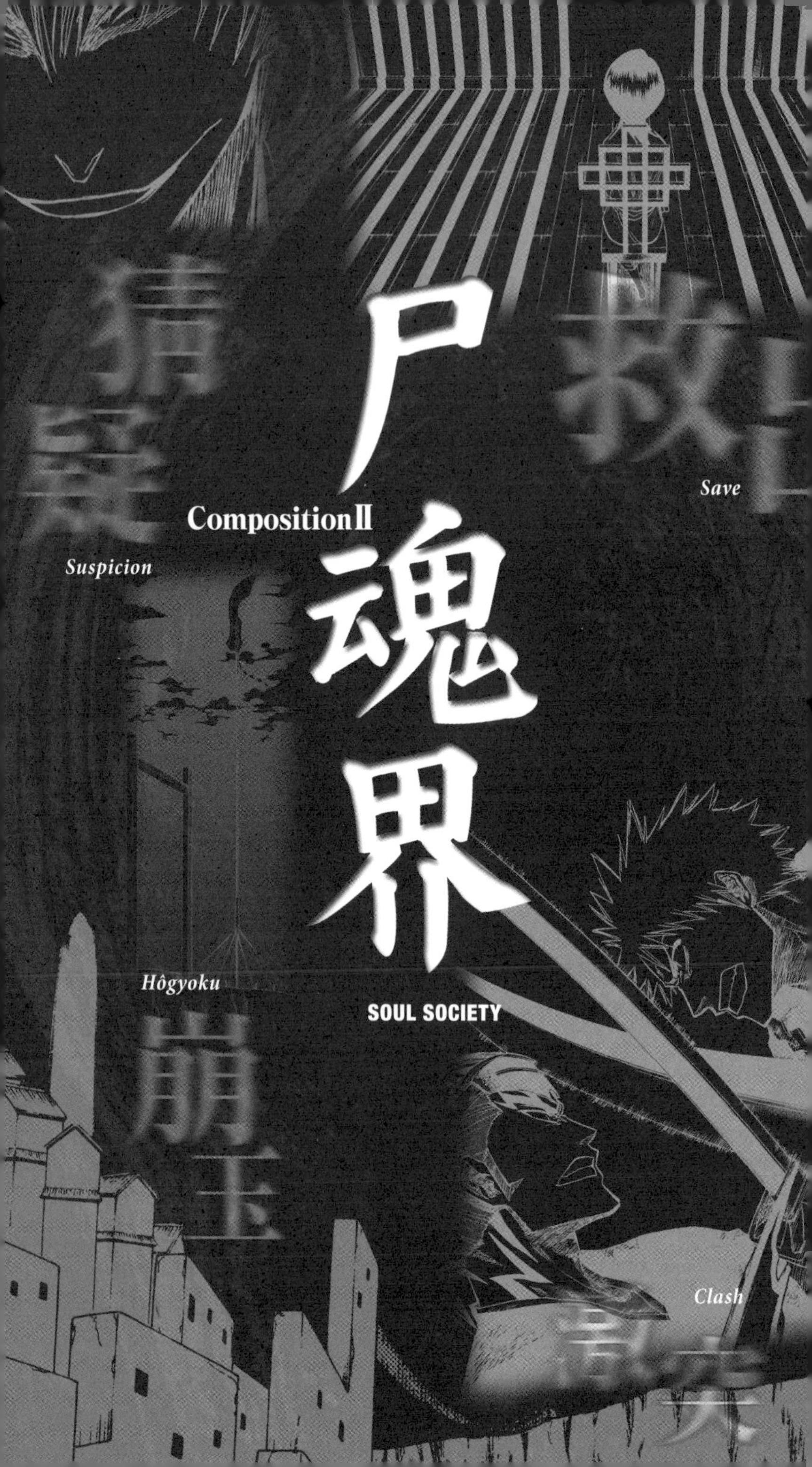
尸魂界
Composition II
SOUL SOCIETY
Save
Suspicion
Hôgyoku
崩玉
Clash

EXPLANATION OF THE SOUL SOCIETY

INTRODUCTION

The Soul Society: The place where souls go after they die. This world consists of the Rukongai, where souls first live when they arrive in the Soul Society, and the Seireitei, which is at the center of the Soul Society. The mode of life here closely resembles that of feudal Japan. It's as Rukia says: "You'll never be hungry (if you don't have spiritual powers), and you'll be happy!" It is a nice place to live, but there are many poverty-stricken people in the lowest level of the Rukongai.

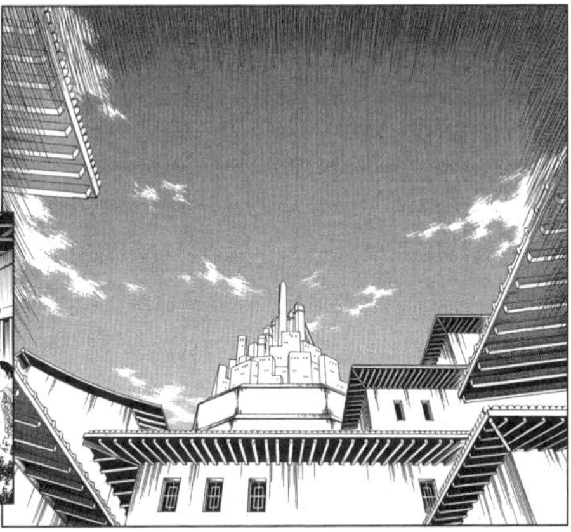

The Rukongai is divided into the four cardinal directions, which are each broken up into 80 areas. There are 320 areas in all. Many souls live here.

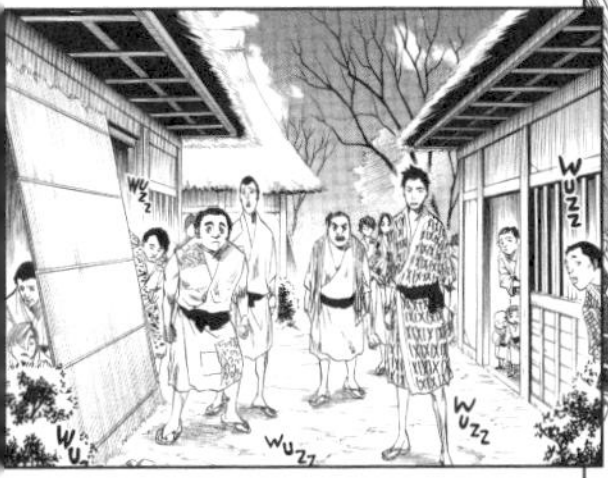
WUZZ
WUZZ
WUZZ
WUZZ

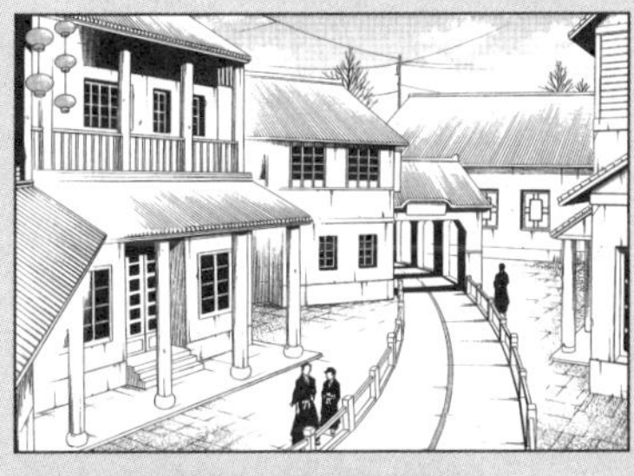

THE MAUSOLEUM WHERE SOUL REAPERS LIVE

SEIREITEI

Seireitei, a peaceful place...the center of the Soul Society. The only people who are allowed to live here are Soul Reapers and the very few existing aristocrats. Aristocrats like the Kuchiki family and the Shihôin family are born in Seireitei. They live their entire lives within the Soul Society. They are refined and are born with strong spiritual powers.

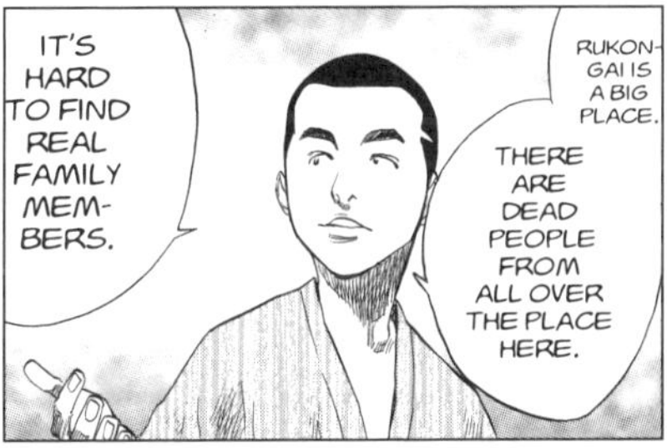
RUKONGAI IS A BIG PLACE.
THERE ARE DEAD PEOPLE FROM ALL OVER THE PLACE HERE.
IT'S HARD TO FIND REAL FAMILY MEMBERS.

THE COEXISTING SPIRITUAL WORLD

The human world is for the living. Dead souls gather in the Soul Society. These two worlds are parallel to each other and are two sides of the same coin. Families separated by death are rarely reunited in the Soul Society. People live nestled together like a family of strangers. Once a soul has spent a certain amount of time in the Soul Society, it is reborn into the human world.

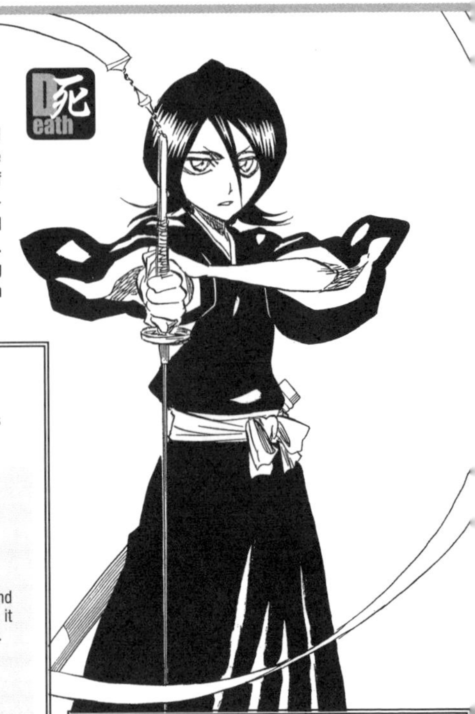

EXPLANATION OF SOUL REAPERS

When souls with exceptional spiritual energy train their bodies, they reach the level of Soul Reaper. The most talented of them become affiliated with various organizations like the Thirteen Court Guard Companies and the Secret Remote Squad. Sometimes, a Soul Reaper is born among the residents of the Rukongai, but such cases are rare.

ZANPAKU-TÔ RELEASE

The following two stages of release greatly change the fighting ability of a Soul Reaper's zanpaku-tô.

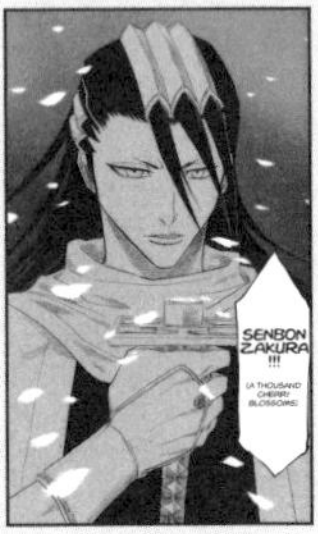
SENBON ZAKURA !!!
(A THOUSAND CHERRY BLOSSOMS)

SHIKAI
The first stage of release. A Soul Reaper is able to activate it by conversing with his zanpaku-tô and harmonizing with it to learn its name.

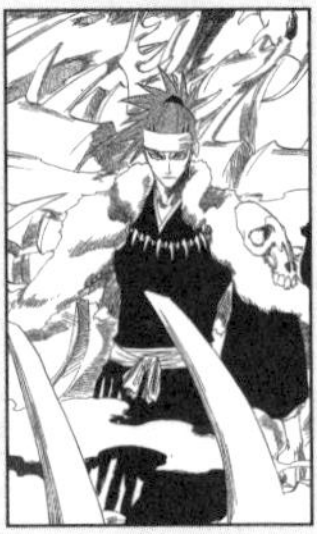

BANKAI
The second stage of release. In order to reach this level, the Soul Reaper needs to materialize the incarnation of the zanpaku-tô and make it yield to him.

THE FOUR BASIC FIGHTING STYLES

The fighting techniques that Soul Reapers use can be broken up into four categories. The abilities of each category will be explained here.

ZANJUTSU
Sword fighting techniques for the zanpaku-tô.The most basic fighting technique.

HOHÔ
The name for all high-speed fighting movements based on the Shunpo or Flash Step.

HAKUDA
An unarmed fighting technique that makes use of one's own body in a fight.

KIDÔ
Advanced spells that require strong spiritual power; Hado and Bakudo.

LIST OF KIDÔ SPELLS

Kidô are fighting spells that can allow the user to gain an advantage in battle. They include direct attack types and battle support types. The main ones are listed here.

TECHNIQUE NAME	EFFECT
Bakudo 1 Sai	Restrains the target's arms and legs.
Bakudo 58 Kakushi	Traces the target's location.
Bakudo 61 Rikujôkôrô	Restrains the target's movement with a spiritual sash of light.
Bakudo 77 Tentei	Transmits the user's voice to several people at the same time.
Bakudo 99 Kin	Restrains the target's arms.
Bakudo 99 Number 2 Bankin	An advanced version of Kin that seals away the target.

TECHNIQUE NAME	EFFECT
Hado 4 Byakurai (Pale Lightning)	Releases a concentrated aura from the user's fingertips.
Hado 31 Shakkaho (Red Flame Cannon)	Sends a fire-type spirit attack from the user's arms.
Hado 33 Sôkatsui	Releases a spirit attack of blue flames from the user's palms.
Hado 63 Raikôhô (Fiery Lightning Howl)	Sends an electrical-type attack at the enemy.
Hado 90 Kurohitsugi (Black Coffin)	Seals away an enemy with a pitch-black coffin.
Hakufuku (details unknown)	Clouds the consciousness of the target.

SOUL SOCIETY ORGANIZATIONAL TREE

A DIAGRAM OF WHAT HAS BEEN REVEALED OF THE SOUL SOCIETY'S ORGANIZATIONAL STRUCTURE.

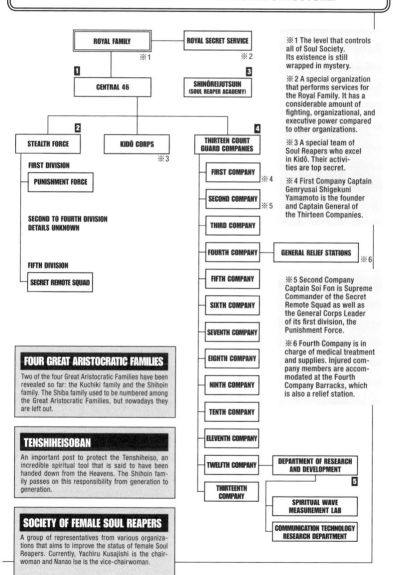

- ROYAL FAMILY ※1 — ROYAL SECRET SERVICE ※2
  - 1 CENTRAL 46
    - 2 STEALTH FORCE
      - FIRST DIVISION: PUNISHMENT FORCE
      - SECOND TO FOURTH DIVISION DETAILS UNKNOWN
      - FIFTH DIVISION: SECRET REMOTE SQUAD
    - KIDÔ CORPS ※3
    - 4 THIRTEEN COURT GUARD COMPANIES
      - FIRST COMPANY ※4
      - SECOND COMPANY ※5
      - THIRD COMPANY
      - FOURTH COMPANY — GENERAL RELIEF STATIONS ※6
      - FIFTH COMPANY
      - SIXTH COMPANY
      - SEVENTH COMPANY
      - EIGHTH COMPANY
      - NINTH COMPANY
      - TENTH COMPANY
      - ELEVENTH COMPANY
      - TWELFTH COMPANY — DEPARTMENT OF RESEARCH AND DEVELOPMENT
        - 5 SPIRITUAL WAVE MEASUREMENT LAB
        - COMMUNICATION TECHNOLOGY RESEARCH DEPARTMENT
      - THIRTEENTH COMPANY
- 3 SHINÔREIJUTSUIN (SOUL REAPER ACADEMY)

※1 The level that controls all of Soul Society. Its existence is still wrapped in mystery.

※2 A special organization that performs services for the Royal Family. It has a considerable amount of fighting, organizational, and executive power compared to other organizations.

※3 A special team of Soul Reapers who excel in Kidô. Their activities are top secret.

※4 First Company Captain Genryusai Shigekuni Yamamoto is the founder and Captain General of the Thirteen Companies.

※5 Second Company Captain Soi Fon is Supreme Commander of the Secret Remote Squad as well as the General Corps Leader of its first division, the Punishment Force.

※6 Fourth Company is in charge of medical treatment and supplies. Injured company members are accommodated at the Fourth Company Barracks, which is also a relief station.

FOUR GREAT ARISTOCRATIC FAMILIES

Two of the four Great Aristocratic Families have been revealed so far: the Kuchiki family and the Shihoin family. The Shiba family used to be numbered among the Great Aristocratic Families, but nowadays they are left out.

TENSHIHEISOBAN

An important post to protect the Tenshiheiso, an incredible spiritual tool that is said to have been handed down from the Heavens. The Shihoin family passes on this responsibility from generation to generation.

SOCIETY OF FEMALE SOUL REAPERS

A group of representatives from various organizations that aims to improve the status of female Soul Reapers. Currently, Yachiru Kusajishi is the chairwoman and Nanao Ise is the vice-chairwoman.

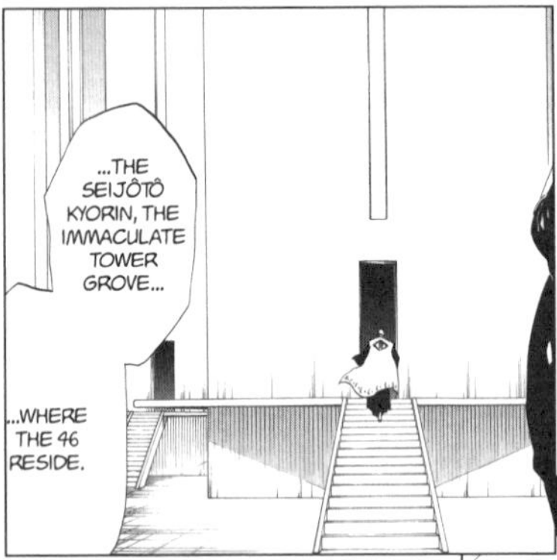
...THE SEIJÔTÔ KYORIN, THE IMMACULATE TOWER GROVE...
...WHERE THE 46 RESIDE.

1 THE SOUL SOCIETY'S SUPREME JUDICIAL ORGANIZATION CENTRAL 46

This supreme judicial organization consists of forty elders and six judges gathered from across the Soul Society. They handle all rulings on Soul Reapers and souls who have violated prohibitions. Their orders are absolute and no decision has been known to be overturned. Some suspect that there is an organization controlling the nature of the legislation and the administration of Central 46.

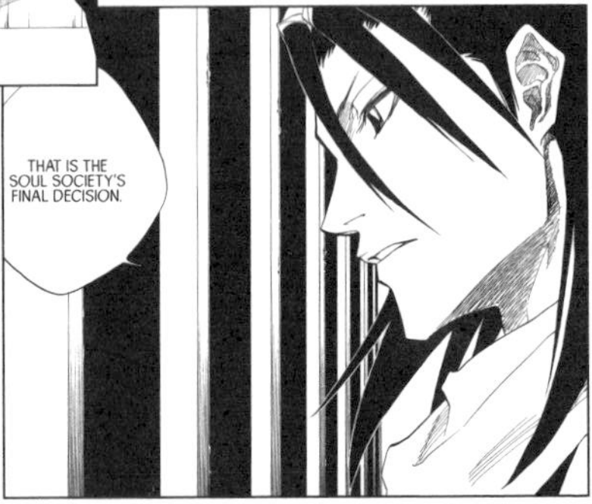
THAT IS THE SOUL SOCIETY'S FINAL DECISION.

COMPLETELY OFF LIMITS

Central 46 is in an off-limits area that is isolated from the public. It is impossible for even high officials to set foot here without permission. The Seijoto Kyorin, the living quarters for the members of Central 46, and the Daireishokairo, the great archive, are also in this area.

2 A STRIKE UNIT THAT WORKS IN SECRECY STEALTH FORCE

A strike unit under the command of the Central 46. Five total divisions handle various missions. Details concerning Second to Fourth division are top secret and aren't talked about much. The Second Company Captain, Soi Fon, succeeded Yoruichi Shihôin as the Supreme Commander after her predecessor suddenly disappeared.

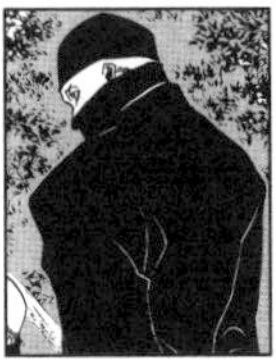

FIRST DIVISION PUNISHMENT FORCE

The black-clad Punishment Force soldiers are known for their cold-bloodedness. They specialize in combat using hakuda.

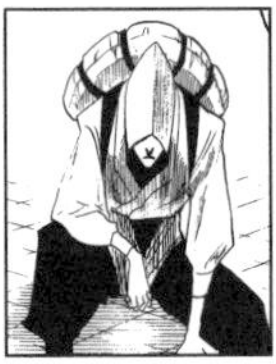

FIFTH DIVISION SECRET REMOTE SQUAD

A special unit sends information within the Soul Society. Their uniforms look like those worn by ancient express messengers and are a time-honored tradition passed down from ancient times.

3 SOUL REAPER TRAINING AND EDUCATION SHINÔREIJUTSUIN

An educational organization with a 2,000-year-old history, founded by Genryusai Shigekuni Yamamoto. It was once called the Soul Reaper Academy. It changed to Spiritual Arts Academy when it developed into an institute for the next generation of the Kidô Corps and Stealth Force as well the Soul Reapers of the Thirteen Court Guard Companies. In the Rukongai, it is still referred to as Soul Reaper Academy.

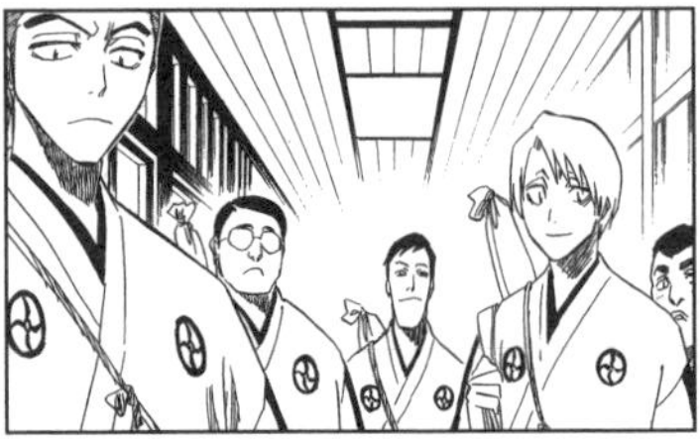

COURT GUARD MEMBERS FROM THE ACADEMY

Currently, most of the members of the Court Guards are alumni of the Spiritual Arts Academy. Most of their relationships within the Spiritual Arts Academy stay with them even after they join the Court Guards.

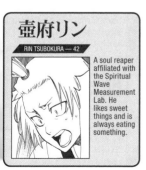

4 DEFENDING THE SEIREITEI AND MANAGING THE MOVEMENT OF SOULS
THIRTEEN COURT GUARD COMPANIES

A division whose main duty is to defend the Seireitei, the center of Soul Society. The companies are assigned to defend different areas of the Seireitei. Each company also has its own unique characteristics. The Fourth Company is in charge of medical treatment as well as supplies, and the Eleventh Company in charge of fighting on the front lines. The company captains all have different abilities, but as a requirement of the position, they have all reached Bankai—except for the Eleventh Captain, Kenpachi Zaraki.

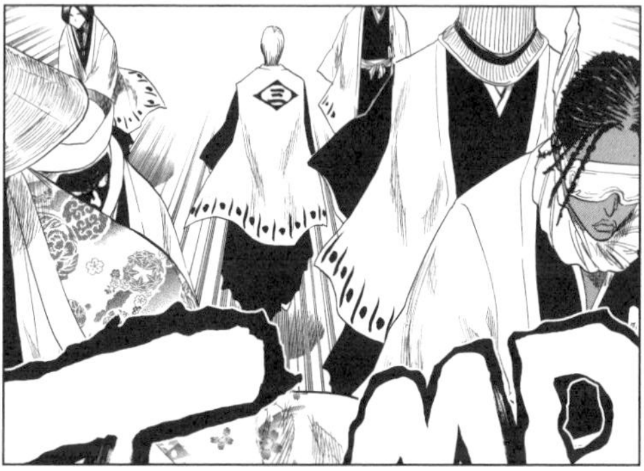
MP

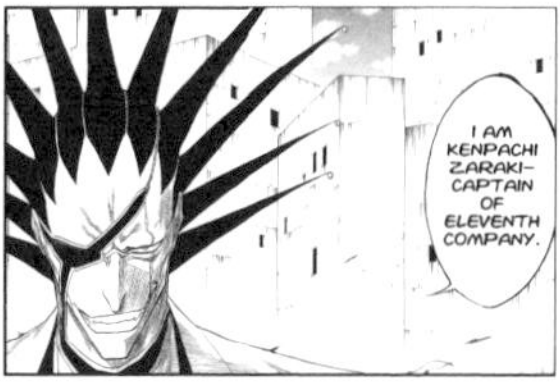
I AM KENPACHI ZARAKI—CAPTAIN OF ELEVENTH COMPANY.

METHOD FOR APPOINTING CAPTAINS

There are three ways to attain the rank of captain: passing the captain's exam, obtaining the recommendation and approval of the other captains, or defeating the current captain in a one-on-one battle.

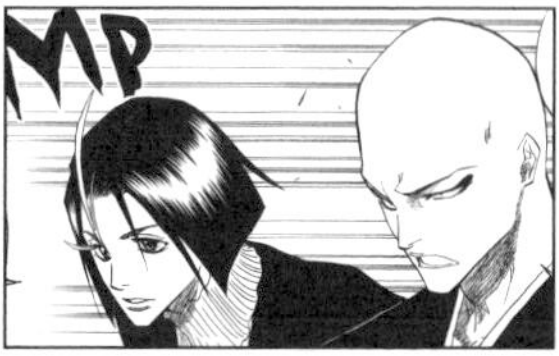
MP

A MERIT SYSTEM! ORDER OF RANK

The Court Guards are an organization with a merit-based hierarchy. They have disposed of the system of rank based on seniority. Abilities are the only means used to determine one's rank.

5 MAYURI KUROTSUCHI'S GROUP OF SOUL REAPERS WITH STRANGE ABILITIES
THE DEPARTMENT OF RESEARCH AND DEVELOPMENT

The department resposible for the development of new technology and spiritual tools. The Twelfth Captain, Mayuri Kurotsuchi, is the bureau chief. The gigai and soul candy were developed here. The staff members have a strange air about them, but they are extremely intelligent. The formation of the current Department of Research and Development is deeply connected with Kisuke Urahara, who is currently exiled from the Soul Society for mysterious reasons. Many male company members come here to use their skills to develop perverted spiritual tools.

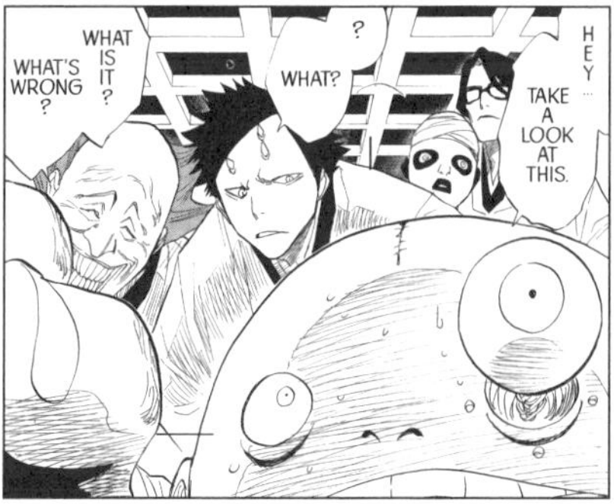
HEY... TAKE A LOOK AT THIS.
?
WHAT?
WHAT IS IT?
WHAT'S WRONG?

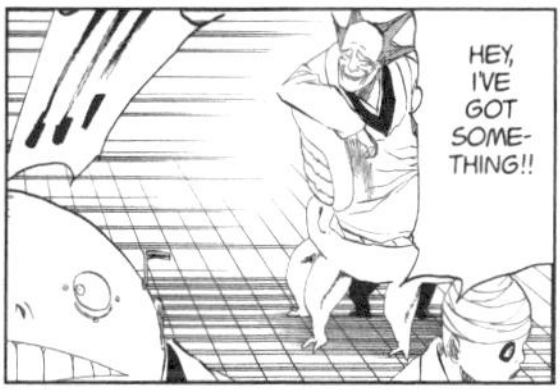
HEY, I'VE GOT SOMETHING!!

KEEPING WATCH OVER THE TRENDS OF THE ARRANCARS

The Spiritual Wave Measurement Lab is always tracking and keeping watch over the actions of the Arrancars.

壺府リン

RIN TSUBOKURA — 42

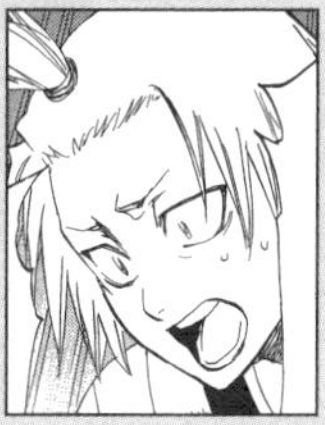

A soul reaper affiliated with the Spiritual Wave Measurement Lab. He likes sweet things and is always eating something.

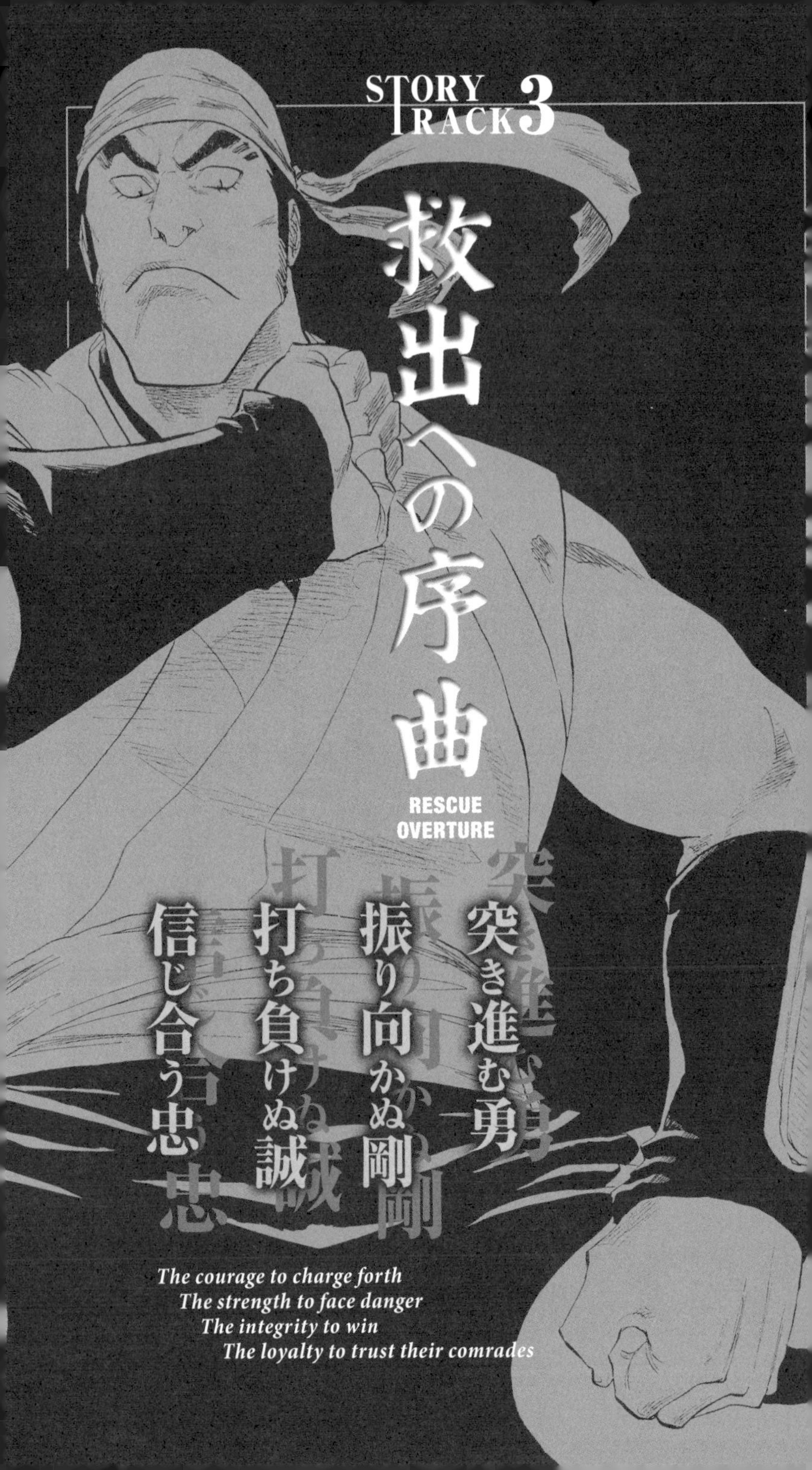
STORY TRACK 3
救出への序曲
RESCUE OVERTURE
突き進む勇
振り向かぬ剛
打ち負けぬ誠
信じ合う忠
The courage to charge forth
The strength to face danger
The integrity to win
The loyalty to trust their comrades

THE GATEKEEPER OF WHITE ROAD GATE

JIDANBÔ — CHARACTER FILE 43

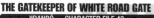

兕丹坊

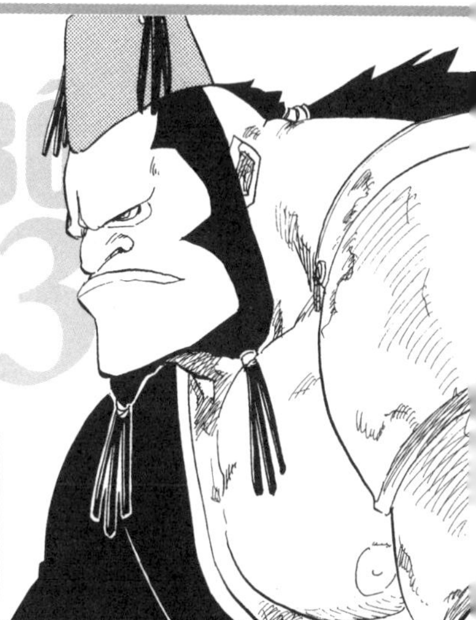

JIDANBÔ
43

MATCHLESS STRENGTH OF THE SOUL SOCIETY

The Gate keeper who defends the White Road Gate, western entrance to the Seireitei. He has incredible strength. It's said that he once defeated thirty Hollows in a single swipe. He stands before Ichigo and his friends when they try to break into the Seireitei without permission.

PROFILE

BIRTHDAY/ JANUARY 10
HEIGHT/ 32′4″
WEIGHT/ 2202 LBS

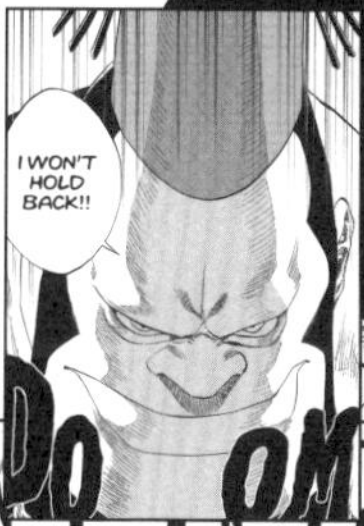

I WON'T HOLD BACK!!

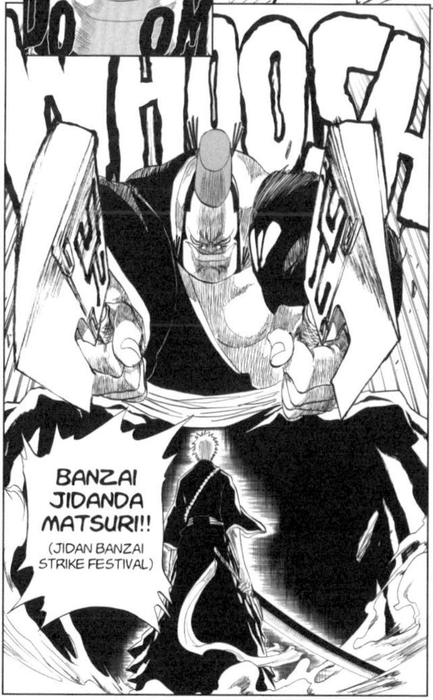

BANZAI JIDANDA MATSURI!!
(JIDAN BANZAI STRIKE FESTIVAL)

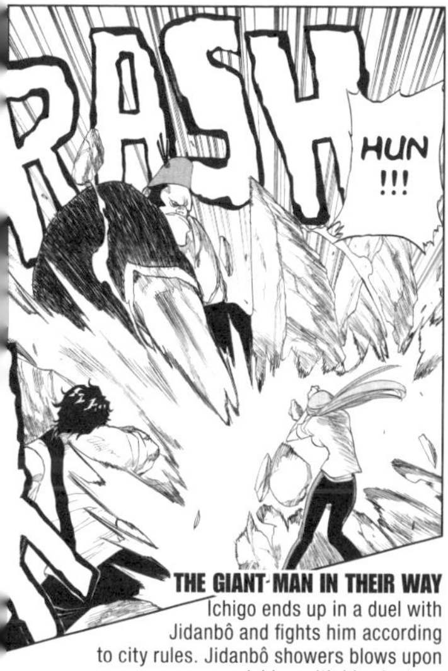

HUN !!!

THE GIANT-MAN IN THEIR WAY
Ichigo ends up in a duel with Jidanbô and fights him according to city rules. Jidanbô showers blows upon Ichigo with his giant ax.

BAD AT MATH?!
The Jidan Ten Strikes Festival Special Attack!! He miscounts and swings more than eleven times.

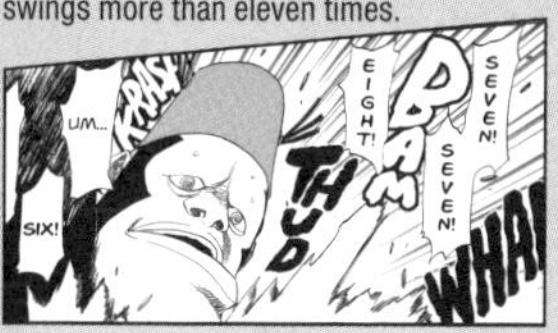

SEVEN!
SEVEN!
EIGHT!
THUD
UM...
SIX!

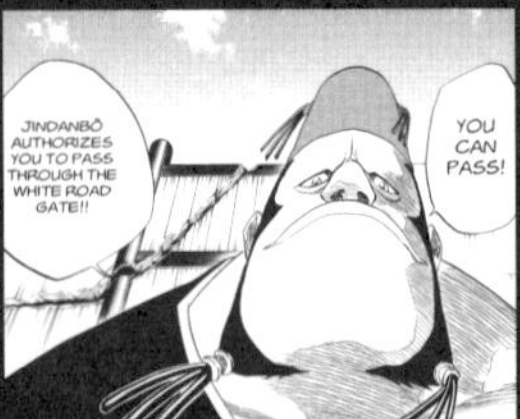
YOU CAN PASS!
JINDANBÔ AUTHORIZES YOU TO PASS THROUGH THE WHITE ROAD GATE!!

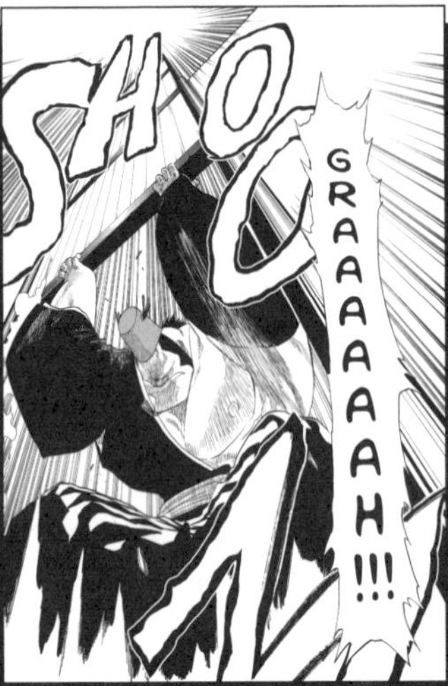
SHOCK
GRAAAAAAAAH!!!

開門

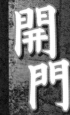

OPEN GATE

The role of a Gatekeeper
VOL. 9-73~74

Jidanbô ends up using his special attack, the Jidan Ten Strikes Festival. But he is no match for Ichigo, who has trained under Urahara. Jidanbô's ax breaks and he quietly accepts his defeat. He allows Ichigo and his friends to enter the Seireitei, but…

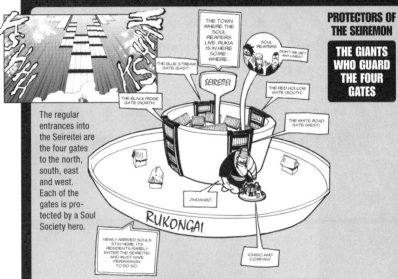

PROTECTORS OF THE SEIREMON

THE GIANTS WHO GUARD THE FOUR GATES

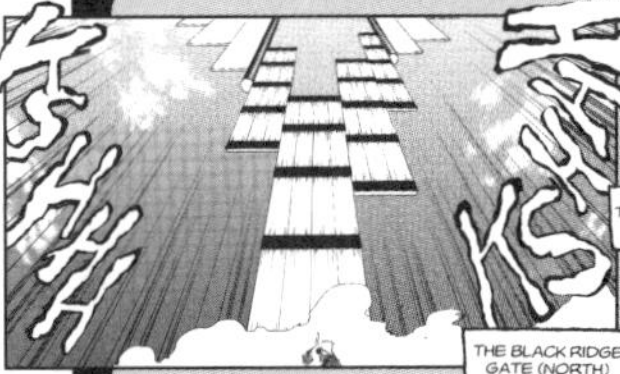

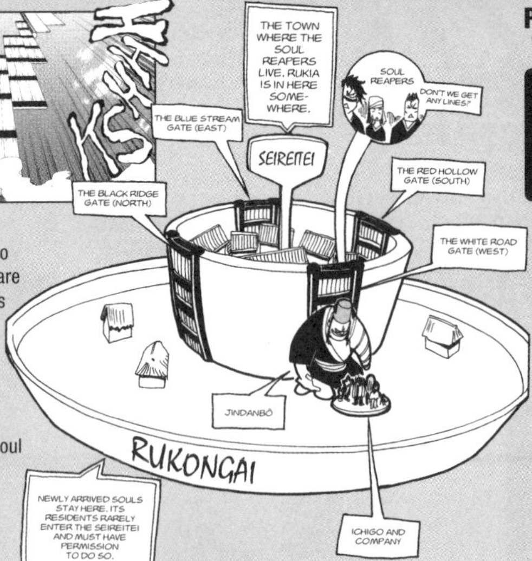
THE TOWN WHERE THE SOUL REAPERS LIVE. RUKIA IS IN HERE SOMEWHERE.
SEIREITEI
SOUL REAPERS
DON'T WE GET ANY LINES?
THE BLUE STREAM GATE (EAST)
THE RED HOLLOW GATE (SOUTH)
THE BLACK RIDGE GATE (NORTH)
THE WHITE ROAD GATE (WEST)
JINDANBÔ
RUKONGAI
NEWLY ARRIVED SOULS STAY HERE. ITS RESIDENTS RARELY ENTER THE SEIREITEI AND MUST HAVE PERMISSION TO DO SO.
ICHIGO AND COMPANY

The regular entrances into the Seireitei are the four gates to the north, south, east and west. Each of the gates is protected by a Soul Society hero.

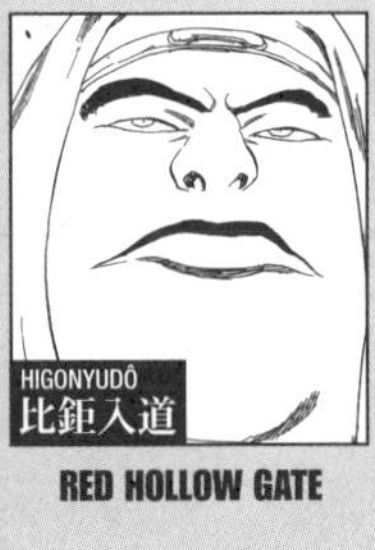
HIGONYUDÔ
比鉅入道

RED HOLLOW GATE

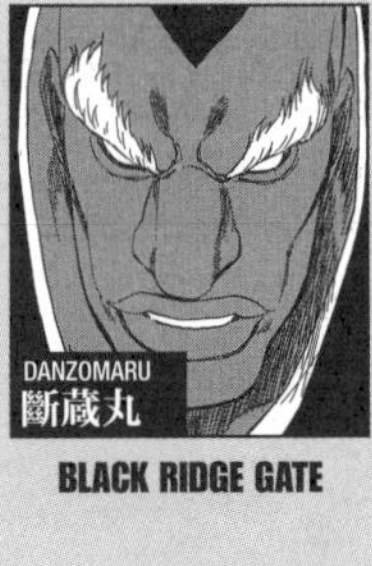
DANZOMARU
斷蔵丸

BLACK RIDGE GATE

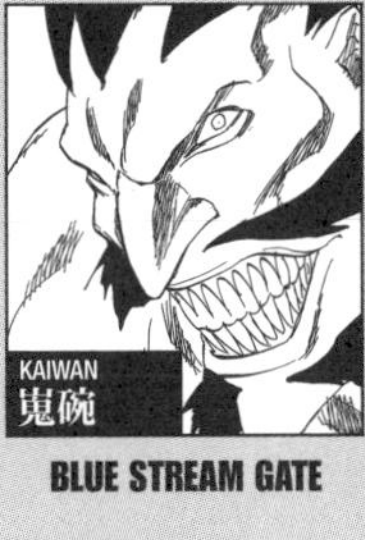
KAIWAN
嵬碗

BLUE STREAM GATE

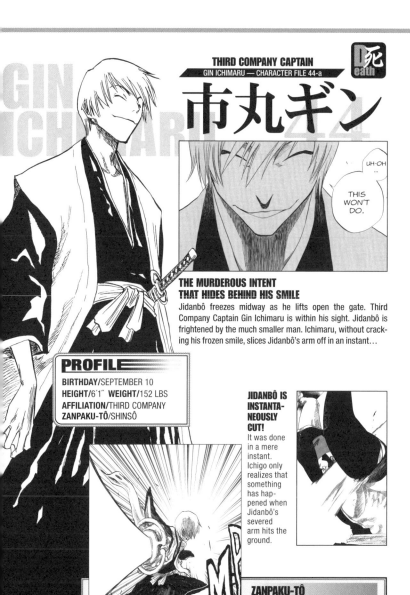

THIRD COMPANY CAPTAIN

GIN ICHIMARU — CHARACTER FILE 44-a

市丸ギン

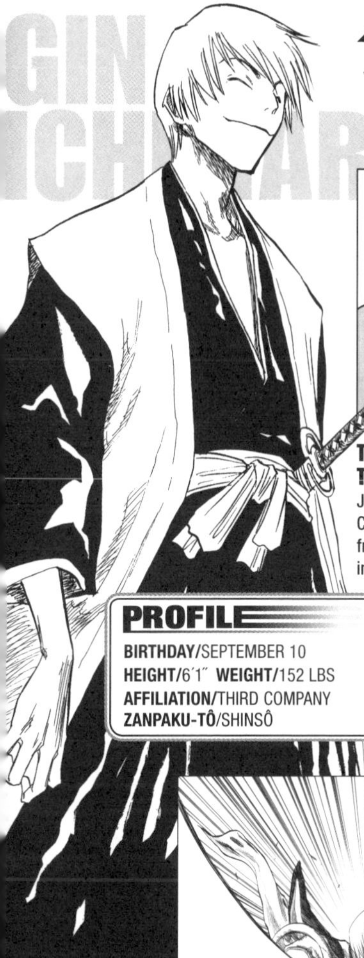

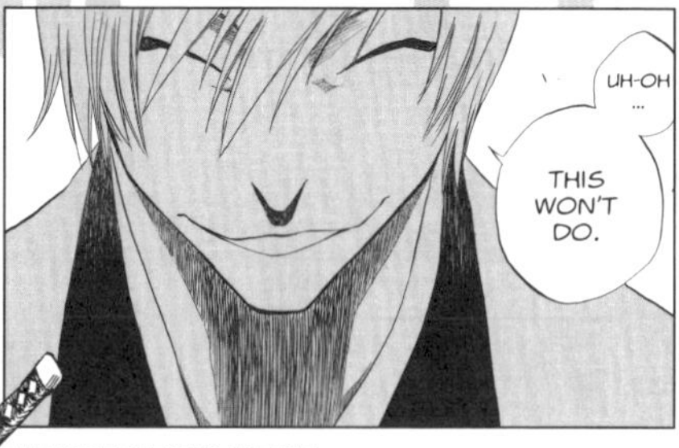
UH-OH ...
THIS WON'T DO.

THE MURDEROUS INTENT THAT HIDES BEHIND HIS SMILE

Jidanbô freezes midway as he lifts open the gate. Third Company Captain Gin Ichimaru is within his sight. Jidanbô is frightened by the much smaller man. Ichimaru, without cracking his frozen smile, slices Jidanbô's arm off in an instant…

PROFILE

BIRTHDAY/SEPTEMBER 10
HEIGHT/6′1″ **WEIGHT/**152 LBS
AFFILIATION/THIRD COMPANY
ZANPAKU-TÔ/SHINSÔ

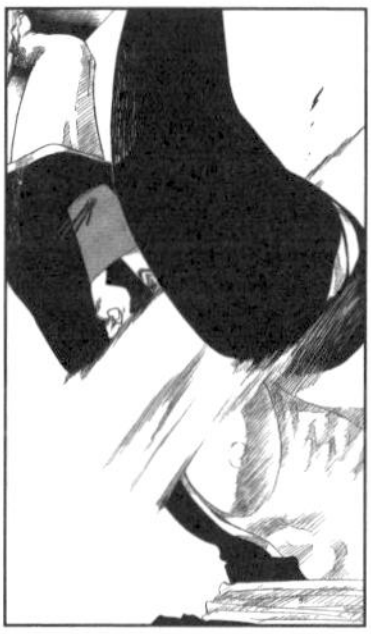

JIDANBÔ IS INSTANTANEOUSLY CUT!

It was done in a mere instant. Ichigo only realizes that something has happened when Jidanbô's severed arm hits the ground.

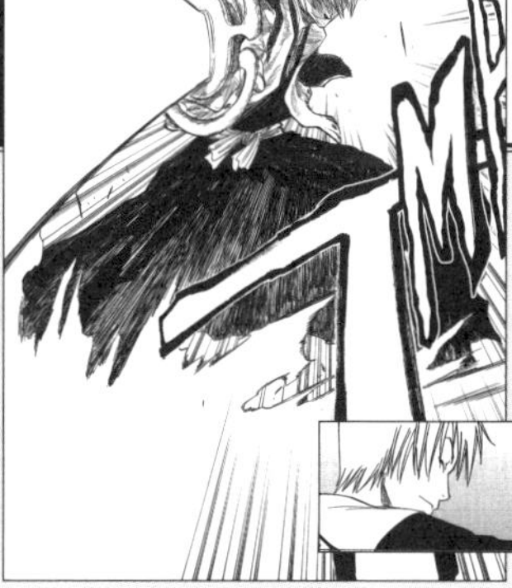

ZANPAKU-TÔ

SHINSÔ

It usually takes the form of a short sword. But when Ichimaru chants, "Shoot'm dead! Shinsô!," its abilities are unleashed, and Ichimaru can shrink and extend its blade at will.

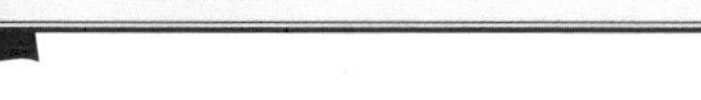

遭遇

ENCOUNTER

The Opened Gat
VOL. 7–75

When Ichigo asks Ichimaru how he plans to use his short sword, Gin displays Shinsô's true abilities.

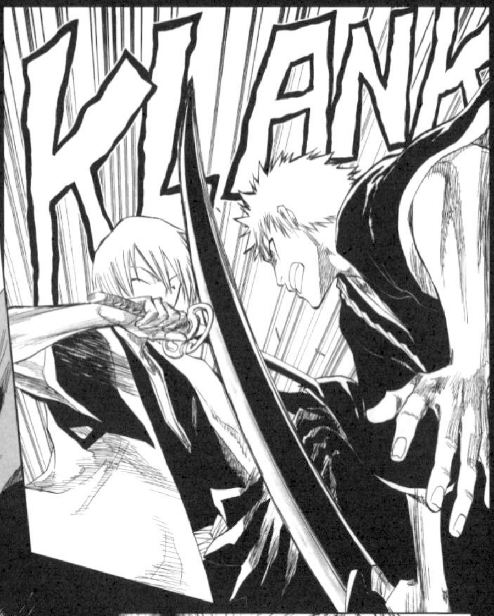
KLANK

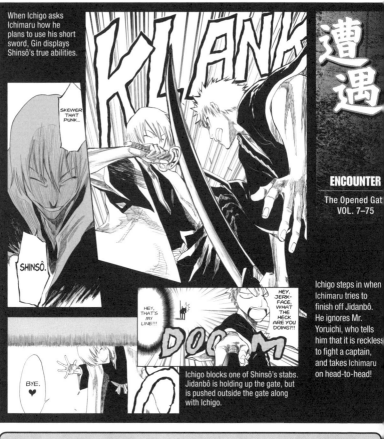

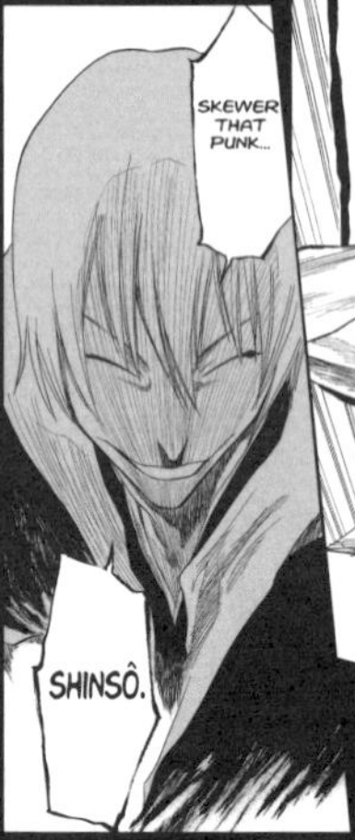
SKEWER THAT PUNK...
SHINSÔ.

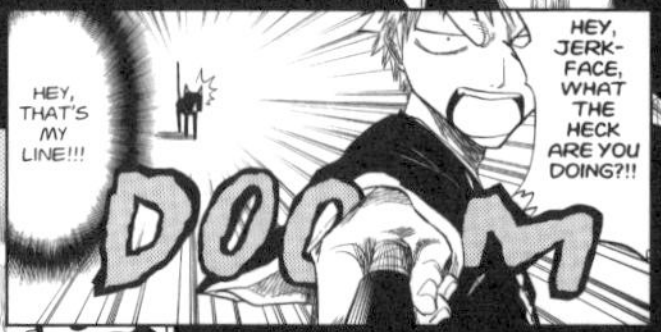
HEY, JERK-FACE, WHAT THE HECK ARE YOU DOING?!!
HEY, THAT'S MY LINE!!!
DOOM

Ichigo blocks one of Shinsô's stabs. Jidanbô is holding up the gate, but is pushed outside the gate along with Ichigo.

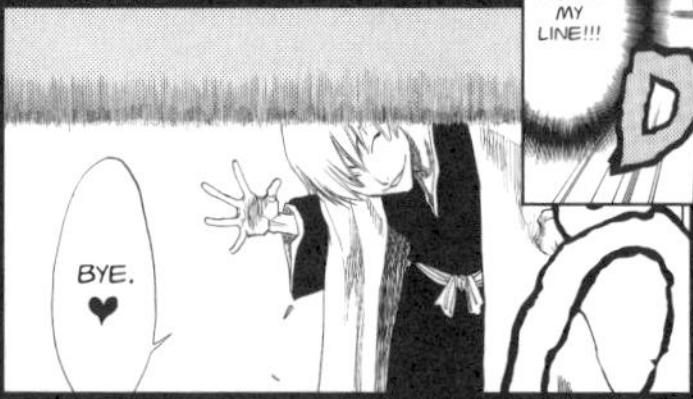
BYE. ❤

Ichigo steps in when Ichimaru tries to finish off Jidanbô. He ignores Mr. Yoruichi, who tells him that it is reckless to fight a captain, and takes Ichimaru on head-to-head!

THE PLACE WHERE SOULS DRIFT

THE RUKONGAI

By chance, Chad meets Yûichi Shibata (the parakeet that he saved) in the Rukongai.

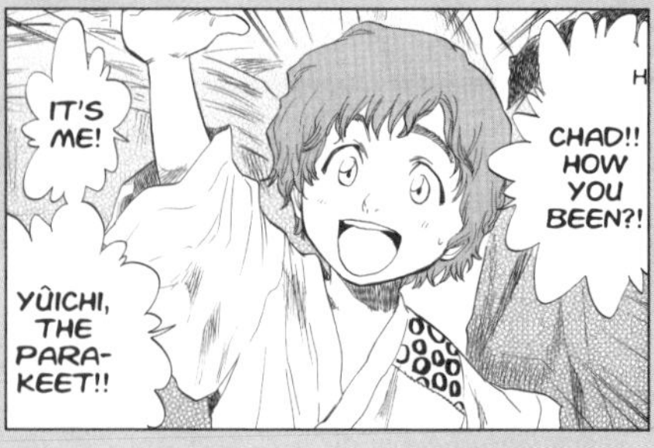
CHAD!! HOW YOU BEEN?!
IT'S ME!
YÛICHI, THE PARAKEET!!

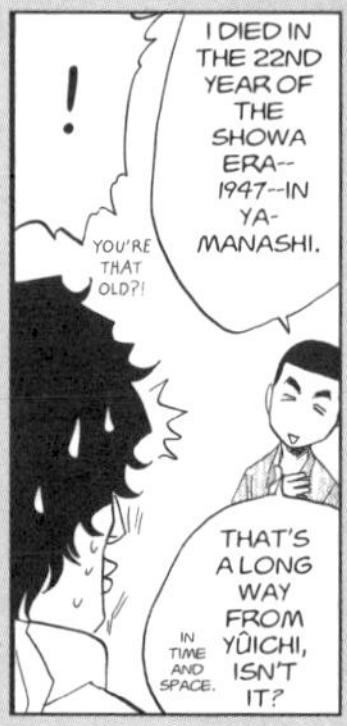
I DIED IN THE 22ND YEAR OF THE SHOWA ERA--1947--IN YA-MANASHI.
!
YOU'RE THAT OLD?!
THAT'S A LONG WAY FROM YÛICHI, ISN'T IT?
IN TIME AND SPACE.

The place to which Soul Reapers deliver souls and the first place souls live. The souls are separated into various zones across the Rukongai regardless of age, sex, or place of death. Reunions with dead family members are rare. People live in family-like communities of strangers.

THE SELF-PROCLAIMED "NUMBER ONE SOUL REAPER HATER OF WEST RUKONGAI."

The man who noisily interrupts Mr. Yoruichi's meeting in the town elder's house. His numerous titles are all self-proclaimed. However, it seems that he really is the "Number One Soul Reaper Hater of West Rukongai." His attitude totally changes when he sees Ichigo's shihakushô.

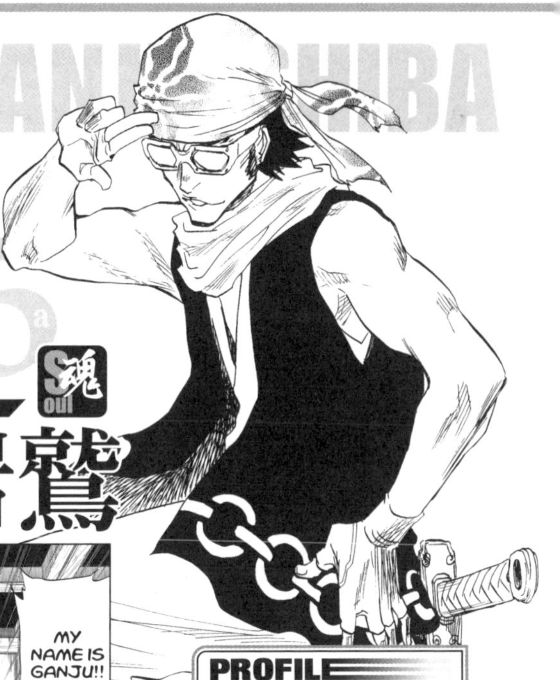

THE MAN OF MANY SELF-PROCLAIMED NAMES

GANJU SHIBA — CHARACTER FILE 45-a

志波岩鷲

PROFILE

BIRTHDAY/OCTOBER 15

HEIGHT/6'0" **WEIGHT**/234 LBS

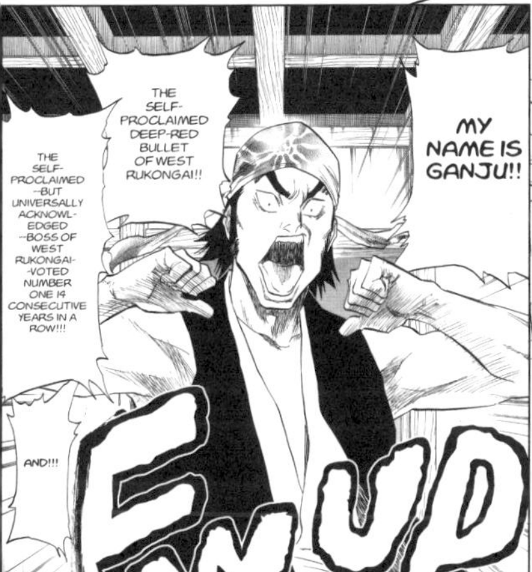
MY NAME IS GANJU!!
THE SELF-PROCLAIMED DEEP-RED BULLET OF WEST RUKONGAI!!
THE SELF-PROCLAIMED --BUT UNIVERSALLY ACKNOWLEDGED --BOSS OF WEST RUKONGAI-VOTED NUMBER ONE 14 CONSECUTIVE YEARS IN A ROW!!!
AND!!!
FWUP

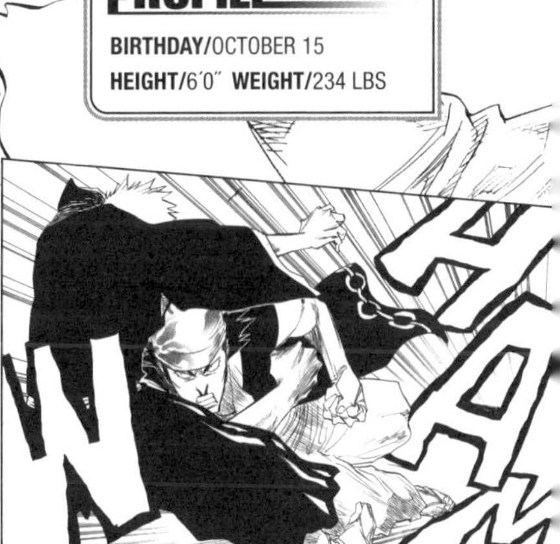

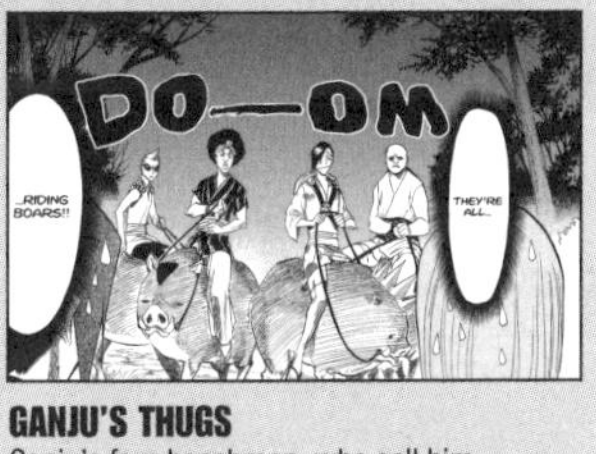
DO—OM
THEY'RE ALL...
...RIDING BOARS!!

GANJU'S THUGS

Ganju's four henchmen, who call him "Boss Man." They ride wild boars.

A BIG CLASH WITH SOUL REAPER ICHIGO

Ichigo and Ganju ignore those around them as things between them heat up. They continue to exchange blows, neither pulling back. But as soon as the bell chimes nine o'clock...

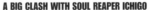

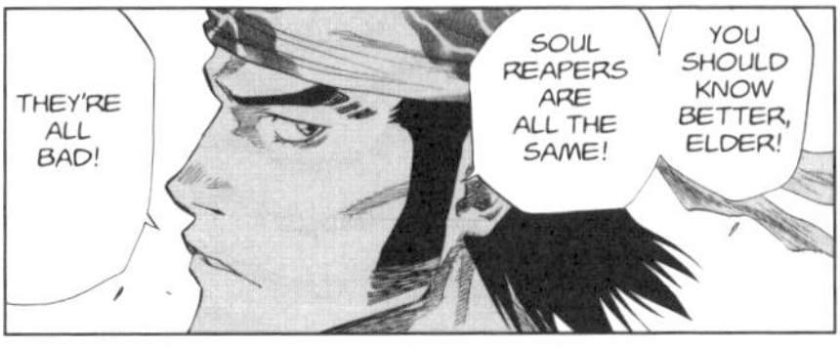
YOU SHOULD KNOW BETTER, ELDER!
SOUL REAPERS ARE ALL THE SAME!
THEY'RE ALL BAD!

訪問

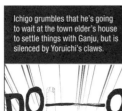

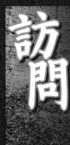

VISIT

Mr. Yoruichi's old friend
VOL. 9-78

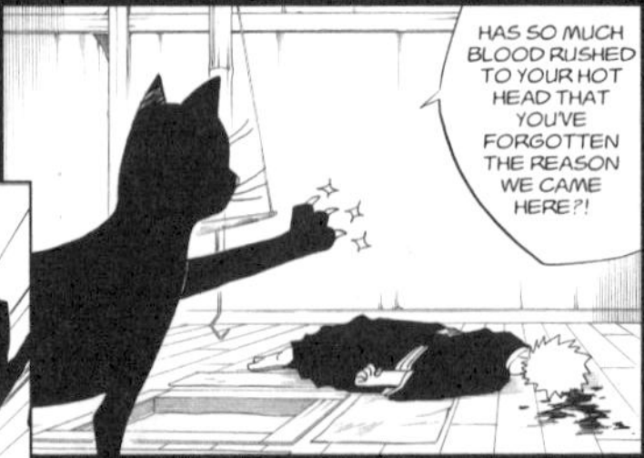
HAS SO MUCH BLOOD RUSHED TO YOUR HOT HEAD THAT YOU'VE FORGOTTEN THE REASON WE CAME HERE?!

Ichigo grumbles that he's going to wait at the town elder's house to settle things with Ganju, but is silenced by Yoruichi's claws.

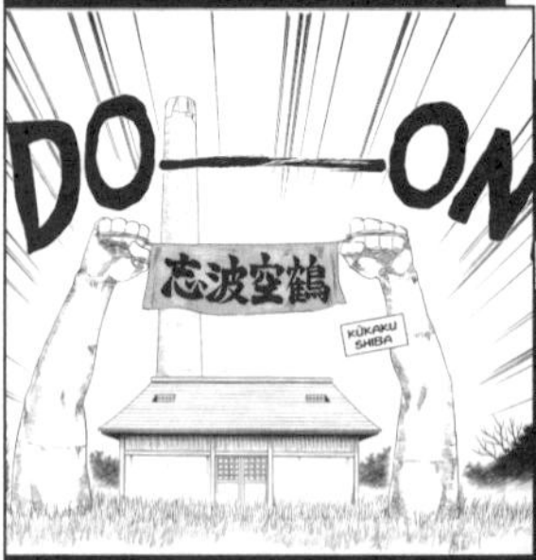
DO—ON
志波空鶴
KÛKAKU SHIBA

The Kukaku residence is a little avant-garde in design.

With entering through the gate no longer an option, Ichigo and his friends go to Kûkaku Shiba to find a way to break into the Seireitei. They meet Kûkaku, the one-armed fireworks wiz, and Ganju, the man that Ichigo got into a fight with the night before. Ichigo and Ganju resume their fight as soon as they see each other. Kûkaku quells their fighting with her fist and begins to explain how they can get into the Seireitei.

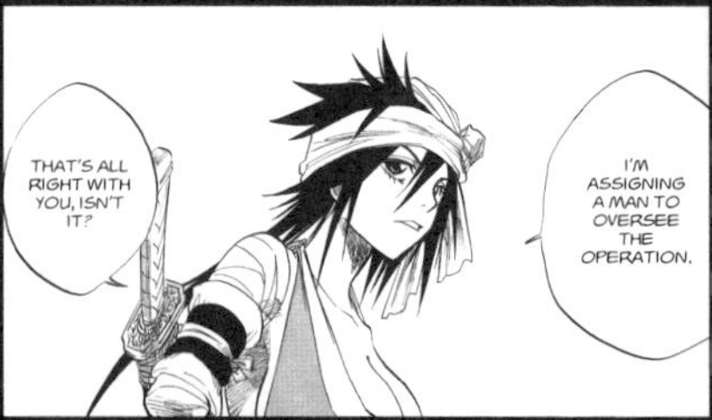
I'M ASSIGNING A MAN TO OVERSEE THE OPERATION.
THAT'S ALL RIGHT WITH YOU, ISN'T IT?

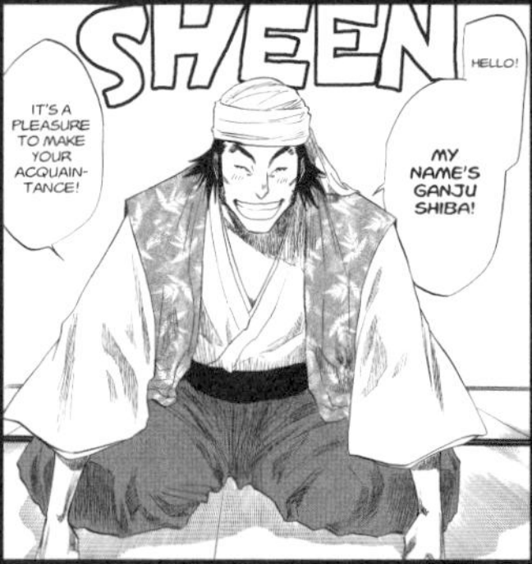
SHEEN
HELLO!
MY NAME'S GANJU SHIBA!
IT'S A PLEASURE TO MAKE YOUR ACQUAINTANCE!

Kûkaku presents her younger brother to Ichigo as a lookout—Ganju Shiba!

THE FASTEST RIDE IN THE RUKONGAI?!

BONNIE, THE GIANT WILD BOAR

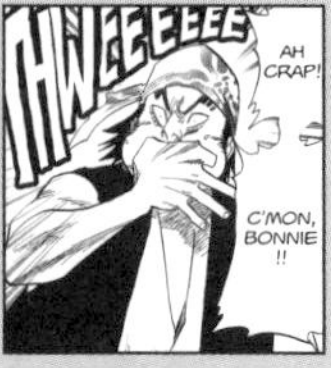
THWEEEEEE
AH CRAP!
C'MON, BONNIE!!

Great at running a straight line, but has a little trouble braking.

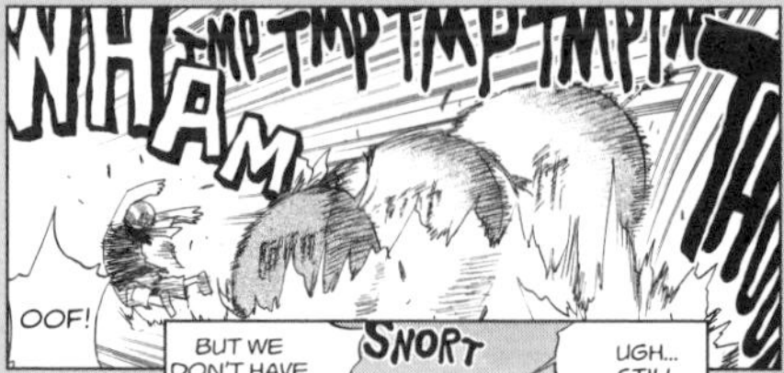
TMP TMP TMP TMP TMP
WHAM
OOF!

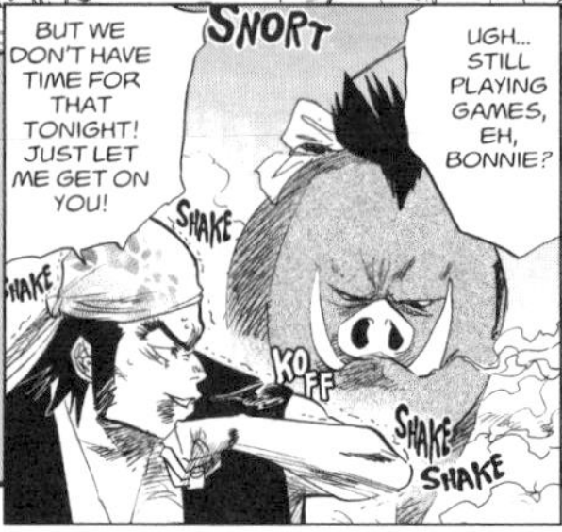
SNORT
UGH... STILL PLAYING GAMES, EH, BONNIE?
BUT WE DON'T HAVE TIME FOR THAT TONIGHT! JUST LET ME GET ON YOU!
SHAKE
SHAKE
KOFF
SHAKE
SHAKE

A dauntless face even when she's run over her master!

One of the giant wild boars that Ganju and his thugs ride. Wild boars are the Soul Society equivalent of motorcycles. Every night, Ganju and his henchmen can be seen riding their wild boars, attacking the slopes and even riding on the paths between the harvested rice fields...

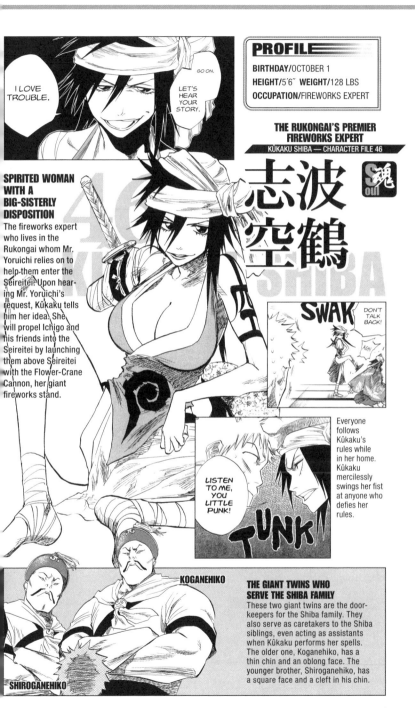

PROFILE

BIRTHDAY/OCTOBER 1

HEIGHT/5′6″ **WEIGHT**/128 LBS

OCCUPATION/FIREWORKS EXPERT

THE RUKONGAI'S PREMIER FIREWORKS EXPERT

KÛKAKU SHIBA — CHARACTER FILE 46

志波空鶴

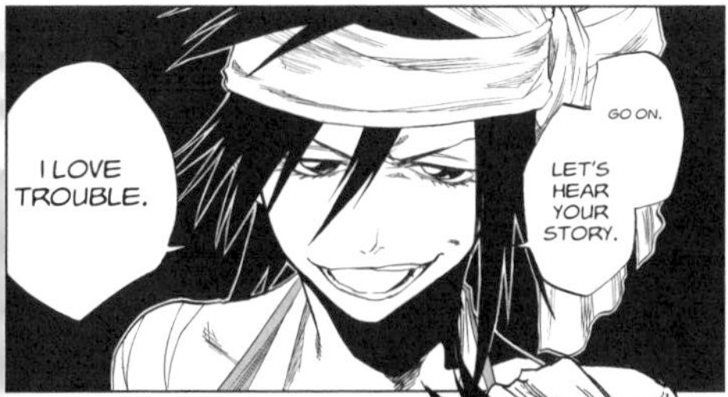
GO ON.
LET'S HEAR YOUR STORY.
I LOVE TROUBLE.

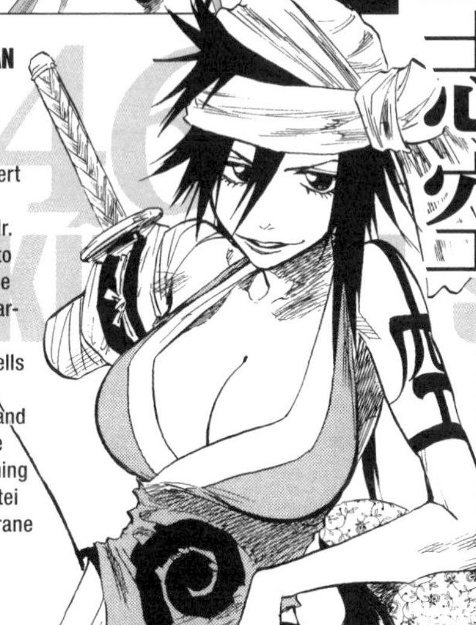
46
KÛKAKU SHIBA

SPIRITED WOMAN WITH A BIG-SISTERLY DISPOSITION

The fireworks expert who lives in the Rukongai whom Mr. Yoruichi relies on to help them enter the Seireitei. Upon hearing Mr. Yoruichi's request, Kûkaku tells him her idea. She will propel Ichigo and his friends into the Seireitei by launching them above Seireitei with the Flower-Crane Cannon, her giant fireworks stand.

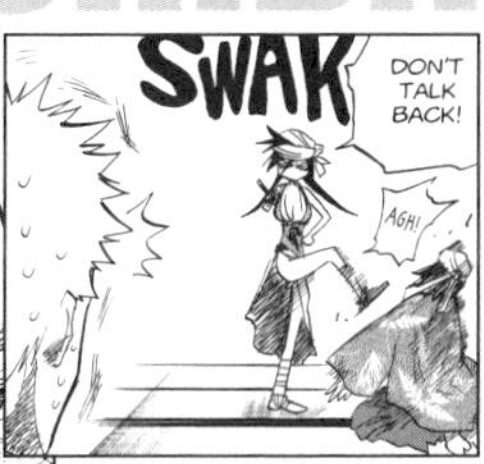
DON'T TALK BACK!
SWAK
AGH!

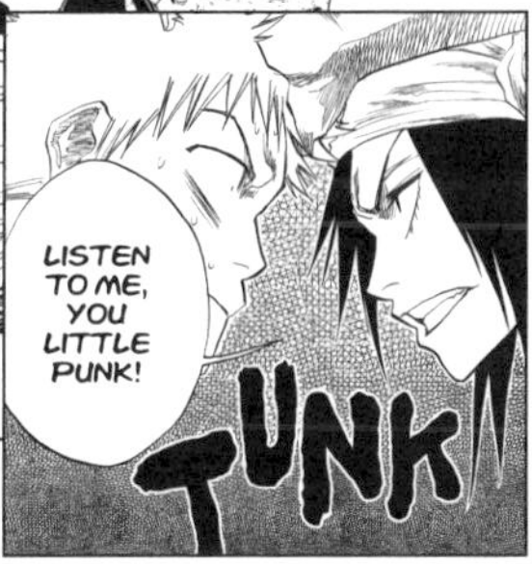
LISTEN TO ME, YOU LITTLE PUNK!
TUNK

Everyone follows Kûkaku's rules while in her home. Kûkaku mercilessly swings her fist at anyone who defies her rules.

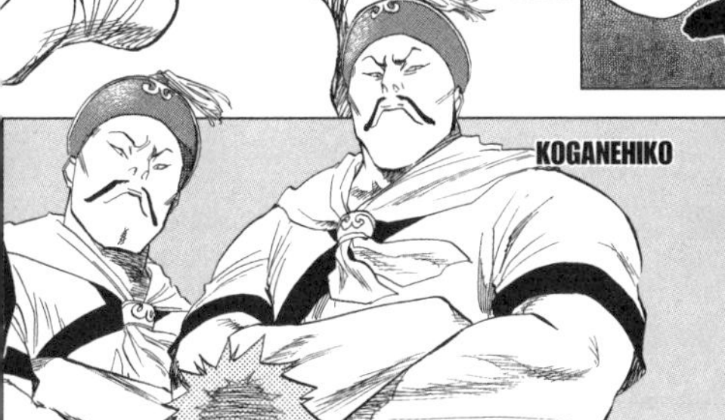
KOGANEHIKO
SHIROGANEHIKO

THE GIANT TWINS WHO SERVE THE SHIBA FAMILY

These two giant twins are the doorkeepers for the Shiba family. They also serve as caretakers to the Shiba siblings, even acting as assistants when Kûkaku performs her spells. The older one, Koganehiko, has a thin chin and an oblong face. The younger brother, Shiroganehiko, has a square face and a cleft in his chin.

集中 CONCENTRATIO

Spirit Core Trainin
VOL. 10-80~82

It isn't about promises or money. Ichigo's only reason for saving Rukia is to return her the favor for saving his life.

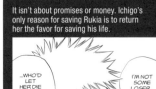

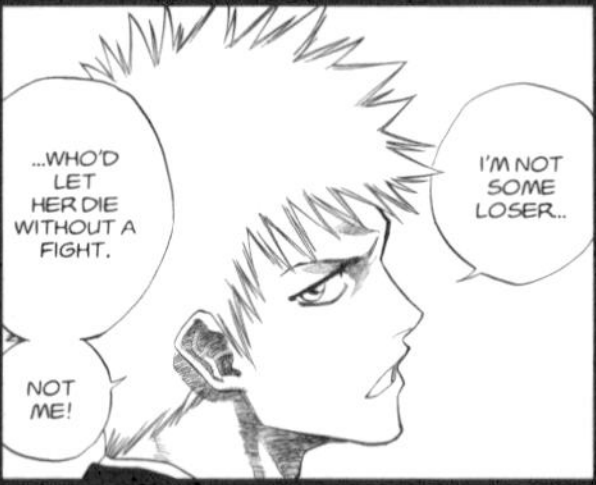
I'M NOT SOME LOSER..
...WHO'D LET HER DIE WITHOUT A FIGHT.
NOT ME!

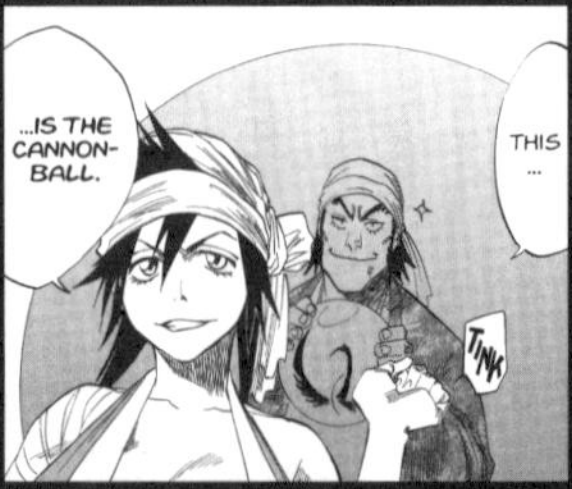
THIS ...
...IS THE CANNON-BALL.
TINK

A person becomes a cannonball by charging their reishu kaku, or spirit core, with spiritual power and creating a wall of reishi around himself.

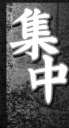

Ichigo and his friends train to create cannonballs out of spirit energy the night before they are to be launched. The only one of them who can't charge his spiritual power is Ichigo. He ends up practicing by himself.

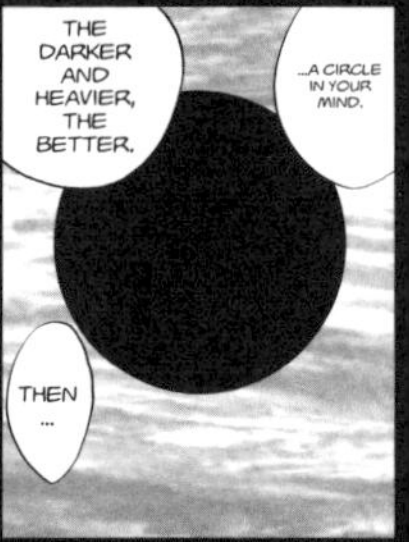
...A CIRCLE IN YOUR MIND.
THE DARKER AND HEAVIER, THE BETTER.
THEN ...

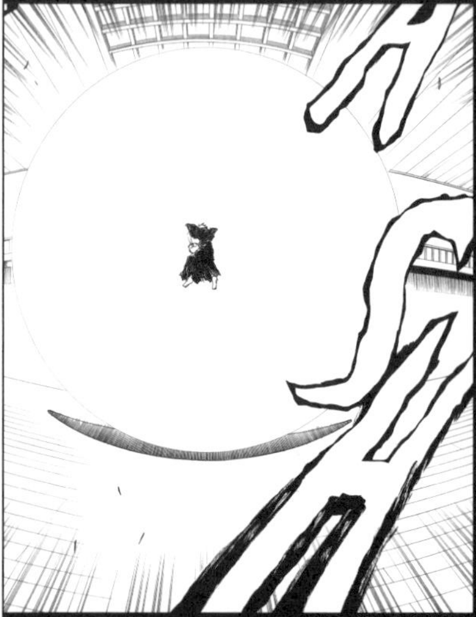

Ganju gives Ichigo a subtle (?) hint. Ichigo tries to charge the spirit core with spiritual energy, but...

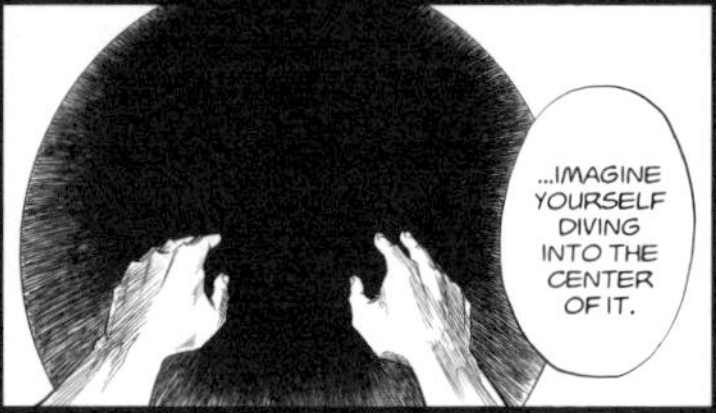
...IMAGINE YOURSELF DIVING INTO THE CENTER OF IT.

THE REASON WHY GANJU HATES SOUL REAPERS

KÛKAKU AND GANJU'S OLDER BROTHER

Ganju doesn't know that his older brother was a Soul Reaper, but his hatred of Soul Reapers is rooted in the fact that his older brother was killed by a fellow Soul Reaper. Ganju has hated Soul Reapers ever since. But he senses that Ichigo is different. He decides to help Ichigo.

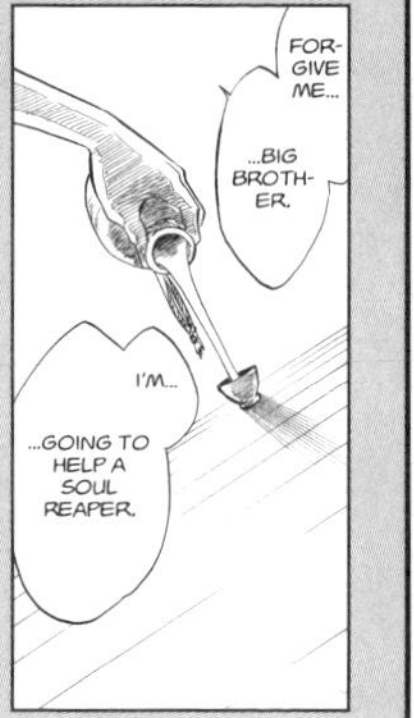
FOR-GIVE ME...
...BIG BROTH-ER.
I'M...
...GOING TO HELP A SOUL REAPER.

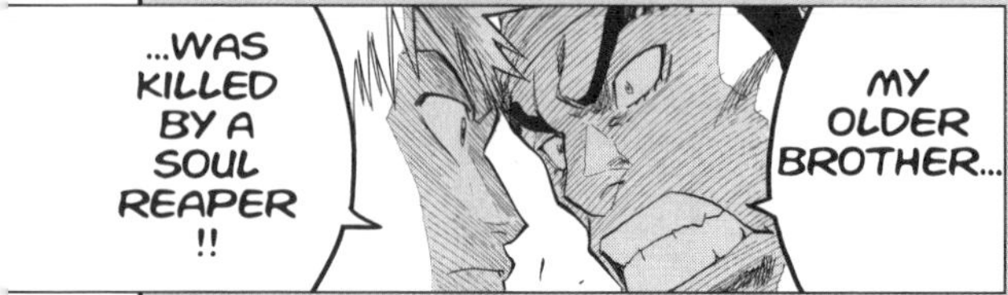
MY OLDER BROTHER...
...WAS KILLED BY A SOUL REAPER !!

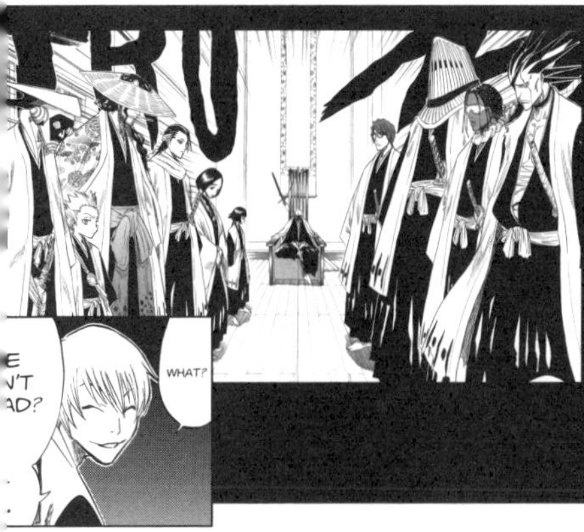
WHAT?

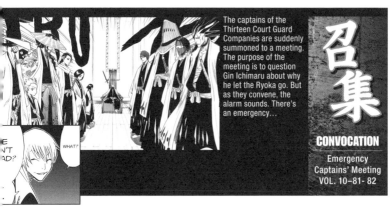

The captains of the Thirteen Court Guard Companies are suddenly summoned to a meeting. The purpose of the meeting is to question Gin Ichimaru about why he let the Ryoka go. But as they convene, the alarm sounds. There's an emergency...

召集

CONVOCATION

Emergency Captains' Meeting
VOL. 10–81- 82

THIRTEEN COURT GUARD COMPANIES' EXECUTIVE ROSTER

Captain General Genryûsai Shigekuni Yamamoto is the leader of the battle division known as the Thirteen Court Guard Companies. Aside from defending their assigned areas of the Seireitei, the companies dispatch Soul Reapers to the human world to perform various jobs. The Guard Companies are a large unit. Each squad is composed of over 200 company members. Altogether, the thirteen companies total at least 3,000 members.

一 FIRST COMPANY

山本元柳斎重國
GENRYÛSAI SHIGEKUNI YAMAMOTO – 49-a

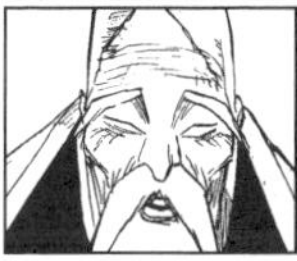
CAPTAIN

雀部長次郎
CHÔJIRO SASAKIBE – 48-a

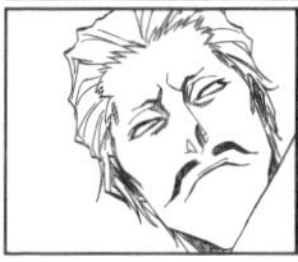
ASSISTANT CAPTAIN

二 SECOND COMPANY

砕蜂
SOI FON – 49-a

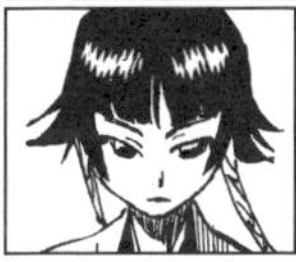
CAPTAIN

大前田希千代
MARECHIYO ÔMAEDA – 50-a

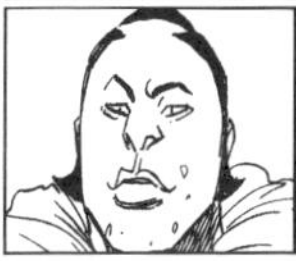
ASSISTANT CAPTAIN

七 SEVENTH COMPANY

狛村左陣
SAJIN KOMAMURA – 56-a

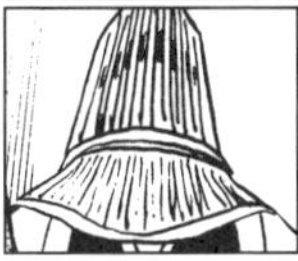
CAPTAIN

射場鉄左衛門
TETSUZAEMON IBA – 57-a

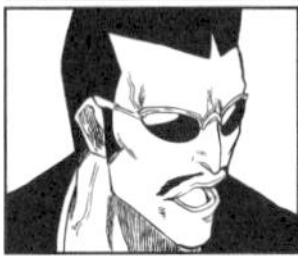
ASSISTANT CAPTAIN

八 EIGHTH COMPANY

京楽春水
SHUNSUI KYÔRAKU – 58-a

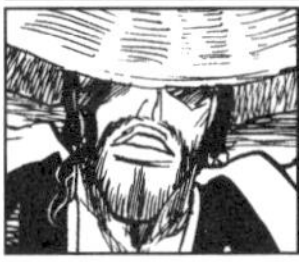
CAPTAIN

伊勢七緒
NANAO ISE – 59-a

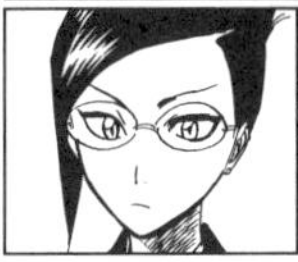
ASSISTANT CAPTAIN

九 NINTH COMPANY

東仙要
KANAME TÔSEN – 60-a

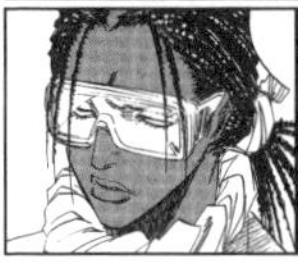
CAPTAIN

檜佐木修兵
SHÛHEI HISAGI – 61-a

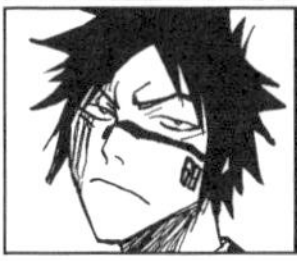
ASSISTANT CAPTAIN

十 TENTH COMPANY

日番谷冬獅郎
TÔSHIRÔ HITSUGAYA – 62-a

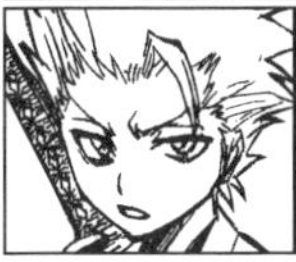
CAPTAIN

松本乱菊
RANGIKU MATSUMOTO – 63-a

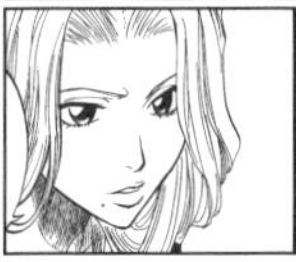
ASSISTANT CAPTAIN

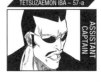

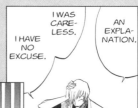

The captains stop questioning Ichimaru when the far too conveniently timed emergency arises. Sôsuke Aizen mentions his suspicions to Ichimaru in passing.

I HAVE NO EXCUSE.

I WAS CARE-LESS.

AN EXPLA-NATION.

OPPOSITION UNDER THE SURFACE?!

GIN AND AIZEN

Aizen forestalls Ichimaru in order to stop his plan. Cold sparks fly.

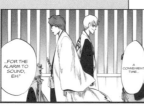

...FOR THE ALARM TO SOUND, EH?"

A CONVENIENT TIME...

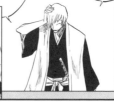

六 **SIXTH COMPANY**	五 **FIFTH COMPANY**	四 **FOURTH COMPANY**	三 **THIRD COMPANY**

朽木白哉
BYAKUYA KUCHIKI — 39-b · CAPTAIN

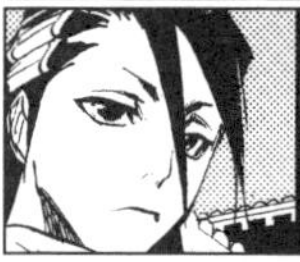

藍染惣右介
SÔSUKE AIZEN — 54-a · CAPTAIN

卯ノ花烈
RETSU UNOHANA — 52-a · CAPTAIN

市丸ギン
GIN ICHIMARU — 44-b · CAPTAIN

阿散井恋次
RENJI ABARAI — 38-b · ASSISTANT CAPTAIN

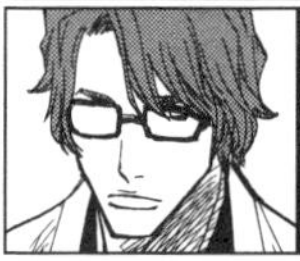

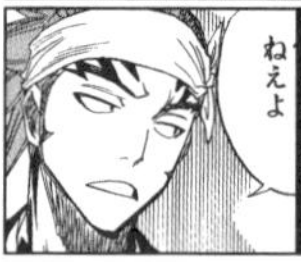

雛森桃
MOMO HINAMORI — 55-a · ASSISTANT CAPTAIN

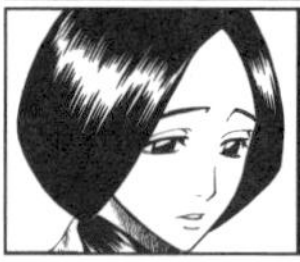

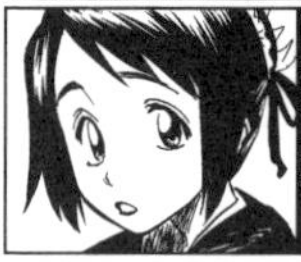

虎徹勇音
ISANE KOTETSU — 53-a · ASSISTANT CAPTAIN

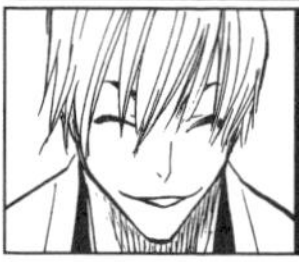

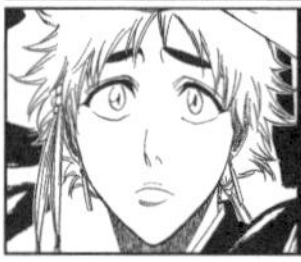

吉良イヅル
IZURU KIRA — 51-a · ASSISTANT CAPTAIN

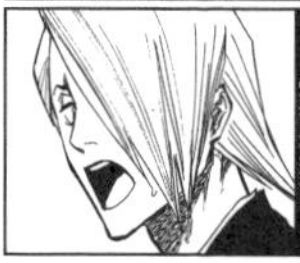

	十三 **THIRTEENTH COMPANY**	十二 **TWELVTH COMPANY**	十一 **ELEVENTH COMPANY**

浮竹十四郎
JÛSHIRÔ UKITAKE — 68-a · CAPTAIN

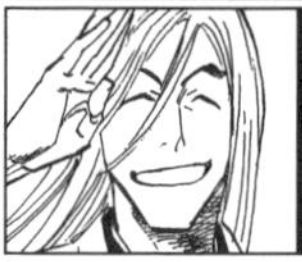

涅マユリ
MAYURI KUROTSUCHI — 66-a · CAPTAIN

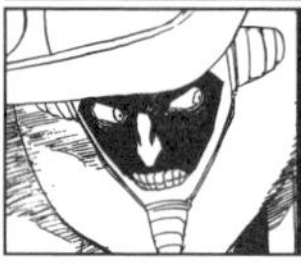

更木剣八
KENPACHI ZARAKI — 64-a · CAPTAIN

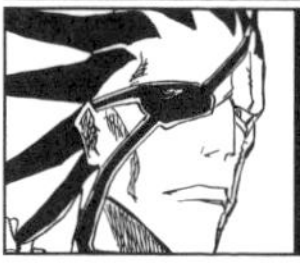

虎徹清音
KIYONE KOTETSU — 70-a · THIRD SEAT

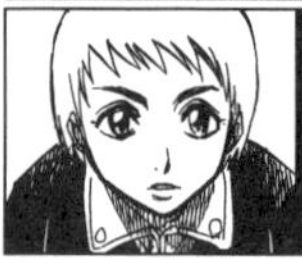

小椿仙太郎
SENTARÔ KOTSUBAKI — 69-a · THIRD SEAT

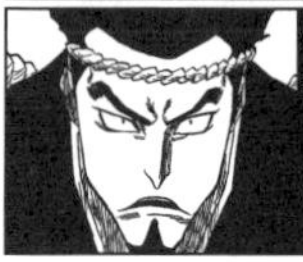

涅ネム
NEMU KUROTSUCHI — 67-a · ASSISTANT CAPTAIN

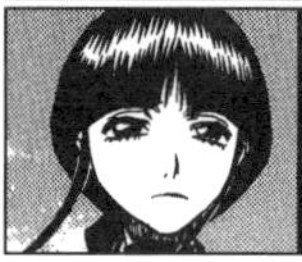

草鹿やちる
YACHIRU KUSAJISHI — 65-a · ASSISTANT CAPTAIN

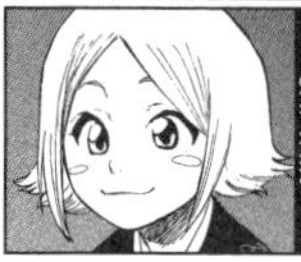

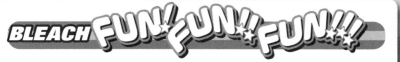

BLEACH FUN! FUN!! FUN!!!

Keigo and Tadanobu

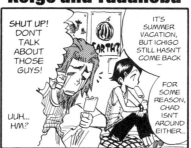

IT'S SUMMER VACATION, BUT ICHIGO STILL HASN'T COME BACK ...
FOR SOME REASON, CHAD ISN'T AROUND EITHER..
EARTH?
SHUT UP! DON'T TALK ABOUT THOSE GUYS!
UUH... HM?
O-OH?!
A
L-LOOK AT THIS, MIZUIRO! A SUMMER ANGEL HAS COME DOWN TO US MISERABLE GUYS!!
ALL RIGHT! WAIT FOR ME, ANGEL!
LICK LICK LICK LICK LICK LICK
ASANO TADANOBU
"A WINNER" POPSICLE STICK WILL GET YOU A FREE POPSICLE.
WOAAAAAAAH!!!
A RARE ONE!!!
STOP FORCING YOURSELF TO BE HAPPY.
YOU'RE JUST BEING TEASED BY THE POPSICLE COMPANY.

2003 *WEEKLY JUMP* COMBINED VOLUMES 37 AND 38

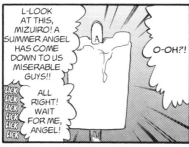

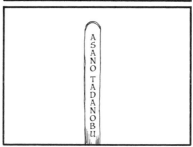

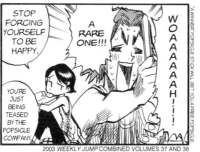

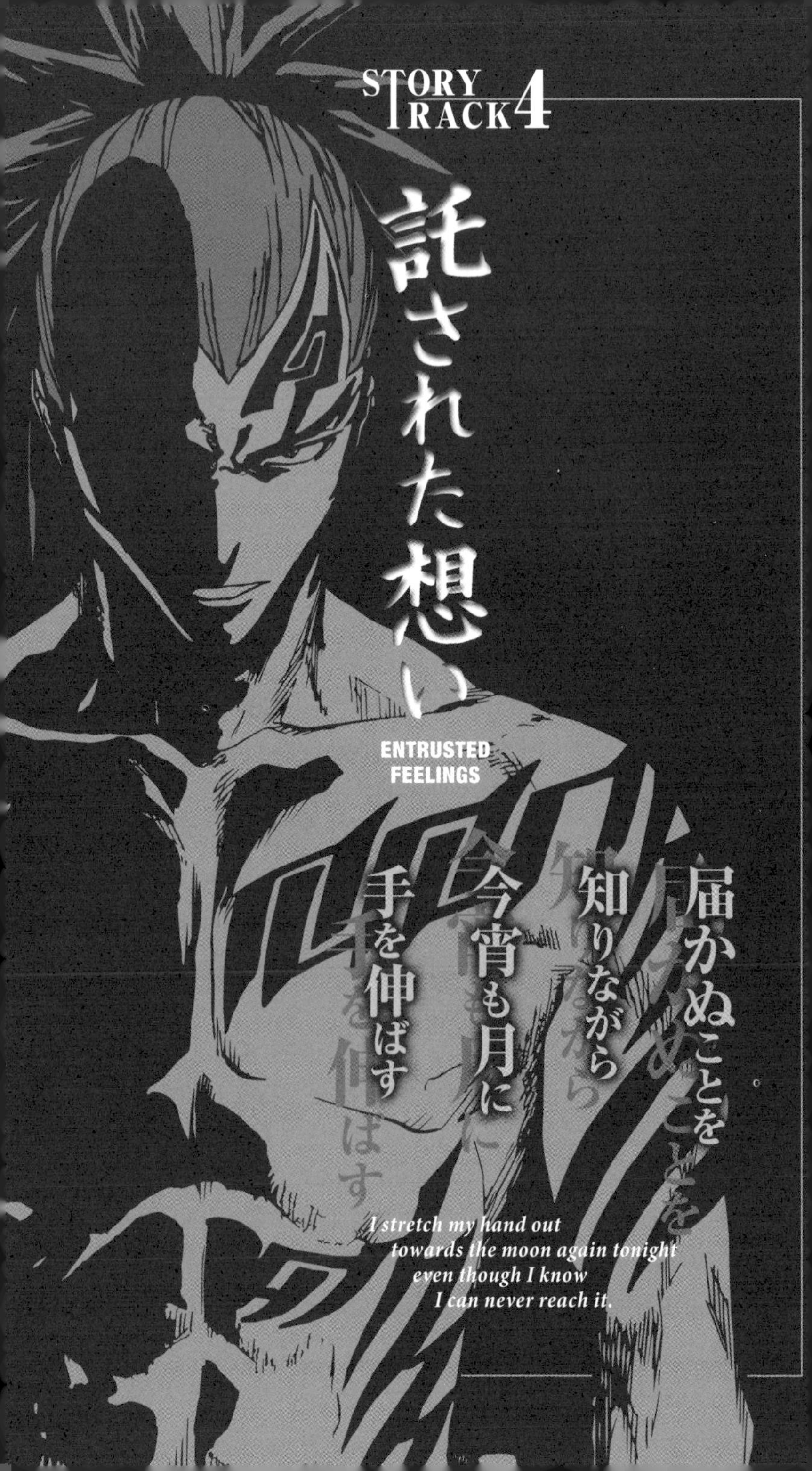
STORY TRACK 4
託された想い
ENTRUSTED FEELINGS
届かぬことを
知りながら
今宵も月に
手を伸ばす
I stretch my hand out
towards the moon again tonight
even though I know
I can never reach it.

花火

FIREWORKS

Beginning Launch
VOL. 10-83~84

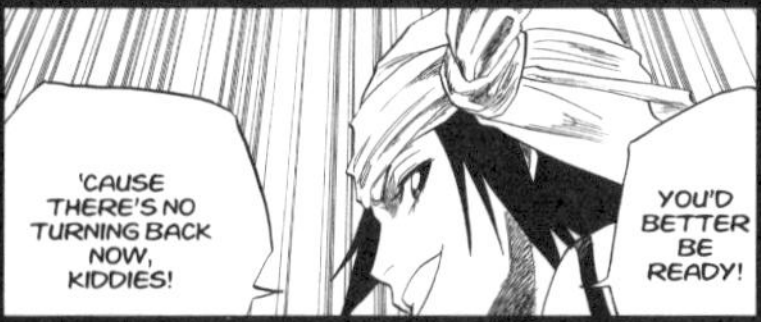
YOU'D BETTER BE READY!
'CAUSE THERE'S NO TURNING BACK NOW, KIDDIES!

Ichigo and his friends get into their spirit core cannonball. Kûkaku, Rukongai's best fireworks expert, launches them high into the air with her personal giant fireworks stand, the Flower Crane Cannon!

Ichigo manages to control his spirit core and complete his cannonball. He falls asleep, having exhausted his spiritual power. Meanwhile, Ganju works hard to master part two of the launch spell. All preparations are made and the launch begins as dawn breaks.

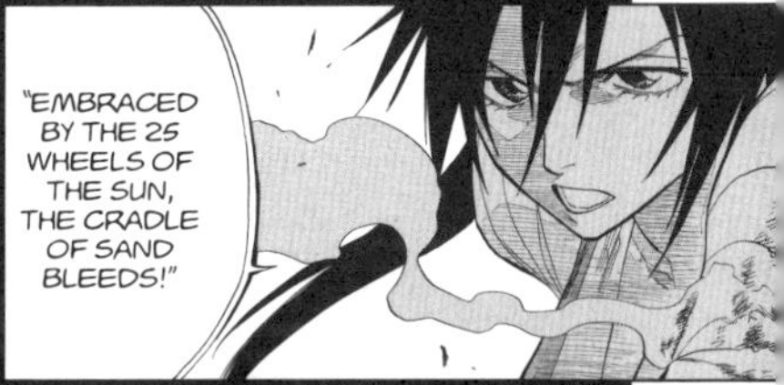
"EMBRACED BY THE 25 WHEELS OF THE SUN, THE CRADLE OF SAND BLEEDS!"

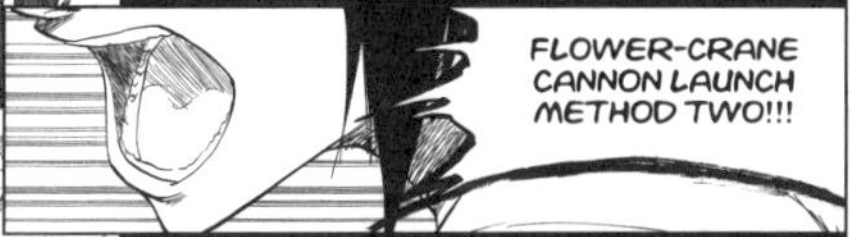
FLOWER-CRANE CANNON LAUNCH METHOD TWO!!!

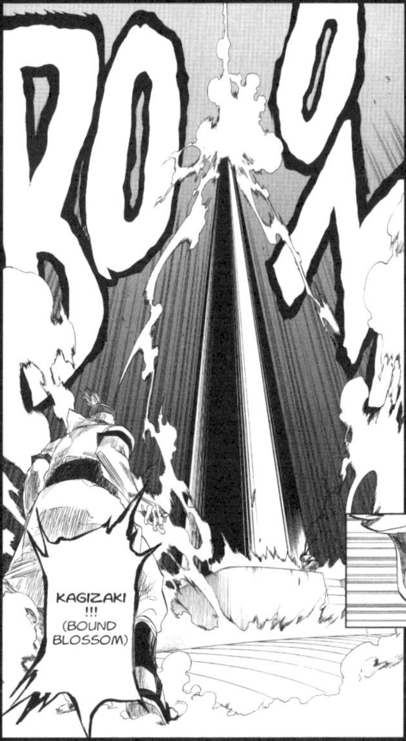
BOOM
KAGIZAKI !!! (BOUND BLOSSOM)

A SHIBA FAMILY SECRET HANDED DOWN THROUGH THE GENERATIONS

THE FLOWER CRANE CANNON LAUNCH

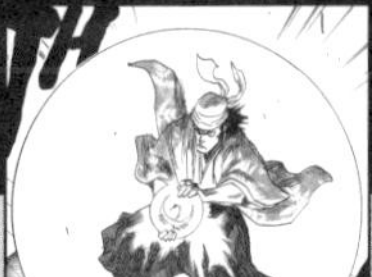

CANNONBALL
A cannon ball is formed by the Special Hard Spiritual Partition Penetration Device that Kûkaku invented.

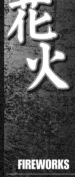

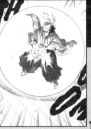

TWO-PART INCANTATION
After the launch details are decided, Ganju controls the cannonball's speed and trajectory from the inside.

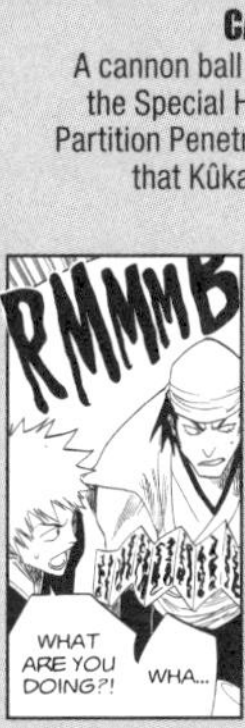
RMMMB
WHA...
WHAT ARE YOU DOING?!

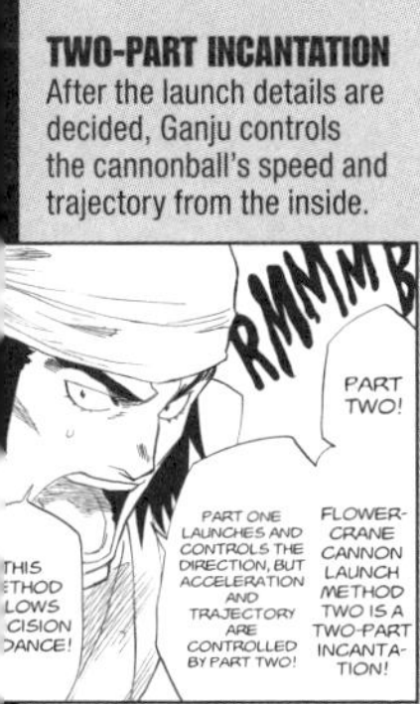
RMMMB
PART TWO!
FLOWER-CRANE CANNON LAUNCH METHOD TWO IS A TWO-PART INCANTATION!
PART ONE LAUNCHES AND CONTROLS THE DIRECTION, BUT ACCELERATION AND TRAJECTORY ARE CONTROLLED BY PART TWO!

The Flower Crane Cannon Launch Number Two is a firing method that shares chanting roles between two casters. This method yields speed and trajectory that are more precise than if a one-person method were used. It also makes it easier to control the point of impact.

衝突 COLLISION

Plow into the Seireitei!
VOL. 10-84~85

Ichigo and his friends have become a cannonball of spiritual power and are flying through the air. Ichigo can't control his spiritual power well, so the cannonball loses control and comes into contact with the Soul Shield Membrane that surrounds the Seireitei!

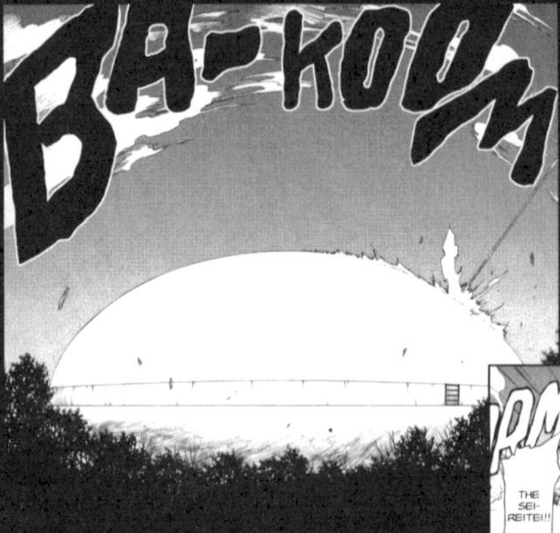
BA-KOOM

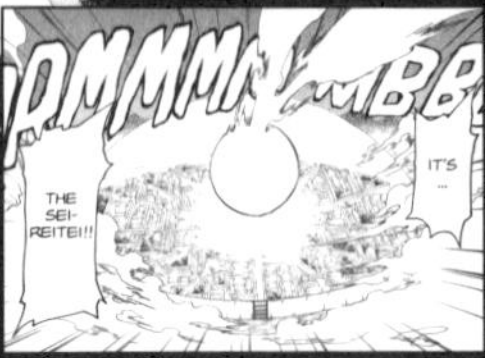
IT'S ...
THE SEI-REITEI!!

The cannonball is very small in comparison to the Soul Shield Membrane, but the shock of the impact shakes the entire Seireitei.

THE BARRIER AROUND SEIREITEI

SHAKONMAKU

Sekki-seki, lethal presence rock, completely blocks spiritual energy. This ore emits radiation waves from its surface that decompose spirit energy. The Soul Shield Membrane, or Shakonmaku, is a barrier formed from this wave. Everything in the Soul Society is made of reishi, and anything made of reishi that tries to pass through the Soul Shield Membrane will turn to dust unless it is of high density.

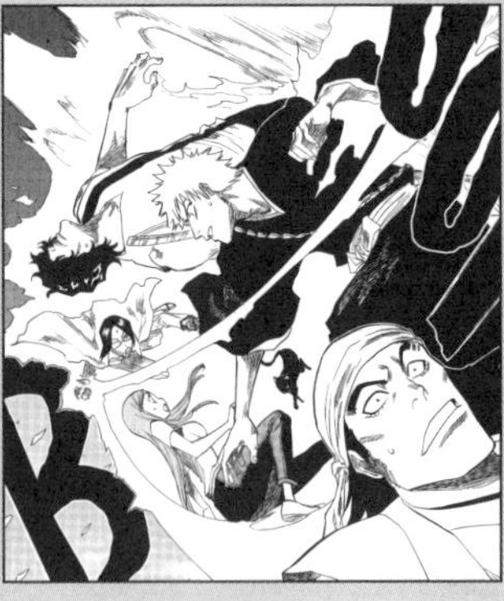

ICHIGO AND HIS FRIENDS SCATTER IN FOUR DIRECTIONS

The cannonball bursts from the impact with the Soul Shield Membrane. The party is scattered into four groups: Uryû and Orihime, Chad, Mr. Yoruichi, and Ichigo and Ganju.

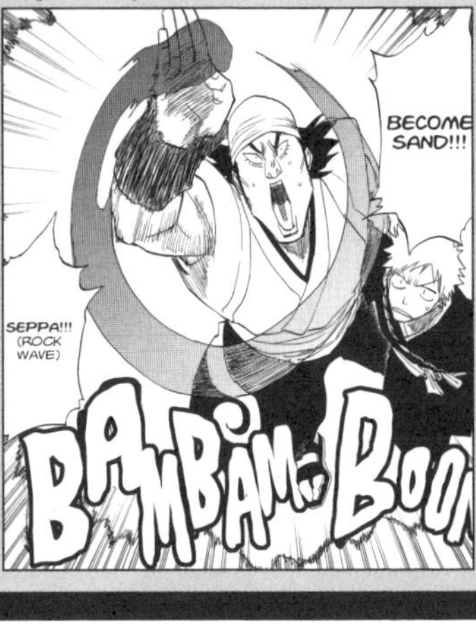
BECOME SAND!!!
SEPPA!!! (ROCK WAVE)

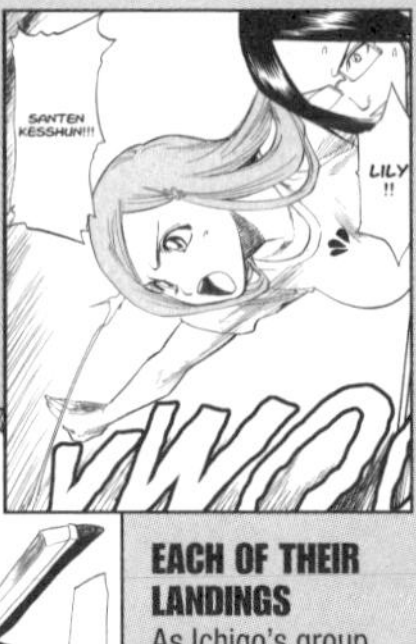
LILY !!
SANTEN KESSHUN!!!

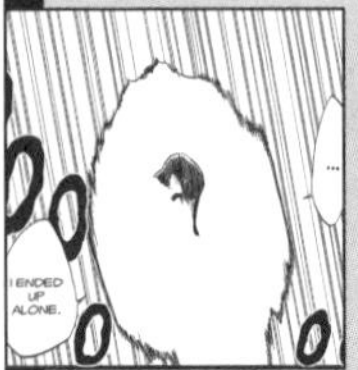
...
I ENDED UP ALONE.

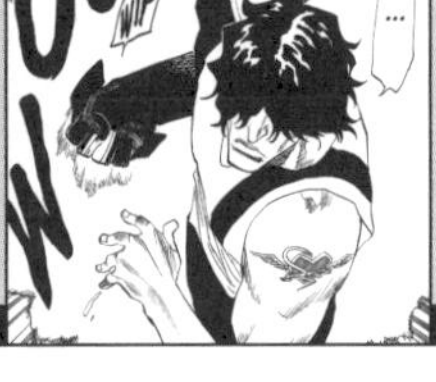
...
WIP

EACH OF THEIR LANDINGS

As Ichigo's group falls from the sky, they all use their abilities to prepare for landing.

ELEVENTH COMPANY THIRD SEAT

IKKAKU MADARAME — CHARACTER FILE 71

Death 死

斑目一角

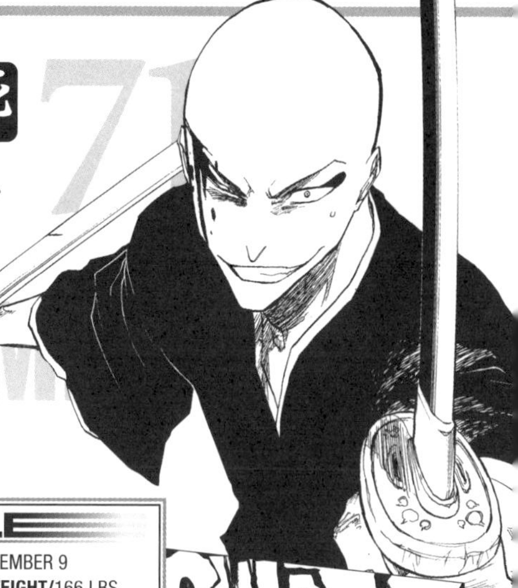

SCRAPPY SOUL REAPER WITH UMBER ONE IN HIS NAME

he Soul Reaper Ichigo and Ganju neet when they fall into the Seireitei. e is very aggressive and has a ough fighting style, but definitely as technical skills. He shows his layful side by performing an odd ance in front of Ichigo and Ganju as ey stand on guard.

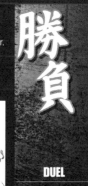

PROFILE

BIRTHDAY/NOVEMBER 9
HEIGHT/6´0˝ **WEIGHT/**166 LBS
AFFILIATION/ELEVENTH COMPANY
ZANPAKU-TÔ/HÔZUKIMARU

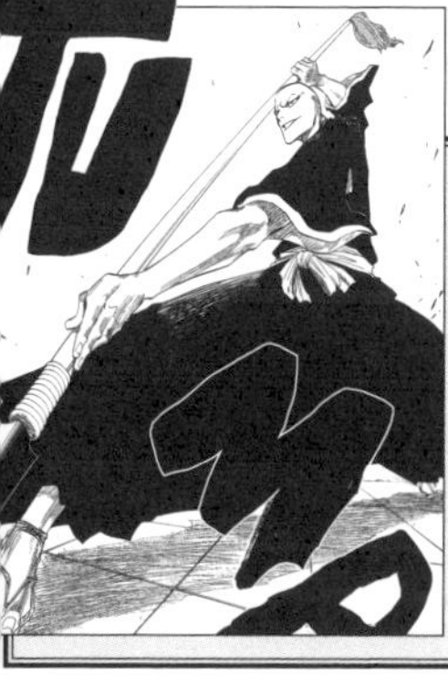

ZANPAKU-TÔ

HÔZUKIMARU

At first glance, it looks like a spear, but by chanting the words, "Extend! Hôzukimaru!" it becomes a three-section staff.

When his zanpaku-tô isn't released, Ikkaku has a unique style where he holds his sword in one hand and his scabbard in the other.

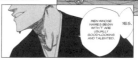

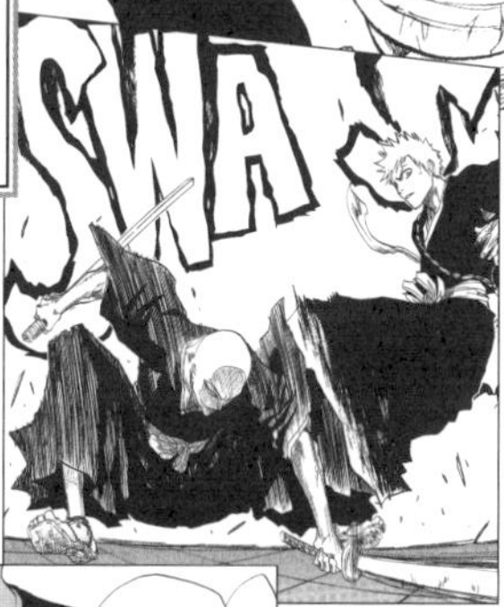
SWA

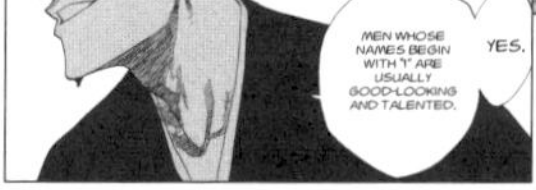
YES.
MEN WHOSE NAMES BEGIN WITH "I" ARE USUALLY GOOD-LOOKING AND TALENTED.

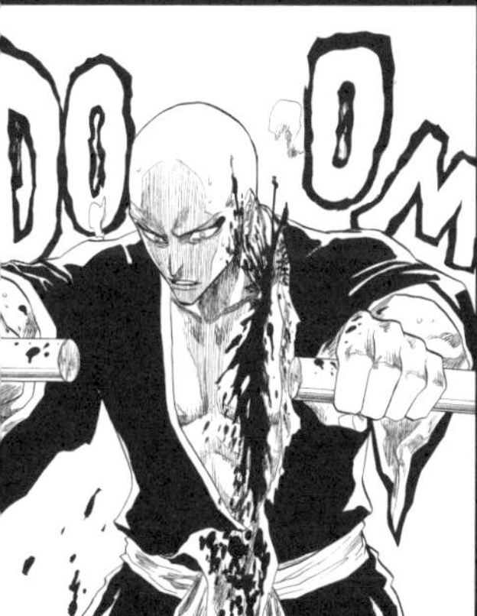
DOOM

Two people with number one in their names go one-on-one. Ikkaku releases his zanpaku-tô when he learns that Urahara is Ichigo's teacher. Ichigo has problems fighting against the ever-changing Hôzukimaru, but he gradually becomes accustomed to its movements.

Ichigo swings Zangetsu. Ikkaku tries to block with Hôzukimaru, but Ichigo slices right through it and mortally wounds Ikkaku.

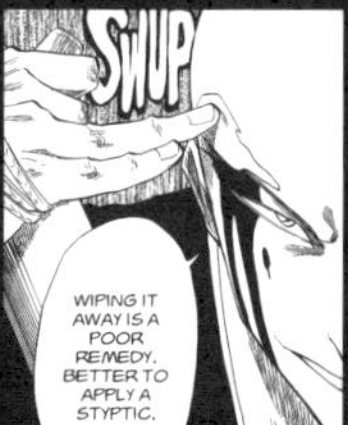
SWUP
WIPING IT AWAY IS A POOR REMEDY. BETTER TO APPLY A STYPTIC.

勝負

DUEL

The first battle in the Seireitei
VOL. 10-86~88

Yumichika slowly closes in on Ganju as he runs away. Yumichika lets his guard down, thinking that Ganju can only do petty tricks. When Ganju trips him, Yumichika is splendidly defeated by an "ugly man."

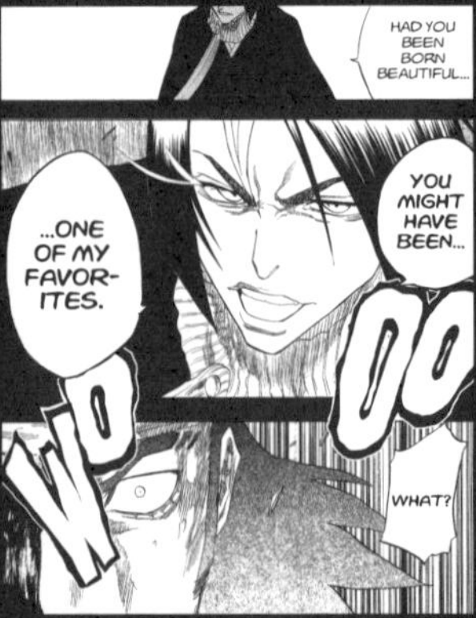
HAD YOU BEEN BORN BEAUTIFUL...
YOU MIGHT HAVE BEEN...
...ONE OF MY FAVORITES.
WHOOO
WHAT?

Yumichika becomes annoyed by Ganju's dogged persistence. He finally shows his serious face!

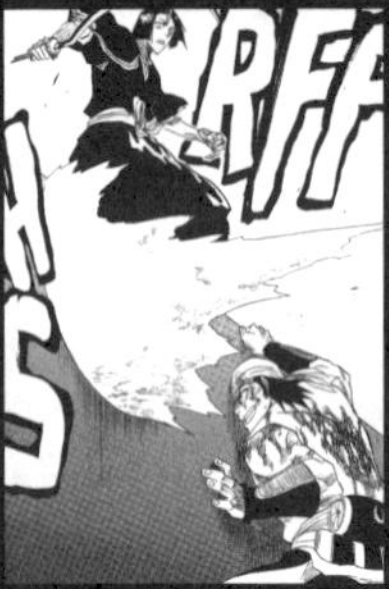

美醜

APPEARANCE

Differences in Aesthetic Sense
VOL. 11-89~90

AN ATTRACTIVE SWORDSMAN WITH A UNIQUE SENSE OF BEAUTY

A Soul Reaper who holds beautiful people and things above everything else. He's full of himself, hates ugly things, and tends to look down on unattractive people. He's in the same company as Ikkaku and often accompanies him.

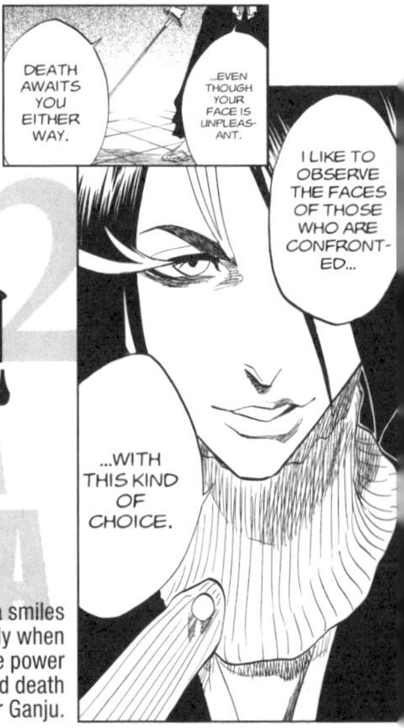
...EVEN THOUGH YOUR FACE IS UNPLEASANT.
DEATH AWAITS YOU EITHER WAY.
I LIKE TO OBSERVE THE FACES OF THOSE WHO ARE CONFRONTED...
...WITH THIS KIND OF CHOICE.

Yumichika smiles sadistically when he has the power of life and death over Ganju.

ELEVENTH COMPANY FIFTH SEAT

YUMICHIKA AYASEGAWA — CHARACTER FILE 72

Death 死 72

綾瀬川弓親

YUMICHIKA AYASEGAWA

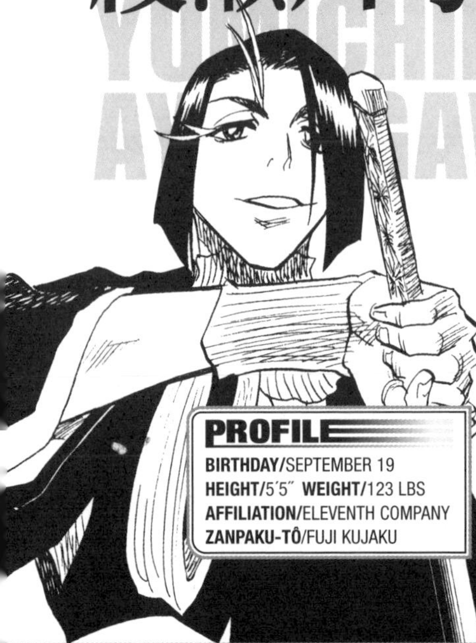

PROFILE

BIRTHDAY/SEPTEMBER 19
HEIGHT/5′5″ **WEIGHT**/123 LBS
AFFILIATION/ELEVENTH COMPANY
ZANPAKU-TÔ/FUJI KUJAKU

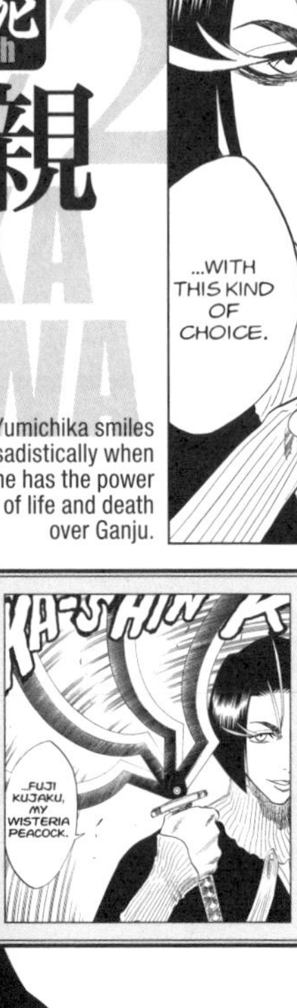
KA-SHIN
...FUJI KUJAKU, MY WISTERIA PEACOCK.

ZANPAKU-TÔ

FUJI KUJAKU

A zanpaku-tô made up of four blades. It seems to have a hidden ability...

ONE OF THE SOUL SOCIETY'S MOST PROMINENT PROJECTILE USERS

The Soul Reaper who Uryû and Orihime fight in the Seireitei. As the Soul Society's strongest projectile user, he holds the title of "Kamaitachi." His zanpaku-tô's ability is appropriate for the title. He is the brother of Jidumbô, the gate-keeper of White Road Gate.

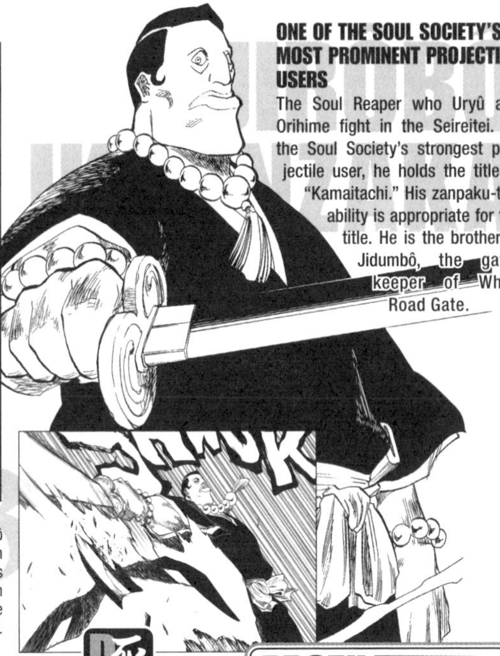
SHAK

Jirôbô knocks down Orihime's Kotenzanshun in a single blow.

ZANPAKU-TÔ

TSUNZAKI GARASU

It splits into countless blades when in Shikai. It attacks the enemy from all directions.

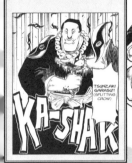

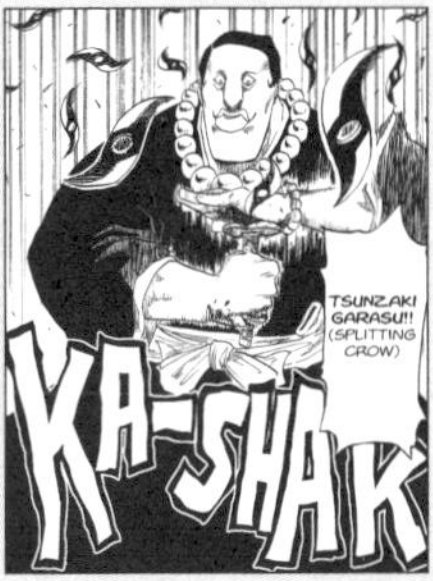
TSUNZAKI GARASU!! (SPLITTING CROW)
KA-SHAK

SEVENTH COMPANY FOURTH SEAT

JIRÔBÔ IKKANZAKA — CHARACTER FILE 73

D死eath

一貫坂慈楼坊

PROFILE

BIRTHDAY/NOVEMBER 9
HEIGHT/7′6″ **WEIGHT**/374 LBS
AFFILIATION/ELEVENTH COMPANY
ZANPAKU-TÔ/TSUNZAKIGARASU

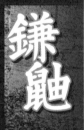

鎌鼬

KAMAITACHI

The strongest projectile user
VOL. 11-91~92

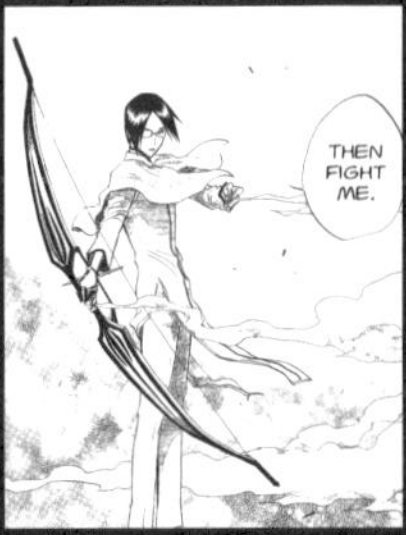
THEN FIGHT ME.

Uryû shoots down all of Jirôbô's blades as soon as he tries to release Tsunzaki Garasu. Jirôbô underhandedly goes after Orihime even though he talks high-mindedly. Uryû quietly burns with anger.

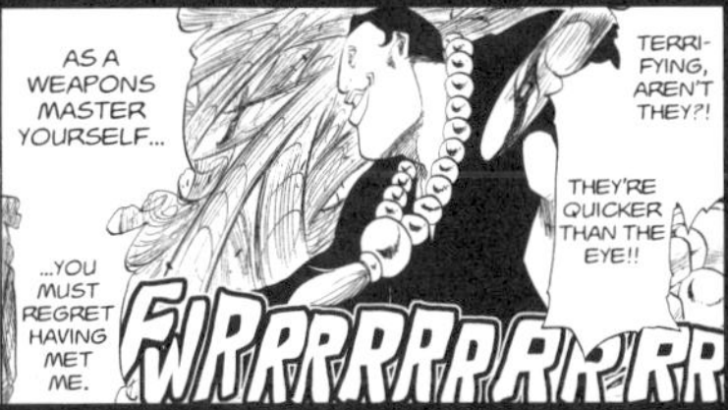
TERRI-FYING, AREN'T THEY?!
THEY'RE QUICKER THAN THE EYE!!
AS A WEAPONS MASTER YOURSELF...
...YOU MUST REGRET HAVING MET ME.
FWRRRRRRRRRRR

With his Quincy training, Uryû gains strength that makes him look like an entirely different person from when he fought Ichigo. Uryû gains an overwhelming victory when he pierces Jirôbô's soul chain and soul sleep.

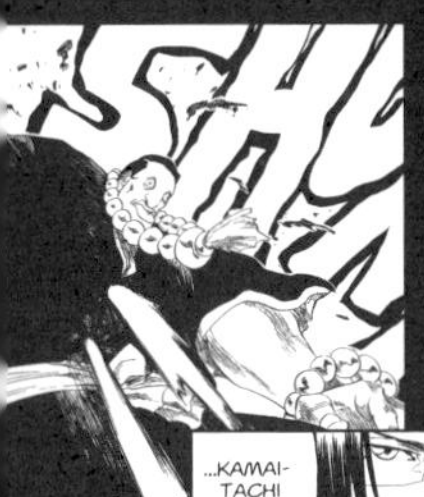
SHA

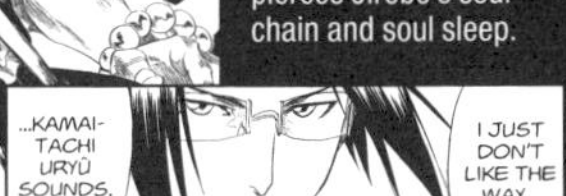
I JUST DON'T LIKE THE WAY...
...KAMAI-TACHI URYÛ SOUNDS.

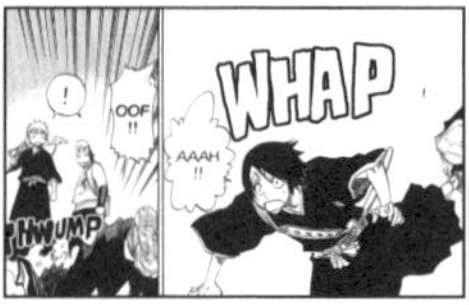
WHAP
AAAH !!
!
OOF !!
THWUMP

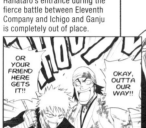

ENDS UP GOING TOGETHER?
Hanatarô's entrance during the fierce battle between Eleventh Company and Ichigo and Ganju is completely out of place.

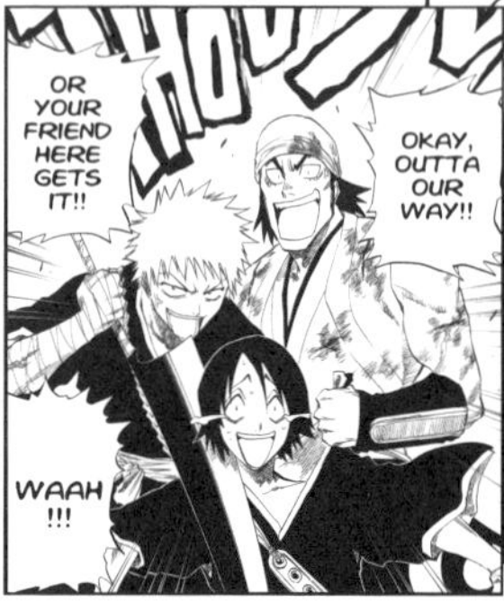
OKAY, OUTTA OUR WAY!!
OR YOUR FRIEND HERE GETS IT!!
WAAH !!!

D 死 eath

FOURTH COMPANY SEVENTH SEAT

HANATARÔ YAMADA — CHARACTER FILE 74

山田花太郎

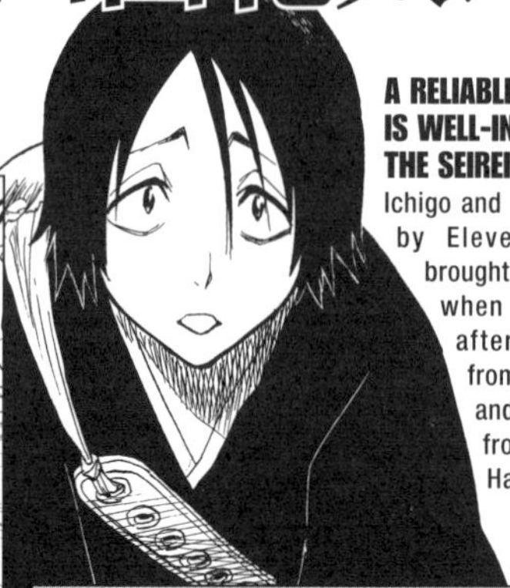

A RELIABLE (?) FRIEND WHO IS WELL-INFORMED ABOUT THE SEIREITEI

Ichigo and Ganju are surrounded by Eleventh Company and brought to a standstill. That's when Hanatarô wanders in after getting separated from his company. Ichigo and Ganju plan to escape from the squad by taking Hanatarô as a hostage,

PROFILE

BIRTHDAY/APRIL 1
HEIGHT/5′0″ **WEIGHT/**99 LBS
AFFILIATION/FOURTH COMPANY
ZANPAKU-TÔ/HISAGOMARU

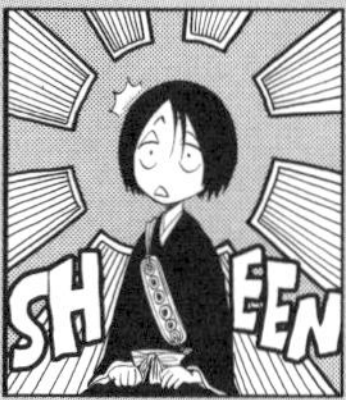
SHEEN

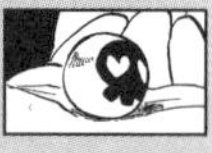

HANATARÔ'S PERSONAL SPECIAL NOURISHMENT TONIC

Hanatarô's Nutritional Fortification Pill is different from that of the other members of his company. The older members pulled a prank on him, so its main component is wheat.

荻堂春信

HARUNOBU OGIDÔ — 76

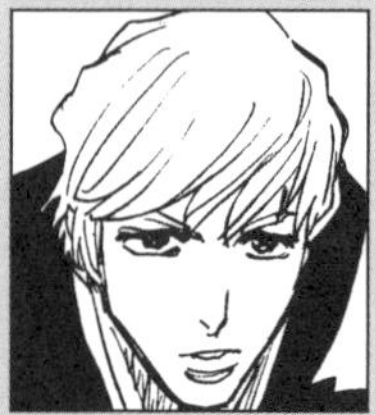

Fourth Company Eighth Seat. Unbeknownst to him, Harunobu is popular amongst female Soul Reapers for his effortless attractiveness.

PROFILE

BIRTHDAY/APRIL 14
HEIGHT/5′7″
WEIGHT/132 LBS

伊江村八十千和

YASOCHIKA IEMURA — 75

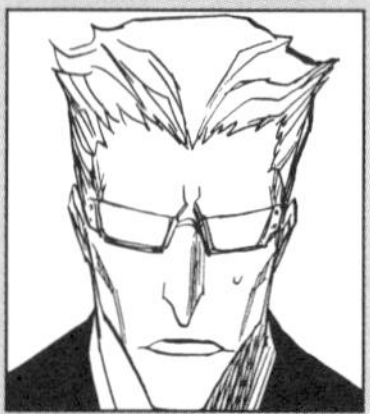

Fourth Company Third Seat. An eyeglasses-wearing Soul Reaper who is not discouraged by the fact that he is in a weaker position than the third seats of other companies.

PROFILE

BIRTHDAY/
FEBRUARY 29
HEIGHT/5′8″
WEIGHT/154 LBS

RELIEF AND SUPPLY UNIT

FOURTH COMPANY

A unique company that specializes in relief and supplies. The ability to heal using spiritual power is rare. However, other companies, particularly Eleventh Company, mock Fourth Company's low fighting abilities.

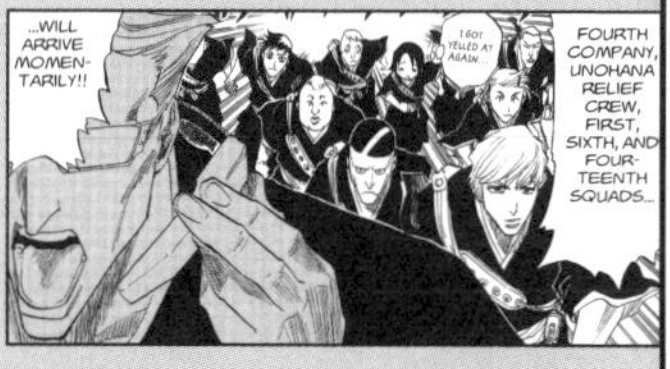
FOURTH COMPANY, UNOHANA RELIEF CREW, FIRST, SIXTH, AND FOURTEENTH SQUADS...
I GOT YELLED AT AGAIN
...WILL ARRIVE MOMENTARILY!!

Fourth Company doesn't participate in battles, but it frequently carries out missions to heal injured company members and send supplies.

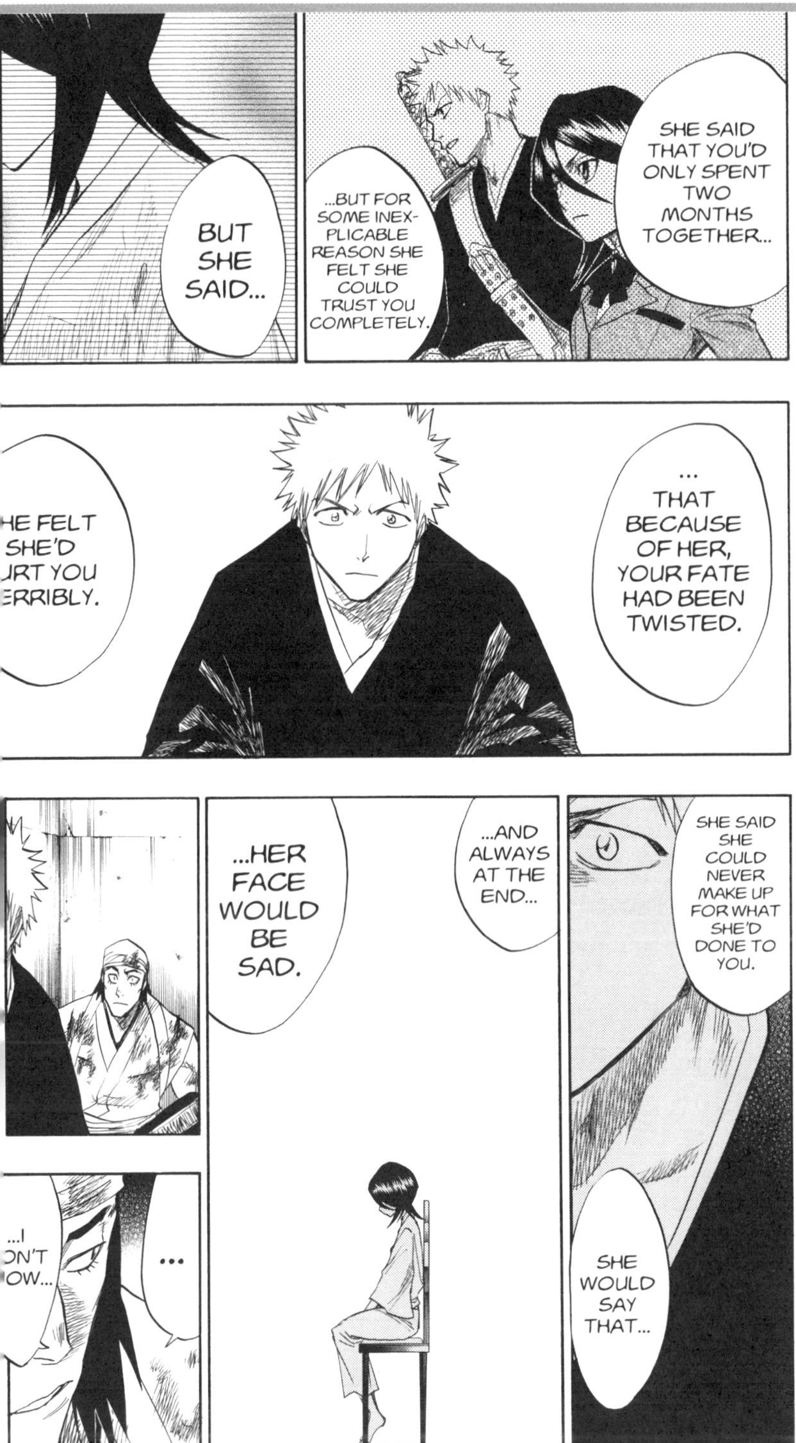
SHE SAID THAT YOU'D ONLY SPENT TWO MONTHS TOGETHER...
...BUT FOR SOME INEX-PLICABLE REASON SHE FELT SHE COULD TRUST YOU COMPLETELY.
BUT SHE SAID...
... THAT BECAUSE OF HER, YOUR FATE HAD BEEN TWISTED.
HE FELT SHE'D URT YOU ERRIBLY.
SHE SAID SHE COULD NEVER MAKE UP FOR WHAT SHE'D DONE TO YOU.
SHE WOULD SAY THAT...
...AND ALWAYS AT THE END...
...HER FACE WOULD BE SAD.
...
...I ON'T OW...

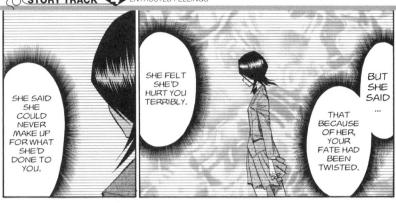

SHE SAID SHE COULD NEVER MAKE UP FOR WHAT SHE'D DONE TO YOU.

SHE FELT SHE'D HURT YOU TERRIBLY.

THAT BECAUSE OF HER, YOUR FATE HAD BEEN TWISTED.

BUT SHE SAID...

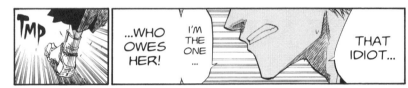

TMP

...WHO OWES HER!

I'M THE ONE...

THAT IDIOT...

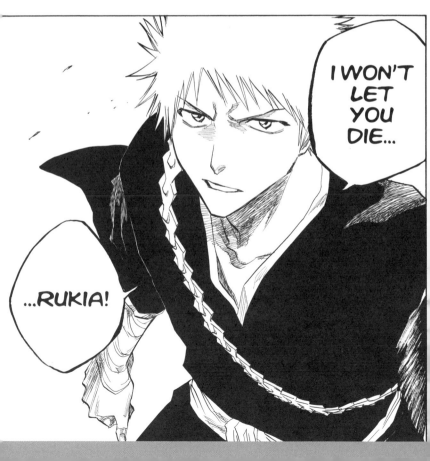

I WON'T LET YOU DIE...

...RUKIA!

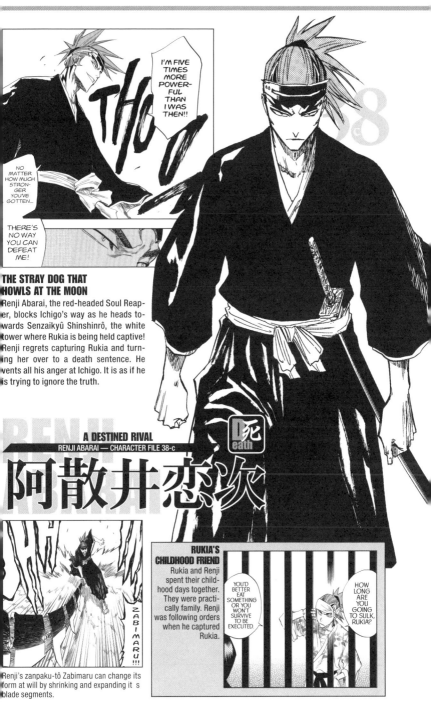

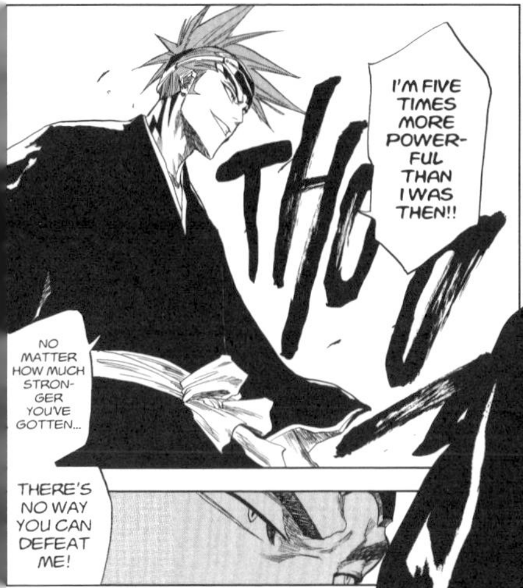
I'M FIVE TIMES MORE POWER-FUL THAN I WAS THEN!!
THOOO
NO MATTER HOW MUCH STRON-GER YOU'VE GOTTEN...
THERE'S NO WAY YOU CAN DEFEAT ME!

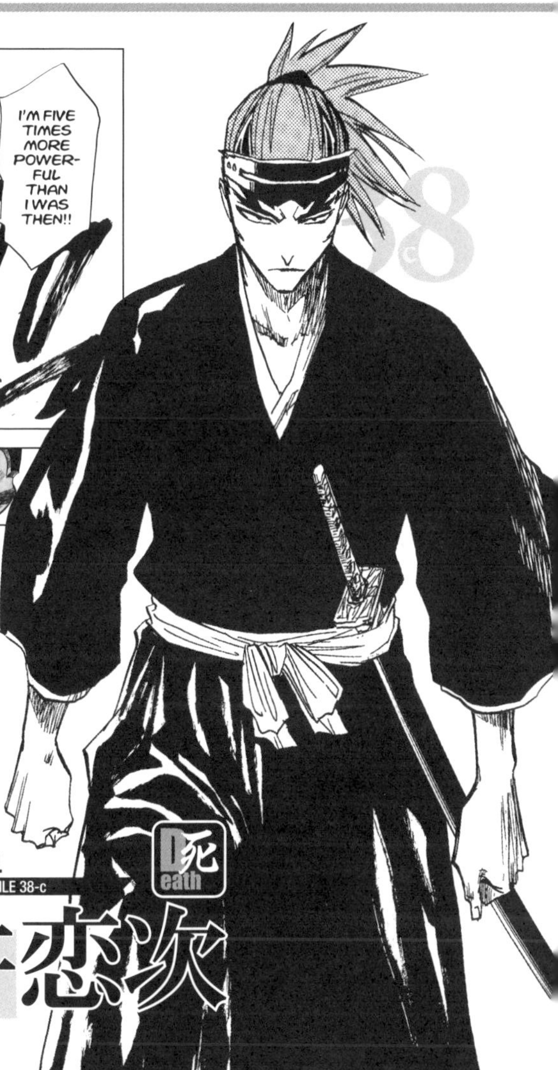

THE STRAY DOG THAT HOWLS AT THE MOON

Renji Abarai, the red-headed Soul Reaper, blocks Ichigo's way as he heads towards Senzaikyû Shinshinrô, the white tower where Rukia is being held captive! Renji regrets capturing Rukia and turning her over to a death sentence. He vents all his anger at Ichigo. It is as if he is trying to ignore the truth.

A DESTINED RIVAL

RENJI ABARAI — CHARACTER FILE 38-c

阿散井恋次

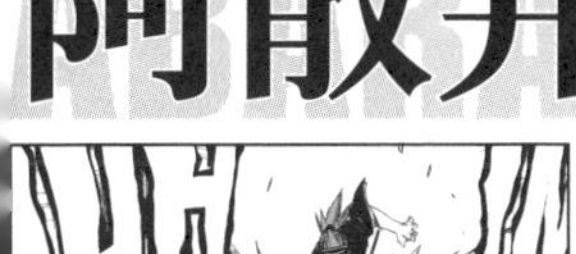
ZABIMARU!!!

Renji's zanpaku-tô Zabimaru can change its form at will by shrinking and expanding it s blade segments.

RUKIA'S CHILDHOOD FRIEND

Rukia and Renji spent their childhood days together. They were practically family. Renji was following orders when he captured Rukia.

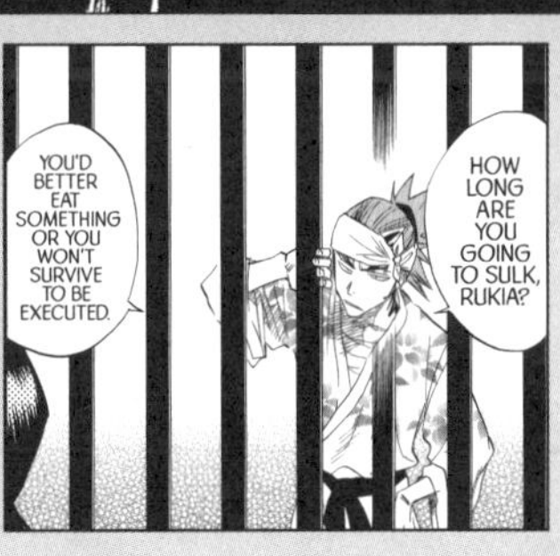
HOW LONG ARE YOU GOING TO SULK, RUKIA?
YOU'D BETTER EAT SOMETHING OR YOU WON'T SURVIVE TO BE EXECUTED.

再戦

REMATCH

Renji Once More
VOL. 11-95~98

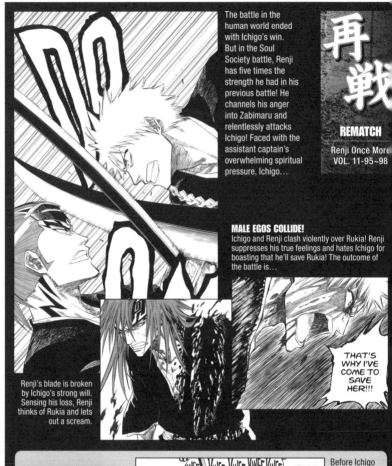

The battle in the human world ended with Ichigo's win. But in the Soul Society battle, Renji has five times the strength he had in his previous battle! He channels his anger into Zabimaru and relentlessly attacks Ichigo! Faced with the assistant captain's overwhelming spiritual pressure, Ichigo...

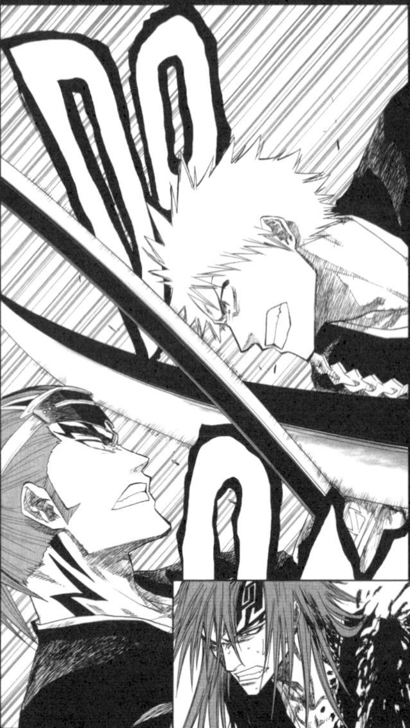

MALE EGOS COLLIDE!

Ichigo and Renji clash violently over Rukia! Renji suppresses his true feelings and hates Ichigo for boasting that he'll save Rukia! The outcome of the battle is...

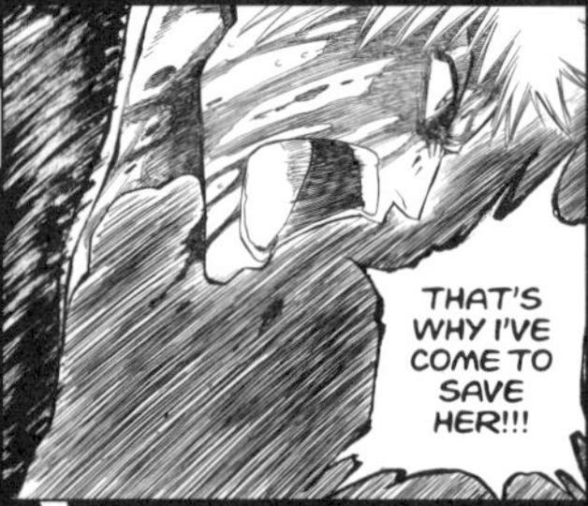
THAT'S WHY I'VE COME TO SAVE HER!!!

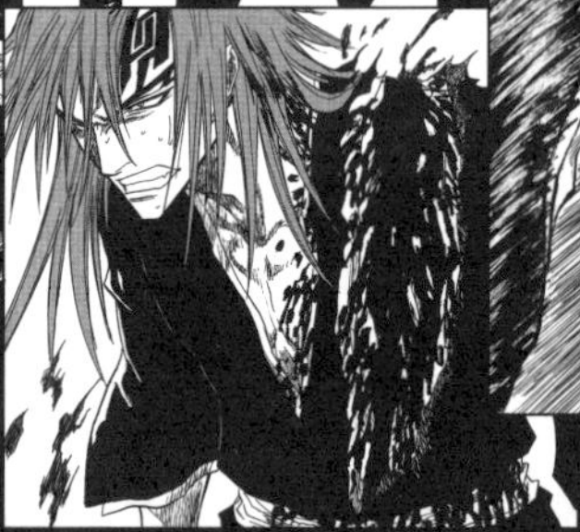

Renji's blade is broken by Ichigo's strong will. Sensing his loss, Renji thinks of Rukia and lets out a scream.

A STRONG UNWAVERING WILL

THE DETERMINATION TO SLICE

Before Ichigo charged into the Soul Society, he had a life-or-death battle with Urahara. It was then that Ichigo learned the terror of swords and the true nature of combat. Ichigo puts his determination to save Rukia into his thrusts and slices Renji!

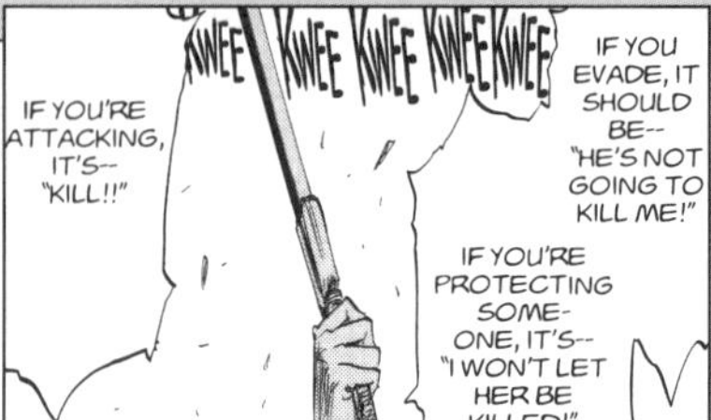
KWEE KWEE KWEE KWEE KWEE
IF YOU EVADE, IT SHOULD BE-- "HE'S NOT GOING TO KILL ME!"
IF YOU'RE ATTACKING, IT'S-- "KILL!!"
IF YOU'RE PROTECTING SOME-ONE, IT'S-- "I WON'T LET HER BE KILLED!"

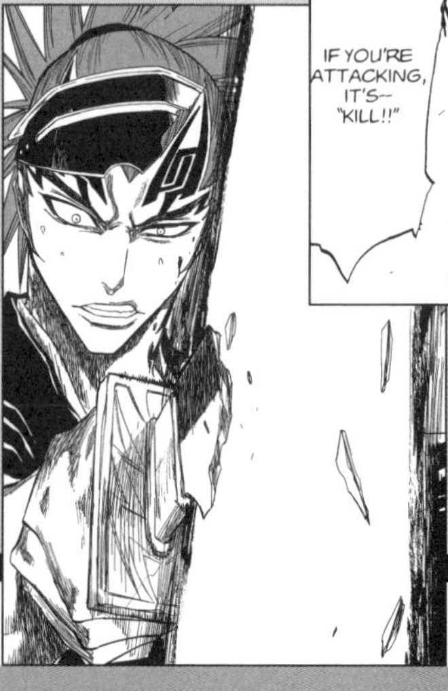

戌吊

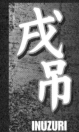

INUZURI

Rukia and Renji
VOL. 11-98

Rukongai Zone 78, Inuzuri (Hanging Dog). One of the most dangerous levels of the Rukongai. Rukia and Renji met here. Orphaned street children gather together like family to survive harsh everyday life.

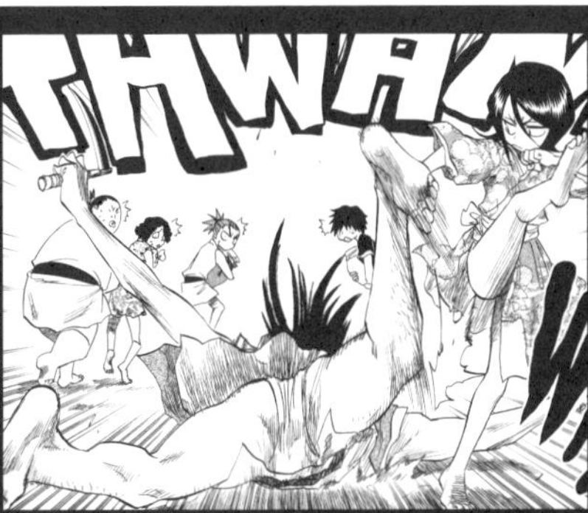
THWAK

A STRONG AND DEEP BOND
It's been ten years since Rukia and Renji met. They lived with death constantly at their side and were the only ones of their group to survive...

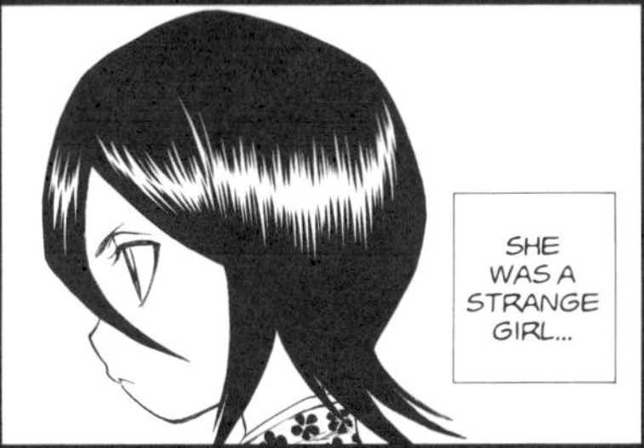
SHE WAS A STRANGE GIRL...

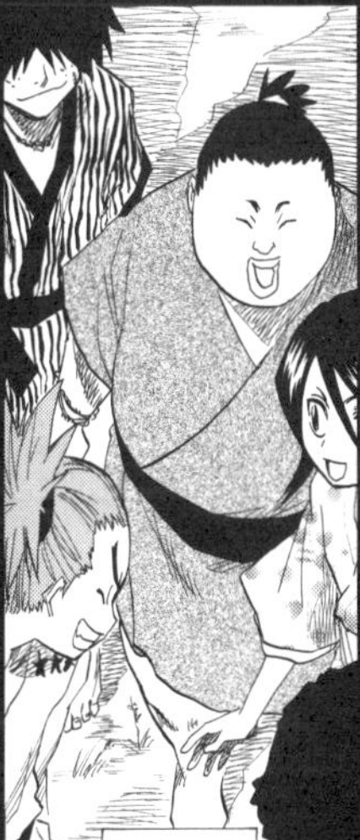
WE WERE A FAMILY.

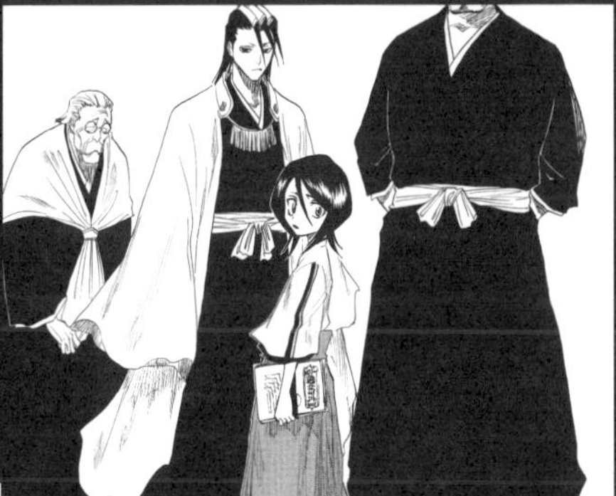

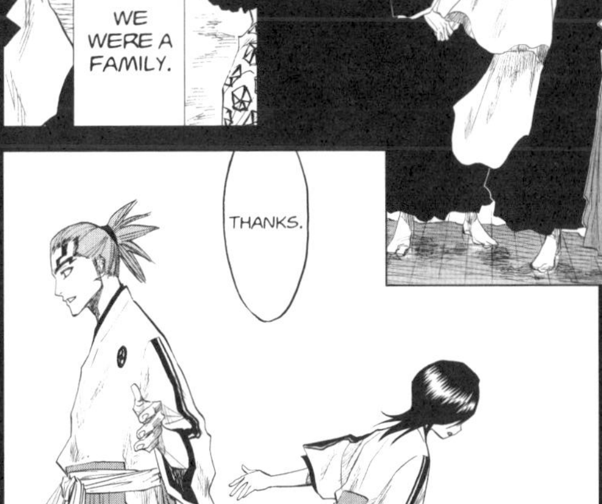
THANKS.

RELEASED HAND
The Kuchiki family offers to adopt Rukia. Renji congratulates her, but their hearts are drawn apart...

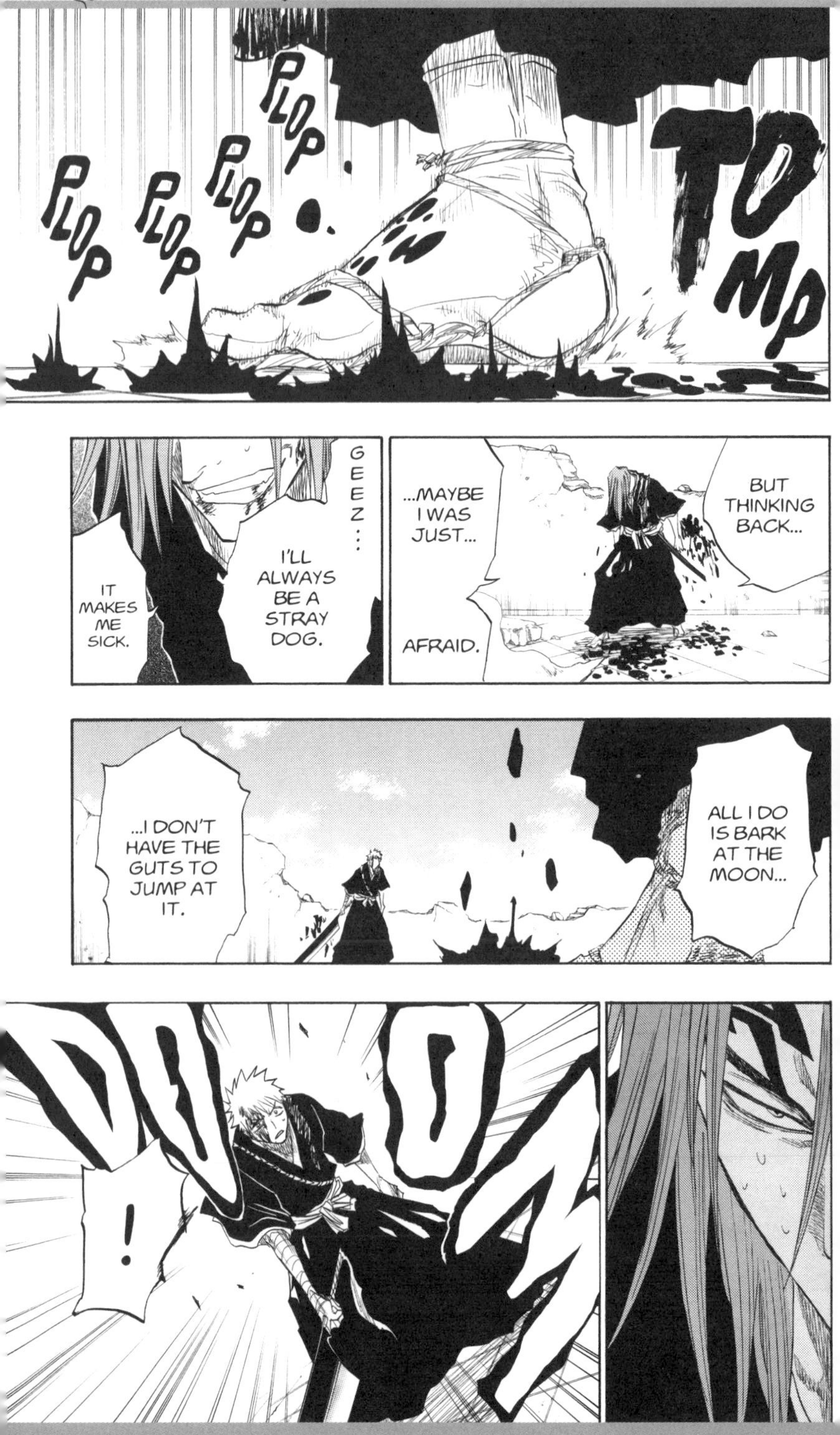
TOMP
PLOP
PLOP
PLOP
PLOP
BUT THINKING BACK...
...MAYBE I WAS JUST...
AFRAID.
GEEZ...
I'LL ALWAYS BE A STRAY DOG.
IT MAKES ME SICK.
ALL I DO IS BARK AT THE MOON...
...I DON'T HAVE THE GUTS TO JUMP AT IT.
!

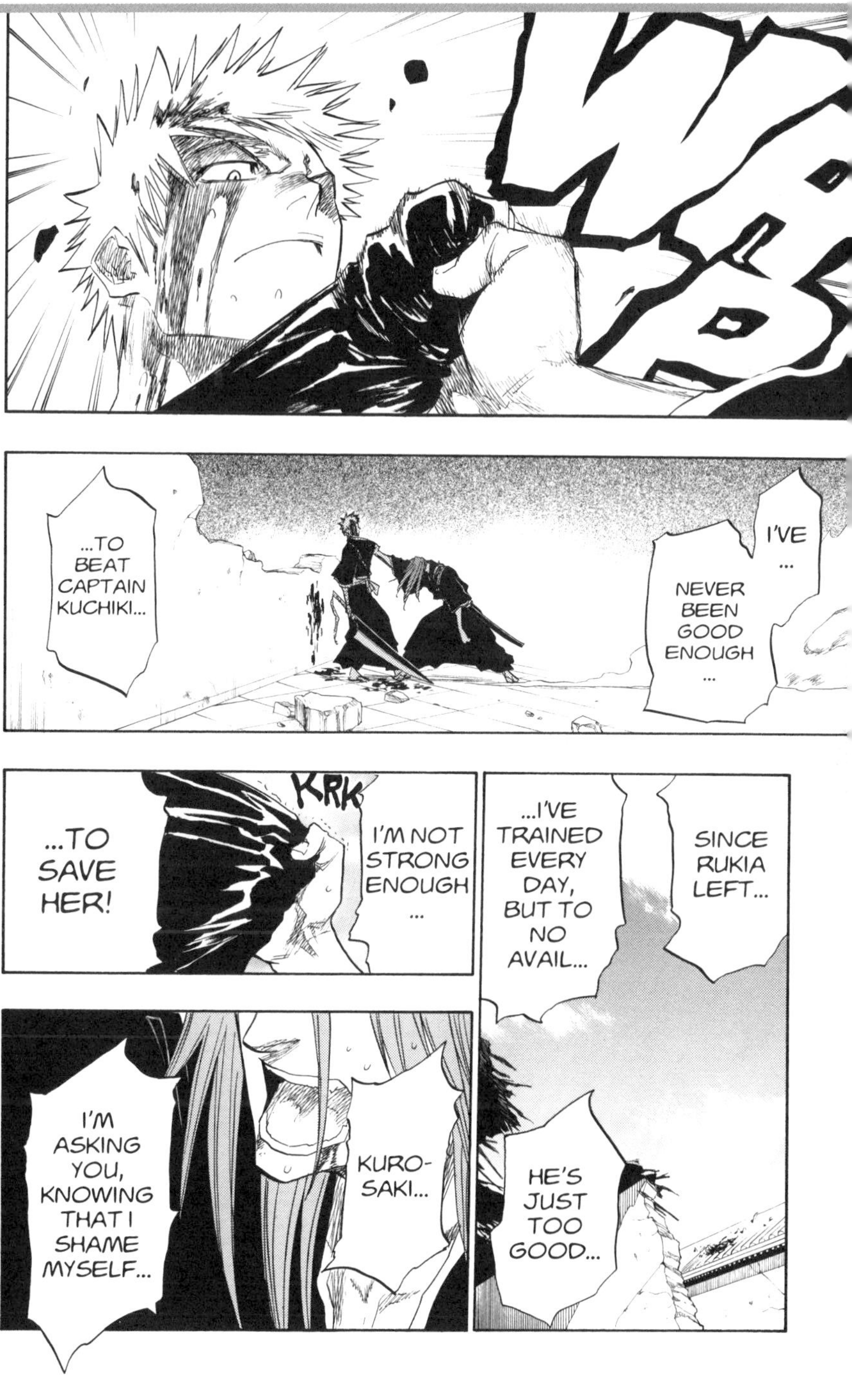

I'VE ... NEVER BEEN GOOD ENOUGH ...
...TO BEAT CAPTAIN KUCHIKI...
SINCE RUKIA LEFT...
...I'VE TRAINED EVERY DAY, BUT TO NO AVAIL...
HE'S JUST TOO GOOD...
KRK
I'M NOT STRONG ENOUGH ...
...TO SAVE HER!
KURO-SAKI...
I'M ASKING YOU, KNOWING THAT I SHAME MYSELF...

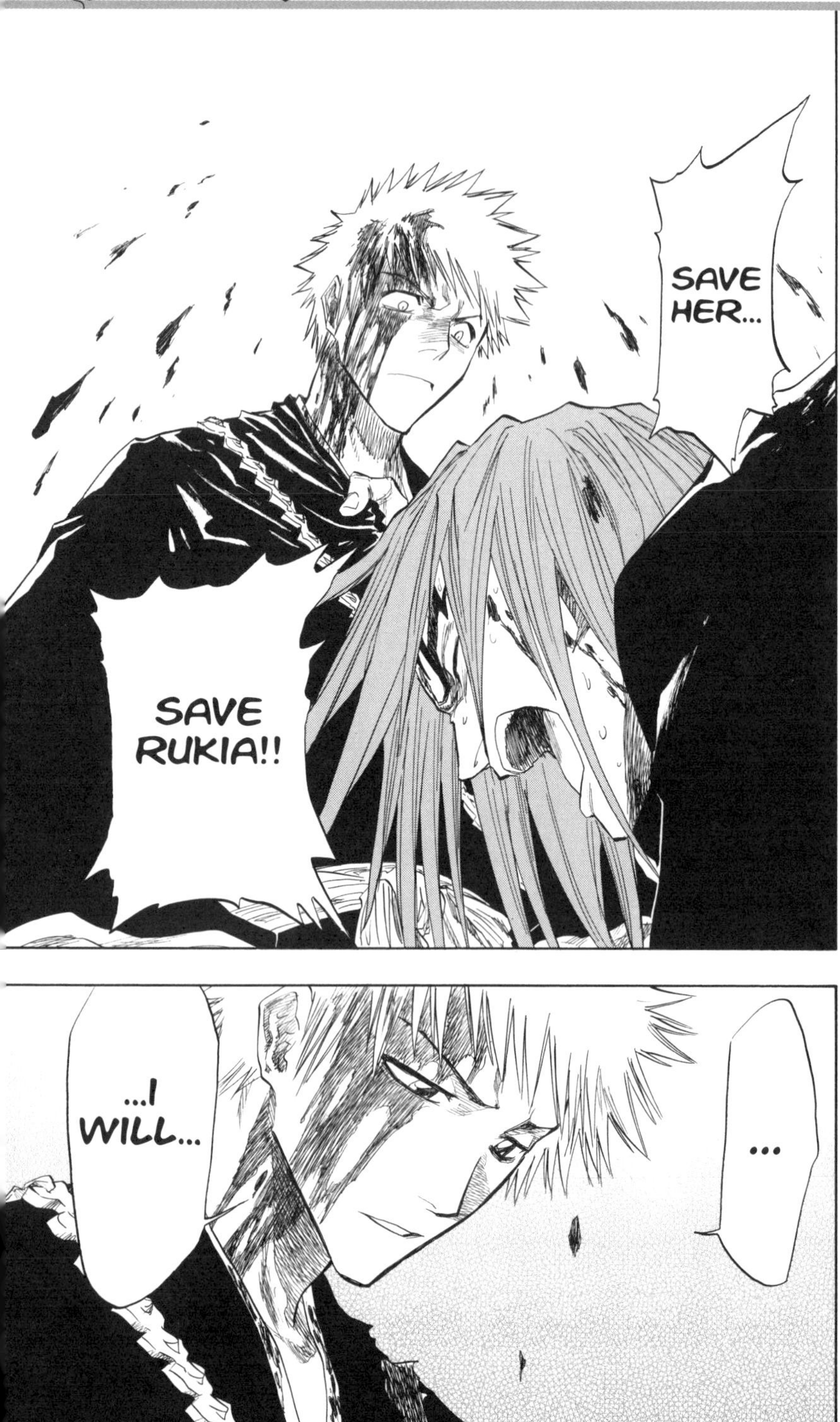
SAVE HER...
SAVE RUKIA!!
...
...I WILL...

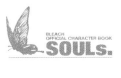
BLEACH
OFFICIAL CHARACTER BOOK
SOULs.

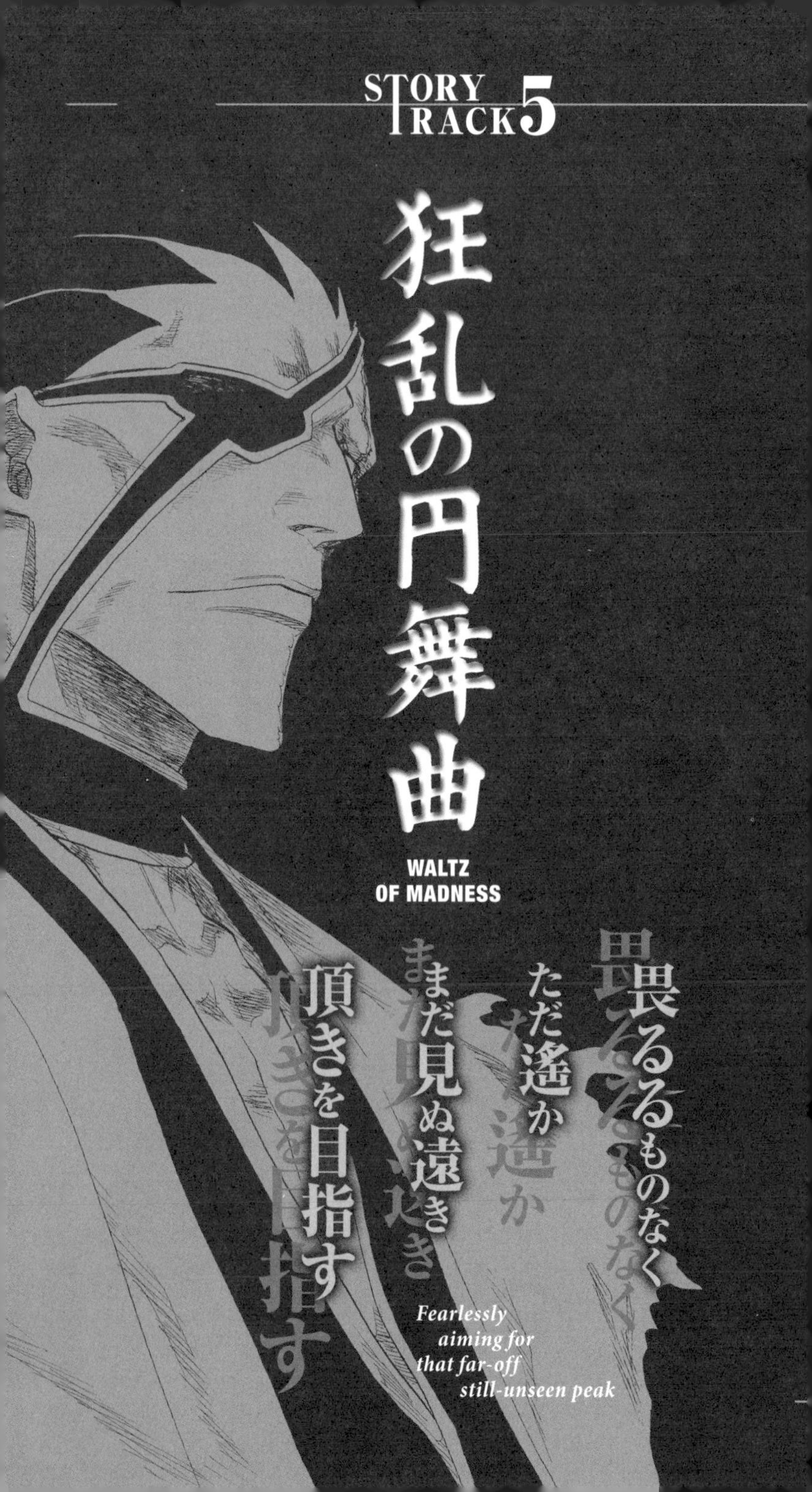
STORY TRACK 5
狂乱の円舞曲
WALTZ OF MADNESS
畏るるものなく
ただ遙か
まだ見ぬ遠き
頂きを目指す
Fearlessly aiming for that far-off still-unseen peak

FIFTH COMPANY CAPTAIN

SŌSUKE AIZEN — CHARACTER FILE 54-b

Death 死

藍染惣右介

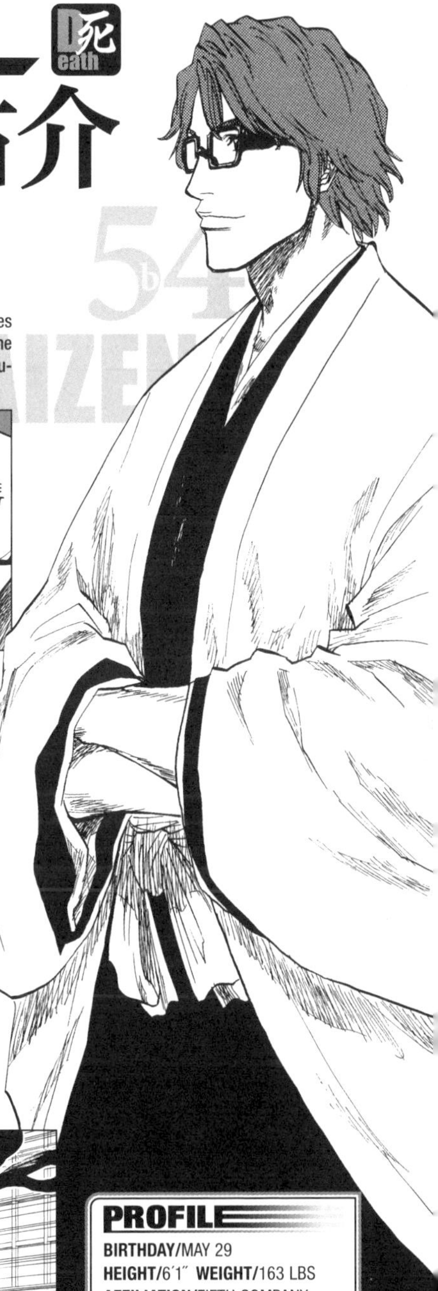

A MAN OF CHARACTER WITH A PEACEFUL GAZE

The Fifth Company captain. His gentle demeanor, kind eyes and genial personality endear him to all the members of the Thirteen Court Guards. He was also Ichimaru and Renji's superior when they were in the Fifth Company.

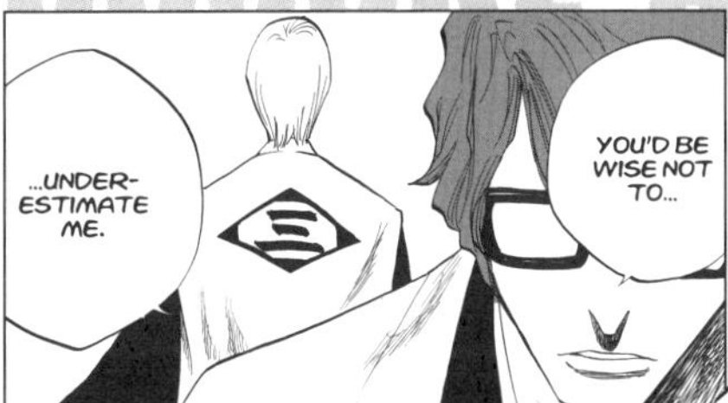
YOU'D BE WISE NOT TO...
...UNDER-ESTIMATE ME.

AIZEN READS ICHIMARU'S EXPECTATIONS?!

The alarm bell rings during the captains' meeting. Aizen gives Ichimaru a warning as he passes him by.

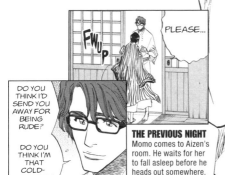

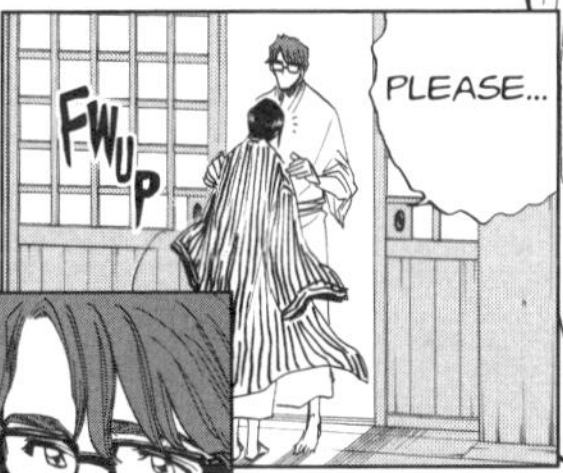
PLEASE...
FWUP

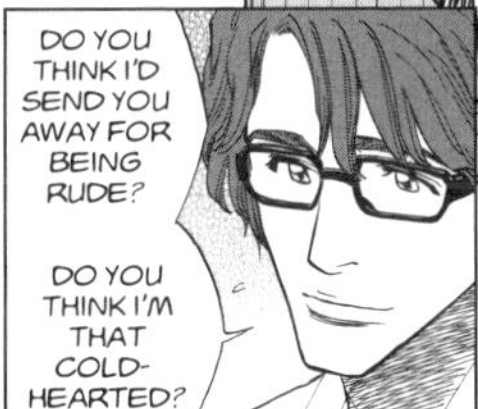
DO YOU THINK I'D SEND YOU AWAY FOR BEING RUDE?
DO YOU THINK I'M THAT COLD-HEARTED?

THE PREVIOUS NIGHT

Momo comes to Aizen's room. He waits for her to fall asleep before he heads out somewhere.

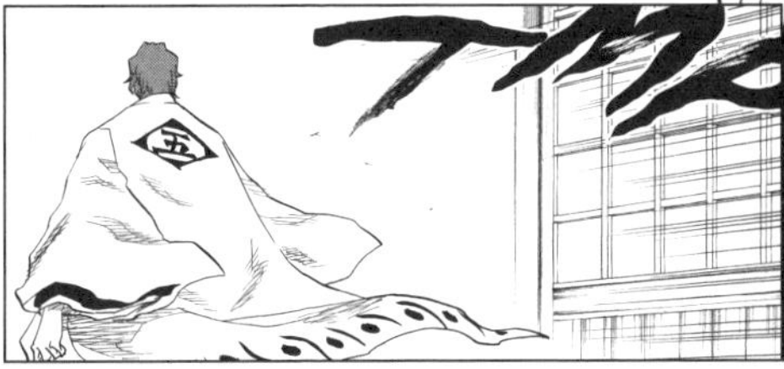

PROFILE

BIRTHDAY/MAY 29

HEIGHT/6′1″ **WEIGHT**/163 LBS

AFFILIATION/FIFTH COMPANY

ZANPAKU-TÔ/?

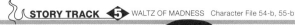

FIFTH COMPANY ASSISTANT CAPTAIN

MOMO HINAMORI — CHARACTER FILE 55-b

雛森桃

D死eath

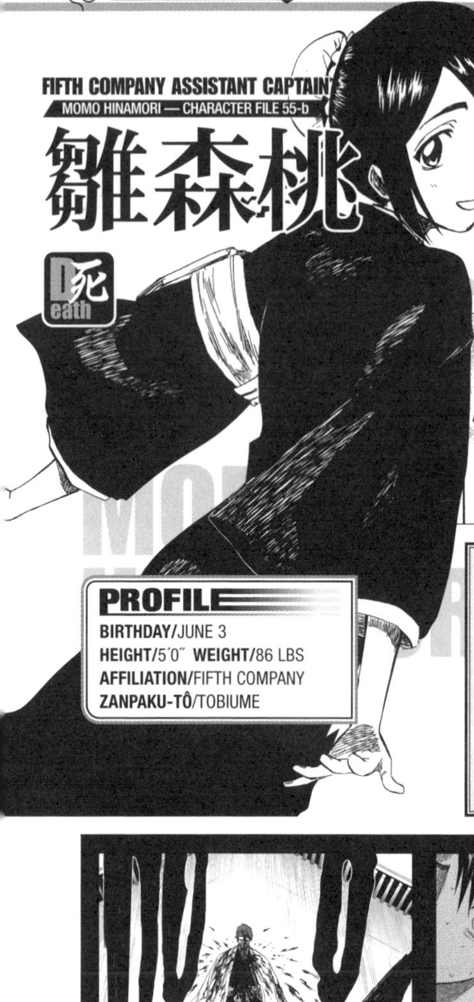

AN ARDENT ADMIRER OF AIZEN

Momo has admired Aizen ever since her days at the Shinôreijutsuin. Her admiration for him has not abated, even though she was named Aizen's assistant captain. She looks young, but she is a master of kidô.

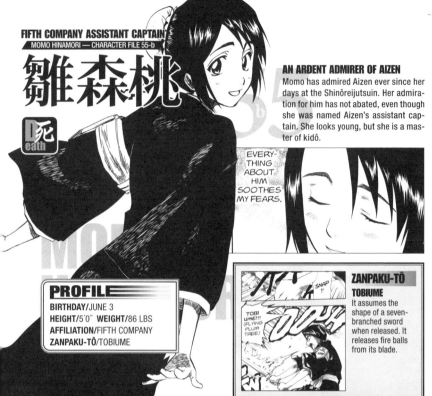

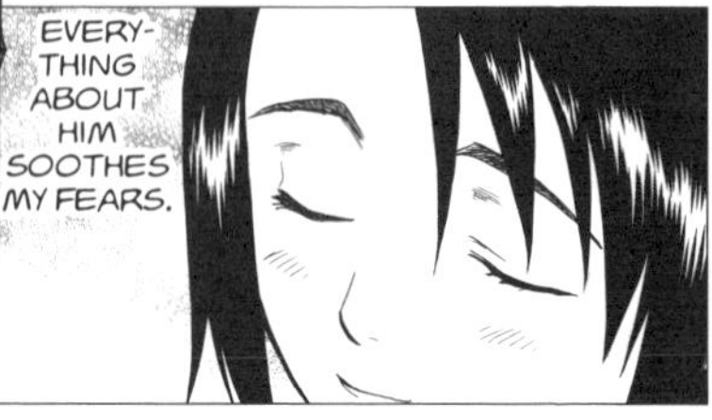
EVERYTHING ABOUT HIM SOOTHES MY FEARS.

PROFILE

BIRTHDAY/JUNE 3
HEIGHT/5′0″ WEIGHT/86 LBS
AFFILIATION/FIFTH COMPANY
ZANPAKU-TÔ/TOBIUME

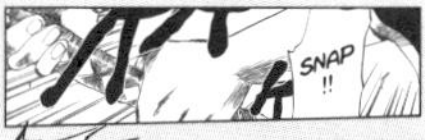
SNAP !!

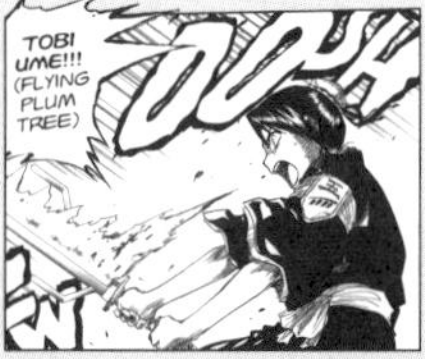
TOBI UME!!! (FLYING PLUM TREE)
DOH

ZANPAKU-TÔ

TOBIUME

It assumes the shape of a seven-branched sword when released. It releases fire balls from its blade.

惨劇

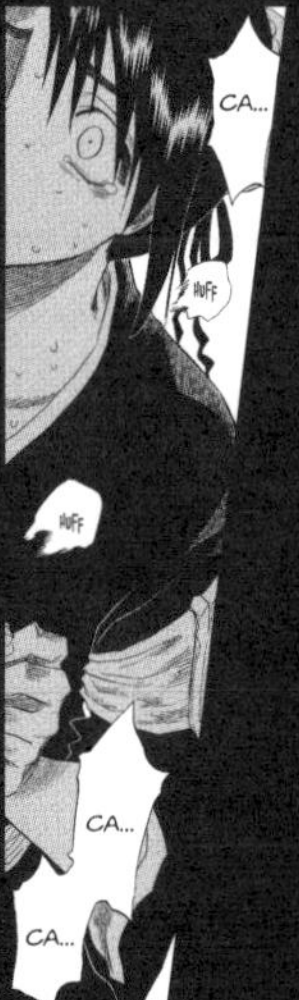
CA...
HUFF
HUFF
CA...
CA...

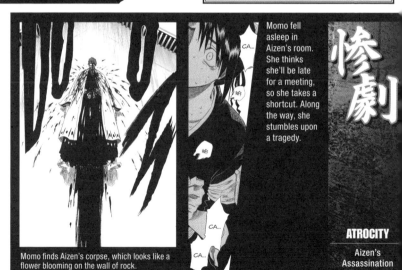

Momo fell asleep in Aizen's room. She thinks she'll be late for a meeting, so she takes a shortcut. Along the way, she stumbles upon a tragedy.

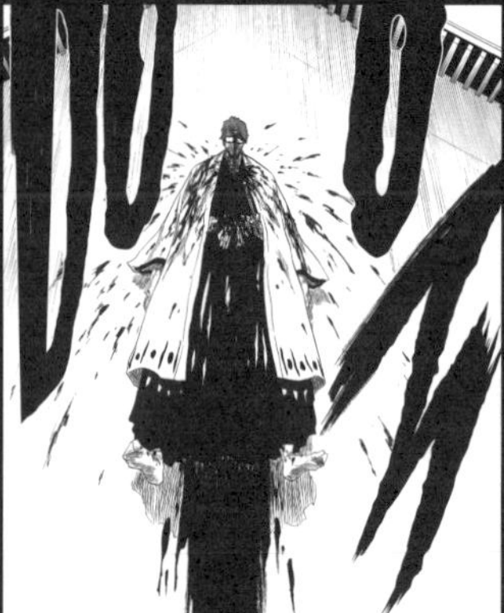

Momo finds Aizen's corpse, which looks like a flower blooming on the wall of rock.

ATROCITY

Aizen's Assassination
VOL. 12-100

暴走

FRENZIED

Momo
goes berserk
VOL. 12–101

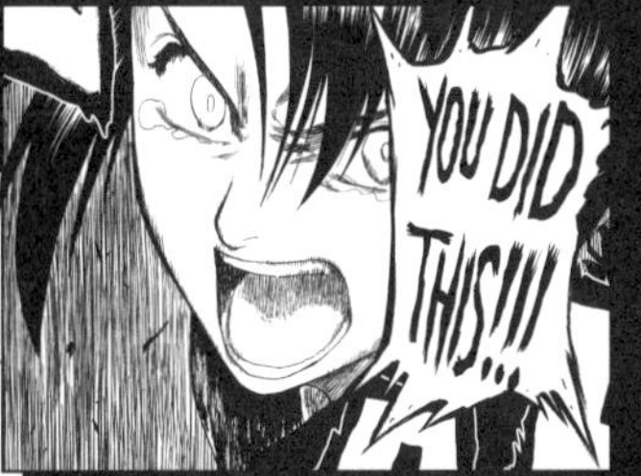

YOU DID THIS!!!

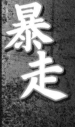

Momo lets out a wail that echoes throughout the Seireitei when she discovers Aizen's corpse. Gin appears and gives her a colorless and transparent smile. Upon seeing this, Momo remembers Hitsugaya's warning. Momo determinedly lashes out at Gin to erase his smile.

Izuru blocks Momo's sword and tries to reason with her. But Momo is in no condition to listen to him.

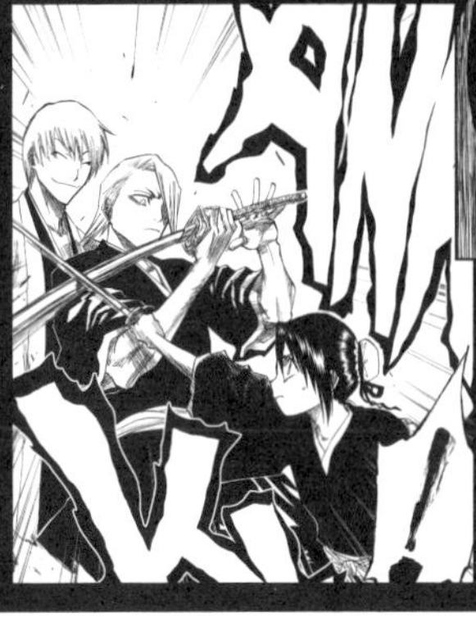

GIN'S FAITHFUL SUBORDINATE

The Third Company Assistant Captain. He puts his duty and orders above all else. If someone, even a friend, tries to harm Captain Ichimaru he will discard his personal feelings on the matter and protect Ichimaru at all costs.

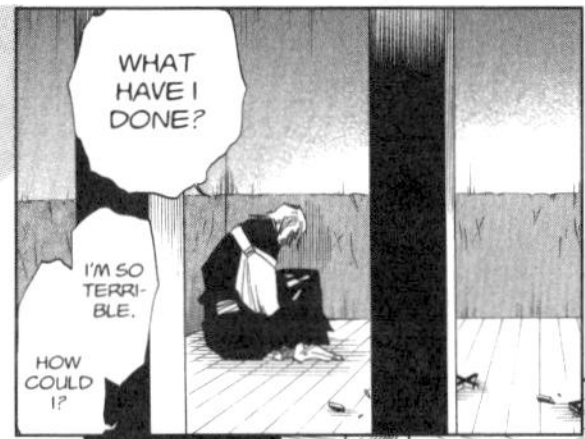

WHAT HAVE I DONE?
I'M SO TERRIBLE.
HOW COULD I?

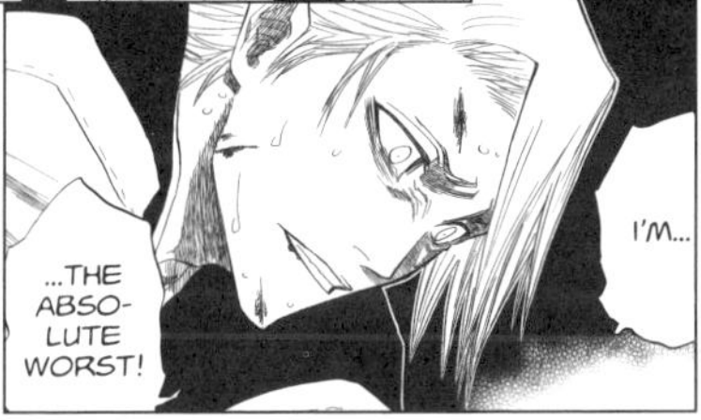

I'M...
...THE ABSOLUTE WORST!

Izuru is tormented with guilt for turning his sword towards Momo.

THIRD COMPANY ASSISTANT CAPTAIN

IZURU KIRA — CHARACTER FILE 51-b

Death 死

吉良イヅル

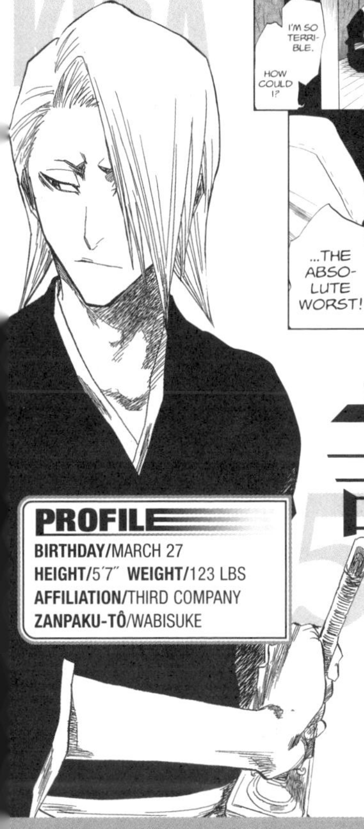

PROFILE

BIRTHDAY/MARCH 27
HEIGHT/5′7″ **WEIGHT/**123 LBS
AFFILIATION/THIRD COMPANY
ZANPAKU-TÔ/WABISUKE

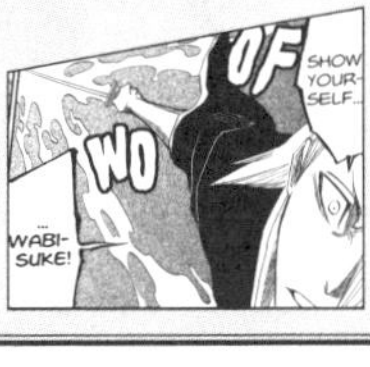

SHOW YOURSELF...
...WABISUKE!
WO
OF

ZANPAKU-TÔ

WABISUKE

It has the power to double the weight of its target each time it strikes.

TENTH COMPANY CAPTAIN

TÔSHIRÔ HITSUGAYA — CHARACTER FILE 62-b

日番谷冬獅郎

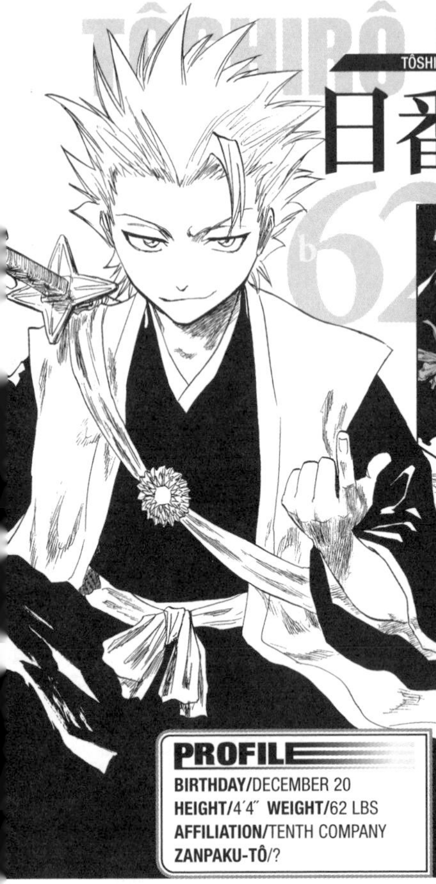

PROFILE

BIRTHDAY/DECEMBER 20
HEIGHT/4′4″ **WEIGHT/**62 LBS
AFFILIATION/TENTH COMPANY
ZANPAKU-TÔ/?

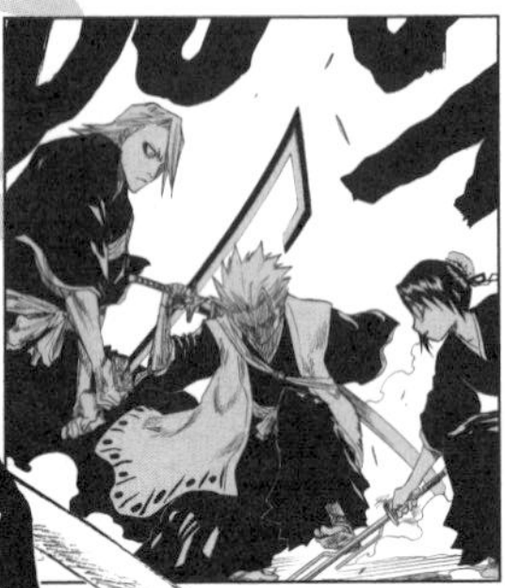

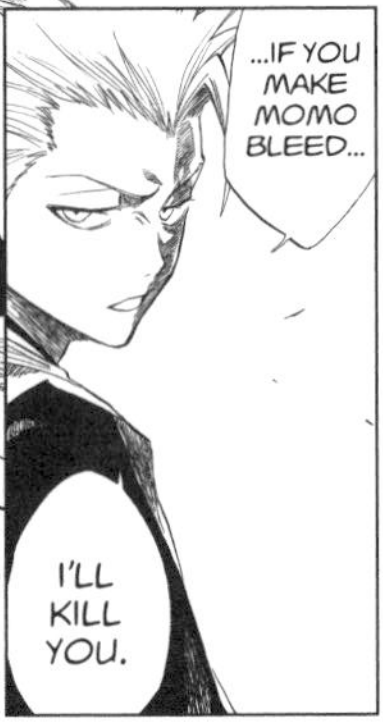
...IF YOU MAKE MOMO BLEED...
I'LL KILL YOU.

THE SILVER-HAIRED CHILD PRODIGY

A Soul Reaper who grew up in the Rukongai. He is a child prodigy with very rare talents, and is the youngest captain in the history of the Soul Society. He has misgivings about Rukia's execution. He becomes wary around Ichimaru when he begins to learn the truth of the circumstances surrounding the execution. He is also friends with Jidanbô. Hitsugaya was the one who taught Jidanbô "the rules of the city."

MOMO'S CHILDHOOD FRIEND

Hitsugaya has familial feelings towards Momo. He makes every effort to protect her.

THE WILL HE LEFT BEHIND

AIZEN'S LETTER

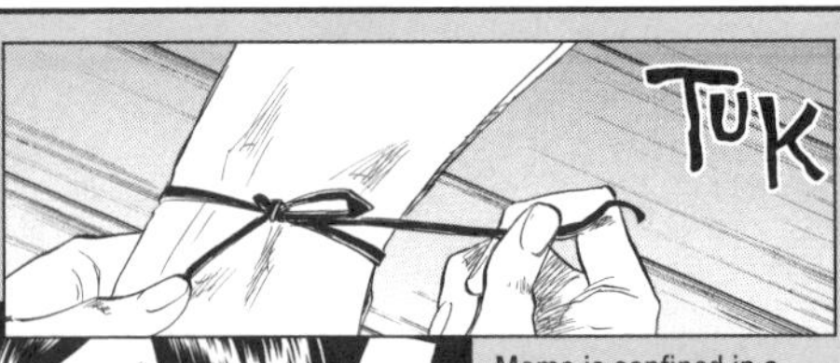
TUK

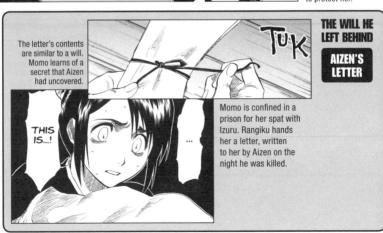

The letter's contents are similar to a will. Momo learns of a secret that Aizen had uncovered.

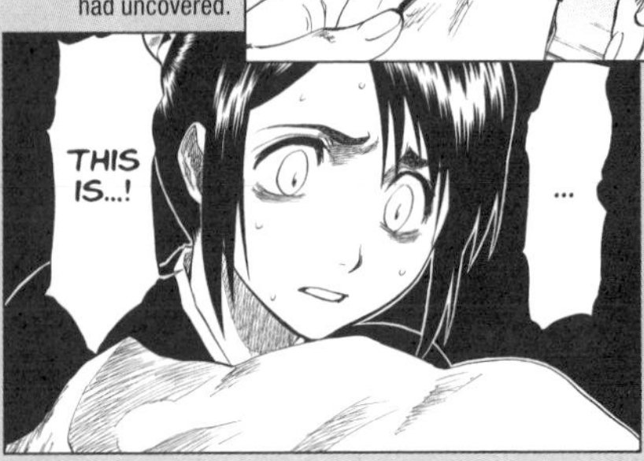
...
THIS IS...!

Momo is confined in a prison for her spat with Izuru. Rangiku hands her a letter, written to her by Aizen on the night he was killed.

H人 uman

TRANSFORMED RIGHT ARM

YASUTORA SADO — CHARACTER FILE 11-c

茶渡泰虎

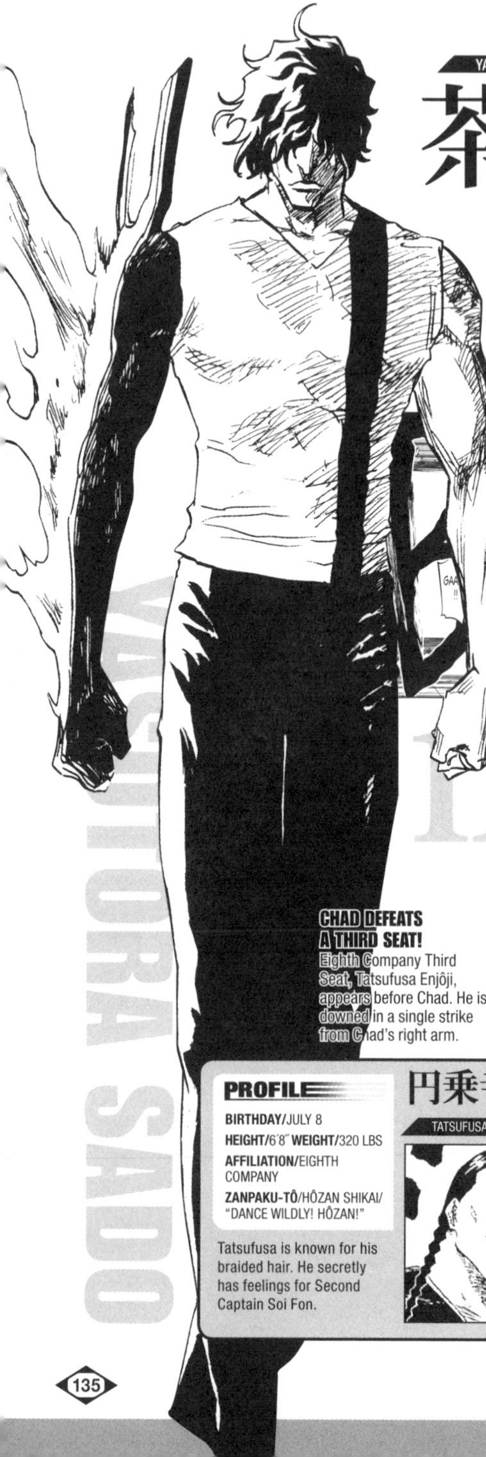

A MAN OF STEEL WHO FIGHTS ALONE

Chad is left all alone after everyone crashes into the Seireitei. But he is rugged and able to fight by himself. He mows down Soul the Reapers in his way and runs towards the Senzaikyû Shishinrô, where Rukia is being held prisoner.

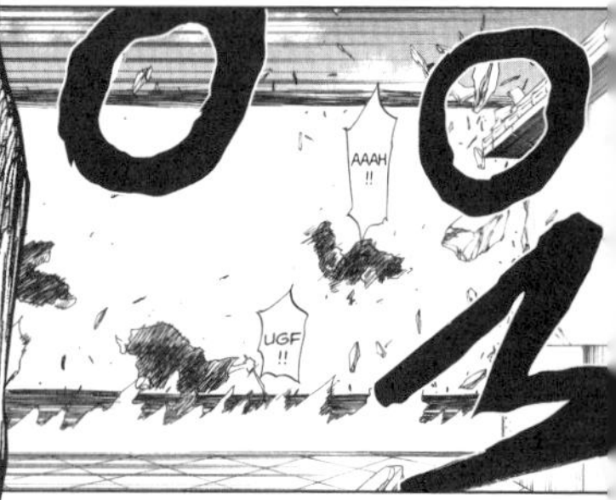
AAAH !!
GAA !!
UGF !!

THE RESULT OF HIS TRAINING

Chad was once only able to use his punch attack two times a day. But after training with Mr. Yoruichi, he can now use it in rapid succession.

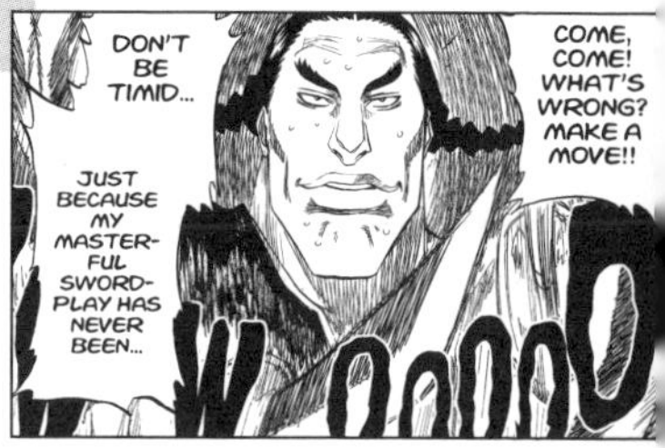
COME, COME! WHAT'S WRONG? MAKE A MOVE!!
DON'T BE TIMID...
JUST BECAUSE MY MASTERFUL SWORDPLAY HAS NEVER BEEN...

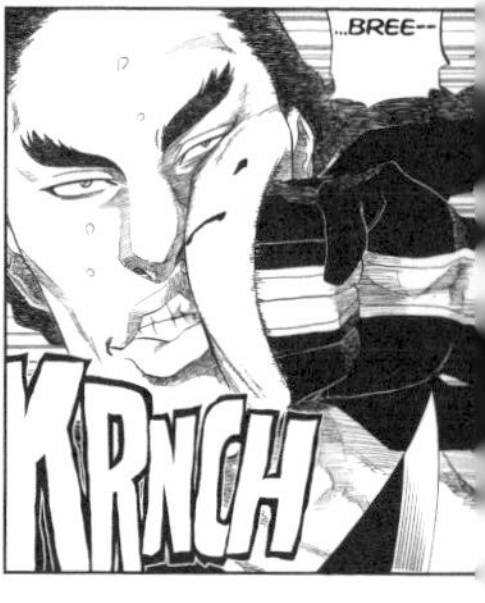
...BREE--
KRNCH

CHAD DEFEATS A THIRD SEAT!

Eighth Company Third Seat, Tatsufusa Enjôji, appears before Chad. He is downed in a single strike from Chad's right arm.

PROFILE

円乗寺辰房

TATSUFUSA ENJÔJI—77

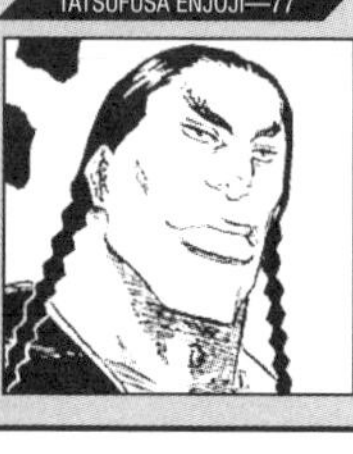

BIRTHDAY/JULY 8

HEIGHT/6′8″ **WEIGHT**/320 LBS

AFFILIATION/EIGHTH COMPANY

ZANPAKU-TÔ/HÔZAN SHIKAI/ "DANCE WILDLY! HÔZAN!"

Tatsufusa is known for his braided hair. He secretly has feelings for Second Captain Soi Fon.

EIGHTH COMPANY CAPTAIN

SHUNSUI KYÔRAKU — CHARACTER FILE 58-b

京楽春水

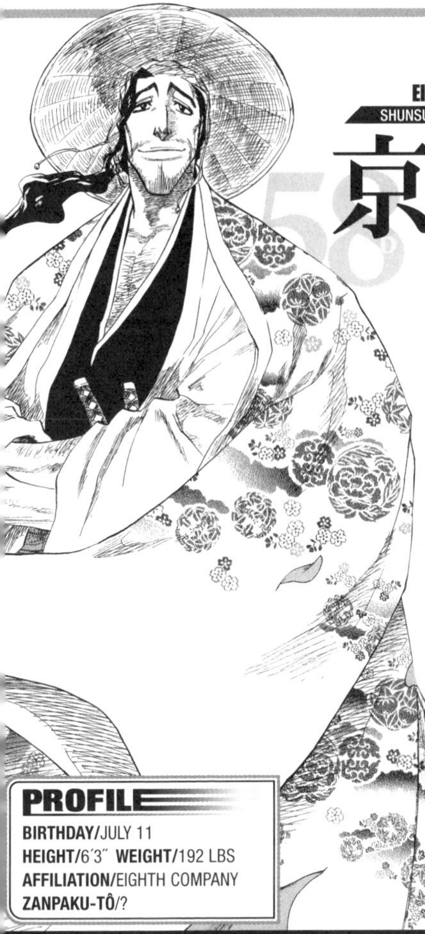

A MAN ABOUT TOWN WHO CAN SEE THE TRUTH

Soul Society's dandiest man. He wears a woman's kimono and loves sake and the ladies. He especially hates missions and jobs that end in bloodshed. He is forced into action this time on "Old Man Yama's" orders.

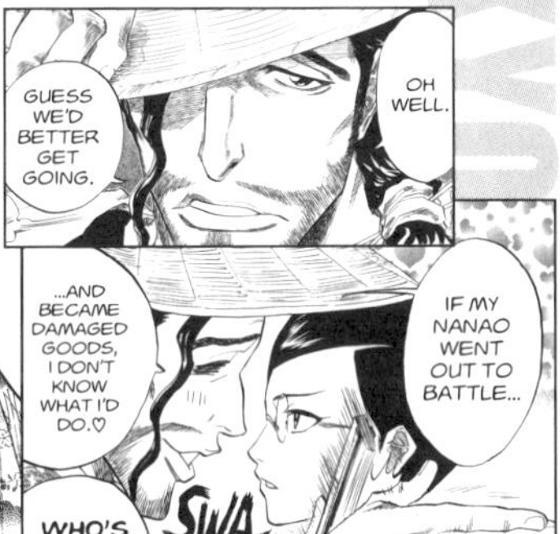
OH WELL.
GUESS WE'D BETTER GET GOING.
IF MY NANAO WENT OUT TO BATTLE...
...AND BECAME DAMAGED GOODS, I DON'T KNOW WHAT I'D DO.♡
SWAK
WHO'S "YOUR" NANAO?

For a captain, he speaks and behaves capriciously, but his abilities are not to be doubted.

PROFILE

BIRTHDAY/JULY 11
HEIGHT/6′3″ **WEIGHT**/192 LBS
AFFILIATION/EIGHTH COMPANY
ZANPAKU-TÔ/?

約束

PROMISE

Reason to Fight
VOL. 12-105~106

There is a reason why Chad cannot retreat. Kyôraku hears his resolution and is obliged to draw his sword.

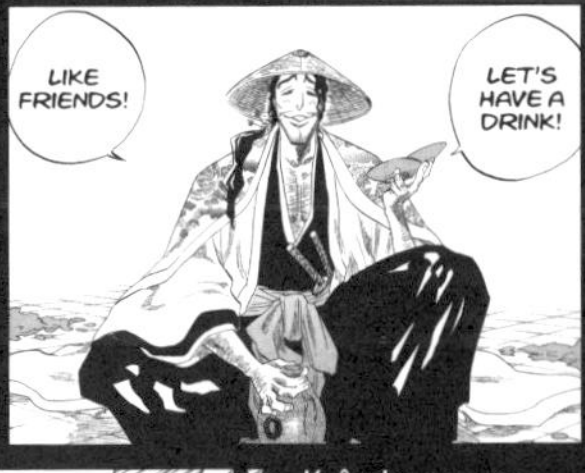
LET'S HAVE A DRINK!
LIKE FRIENDS!

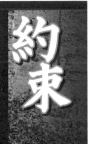

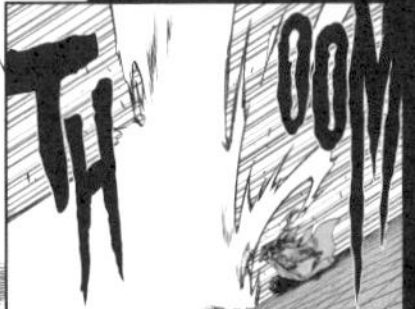
TH OOM

Kyôraku appears before Chad. Neither wants to fight, but neither can retreat. That's when Kyôraku suggests...

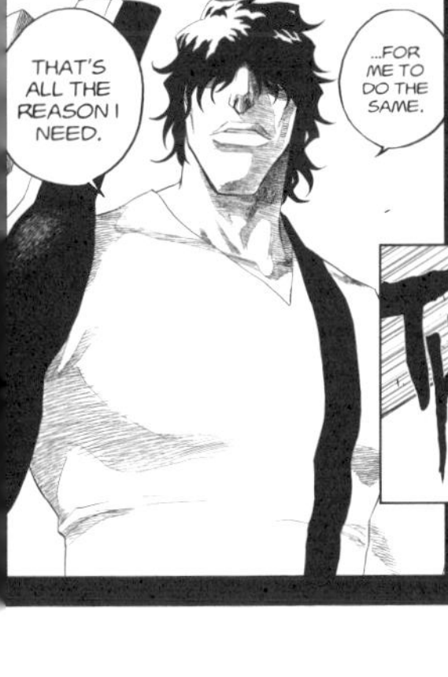
...FOR ME TO DO THE SAME.
THAT'S ALL THE REASON I NEED.

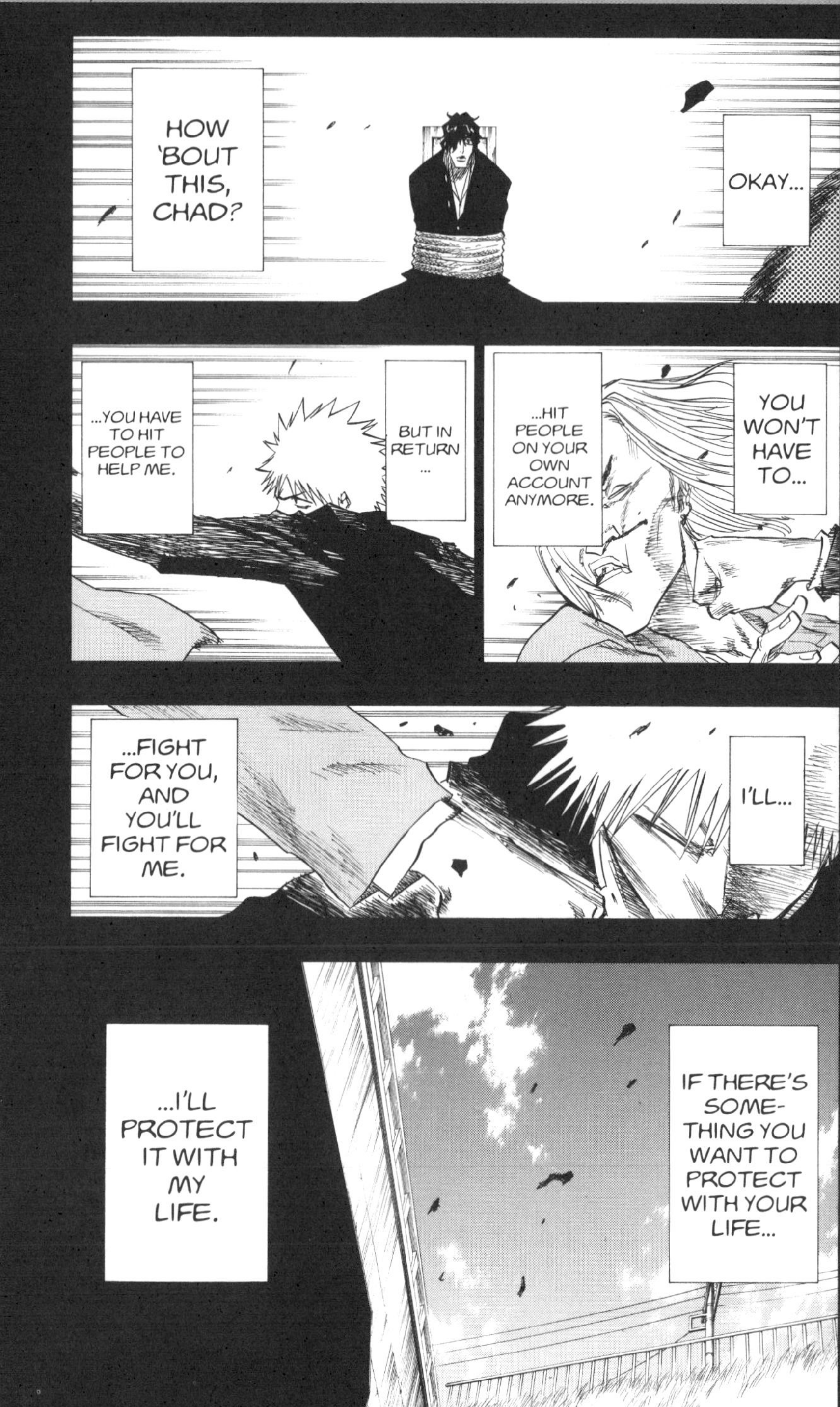
OKAY...
HOW 'BOUT THIS, CHAD?
YOU WON'T HAVE TO...
...HIT PEOPLE ON YOUR OWN ACCOUNT ANYMORE.
BUT IN RETURN...
...YOU HAVE TO HIT PEOPLE TO HELP ME.
I'LL...
...FIGHT FOR YOU, AND YOU'LL FIGHT FOR ME.
IF THERE'S SOME-THING YOU WANT TO PROTECT WITH YOUR LIFE...
...I'LL PROTECT IT WITH MY LIFE.

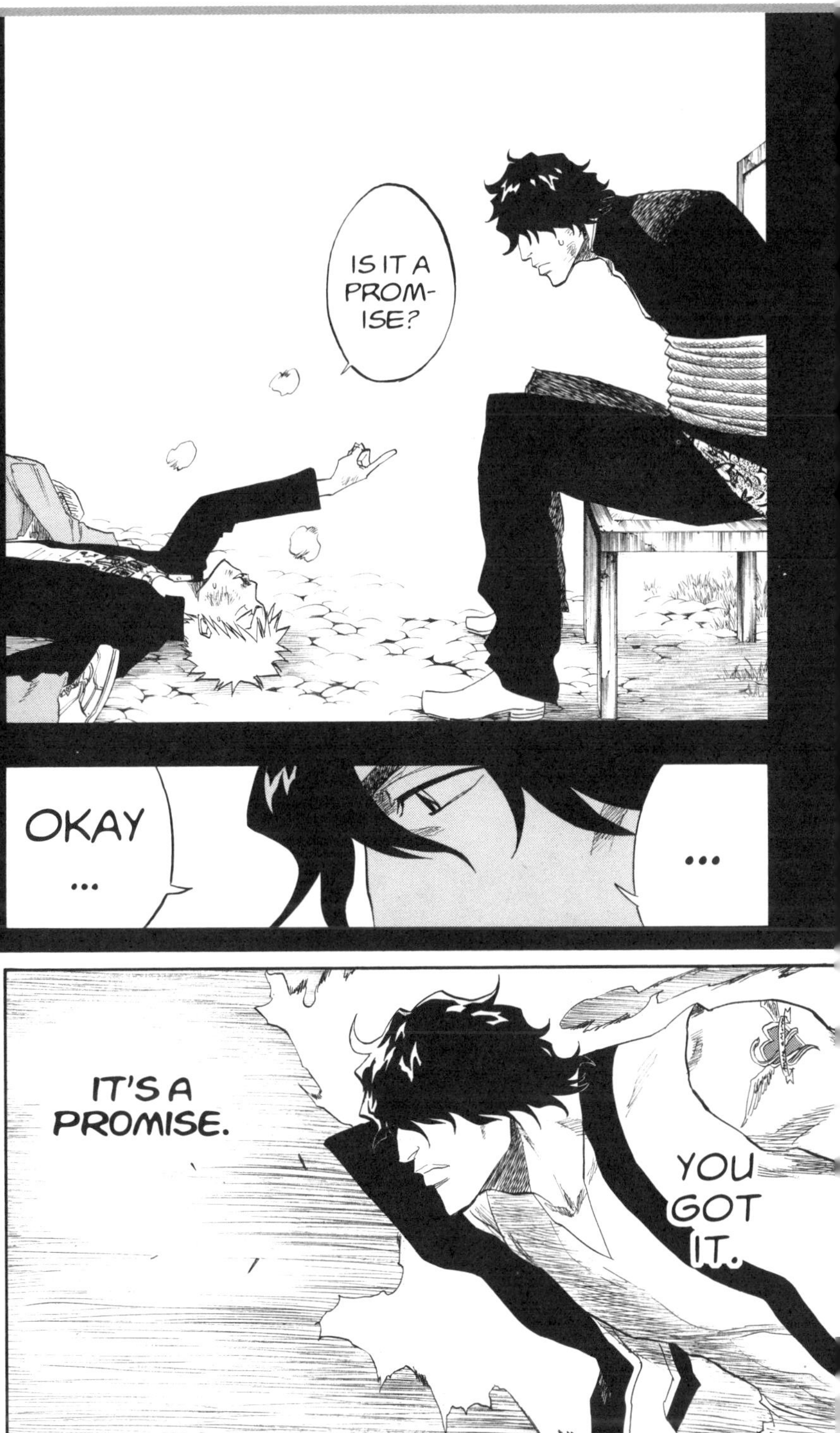
IS IT A PROM-ISE?
...
OKAY ...
IT'S A PROMISE.
YOU GOT IT.

In a single stroke, a straight red line is drawn.

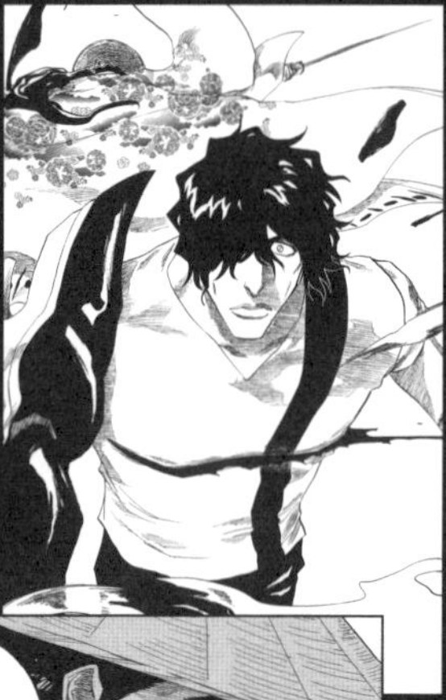

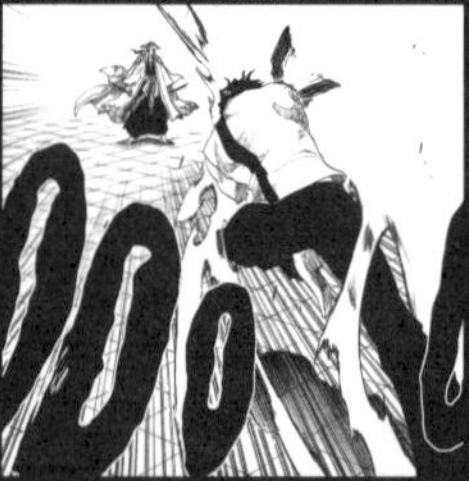

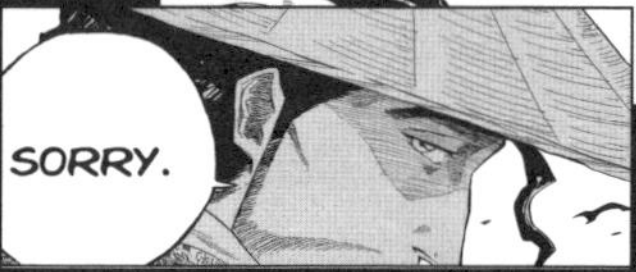
SORRY.

Because "Ichigo wants to save her" is a very simple and absolute reason. Chad's only reason for fighting is his promise to Ichigo. To fulfill his promise, Chad stores all of his spiritual power in his right arm and charges at Shunsui, the enemy before him!

一閃

FLASH

A Broken Promi
VOL. 12-107

EIGHTH COMPANY ASSISTANT CAPTAIN

NANAO ISE — CHARACTER FILE 59-b

伊勢七緒

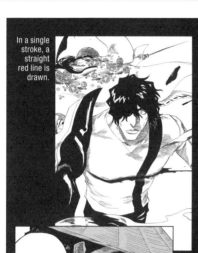

CAPTAIN KYÔRAKU'S SUPERVISOR

The bespectacled female assistant captain who aids Kyôraku. Every day, she coldly brushes off Shunsui's irritating comments. She treats Kyôraku as if he were an overgrown child who needs minding. Deep down though, she respects him.

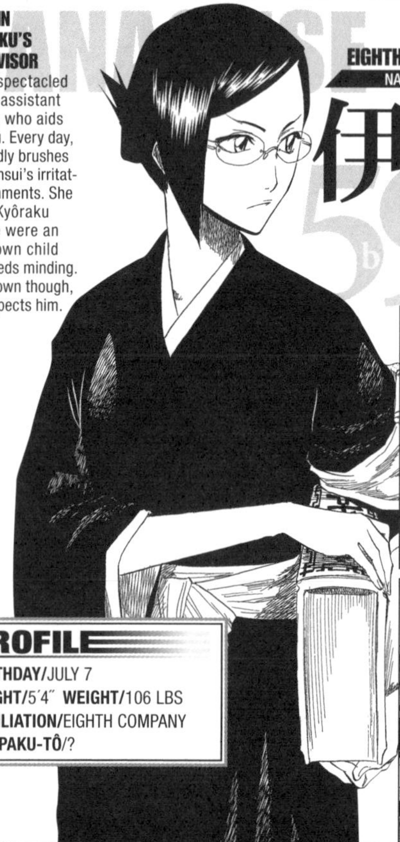

PROFILE

BIRTHDAY/JULY 7
HEIGHT/5′4″ **WEIGHT/**106 LBS
AFFILIATION/EIGHTH COMPANY
ZANPAKU-TÔ/?

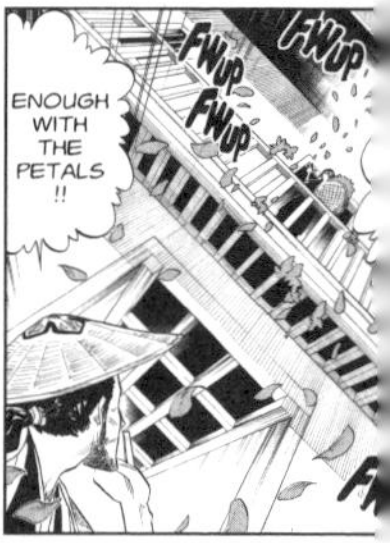
FWUP
FWUP
FWUP
ENOUGH WITH THE PETALS!!

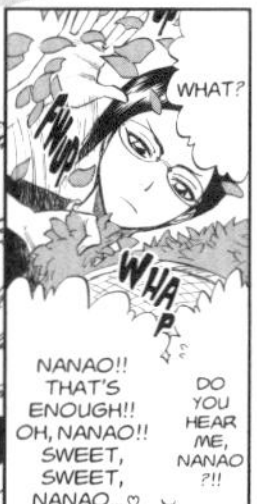
WHAT?
FWUP
WHAP
NANAO!! THAT'S ENOUGH!! OH, NANAO!! SWEET, SWEET, NANAO...♡
DO YOU HEAR ME, NANAO?!!

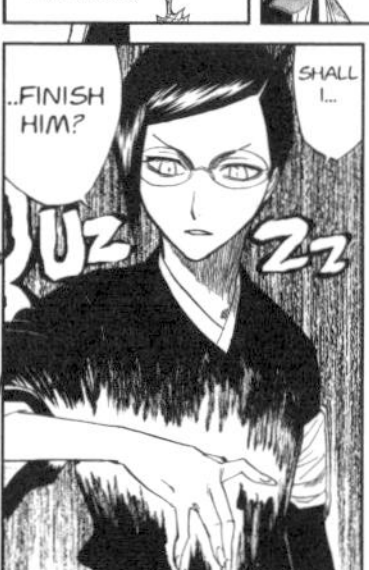
SHALL I...
..FINISH HIM?
BUZ
ZZ

Nanao doesn't show much enthusiasm for Kyôraku's jokes, but goes along with them. But she shows a cold-hearted side in front of enemies.

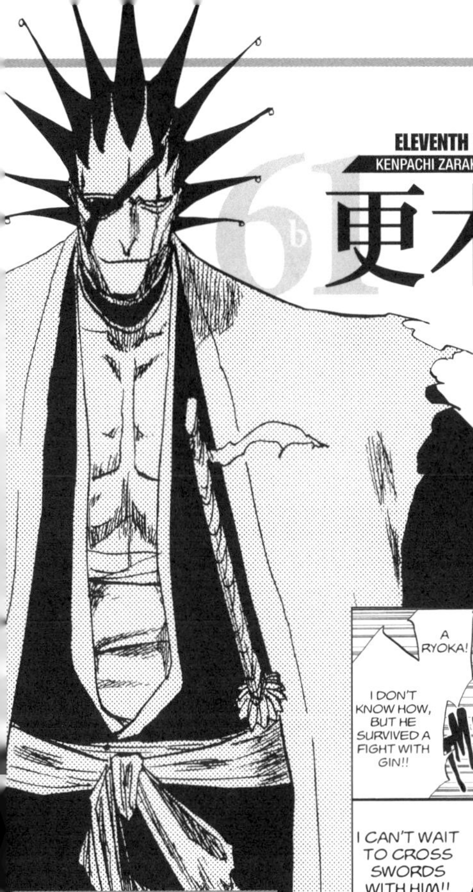

ELEVENTH COMPANY CAPTAIN

KENPACHI ZARAKI — CHARACTER FILE 64-b

D死eath

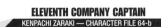

更木剣八

SOUL SOCIETY'S MOST SINISTER BATTLE MANIAC

A ruffian who leads other ruffians. His fighting power is tremendous and, though his swordsmanship is unpolished, he more than makes up for it with his overwhelming power and resilience. He obtained his captaincy by the sword—he killed his predecessor in battle.

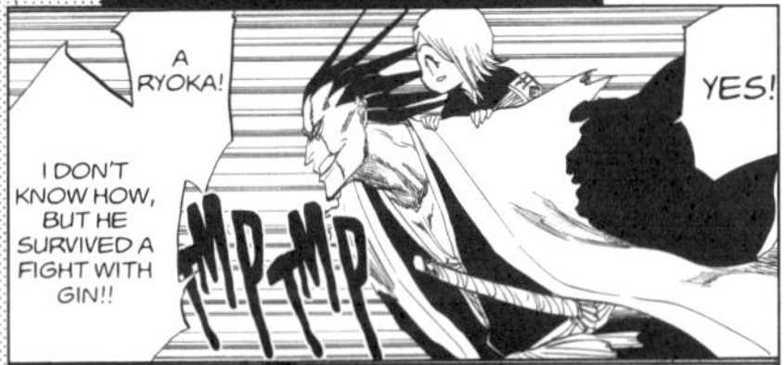
YES!
A RYOKA!
I DON'T KNOW HOW, BUT HE SURVIVED A FIGHT WITH GIN!!
TMP TMP

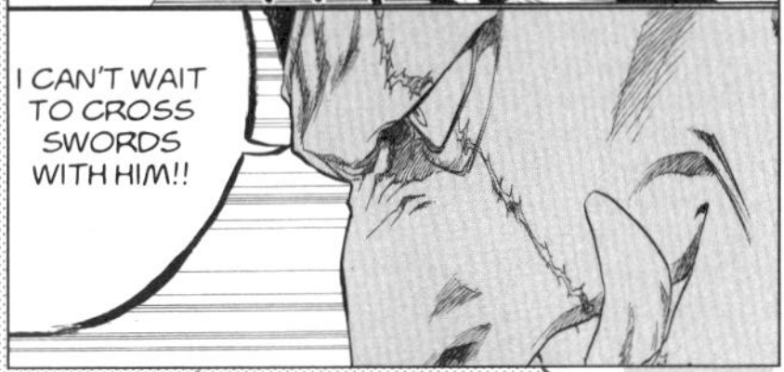
I CAN'T WAIT TO CROSS SWORDS WITH HIM!!

PROFILE

BIRTHDAY/NOVEMBER 19
HEIGHT/6′6″ **WEIGHT/**198 LBS
AFFILIATION/ELEVENTH COMPANY
ZANPAKU-TÔ/UNKNOWN

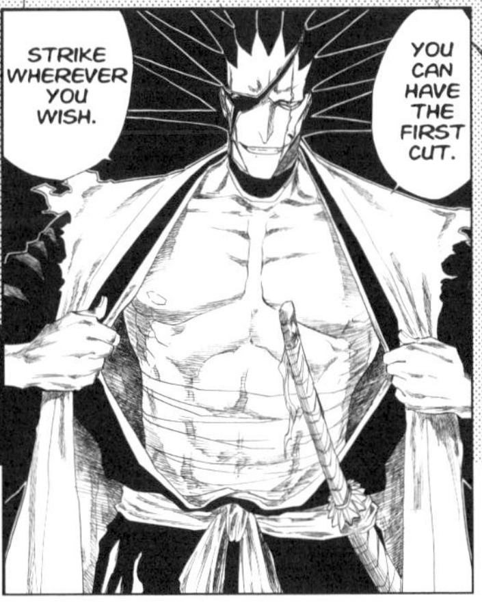
YOU CAN HAVE THE FIRST CUT.
STRIKE WHEREVER YOU WISH.

A CRAVING TO FIGHT STRONG PEOPLE!

Zaraki has an unnaturally aggressive disposition. Even in the midst of the riot, he seeks out Ichigo just for the opportunity to fight a strong opponent, not out of any sense of duty.

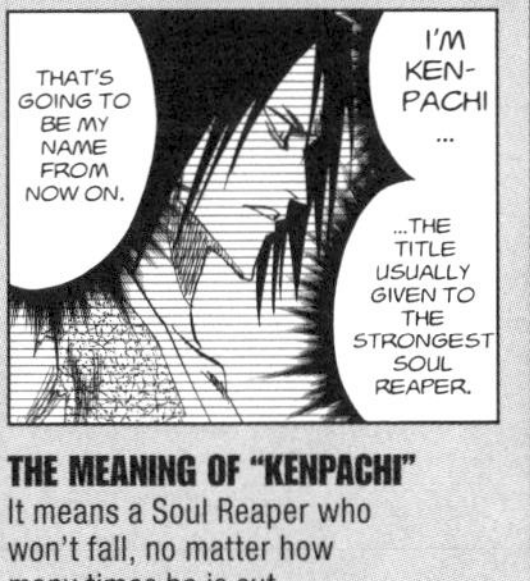
I'M KEN-PACHI ...
THAT'S GOING TO BE MY NAME FROM NOW ON.
...THE TITLE USUALLY GIVEN TO THE STRONGEST SOUL REAPER.

THE MEANING OF "KENPACHI"

It means a Soul Reaper who won't fall, no matter how many times he is cut.

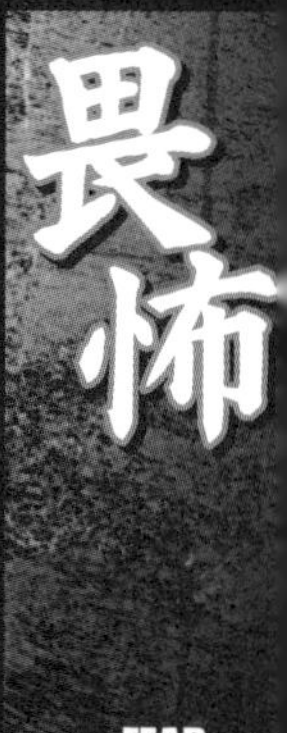
畏怖

FEAR

An overwhelmin[g] difference in pow[er]
VOL. 12-102~
VOL. 13-110

Ichigo has recovered from the wounds that he received from his fight with Renji and heads towards the Senzaikyû Shishinrô with Ganju and Hanatarô. Along the way they are discovered by Kenpachi Zaraki, a wild beast of a captain. Ganju and Hanatarô have trouble breathing because of the immense, ominous spiritual pressure emanating from Zaraki. Ichigo lets Ganju and Hanatarô escape ahead of him and takes on Zaraki by himself!

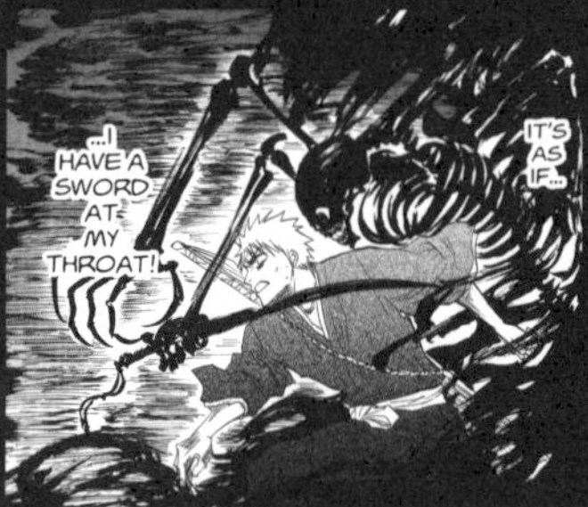
IT'S AS IF...
...I HAVE A SWORD AT MY THROAT!

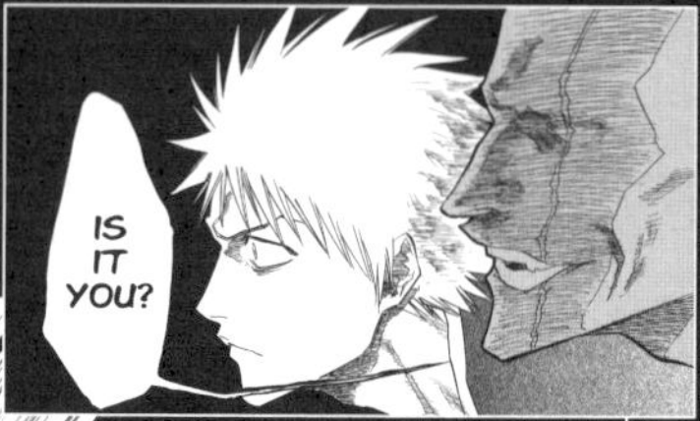
IS IT YOU?

UNSHAKABLE KILLING INTENT
In the terrible atmosphere generated by Zaraki, Ichigo hallucinates that he has been killed.

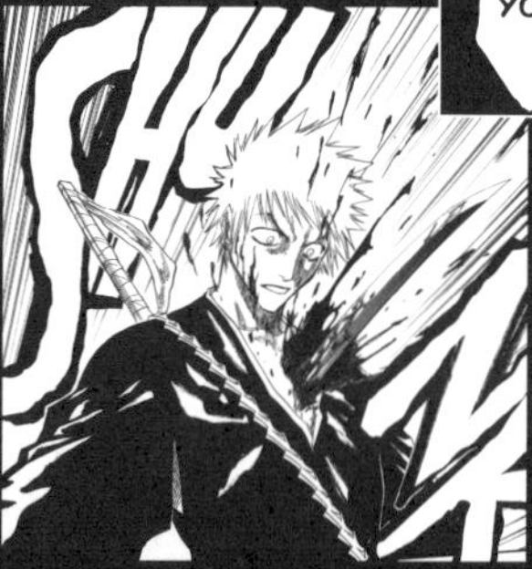

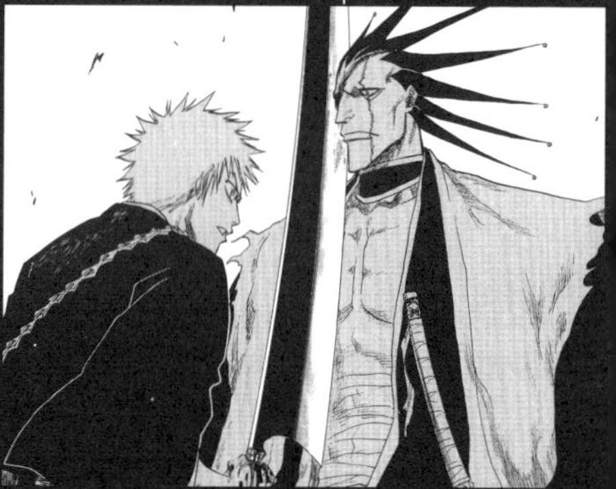

AN INVULNERABLE BODY
Ichigo freezes with fear. He cannot breech Zaraki's defenses.

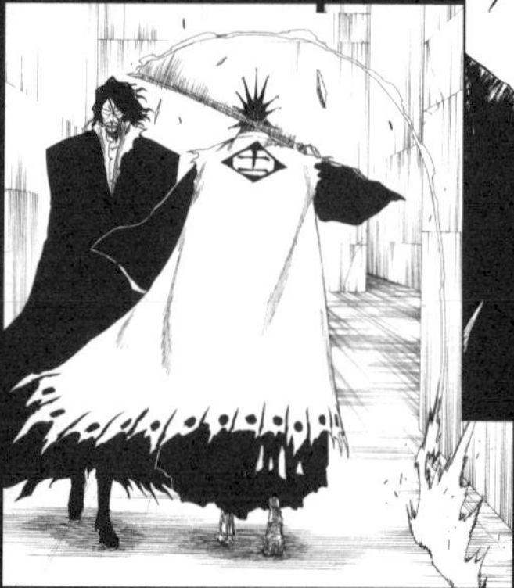

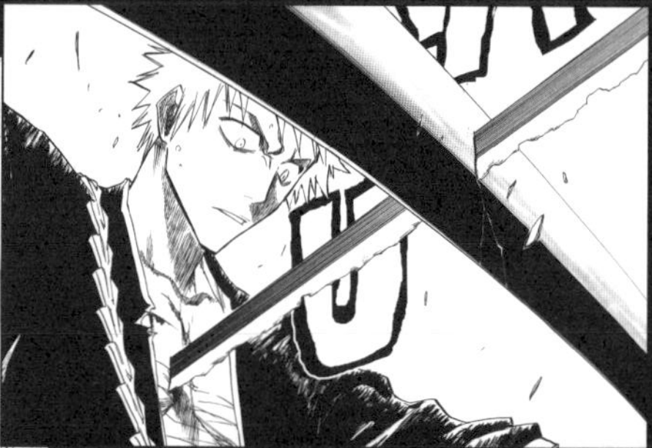

THE THING HE SAW AT THE END
Ichigo's sword breaks through his own carelessness, and he lands face down on the ground. As Zaraki leaves, Ichigo sees Zangetsu.

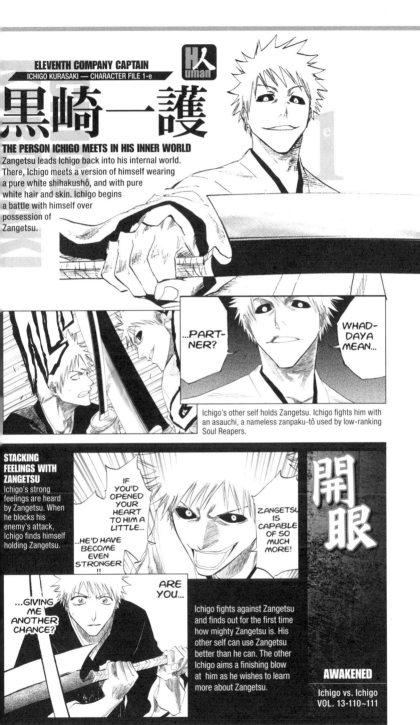

ELEVENTH COMPANY CAPTAIN

ICHIGO KURASAKI — CHARACTER FILE 1-e

黒崎一護

THE PERSON ICHIGO MEETS IN HIS INNER WORLD

Zangetsu leads Ichigo back into his internal world. There, Ichigo meets a version of himself wearing a pure white shihakushô, and with pure white hair and skin. Ichigo begins a battle with himself over possession of Zangetsu.

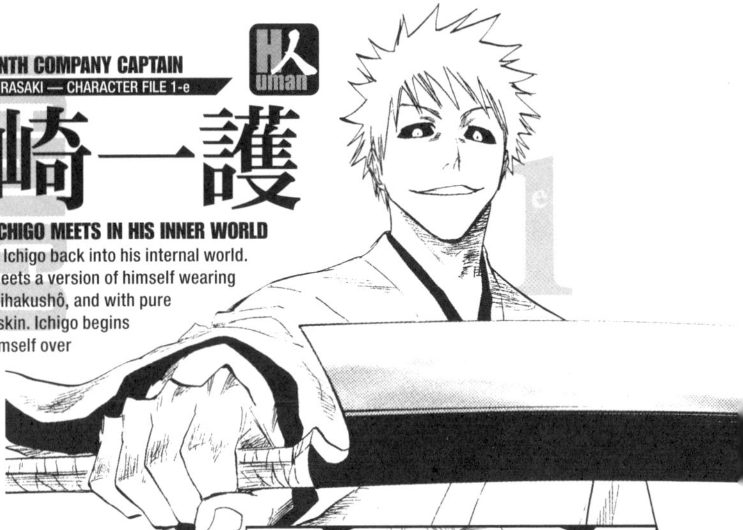

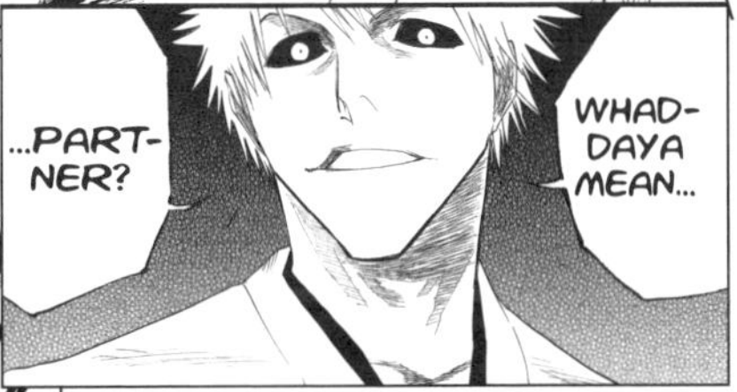
WHAD-
DAYA
MEAN...
...PART-
NER?

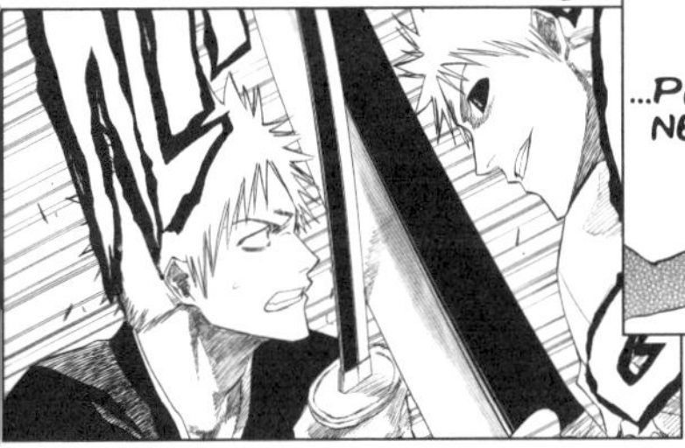

Ichigo's other self holds Zangetsu. Ichigo fights him with an asauchi, a nameless zanpaku-tô used by low-ranking Soul Reapers.

STACKING FEELINGS WITH ZANGETSU

Ichigo's strong feelings are heard by Zangetsu. When he blocks his enemy's attack, Ichigo finds himself holding Zangetsu.

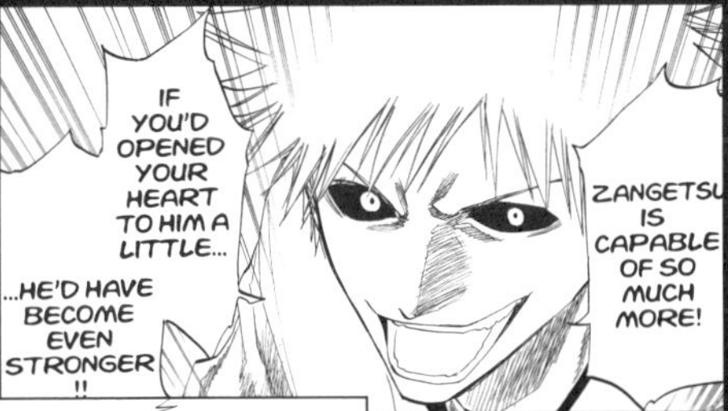
ZANGETSU IS CAPABLE OF SO MUCH MORE!
IF YOU'D OPENED YOUR HEART TO HIM A LITTLE...
...HE'D HAVE BECOME EVEN STRONGER!!

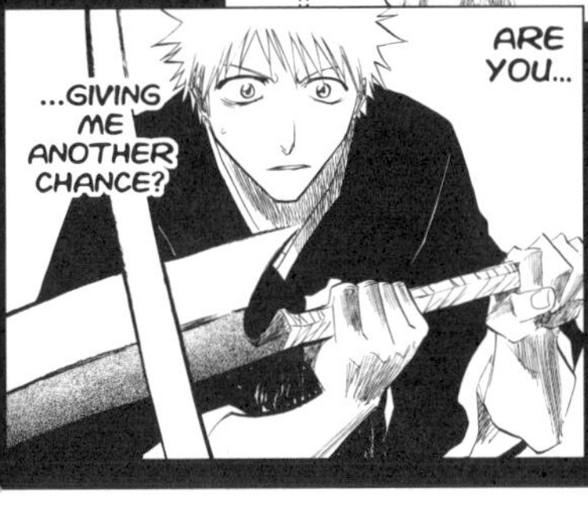
ARE YOU...
...GIVING ME ANOTHER CHANCE?

Ichigo fights against Zangetsu and finds out for the first time how mighty Zangetsu is. His other self can use Zangetsu better than he can. The other Ichigo aims a finishing blow at him as he wishes to learn more about Zangetsu.

開眼

AWAKENED

Ichigo vs. Ichigo
VOL. 13-110~111

血煙 SPURTING BLOO

Battle resumed
VOL. 13-111~113

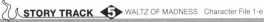

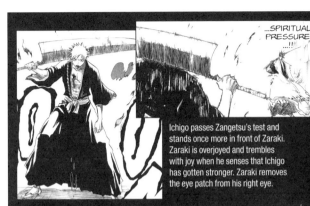

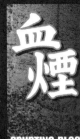

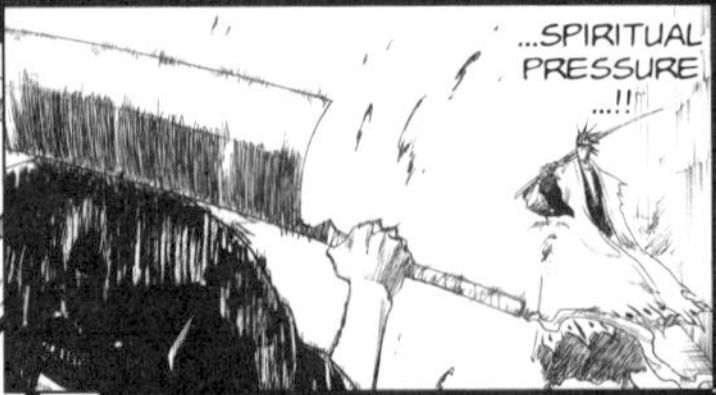
...SPIRITUAL PRESSURE ...!!

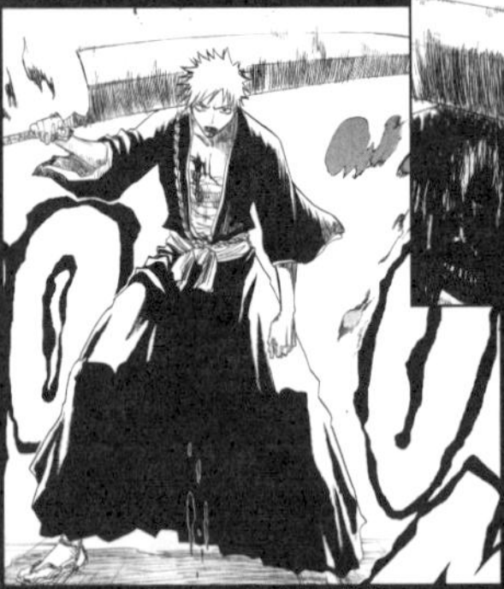

Ichigo passes Zangetsu's test and stands once more in front of Zaraki. Zaraki is overjoyed and trembles with joy when he senses that Ichigo has gotten stronger. Zaraki removes the eye patch from his right eye.

ZARAKI'S TRUE STRENGTH
Zaraki's eye patch is a monster that continuously devours spiritual energy. Zaraki attains his true strength when it is removed.

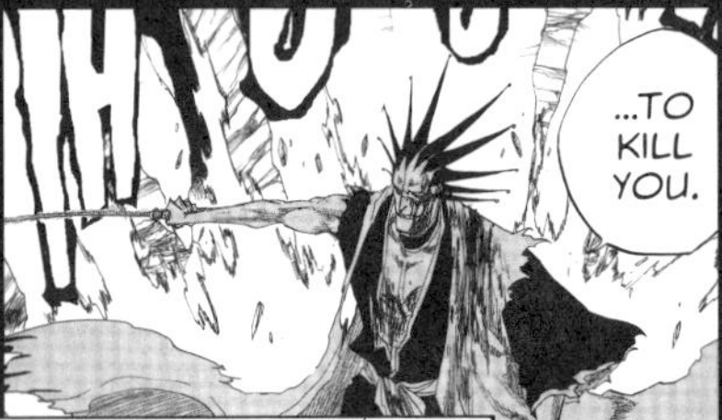
...TO KILL YOU.

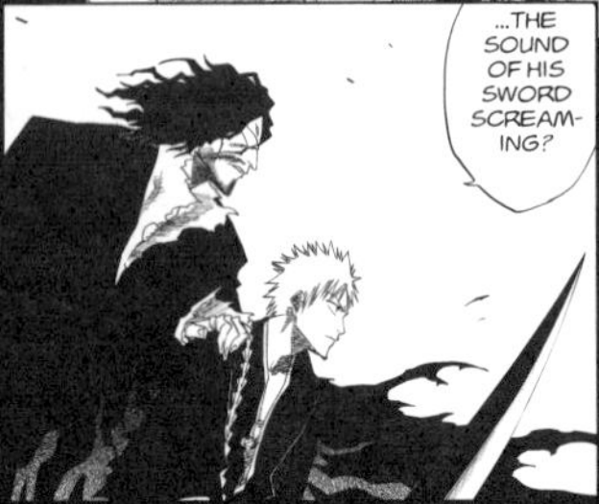
...THE SOUND OF HIS SWORD SCREAMING?

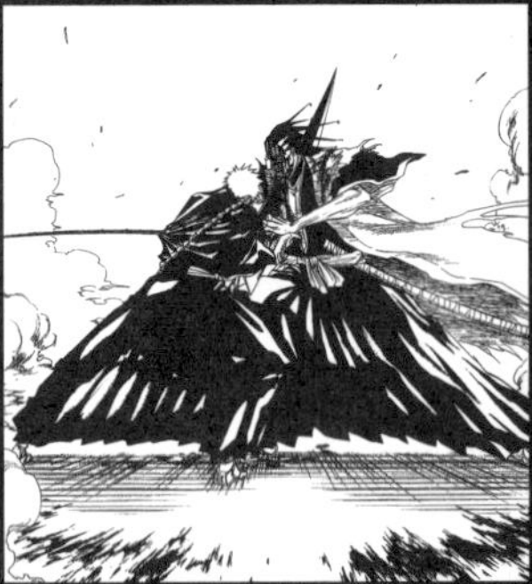

TOGETHER WITH ZANGETSU
Zaraki fights against himself and Ichigo fights with Zangetsu. Two giant powers are about to clash.

TO ENJOY BATTLE

BELLS AND AN EYE PATCH

AN ITEM CUSTOM-MADE FOR ZARAKI
A specially made eye patch created by the Department of Research and Development. It is a monster that continually eats spiritual energy.

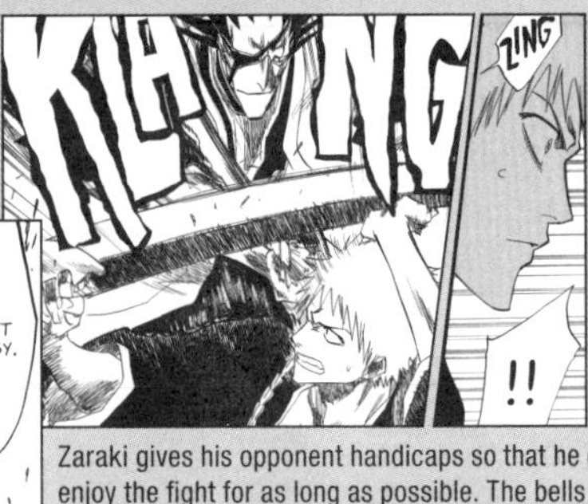
ZING
!!

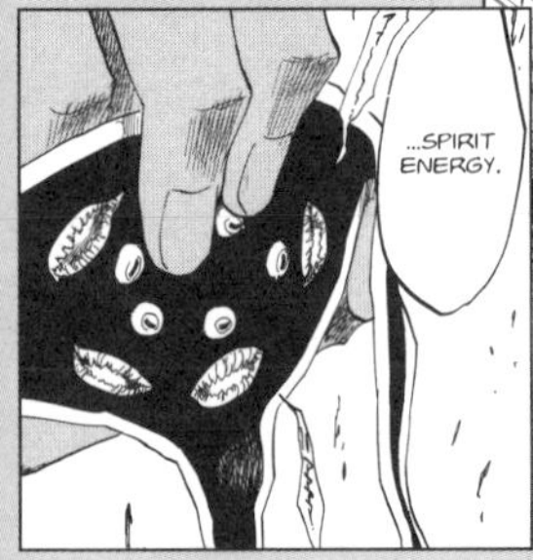
...SPIRIT ENERGY.

Zaraki gives his opponent handicaps so that he can enjoy the fight for as long as possible. The bells tell his opponent where he is and in which direction he's moving. The eye patch reduces his field of vision and also suppresses his spiritual energy.

YACHIRU'S SPECIAL SEAT
Yachiru rides on Zaraki's shoulder when she's with him. It's a special privilege reserved only for Yachiru.

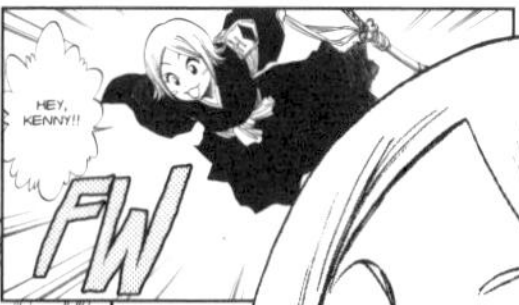
HEY, KENNY!!
FW

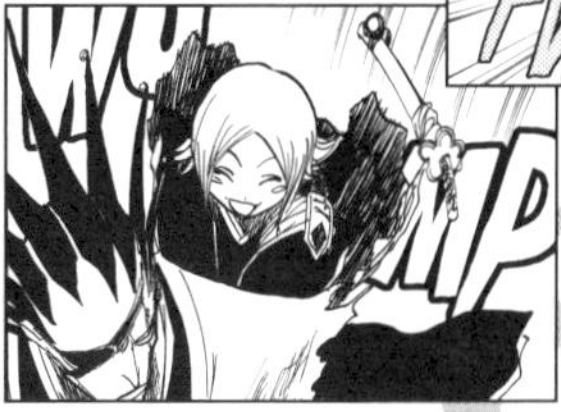

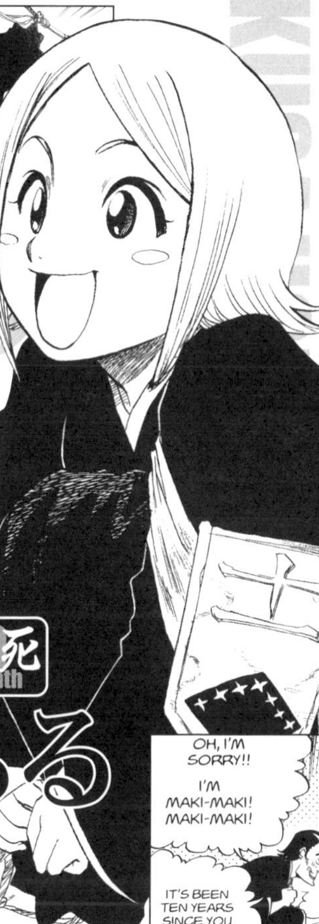

THE GIRL WHO FOLLOWS KENPACHI
She immediately became assistant captain without taking the entrance exam—the same way Zaraki became captain. She looks and acts like a little girl, but she carries Zaraki away after he is injured in his battle with Ichigo. She is compact and high powered.

ELEVENTH COMPANY ASSISTANT CAPTAIN
YACHIRU KUSAJISHI — CHARACTER FILE 65-b

草鹿やちる

PROFILE
BIRTHDAY/FEBRUARY 12
HEIGHT/3′6″ **WEIGHT**/34 LBS
AFFILIATION/ELEVENTH COMPANY
ZANPAKU-TÔ/?

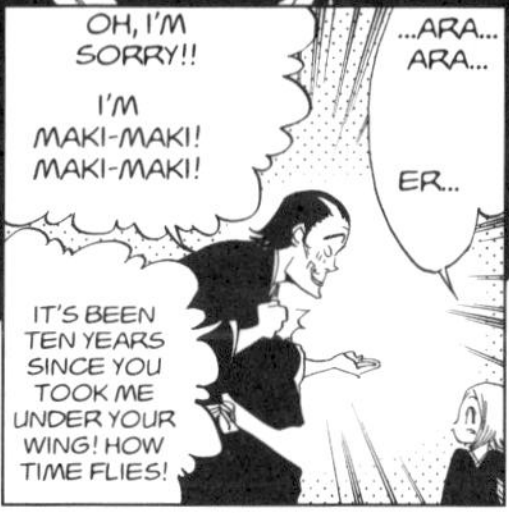
...ARA... ARA...
OH, I'M SORRY!!
I'M MAKI-MAKI! MAKI-MAKI!
ER...
IT'S BEEN TEN YEARS SINCE YOU TOOK ME UNDER YOUR WING! HOW TIME FLIES!

She's an assistant captain who gives people nicknames and then forgets them.

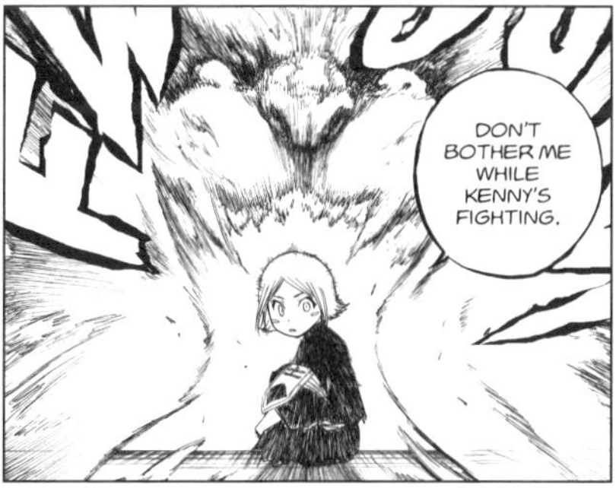
DON'T BOTHER ME WHILE KENNY'S FIGHTING.

She shows a glimpse of her power as she watches Zaraki's battle.

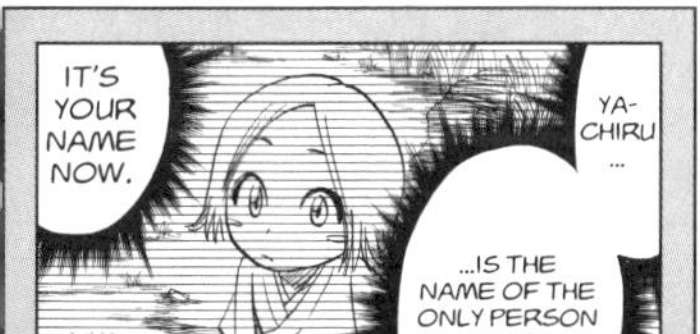
YA-CHIRU ...
...IS THE NAME OF THE ONLY PERSON I EVER ADMIRED.
IT'S YOUR NAME NOW.

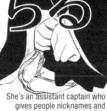

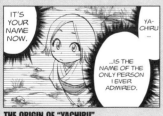

THE ORIGIN OF "YACHIRU"
Zaraki named Yachiru. It is apparently the name of the one person that Zaraki admires. Yachiru's name is written as 八千流 in kanji.

追憶

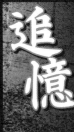

RECOLLECTION

Their encounter
VOL. 13-114

Zaraki and Yachiru met in North Rukongai Zone 79, Kusajishi, a place filled with blood and violence. The two lonesome souls were drawn together and have been together ever since.

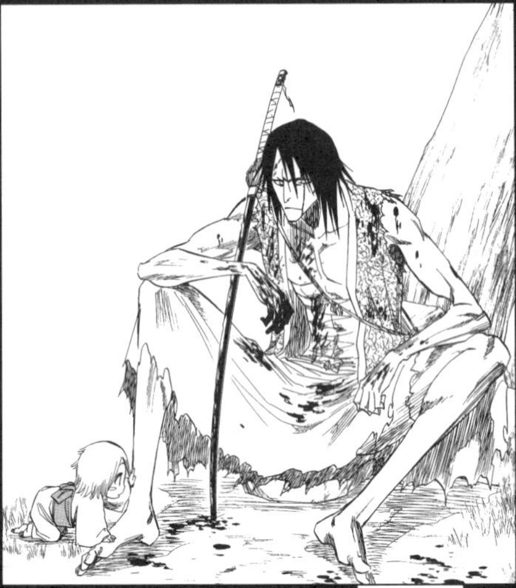

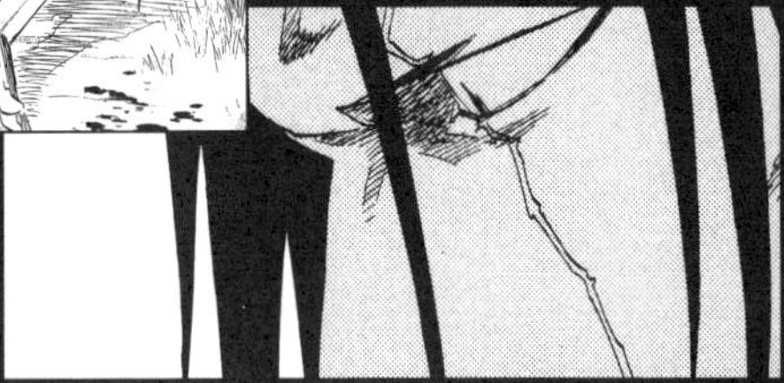

KID, WHAT'S YOUR NAME? DON'T YOU HAVE ONE? NEITHER DO I.

THAT'S RIGHT. EVER SINCE THAT DAY, YOU'VE BEEN MY EVERYTHING.

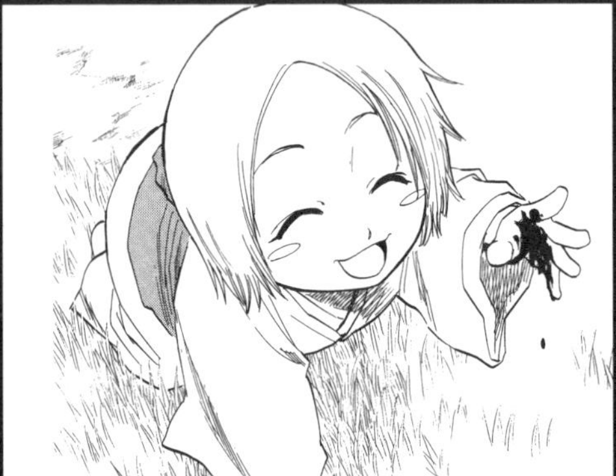

BOTH OF THEIR NAMES
Zaraki gave himself and Yachiru their names. It was the moment at which they were "born" into the world.

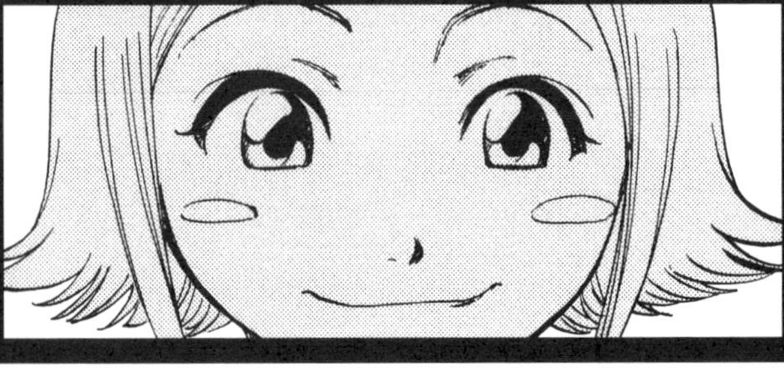

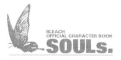

BLEACH
OFFICIAL CHARACTER BOOK
SOULs.

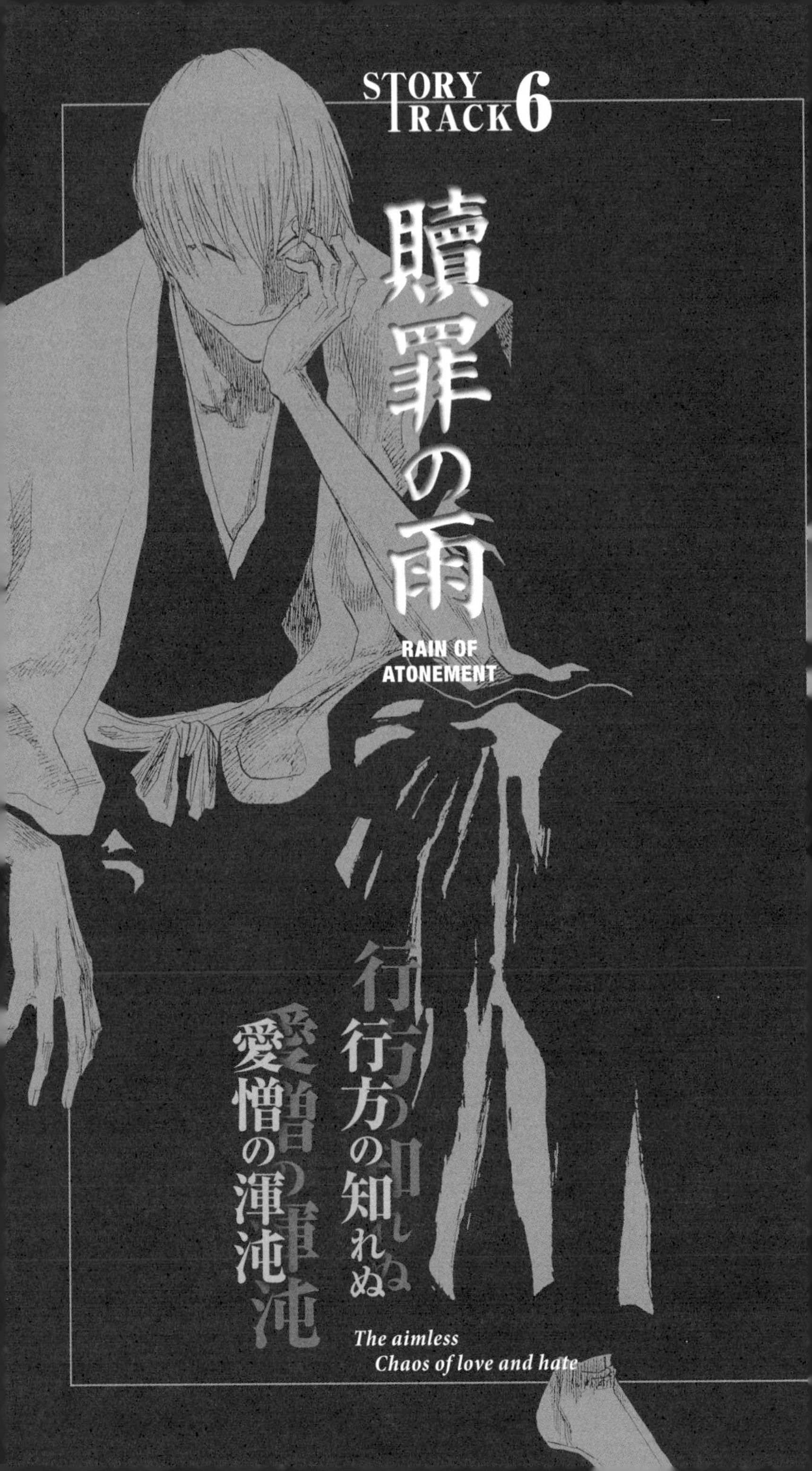
STORY TRACK 6
贖罪の雨
RAIN OF ATONEMENT
行方の知れぬ
愛憎の渾沌
The aimless
Chaos of love and hate

奇縁

A STRANGE COINCIDENCE

An unforgettable enemy
VOL. 13-115

Once she sees the Shiba family crest, Rukia understands everything. She acknowledges that she is Ganju's enemy.

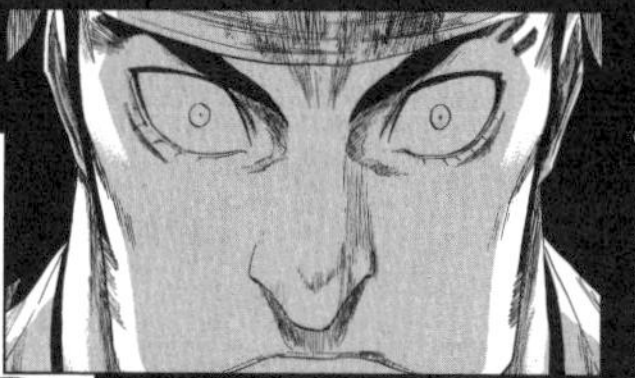

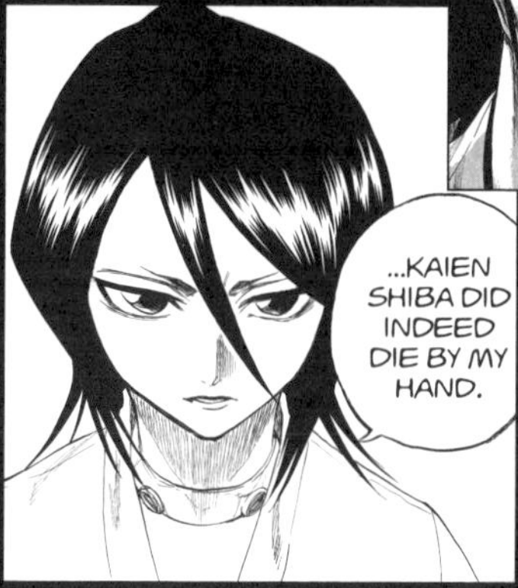
...KAIEN SHIBA DID INDEED DIE BY MY HAND.

Ganju and Hanataro escape from Kenpachi and arrive at the Senzaikyû Shishinrô before Ichigo. Ganju opens the cell with the key that Hanataro borrowed. When he does, he is greeted by an unbelievable sight: Rukia Kuchiki, a person he could never forget.

AN ENTRUSTED RESOLUTION

Ganju roughly grabs Rukia, his brother's enemy. Hanatarô desperately tries to stop him. As they jostle each other, they sense an enormous spiritual pressure. It is Byakuya Kuchiki. Hanataro tries to sacrifice himself for Rukia, but Ganju restrains him and personally confronts Byakuya.

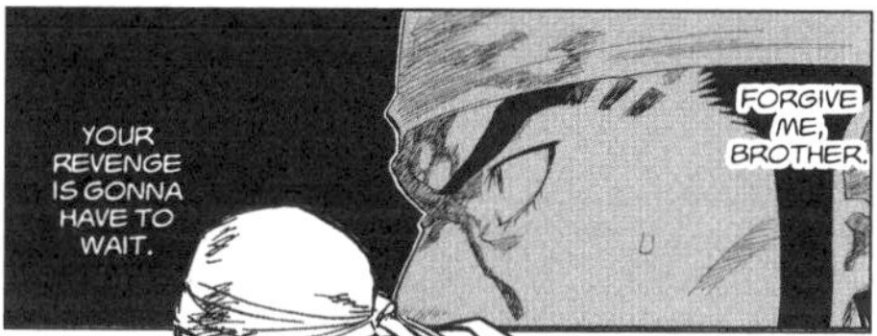
FORGIVE ME, BROTHER.
YOUR REVENGE IS GONNA HAVE TO WAIT.

BATTLE ATTIRE

GANJU SHIBA — CHARACTER PROFILE 45-b

志波岩鷲

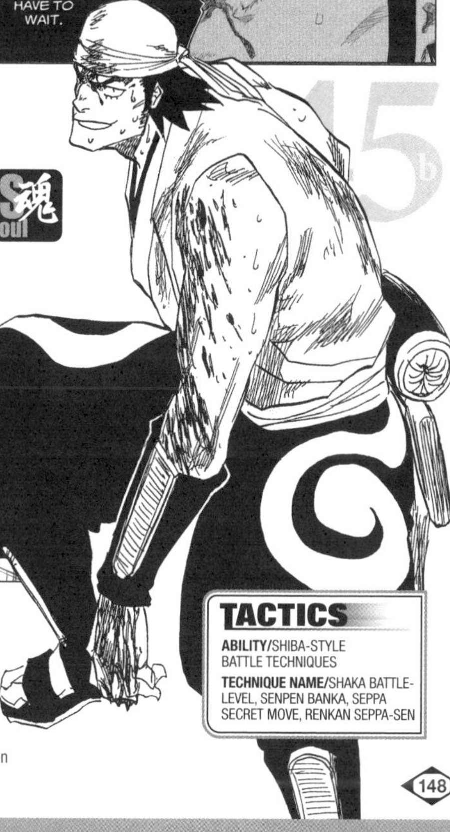

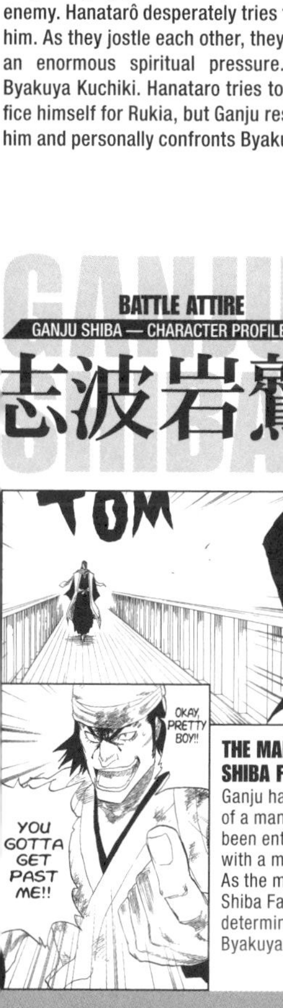
TOM
OKAY, PRETTY BOY!!
YOU GOTTA GET PAST ME!!

THE MAN OF THE SHIBA FAMILY

Ganju has the pride of a man who has been entrusted with a mission. As the man of the Shiba Family, he determinedly takes on Byakuya.

TACTICS

ABILITY/SHIBA-STYLE BATTLE TECHNIQUES

TECHNIQUE NAME/SHAKA BATTLE-LEVEL, SENPEN BANKA, SEPPA SECRET MOVE, RENKAN SEPPA-SEN

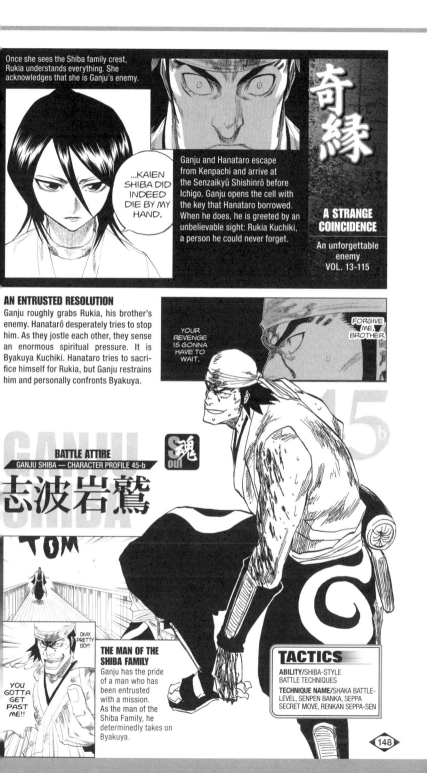

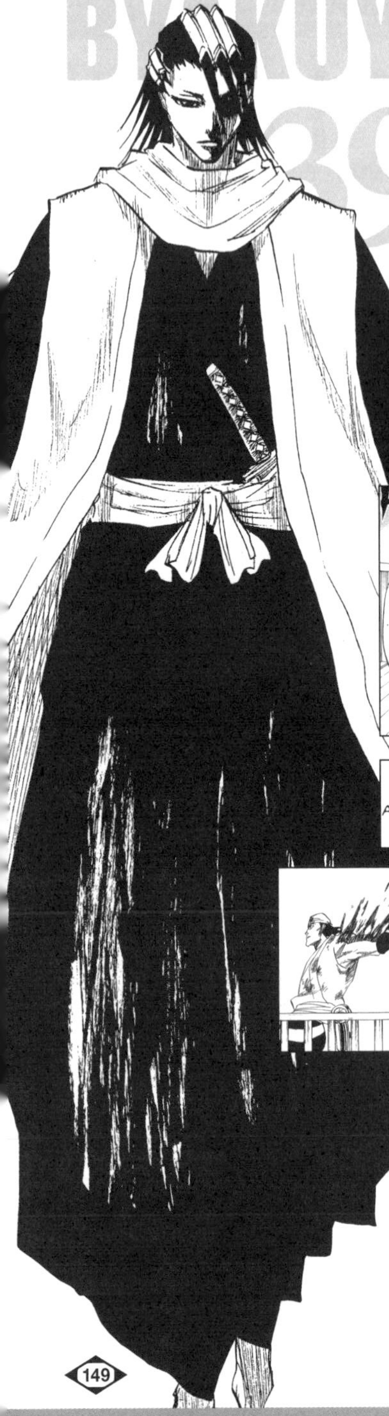
BYAKUYA KUCHIKI
39

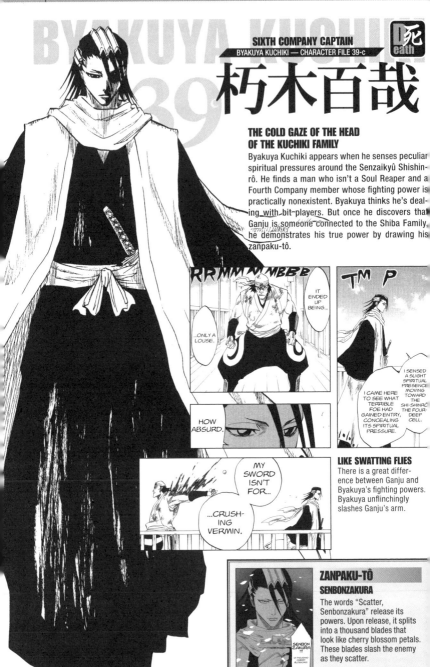

SIXTH COMPANY CAPTAIN

BYAKUYA KUCHIKI — CHARACTER FILE 39-c

D死eath

朽木百哉

THE COLD GAZE OF THE HEAD OF THE KUCHIKI FAMILY

Byakuya Kuchiki appears when he senses peculiar spiritual pressures around the Senzaikyû Shishinrô. He finds a man who isn't a Soul Reaper and a Fourth Company member whose fighting power is practically nonexistent. Byakuya thinks he's dealing with bit-players. But once he discovers that Ganju is someone connected to the Shiba Family, he demonstrates his true power by drawing his zanpaku-tô.

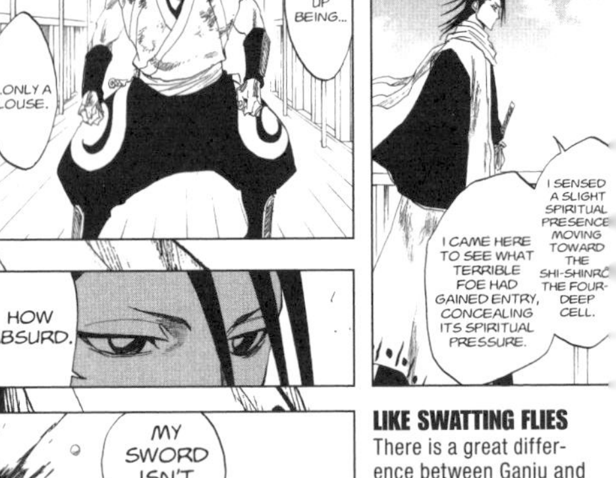
TM P
I SENSED A SLIGHT SPIRITUAL PRESENCE MOVING TOWARD THE SHI-SHINRÔ THE FOUR-DEEP CELL.
I CAME HERE TO SEE WHAT TERRIBLE FOE HAD GAINED ENTRY, CONCEALING ITS SPIRITUAL PRESSURE.
RRMMMMMBBB
IT ENDED UP BEING...
...ONLY A LOUSE.
HOW ABSURD.

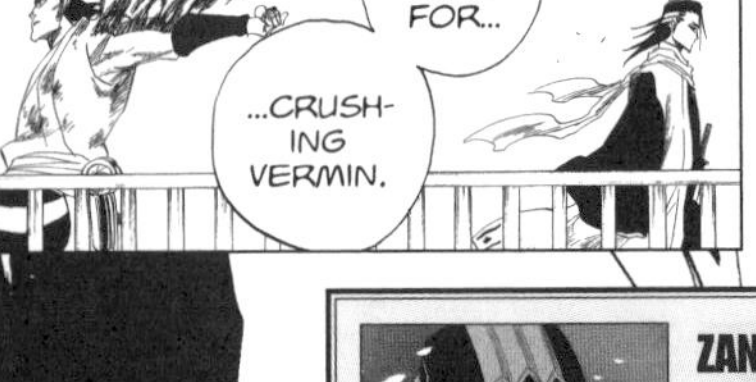
MY SWORD ISN'T FOR...
...CRUSHING VERMIN.

LIKE SWATTING FLIES

There is a great difference between Ganju and Byakuya's fighting powers. Byakuya unflinchingly slashes Ganju's arm.

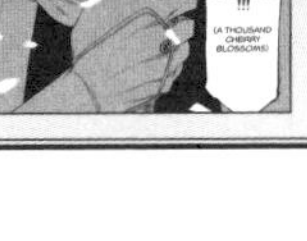
SENBON ZAKURA !!!
(A THOUSAND CHERRY BLOSSOMS)

ZANPAKU-TÔ

SENBONZAKURA

The words "Scatter, Senbonzakura" release its powers. Upon release, it splits into a thousand blades that look like cherry blossom petals. These blades slash the enemy as they scatter.

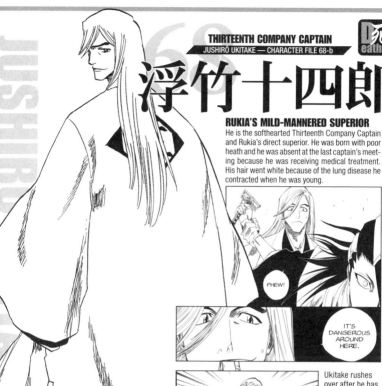

THIRTEENTH COMPANY CAPTAIN

JUSHIRÔ UKITAKE — CHARACTER FILE 68-b

浮竹十四郎

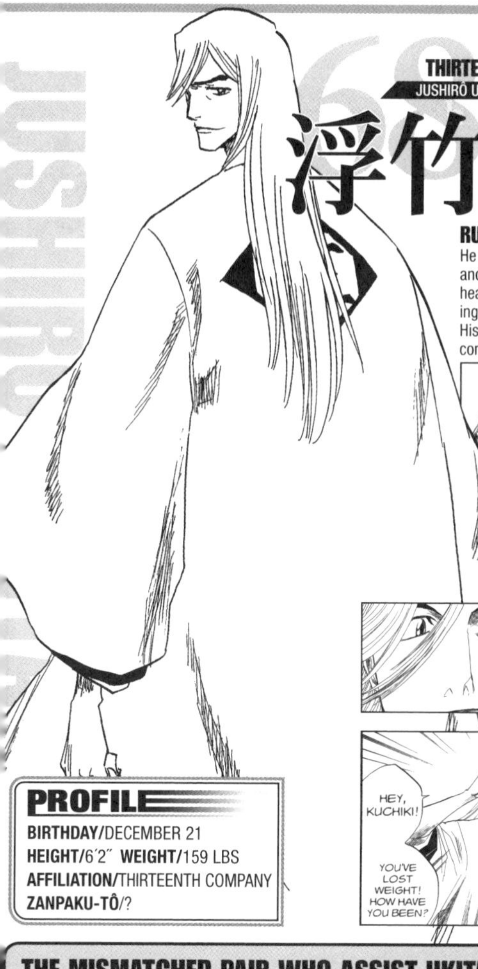

RUKIA'S MILD-MANNERED SUPERIOR

He is the softhearted Thirteenth Company Captain and Rukia's direct superior. He was born with poor heath and he was absent at the last captain's meeting because he was receiving medical treatment. His hair went white because of the lung disease he contracted when he was young.

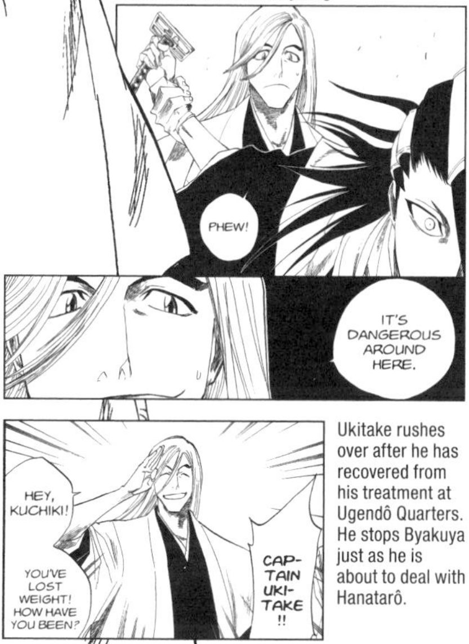
PHEW!
IT'S DANGEROUS AROUND HERE.
CAPTAIN UKITAKE !!
HEY, KUCHIKI!
YOU'VE LOST WEIGHT! HOW HAVE YOU BEEN?

Ukitake rushes over after he has recovered from his treatment at Ugendô Quarters. He stops Byakuya just as he is about to deal with Hanatarô.

PROFILE

BIRTHDAY/DECEMBER 21
HEIGHT/6′2″ **WEIGHT**/159 LBS
AFFILIATION/THIRTEENTH COMPANY
ZANPAKU-TÔ/?

THE MISMATCHED PAIR WHO ASSIST UKITAKE!!

虎徹清音

KIYONE KOTETSU — 70-b

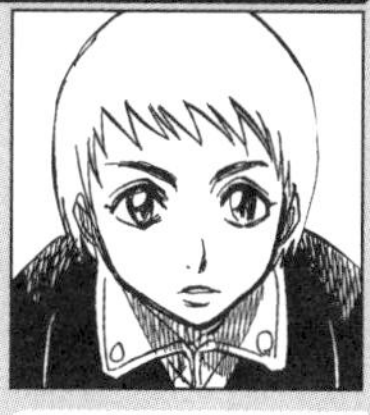

PROFILE

BIRTHDAY/SEPTEMBER 22
HEIGHT/5′1″
WEIGHT/95 LBS

Sentarô calls her a "Booger Girl." She is Isane Kotetsu's younger sister.

小椿仙太郎

SENTARÔ KOTSUBAKI — 69-b

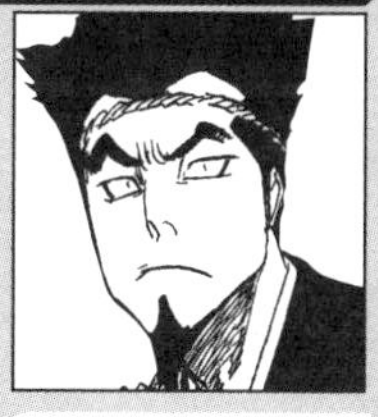

PROFILE

BIRTHDAY/SEPTEMBER 22
HEIGHT/6′0″
WEIGHT/165 LBS

Kiyone Kotetsu calls him an "Armpit-smelling Goatee Monkey."

THEY STRONGLY SUPPORT UKITAKE!!

THE TWO THIRD SEATS

These two greatly respect Ukitake. They have remarkably heated arguments over who respects Ukitake more.

THE BLACK CAT'S TRUE FORM

Ichigo loses consciousness and collapses after his battle with Kenpachi. When he wakes up, he finds that Mr. Yoruichi has moved them to a safe place and treated his wounds. He is puzzled by how Mr. Yoruichi, a cat, could have done that. Mr. Yoruichi reveals to him his true form.

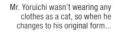

Mr. Yoruichi wasn't wearing any clothes as a cat, so when he changes to his original form...

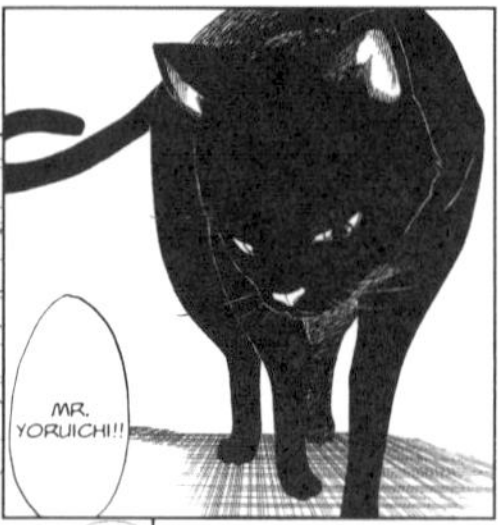
MR. YORUICHI!!

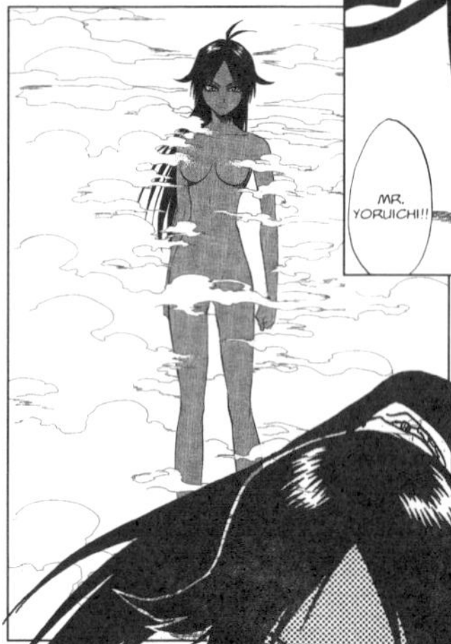

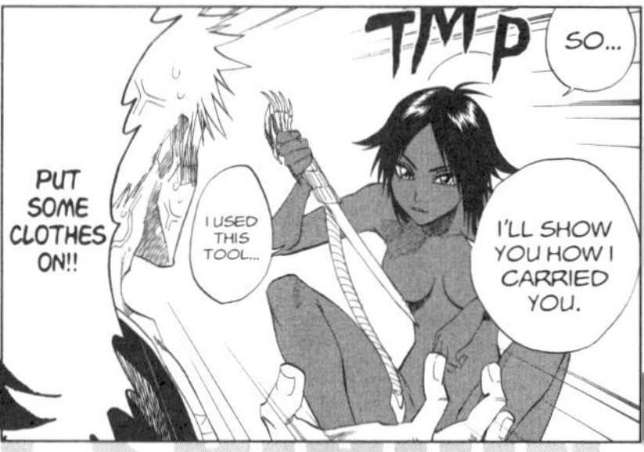
SO...
I'LL SHOW YOU HOW I CARRIED YOU.
I USED THIS TOOL...
TMP
PUT SOME CLOTHES ON!!

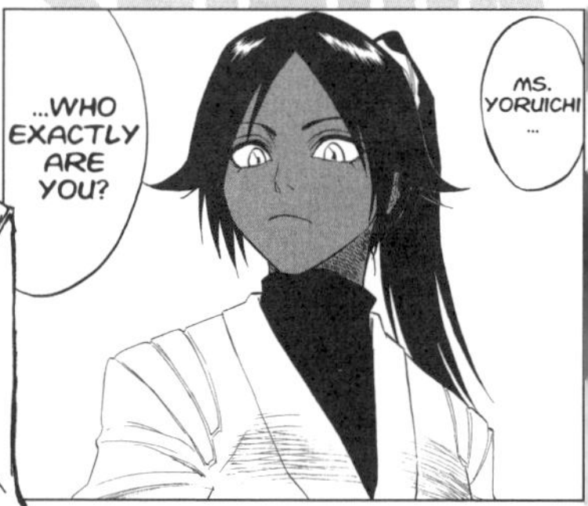
MS. YORUICHI ...
...WHO EXACTLY ARE YOU?

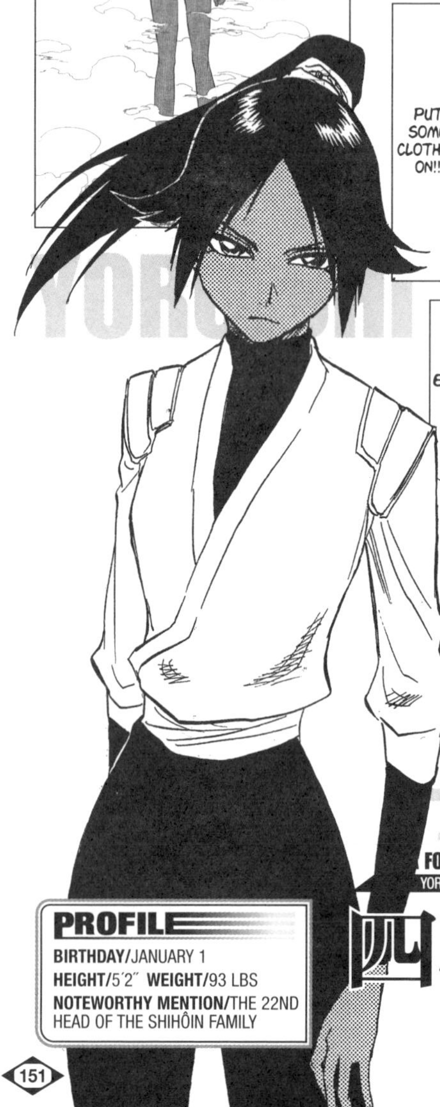

THE PREVIOUS SUPREME COMMANDER OF THE SECRET REMOTE SQUAD

Yoruichi's true form. She is a veteran soldier who was once the Supreme Commander of the Secret Remote Squad as well as the General Corps Leader of the Punishment Force.

FORMERLY INFLUENTIAL PERSON

YORUICHI SHIHÔIN — CHARACTER FILE 41-b

Death 死

四楓院夜一

PROFILE

BIRTHDAY/JANUARY 1
HEIGHT/5′2″ **WEIGHT/**93 LBS
NOTEWORTHY MENTION/THE 22ND HEAD OF THE SHIHÔIN FAMILY

疾駆

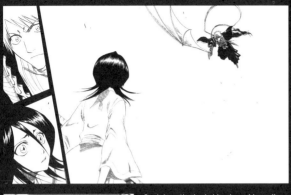

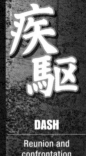

DASH

Reunion and confrontation
VOL. 14-116~117

Ganju's entire body bleeds and he collapses when Byakuya mercilessly slashes him with his Senbonzakura. Byakuya then turns his attack towards Hanataro... But Thirteenth Captain Ukitake appears on the scene and stops Byakuya out of kindness. Suddenly, enormous spiritual pressure approaches them at high speed. At the middle of the spiritual pressure is Ichigo, who is zooming through the air.

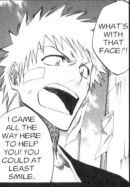

WHAT'S WITH THAT FACE?!
I CAME ALL THE WAY HERE TO HELP YOU! YOU COULD AT LEAST SMILE.

I TOLD YOU NOT TO COME.
I TOLD YOU...
...NOT TO COME AFTER ME!

Reunion. Rukia tears up even though she scolds him for coming after her.

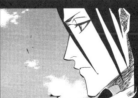

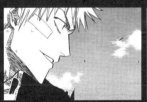

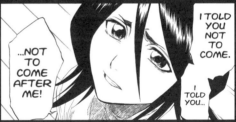

POISE AND PASSION CLASH
Ichigo confronts Byakuya once more to get back at him and save Rukia.

THE TOOL HANDED DOWN FROM THE HEAVENS

TENTÔKEN

The tentôken is a very valuable and powerful weapon and tool. It is usually entrusted and sealed away by the Shihôin family.

MP

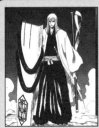

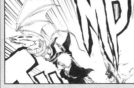

Yoruichi is the head of the Shihôin family, a prestigious family that has passed on the responsibility of the Tenshiheisoban from generation to generation.

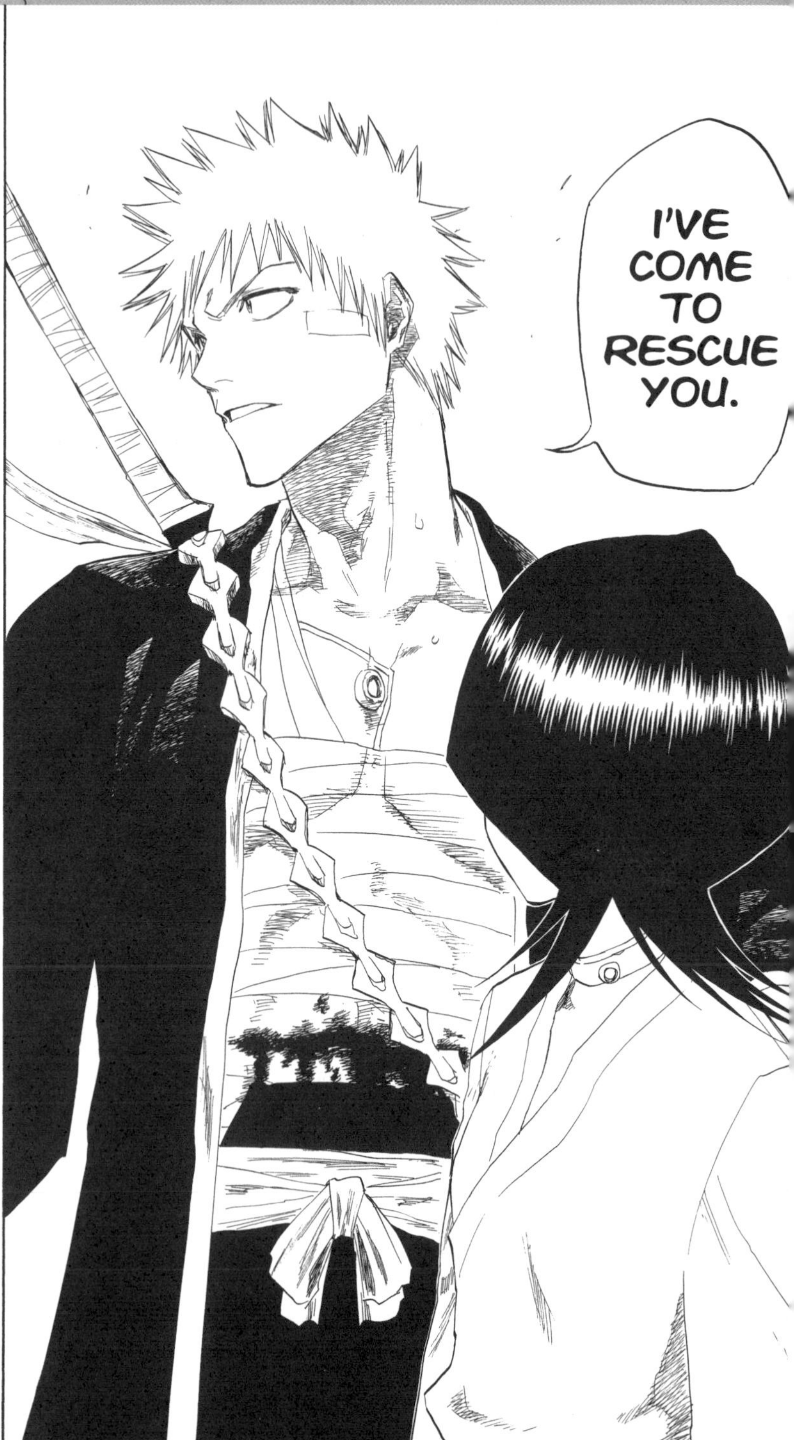
I'VE COME TO RESCUE YOU.

鬼事

TAG

Byakuya and Yoruichi
VOL. 14-117~118

Yoruichi interferes when Byakuya tries to release his Senbonzakura. Yoruichi doesn't treat Byakuya with special respect, even though he's a nobleman and Captain.

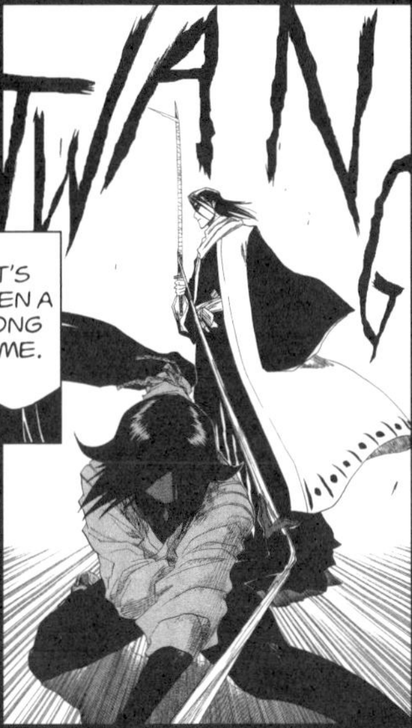
TWANG

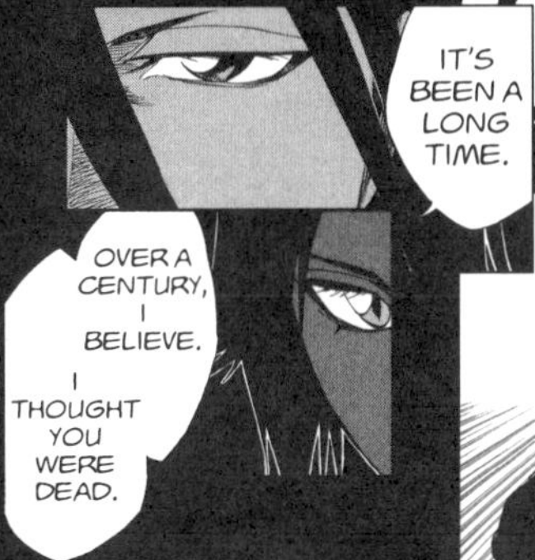
IT'S BEEN A LONG TIME.
OVER A CENTURY, I BELIEVE.
I THOUGHT YOU WERE DEAD.

Yoruichi was gone for a hundred years. Even so, her fame has not faded.

YORUICHI'S TRUE INTENT
Yoruichi has determined that Ichigo has no chance of winning. She drives an anesthetic into Ichigo with a stab of her hand and attempts to carry him away while he's unconscious.

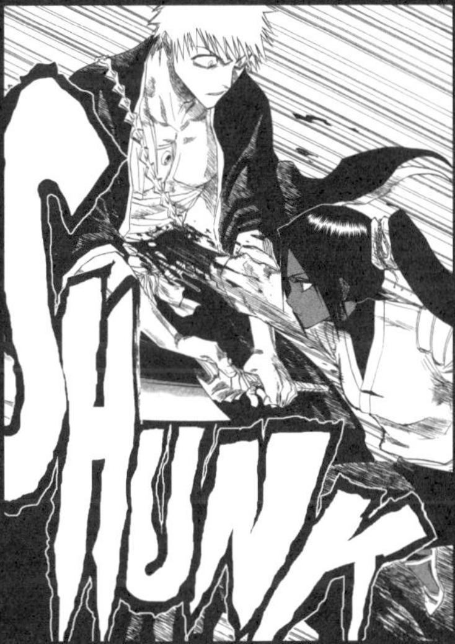
SHUNK

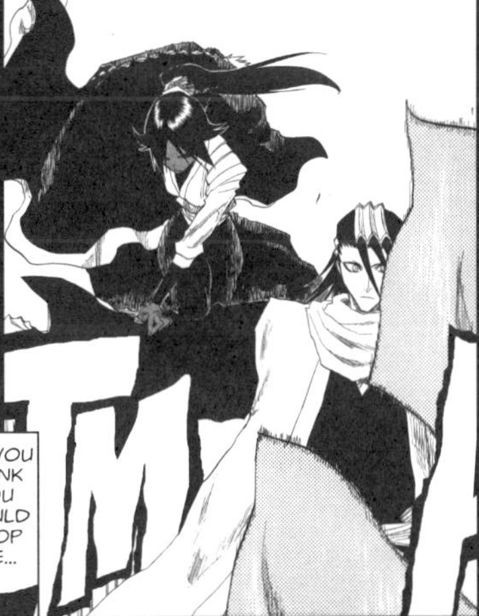
TM

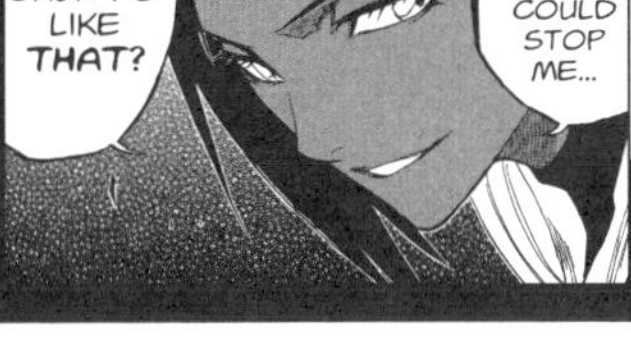
DID YOU THINK YOU COULD STOP ME...
...WITH A SHUN-PO LIKE **THAT?**

Yoruichi is nicknamed "Flash Master." Her incredible god-like speed makes her difficult even for Byakuya to catch.

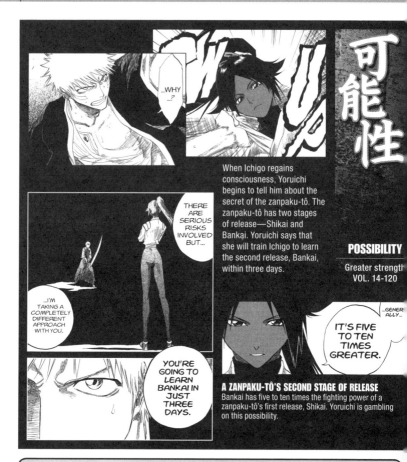

可能性

POSSIBILITY

Greater strength
VOL. 14-120

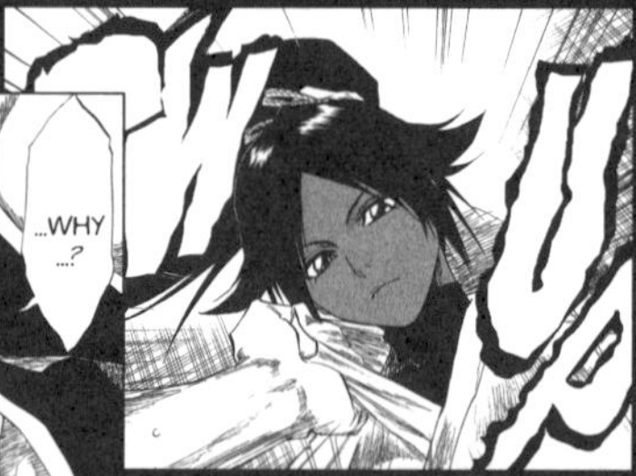

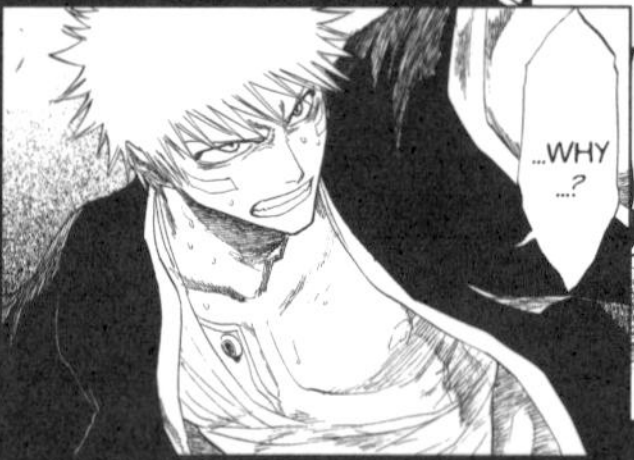
...WHY ...?

When Ichigo regains consciousness, Yoruichi begins to tell him about the secret of the zanpaku-tô. The zanpaku-tô has two stages of release—Shikai and Bankai. Yoruichi says that she will train Ichigo to learn the second release, Bankai, within three days.

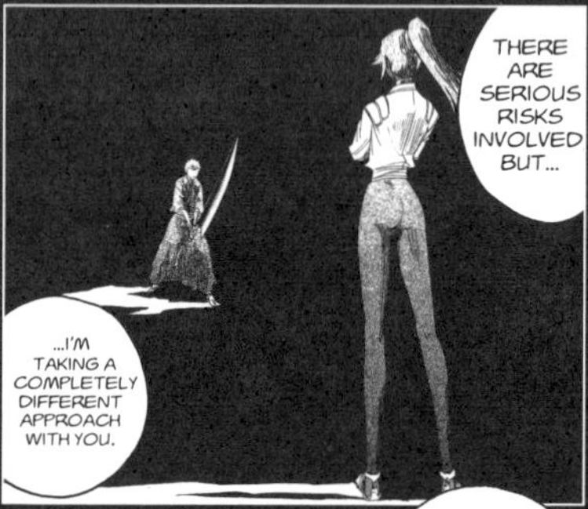
THERE ARE SERIOUS RISKS INVOLVED BUT...
...I'M TAKING A COMPLETELY DIFFERENT APPROACH WITH YOU.

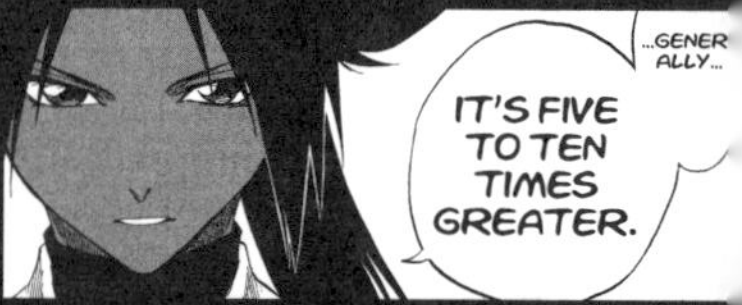
...GENERALLY...
IT'S FIVE TO TEN TIMES GREATER.

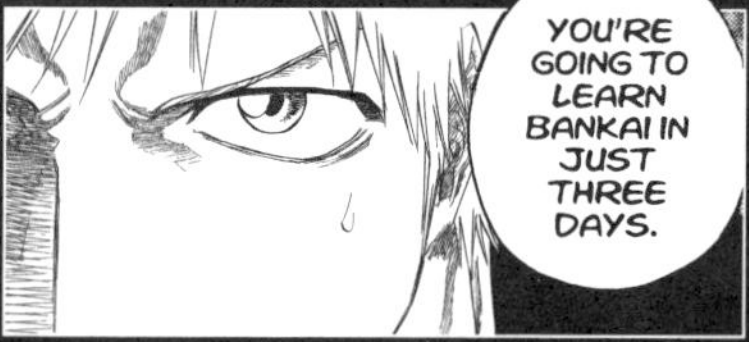
YOU'RE GOING TO LEARN BANKAI IN JUST THREE DAYS.

A ZANPAKU-TÔ'S SECOND STAGE OF RELEASE
Bankai has five to ten times the fighting power of a zanpaku-tô's first release, Shikai. Yoruichi is gambling on this possibility.

RUKIA'S LINGERING MEMORIES...

THE MAN WHO LOOKS LIKE ICHIGO

Ukitake is surprised when he sees Ichigo's face and cries out, "Who is he?" Byakuya says he's no one important, and he'll soon be disposed of anyway. Rukia also recalls seeing a man who looks like Ichigo. Who is this man they are thinking of? And what is the as-yet untold relationship between him and Rukia?

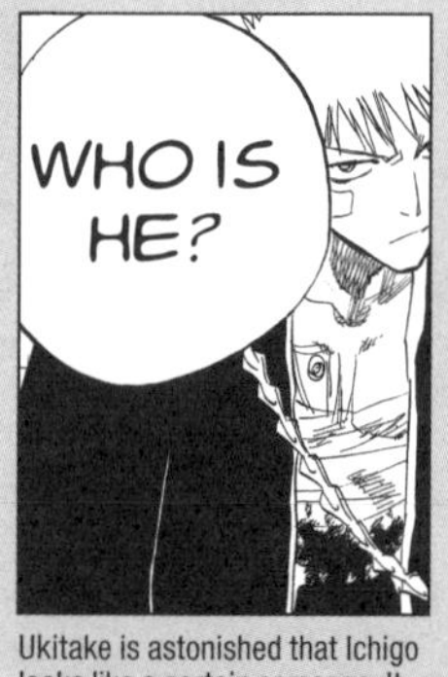
WHO IS HE?

Ukitake is astonished that Ichigo looks like a certain someone. It seems that it is someone who is deeply connected with Thirteenth Company...

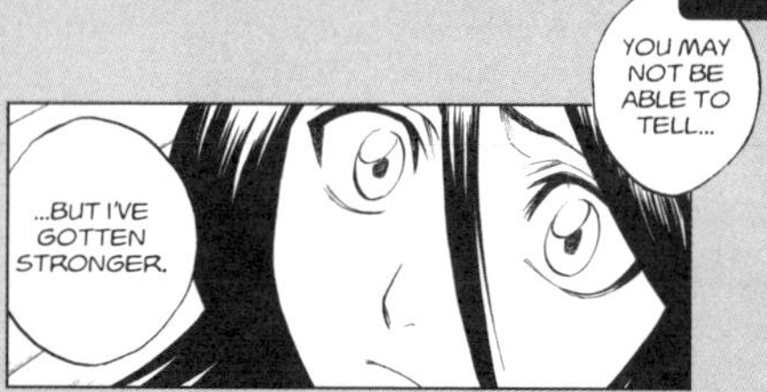
YOU MAY NOT BE ABLE TO TELL...
...BUT I'VE GOTTEN STRONGER.

Ichigo's abrupt words and actions bring back Rukia's memories.

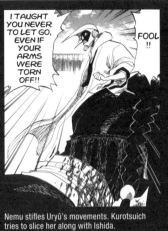

外道

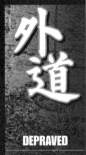

DEPRAVED

His demonic deeds
VOL. 14-120~123

Uryû and Orihime dress up as Soul Reapers and head to the Senzaikyû Shishinrô, where Rukia is being held captive. Mayuri Kurotsuchi, a peculiar Soul Reaper, appears before them. Orihime uses the Shunshunrikka when Kurotsuchi blows up one of his subordinates. Kurotsuchi is intrigued by Orihime's unusual technique and attempts to capture her as research material. Uryû tries to prevent this by letting Orihime escape and taking on Kurotsuchi himself.

FOOL!!
I TAUGHT YOU NEVER TO LET GO, EVEN IF YOUR ARMS WERE TORN OFF!!

Nemu stifles Uryû's movements. Kurotsuich tries to slice her along with Ishida.

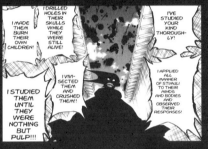

I'VE STUDIED YOUR KIND THOROUGH-LY!
I DRILLED HOLES IN THEIR SKULLS WHILE THEY WERE STILL ALIVE!
I MADE THEM BURN THEIR OWN CHILDREN!
I APPLIED ALL MANNER OF STIMULI TO THEIR MINDS AND BODIES AND OBSERVED THEIR RESPONSES!
I VIVI-SECTED THEM AND CRUSHED THEM!!
I STUDIED THEM UNTIL THEY WERE NOTHING BUT PULP!!!

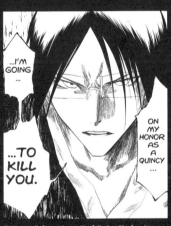

...I'M GOING ...
ON MY HONOR AS A QUINCY ...
...TO KILL YOU.

Ashisogi Jizô paralyzes Uryû limbs. Uryû gets up by using the Ransô Tengai!

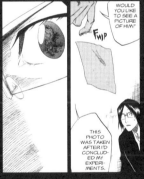

WOULD YOU LIKE TO SEE A PICTURE OF HIM?
FWIP
THIS PHOTO WAS TAKEN AFTER I'D CONCLUD-ED MY EXPERI-MENTS.

THE PEAK OF ANGER
Kurotsuchi shows Uryû a photograph. It is a picture of the dead body of Uryû's master, Sôken Ishida.

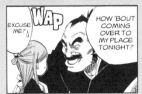

ABUSE OF AUTHORITY?!

TOSHIMORI UMESADA

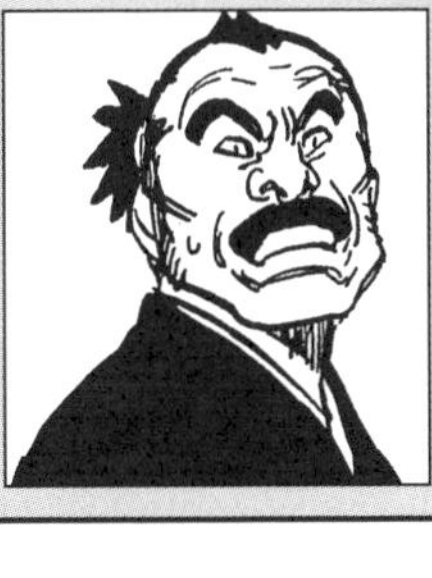

One of the 15 twentieth seats of Ninth Company. He meets Uryû and Orihime by chance when they sneak into a company while dressed as Soul Reapers. His speech and actions are despotic.

HOW 'BOUT COMING OVER TO MY PLACE TONIGHT?
WAP
EXCUSE ME?

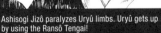

Umesada makes this comment during the turmoil. He seems to like Orihime a lot.

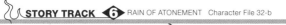

SANREI SHUTÔ RELEASED

URYÛ ISHIDA — CHARACTER FILE 32-b

石田雨竜

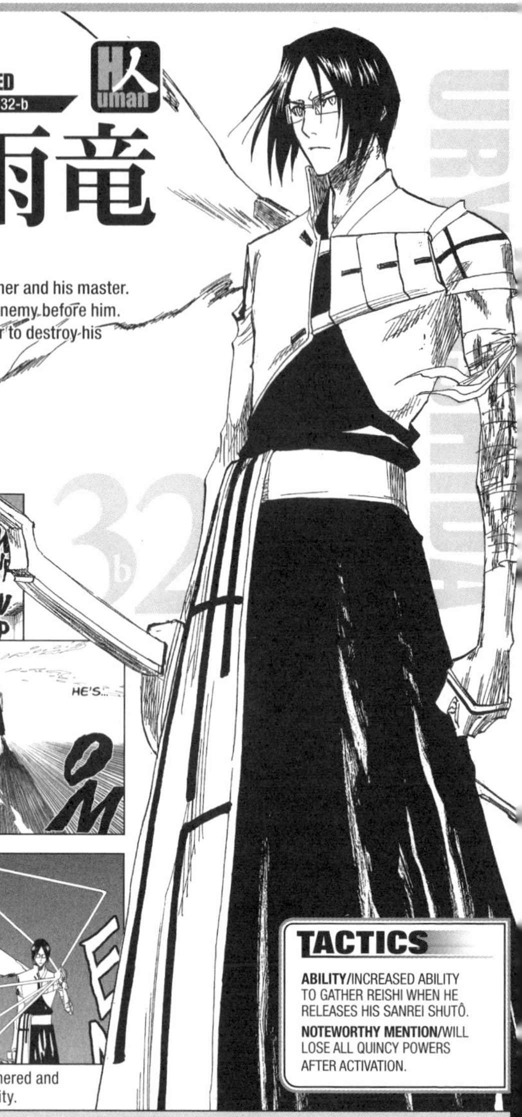

DO NOT HATE MYSELF

Uryû gets up and remembers his father and his master. He takes a look at the unforgivable enemy before him. He removes his Sanrei Shutô in order to destroy his master's enemy.

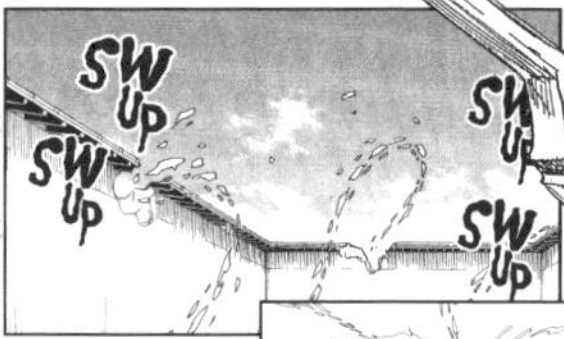
SW UP
SW UP
SW UP
SW UP

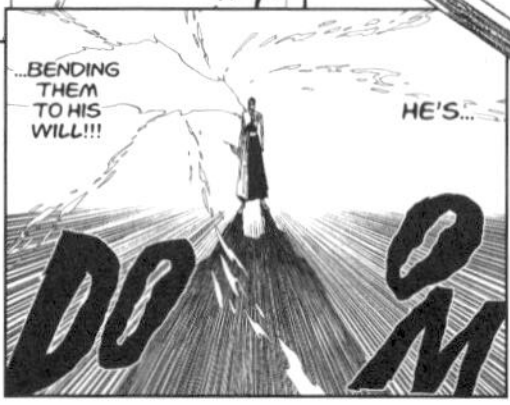
HE'S...
...BENDING THEM TO HIS WILL!!!
DOOM

The release of the Sanrei Shutô breaks down the surrounding structures and allows Uryû to absorb the reishi they are made of.

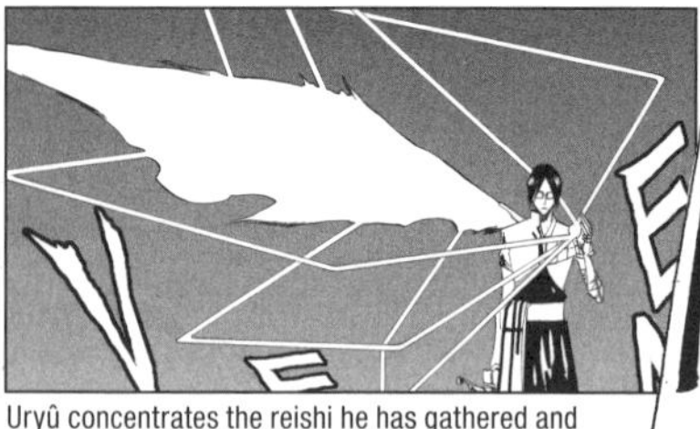

Uryû concentrates the reishi he has gathered and creates an arrow of high spiritual intensity.

TACTICS

ABILITY/INCREASED ABILITY TO GATHER REISHI WHEN HE RELEASES HIS SANREI SHUTÔ.

NOTEWORTHY MENTION/WILL LOSE ALL QUINCY POWERS AFTER ACTIVATION.

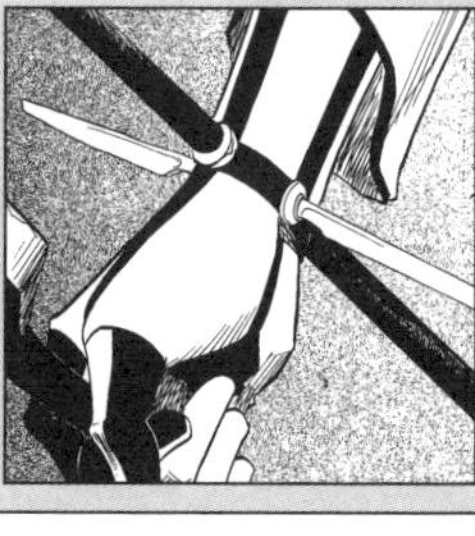

SANREI SHUTÔ

A Quincy can attain nearly peak-level power if he trains with this glove for seven days and seven nights.

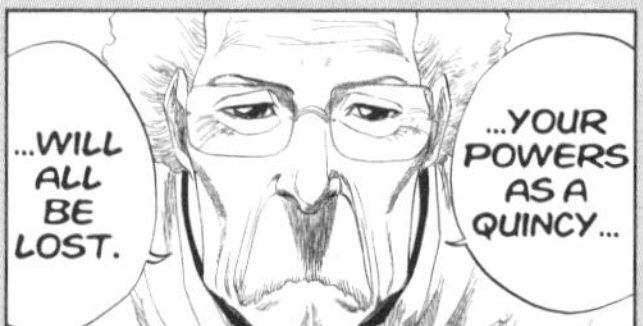
...YOUR POWERS AS A QUINCY...
...WILL ALL BE LOST.

After gaining power and taking off the glove, a Quincy can gain immense power, but...

A MAD SCIENTIST WHO PLAYS WITH LIVES

The Twelfth Company Captain and the second Head of the Department of Research and Development. His motives are pure but because of that he has an insidiously inquiring mind. He thinks nothing of others in his pursuit to satisfy his intellectual curiosity. His interest has even extended to his own body, which he has modified.

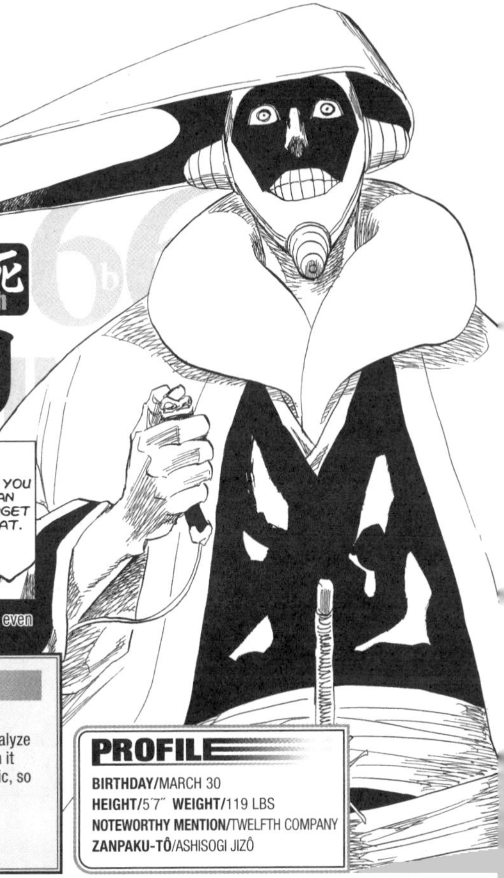

TWELFTH COMPANY CAPTAIN

MAYURI KUROTSUCHI — CHARACTER FILE 66-b

Death 死

涅マユリ

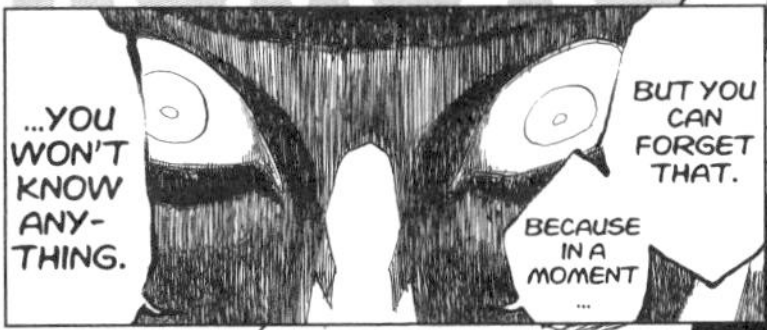

BUT YOU CAN FORGET THAT.
BECAUSE IN A MOMENT ...
...YOU WON'T KNOW ANY-THING.

Kurotsuchi has a strange appearance. His whole body, even his face and hands, has been painted black and white.

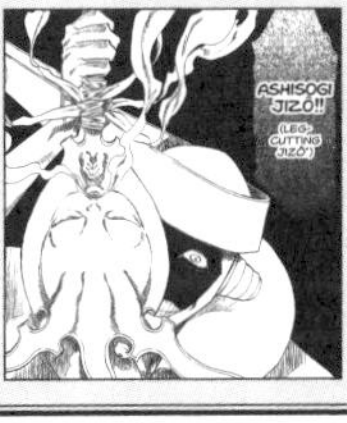

ASHISOGI JIZÔ!!
(LEG-CUTTING JIZÔ!)

ZANPAKU-TÔ

ASHISOGI JIZÔ

It has the ability to paralyze the limbs of the person it cuts. It is not anesthetic, so the pain still remains.

PROFILE

BIRTHDAY/MARCH 30
HEIGHT/5′7″ **WEIGHT/**119 LBS
NOTEWORTHY MENTION/TWELFTH COMPANY
ZANPAKU-TÔ/ASHISOGI JIZÔ

KUROTSUCHI'S GREATEST CREATION

Nemu is a Soul Reaper who was created through the combination of Kurotsuchi's gigai technology and substitute soul technology. Nemu considers Kurotsuchi to be her father. Kurotsuchi's orders are absolute, and Nemu would gladly give her life to defeat his enemy.

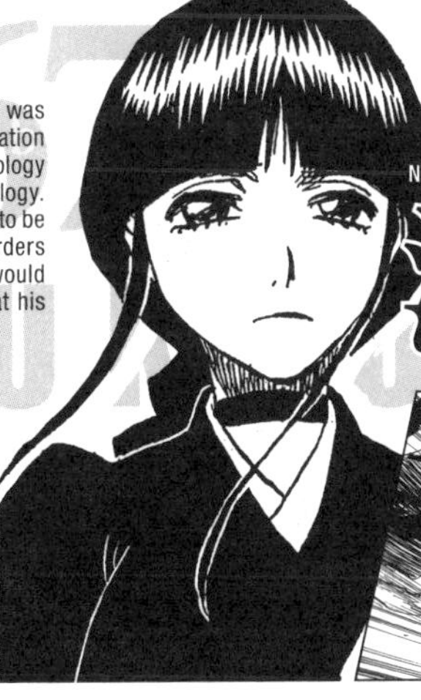

TWELFTH COMPANY ASSISTANT CAPTAIN

NEMU KUROTSUCHI — CHARACTER FILE 67-b

Death 死

涅ネム

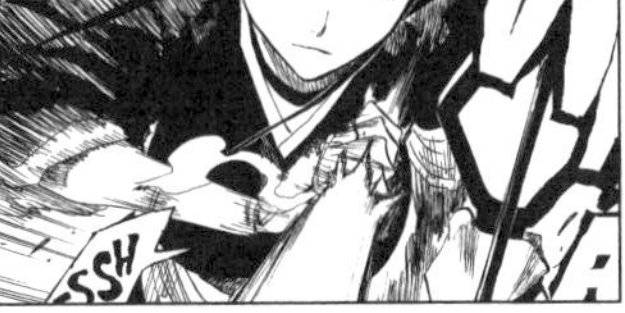

SSH

PROFILE

BIRTHDAY/MARCH 30
HEIGHT/5′5″
WEIGHT/115 LBS

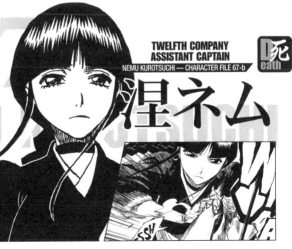

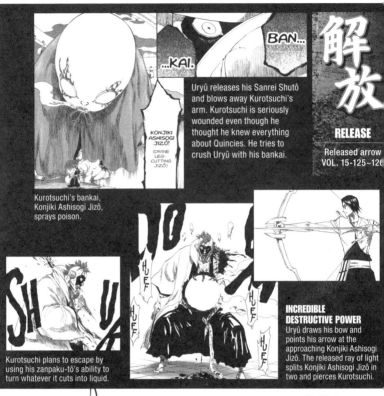

解放

RELEASE

Released arrow
VOL. 15-125~126

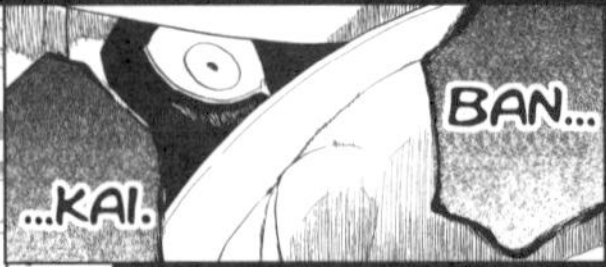
BAN...
...KAI.

Uryû releases his Sanrei Shutô and blows away Kurotsuchi's arm. Kurotsuchi is seriously wounded even though he thought he knew everything about Quincies. He tries to crush Uryû with his bankai.

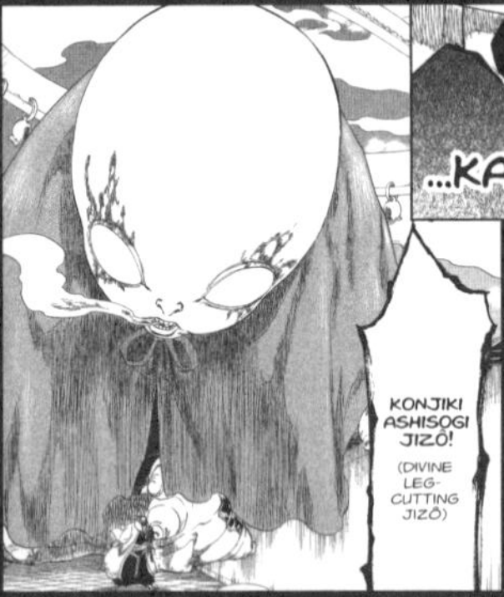
KONJIKI ASHISOGI JIZÔ!
(DIVINE LEG-CUTTING JIZÔ)

Kurotsuchi's bankai, Konjiki Ashisogi Jizô, sprays poison.

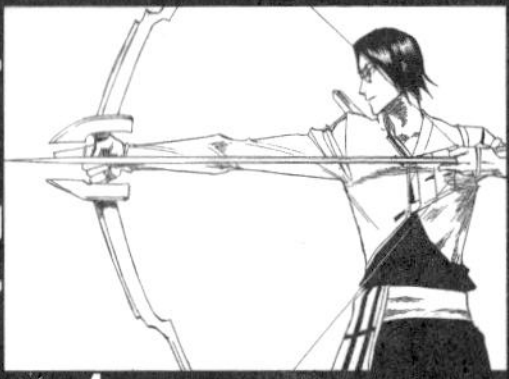

INCREDIBLE DESTRUCTIVE POWER
Uryû draws his bow and points his arrow at the approaching Konjiki Ashisogi Jizô. The released ray of light splits Konjiki Ashisogi Jizô in two and pierces Kurotsuchi.

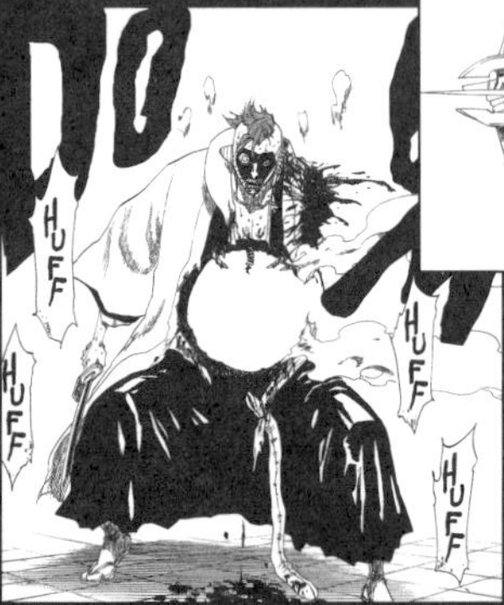
HUFF
HUFF
HUFF
HUFF

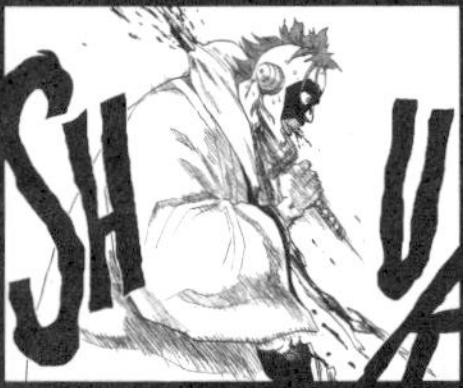

Kurotsuchi plans to escape by using his zanpaku-tô's ability to turn whatever it cuts into liquid.

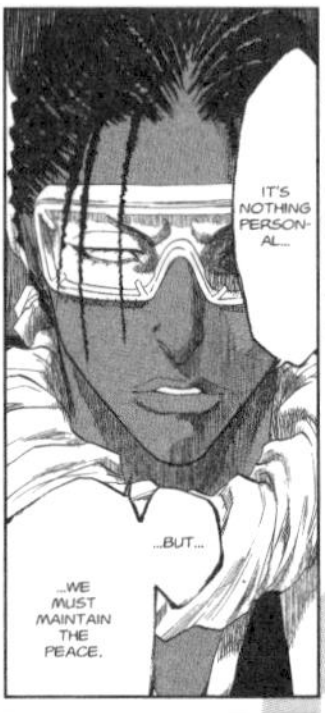
IT'S NOTHING PERSONAL...
...BUT...
...WE MUST MAINTAIN THE PEACE.

A DISPASSIONATE PACIFIST
Tôsen is the blind Soul Reaper who stands in Uryû's way to the Senzaikyû Shishinrô. He has abandoned all self-interest and wields his sword solely in the name of justice.

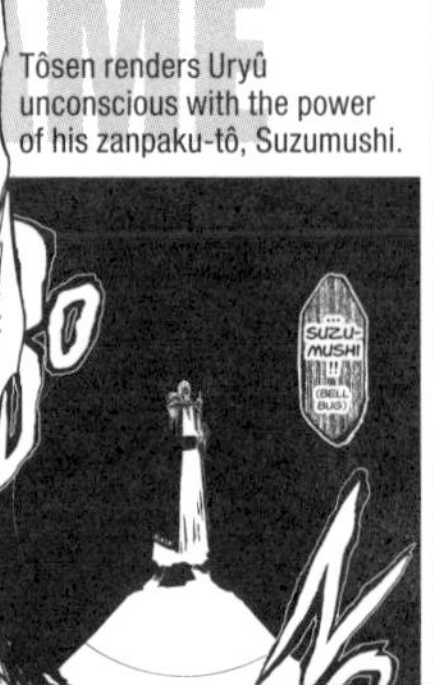
...SUZUMUSHI!!
(BELL BUG)

Tôsen renders Uryû unconscious with the power of his zanpaku-tô, Suzumushi.

KANAME

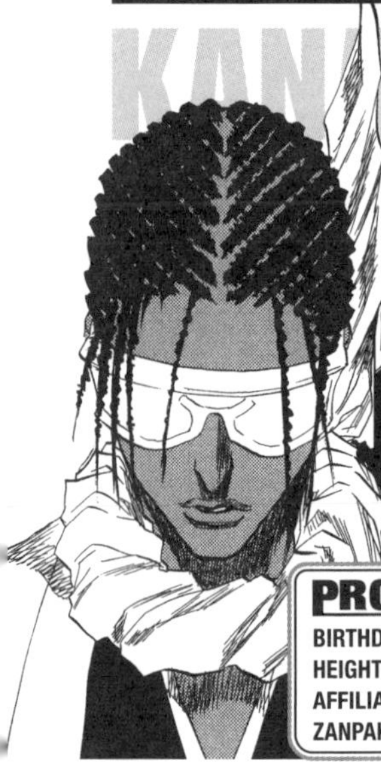

PROFILE
BIRTHDAY/NOVEMBER 13
HEIGHT/5′8″ **WEIGHT**/134 LBS
AFFILIATION/NINTH COMPANY
ZANPAKU-TÔ/SUZUMUSHI

60 b

Death 死

NINTH COMPANY CAPTAIN
KANAME TÔSEN — CHARACTER FILE 60-b

東仙要

ZANGETSU'S INCARNATION

ZANGETSU — CHARACTER FILE 40-b

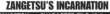

斬月

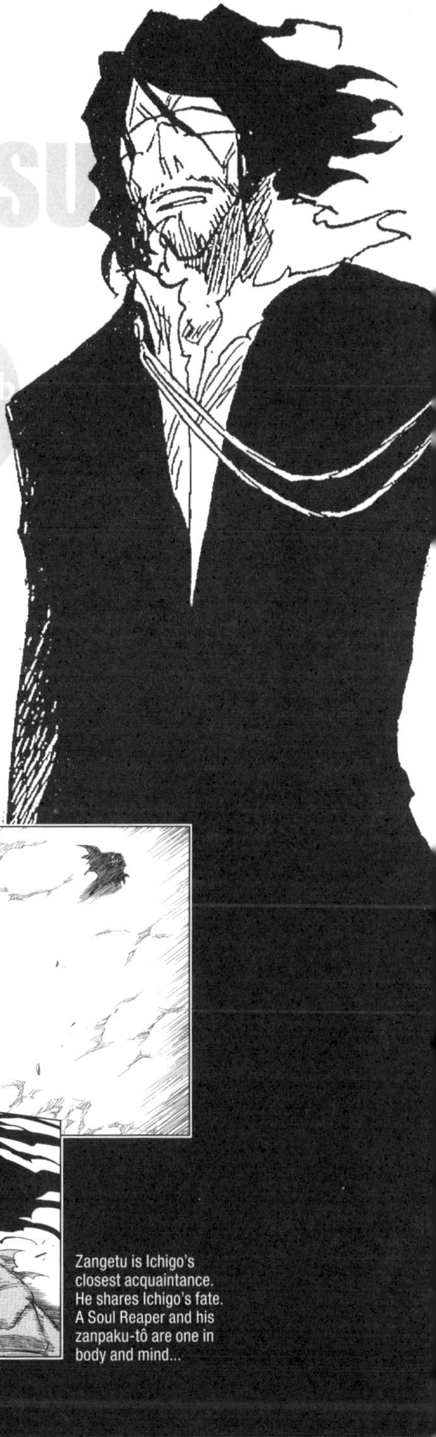

A TALL, THIN, GREAT MAN

A person needs more than ten years of training to achieve bankai. In order to defeat Byakuya, Ichigo needs to learn to use it in just three days. Ichigo has already learned how to converse and harmonize with his zanpaku-tô in order to use shikai. He must take the next step and learn how to externalize and subjugate. He must do this with Zangetsu, the man in black.

Ichigo is throwing himself into a tough battle. Zangetsu tells him that he is not alone.

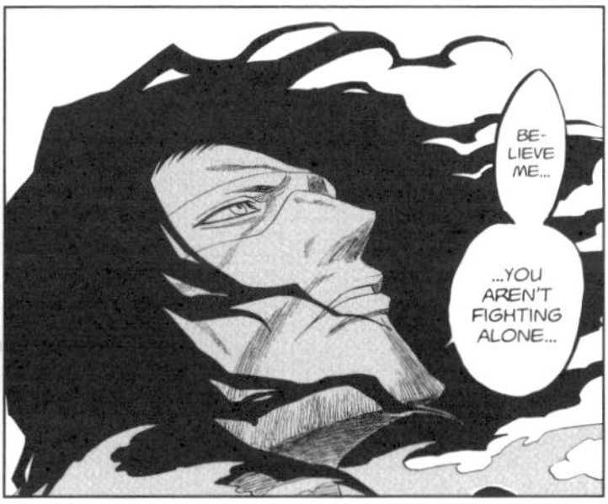
BE-LIEVE ME...
...YOU AREN'T FIGHTING ALONE...

ENDLESS BATTLE

In order to learn the bankai, Ichigo begins a fierce battle with Zangetsu, who has materialized.

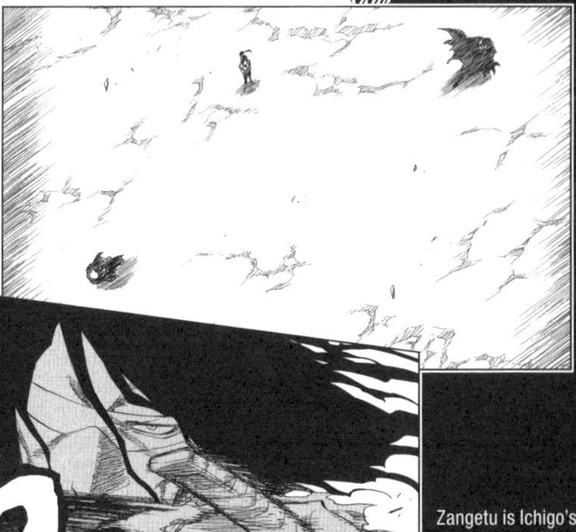

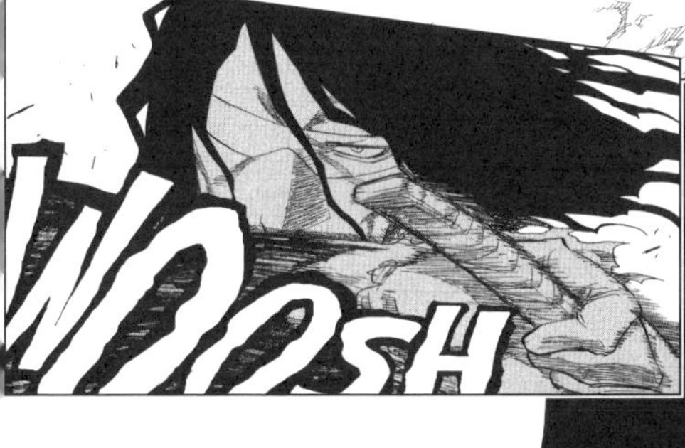
WOOSH

Zangetu is Ichigo's closest acquaintance. He shares Ichigo's fate. A Soul Reaper and his zanpaku-tô are one in body and mind...

卍解

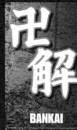

BANKAI

Desperate struggl
with Zangetsu
VOL. 15-126~130

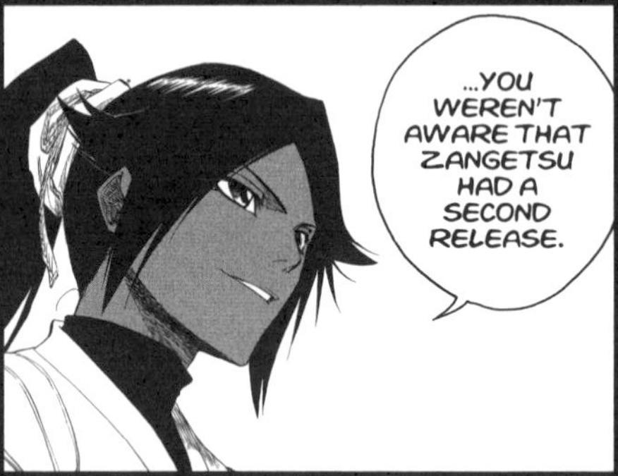
...YOU WEREN'T AWARE THAT ZANGETSU HAD A SECOND RELEASE.

A person needs to externalize and subjugate the spirit of their zanpaku-tô in order to learn bankai, the second stage of release. Ichigo is told to fight Zangetsu and cut him down... A long battle begins.

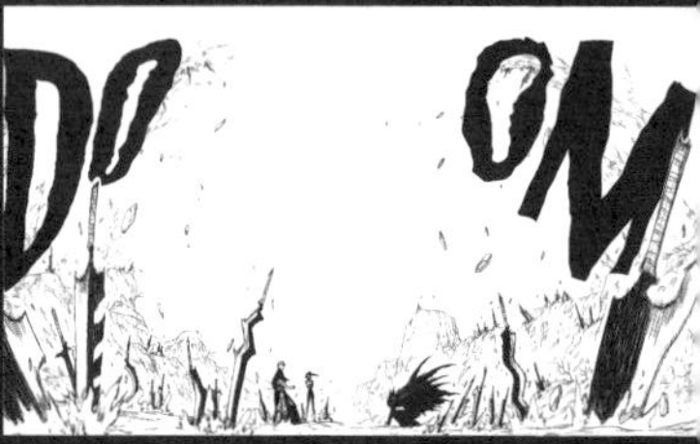
DO OM

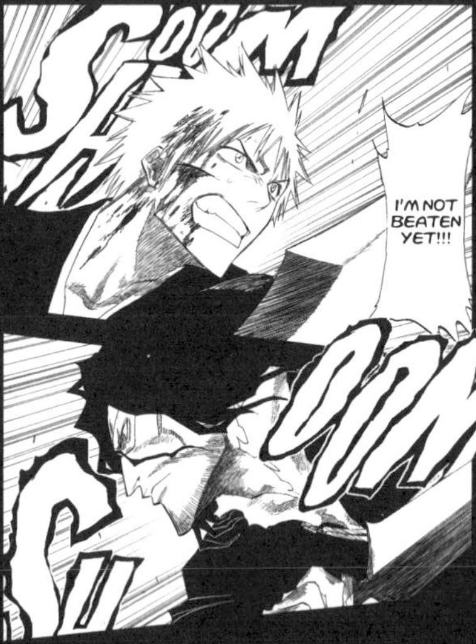
I'M NOT BEATEN YET!!!

THE REAL ZANGETSU
The only way that Ichigo can defeat Zangetsu is by using the real Zangetsu hidden among countless swords.

DEFEAT ZANGETSU!!
Even though every sword he picks gets smashed, Ichigo picks up another sword and continues to attack Zangetsu!!

SPECIAL SPIRIT TOOL

TENSHINTAI

One of the most important spirit tools of the Stealth Force. It can force a zanpaku-tô to shift into its materialized form. Ichigo trains with this spirit tool.

Yoruichi helps Ichigo with various spirit items. The Tenshintai is an emergency item that she reveals three days before Ichigo's final showdown with Byakuya.

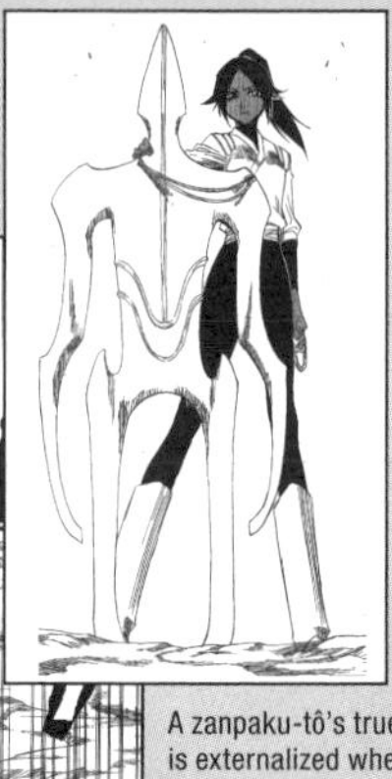

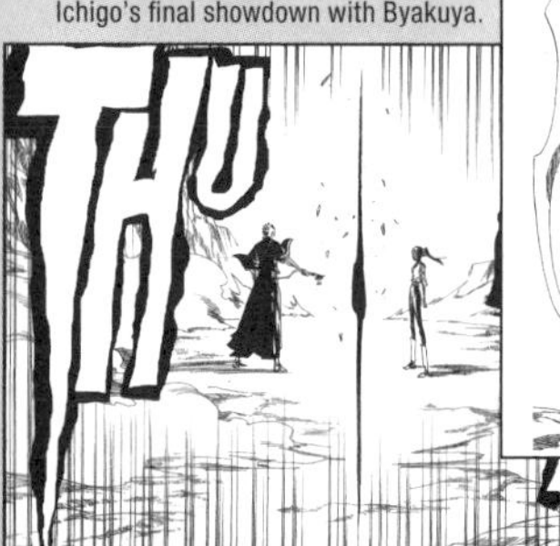
THU

A zanpaku-tô's true form is externalized when it is stabbed into the tenshintai.

休息

REST

Confessed past
VOL. 15-130

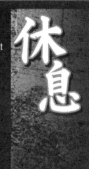

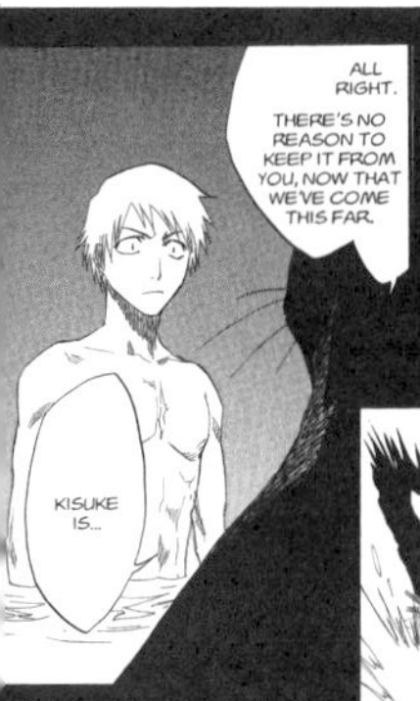
ALL RIGHT. THERE'S NO REASON TO KEEP IT FROM YOU, NOW THAT WE'VE COME THIS FAR.
KISUKE IS...

After the first day of training, Ichigo and Yoruichi go to a hot spring gushing from a subterranean nook to relieve their exhaustion. There, Yoruichi tells Ichigo about her relationship with Urahara, and the fact that Urahara was the previous Twelfth Company Captain and founder of the Department of Research and Development...

chigo had been wondering bout Urahara's identity for while, but it was nothing ke he had expected...

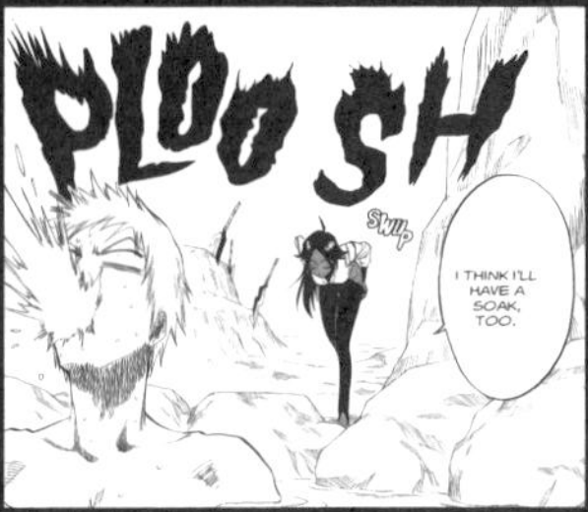
PLOOSH
SWIP
I THINK I'LL HAVE A SOAK, TOO.

Intentional or not, Yoruichi's actions fluster Ichigo. Is she showing an unexpectedly mischievous side?!

REVEALED IDENTITY

KISUKE URAHARA — CHARACTER FILE 15-c

Death 死

浦原喜助

FORMER TWELFTH COMPANY CAPTAIN AND THE FIRST HEAD OF THE DEPARTMENT OF RESEARCH AND DEVELOPMENT

Urahara saved Rukia when she was in the Human World and trained Ichigo and his friends when they were headed to Soul Society. These weren't just simple acts of kindness. It seems that Urahara played a significant role in forming the Department of Research and Development.

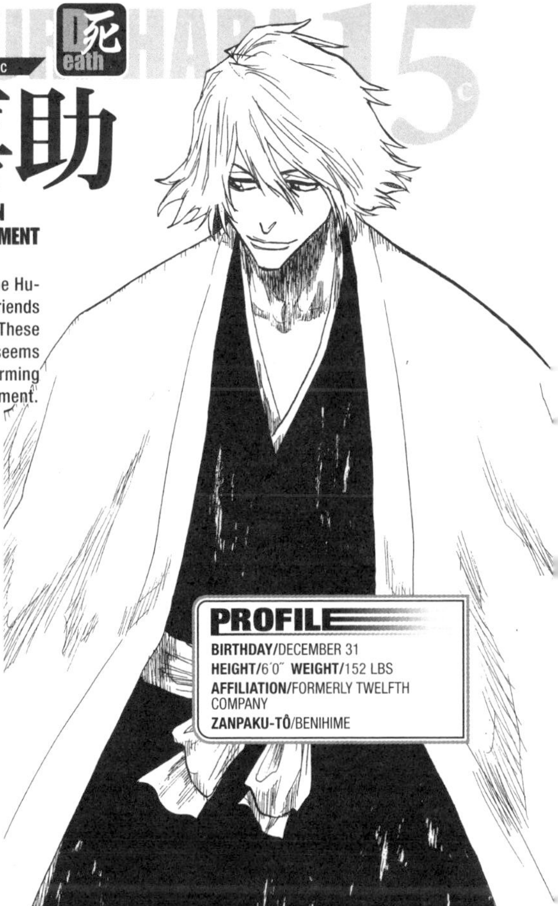

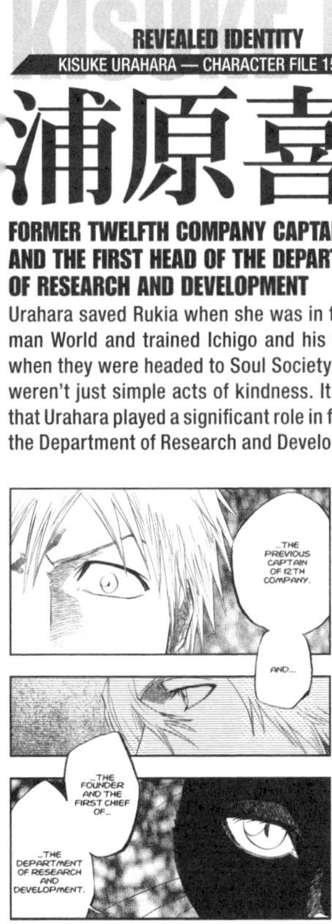
...THE PREVIOUS CAPTAIN OF 12TH COMPANY.
AND...
...THE FOUNDER AND THE FIRST CHIEF OF...
...THE DEPARTMENT OF RESEARCH AND DEVELOPMENT.

What kinds of secrets are in Urahara's past...?!

PROFILE

BIRTHDAY/DECEMBER 31
HEIGHT/6′0″ **WEIGHT**/152 LBS
AFFILIATION/FORMERLY TWELFTH COMPANY
ZANPAKU-TÔ/BENIHIME

決起

RISE TO ACTIO

Soul Society Goes into Actio
VOL. 15-127

Renji, Hinamori, and Izuru, who have been detained as traitors, go into action. Their desires intertwine, and further increase the disorder in conflict-ridden Soul Society...

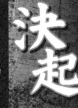

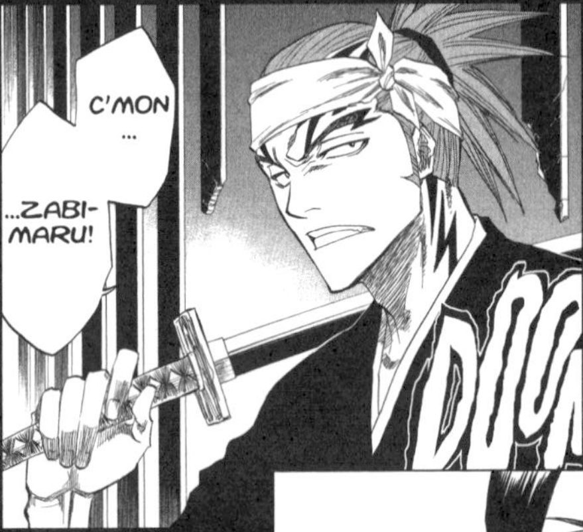
C'MON
...
...ZABI-MARU!

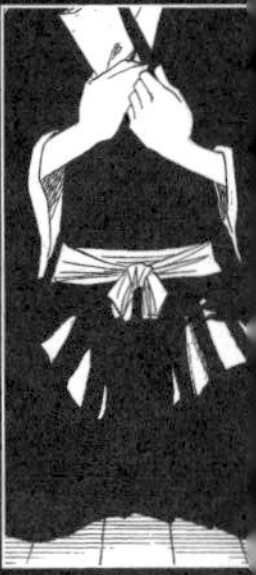

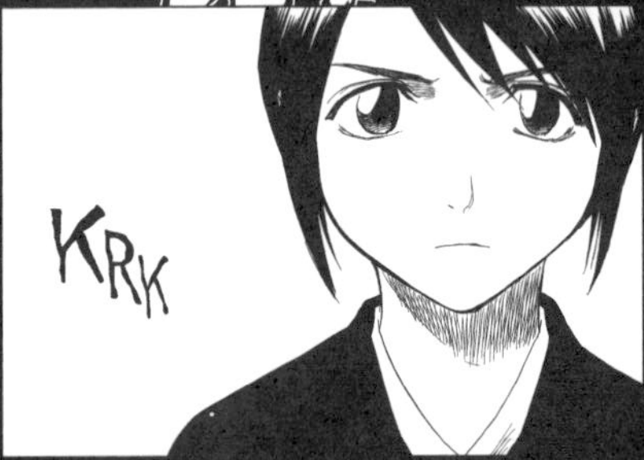
KRK

THEIR DESIRES

Renji and Hinamori go beyond their roles and status and stand up for what they believe in. Renji wants to save Rukia, and Hinamori wants to confirm the things that the late Captain Aizen uncovered...

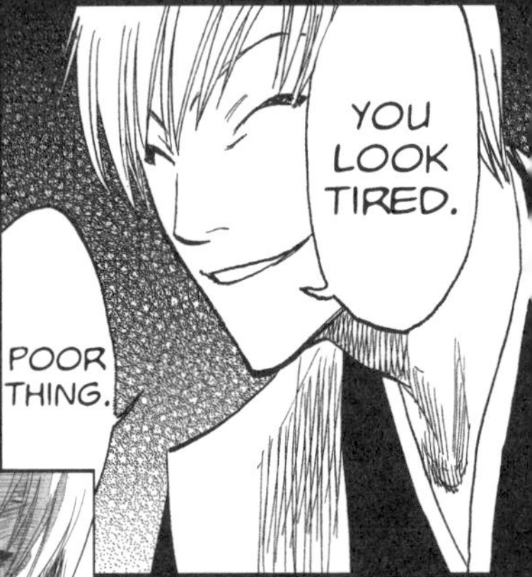
YOU LOOK TIRED.
POOR THING.

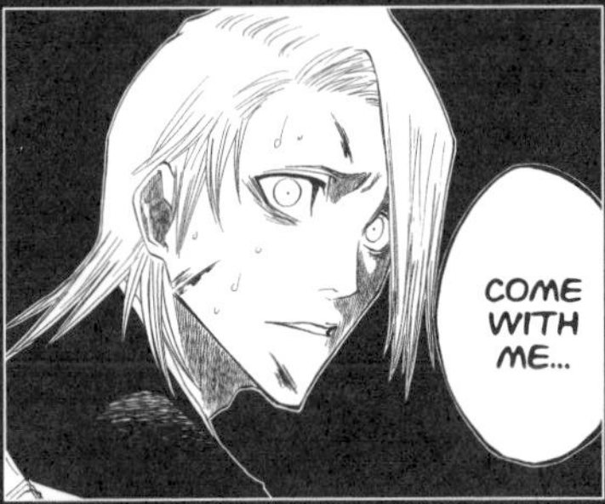
COME WITH ME...

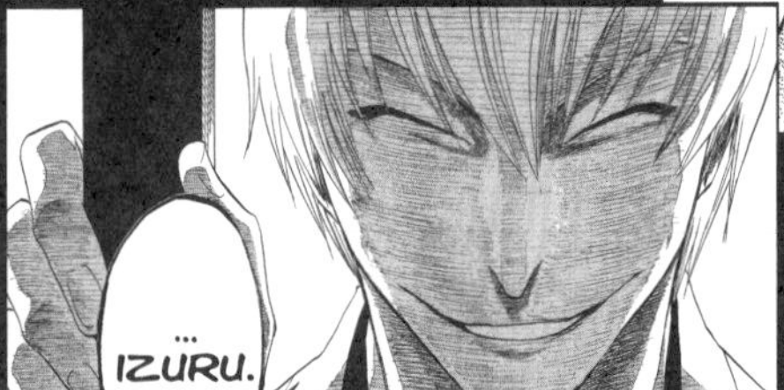
... IZURU.

ICHIMARU'S MANEUVERS

Izuru is imprisoned for striking back at Momo when she lost herself after Aizen's death. Izuru's superior, Third Company Captain Gin Ichimaru, suddenly asks Izuru to go somewhere with him. Is his smile good or evil? What is Ichimaru's true intent?

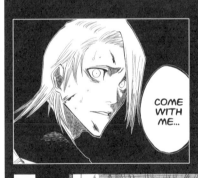

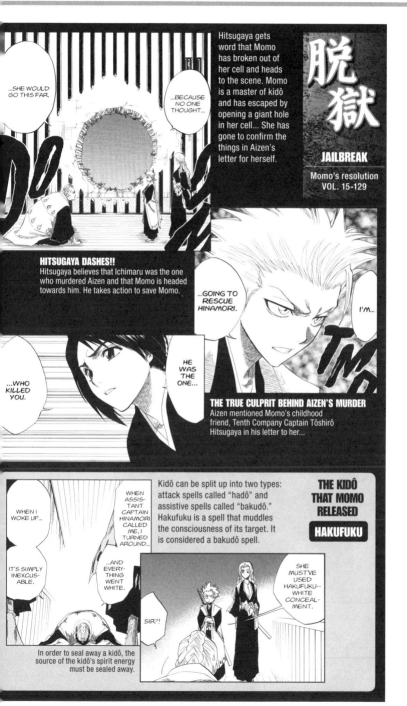

脱獄

JAILBREAK

Momo's resolution
VOL. 15-129

Hitsugaya gets word that Momo has broken out of her cell and heads to the scene. Momo is a master of kidô and has escaped by opening a giant hole in her cell... She has gone to confirm the things in Aizen's letter for herself.

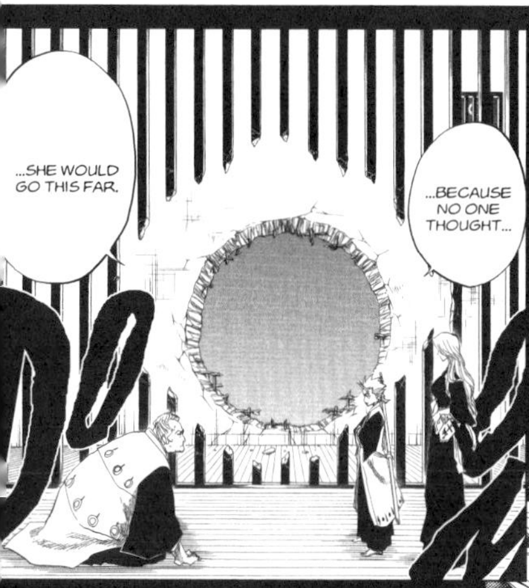
...BECAUSE NO ONE THOUGHT...
...SHE WOULD GO THIS FAR.

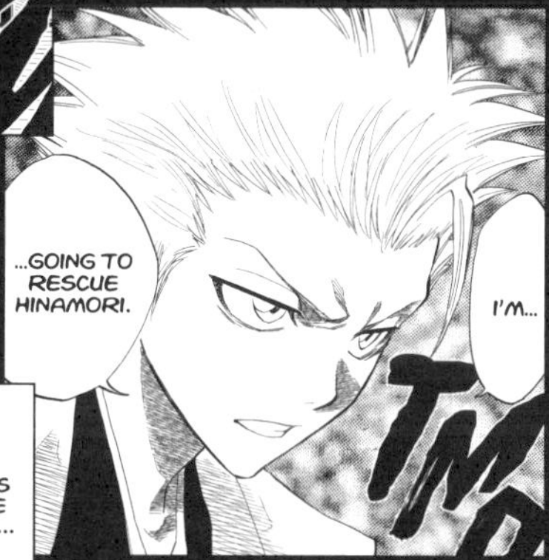
I'M...
...GOING TO RESCUE HINAMORI.

HITSUGAYA DASHES!!
Hitsugaya believes that Ichimaru was the one who murdered Aizen and that Momo is headed towards him. He takes action to save Momo.

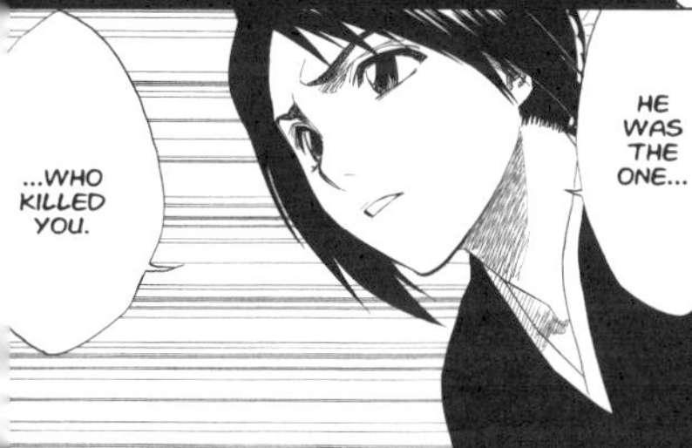
HE WAS THE ONE...
...WHO KILLED YOU.

THE TRUE CULPRIT BEHIND AIZEN'S MURDER
Aizen mentioned Momo's childhood friend, Tenth Company Captain Tôshirô Hitsugaya in his letter to her...

THE KIDÔ THAT MOMO RELEASED

HAKUFUKU

Kidô can be split up into two types: attack spells called "hadô" and assistive spells called "bakudô." Hakufuku is a spell that muddles the consciousness of its target. It is considered a bakudô spell.

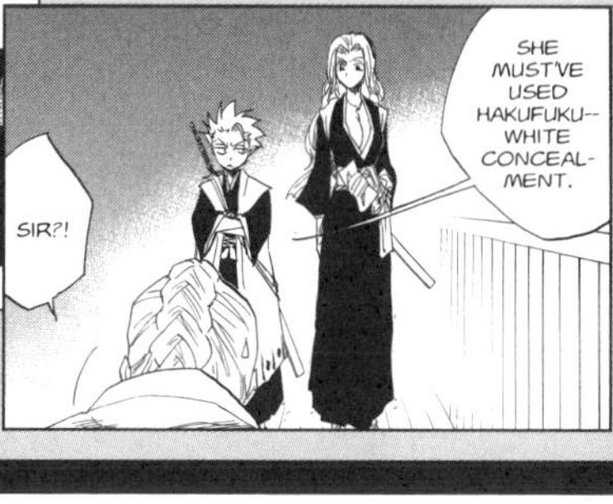
SHE MUST'VE USED HAKUFUKU--WHITE CONCEALMENT.
SIR?!

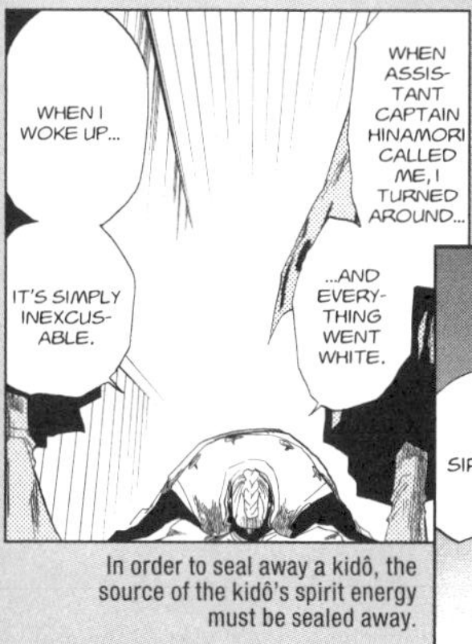
WHEN ASSISTANT CAPTAIN HINAMORI CALLED ME, I TURNED AROUND...
WHEN I WOKE UP...
...AND EVERYTHING WENT WHITE.
IT'S SIMPLY INEXCUSABLE.

In order to seal away a kidô, the source of the kidô's spirit energy must be sealed away.

THE YOUNGEST CAPTAIN OF THE THIRTEEN COURT GUARD COMPANIES

Death 死

TÔSHIRÔ HITSUGAYA — CHARACTER FILE 62-c

日番谷冬獅郎

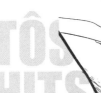

"I'M GOING TO KILL YOU BEFORE SHE GETS HERE."
Hitsugaya discovers Ichimaru and Izuru before Momo does. Determined to finish Ichimaru off before Momo arrives, he reaches for his sword. But before he can, a grimly determined Hinamori blocks his way with her zanpaku-tô.

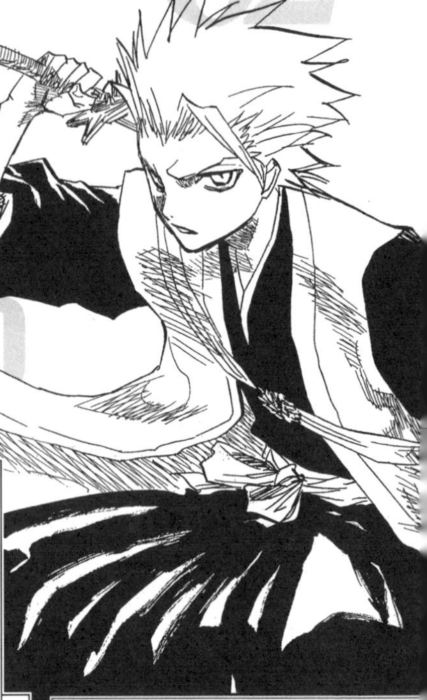

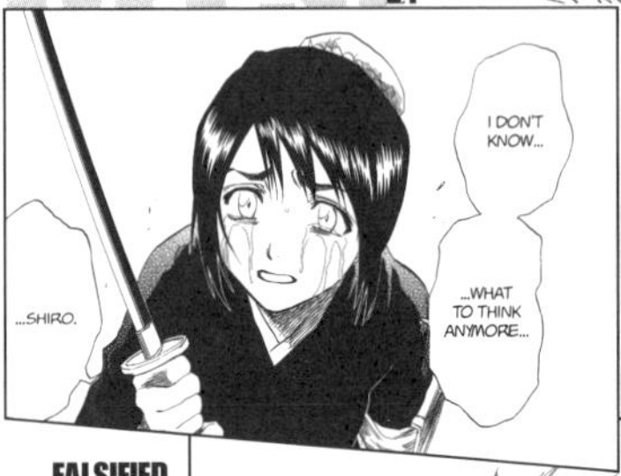
I DON'T KNOW...
...WHAT TO THINK ANYMORE...
...SHIRO.

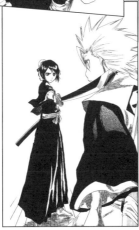

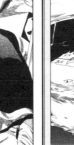

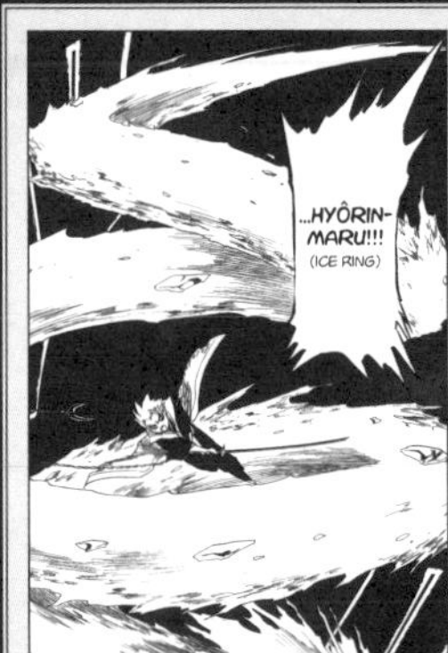
...HYÔRINMARU!!!
(ICE RING)

ZANPAKU-TÔ
HYÔRINMARU
The strongest ice-type zanpaku-tô. It has the ability to create an enormous dragon out of water and snow, and can even control the weather.

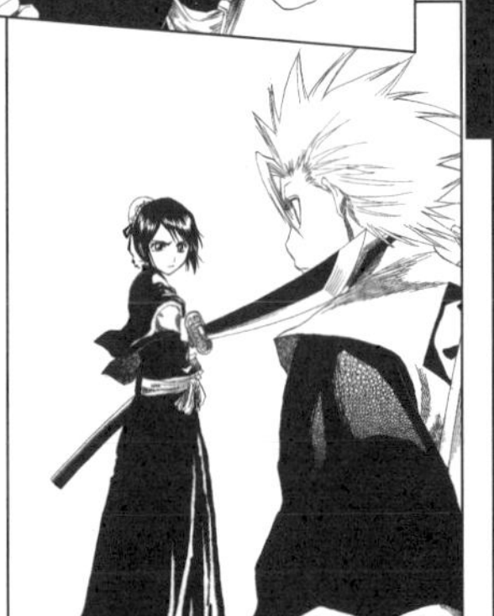

FALSIFIED LETTER
Aizen wrote in his letter, "...if I die, Hinamori, please carry on for me and kill him."

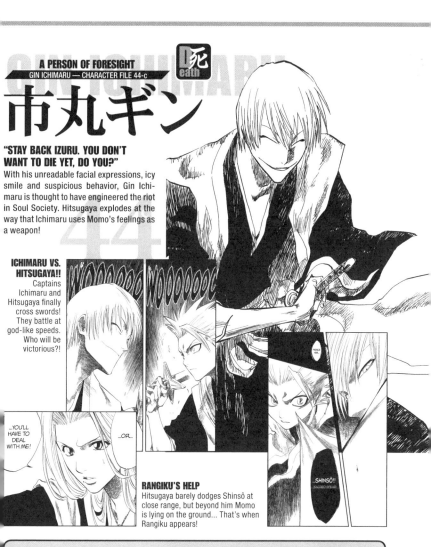

A PERSON OF FORESIGHT

GIN ICHIMARU — CHARACTER FILE 44-c

Death 死

市丸ギン

GIN ICHIMARU

44c

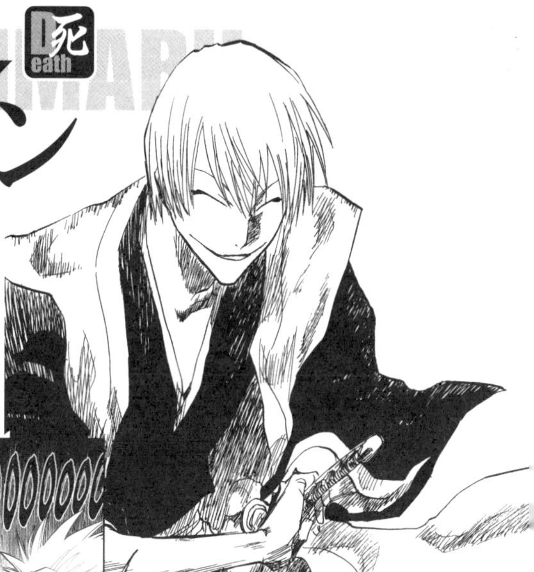

"STAY BACK IZURU. YOU DON'T WANT TO DIE YET, DO YOU?"

With his unreadable facial expressions, icy smile and suspicious behavior, Gin Ichimaru is thought to have engineered the riot in Soul Society. Hitsugaya explodes at the way that Ichimaru uses Momo's feelings as a weapon!

ICHIMARU VS. HITSUGAYA!!

Captains Ichimaru and Hitsugaya finally cross swords! They battle at god-like speeds. Who will be victorious?!

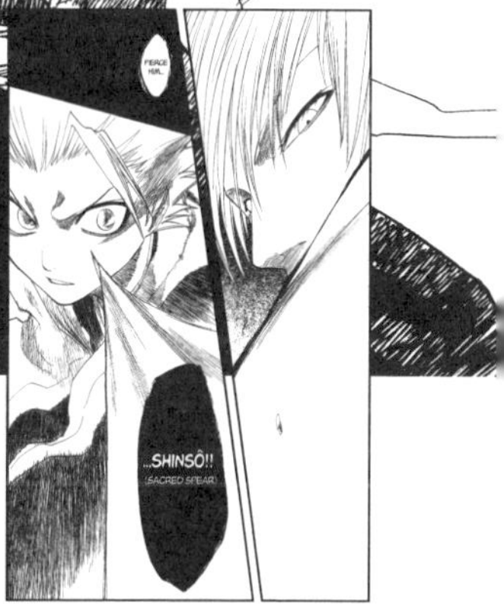
PIERCE HIM...
...SHINSÔ!!
(SACRED SPEAR)

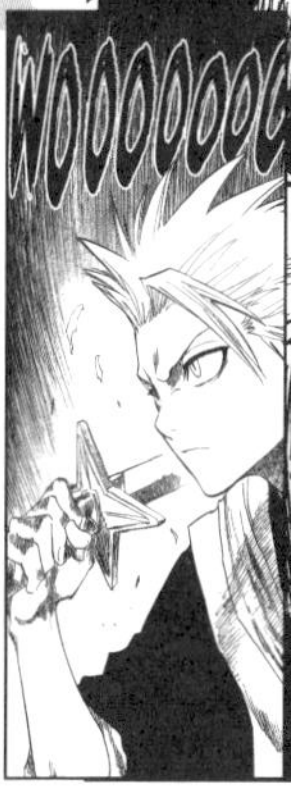
WOOOOOO

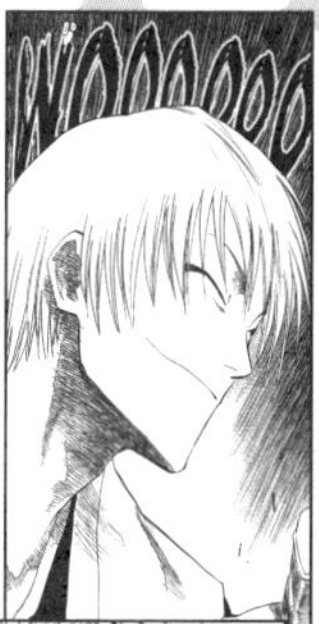
WOOOOOO

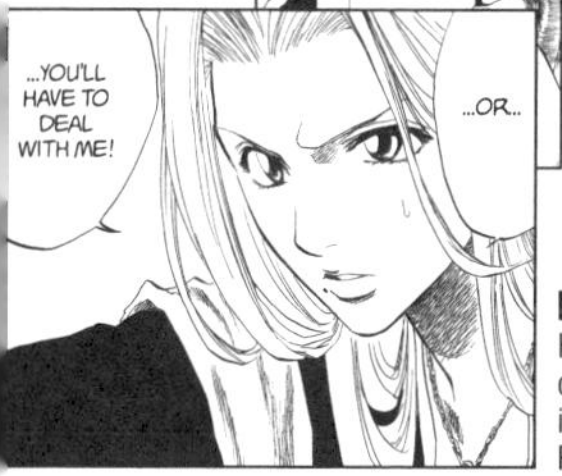
...OR...
...YOU'LL HAVE TO DEAL WITH ME!

RANGIKU'S HELP

Hitsugaya barely dodges Shinsô at close range, but beyond him Momo is lying on the ground... That's when Rangiku appears!

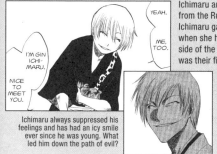

UNSPOKEN RELATIONSHIP

ICHIMARU AND RANGIKU

Ichimaru and Rangiku are both from the Rukongai. As a boy, Ichimaru gave food to Rangiku when she had collapsed on the side of the road from hunger. That was their first meeting. They've been together ever since, but Ichimaru often disappears without explanation.

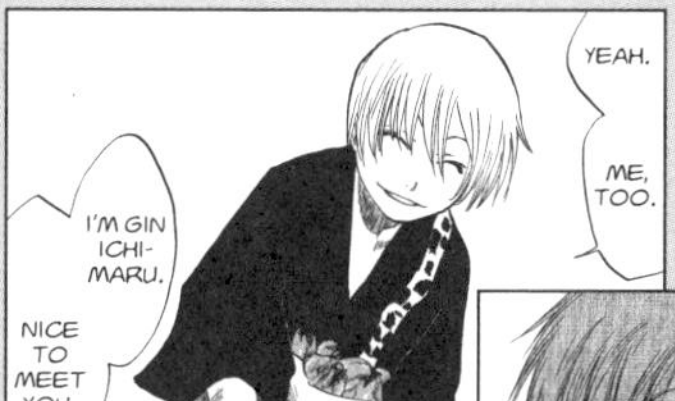
YEAH.
ME, TOO.
I'M GIN ICHIMARU.
NICE TO MEET YOU.

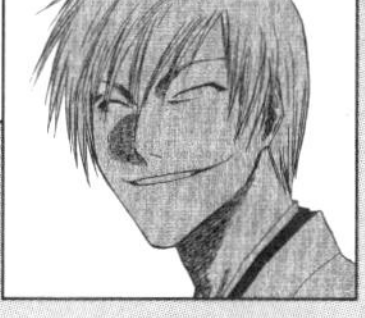

Ichimaru always suppressed his feelings and has had an icy smile ever since he was young. What led him down the path of evil?

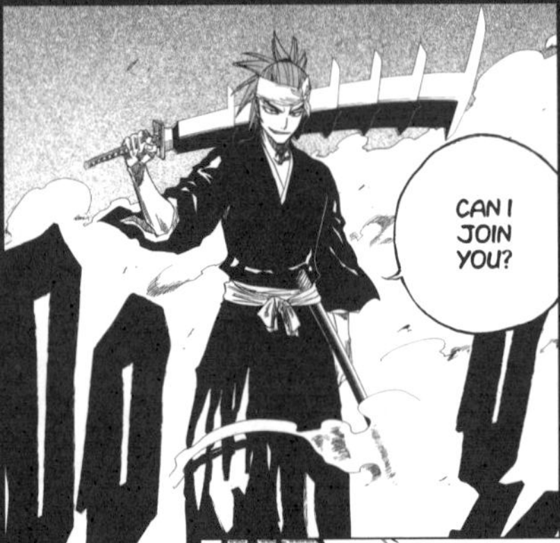
CAN I JOIN YOU?

The date of Rukia's execution is suddenly advanced. Renji heads to the place where Ichigo is training for bankai to save Rukia. Ichigo strives even harder to learn the bankai when he learns that the execution has been accelerated.

変更

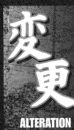

ALTERATION

Execution date advanced
VOL. 16-133

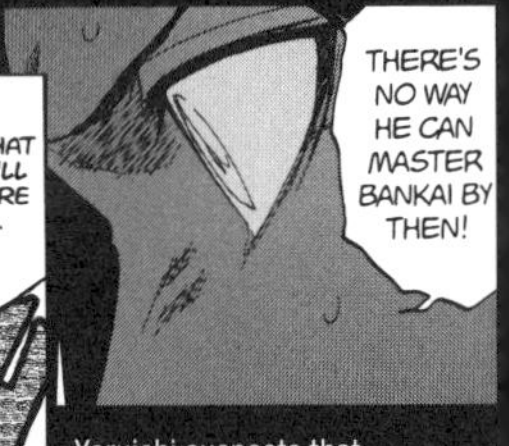
THERE'S NO WAY HE CAN MASTER BANKAI BY THEN!

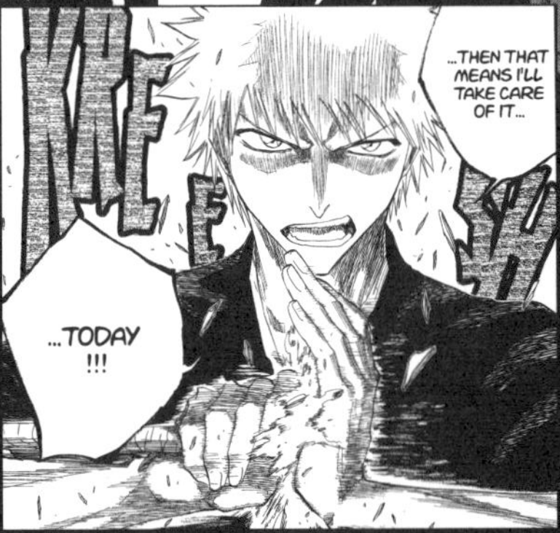
...THEN THAT MEANS I'LL TAKE CARE OF IT...
...TODAY !!!

UNWAVERING INSTINCT

On a hunch, Ichigo decides to try the bankai one more time. His gut tells him that it is the right thing to do.

Yoruichi suspects that Ichigo and Renji do not have enough time to train. Ichigo refuses to give up, though, and determinedly rises to the challenge!

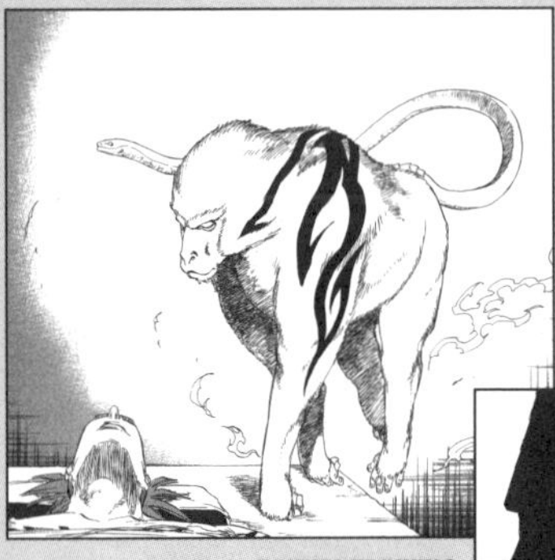

Renji's zanpaku-tô Zabimaru manifests in the form of a Nue demon. Its monkey head and snake tail have their own personalities and make demands upon Renji. They always voice their opinions to him, and they ardently desire a rematch with Zangetsu to whom Zabimaru lost a match.

RENJI'S ZANPAKU-TÔ

ZABIMARU

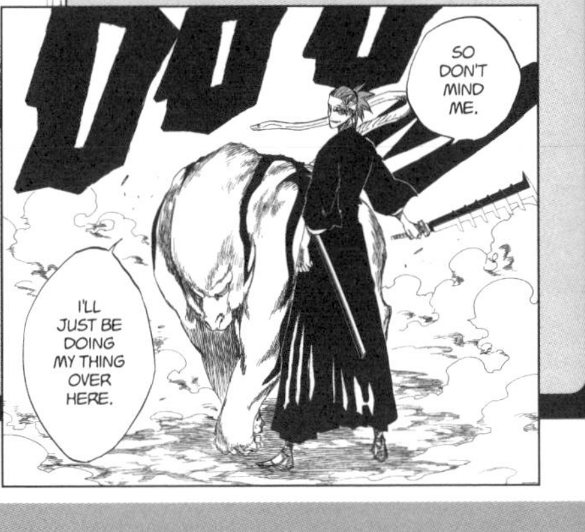
SO DON'T MIND ME.
I'LL JUST BE DOING MY THING OVER HERE.

BANKAI TRAINING

Renji, like Ichigo, also wants his bankai to get stronger. He wants to surpass that of Byakuya, the infinitely high barrier that stands before him, and to save Rukia. Renji's training begins.

THE DEATH ROW INMATE WHO IS INCARCERATED IN SENZAIKYÛ SHISHINRÔ

RUKIA KUCHIKI — CHARACTER FILES 2-b

朽木ルキア

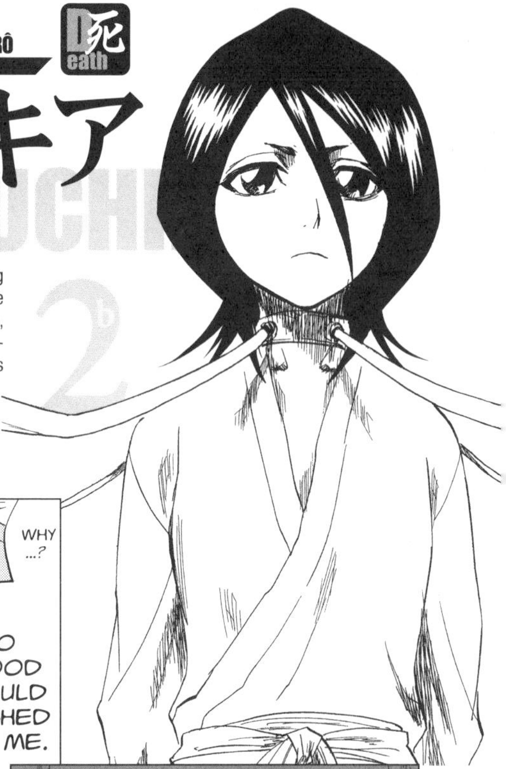

SELF-REPROACH AND REGRET

Rukia has committed a serious crime by transferring her Soul Reaper powers to Ichigo in order to save his family. While captive in the Senzaikyû Shishinrô, she thinks about the passing days and an unforgettable memory... Rukia quietly talks to herself. She is tormented by self-reproach.

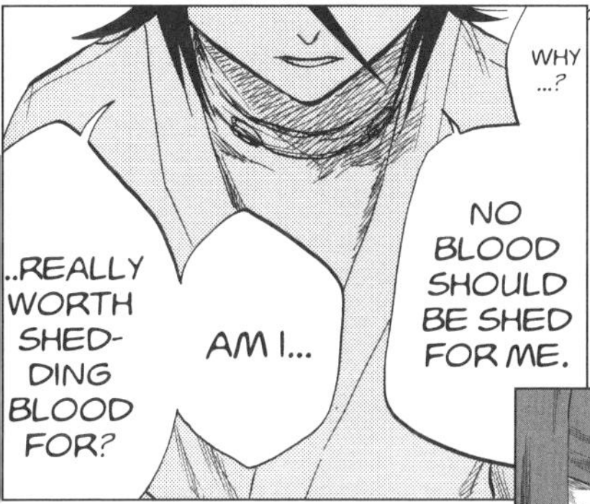
WHY ...?
NO BLOOD SHOULD BE SHED FOR ME.
AM I...
..REALLY WORTH SHED-DING BLOOD FOR?

Rukia feels responsible for the fact that people are getting hurt for her.

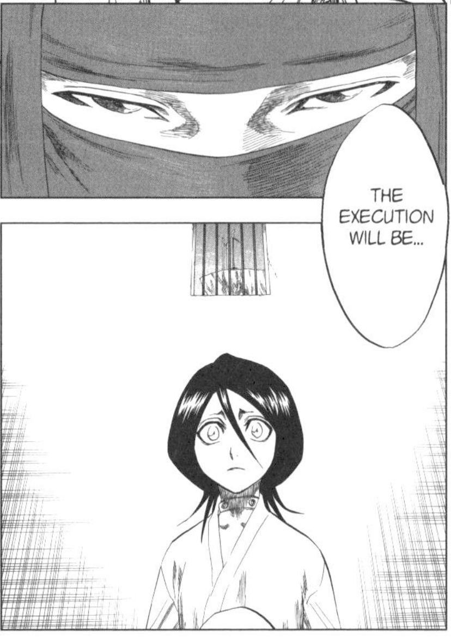
THE EXECUTION WILL BE...

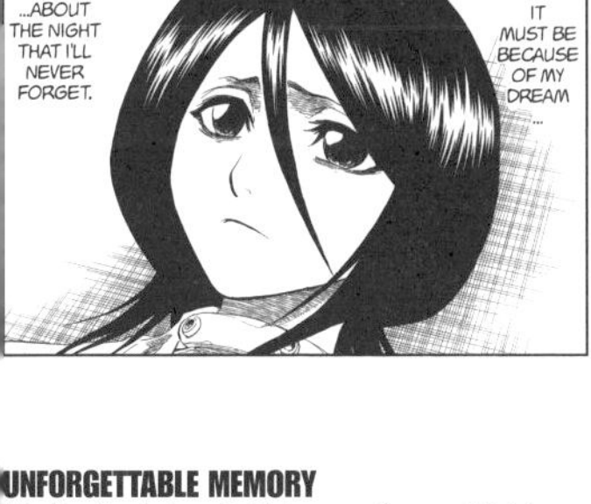
IT MUST BE BECAUSE OF MY DREAM ...
...ABOUT THE NIGHT THAT I'LL NEVER FORGET.

UNFORGETTABLE MEMORY

It is the day before Rukia's execution, and Rukia is lost in the depths of her memories. She has a dream of the rain that fell on that unforgettable day. Even now, that rain continues to fall coldly on Rukia.

雨

RAIN

Undying rain
VOL. 16-133

Rukia's memory of rain...It is a memory of long ago when she had just become a Soul Reaper and was assigned to the Thirteenth Company... Rukia repeatedly screams the name of the bleeding man she is embracing in the pouring rain...

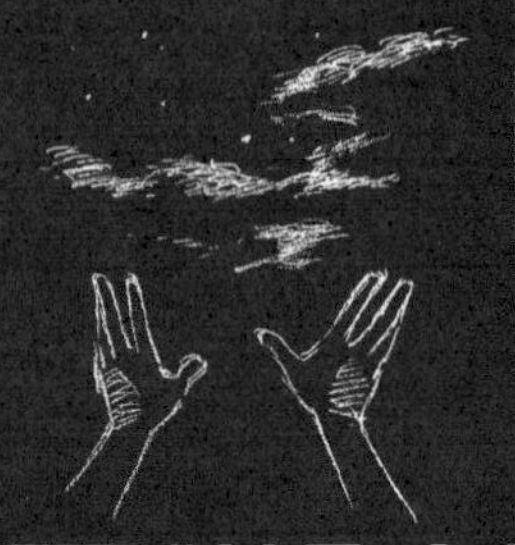

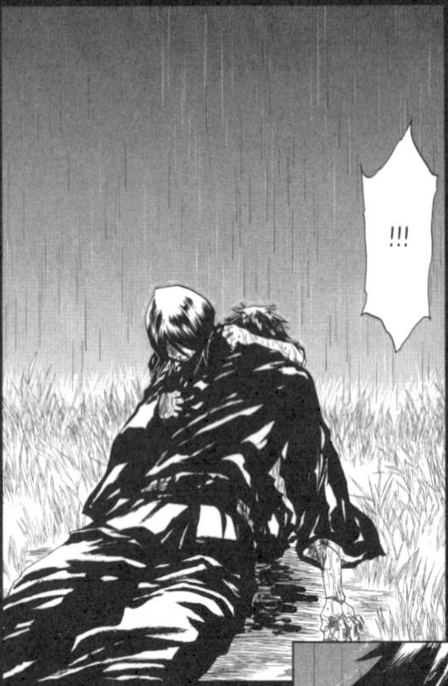
!!!

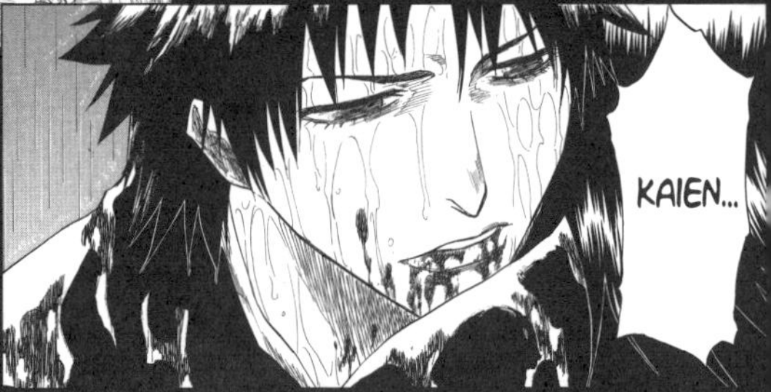
KAIEN...

MOURNING KAIEN
Rukia is embracing Kaien, the man who looks like Ichigo. Kaien is Rukia's superior and the man whose life Rukia ended. The memory of that day left a deep scar in Rukia's heart.

THE RAIN FALLING IN THEIR HEARTS

ICHIGO AND RUKIA

Cold rain was falling when Ichigo's mother Masaki died and when Rukia killed Kaien. It was as if the sky was crying in response to Ichigo and Rukia's sad hearts... Even now, it still rains in their hearts.

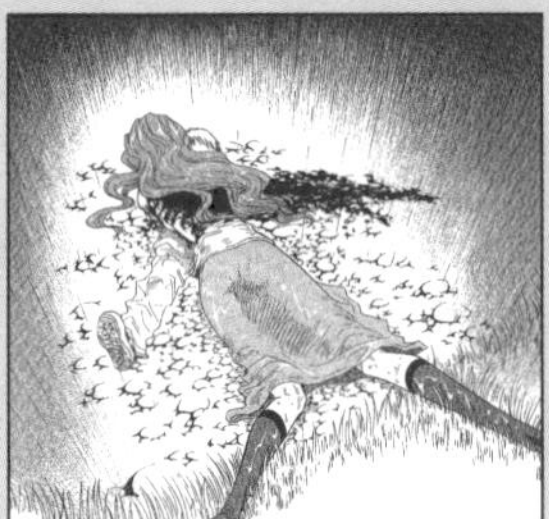

Masaki died when she risked her life to save young Ichigo from Grand Fisher.

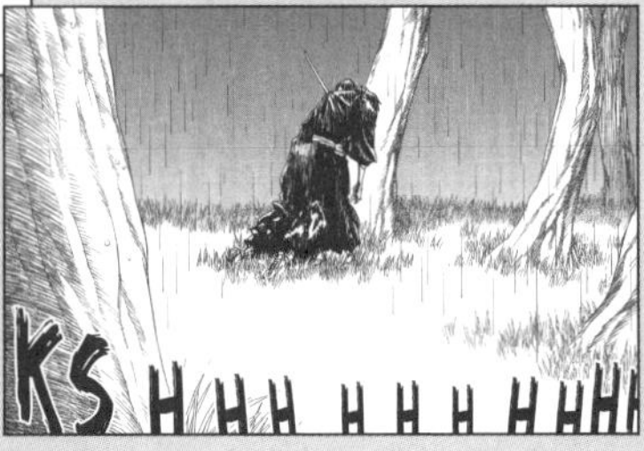
KSHHHHHHHHHH

ORIGINAL SIN AND ATONEMENT
Guilt has sunk deep into Ichigo and Rukia's hearts. Ichigo took his beloved mother from his family. Rukia took the life of her adored and respected mentor. Ichigo and Rukia live their lives atoning for their sins.

KAIEN SHIBA

THIRTEENTH COMPANY ASSISTANT CAPTAIN

KAIEN SHIBA — CHARACTER FILE 78-a

Death 死

志波海燕

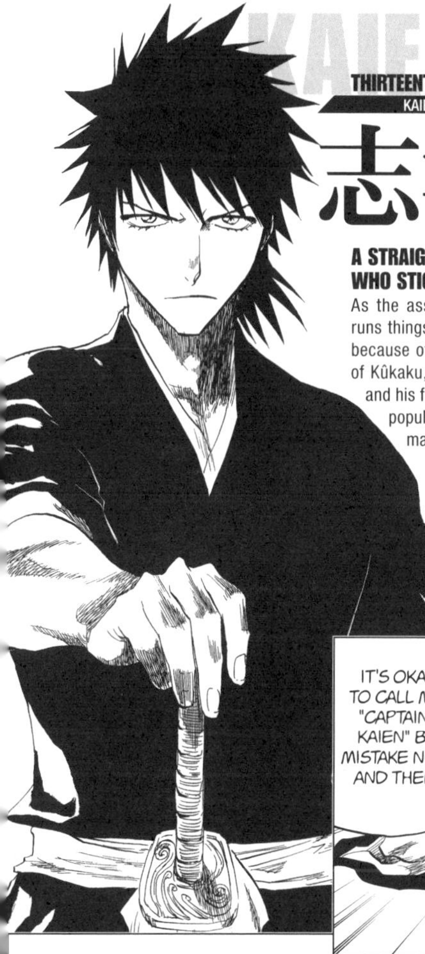

A STRAIGHTFORWARD MAN WHO STICKS TO HIS BELIEFS

As the assistant captain of Thirteenth Company, he runs things in Ukitake's stead, when Ukitake is absent because of his poor health. Kaien is the older brother of Kûkaku, the pyrotechnics expert who helped Ichigo and his friends break into Seireitei, and Ganju. He is a popular man who is very ethical and is adored by many company members.

PROFILE

BIRTHDAY/OCTOBER 27
HEIGHT/6′0″ **WEIGHT/**150 LBS
AFFILIATION/THIRTEENTH COMPANY
ZANPAKU-TÔ/NEJIBANA

OUR CAPTAIN'S IN POOR HEALTH...
...SO I BASICALLY RUN THE SHOW!
IT'S OKAY TO CALL ME "CAPTAIN KAIEN" BY MISTAKE NOW AND THEN.

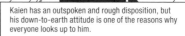

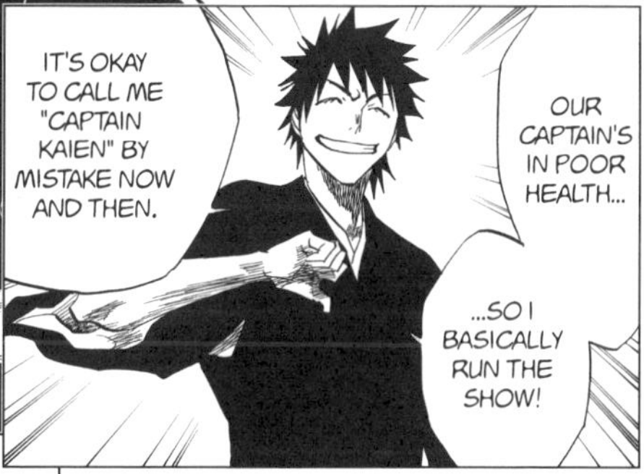

Kaien has an outspoken and rough disposition, but his down-to-earth attitude is one of the reasons why everyone looks up to him.

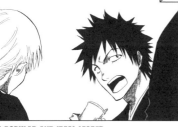

A POPULAR AND IDEAL LEADER

Kaien treats his fellow company members indiscriminately, regardless of their social standing and rank. His fair attitude is popular among both aristocrats and commoners in the company.

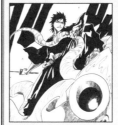

ZANPAKU-TÔ

NEJIBANA

Its true form has not made an appearance, but it changes into a three-pronged pike when it goes into shikai.

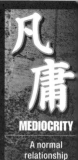

凡庸

MEDIOCRITY

A normal relationship
VOL. 16-134

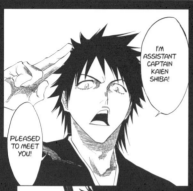

I'M ASSISTANT CAPTAIN KAIEN SHIBA!
PLEASED TO MEET YOU!

Things changed drastically for Rukia when she was adopted into the Kuchiki family. No one would treat her normally. When she joined the Thirteen Court Guard Companies and was assigned to Thirteenth Company, Kaien was the only one who treated her like everyone else.

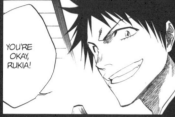

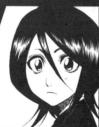

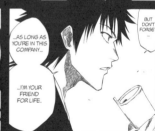

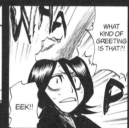

WHAT KIND OF GREETING IS THAT?!
EEK!!
GOOD!
YOU'RE OKAY, RUKIA!

WHAT RUKIA WANTED
Since Rukia was from the Rukongai, being treated with deference was painful to her. Kaien's attitude was refreshing.

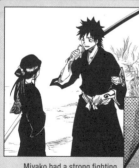

BUT DON'T FORGET...
...AS LONG AS YOU'RE IN THIS COMPANY...
...I'M YOUR FRIEND FOR LIFE.

THE PERSON RUKIA ADORED

MIYAKO SHIBA

Kaien's wife Miyako was a heroic woman who rose to the ranks of third seat despite her gender. She was wise and kind, and a perfect Soul Reaper and woman. Rukia idolized her.

SHE WAS...
...MY IDOL.

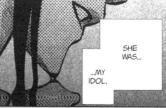

Miyako had a strong fighting power and a lot of combat experience. She often took dangerous missions on the front lines.

Thirteenth Company receives word that the reconnaissance team sent to gather information in order to subdue a new Hollow has been annihilated. It was the team that Kaien's wife Miyako was leading. Kaien, upon hearing this...

兇変

CALAMITY

A sudden loss
VOL. 16-134~135

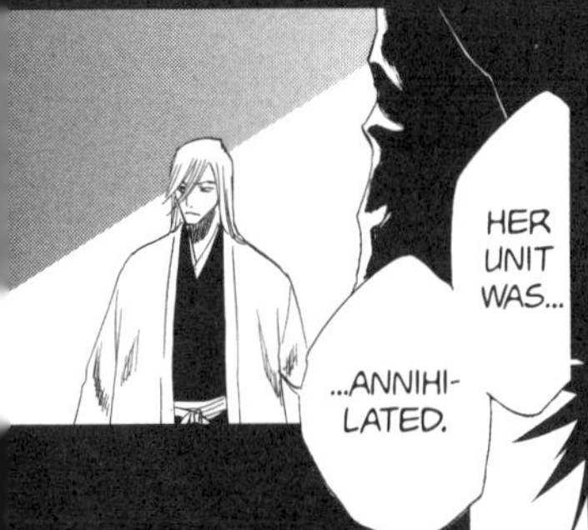
HER UNIT WAS...
...ANNIHI-LATED.

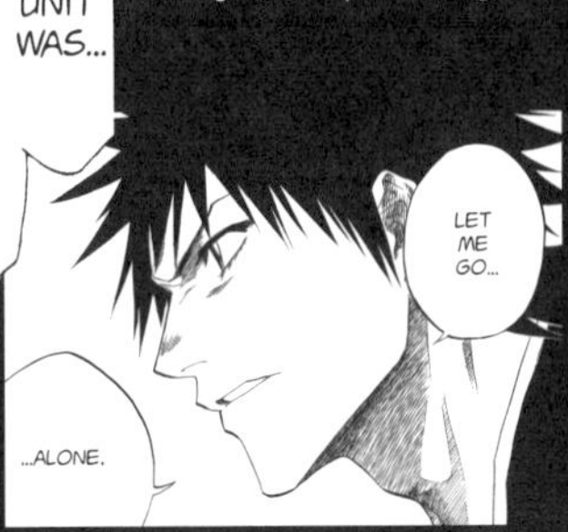
LET ME GO...
...ALONE.

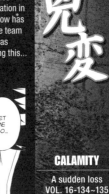

A BATTLE OF VENGEANCE
Kaien is furious that his wife has been killed and asks to join the assault team. Knowing Kaien's motives, Thirteenth Company Captain Ukitake tells Kaien where he can find the Hollow.

A NEST-BUILDING PARASITIC HOLLOW

PARASITIC HOLLOW — CHARACTER FILE 79

H虚ollow

寄生型虚

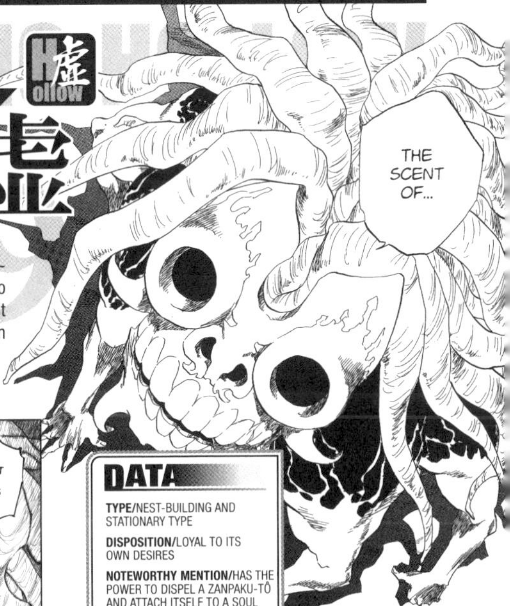
THE SCENT OF...

A WICKED MONSTER

This Hollow has the unusual ability to fuse its spiritual body to that of its victim, thus enabling it to control the victim's physical body. Likely as a result of this ability, it can build its nest in a set location and feed on passing Soul Reapers.

Once a night, this Hollow can activate its special ability to dissolve any zanpaku-tô it touches!

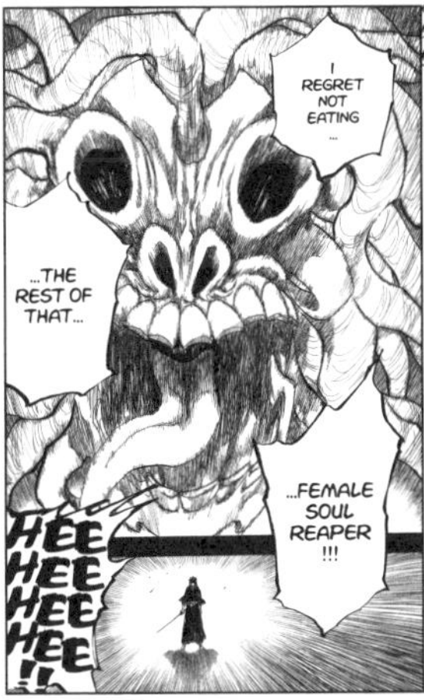
I REGRET NOT EATING...
...THE REST OF THAT...
...FEMALE SOUL REAPER!!!
HEE HEE HEE HEE!!

DATA

TYPE/NEST-BUILDING AND STATIONARY TYPE

DISPOSITION/LOYAL TO ITS OWN DESIRES

NOTEWORTHY MENTION/HAS THE POWER TO DISPEL A ZANPAKU-TÔ AND ATTACH ITSELF TO A SOUL

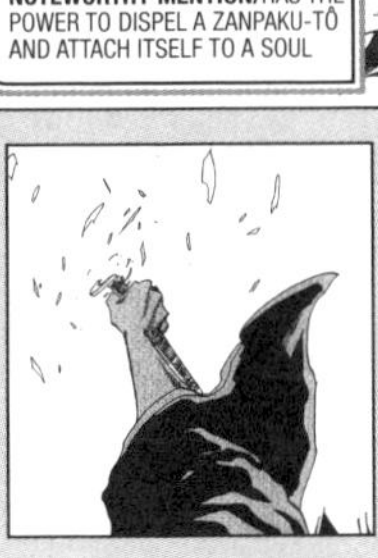

ZANPAKU-TÔ DISSOLVES
"I regret not eating the rest of that female Soul Reaper!" the Hollow roars. He talks of his previous night's activities to goad Kaien.

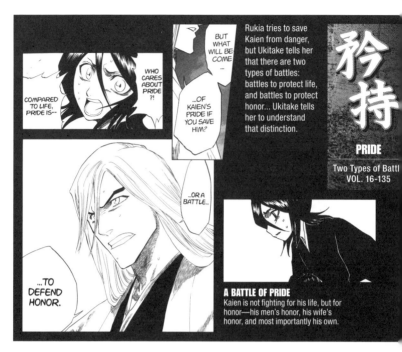

矜持
PRIDE

Two Types of Battl
VOL. 16-135

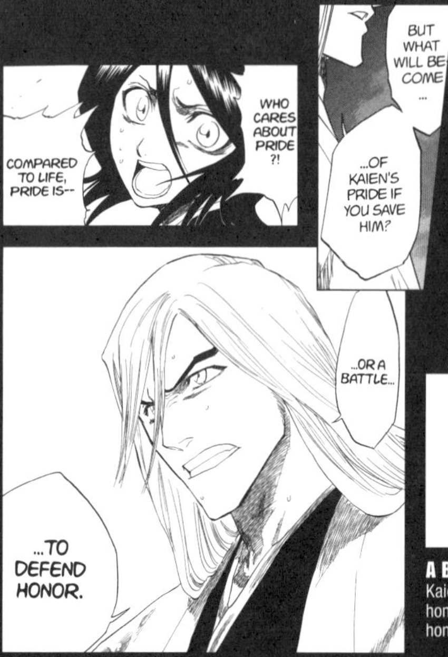
BUT WHAT WILL BECOME ...
...OF KAIEN'S PRIDE IF YOU SAVE HIM?
WHO CARES ABOUT PRIDE ?!
COMPARED TO LIFE, PRIDE IS--
...OR A BATTLE...
...TO DEFEND HONOR.

Rukia tries to save Kaien from danger, but Ukitake tells her that there are two types of battles: battles to protect life, and battles to protect honor... Ukitake tells her to understand that distinction.

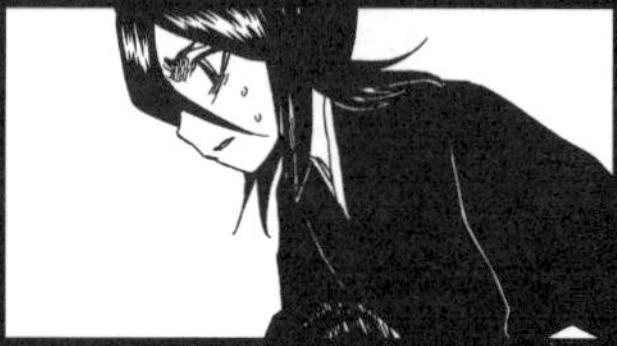

A BATTLE OF PRIDE
Kaien is not fighting for his life, but for honor—his men's honor, his wife's honor, and most importantly his own.

KAIEN SHIBA

PARASITIC FORM
KAIEN SHIBA — CHARACTER FILE 78-b

虚 Hollow

志波海燕

78

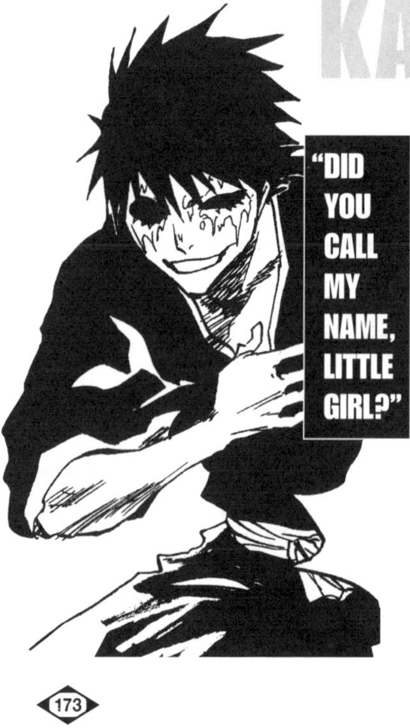

"DID YOU CALL MY NAME, LITTLE GIRL?"

KAIEN'S HIJACKED BODY

Kaien's body is wrested from him when the Hollow enters his spiritual body and soul. His body keeps its original form, but everything else about it is controlled by the Hollow. Rukia is in a panic and Ukitake orders her to retreat.

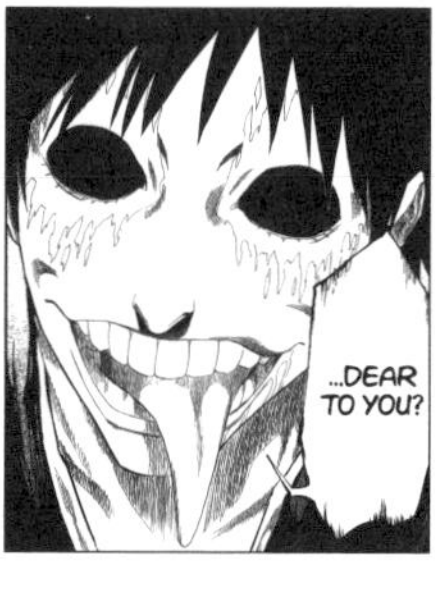
...DEAR TO YOU?

Kaien turns towards Rukia's screams... He is no longer the Kaien that Rukia knew.

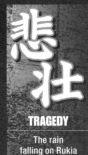

悲壮

TRAGEDY

The rain falling on Rukia
VOL. 16-136

Ukitake tries to think of a way to save Kaien, but it is not possible to split two fused spiritual bodies. Kaien can only be saved if he is killed along with the Hollow. Ukitake gives Rukia the order to kill Kaien, who is coming after her...

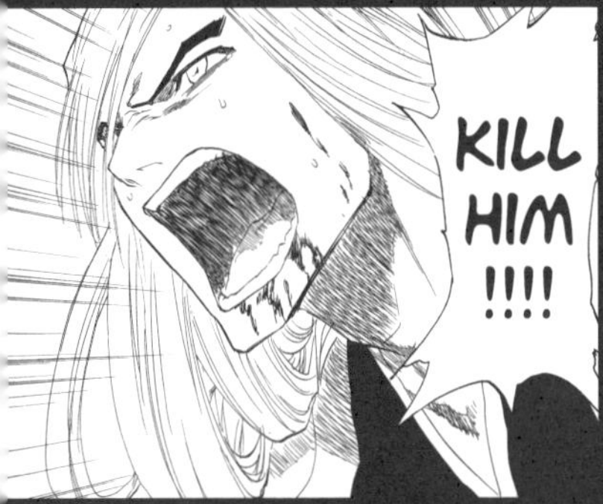
KILL HIM !!!!

Rukia stabs Kaien through the chest to save him. Kaien's blood falls on her along with the cold rain...

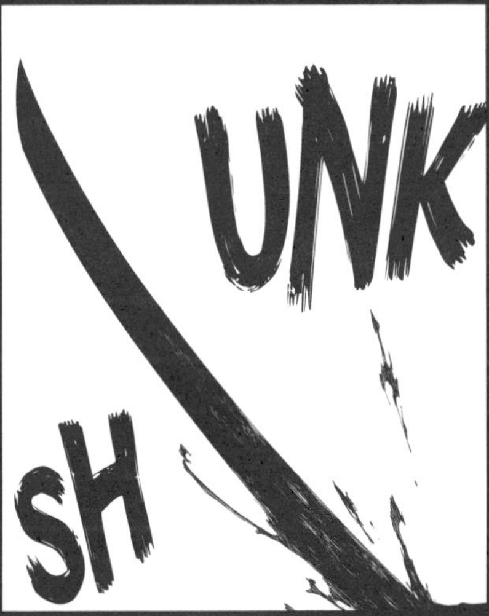
SH
UNK

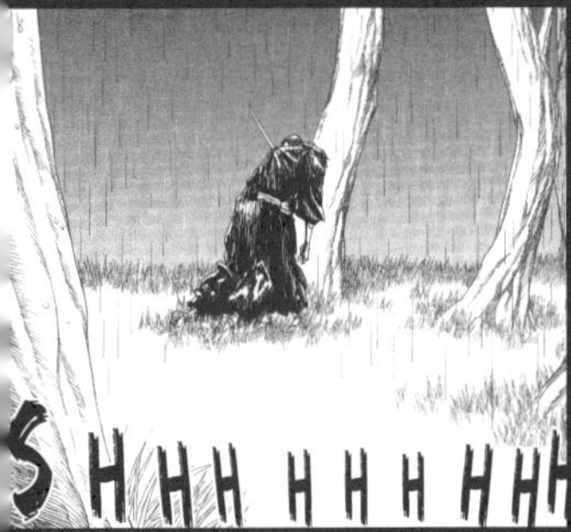
SHHHHHHHHH

Just before he dies, Kaien regains consciousness. As he fades, Kaien gives Rukia a heartfelt apology and his thanks.

"THANK YOU. NOW I CAN LEAVE MY HEART BEHIND."

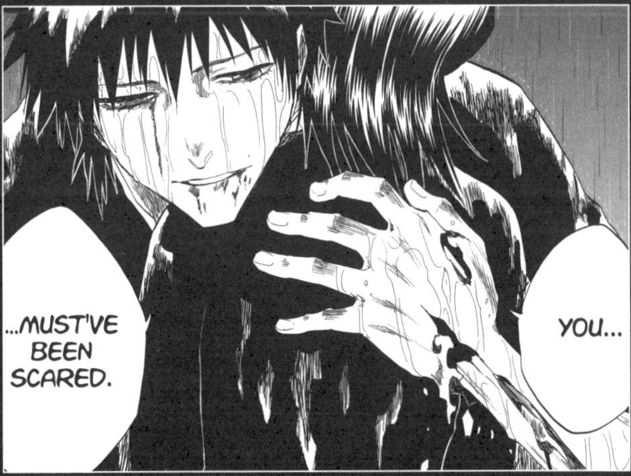
YOU...
...MUST'VE BEEN SCARED.

苛責

NERVE-RACKIN RESPONSIBILIT

Rukia's sin
VOL. 16-136

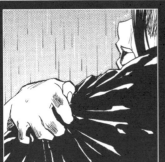

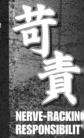

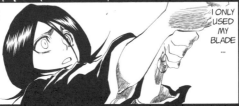

Rukia is bewildered by Kaien's thanks. She ran away because she was afraid to fight Kaien. She came back because she couldn't stand her own cowardice. And she killed Kaien because she couldn't bear to see him suffer... Rukia is full of self-reproach because everything she did was for herself.

I ONLY USED MY BLADE ...
...BECAUSE I COULDN'T BEAR TO SEE YOU SUFFER.

I DID IT ALL FOR...
...MYSELF.

"PATHETIC... I'M NOT WORTH SAVING..."

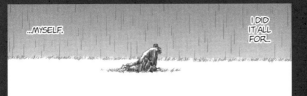

THE UNTOLD TRUTH

FEUD WITH THE SHIBA FAMILY

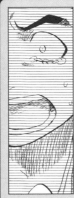

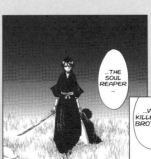

Ganju Shiba hates Soul Reapers because a Soul Reaper killed his older brother Kaien. But another bitter event occurs after Kaien's death. Rukia delivers Kaien's body to the Shiba family without revealing what happened. It is as if she is inflicting punishment upon herself...

No matter how much time passes, Rukia cannot forget Kaien. His memory makes her suffer.

The face of the bloody Soul Reaper Ganju saw when he was young... That hate-filled memory of the Soul Reapers remains with Ganju even now.

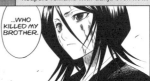

...WHO KILLED MY BROTHER.
...THE SOUL REAPER ...

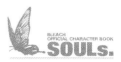

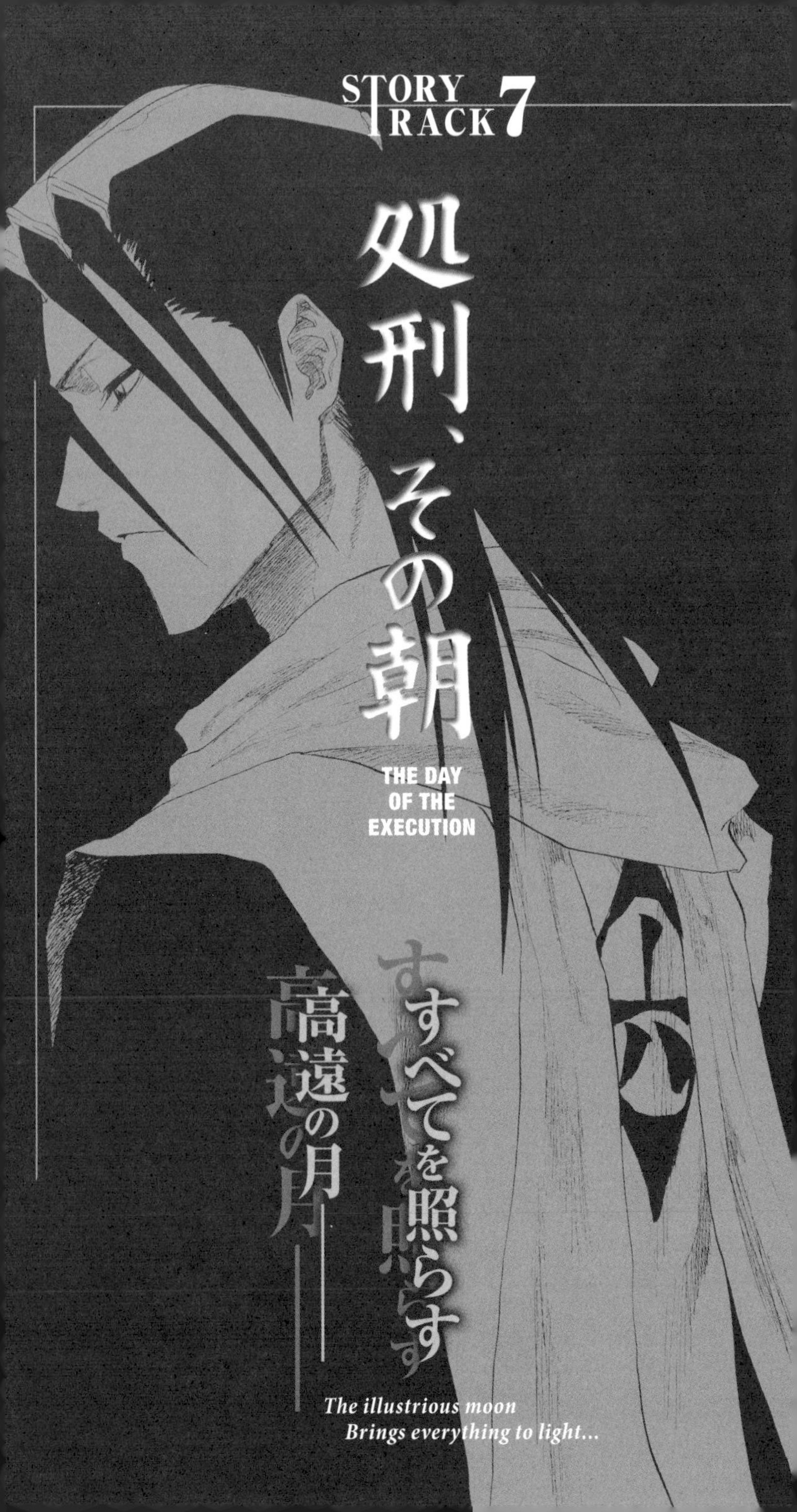
STORY TRACK 7
処刑、その朝
THE DAY OF THE EXECUTION
すべてを照らす
高遠の月——
The illustrious moon
Brings everything to light...

再起

RECOVERY

Kenpachi Zaraki makes his move VOL. 15-128~ VOL.16-137

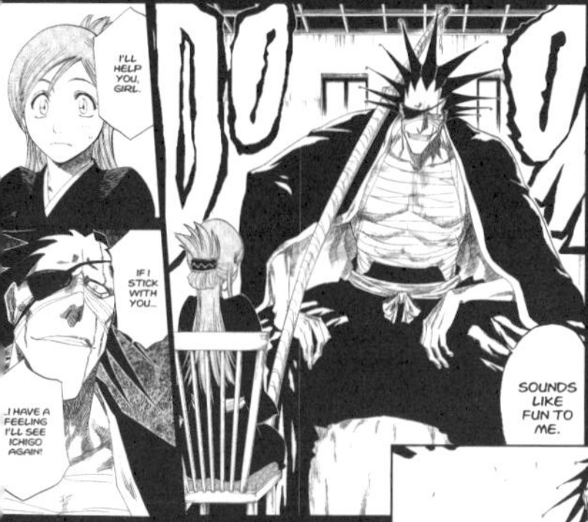
DO
OM
SOUNDS LIKE FUN TO ME.
IF I STICK WITH YOU...
...I HAVE A FEELING I'LL SEE ICHIGO AGAIN!
I'LL HELP YOU, GIRL.

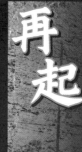

Yachiru picks up Orihime, who was running away with Aramaki, and together they meet Kenpachi. Kenpachi figures if he is with one of the ryoka, he can fight Ichigo again... It is the only reason why Kenpachi helps Orihime search the Seireitei for Ichigo.

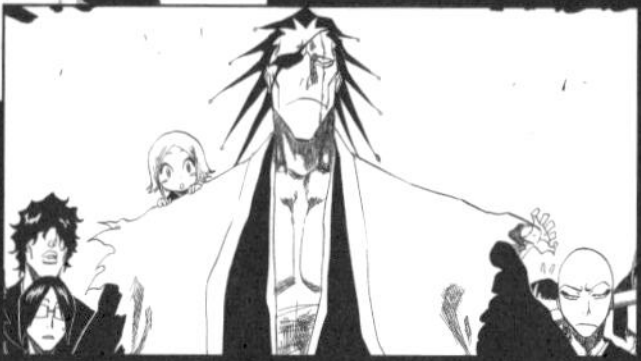

HE ZARAKI COMPANY'S NITED EFFORTS!

/hile searching for Ichigo, Kenpachi ıanages to get Chad, Uryû, and Ganju ut of prison, and persuades them to ork with him.

THE THIRTEEN COURT GUARD COMPANY'S NUMBER ONE FIGHTING TEAM

THE ZARAKI COMPANY

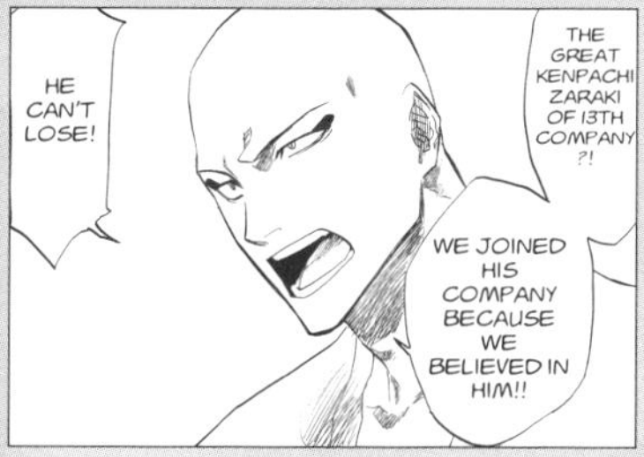
THE GREAT KENPACHI ZARAKI OF 13TH COMPANY ?!
WE JOINED HIS COMPANY BECAUSE WE BELIEVED IN HIM!!
HE CAN'T LOSE!

The Eleventh Company members always call themselves the "Zaraki Company." Nobody outside of the company calls them that. That is how unique Kenpachi Zaraki is.

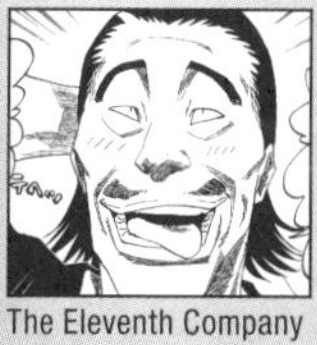

The Eleventh Company member with a mustache. His nickname is Maki-maki.

MAKIZO ARAMAKI

It could be because they are primarily a combat company, but the Soul Reapers of Zaraki Company are fundamentally of poor character. Moreover, they don't get along with the Fourth Company.

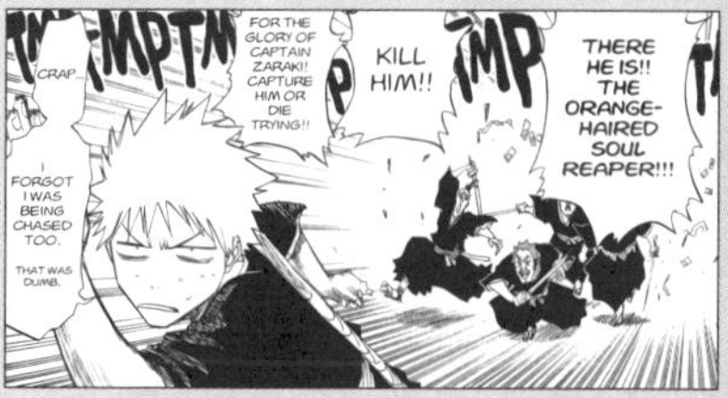
THERE HE IS!! THE ORANGE-HAIRED SOUL REAPER!!!
TMP
KILL HIM!!
FOR THE GLORY OF CAPTAIN ZARAKI! CAPTURE HIM OR DIE TRYING!!
MPTM
CRAP...
I FORGOT I WAS BEING CHASED TOO.
THAT WAS DUMB.

射場鉄左衛門

TETSUZAEMON IBA — 57-b

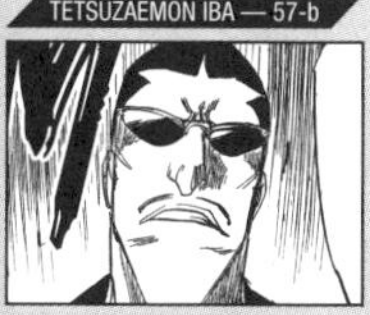

He is currently Seventh Company's assistant captain. He was Ikkaku's senior.

阿散井恋次

RENJI ABARAI — 38-d

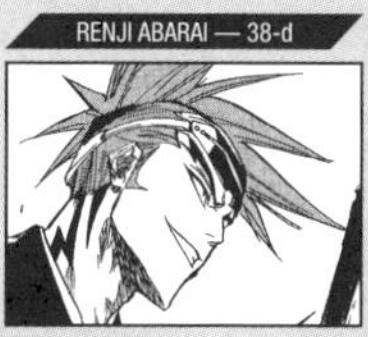

He is currently Sixth Company's assistant captain. He taught Ikkaku how to fight.

FORMER ZARAKI COMPANY MEMBERS

Renji Abarai and Tetsuzaemon Iba were formerly assigned to Zaraki Company. Currently, they hold the rank of assistant captains in other squads. Even though they've moved on to different squads, there are times when their actions, speech and aggressiveness remind people that they were from Zaraki Squad.

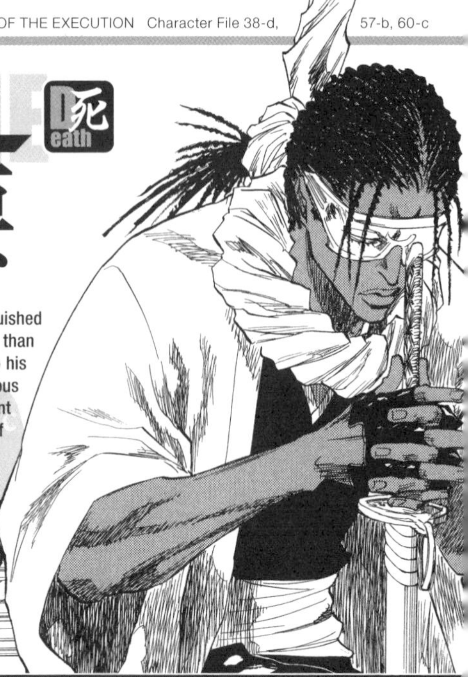

Death 死

NINTH COMPANY CAPTAIN

KANAME TÔSEN — CHAPTER FILE 60-c

東仙要

RISKING ALL OF HIS IDEALS

Ninth Company's blind captain, distinguished by his dreadlocks. He loves peace more than anything, but he won't hesitate to pick up his sword to maintain it. Tôsen has been cautious of Kenpachi ever since he gained his current position by killing the former captain of Eleventh Company.

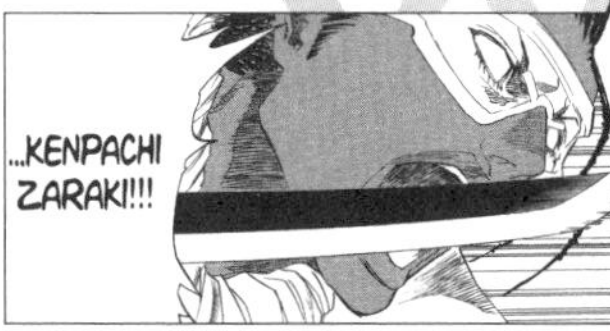
...KENPACHI ZARAKI!!!

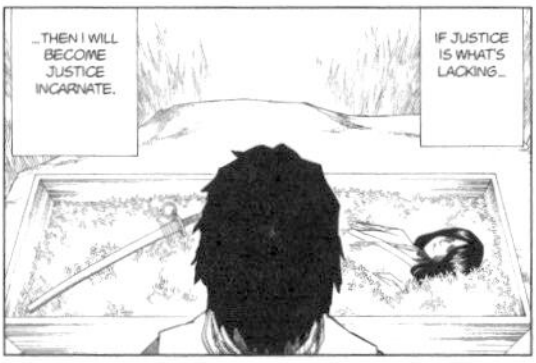
IF JUSTICE IS WHAT'S LACKING...
...THEN I WILL BECOME JUSTICE INCARNATE.

TO BRUSH AWAY THE CLOUDS

Tôsen wishes for peace. He takes up the sword to gain the power to make it a reality.

SUZUMUSHI TSUISHIKI ENMA KÔROGI

卍解 BANKAI

This creates a vacuum that nullifies the senses of spiritual energy, sight, sound, and scent to everyone but the person holding Suzumushi.

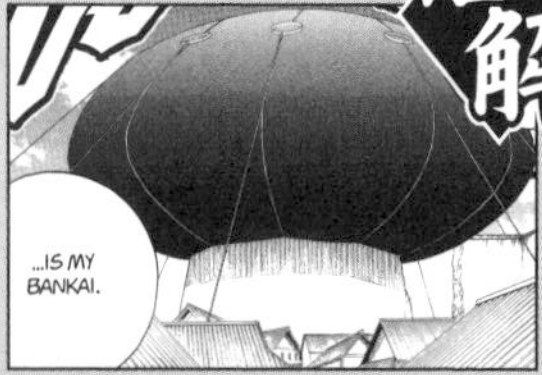
...IS MY BANKAI.

剣鬼

A DEMON O
SWORDS

Four against Or
VOL. 16-138~1

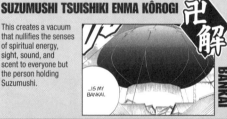

It is the day of Rukia's execution. Kenpachi's team is busily looking for Ichigo. But Komamura and Tôsen stop them. They accuse Kenpachi of conducting himself in a manner unbecoming of a captain of the Thirteen Court Guard Companies. Kenpachi provokes them in response!

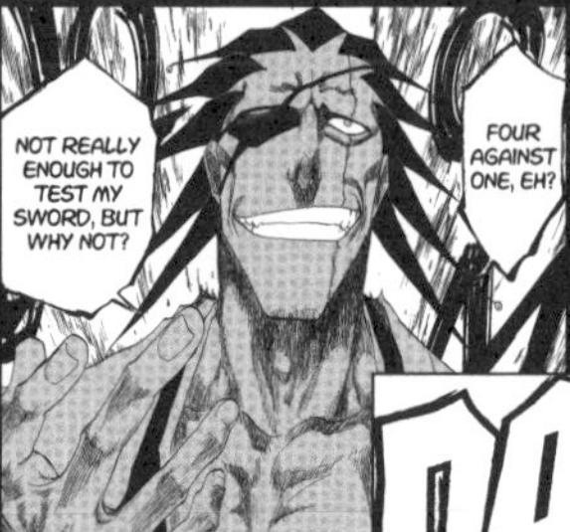
FOUR AGAINST ONE, EH?
NOT REALLY ENOUGH TO TEST MY SWORD, BUT WHY NOT?

Dismissing the four captain class officers as "not really enough to test" his sword, Kenpachi smiles viciously.

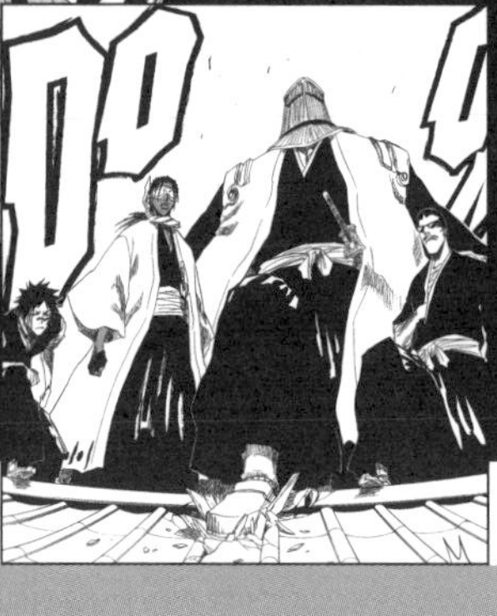

Seventh Company and Ninth Company's captains and assistant captains stand in Kenpachi's way. Their aura of dignity overwhelms their surroundings.

SEVENTH COMPANY CAPTAIN

SAJIN KOMAMURA — CHARACTER FILE 56-b

D死eath

狛村左陣

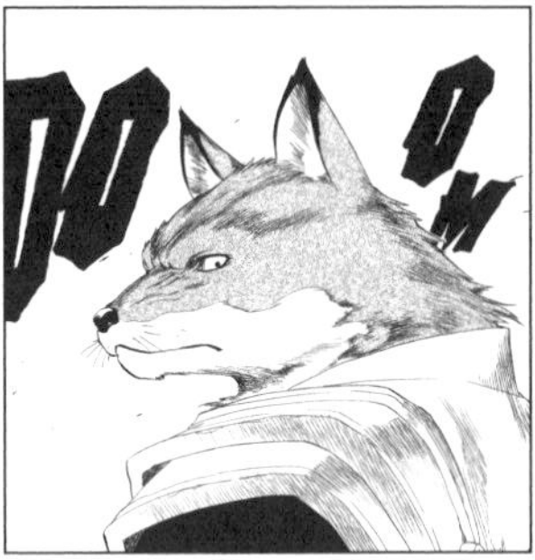
DO
OM

A wolf face appears from Komamura's helmet when it is split open.

A LARGE MAN WITH A BEAST FORM

Komamura usually wears a mask and helmet in order to hide his beast-like form. He is a wolf-man. Those around him shunned him, but Genryûsai Shigekuni Yamamoto adopted him anyway. Thus, everything he does is in gratitude and loyalty to Genryûsai.

SAJIN KOMAMURA 56 b

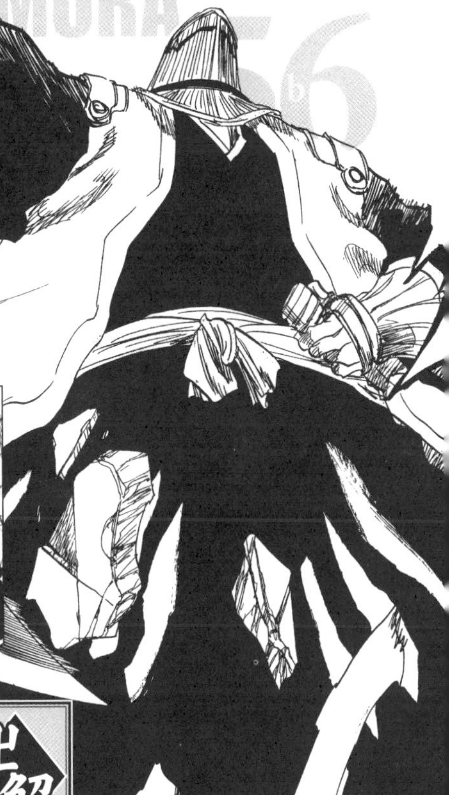

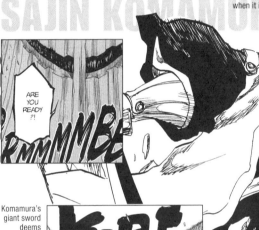

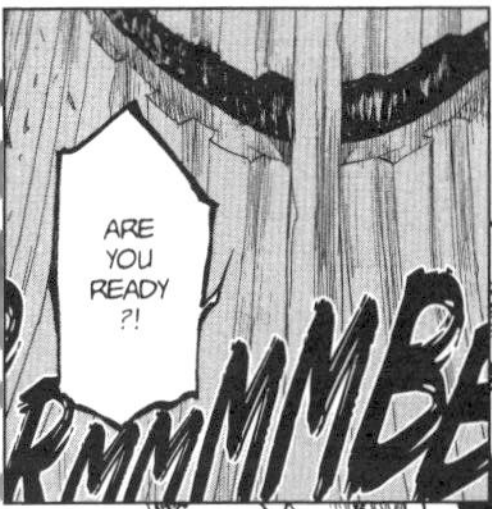
ARE YOU READY ?!
RMMMMBE

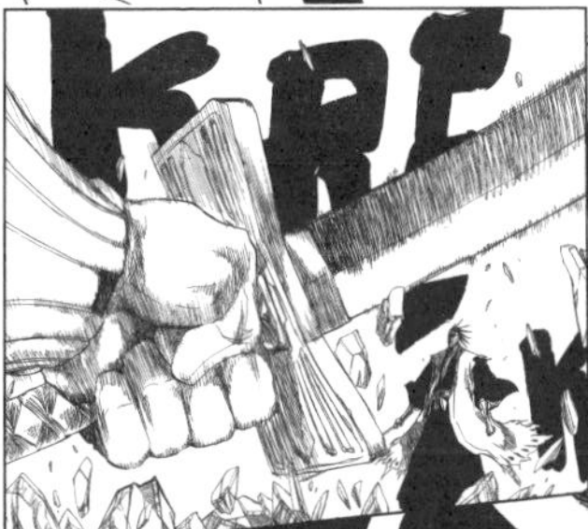

Komamura's giant sword deems Kenpachi a traitor for helping the ryoka, and gives out a roar.

KOKUJÔ TENGEN MYÔ-OH

When Komamura performs his bankai, a giant tall enough to reach the clouds appears behind him. This giant moves in synch with Komamura's movements.

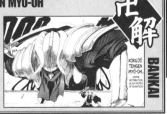

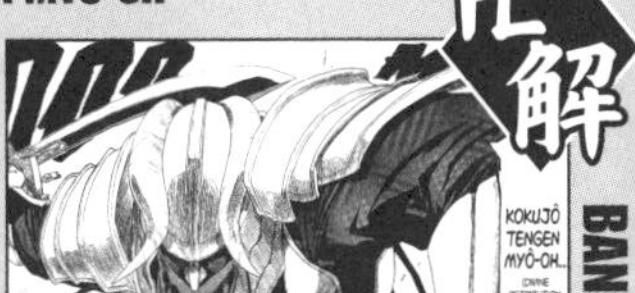
KOKUJÔ TENGEN MYÔ-OH...
(DIVINE RETRIBUTION, BLACK ROPES OF RUINATION)

卍解 BANKAI

PROFILE

BIRTHDAY/AUGUST 23
HEIGHT/9´4˝ **WEIGHT**/664 LBS
AFFILIATION/SEVENTH COMPANY
ZANPAKU-TÔ/TENKEN

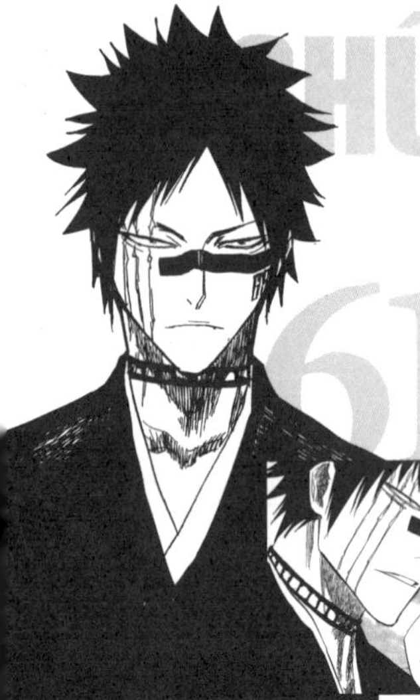

NINTH COMPANY ASSISTANT CAPTAIN

SHÛHEI HISAGI — CHARACTER FILE 61-b

檜佐木修兵

THE BRILLIANT MAN FROM SHINÔREIJUTSUIN

Shûhei was an exemplary student who was expected to graduate from the academy as a seated officer in the Thirteen Court Guard Companies. On the day of the execution, he goes with Tôsen and crosses swords with Eleventh Company Fifth Seat Yumichika.

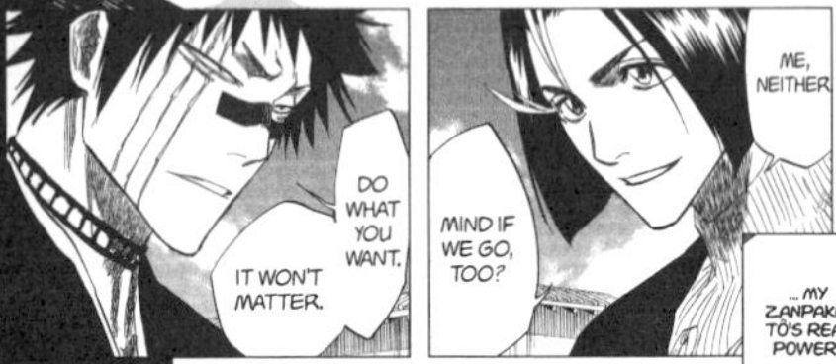
ME, NEITHER
MIND IF WE GO, TOO?
DO WHAT YOU WANT.
IT WON'T MATTER.

PROFILE

BIRTHDAY/AUGUST 14
HEIGHT/5′9″ **WEIGHT/**148 LBS
AFFILIATION/NINTH COMPANY
ZANPAKU-TÔ/?

YUMICHIKA'S SECRET

Shûhei corners Yumichika, but he is defeated when his spiritual power is absorbed by Fuji Kujaku's true power.

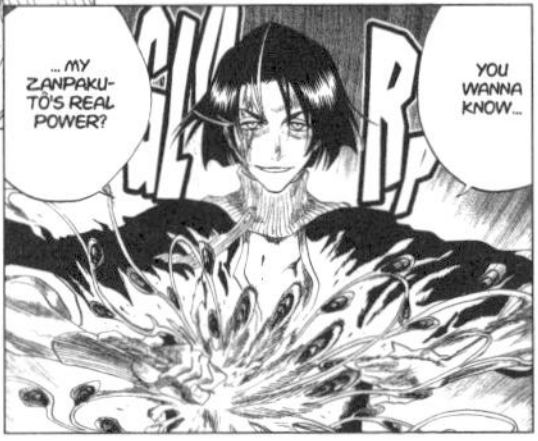
YOU WANNA KNOW...
...MY ZANPAKU-TÔ'S REAL POWER?

A JACK OF ALL TRADES WHO USES ALL FOUR BASIC FIGHTING STYLES.

Despite his intimidating appearance, Iba is a multi-talented man who trained in the four basic fighting techniques (zanjutsu, hakuda, hohô, kidô) in order to become an assistant captain. It is rumored that he became versatile so that he could get promoted and make things easier on his mother, but he denies this.

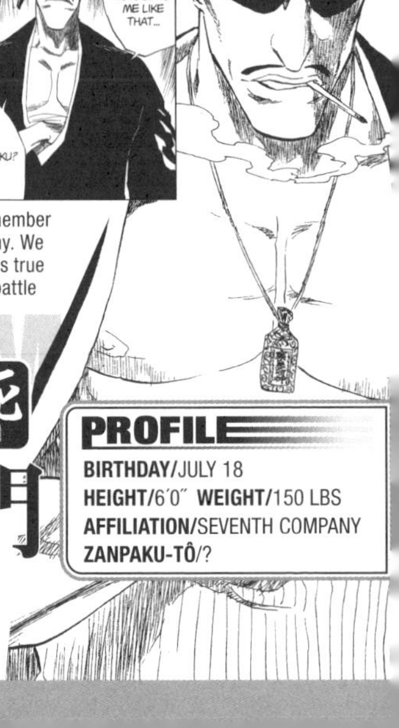

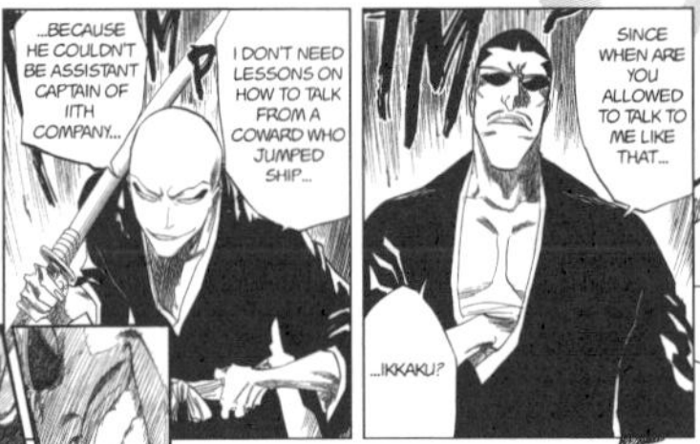
SINCE WHEN ARE YOU ALLOWED TO TALK TO ME LIKE THAT...
...IKKAKU?
I DON'T NEED LESSONS ON HOW TO TALK FROM A COWARD WHO JUMPED SHIP...
...BECAUSE HE COULDN'T BE ASSISTANT CAPTAIN OF 11TH COMPANY...

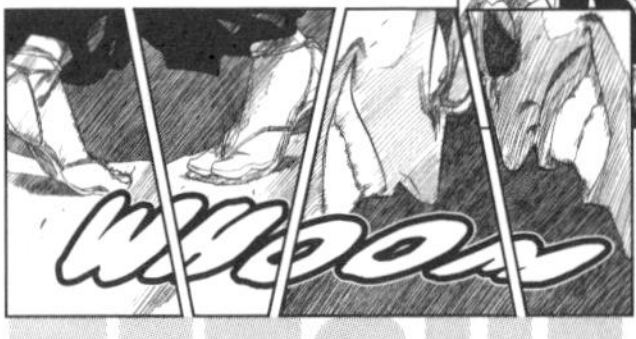

Iba is formerly a member of Eleventh Compny. We get a glimpse of his true disposition in his battle with Ikkaku.

SEVENTH COMPANY ASSISTANT CAPTAIN

TETSUZAEMON IBA — CHARACTER FILE 57-c

射場鉄左衛門

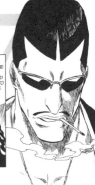

PROFILE

BIRTHDAY/JULY 18
HEIGHT/6′0″ **WEIGHT/**150 LBS
AFFILIATION/SEVENTH COMPANY
ZANPAKU-TÔ/?

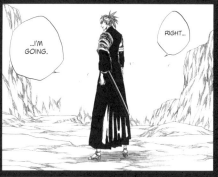

月吼

MOON HOWL

Renji's rebellion
VOL. 17-140

RIGHT...
...I'M GOING.

Renji wants the power to save Rukia... His desire allows him to reach bankai, the second stage of zanpaku-tô release. With his sword Zabimaru in hand, he heads to the Sokyoku Hill, the execution grounds!

Renji has been denying his feelings. But now he follows his instincts and he runs to Rukia, the person he truly wants to protect!!

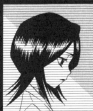

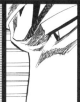

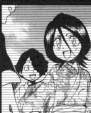

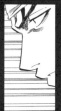

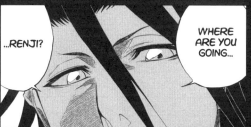

WHERE ARE YOU GOING...
...RENJI?

THE TOWERING BARRIER

Byakuya is the illustrious moon that Renji adored and wished to surpass... Now Renji's battle to surpass Byakuya and save Rukia begins!

SOMEONE WHO UNDERSTANDS RENJI WELL

SIXTH COMPANY MEMBER RIKICHI

A rookie Sixth Company member who strongly admires and respects Renji. He copies Renji's looks, and even has the same tattoo on his forehead.

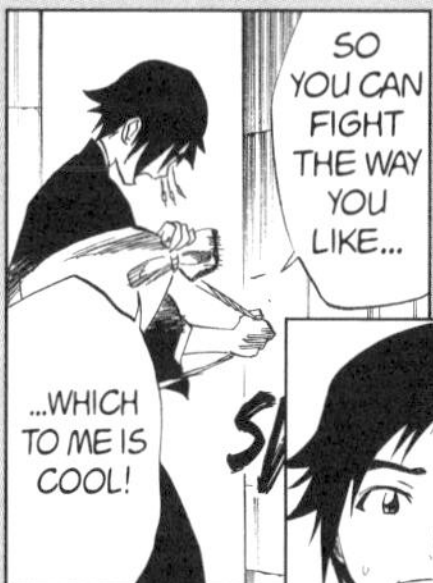

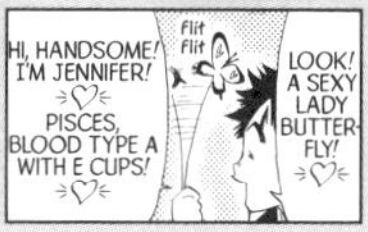

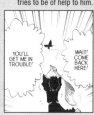

SO YOU CAN FIGHT THE WAY YOU LIKE...
...WHICH TO ME IS COOL!

...THAT I...
...JOINED THE 13 COURT GUARDS BECAUSE OF YOU!

Rikichi is surprised by Renji's sudden rebellion, but accepts everything and tries to be of help to him.

WAIT! COME BACK HERE!
YOU'LL GET ME IN TROUBLE!

LOOK! A SEXY LADY BUTTER-FLY! ♡
Flit Flit
HI, HANDSOME! I'M JENNIFER! ♡ PISCES, BLOOD TYPE A WITH E CUPS! ♡

Rikichi is a low ranking member who is timid and terrible at getting things done. He has a gentle disposition and is a hard worker.

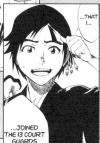

BYAKUYA KUCHIKI

Death 死

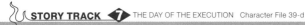

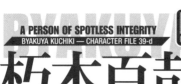

A PERSON OF SPOTLESS INTEGRITY

BYAKUYA KUCHIKI — CHARACTER FILE 39-d

朽木白哉

39-d

THE ILLUSTRIOUS MOON THAT SHINES IN THE HEAVENS

Byakuya is pure. He has a cold stare and an unwavering conviction. Renji wants to save Rukia, but Byakuya stands in his way to break his fangs. Byakuya's imperious gaze pierces Renji's body.

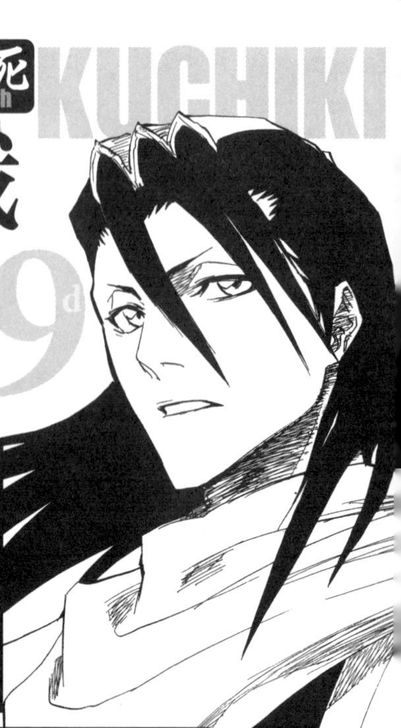

"YOU COULDN'T EVEN FORCE ME TO ONE KNEE."

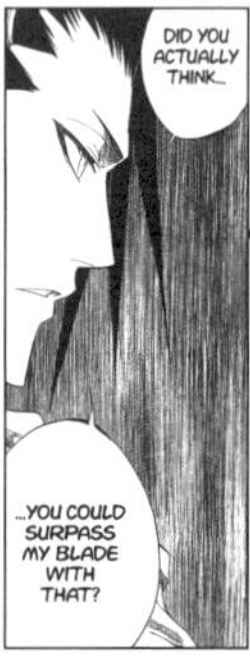
DID YOU ACTUALLY THINK...
...YOU COULD SURPASS MY BLADE WITH THAT?

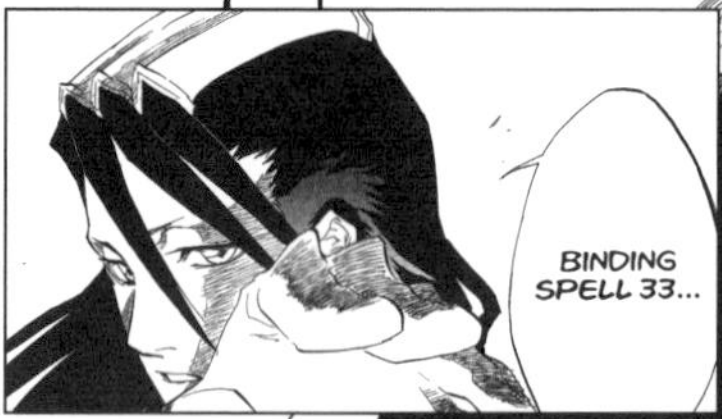
BINDING SPELL 33...

Senka is a technique where Byakuya strikes his opponent from behind using shunpo and destroys the opponent's saketsu chain and hakusui soul sleep with a single thrust. Byakuya murmurs tauntingly to Renji when Renji is able to defend himself against it.

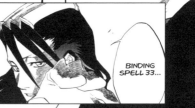

卍解

BANKAI

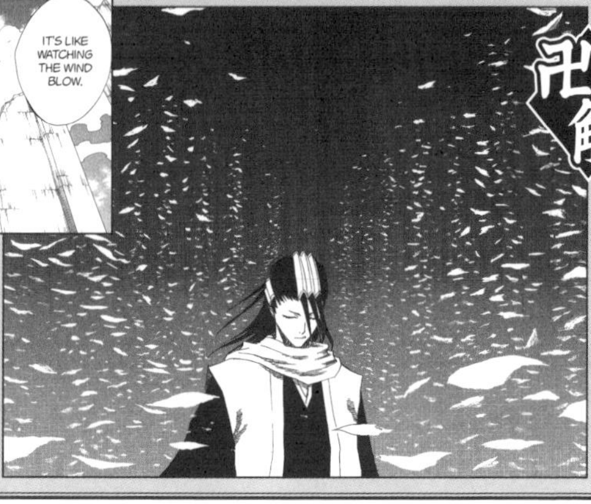

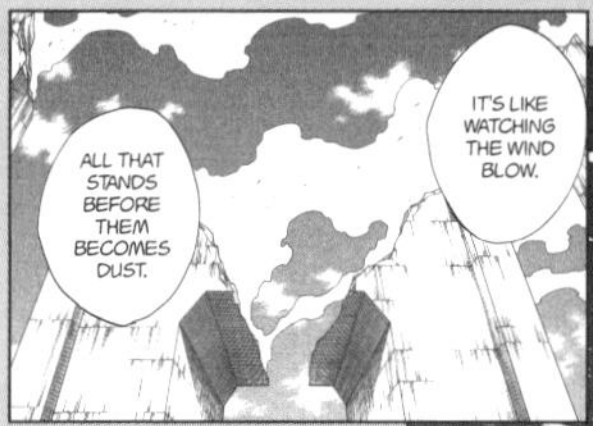
IT'S LIKE WATCHING THE WIND BLOW.
ALL THAT STANDS BEFORE THEM BECOMES DUST.

SENBONZAKURA KAGEYOSHI

When Byakuya performs his bankai, a row of swords rise from the ground and scatter like petals in their full glory. Its countless blades have no blind spots and can attack from all directions.

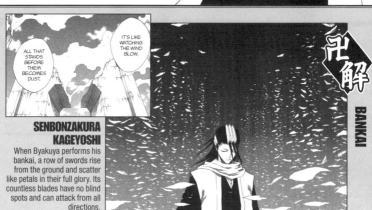

"I'M GOING TO SURPASS YOU, CAPTAIN KUCHIKI."

HIHIÔ ZABIMARU

RENJI ABARAI — CHARACTER FILE 38-e

Death 死

阿散井恋次

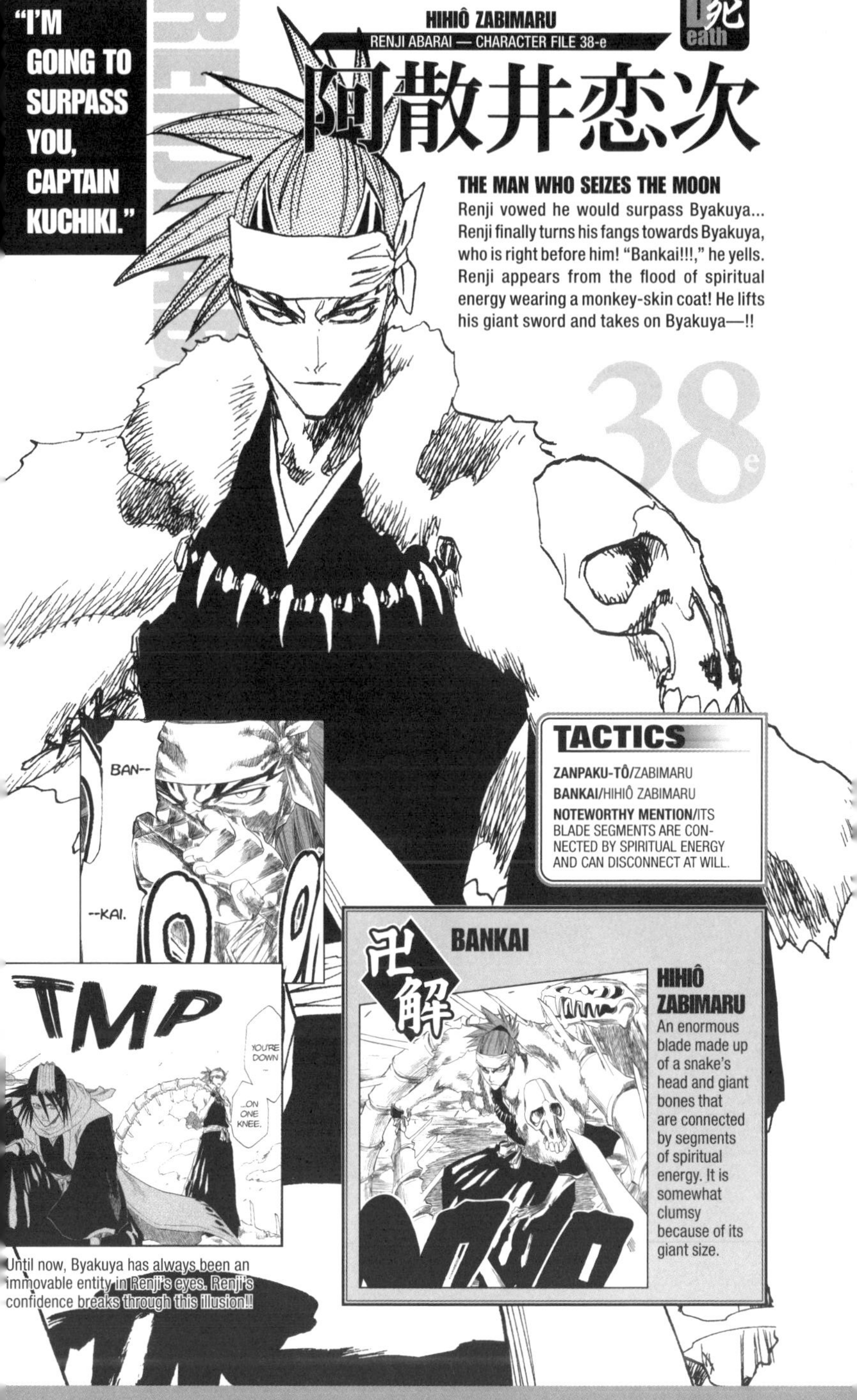

THE MAN WHO SEIZES THE MOON

Renji vowed he would surpass Byakuya... Renji finally turns his fangs towards Byakuya, who is right before him! "Bankai!!!," he yells. Renji appears from the flood of spiritual energy wearing a monkey-skin coat! He lifts his giant sword and takes on Byakuya—!!

38e

TACTICS

ZANPAKU-TÔ/ZABIMARU

BANKAI/HIHIÔ ZABIMARU

NOTEWORTHY MENTION/ITS BLADE SEGMENTS ARE CONNECTED BY SPIRITUAL ENERGY AND CAN DISCONNECT AT WILL.

BAN--
--KAI.
TMP
YOU'RE DOWN
...ON ONE KNEE.

Until now, Byakuya has always been an immovable entity in Renji's eyes. Renji's confidence breaks through this illusion!!

BANKAI

卍解

HIHIÔ ZABIMARU

An enormous blade made up of a snake's head and giant bones that are connected by segments of spiritual energy. It is somewhat clumsy because of its giant size.

誓い

OATH

At the limit
VOL. 17-142~14

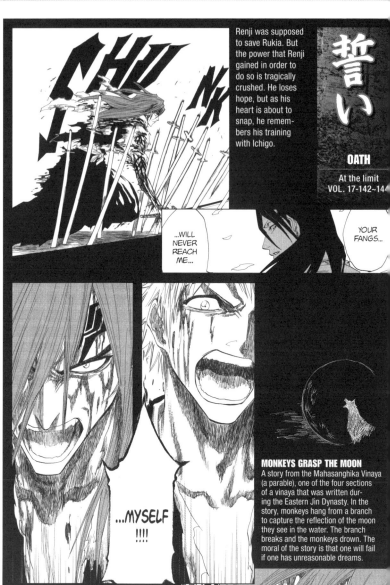

Renji was supposed to save Rukia. But the power that Renji gained in order to do so is tragically crushed. He loses hope, but as his heart is about to snap, he remembers his training with Ichigo.

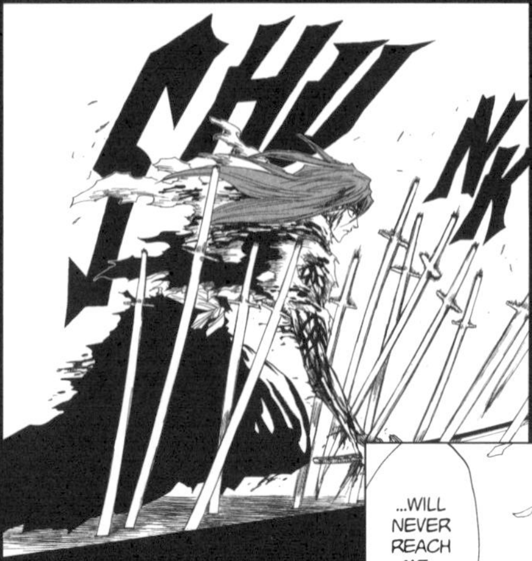
CHUNK

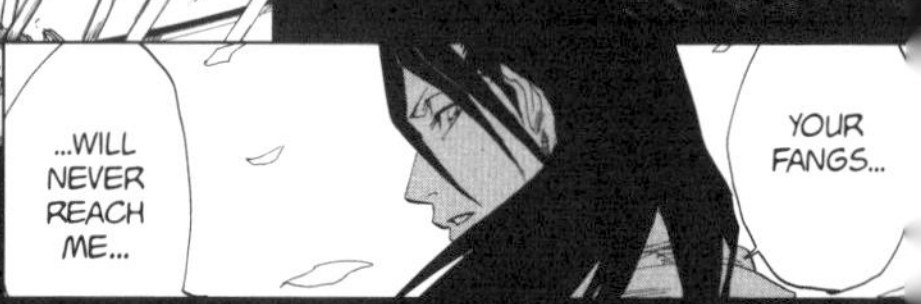
YOUR FANGS...
...WILL NEVER REACH ME...

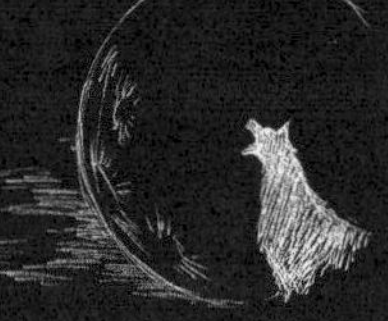

MONKEYS GRASP THE MOON
A story from the Mahasanghika Vinaya (a parable), one of the four sections of a vinaya that was written during the Eastern Jin Dynasty. In the story, monkeys hang from a branch to capture the reflection of the moon they see in the water. The branch breaks and the monkeys drown. The moral of the story is that one will fail if one has unreasonable dreams.

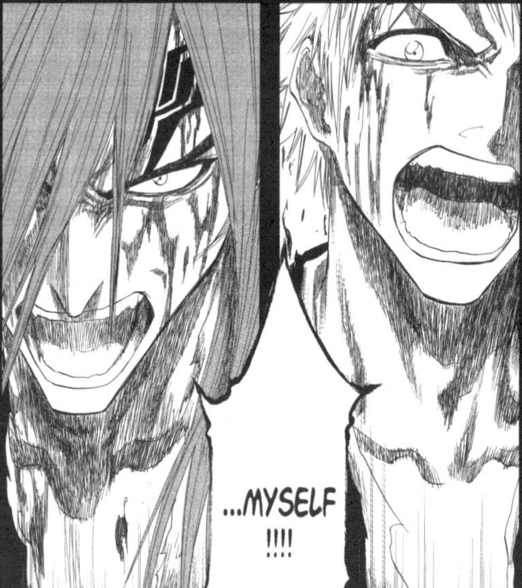
...MYSELF !!!!

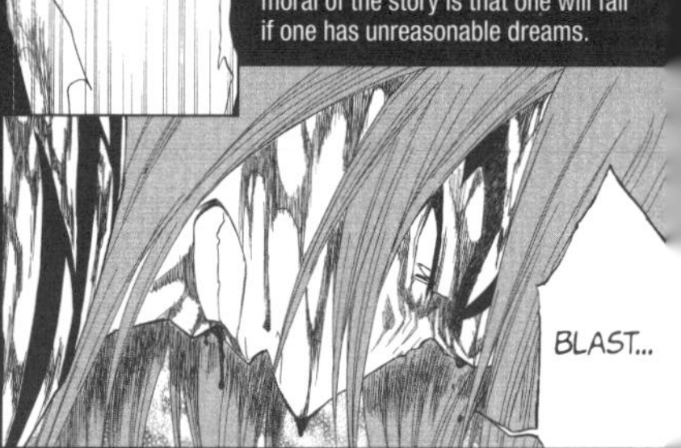
BLAST...

SOMETHING HE CANNOT GIVE
Renji vowed that he would save Rukia. It wasn't a promise to her, but to his soul. Renji gathers his remaining strength to defend his vow and stabs his blade into Byakuya's chest!!

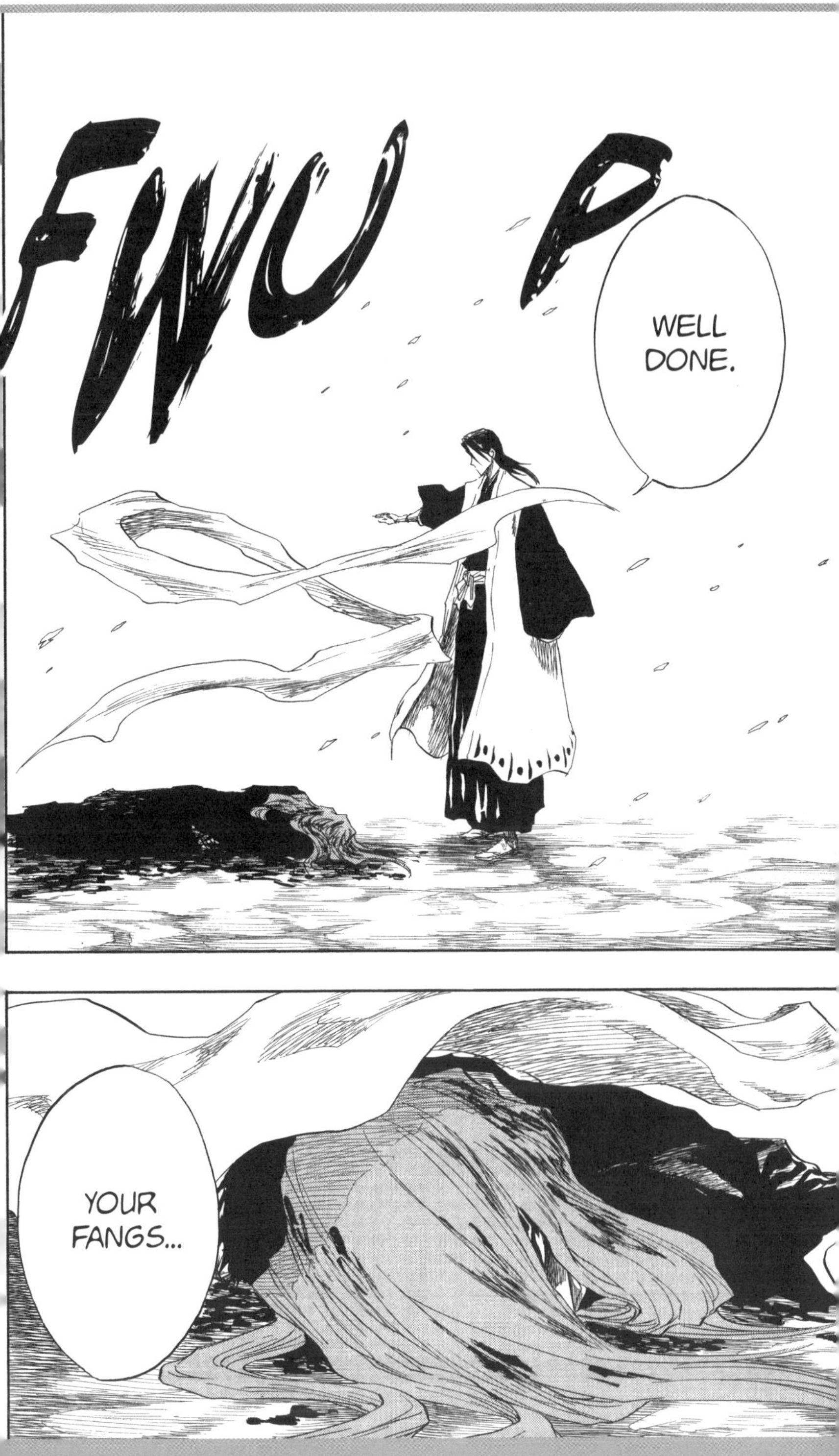
FWUP
WELL DONE.
YOUR FANGS...

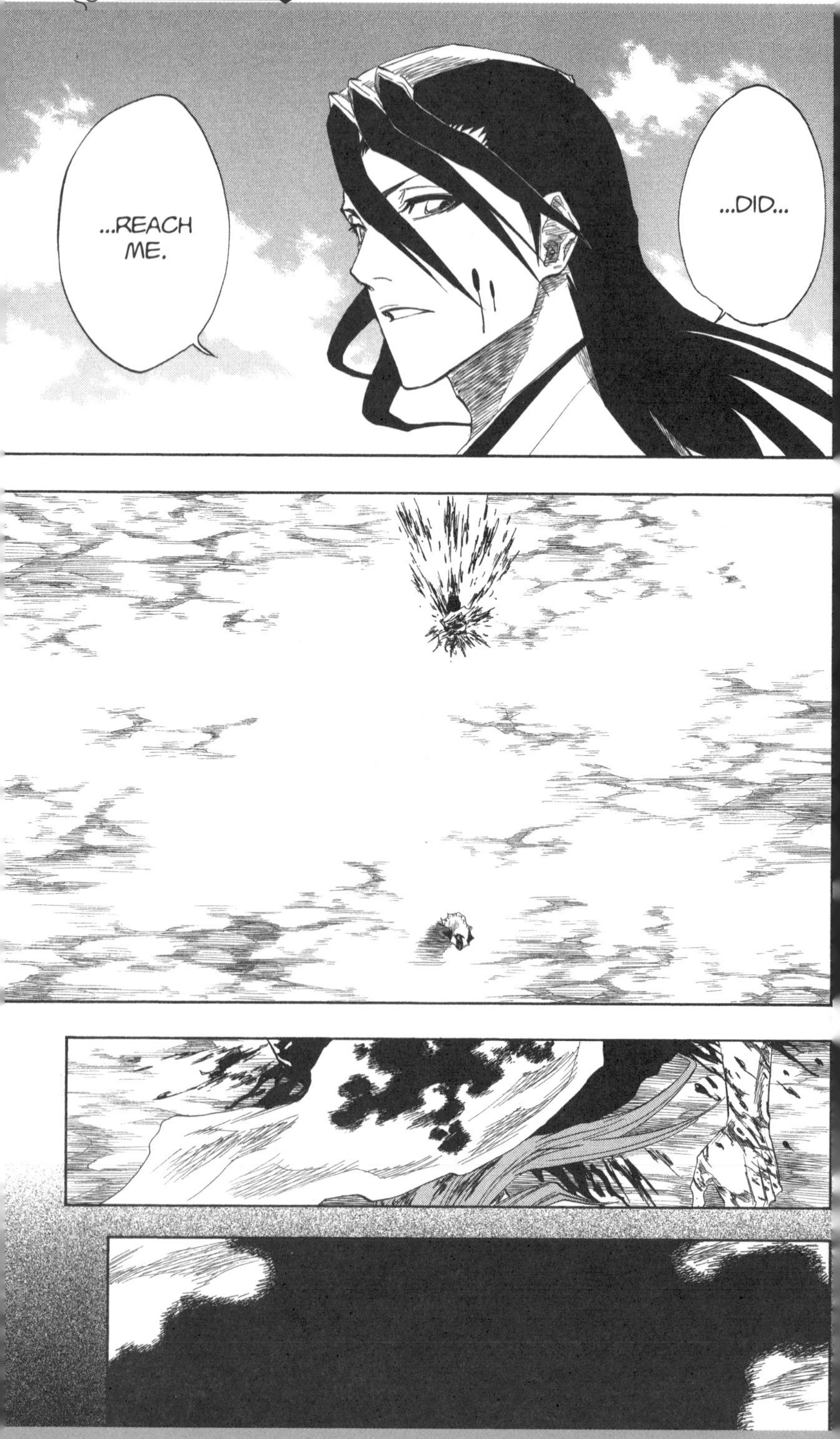
...DID...
...REACH ME.

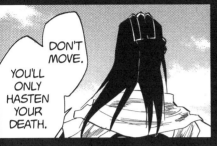

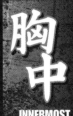

胸中

INNERMOST FEELINGS

Byakuya's Desire
VOL. 17-144

Byakuya slashes Renji's body with his Senbonzakura Kageyoshi. He tries to stop Renji from rising... It is as if Byakuya is worried about him.

DON'T MOVE.
YOU'LL ONLY HASTEN YOUR DEATH.

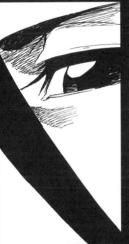

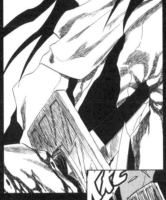

THE FANG THAT HIT ITS MARK
Renji stabs with the last of his strength... Byakuya takes a square hit and senses Renji's fervor.

Renji's fang finally reaches Byakuya. Byakuya shows his feelings for the first time as he watches Renji fall. It's as if his eyes reflect the trembling of his heart.

EVIDENCE THAT HE IS HEAD OF THE KUCHIKI FAMILY

SILVER-WHITE WINDFLOWER-SILK GAUZE

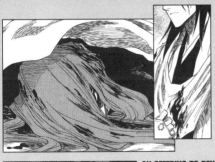

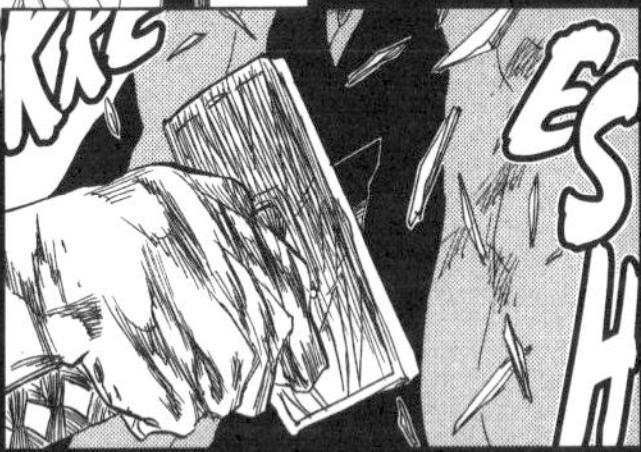

An unusual scarf worn by the heads of the Kuchiki family. The scarf alone is worth enough to buy ten mansions in the Seireitei. Byakuya covers Renji with this scarf out of respect.

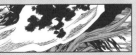

AN OFFERING TO RENJI
Byakuya gives Renji a valuable offering in recognition of Renji's strength.

双殛

SÔKYOKU

Fateful momen
VOL. 18-150

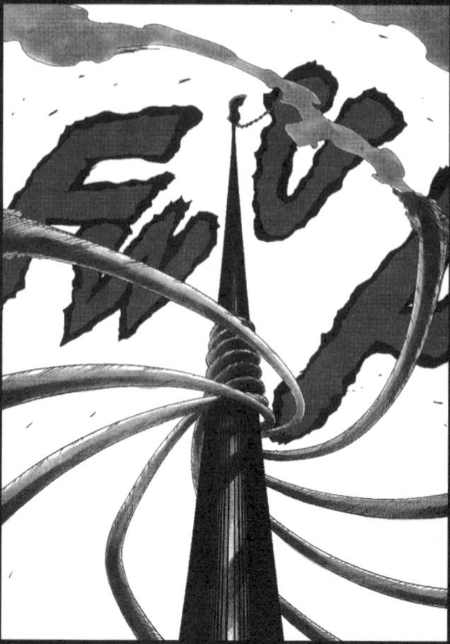

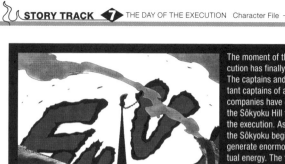

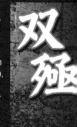

The moment of the execution has finally arrived. The captains and assistant captains of all the companies have come to the Sôkyoku Hill to watch the execution. As they do, the Sôkyoku begins to generate enormous spiritual energy. The fateful moment is approaching. Byakuya stays silent and doesn't voice his feelings.

KIKÔ OH, THE ULTIMATE EXECUTIONER

The Sôkyoku reveals its true form to perform the execution. Surrounded by crimson flames, it transforms into a grand phoenix. The phoenix hovers before Rukia, the criminal it is about to pierce!

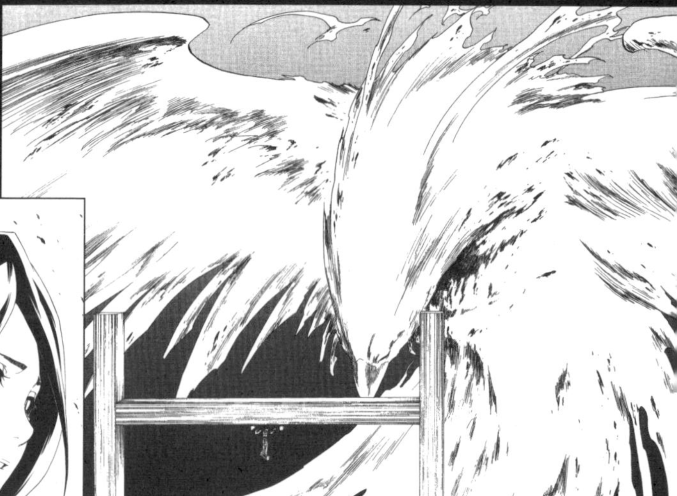

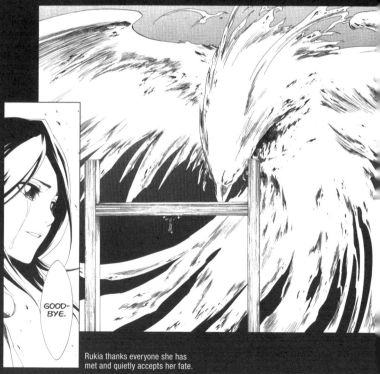

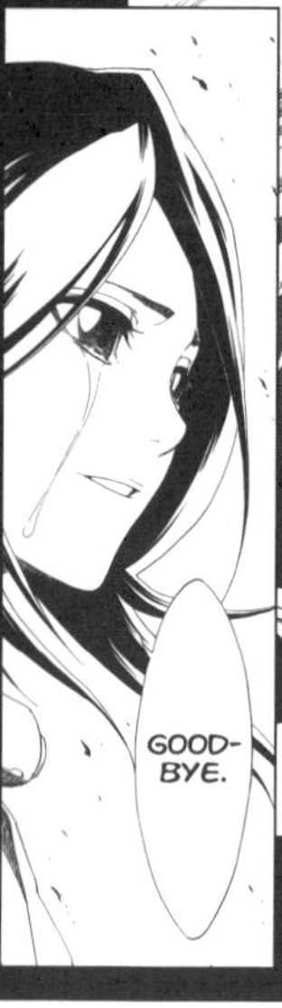
GOOD-BYE.

Rukia thanks everyone she has met and quietly accepts her fate.

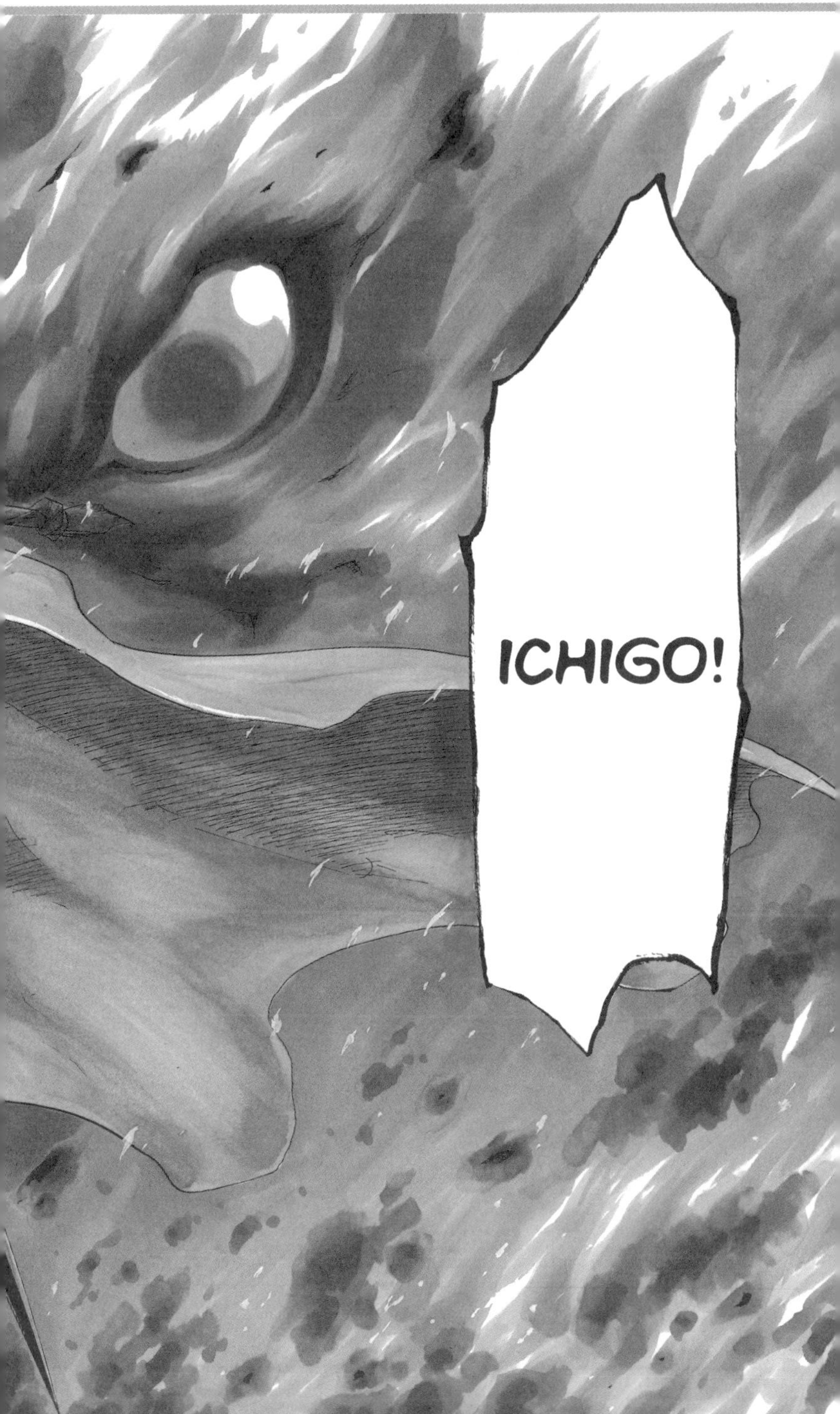
ICHIGO!

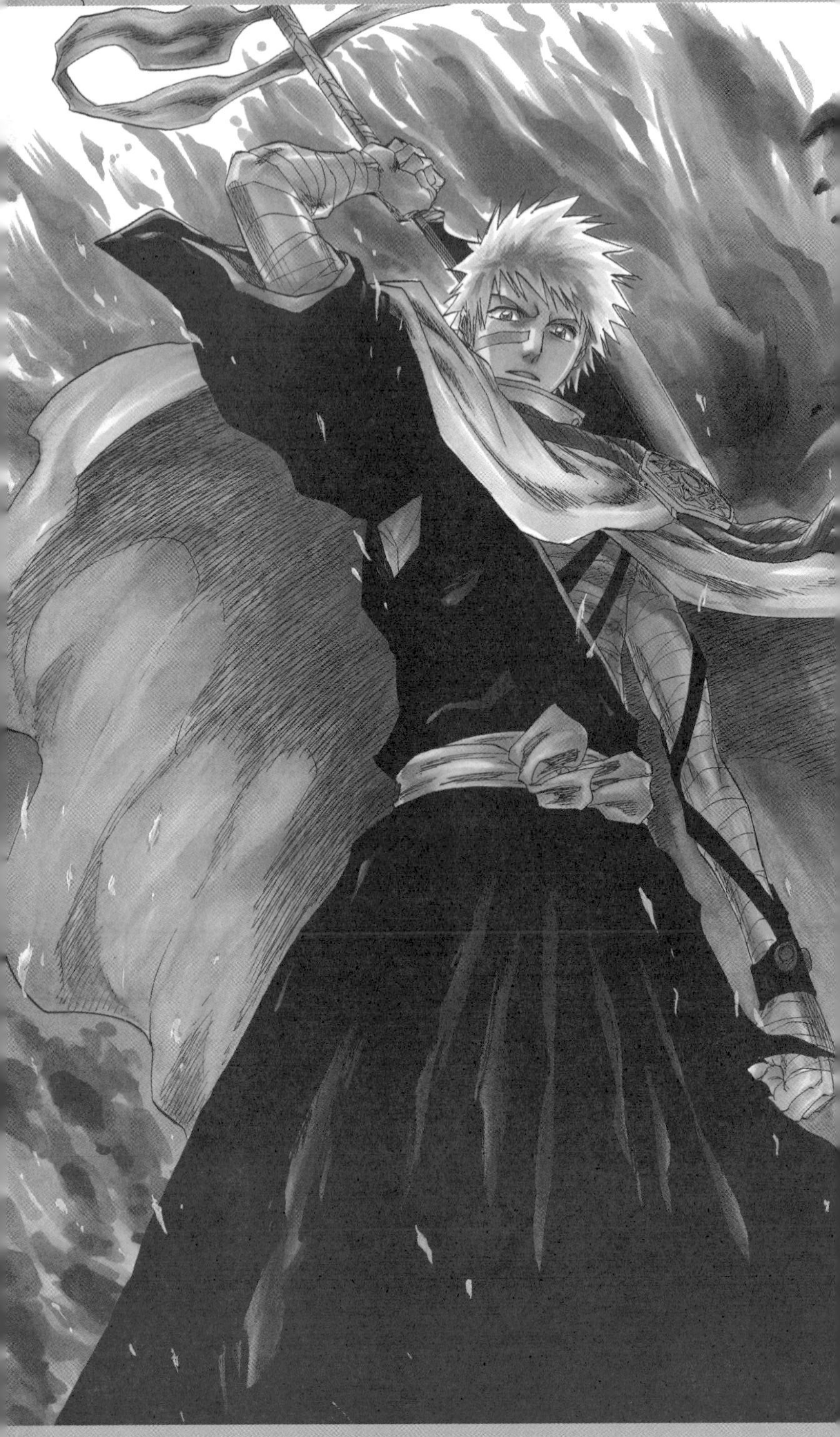

奪還

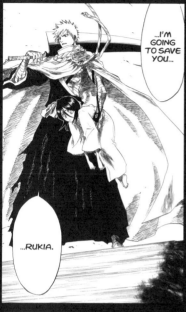

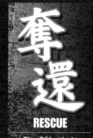

RESCUE

The Sôkyoku's destruction
VOL. 18-151~152

Kikô Oh's attack draws near... As soon as it looks like Rukia is about to be executed, Ichigo appears before everyone shouldering Zangetsu! Kikô Oh has the power of a million zanpaku-tô, but Ichigo stops its attack with his back. Ichigo shouts at Rukia, "Hey!"

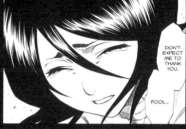

DON'T EXPECT ME TO THANK YOU.
FOOL...

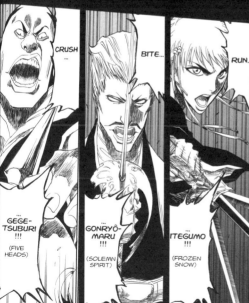

...I'M GOING TO SAVE YOU...
...RUKIA.

RUN...
...ITEGUMO !!!
(FROZEN SNOW)
BITE...
...GONRYÔ-MARU !!!
(SOLEMN SPIRIT)
CRUSH ...
...GEGE-TSUBURI !!!
(FIVE HEADS)

Ichigo destroys the Sôkyoku and leaves Rukia with Renji. Three assistant captains try to go after Renji, but Ichigo stands in their way and defeats all three of them instantaneously! Ichigo's power exceeds that of the three captains. He has reached Bankai level!!

FOURTH COMPANY ASSISTANT CAPTAIN

ISANE KOTETSU — 53-b

虎徹勇音

PROFILE

BIRTHDAY/AUGUST 2
HEIGHT/6′1″ **WEIGHT/**154 LBS
AFFILIATION/FOURTH COMPANY
ZANPAKU-TÔ/ITEGUMO

FIRST COMPANY ASSISTANT CAPTAIN

CHOJIRO SASAKIBE — 48-b

雀部長次郎

PROFILE

BIRTHDAY/NOVEMBER 4
HEIGHT/5′9″ **WEIGHT/**146 LBS
AFFILIATION/FIRST SQUAD
ZANPAKU-TÔ/GONRYÔMARU

SECOND COMPANY ASSISTANT CAPTAIN

MARECHIYO ÔMAEDA — 50-b

大前田希千代

PROFILE

BIRTHDAY/MAY 5
HEIGHT/6′9″ **WEIGHT/**333 LBS
AFFILIATION/SECOND SQUAD
ZANPAKU-TÔ/GEGETSUBURI

Death 死

FOURTH COMPANY CAPTAIN

RETSU UNOHANA — CHARACTER FILES 52-b

卯ノ花烈

52b

HER MILD-MANNERED SMILE AND STRONG WILL

The captain of Fourth Company, a company that specializes in giving aid to wounded Court Guard members. Her measured looks, words, and actions soothe and give piece of mind to those around her. She doesn't participate in battle, but she is a daring and talented woman who is always calm, composed and makes apt judgments.

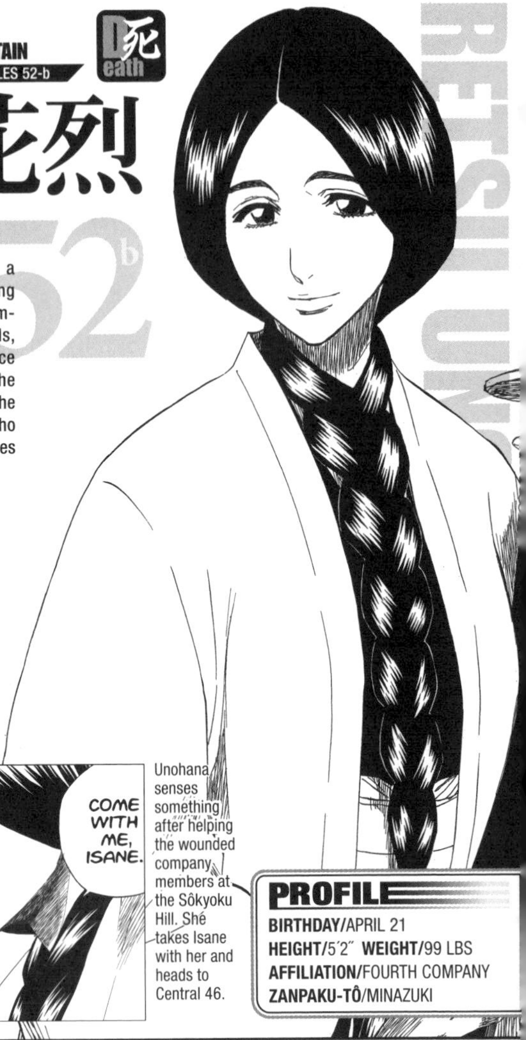

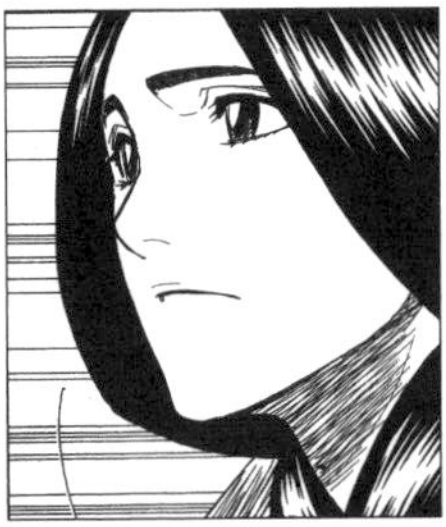

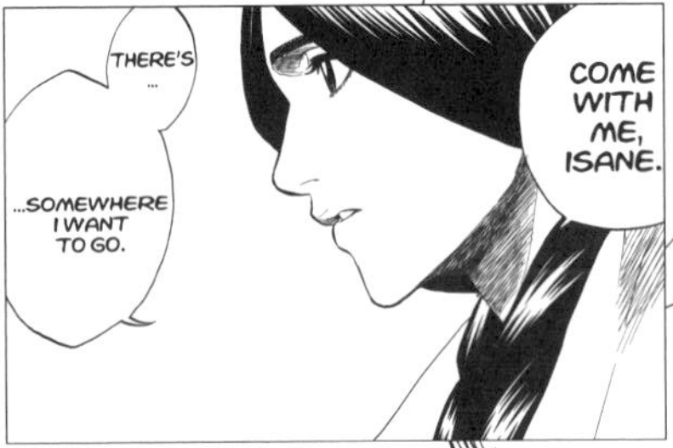
COME WITH ME, ISANE.
THERE'S ...
...SOMEWHERE I WANT TO GO.

Unohana senses something after helping the wounded company members at the Sôkyoku Hill. She takes Isane with her and heads to Central 46.

PROFILE

BIRTHDAY/APRIL 21

HEIGHT/5′2″ **WEIGHT**/99 LBS

AFFILIATION/FOURTH COMPANY

ZANPAKU-TÔ/MINAZUKI

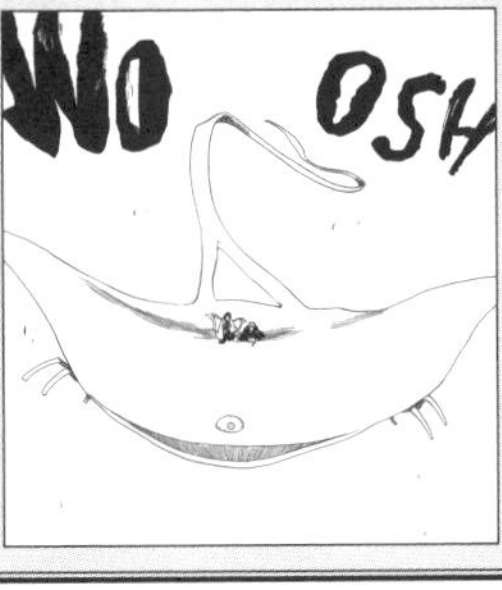

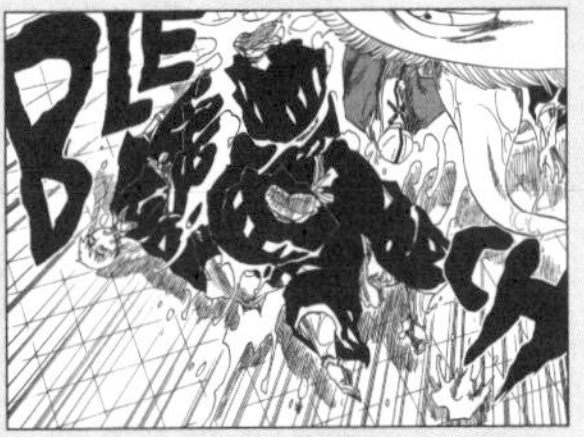

Minazuki has the ability to heal injured company members, by leaving them in its stomach for a few minutes.

ZANPAKU-TÔ

MINAZUKI

It usually takes the form of a falchion, but when it is released it transforms into a giant, rideable creature that heals those it engulfs.

分掌

DIVISION OF DUTIES

Reason for getting stronger
VOL. 18-155

Rukia is saved by Ichigo and is carried away by Renji. Rukia feels guilty that Ichigo is getting hurt and tells Renji to let her go. Renji begins to tell Rukia about Ichigo's true feelings.

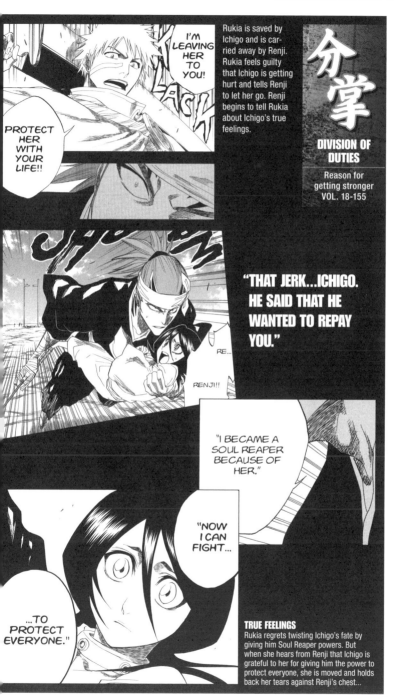

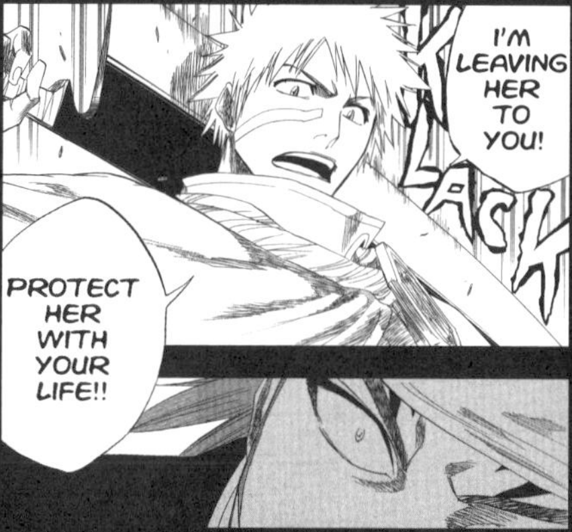
I'M LEAVING HER TO YOU!
PROTECT HER WITH YOUR LIFE!!

"THAT JERK...ICHIGO. HE SAID THAT HE WANTED TO REPAY YOU."

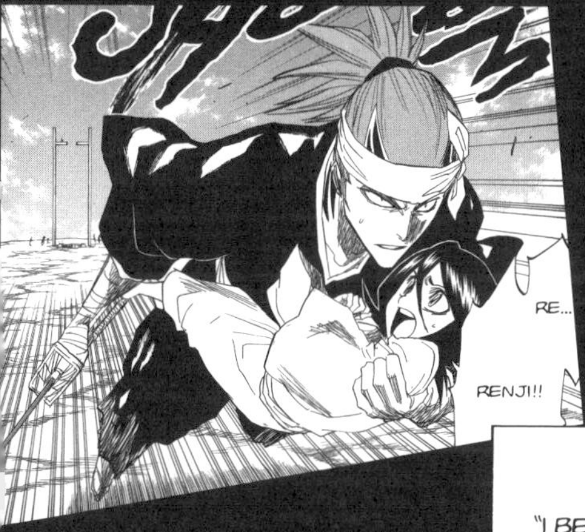
RE...
RENJI!!

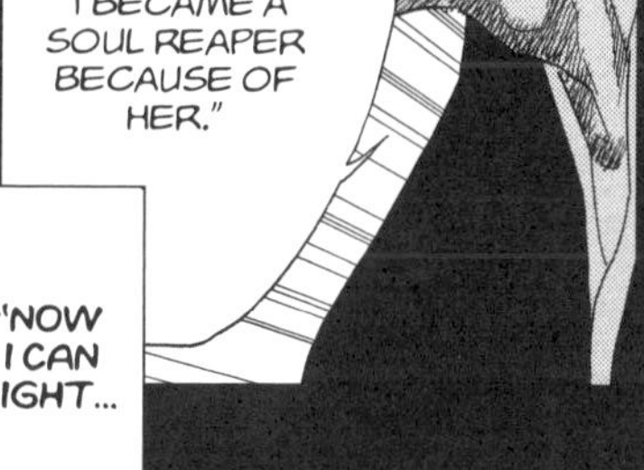
"I BECAME A SOUL REAPER BECAUSE OF HER."

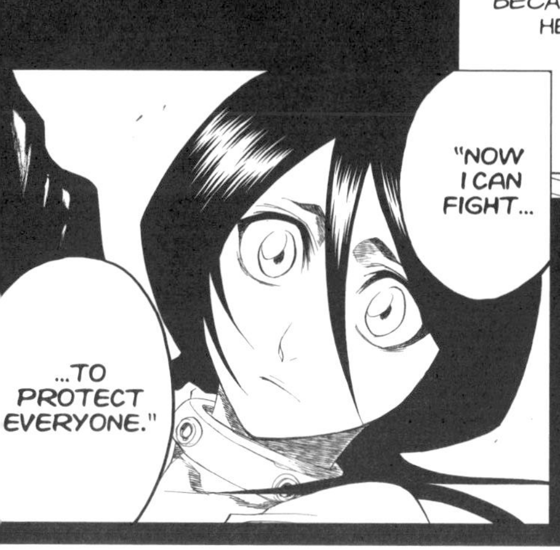
"NOW I CAN FIGHT...
...TO PROTECT EVERYONE."

TRUE FEELINGS

Rukia regrets twisting Ichigo's fate by giving him Soul Reaper powers. But when she hears from Renji that Ichigo is grateful to her for giving him the power to protect everyone, she is moved and holds back her tears against Renji's chest...

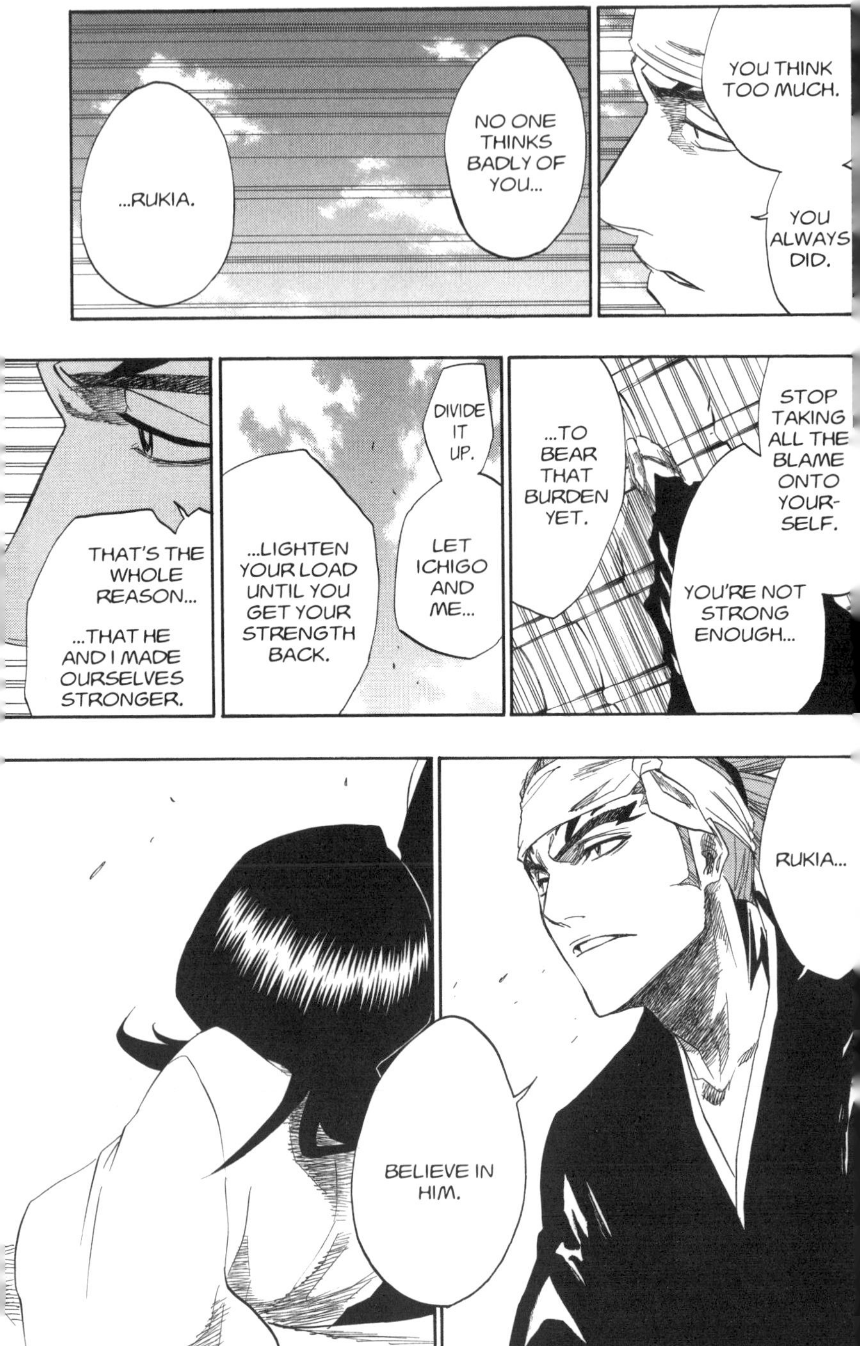
YOU THINK TOO MUCH.
YOU ALWAYS DID.
NO ONE THINKS BADLY OF YOU...
...RUKIA.
STOP TAKING ALL THE BLAME ONTO YOURSELF.
YOU'RE NOT STRONG ENOUGH...
...TO BEAR THAT BURDEN YET.
DIVIDE IT UP.
LET ICHIGO AND ME...
...LIGHTEN YOUR LOAD UNTIL YOU GET YOUR STRENGTH BACK.
THAT'S THE WHOLE REASON...
...THAT HE AND I MADE OURSELVES STRONGER.
RUKIA...
BELIEVE IN HIM.

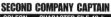

SECOND COMPANY CAPTAIN

SOI FON — CHARACTER FILE 49-b

Death 死

砕蜂

49b

SOI FON

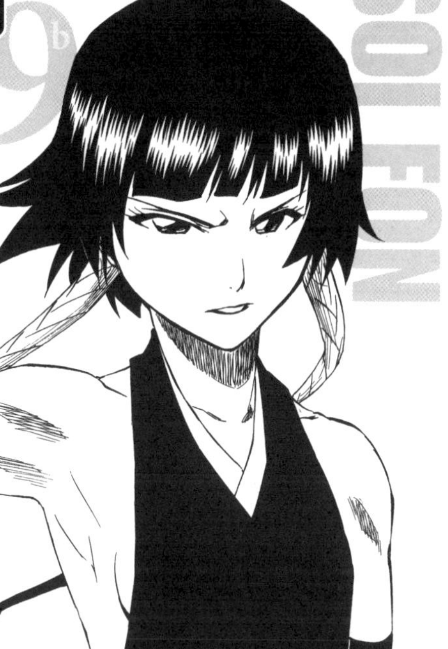

YORUICHI'S FORMER SUBORDINATE WHO IS NOW HOSTILE TOWARDS HER

The ninth head of the Fon family, a family that makes its living as executioners and assassins. She unified the Secret Remote Squad as well as the Punishment Force after Yoruichi disappeared. She is devoted to her missions as a member of the Thirteen Court Guard Companies and is merciless to those who get in her way, even if they are former superiors.

PROFILE

BIRTHDAY/FEBRUARY 11
HEIGHT/4′9″ **WEIGHT/**84 LBS
AFFILIATION/SECOND COMPANY
ZANPAKU-TÔ/SUZUMEBACHI

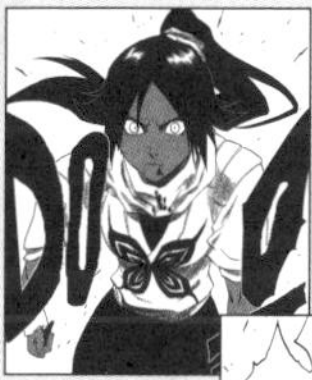
DO
O

ZANPAKU-TÔ

SUZUMEBACHI

Suzumebachi will kill those it strikes twice in the same place.

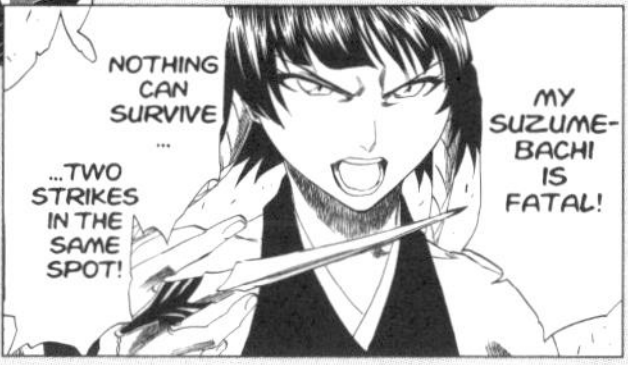
MY SUZUME-BACHI IS FATAL!
NOTHING CAN SURVIVE ...
...TWO STRIKES IN THE SAME SPOT!

A Homonka death mark appears on the body of Soi Fon's victims with her first strike.

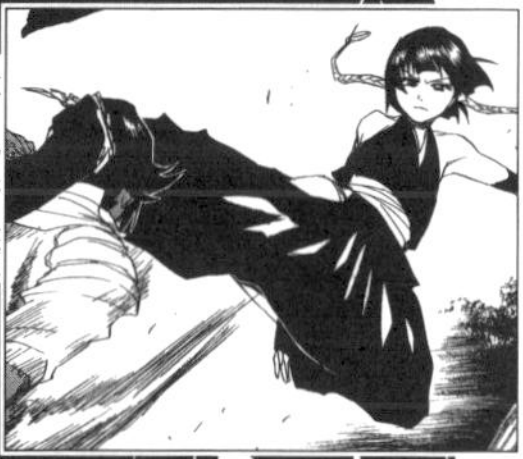

Soi Fon's close combat skills rival or even surpass those of Yoruichi's.

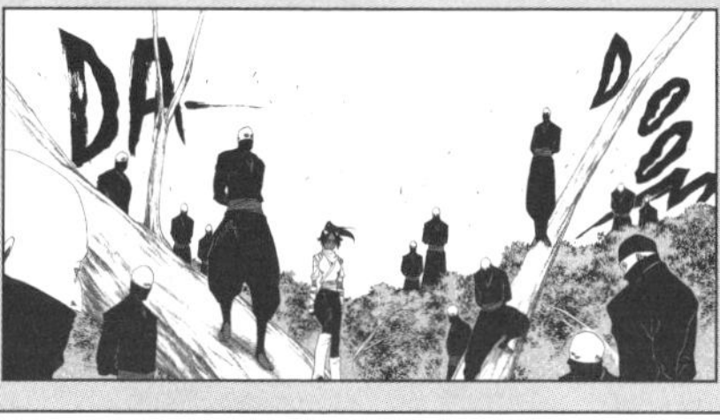
DOOM
DA

They carry out the executions and assassinations of Soul Reapers who have turned against the law, and serve as scouts and guards against Hollows. If the Thirteen Court Guard Companies are the exterior guard, the Secret Remote Squad is an interior, covert guard.

SEIREITEI'S ASSASSIN SQUAD

SECRET REMOTE SQUAD

瞬撃

FLASH ATTAC

The hindrance
of a hundred yea
VOL. 18–153~15
& 157~158

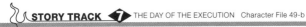

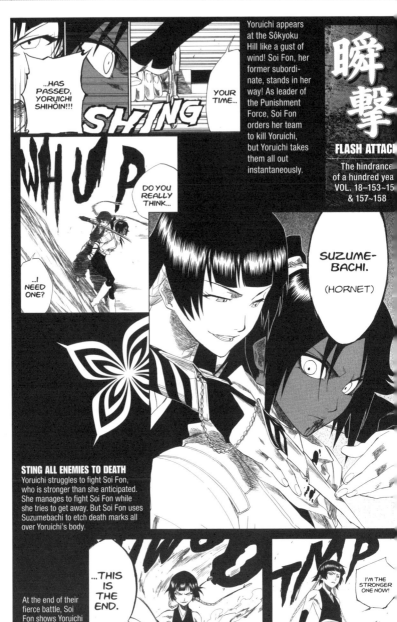

Yoruichi appears at the Sôkyoku Hill like a gust of wind! Soi Fon, her former subordinate, stands in her way! As leader of the Punishment Force, Soi Fon orders her team to kill Yoruichi, but Yoruichi takes them all out instantaneously.

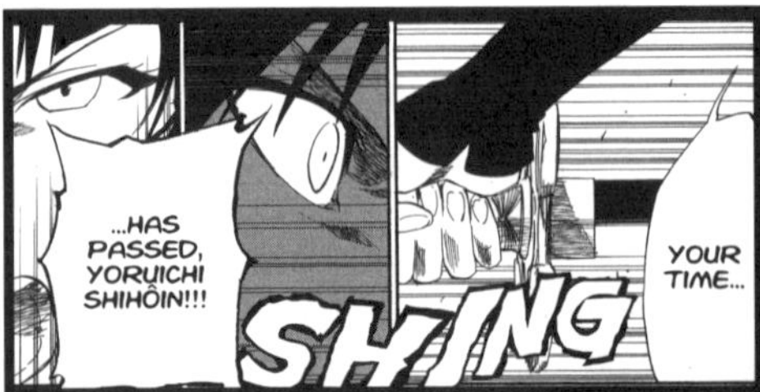
YOUR TIME...
SHING
...HAS PASSED, YORUICHI SHIHÔIN!!!

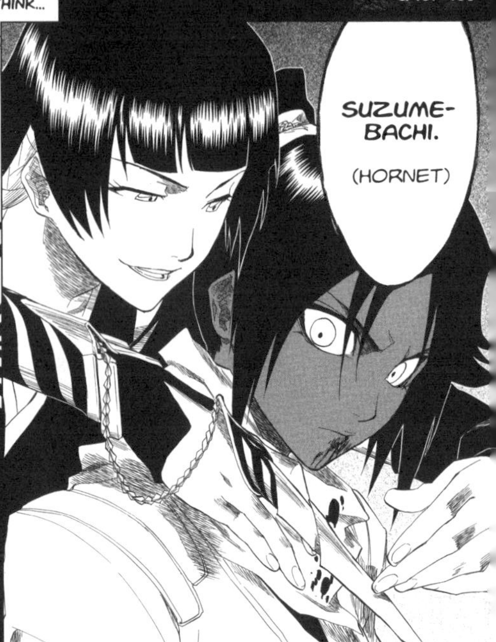
SUZUME-BACHI.
(HORNET)

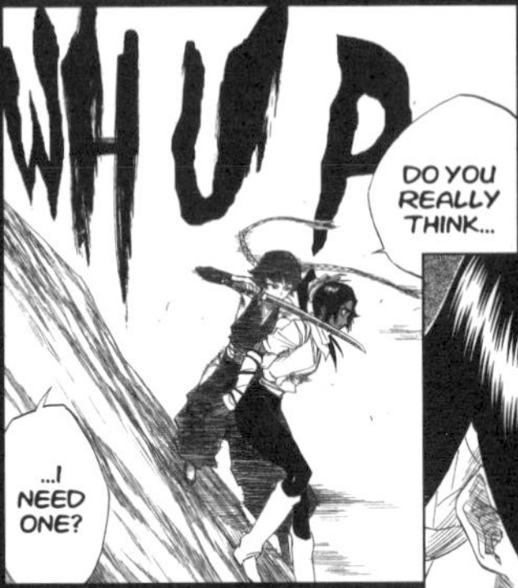
WHUP
DO YOU REALLY THINK...
...I NEED ONE?

STING ALL ENEMIES TO DEATH

Yoruichi struggles to fight Soi Fon, who is stronger than she anticipated. She manages to fight Soi Fon while she tries to get away. But Soi Fon uses Suzumebachi to etch death marks all over Yoruichi's body.

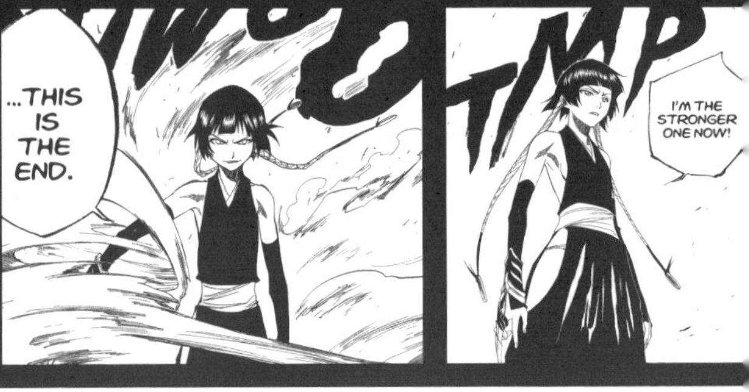
TMP
I'M THE STRONGER ONE NOW!
...THIS IS THE END.

At the end of their fierce battle, Soi Fon shows Yoruichi the technique she will finish her with. It is a new technique that Soi Fon has created that fuses hakuda with kidô, but..

死
ath

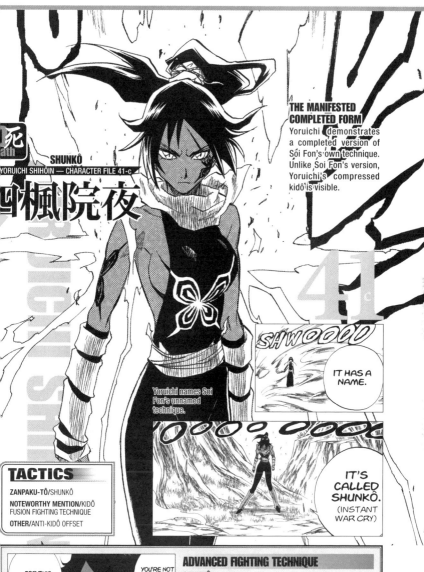

SHUNKÔ

YORUICHI SHIHÔIN — CHARACTER FILE 41-c

四楓院夜

41c

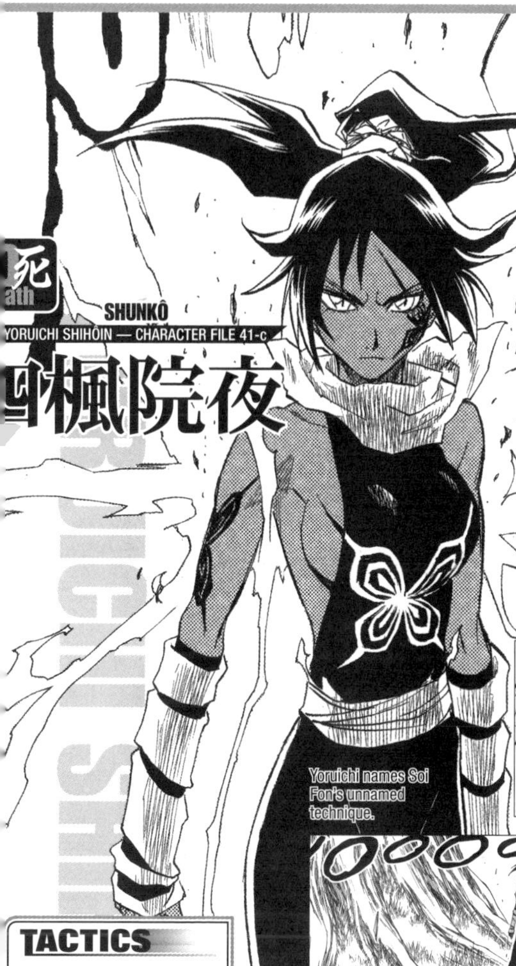

THE MANIFESTED COMPLETED FORM

Yoruichi demonstrates a completed version of Soi Fon's own technique. Unlike Soi Fon's version, Yoruichi's compressed kidô is visible.

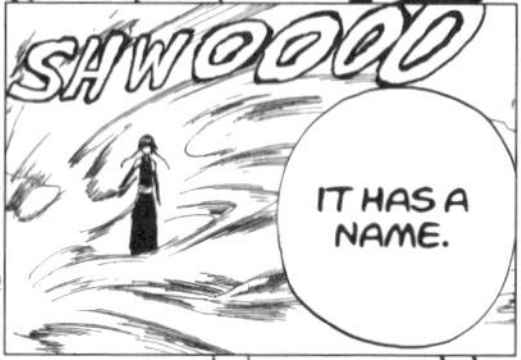
SHWOOOOO
IT HAS A NAME.

Yoruichi names Soi Fon's unnamed technique.

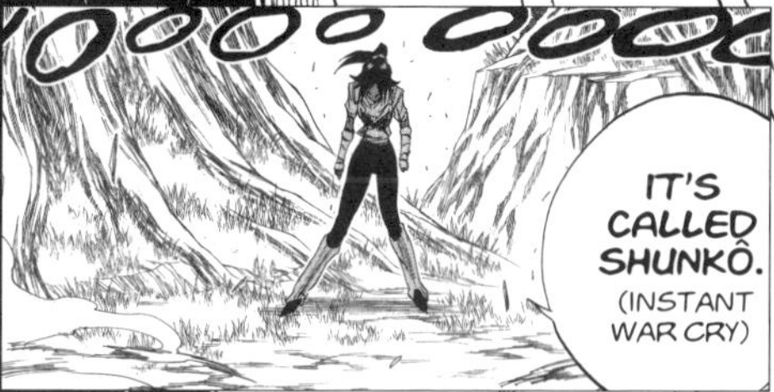
OOOOOO OOOOO
IT'S CALLED SHUNKÔ. (INSTANT WAR CRY)

TACTICS

ZANPAKU-TÔ/SHUNKÔ

NOTEWORTHY MENTION/KIDÔ FUSION FIGHTING TECHNIQUE

OTHER/ANTI-KIDÔ OFFSET

ADVANCED FIGHTING TECHNIQUE

SHUNKÔ

An advanced fighting technique that combines hakuda and kidô. The user fights by surrounding his back and arms with pressurized kidô. The keisen uniform has no back or sleeves because they will rip apart when this technique is activated.

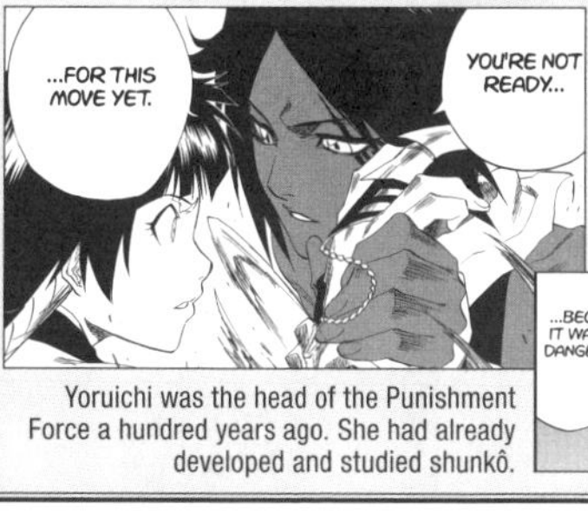
YOU'RE NOT READY...
...FOR THIS MOVE YET.

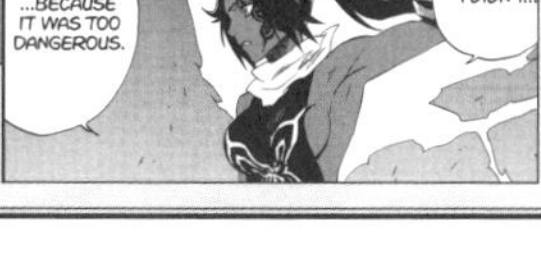
I DIDN'T...
...BECAUSE IT WAS TOO DANGEROUS.

Yoruichi was the head of the Punishment Force a hundred years ago. She had already developed and studied shunkô.

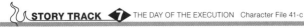

本心

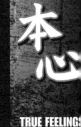

TRUE FEELINGS

Soi Fon's desire
VOL. 19-159

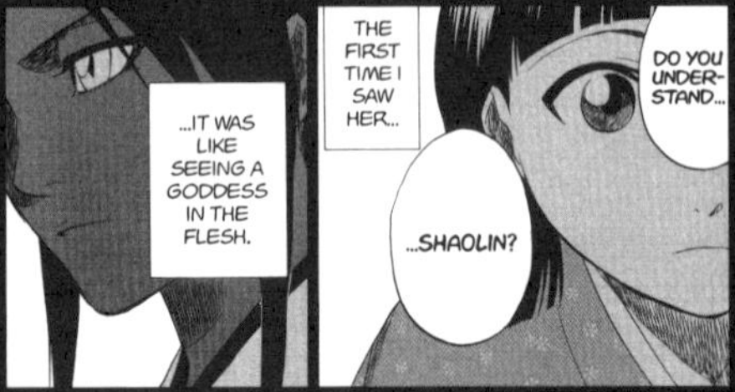
THE FIRST TIME I SAW HER...
DO YOU UNDERSTAND...
...SHAOLIN?
...IT WAS LIKE SEEING A GODDESS IN THE FLESH.

Soi Fon is overwhelmed by the power of the completed shunkô. She screams that she is stronger than Yoruichi, as if to convince herself that she is.

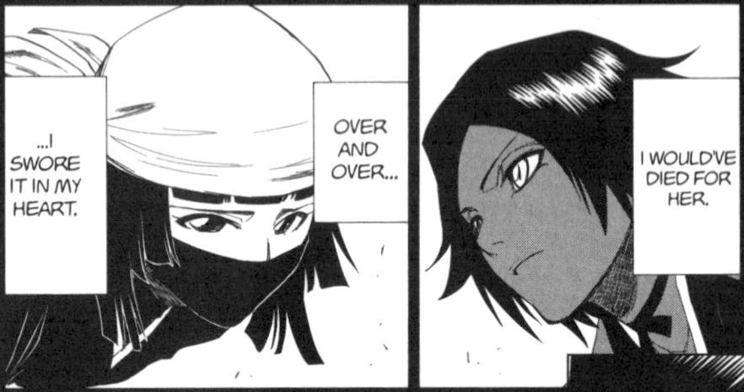
I WOULD'VE DIED FOR HER.
OVER AND OVER...
...I SWORE IT IN MY HEART.

SUDDEN BETRAYAL
Soi Fon worships and respects Yoruichi as if she were a god. She felt betrayed when Yoruichi disappeared.

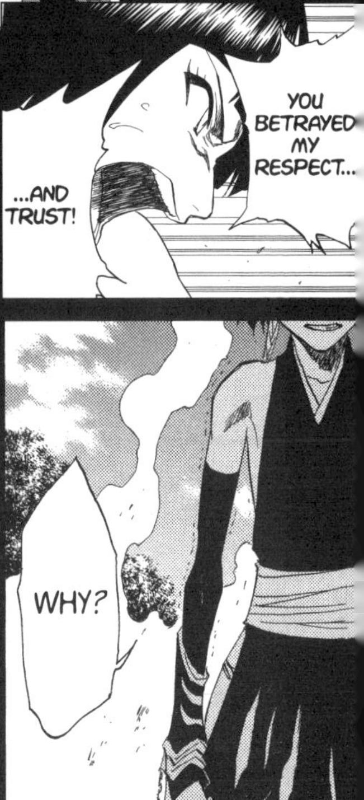
YOU BETRAYED MY RESPECT...
...AND TRUST!
WHY?

Soi Fon weeps as she states the desire she has suppressed for a hundred years...

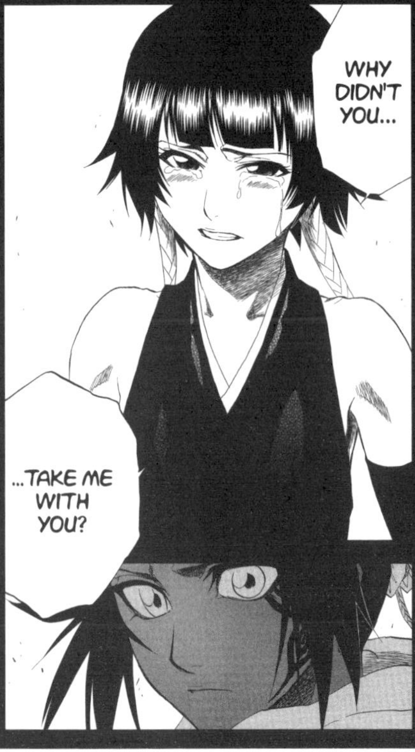
WHY DIDN'T YOU...
...TAKE ME WITH YOU?

FIRST COMPANY CAPTAIN

GENRYÛSAI SHIGEKUNI YAMAMOTO — CHARACTER FILE 47-b

D死eath

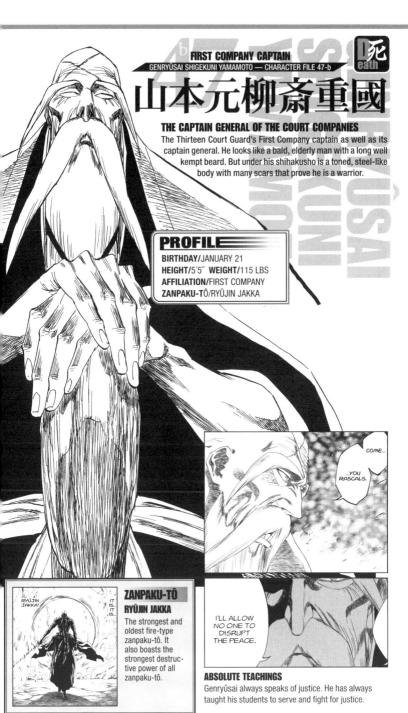

山本元柳斎重國

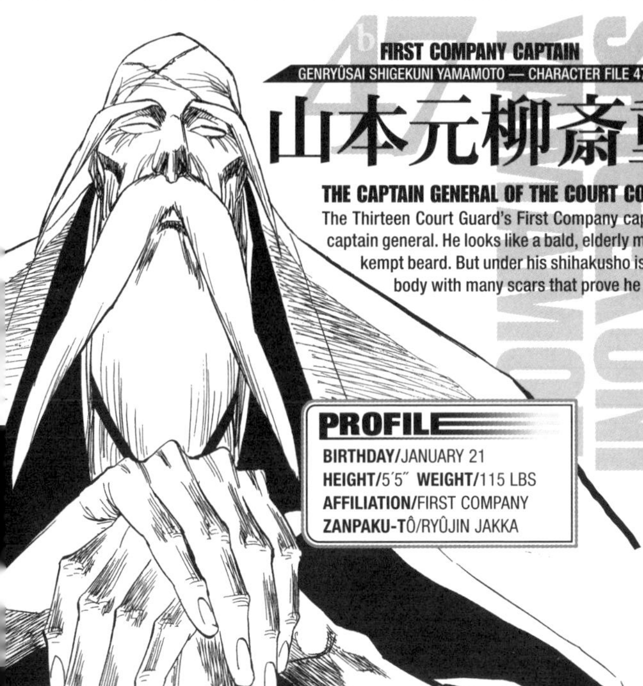

THE CAPTAIN GENERAL OF THE COURT COMPANIES

The Thirteen Court Guard's First Company captain as well as its captain general. He looks like a bald, elderly man with a long well kempt beard. But under his shihakusho is a toned, steel-like body with many scars that prove he is a warrior.

PROFILE

BIRTHDAY/JANUARY 21
HEIGHT/5′5″ **WEIGHT/**115 LBS
AFFILIATION/FIRST COMPANY
ZANPAKU-TÔ/RYÛJIN JAKKA

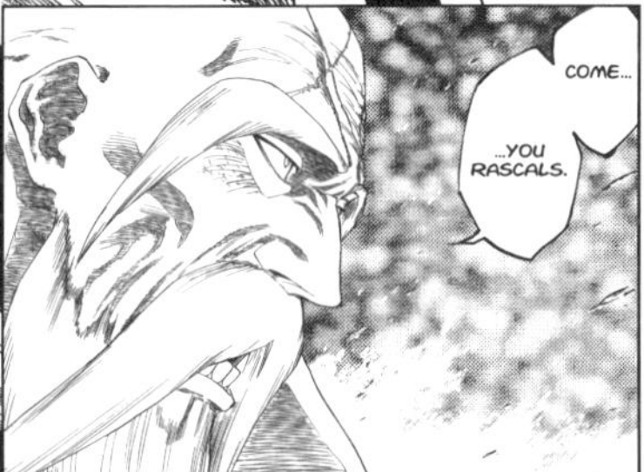
COME...
...YOU RASCALS.

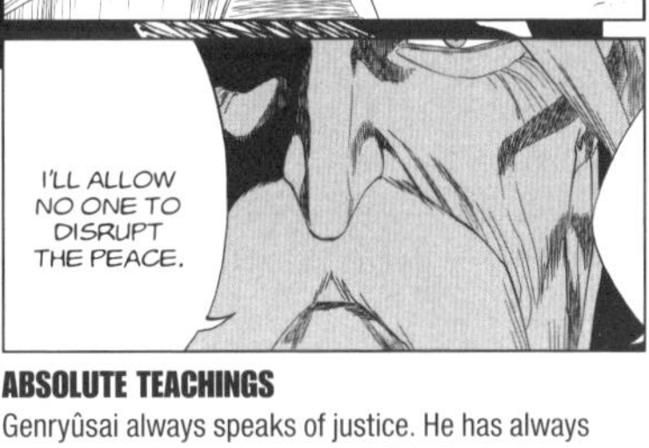
I'LL ALLOW NO ONE TO DISRUPT THE PEACE.

ABSOLUTE TEACHINGS

Genryûsai always speaks of justice. He has always taught his students to serve and fight for justice.

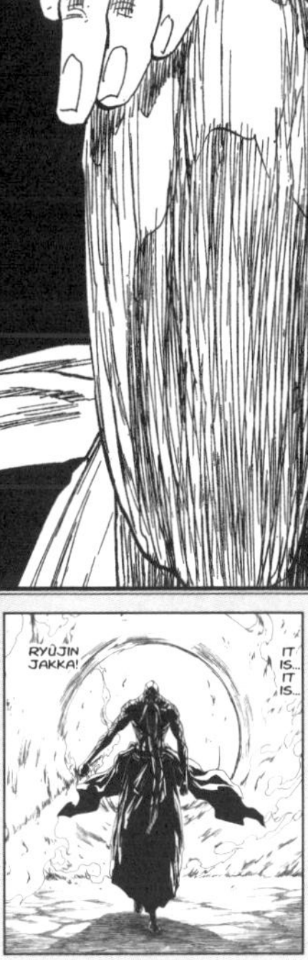
IT IS... IT IS...
RYÛJIN JAKKA!

ZANPAKU-TÔ

RYÛJIN JAKKA

The strongest and oldest fire-type zanpaku-tô. It also boasts the strongest destructive power of all zanpaku-tô.

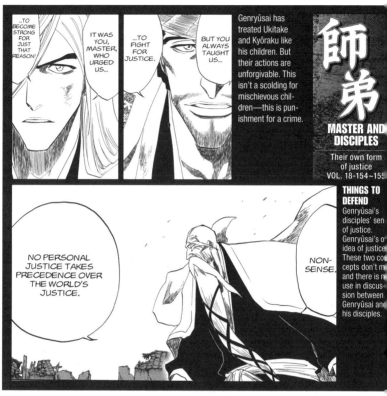

師弟 MASTER AND DISCIPLES

Their own form of justice
VOL. 18-154~155

BUT YOU ALWAYS TAUGHT US...
...TO FIGHT FOR JUSTICE.

IT WAS YOU, MASTER, WHO URGED US...
...TO BECOME STRONG FOR JUST THAT REASON!

Genryûsai has treated Ukitake and Kyôraku like his children. But their actions are unforgivable. This isn't a scolding for mischievous children—this is punishment for a crime.

NON-SENSE.
NO PERSONAL JUSTICE TAKES PRECEDENCE OVER THE WORLD'S JUSTICE.

THINGS TO DEFEND

Genryûsai's disciples' sen of justice. Genryûsai's o idea of justice These two co cepts don't m and there is n use in discus-sion between Genryûsai an his disciples.

SOUL REAPER TRAINING ORGANIZATION

SOUL REAPER ACADEMY

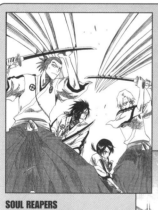

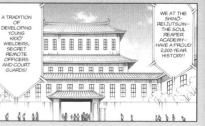

The educational organization that Genryûsai established 2,000 years ago that was meant to train future members of the Kidô Corps, the Stealth Force, and the Thirteen Court Guard Companies. Its lessons range from training in all four basic fighting techniques to practicing soul funerals in the world of the living. It normally takes six years to graduate, but gifted students can graduate sooner by skipping years. It's always wide open, and the school will even admit those from the Rukongai, so long as they pass the entrance exam.

SOUL REAPERS FROM THE ACADEMY

Most of the Soul Reapers from the Rukongai are graduates of the academy. Incidentally, Ukitake and Kyôraku are the first graduates of the Academy to become captains of the Thirteen Court Guard Companies.

WE AT THE SHINÔ-REIJUTSUIN--THE SOUL REAPER ACADEMY--HAVE A PROUD 2,000-YEAR HISTORY!
A TRADITION OF DEVELOPING YOUNG KIDÔ WIELDERS, SECRET REMOTE OFFICERS AND COURT GUARDS!
WE HOPE THAT EACH OF YOU WILL HONOR THAT TRADITION!

SÔGYO NO KOTOWARI

JÛSHIRÔ UKITAKE — CHARACTER FILE 68-c

Death 死

浮竹十四郎

JÛSHIRÔ UKITAKE

c 68

"WAVE, BECOME MY SHIELD! LIGHTNING, BECOME MY BLADE!"

Ukitake's beliefs tell him that Rukia's execution is wrong and must be stopped. To serve his sense of justice, he and Kyôraku destroy Kikô Oh and release their zanpaku-tô to challenge their teacher, Genryûsai.

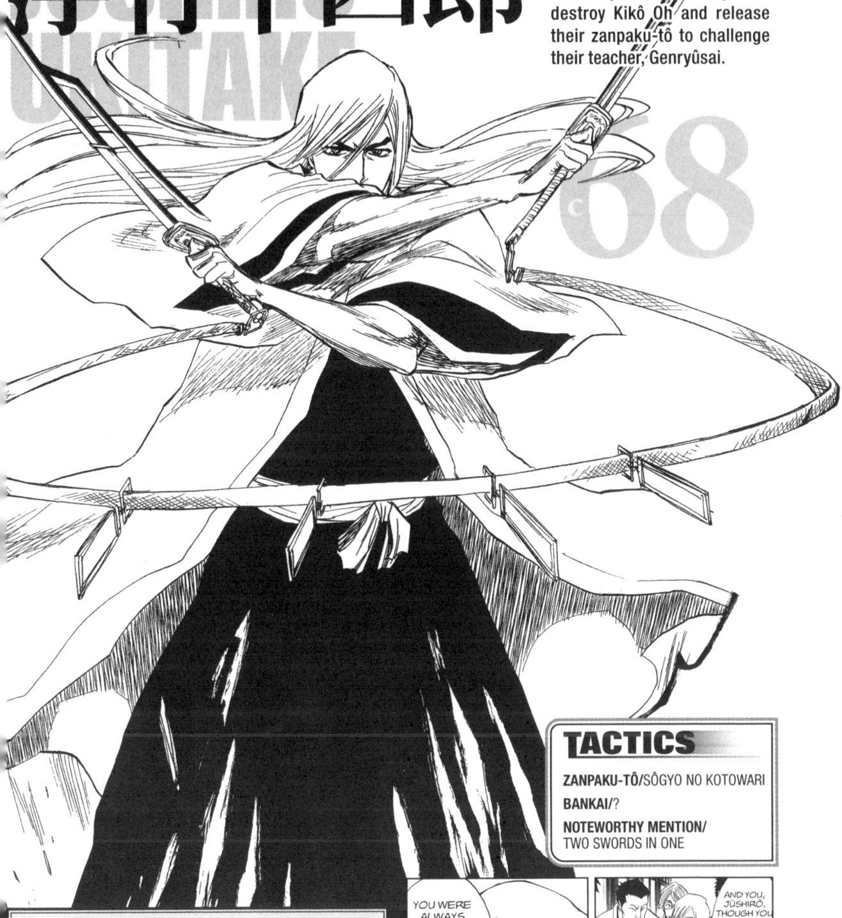

TACTICS

ZANPAKU-TÔ/SÔGYO NO KOTOWARI

BANKAI/?

NOTEWORTHY MENTION/
TWO SWORDS IN ONE

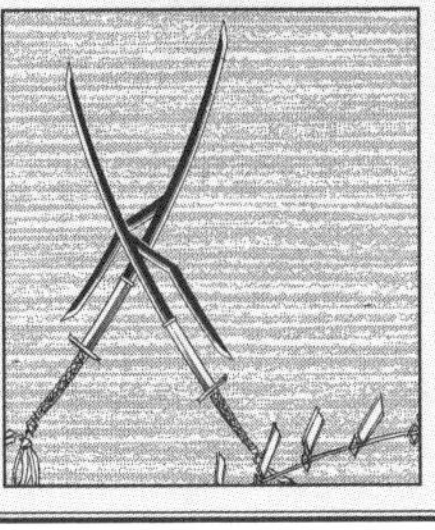

ZANPAKU-TÔ

SÔGYO NO KOTOWARI

When released, this zanpaku-tô splits into two swords.

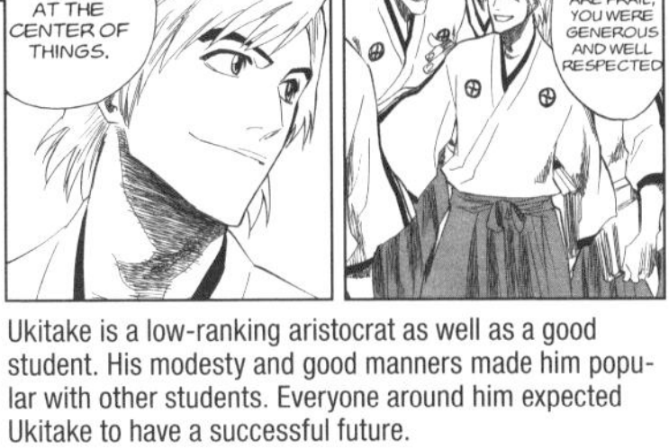
AND YOU, JŪSHIRŌ, THOUGH YOU ARE FRAIL, YOU WERE GENEROUS AND WELL RESPECTED.
YOU WERE ALWAYS AT THE CENTER OF THINGS.

Ukitake is a low-ranking aristocrat as well as a good student. His modesty and good manners made him popular with other students. Everyone around him expected Ukitake to have a successful future.

KATEN KYÔKOTSU

SHÛNSUI KYÔRAKU — CHARACTER FILE 58-c

京楽春水

"WHEN THE FLOWER WIND RAGES, THE FLOWER GOD ROARS. WHEN THE WIND OF HEAVEN RAGES, THE GOD OF THE UNDERWORLD SNEERS…"

Kyôraku thinks it's strange to brand the ryoka as enemies without hearing their story...He also has misgivings about recent events. Though their lines of reasoning were different, Kyôraku reaches the same conclusion as Ukitake. The two of them work together to take on their teacher, "Old Man Yama."

TACTICS

ZANPAKU-TÔ/KATEN KYÔKOTSU

BANKAI/?

NOTEWORTHY MENTION/
TWO SWORDS IN ONE

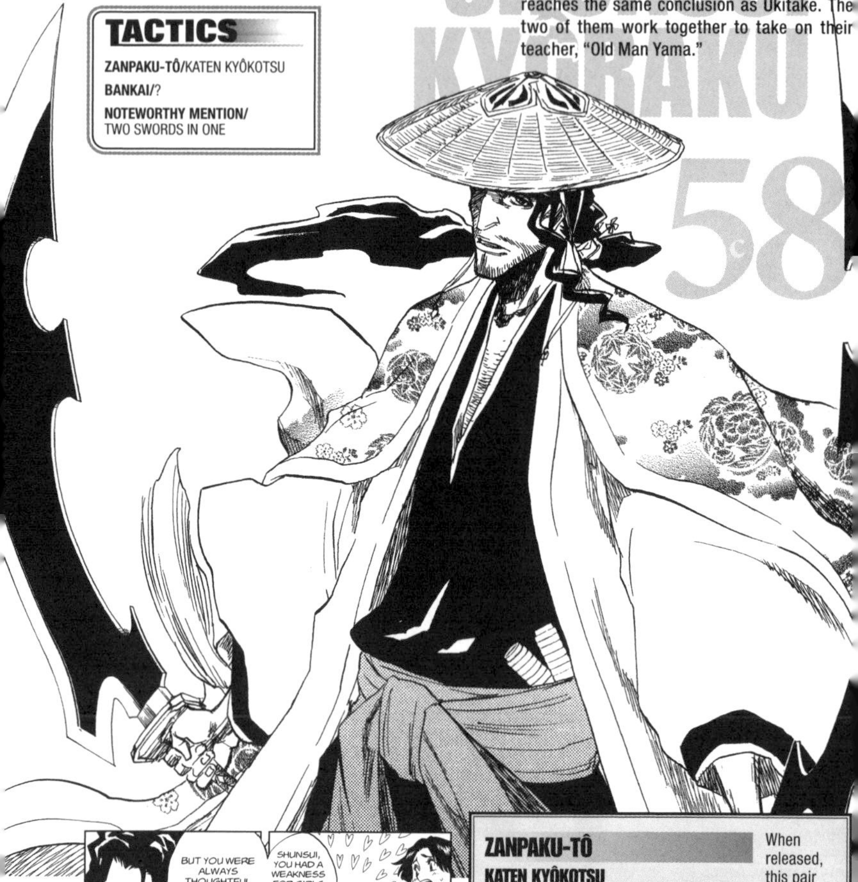

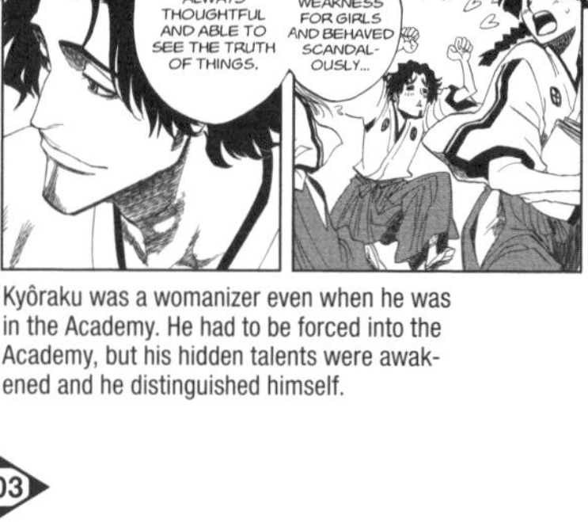
SHUNSUI, YOU HAD A WEAKNESS FOR GIRLS AND BEHAVED SCANDAL-OUSLY...
BUT YOU WERE ALWAYS THOUGHTFUL AND ABLE TO SEE THE TRUTH OF THINGS.

Kyôraku was a womanizer even when he was in the Academy. He had to be forced into the Academy, but his hidden talents were awakened and he distinguished himself.

ZANPAKU-TÔ

KATEN KYÔKOTSU

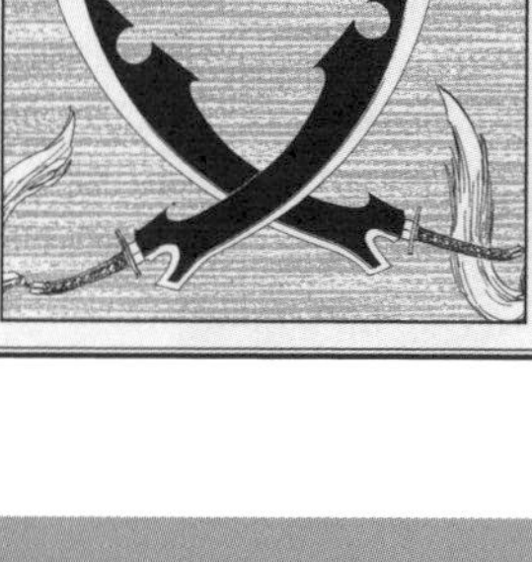

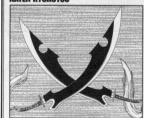

When released, this pair of long and short swords transforms into swords that resemble Chinese falchions.

激突

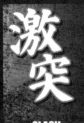

CLASH

Ichigo vs. Byakuya
VOL. 18-152~153

The Sôkyoku is destroyed and Ichigo finally manages to save Rukia. Byakuya stands before him and asks Ichigo why he wants to save Rukia. In return, Ichigo asks Byakuya why he won't save Rukia, even though he's her older brother.

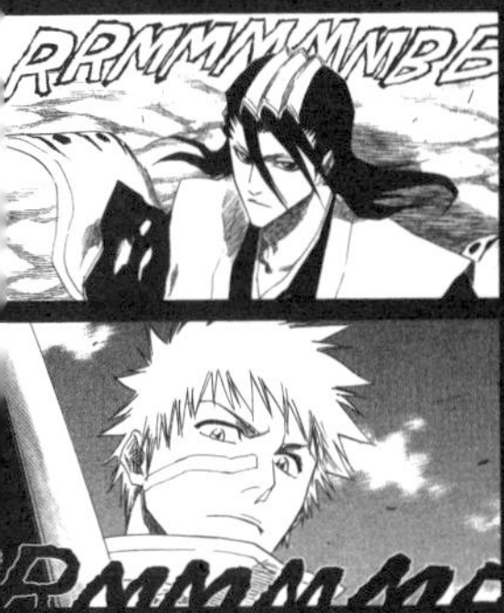

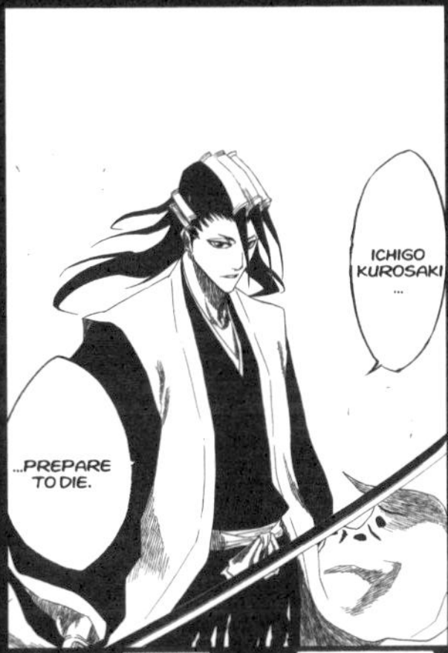
ICHIGO KUROSAKI...
...PREPARE TO DIE.

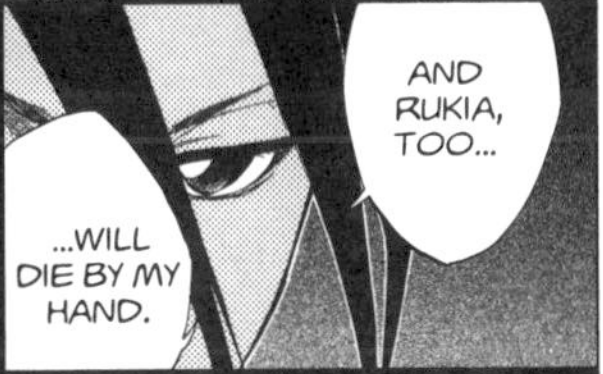
AND RUKIA, TOO...
...WILL DIE BY MY HAND.

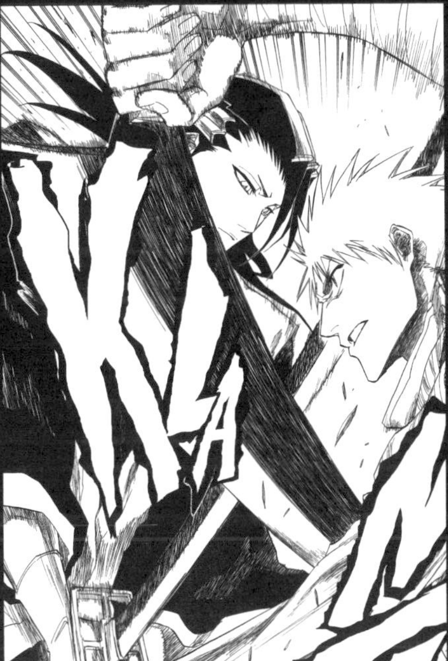

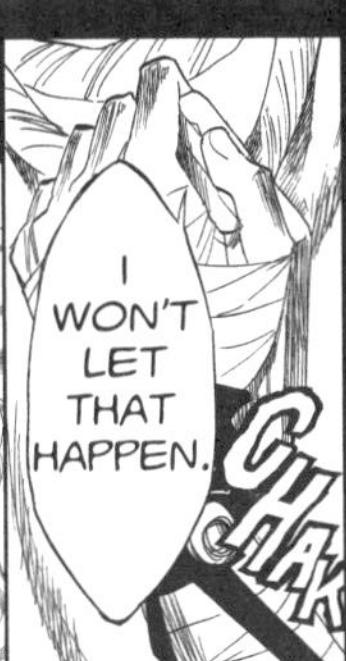
I WON'T LET THAT HAPPEN.
CHAK

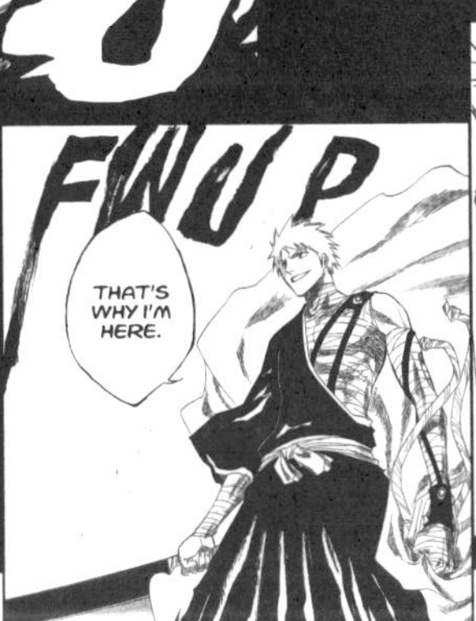
FWUP
THAT'S WHY I'M HERE.

THE TIME OF SETTLEMENT
Ichigo and Byakuya's different motives cannot be resolved with discussion. They both release their spiritual energy... There is no other way to stop Rukia's execution aside from shattering Byakuya's will... Ichigo has made up his mind. He removes his tentoken and firmly grips Zangetsu!!

挑発

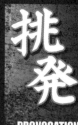

PROVOCATION

Byakuya's bankai
VOL. 19-160~161

Ichigo seethes when Byakuya says that he will execute Rukia himself. As an older brother, as someone with the character for "protect" in his name (the "go" in Ichigo), Ichigo declares that he will give it his all to crush Byakuya. Ichigo tells Byakuya to show his bankai. He defeats Byakuya's Senbonzakura with his Getsuga Tenshô. Byakuya is forced to take the fight seriously.

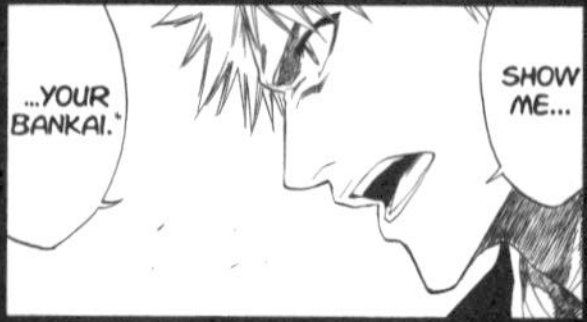
SHOW ME...
...YOUR BANKAI.*

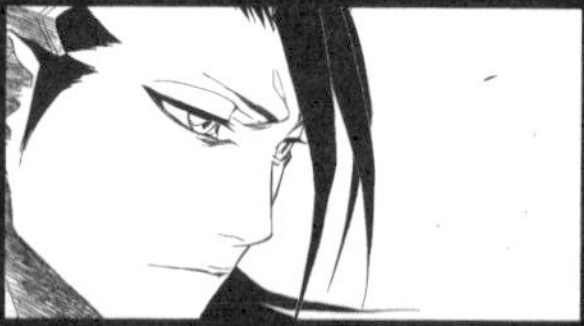

Byakuya releases his bankai, Senbonzakura Kageyoshi. A stream of cherry blossom-like blades pierce Ichigo's body and slam him into the ground.

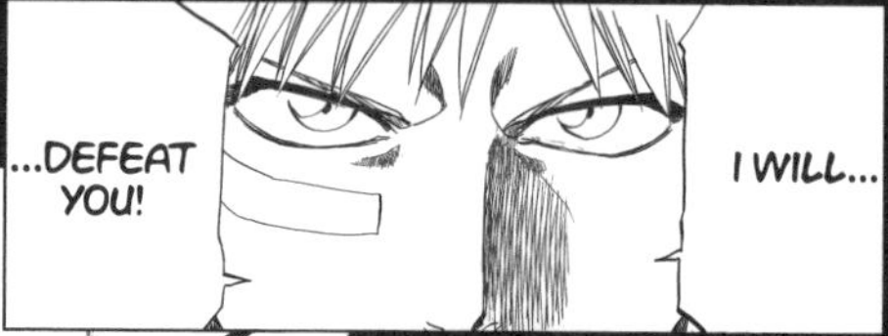
I WILL...
...DEFEAT YOU!

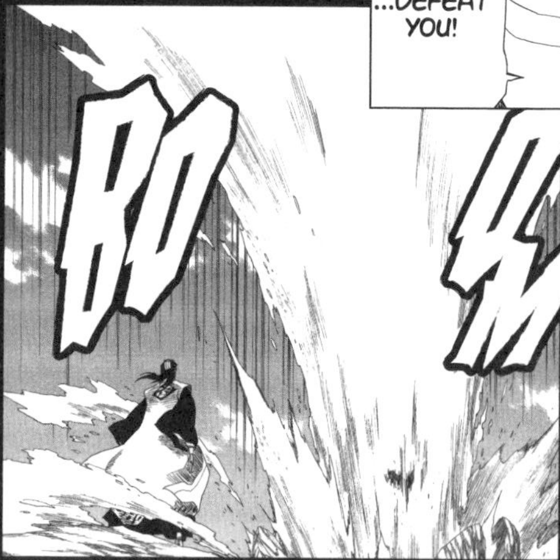
BO
OM

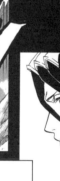

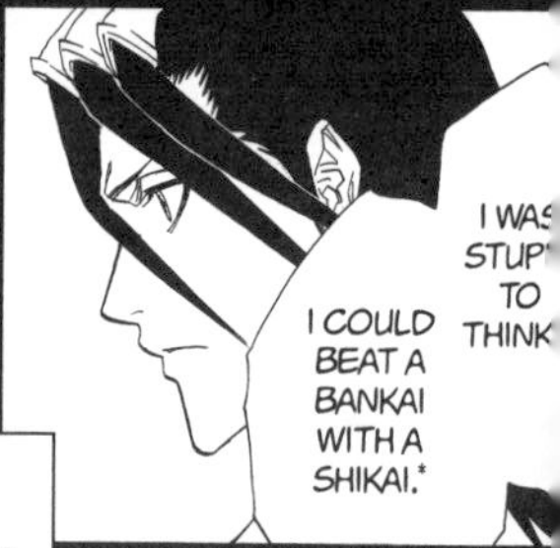
I WAS STUP TO THINK
I COULD BEAT A BANKAI WITH A SHIKAI.*

SECOND STAGE OF RELEASE

Ichigo's body is slashed. Lying on the ground, he says he was foolish to try and beat a bankai with a shikai. Byakuya coldly tells him to watch his tongue, since he makes it sound like he has achieved bankai. Ichigo makes up his mind and yells, "That's exactly what I'm saying, Byakuya Kuchiki!!!"

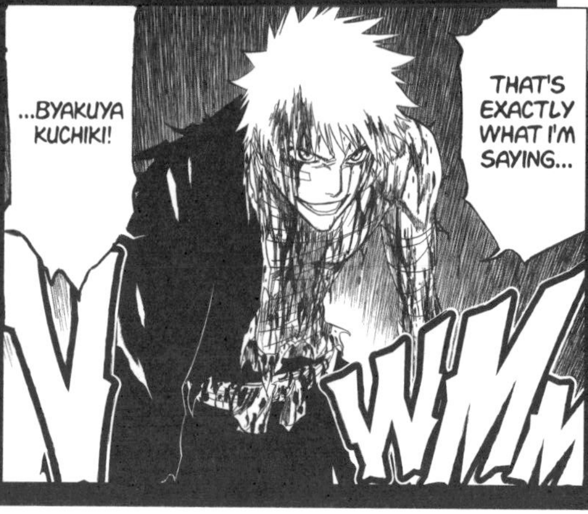
THAT'S EXACTLY WHAT I'M SAYING...
...BYAKUYA KUCHIKI!
WM

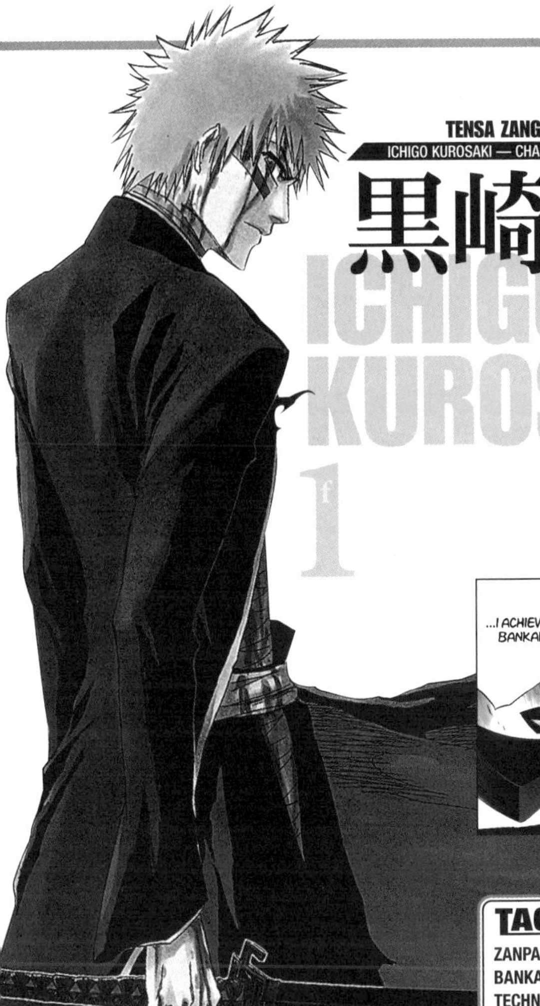

D
死
eath

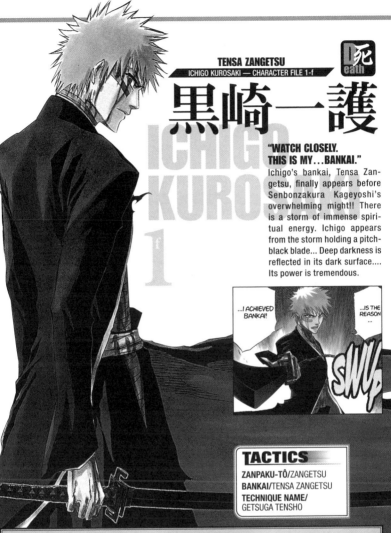

TENSA ZANGETSU

ICHIGO KUROSAKI — CHARACTER FILE 1-f

黒崎一護

ICHIGO KUROSAKI 1 f

"WATCH CLOSELY. THIS IS MY...BANKAI."

Ichigo's bankai, Tensa Zangetsu, finally appears before Senbonzakura Kageyoshi's overwhelming might!! There is a storm of immense spiritual energy. Ichigo appears from the storm holding a pitch-black blade... Deep darkness is reflected in its dark surface.... Its power is tremendous.

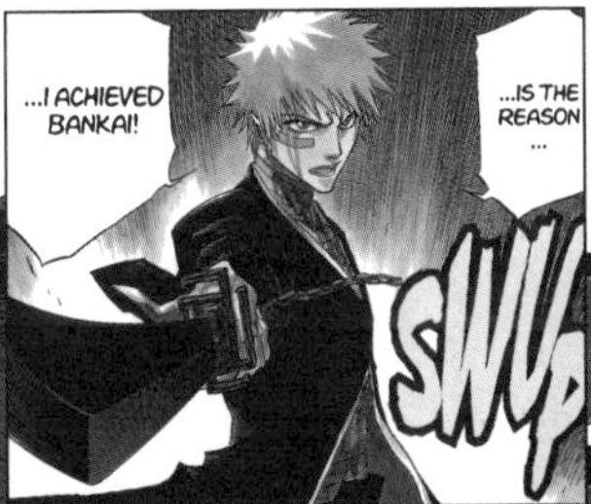

...IS THE REASON ...
...I ACHIEVED BANKAI!
SWUP

TACTICS

ZANPAKU-TÔ/ZANGETSU
BANKAI/TENSA ZANGETSU
TECHNIQUE NAME/
GETSUGA TENSHO

BANKAI
TENSA ZANGETSU

Tensa Zangetsu is the ultimate power Ichigo gained after a long deadly battle with Zangetsu. It channels all of the bankai power into speed, thus allowing the user to battle at a feverish pace. It is small compared to other bankai.

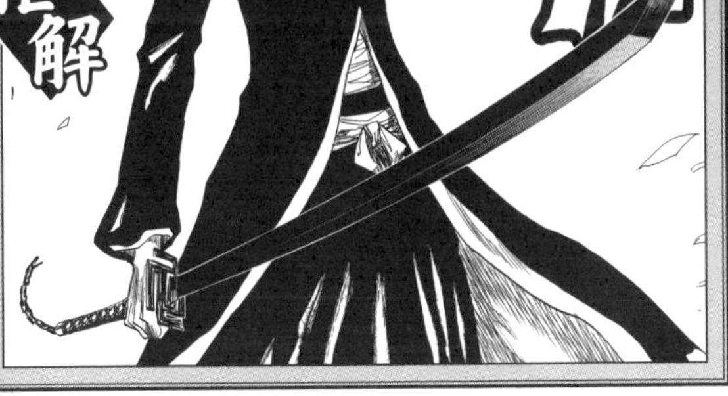

卍解

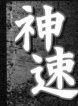

神速

GOD-LIKE SPEE

Fastest Bankai Fighting Speed
VOL. 19-163

Like lightning, Ichigo pressures Byakuya with god-like speed and attacks him at close range!

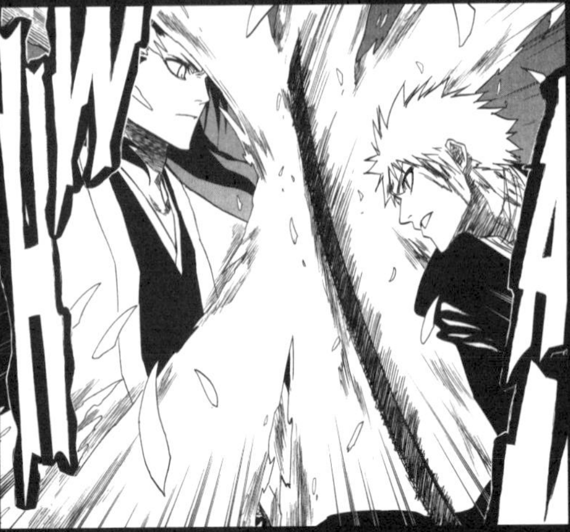

Byakuya's Senbonzakura Kageyoshi constantly changes its form as it attacks. Ichigo dodges it with his fastest bankai fighting speed. Byakuya is able to increase his Senbonzakura's speed by manipulating it with the palms of his hands. But just as it looks as if he will triumph, Ichigo intensely swipes away all of the blades coming at him... Ichigo's speed is beyond what Byakuya imagined.

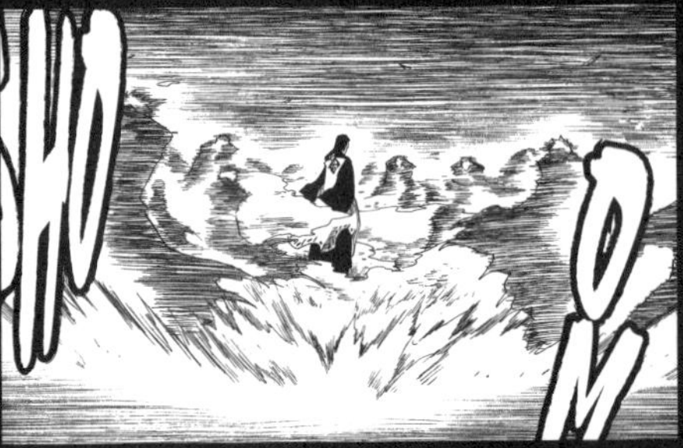

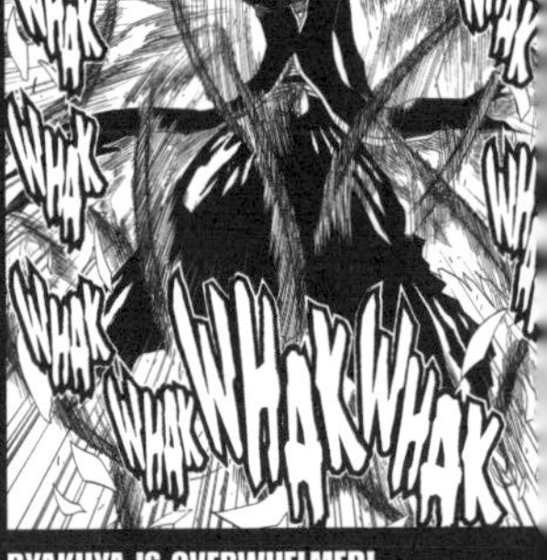
WHAK WHAK WHAK WHAK WHAK

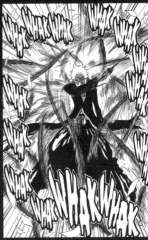

BYAKUYA IS OVERWHELMED!
Ichigo reminds Byakuya that miracles happen only once. Byakuya allowed Ichigo to get close to him twice. Byakuya burns with anger at his shattered confidence and pride! He decides to give it his all and release Senbonzakura's true power to defeat Ichigo.

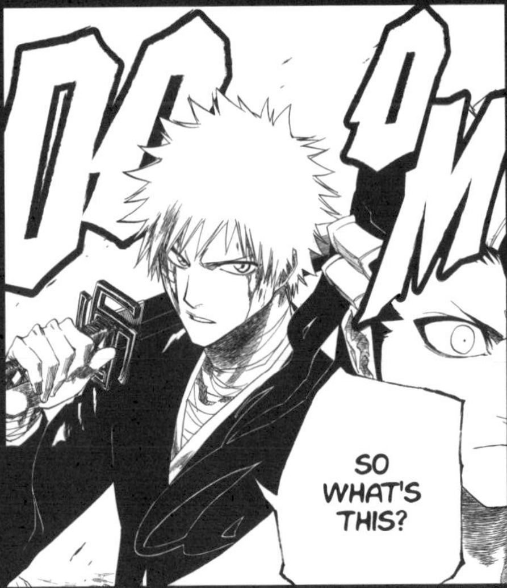
DOOM
SO WHAT'S THIS?

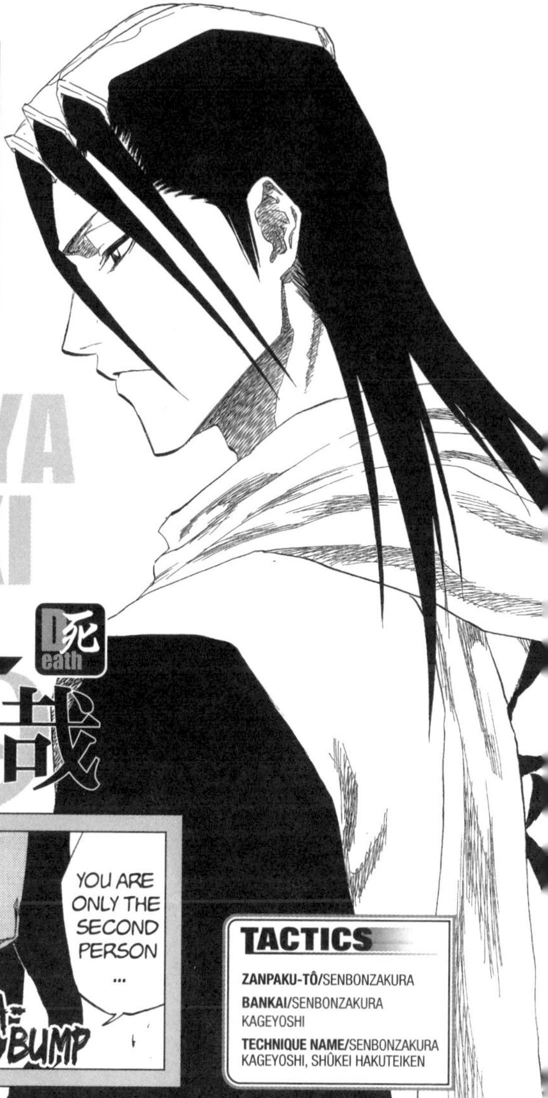

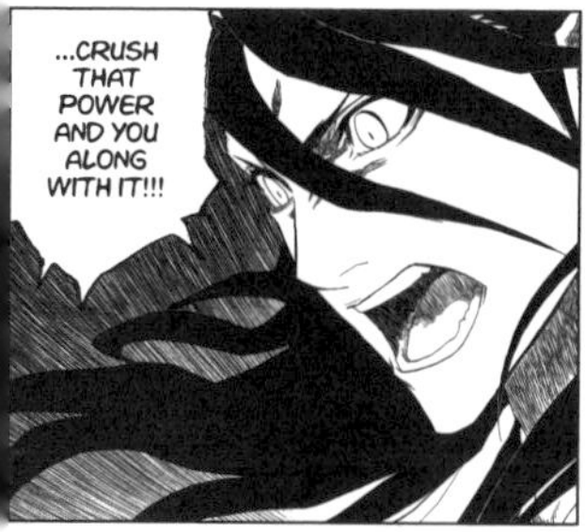
...CRUSH THAT POWER AND YOU ALONG WITH IT!!!

AN ILLUSTRIOUS GAZE FILLED WITH ANXIETY

Perhaps it is his pride as the head of the Kuchiki family, but Byakuya always suppresses his feelings and acts calmly. But with his pride crushed, he explodes in anger! He says, "Behold, Ichigo Kurasaki. This is the true form of Senbonzakura." The falling blades gather and a thousand blades appear in the air... It is Senkei Senbonzakura Kageyoshi!

BYAKUYA KUCHIKI

SENKEI SENBONZAKURA KAGEYOSHI

BYAKUYA KUCHIKI — CHARACTER FILE 39-e

Death 死

朽木百哉

39 e

Byakuya says that Ichigo is the second person he has activated his Senkei against. Who is the first person?!

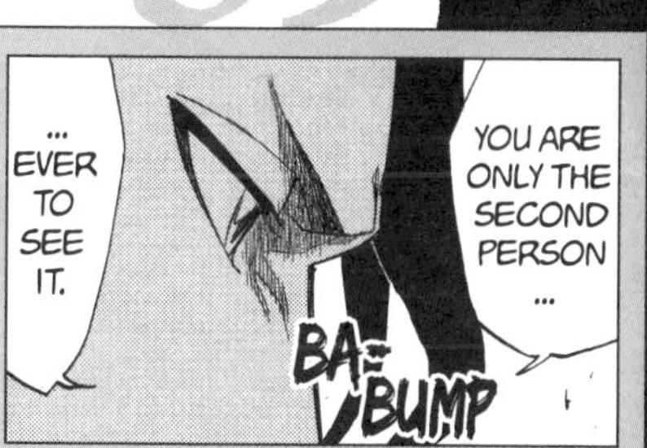
YOU ARE ONLY THE SECOND PERSON ...
... EVER TO SEE IT.
BA-BUMP

TACTICS

ZANPAKU-TÔ/SENBONZAKURA

BANKAI/SENBONZAKURA KAGEYOSHI

TECHNIQUE NAME/SENBONZAKURA KAGEYOSHI, SHÛKEI HAKUTEIKEN

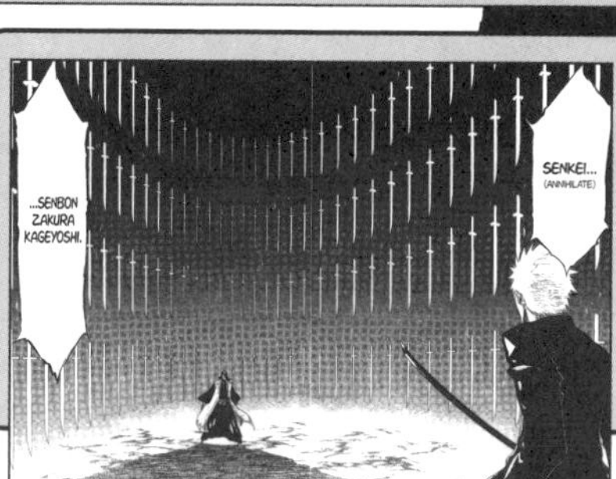
SENKEI... (ANNIHILATE)
...SENBON ZAKURA KAGEYOSHI.

SENBONZAKURA'S TRUE FORM

SENKEI SENBONZAKURA KAGEYOSHI

Byakuya only shows Senbonzakura's true form to people he vows he will slice. Its form disregards defense and specializes in death. Its ability to kill is double that of Senbonzakura Kageyoshi.

決断

DECISION

Serious battle
VOL. 19-164

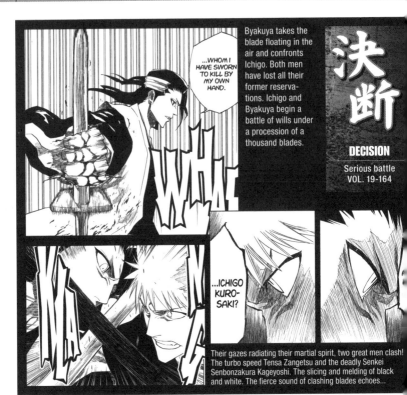

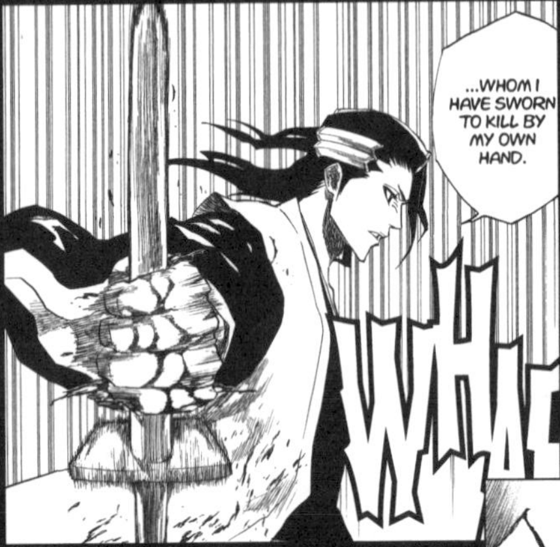
...WHOM I HAVE SWORN TO KILL BY MY OWN HAND.

Byakuya takes the blade floating in the air and confronts Ichigo. Both men have lost all their former reservations. Ichigo and Byakuya begin a battle of wills under a procession of a thousand blades.

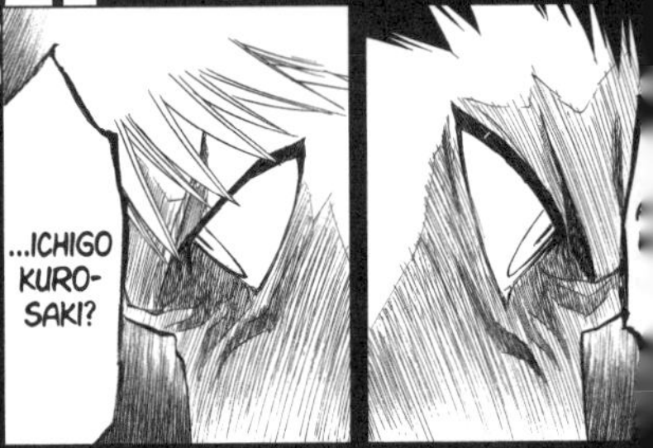
...ICHIGO KURO-SAKI?

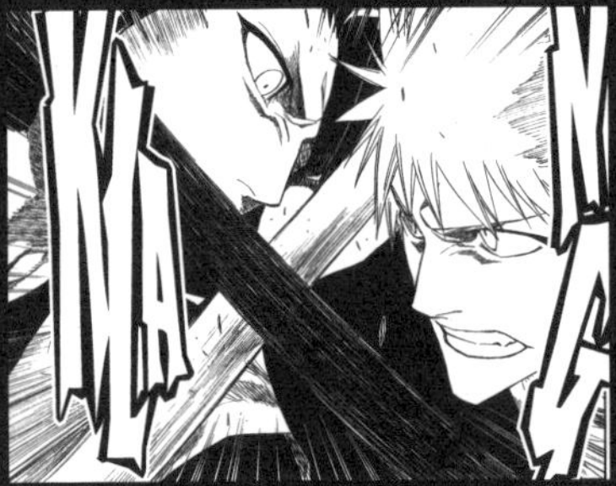

Their gazes radiating their martial spirit, two great men clash! The turbo speed Tensa Zangetsu and the deadly Senkei Senbonzakura Kageyoshi. The slicing and melding of black and white. The fierce sound of clashing blades echoes...

URYÛ AND ORIHIME...

THE FEELINGS OF THOSE FROM THE WORLD OF THE LIVING

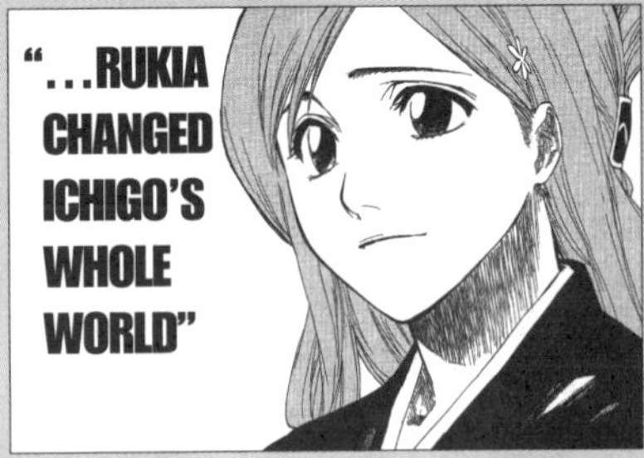

"...RUKIA CHANGED ICHIGO'S WHOLE WORLD"

Ichigo is no ordinary friend... Orihime understands Ichigo's concern for Rukia. Her heart is pained. Uryû has recurring insecurities... He doesn't want Orihime to be sad, so he hopes that Ichigo will be victorious in his struggle.

Those from the world of the living fight because their hearts are overflowing with feelings for Ichigo.

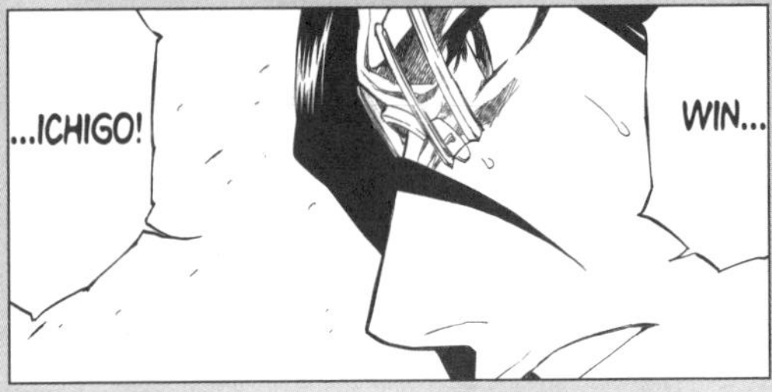
WIN...
...ICHIGO!

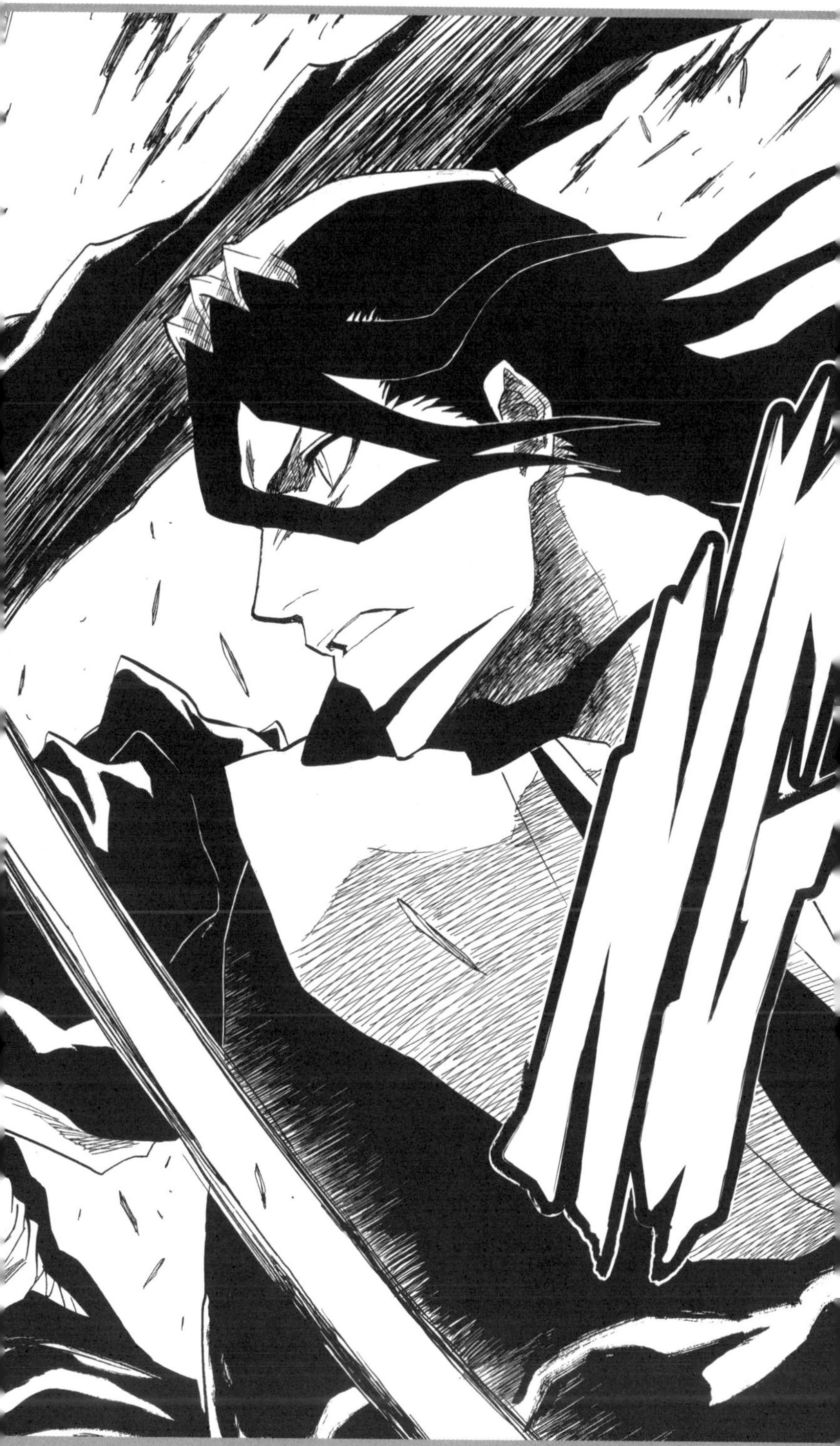

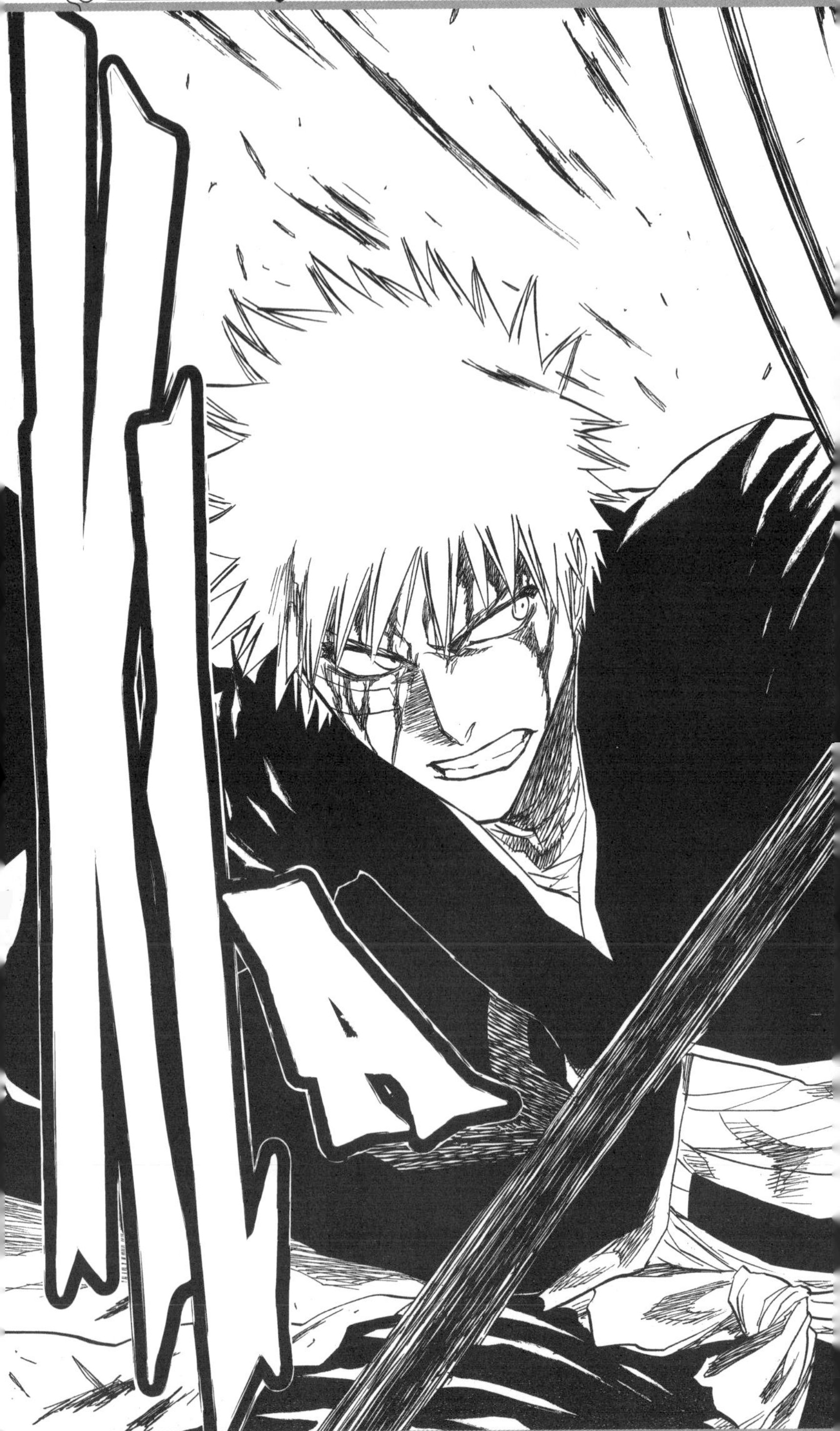

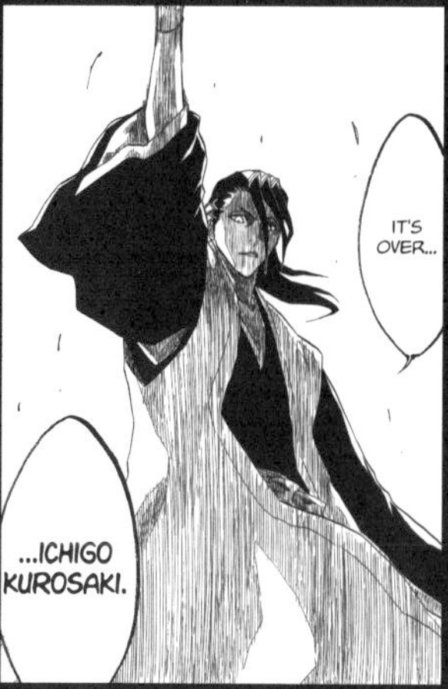
IT'S OVER...
...ICHIGO KUROSAKI.

Ichigo thinks that Byakuya is gradually gaining speed as he crosses blades with him... But Byakuya's speed hasn't changed at all. Ichigo's speed has begun to rapidly decline! Ichigo has been fighting fierce battles ever since he infiltrated the Soul Society. His physical body has already reached its limit and his muscles and bones are screaming. At that moment...

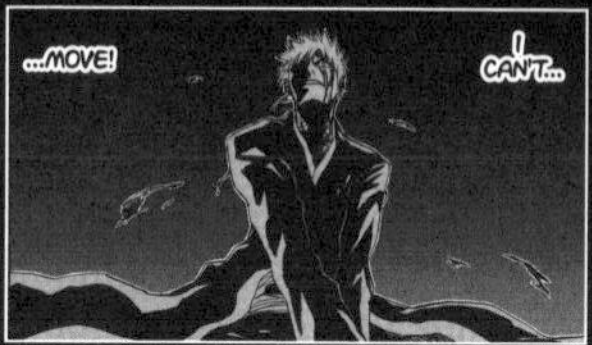
I CAN'T...
...MOVE!

虚化

HOLLOW TRANSFORMATION

The emergent mask
VOL. 19-165

HOLLOW MASK

ICHIGO KUROSAKI — CHARACTER FILE 1-g

Death 死

黒崎一護

"WHO AM I? I HAVE NO NAME."

Another Ichigo whose face is half-covered by a Hollow mask. He stops Byakuya's sword with his hand and easily crushes it! His fighting power far exceeds that of the usual Ichigo.

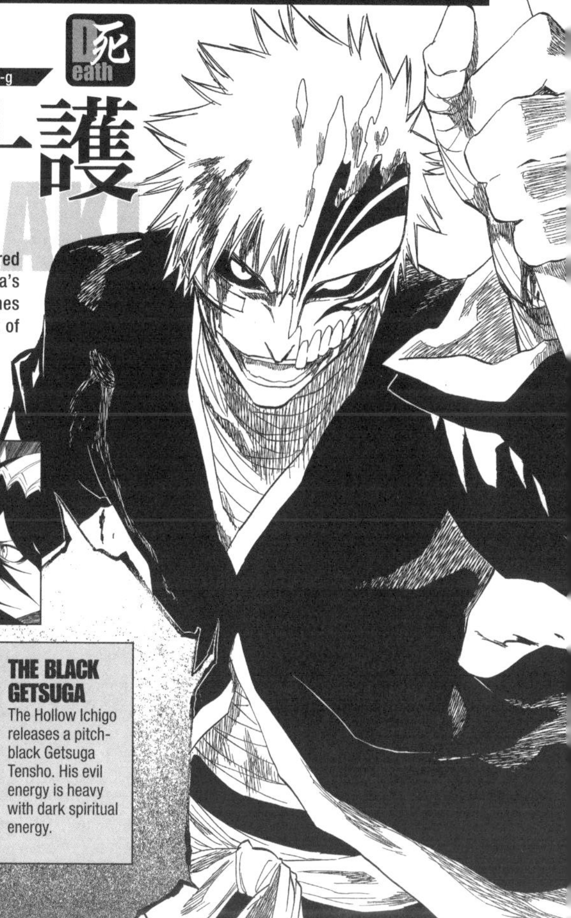

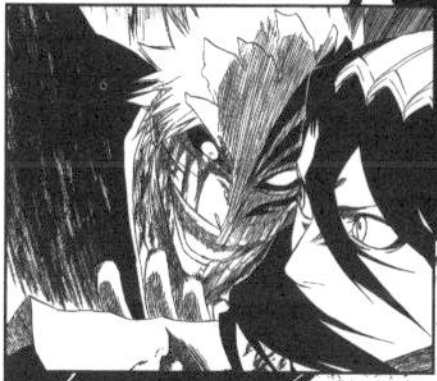

The Hollow Ichigo drives Byakuya back with incredible speed. Byakuya senses something ominous behind him!

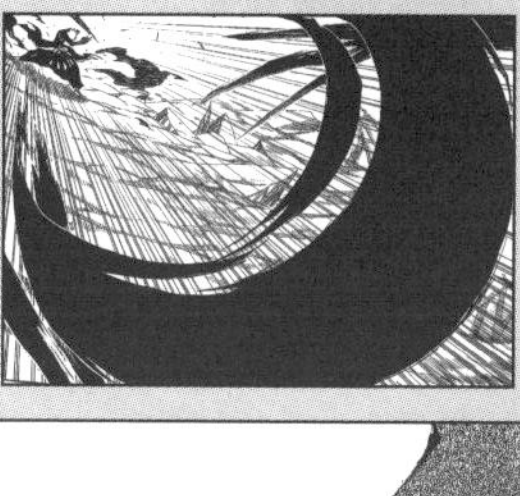

THE BLACK GETSUGA

The Hollow Ichigo releases a pitch-black Getsuga Tensho. His evil energy is heavy with dark spiritual energy.

黒と白

BLACK AND WH

The final strike
VOL. 19-166

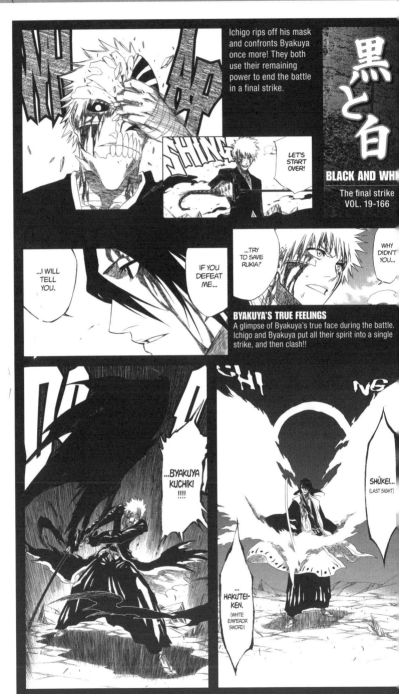

Ichigo rips off his mask and confronts Byakuya once more! They both use their remaining power to end the battle in a final strike.

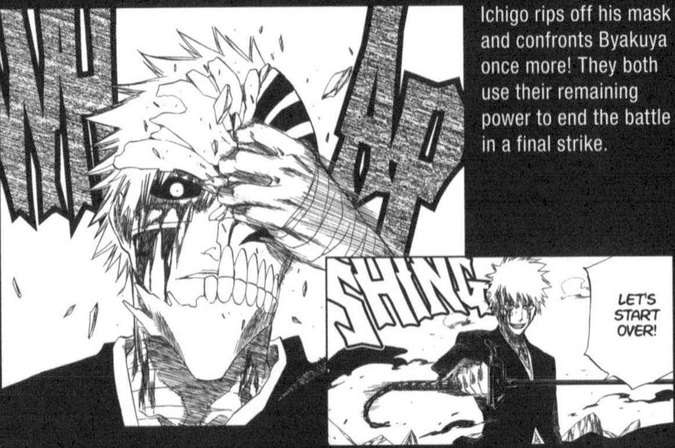
WHAP
SHING
LET'S START OVER!

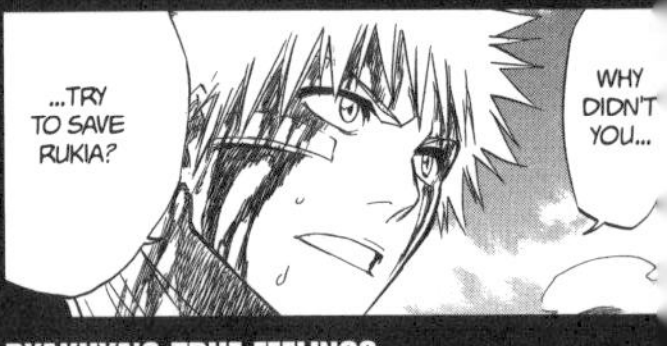
WHY DIDN'T YOU...
...TRY TO SAVE RUKIA?

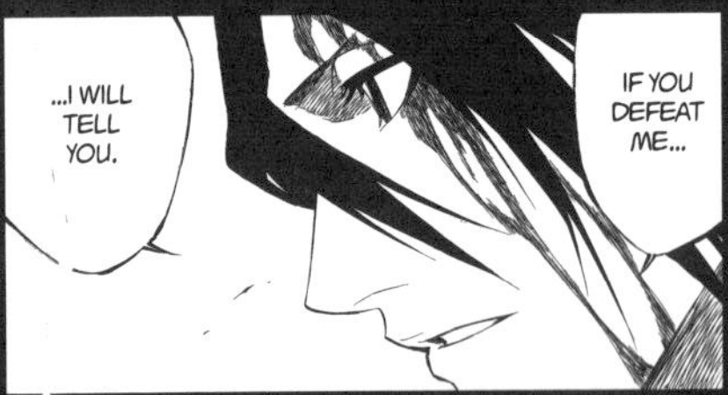
IF YOU DEFEAT ME...
...I WILL TELL YOU.

BYAKUYA'S TRUE FEELINGS
A glimpse of Byakuya's true face during the battle. Ichigo and Byakuya put all their spirit into a single strike, and then clash!!

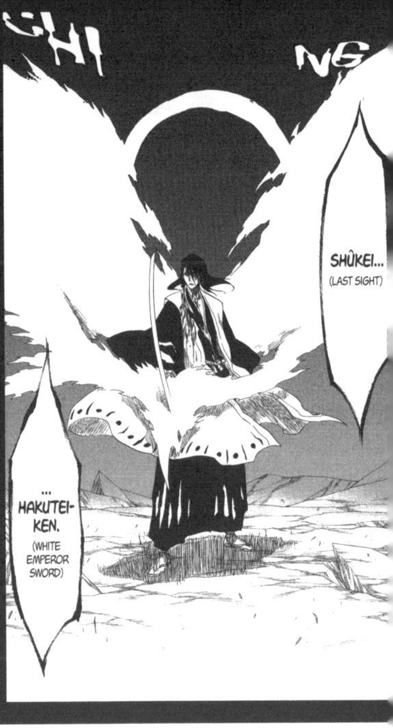
CHI
NG
SHÛKEI...
(LAST SIGHT)
...HAKUTEI-KEN.
(WHITE EMPEROR SWORD)

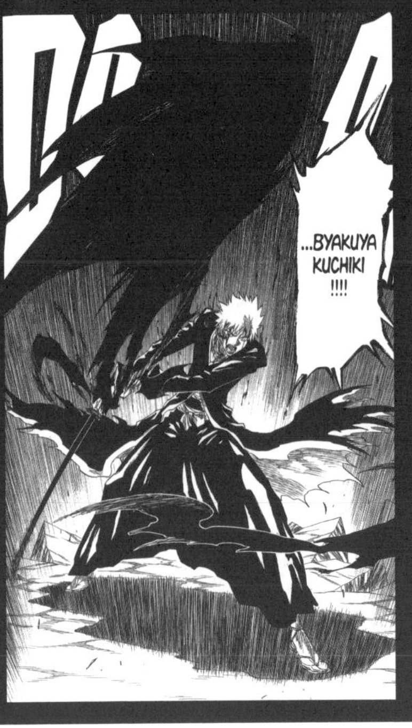
...BYAKUYA KUCHIKI !!!!

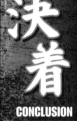

決着

CONCLUSION

The outcome
VOL. 19-166~167

There is a black wing and a white wing flapping on the Sôkyoku Hill. Shûkei Hakuteiken, Senbonzakura's final form, and Tensa Zangetsu's black spiritual energy clash head-on!!! A shockwave reverberates throughout the Seireitei. A long battle has finally come to an end.

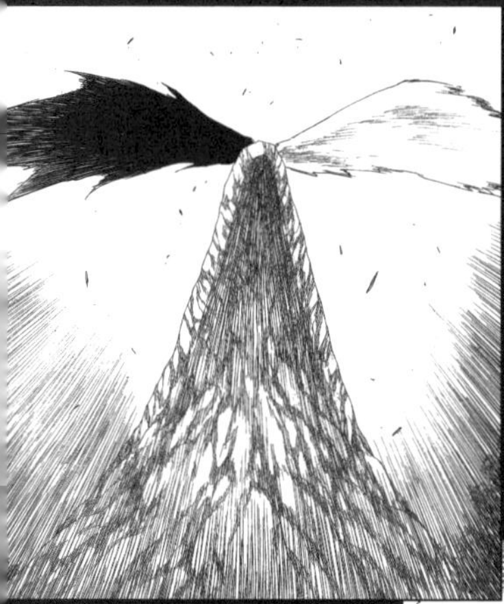

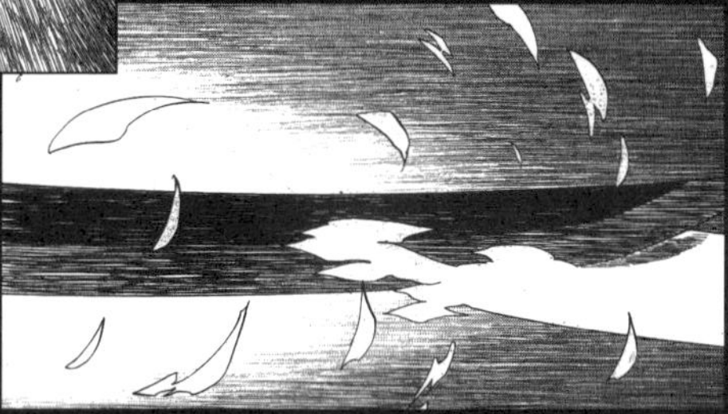

SMASHED WHITE BLADE
The pitch-black blade smashes through the pure white blade... Ichigo is covered in wounds and can barely stand, but the same goes for Byakuya. As he promised, Byakuya quietly begins to tell the innermost feelings hidden in his heart...

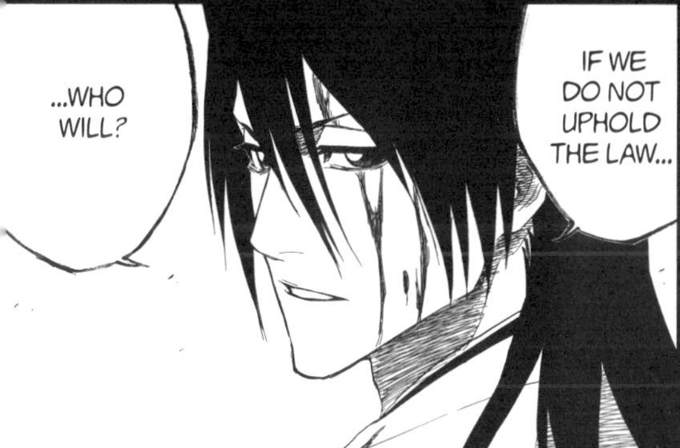
IF WE DO NOT UPHOLD THE LAW...
...WHO WILL?

HIS INNERMOST FEELINGS SPOKEN
Byakuya says that, as the head of the Kuchiki family, he cannot go against the laws of the Soul Society. He wouldn't save Rukia because her execution was legally sanctioned.

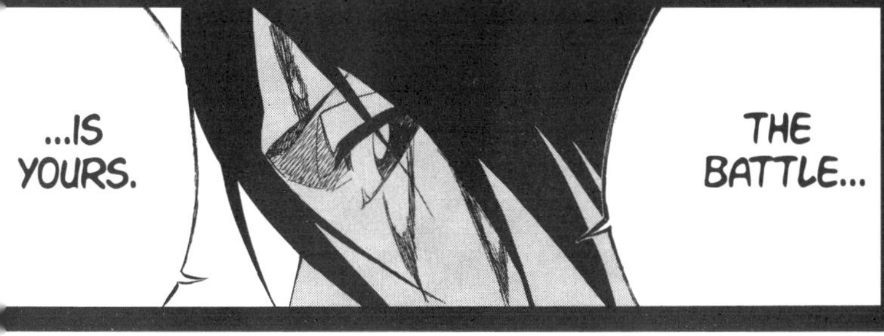
THE BATTLE...
...IS YOURS.

終幕 THE LAST SCEN

The end of the fierce battle
VOL. 19-167

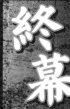

Byakuya admits defeat and disappears. Ichigo gives a joyful shout as if to taste his victory. He is reunited with Orihime, Uryû, and Chad and they celebrate.

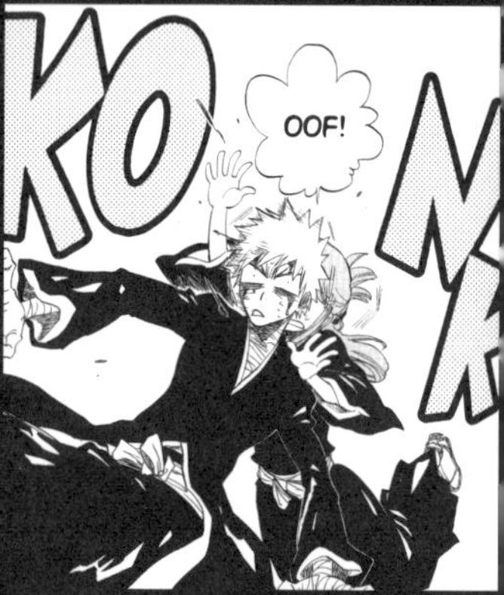
KO
OOF!

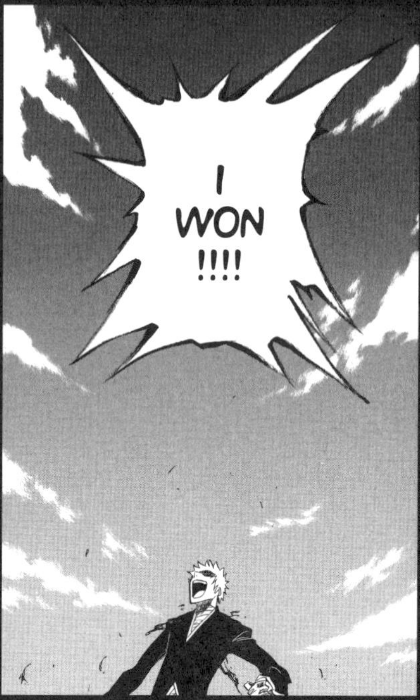
I WON !!!!

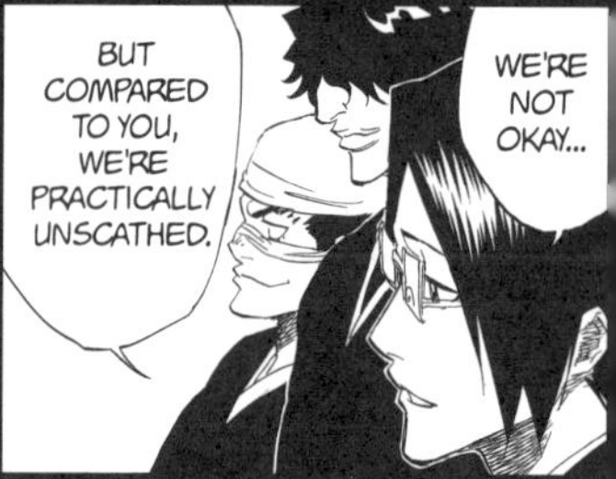
WE'RE NOT OKAY...
BUT COMPARED TO YOU, WE'RE PRACTICALLY UNSCATHED.

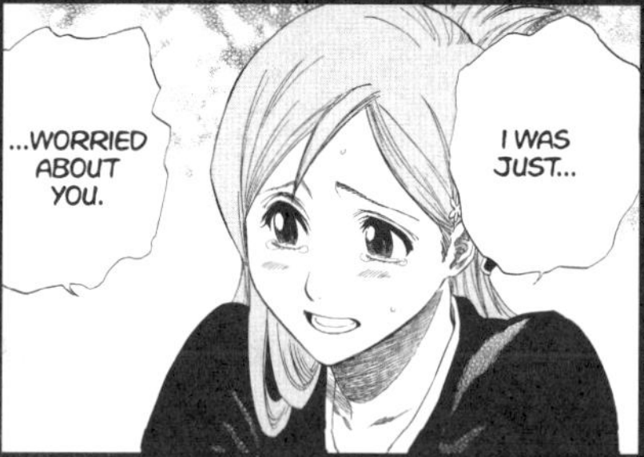
I WAS JUST...
...WORRIED ABOUT YOU.

Orihime's eyes are brimming with large tears. She is overjoyed that Ichigo is safe. Ichigo accepts Orihime's feelings and thanks her.

A MATERIAL FULL OF MYSTERY

HOLLOW MASK

Ever since his Soul Reaper training with Urahara, a mysterious Hollow mask has appeared whenever Ichigo is in danger. Why is still a mystery, but it definitely has a connection with Ichigo's Hollow transformation during his fight with Byakuya.

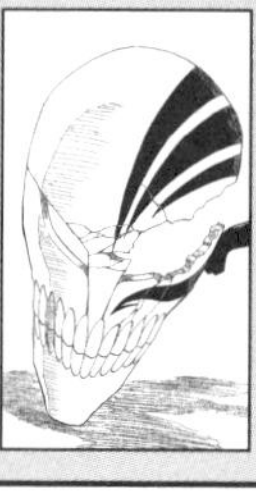

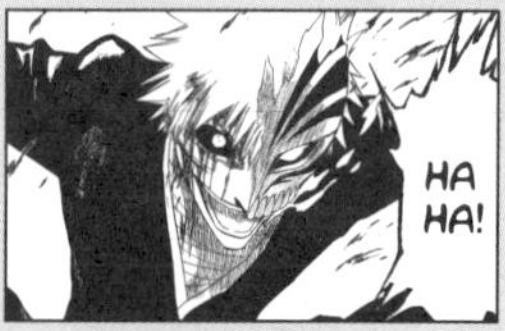
HA HA!

The Hollow Ichigo, whose personality is different from the real Ichigo. He has a cruel and vicious temperament.

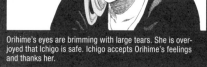

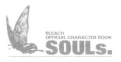

STORY TRACK 8

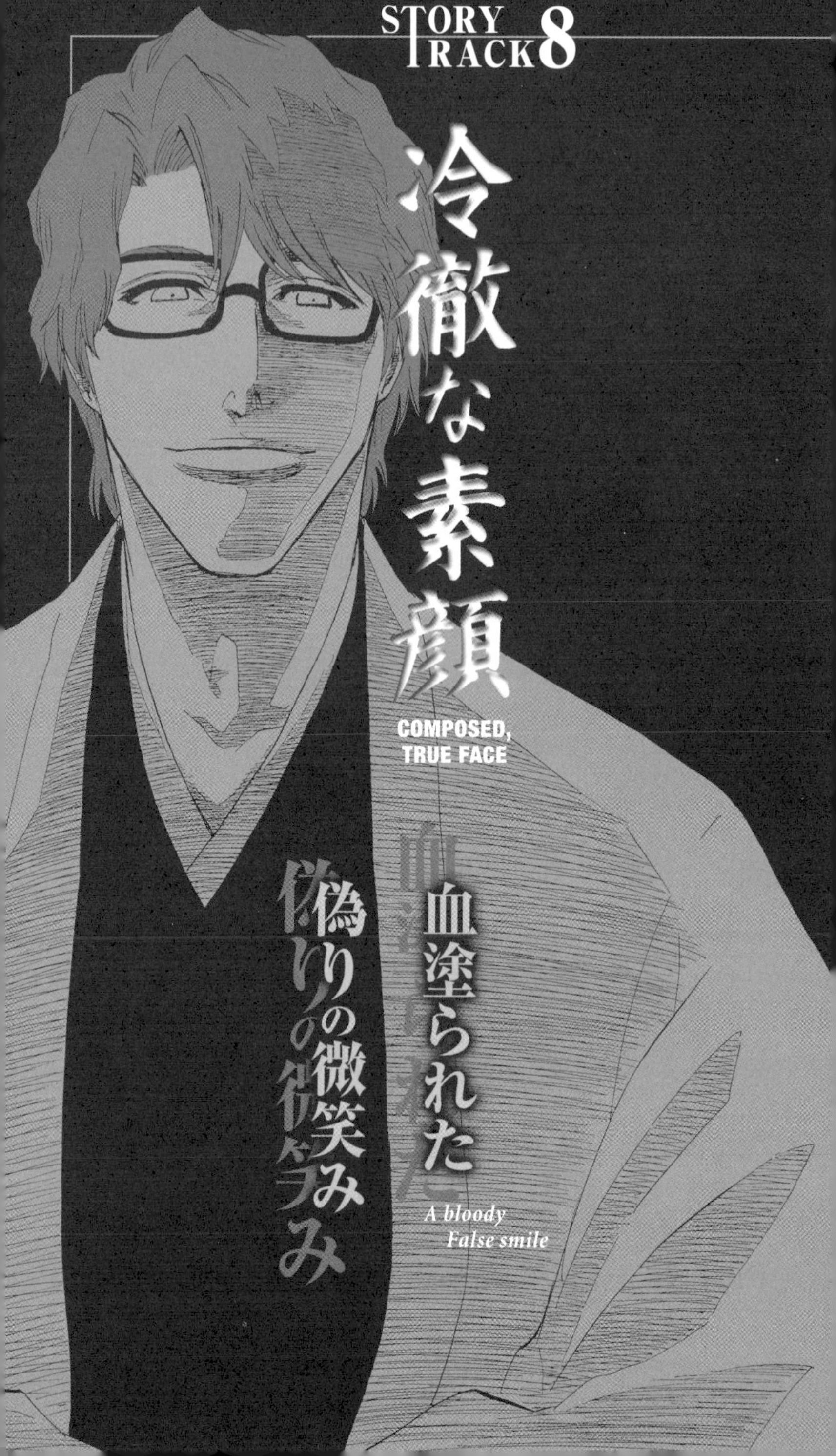

冷徹な素顔

COMPOSED, TRUE FACE

血塗られた偽りの微笑み

A bloody False smile

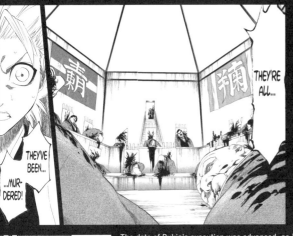

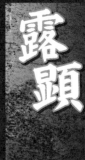

露顕

EXPOSED

The Central 46 are murdered
VOL. 19-167~168

THEY'RE ALL...
THEY'VE BEEN...
...MUR-DERED!

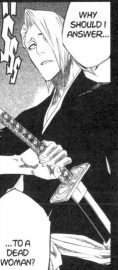

The date of Rukia's execution was advanced, as if in response to Ichimaru's alarming behavior. Hitsugaya learns from Aizen's letter that the person responsible for the conflict in Soul Society wants something from the Sôkyoku. He enters a prohibited area in order to convince the Central 46 to call off the execution. But when he gets there, he sees forty-six bloody bodies. That's when Izuru Kira, who has been working with Ichimaru, appears.

IZURU'S TAUNT

Hitsugaya chases after Izuru. And Izuru turns around to tell Hitsugaya, "There's something else you should be worried about... instead of chasing me..."

SHOULDN'T YOU BE...
...PROTECTING MOMO?

WHY SHOULD I ANSWER...
...TO A DEAD WOMAN?

THE SOUL SOCIETY'S SUPREME JUDICIAL ORGANIZATION

THE CENTRAL 46

The organization that controls the Soul Society's legal system. Soul Reaper crimes are judged here, regardless if they were committed in the Soul Society or the world of the living. In the event of a Soul Reaper's execution, they even give leave for the Secret Remote Squad and the Thirteen Court Guard Companies to use lethal force.

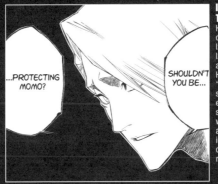

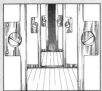

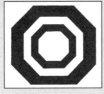

The Central 46's crest is based on the shape of their assembly hall, the Seijôtô Kyorin.

The hall leading to the Central 46 is heavily defended by thirteen layers of protective walls.

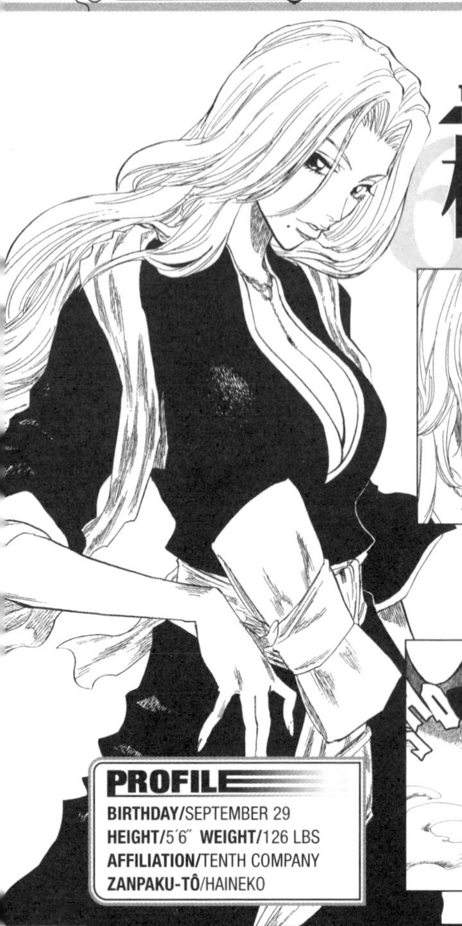

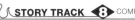

TENTH COMPANY ASSISTANT CAPTAIN

RANGIKU MATSUMOTO — CHARACTER FILE 63-b

Death 死

松本乱菊

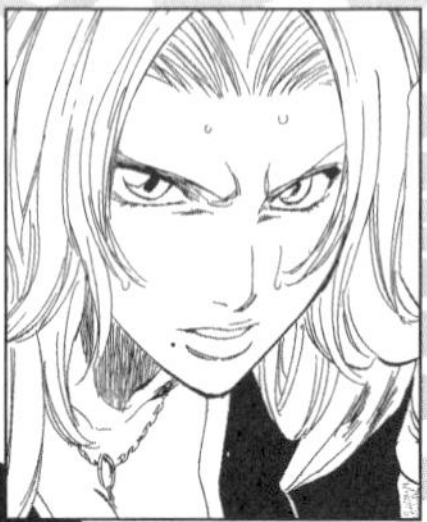

THE LARGE FLOWER BLOOMING ON THE BATTLEFIELD

Hitsugaya goes back to the Central 46 out of concern for Momo. Izuru goes after him, but comes face-to-face with Rangiku! Izuru's zanpaku-tô Wabisuke can freely control gravity. Facing Izuru's zanpaku-tô, Rangiku fights back by releasing hers.

ZANPAKU-TÔ

HAINEKO

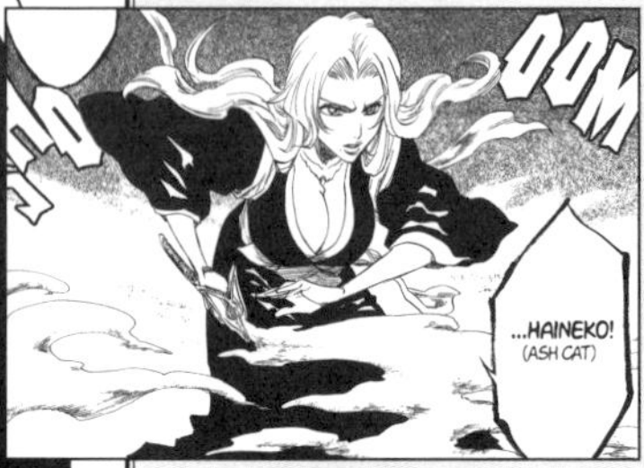
DOOM
...HAINEKO!
(ASH CAT)

Its blade scatters like ashes and drifts around the surrounding area... Its ability is still unknown.

PROFILE

BIRTHDAY/SEPTEMBER 29
HEIGHT/5′6″ **WEIGHT/**126 LBS
AFFILIATION/TENTH COMPANY
ZANPAKU-TÔ/HAINEKO

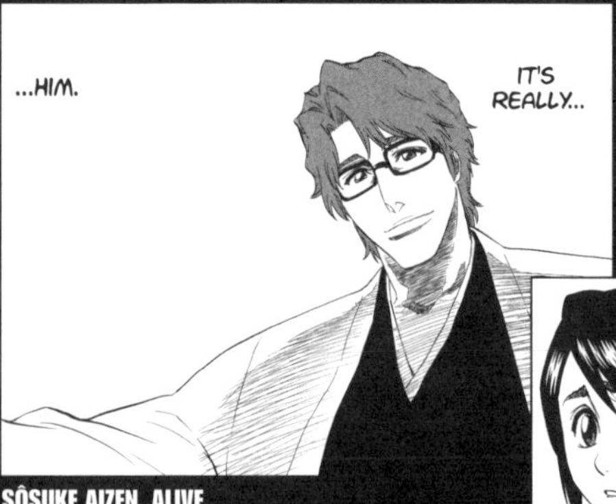
IT'S REALLY...
...HIM.

SÔSUKE AIZEN, ALIVE

Ichimaru tells Momo that there is someone that he wants her to meet. When they arrive...Momo is reunited with Aizen, a man who is supposed to be dead.

Momo follows Hitsugaya to the Central 46. The horrible spectacle before her renders her speechless. Gin Ichimaru creeps up behind her.

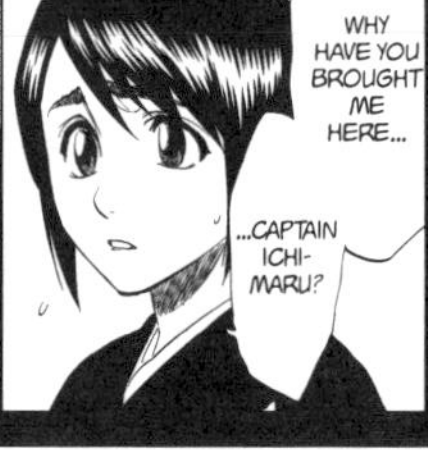
WHY HAVE YOU BROUGHT ME HERE...
...CAPTAIN ICHIMARU?

引見

AUDIENCE

Reunion with Aiz

VOL. 20-169

A LATE ARRIVAL

Hitsugaya arrives to find Momo in a pathetic state—Momo, the person he most wanted to protect... He is stunned and realizes Aizen's true hidden character.

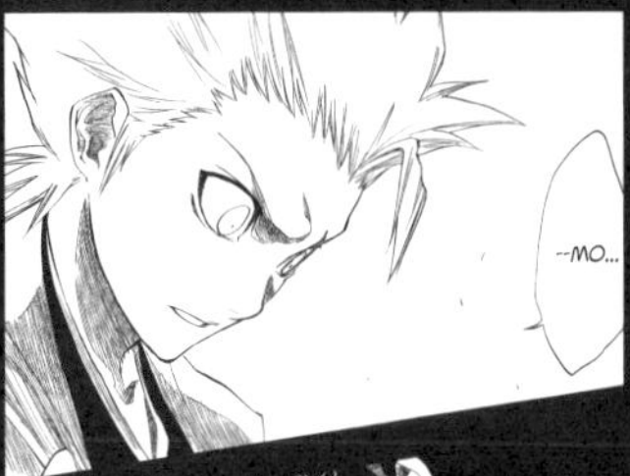
--MO...

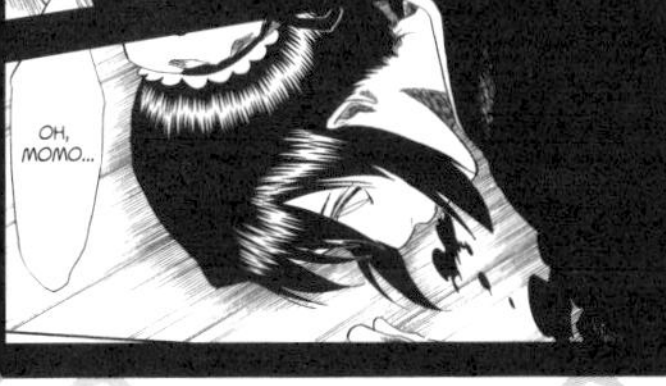
OH, MOMO...

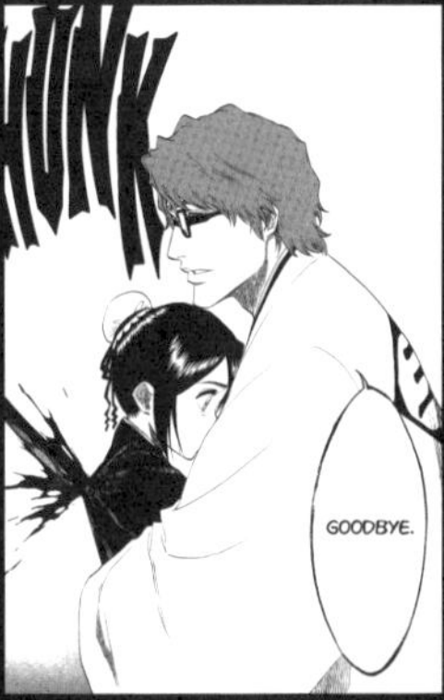
THUNK
GOODBYE.

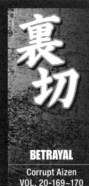

裏切

BETRAYAL

Corrupt Aizen
VOL. 20-169~170

Momo can only cry when she learns that Aizen is alive. Aizen tenderly gives her a hug. He sympathizes with Momo's concern for him and kindly shows his appreciation. Suddenly, a cruel blade is stabbed into Momo's chest. Momo cries out in disbelief.

DAIGUREN HYÔRINMARU

TÔSHIRÔ HITSUGAYA — CHARACTER FILE 62-d

Death 死

日番谷冬獅郎

TACTICS

ZANPAKU-TÔ/HYÔRINMARU

BANKAI/DAIGUREN HYÔRINMARU

NOTEWORTHY MENTION/THE STRONGEST ICE-TYPE

THE BRIGHT RED FLAMING ICE-COLD MOON

Hitsugaya explodes with anger at the way that Aizen has tricked everyone and betrayed Momo, who adored and respected Aizen. He screams, "Bankai!!!" Cold air flows out and enormous wings of ice form on his shoulders... It is Hitsugaya's bankai, Daiguren Hyôrinmaru!! His raging anger becomes his blade. He attacks Aizen with his freezing fighting spirit!!

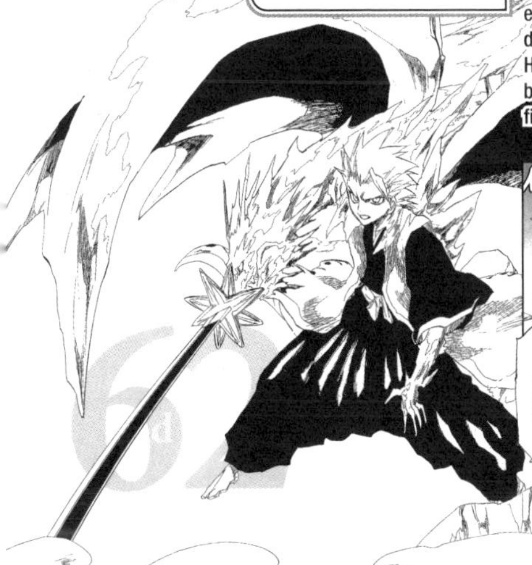

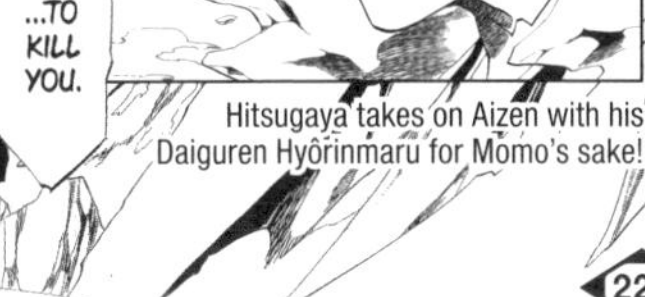
KRAK
AIZEN...
I'M GOING...
...TO KILL YOU.

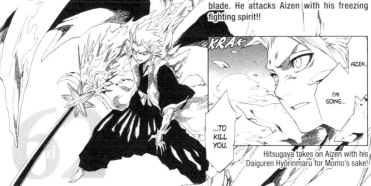

Hitsugaya takes on Aizen with his Daiguren Hyôrinmaru for Momo's sake!

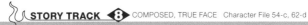

THE CAUSE OF THE MISFORTUNES AFFLICTING THE SOUL SOCIETY

SÔSUKE AIZEN — CHARACTER FILE 54-c

Death 死

藍染惣右介

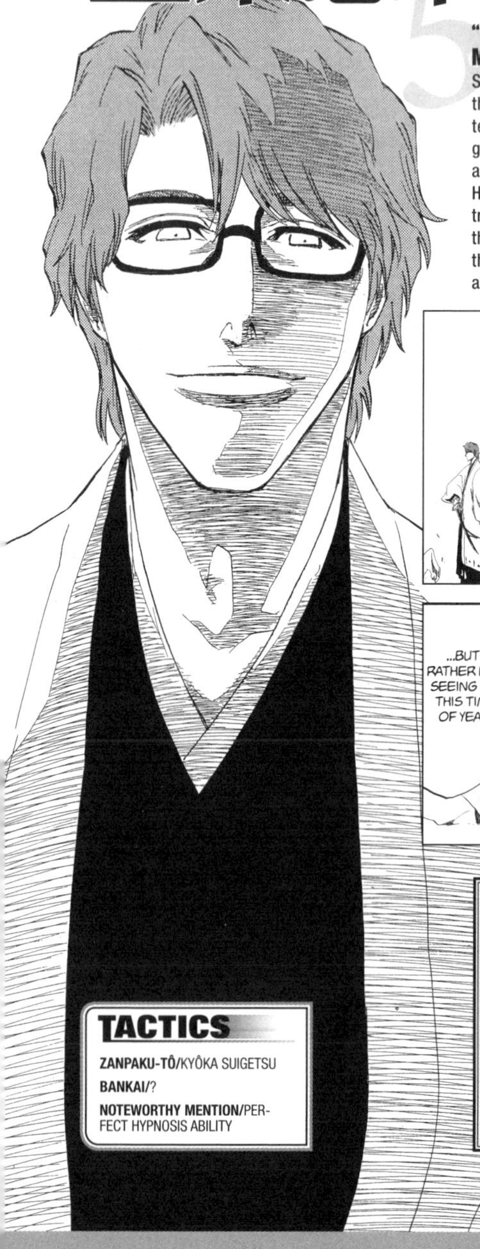

"...NONE OF YOU RECOGNIZED MY TRUE IDENTITY."

Sôsuke Aizen gained popularity with those around him because of his character, his gentle smile, and his affectionate gaze... When he was alive, he projected an illusion to deceive those around him. Hitsugaya is angry when Aizen shows his true nature. Aizen tells Hitsugaya that rash threats will just make him look weak. With that, Hitsugaya swings down Hyôrinmaru at Aizen. And then...

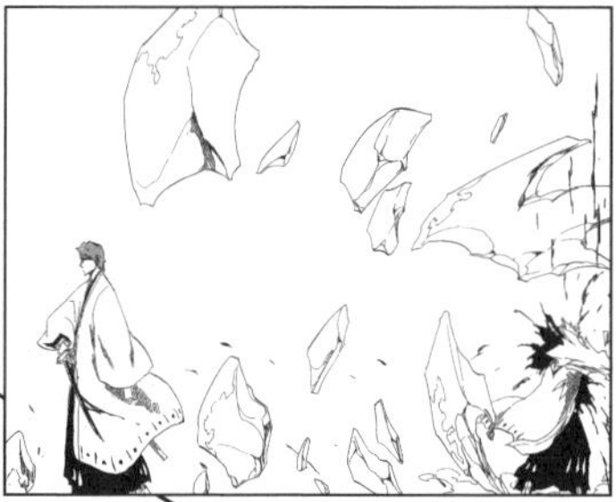

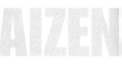

HITSUGAYA DEFEATED IN A FLASH

Aizen defeats Hitsugaya's whole-hearted attack as if it were nothing. It is an overwhelming victory.

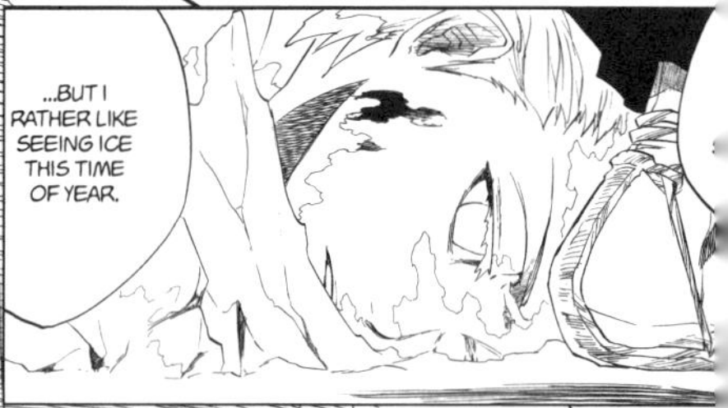
...BUT I RATHER LIKE SEEING ICE THIS TIME OF YEAR.

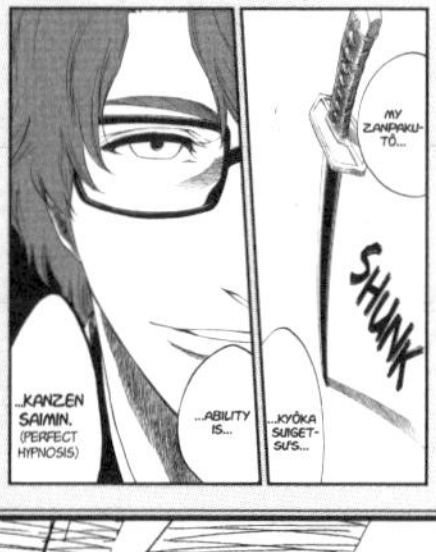
MY ZANPAKU-TÔ...
SHUNK
...KYÔKA SUIGETSU'S...
...ABILITY IS...
...KANZEN SAIMIN. (PERFECT HYPNOSIS)

ZANPAKU-TÔ

KYÔKA SUIGETSU

Whoever sees its release will have all their senses disrupted and succumb to illusions.

TACTICS

ZANPAKU-TÔ/KYÔKA SUIGETSU

BANKAI/?

NOTEWORTHY MENTION/PERFECT HYPNOSIS ABILITY

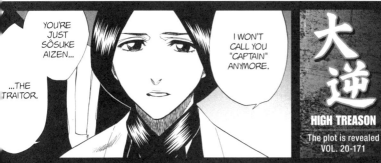

大逆

HIGH TREASON

The plot is revealed
VOL. 20-171

I WON'T CALL YOU "CAPTAIN" ANYMORE.
YOU'RE JUST SÔSUKE AIZEN...
...THE TRAITOR.

Unohana had suspicions about Aizen's death and has taken her own line of action. When she arrives at the Seijôtô Kyôrin, she asks Aizen for the truth. He tells her about his complete, all-encompassing hypnosis abilities, and about Ninth Captain Tôsen's betrayal... He then disappears to the site of the former Sôkyoku, where Rukia will fulfill his long-cherished ambition.

KYÔKA SUIGETSU'S ABILITY
The Kyôka Suigetsu has the power of perfect hypnosis. It can control all of an enemy's senses and make him misidenitfy looks, shapes, quantity, feeling, and even smell.

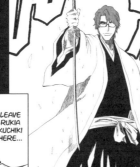

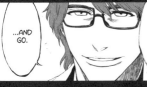

LEAVE RUKIA KUCHIKI HERE...
...AND GO.

EMERGENCY TRANSMISSION

TENTEI KÛRA

All of the Soul Reapers find out about Aizen's betrayal through Isane's Tentei Kûra bakudô. This astonishing news is also sent to Ichigo and his friends...

WHAT I'M ABOUT TO TELL YOU...
...IS THE TRUTH.

...WANTS RUKIA...
...DEAD!

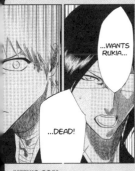

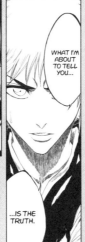

AIZEN'S GOAL
Ichigo and his friends grasp everything that is happening through Isane's transmission. About the annihilation of Central 46, Aizen's faked death, and the advancement of the date of Rukia's execution... The intricately intertwined threads become one. Aizen's goal was Rukia's execution.

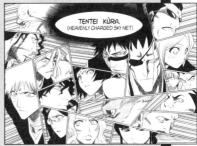

TENTEI KÛRA.
(HEAVENLY CHARGED SKY NET)

卓絶

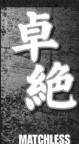

MATCHLESS

Aizen's fighting abilit
VOL. 20-172~175

Renji protects Rukia as he carries her. Aizen orders him to leave her behind. Renji refuses. Aizen points his blade at Renji and tells him that his refusal is unfortunate.

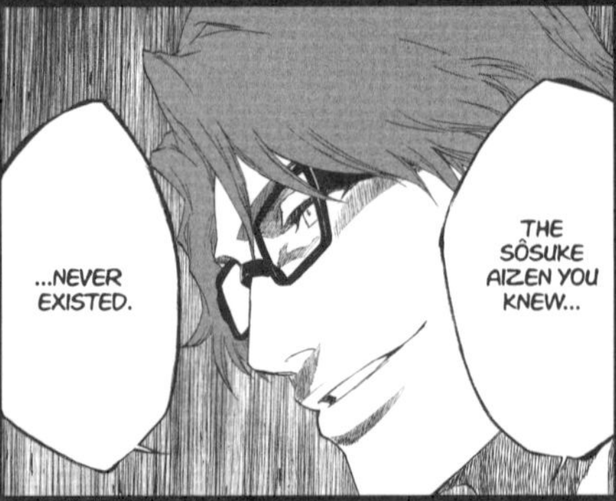
THE SÔSUKE AIZEN YOU KNEW...
...NEVER EXISTED.

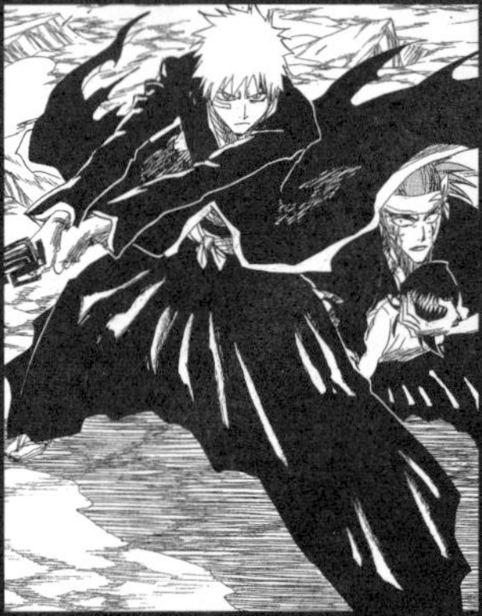

SPEEDY HELP
Aizen swings his blade at Renji... At that moment, Ichigo blocks his attack. Ichigo and Renji both want to protect Rukia. They team up to fight against Aizen.

OVERWHELMING DIFFERENCE IN STRENGTH
Aizen blocks Tensa Zangetsu with his pointer finger and slashes Ichigo's body... It is a hopeless loss.

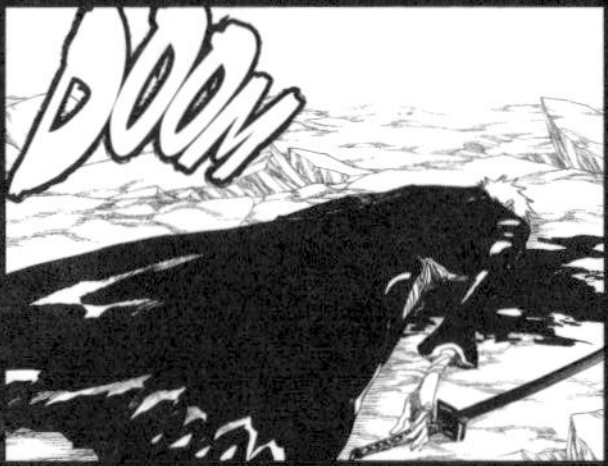
DOOM

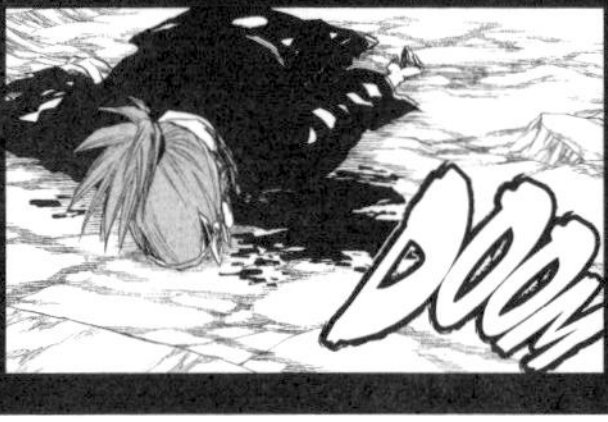
DOOM

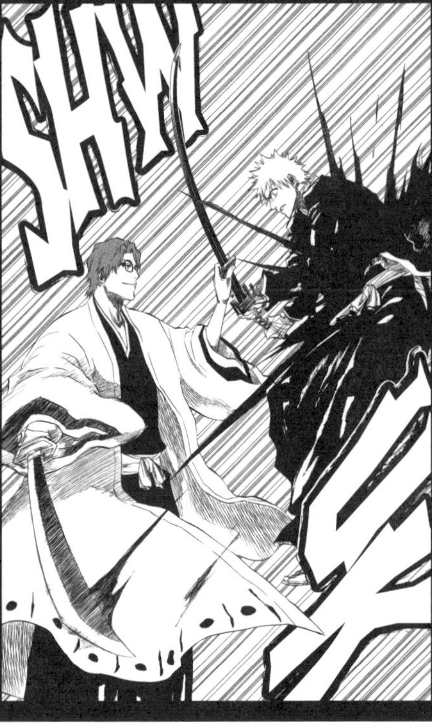

独白 MONOLOGUE

The full account of the riot
VOL. 20-175

"YOUR PART IN ALL THIS... IS OVER."

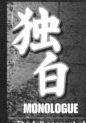

Ichigo and Renji are defeated by Aizen's blade... Aizen begins to tell them the full details of his grand plot. It all started when the first head of the Department of Research and Development, Kisuke Urahara, created a certain material, Hôgyoku. It is a forbidden orb that can dramatically increase Soul Reapers' abilities by removing the barrier between Soul Reaper and Hollow. Aizen's true goal was to obtain the Hôgyoku.

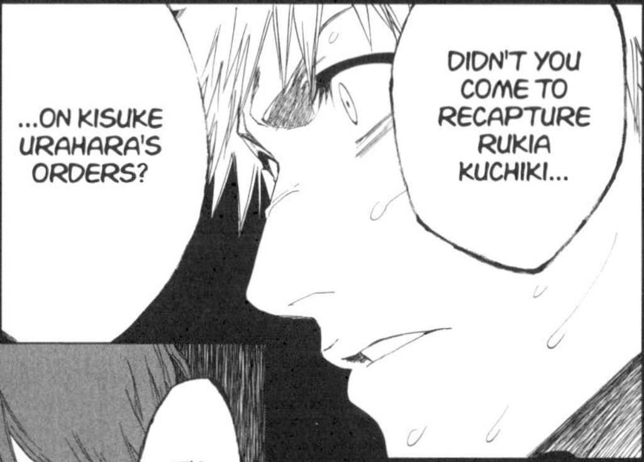
DIDN'T YOU COME TO RECAPTURE RUKIA KUCHIKI...
...ON KISUKE URAHARA'S ORDERS?

THE TRUTH IS REVEALED
Kisuke Urahara helped Ichigo and his friends get to the Soul Society. Urahara's true goal was to get the Hôgyoku back, as well as save Rukia, who functions as its hiding place.

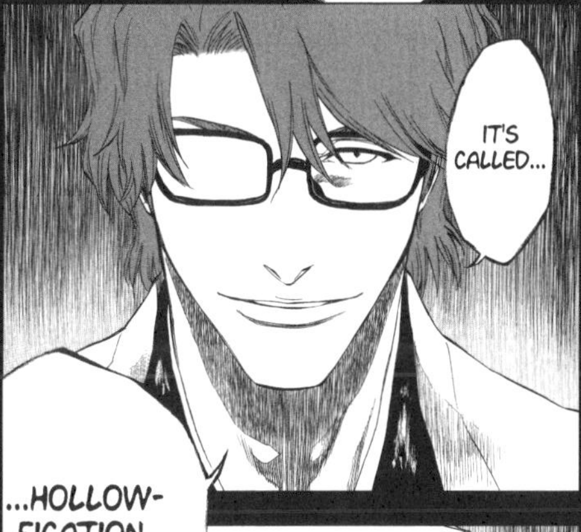
IT'S CALLED...
...HOLLOW-FICATION.

THE LOCATION OF THE HÔGYOKU
Urahara realized the that the Hôgyoku was dangerous and tried to destroy it, but he failed. So he placed a barrier around it and tried to hide its whereabouts by placing it in another's soul. He chose Rukia as his hiding place.

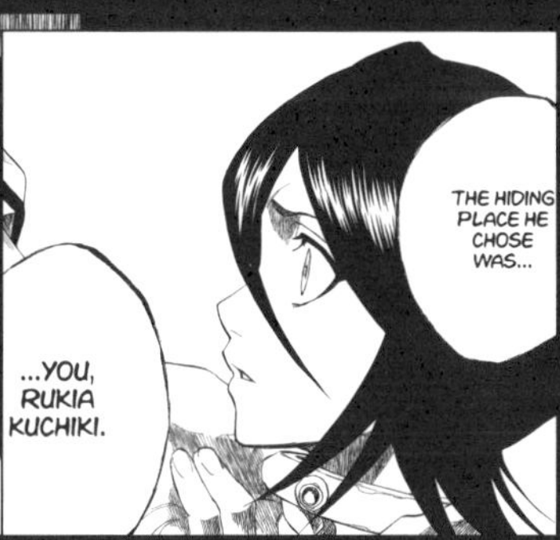
THE HIDING PLACE HE CHOSE WAS...
...YOU, RUKIA KUCHIKI.

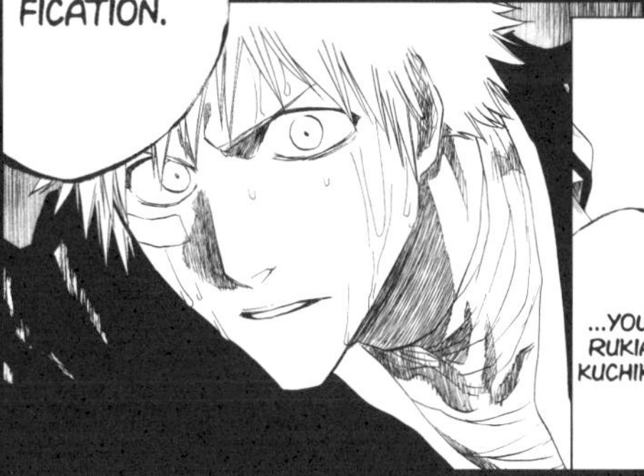

宿望
LONG-CHERISH DREAM
Accomplished ambition
VOL. 20-176

Urahara had implanted the Hôgyoku in Rukia's soul, and so Aizen planned her execution. The Sôgyoku had enough destructive power to remove the Hôgyoku from its host... Ichigo and Renji are at a loss for words when they hear Aizen's plans. Aizen finally removes the Hôgyoku from Rukia's body and fulfills his dream.

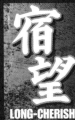

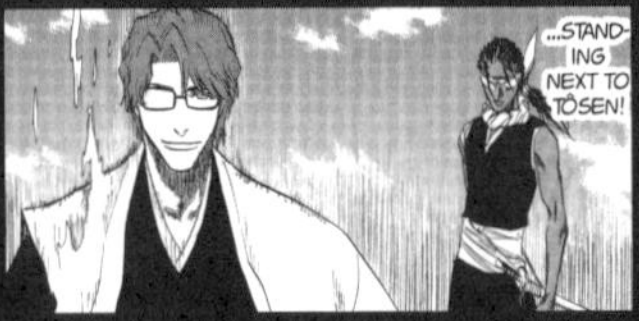
...STANDING NEXT TO TÔSEN!

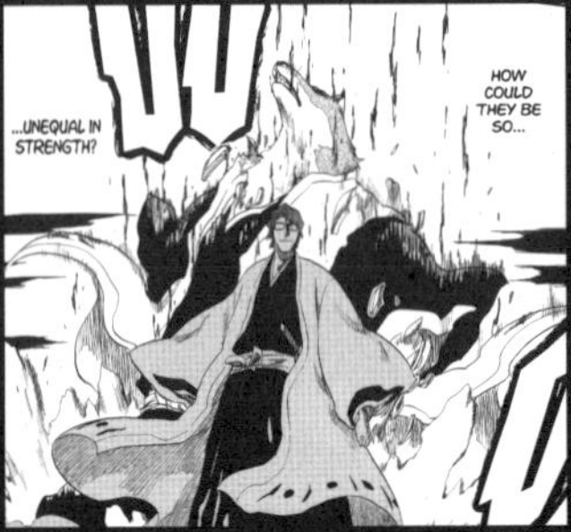
HOW COULD THEY BE SO...
...UNEQUAL IN STRENGTH?

Komamura is angered at Tôsen's betrayal, but Aizen slashes him instantaneously...

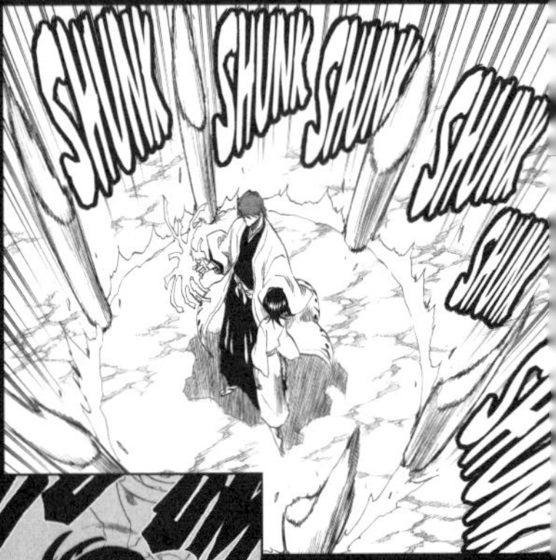
SHUNK
SHUNK
SHUNK

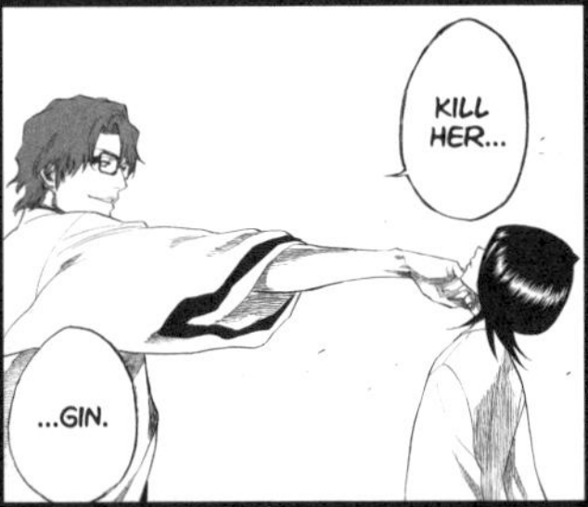
KILL HER...
...GIN.

Rukia turns into an empty shell once the Hôgyoku is removed... Aizen orders her death.

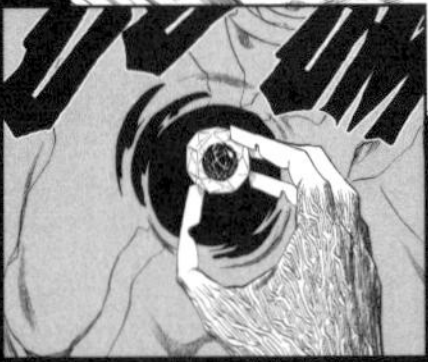

Aizen examined Urahara's research records in the Daireishokairo archives after he faked his death. There he discovered a method to extrac objects buried in souls.

AIZEN'S TRUE GOAL

HÔGYOKU, THE BREAKDOWN SPHERE

The strength of a soul is determined by its physical potential. The abilities of Soul Reapers and Hollows cannot go beyond that limit. However, it is possible to exceed one's limits by removing the barrier that separates Soul Reapers and Hollows. This can be done with the Hôgyoku, the material that Urahara created.

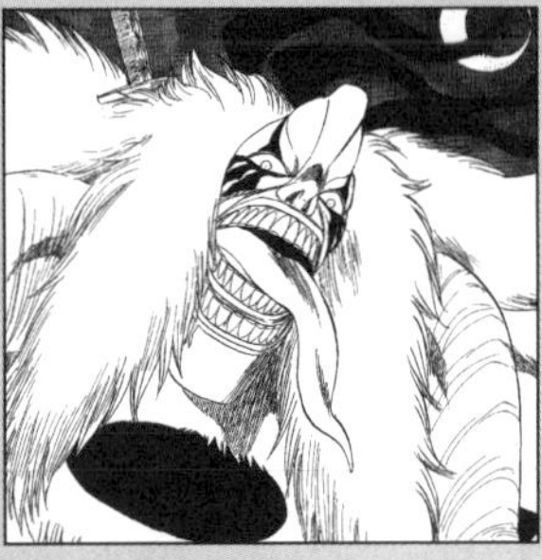

THE SOUL REAPERFICATION OF HOLLOWS
Aizen wants to Soul Reaperfy Hollows. His experiments produced the Hollow that killed Kaien and the Huge Hollows that can hide their spiritual pressure.

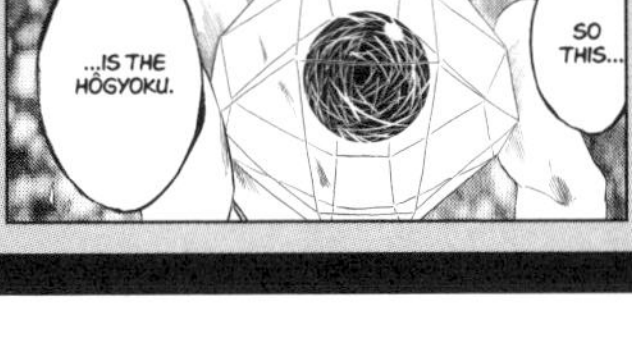
SO THIS...
...IS THE HÔGYOKU.

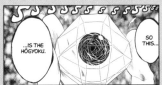

終局

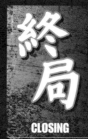

CLOSING

Conclusion to the uprising
VOL. 20-176~178

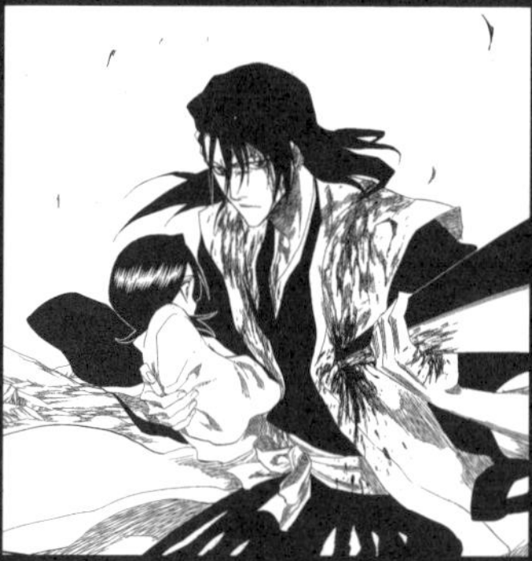

"Shoot him dead, Shinso!" Ichimaru says. His blade extends towards Rukia... But Byakuya blocks Ichimaru's blade with his body! At the same time, all the Court Guards in the Seireitei appear on Sôkyoku Hill! It looks as if Aizen is out of luck, but Aizen gives a undaunted smile.

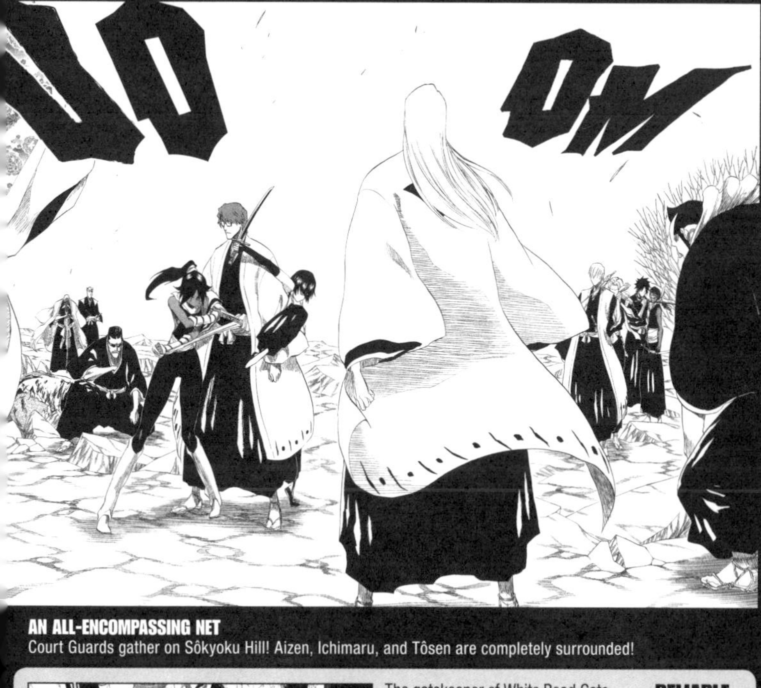

AN ALL-ENCOMPASSING NET
Court Guards gather on Sôkyoku Hill! Aizen, Ichimaru, and Tôsen are completely surrounded!

RELIABLE HELPERS

KUKAKU AND JIDANBÔ

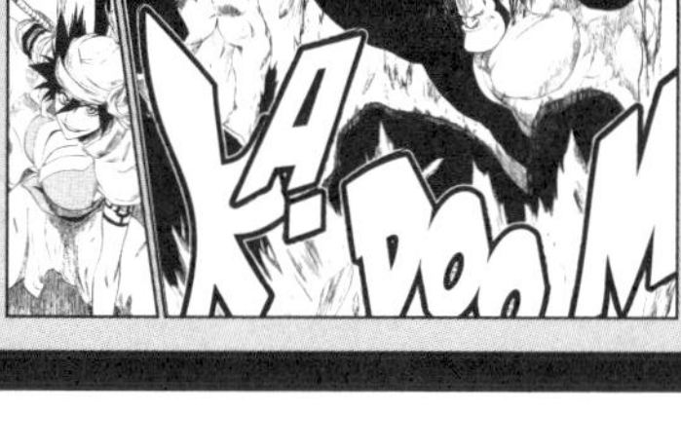

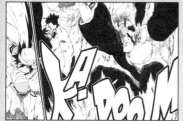

The gatekeeper of White Road Gate, whom Ichigo fought in the Rukongain, and the Rukongai's best fireworks expert, who helped Ichigo get into the Seireitei, have arrived! Jidanbô and Kûkaku have come to help!

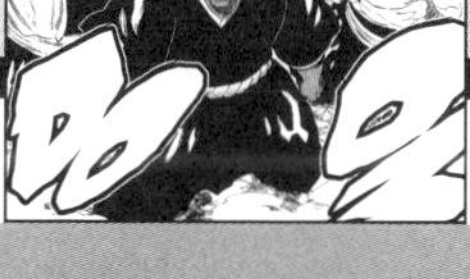

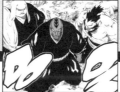

THE INFERNAL GATE OPENS

Just when everyone thinks that Aizen has been caught, the sky splits open and countless Menos Grande appear. The Menos emit a Negación, a beam they use to save their brethren, and welcome Aizen's group.

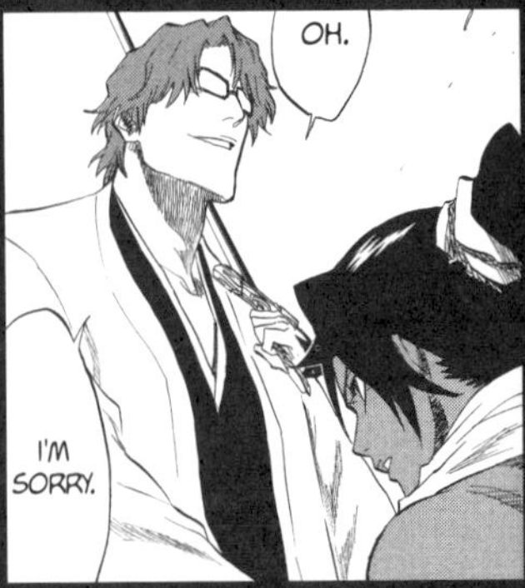
OH.
I'M SORRY.

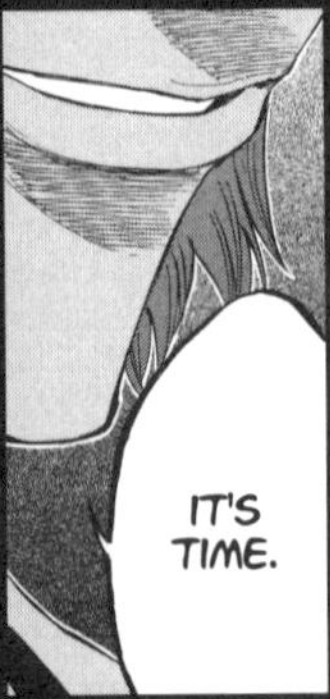
IT'S TIME.

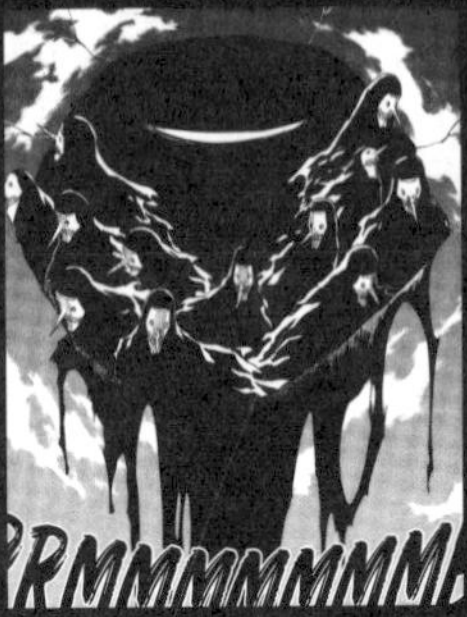
RMMMMMMMM

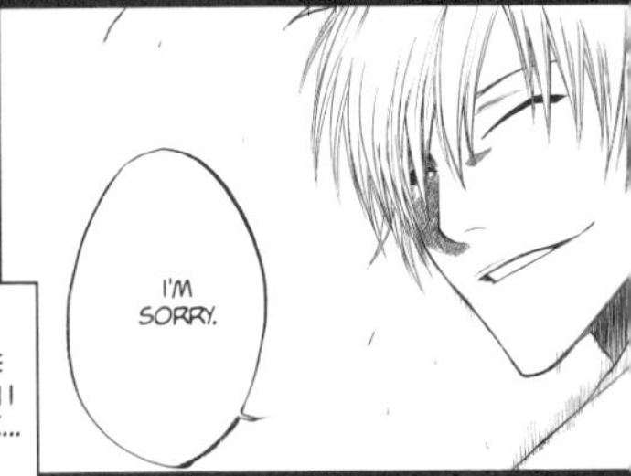
I'M SORRY.

Ichimaru and Tôsen rise into the sky surrounded by the Negación. What are their true motives?!

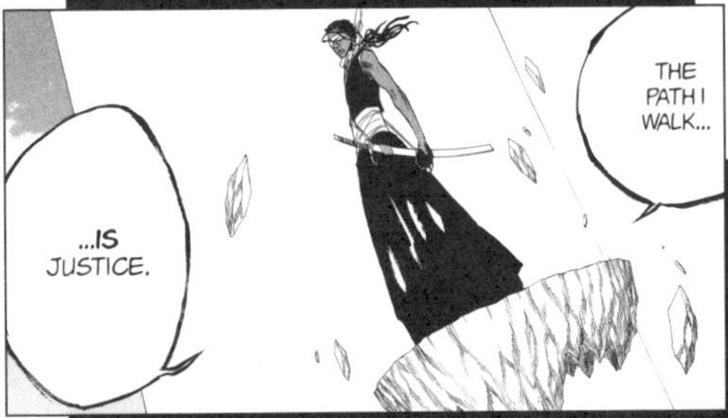
THE PATH I WALK...
...IS JUSTICE.

AIZEN ESCAPES

Aizen declares, "...the unbearable vacancy of heaven's throne ends now... From now on, I will stand atop the heavens." He and the Menos Grande go through the entrance to Hueco Mundo. Aizen has a dark madness to his gaze...

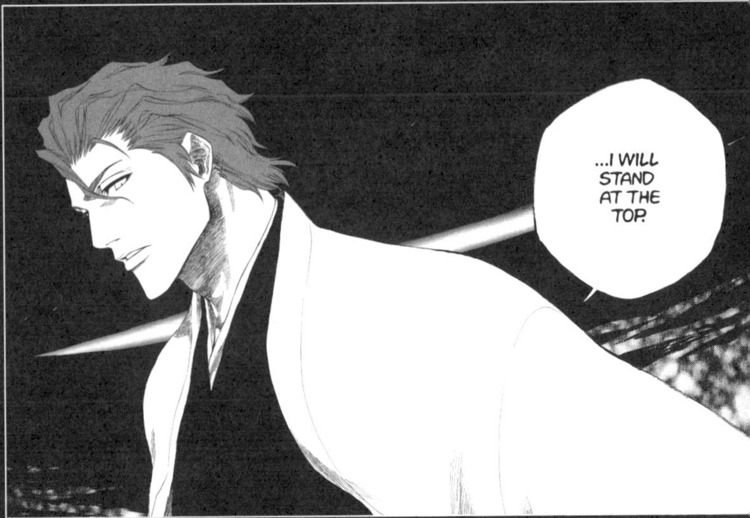
...I WILL STAND AT THE TOP.

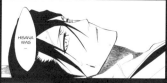

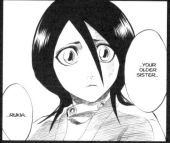

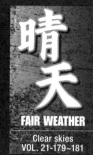

晴天

FAIR WEATHER

Clear skies
VOL. 21-179~181

Aizen has left. Unohana, the Captain of Fourth Company, makes efforts to attend to the injured. She calls Rukia. Byakuya tells Rukia that his wife Hisana was her older sister. He describes how he promised Hisana that he would protect Rukia, and how he vowed before Hisana's grave to defend the law. Byakuya says that his long conflict has come to an end.

HISANA WAS ...

...YOUR OLDER SISTER...
...RUKIA.

... FORGIVE ME.

THE VOW BEFORE HER GRAVE

Byakuya welcomes Rukia into the Kuchiki family. He vows before Hisana's grave that he will never break the law again.

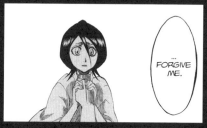

I'M SORRY!

SO ...
I DECIDED A LONG TIME AGO...
IF YOU EVER APOLO-GIZED ...
...I'D FORGIVE YOU.

RUKIA'S APOLOGY

Rukia apologizes. She finally says the things that she has wanted to say for a long time.

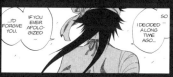

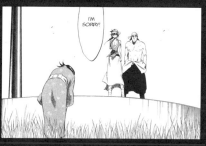

RUKIA'S OLDER SISTER

HISANA KUCHIKI

Hisana Kuchiki is Byakuya's deceased wife. She and Rukia shared a resemblance. Hisana regretted leaving Rukia behind as a baby. While on her deathbed, she asked Byakuya to protect and watch over Rukia.

I ABAN-DONED HER..
I HAVE NO RIGHT TO CALL HER MY SISTER.
BUT, PLEASE, ALLOW HER..
...TO CALL YOU "BROTHER" ...

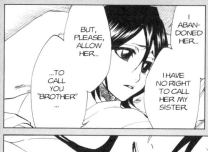

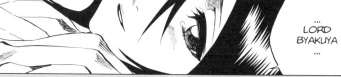

... LORD BYAKUYA ...

RUKIA'S RESOLUTION
Rukia looks straight at Ichigo and tells him that she has decided to stay in the Soul Society.

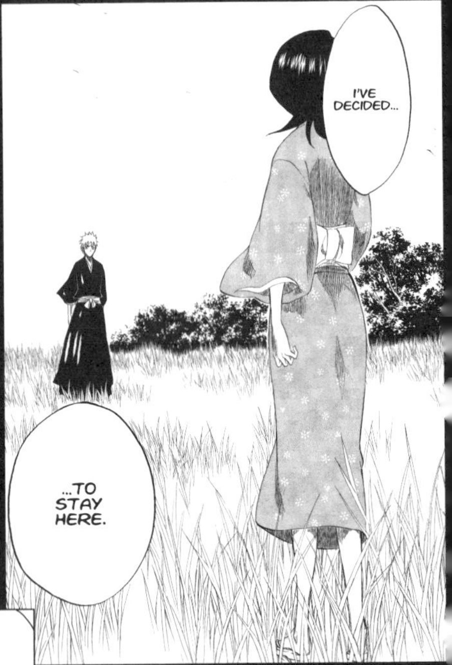
I'VE DECIDED...
...TO STAY HERE.

"I REMEMBERED NOW WHY I WANTED TO SAVE YOU SO BAD..."

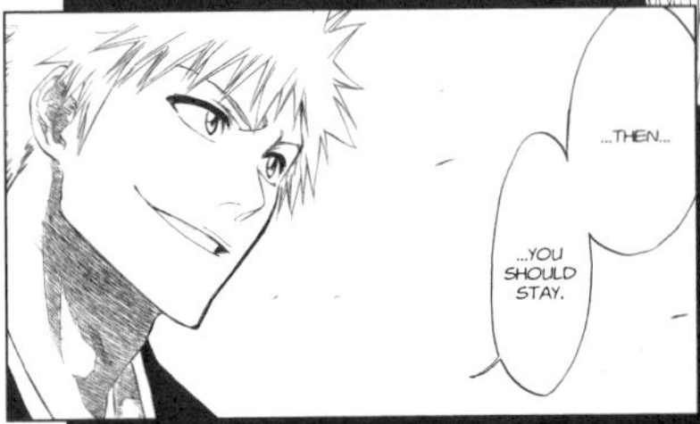
...THEN...
...YOU SHOULD STAY.

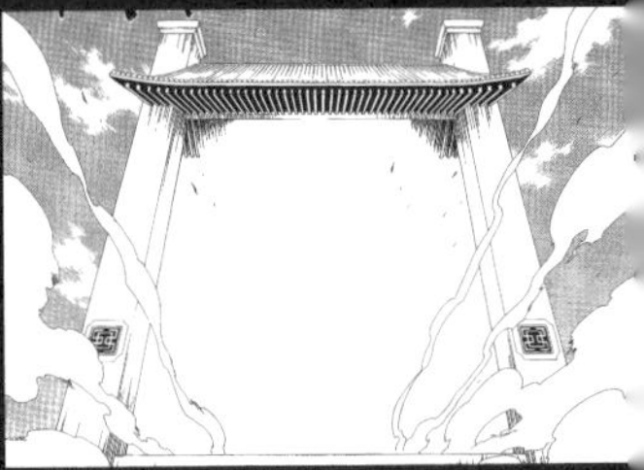

"THANKS, RUKIA. BECAUSE OF YOU, THE RAIN HAS FINALLY STOPPED."

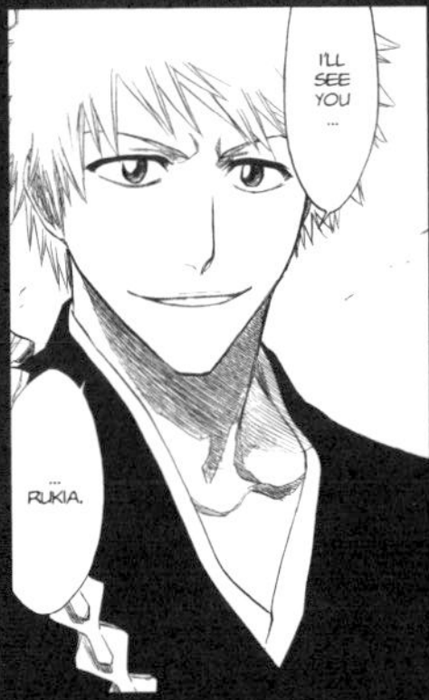
I'LL SEE YOU ...
... RUKIA.

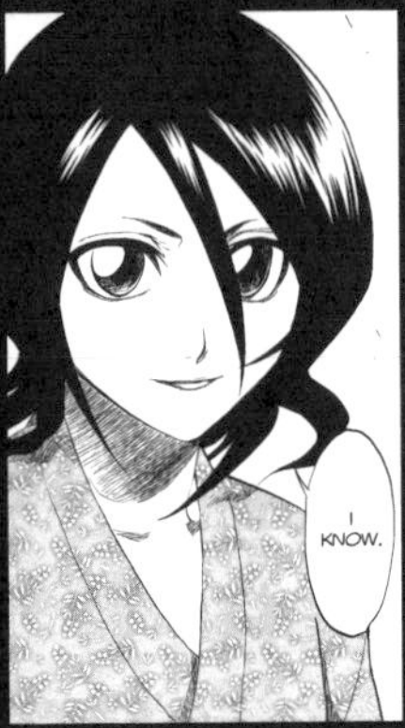
I KNOW.

RETURN TO THE WORLD OF THE LIVING
Ichigo and Rukia remember what it's like to be protected. The rain clouds in their hearts have finally cleared... It all happened in a single summer. The seasons change, and a new day begins.

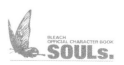

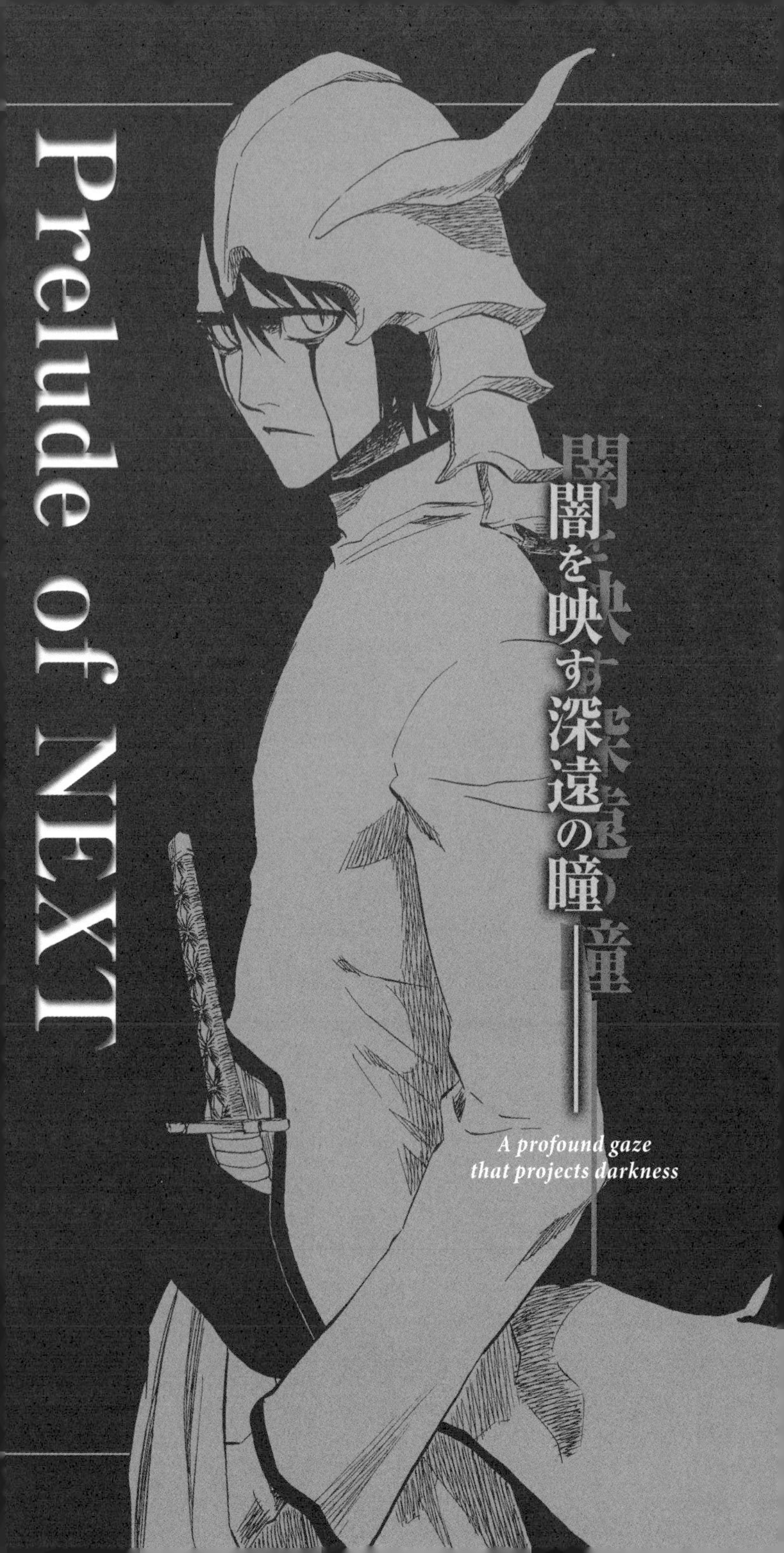
Prelude of NEXT
闇を映す深遠の瞳――
A profound gaze
that projects darkness

仮面の軍勢
The Masked Army

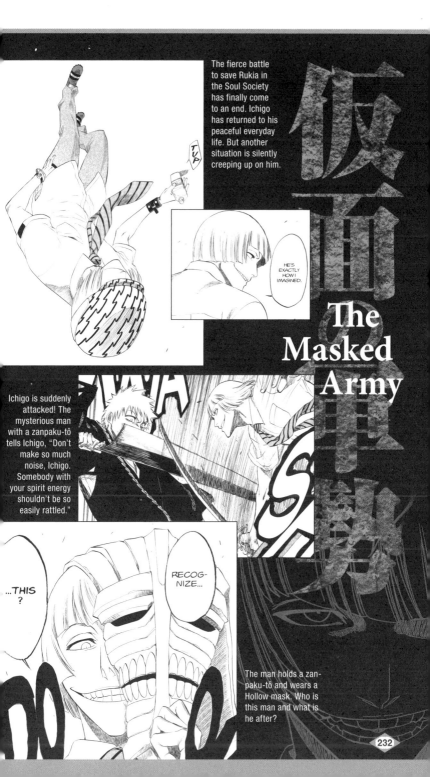

The fierce battle to save Rukia in the Soul Society has finally come to an end. Ichigo has returned to his peaceful everyday life. But another situation is silently creeping up on him.

TUP

HE'S EXACTLY HOW I IMAGINED.

Ichigo is suddenly attacked! The mysterious man with a zanpaku-tô tells Ichigo, "Don't make so much noise, Ichigo. Somebody with your spirit energy shouldn't be so easily rattled."

RECOG- NIZE...
...THIS ?

The man holds a zan-paku-tô and wears a Hollow mask. Who is this man and what is he after?

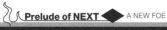

Uryû sees his father Ryûken after a long absence. But there is no affection between them, only cold words... Ryûken tells Uryû not to get involved with the Soul Reapers.

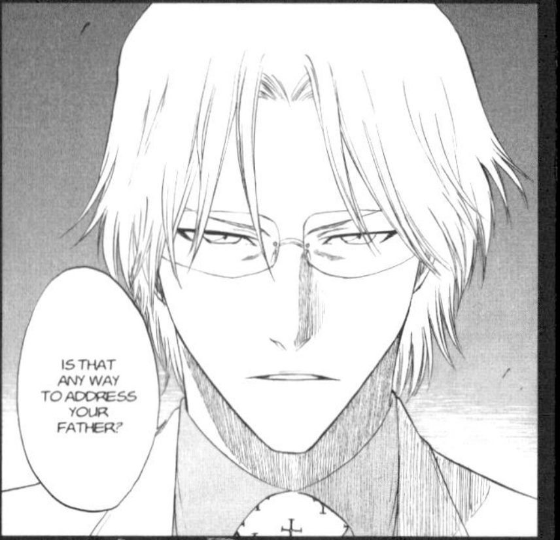
IS THAT ANY WAY TO ADDRESS YOUR FATHER?

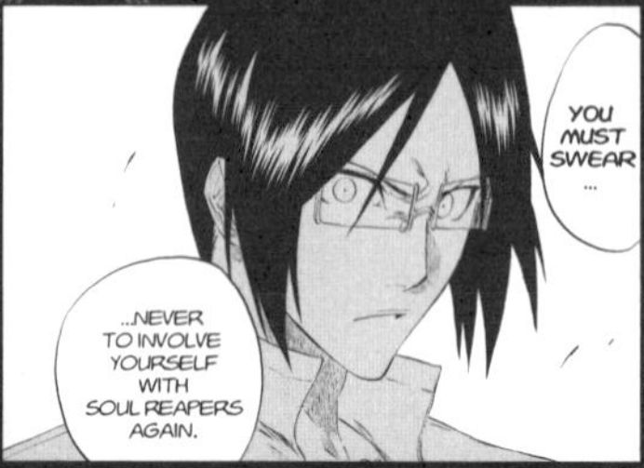
YOU MUST SWEAR ...
...NEVER TO INVOLVE YOURSELF WITH SOUL REAPERS AGAIN.

Broken Mask

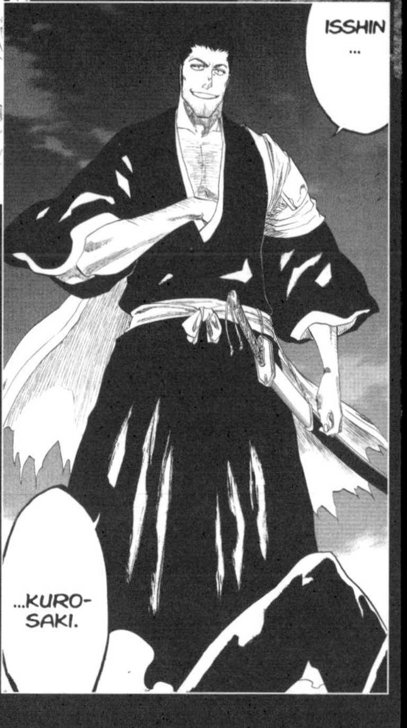
ISSHIN ...
...KURO-SAKI.

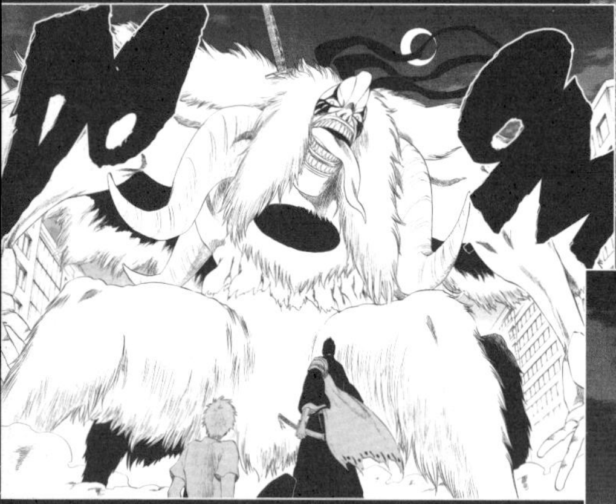

A monstrosity with a hole in its chest and a zanpaku-tô on its back appears... And why is Ichigo's father Isshin wearing a shihakushô?

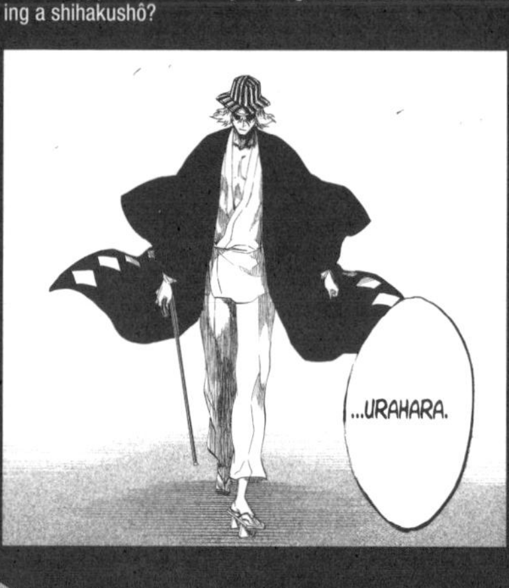
...URAHARA.

With the Hôgyoku in hand, Sôsuke Aizen seeks to reign in heaven. In order to stop Aizen, Ichigo's father Isshin Kurosaki gives aid to Kisuke Urahara!!

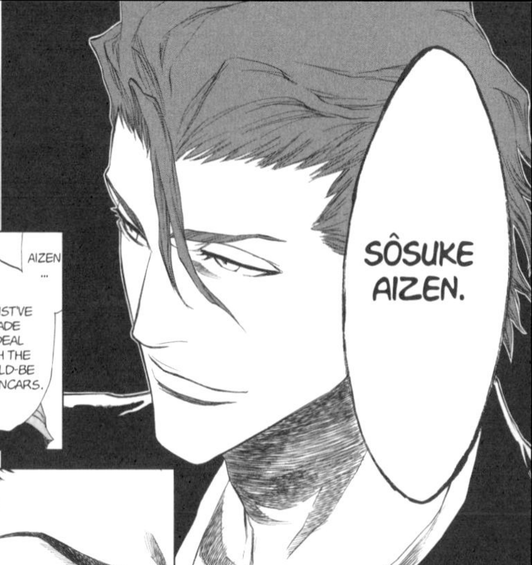
SÔSUKE AIZEN.

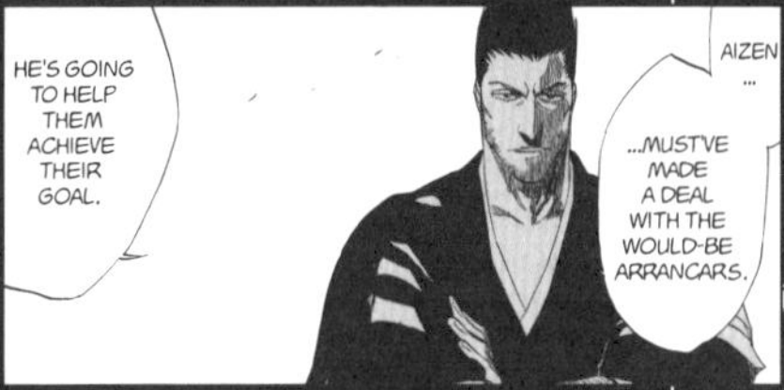
AIZEN...
...MUST'VE MADE A DEAL WITH THE WOULD-BE ARRANCARS.
HE'S GOING TO HELP THEM ACHIEVE THEIR GOAL.

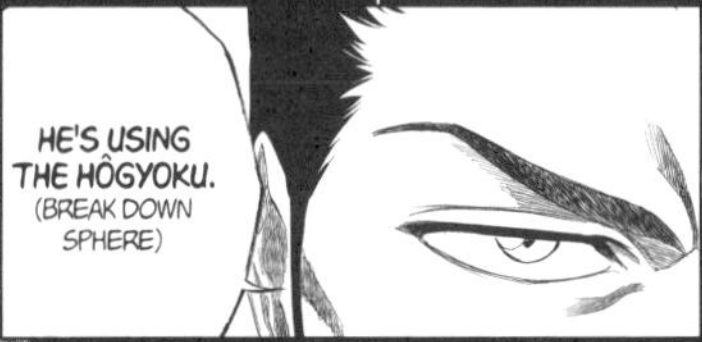
HE'S USING THE HÔGYOKU.
(BREAK DOWN SPHERE)

深謀 Careful Plan

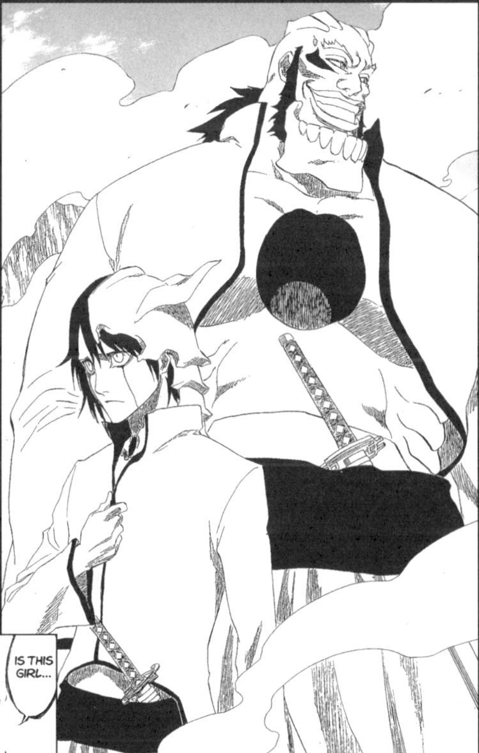

A strange-looking pair suddenly appears in Karakura Town... They have holes in their chests, zanpaku-tô, and the remains of Hollow masks... One of them has a vicious smile as he extends his bloody hands towards Orihime. At that moment...

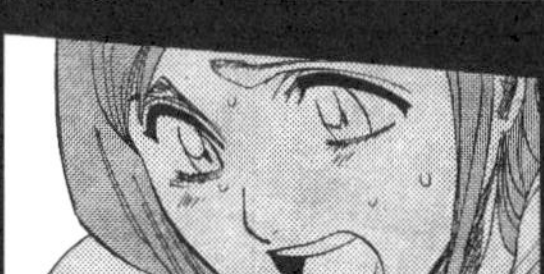

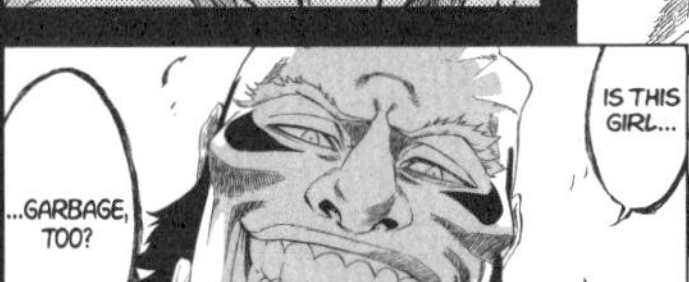
IS THIS GIRL...
...GARBAGE, TOO?

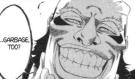

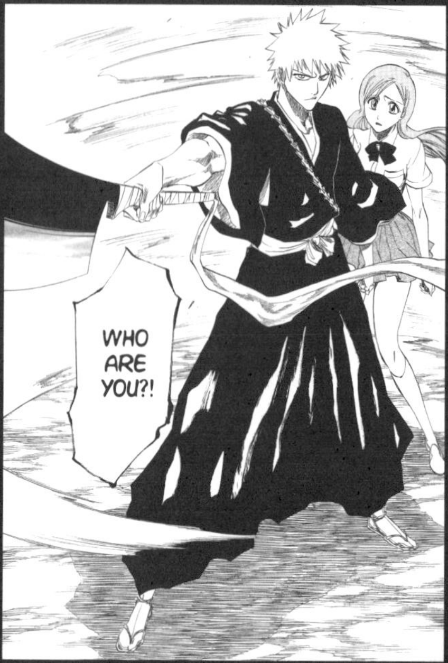
WHO ARE YOU?!

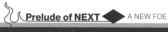

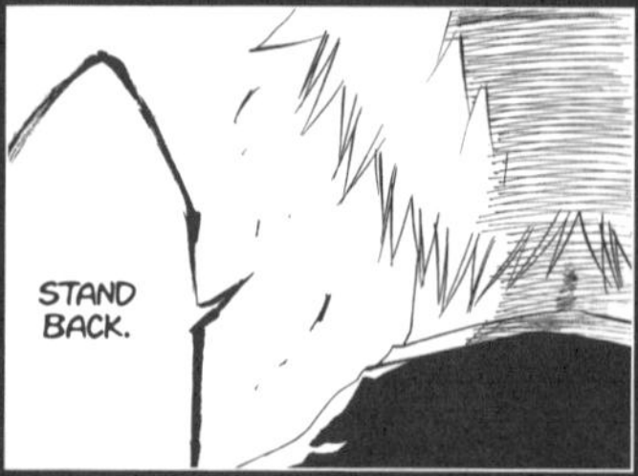
STAND BACK.

Ichigo saves Orihime just in time. He coldly tells the Hollow to let go of Orihime. Enormous power begins to build up in Ichigo... when suddenly, something unexpected happens to his body!! His inner Hollow goes out of control and infiltrates his mind!!

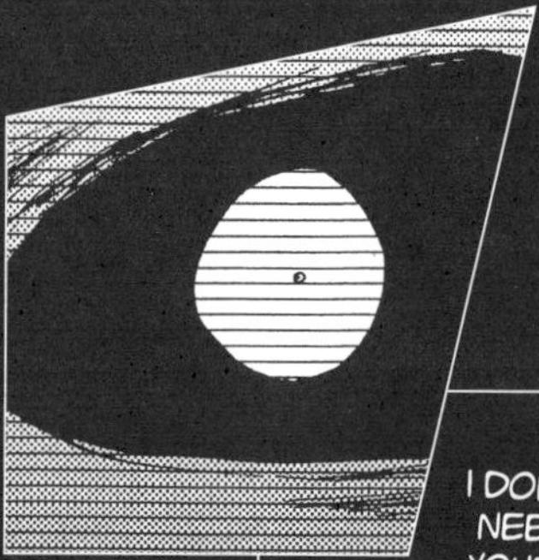

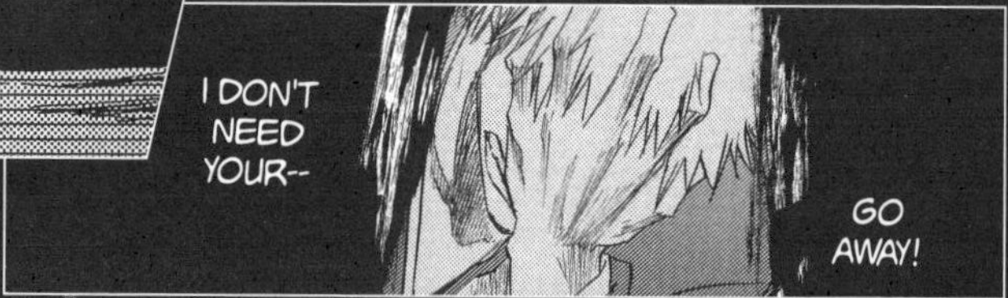
GO AWAY!
I DON'T NEED YOUR--

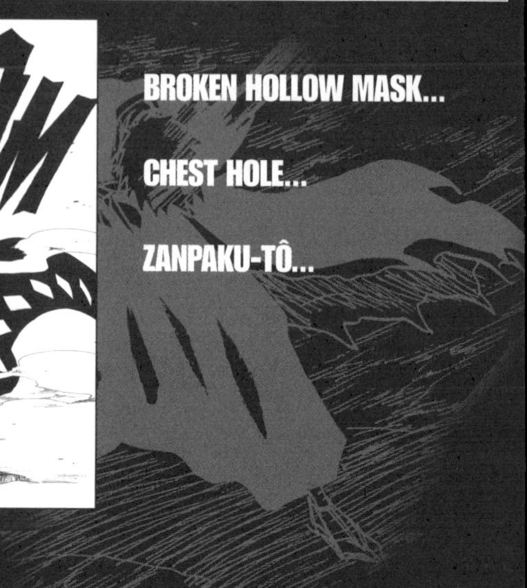
BROKEN HOLLOW MASK...
CHEST HOLE...
ZANPAKU-TÔ...

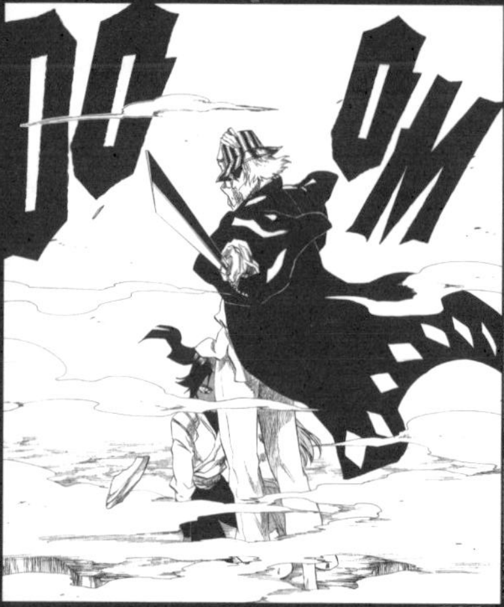
DOOM

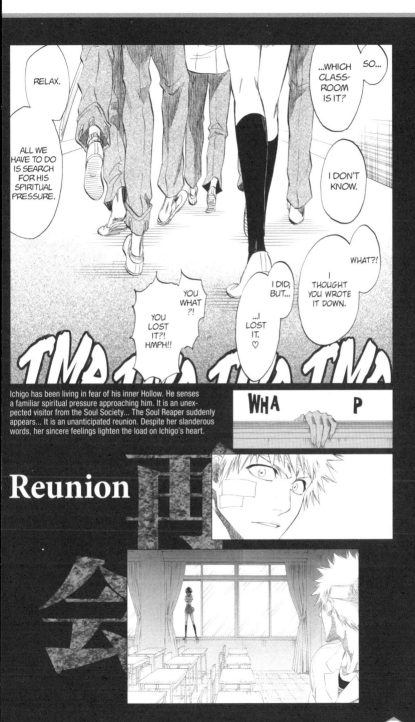

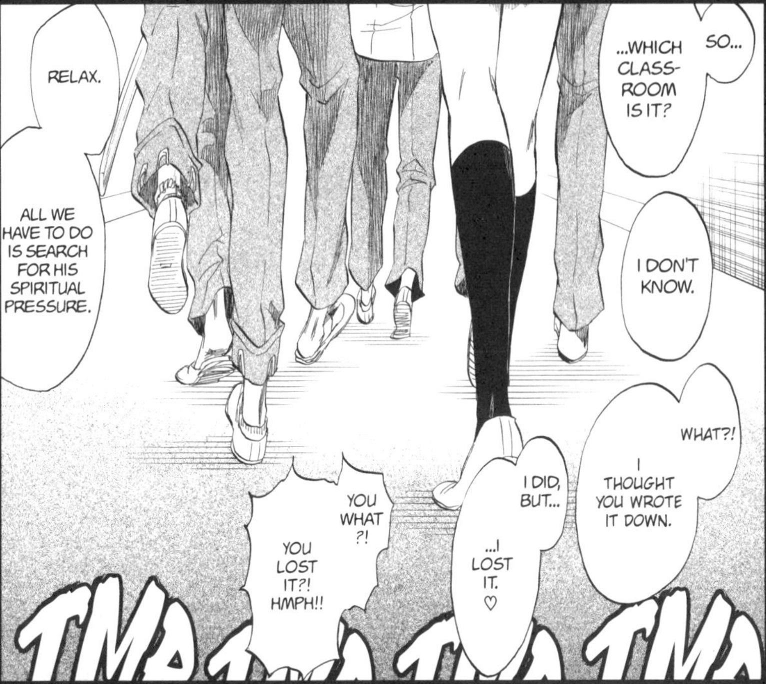
SO...
...WHICH CLASSROOM IS IT?
RELAX.
ALL WE HAVE TO DO IS SEARCH FOR HIS SPIRITUAL PRESSURE.
I DON'T KNOW.
WHAT?!
I THOUGHT YOU WROTE IT DOWN.
I DID, BUT...
...I LOST IT. ♡
YOU WHAT?!
YOU LOST IT?! HMPH!!
TMP

Ichigo has been living in fear of his inner Hollow. He senses a familiar spiritual pressure approaching him. It is an unexpected visitor from the Soul Society... The Soul Reaper suddenly appears... It is an unanticipated reunion. Despite her slanderous words, her sincere feelings lighten the load on Ichigo's heart.

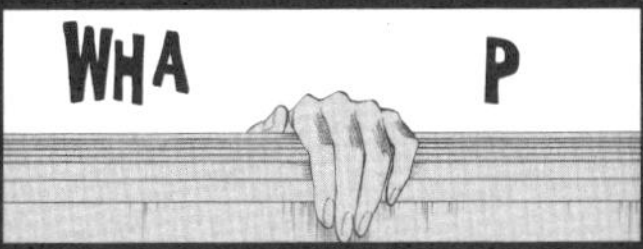
WHA P

Reunion

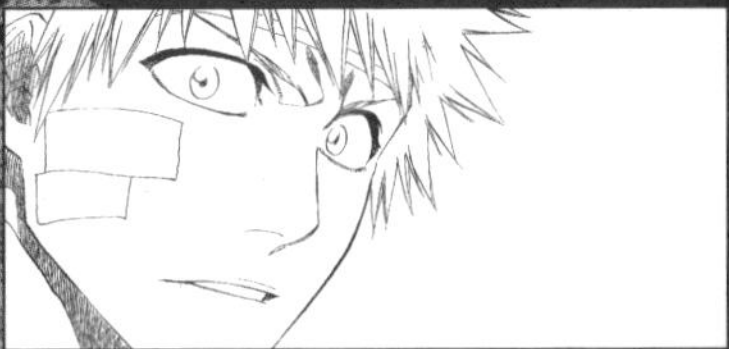

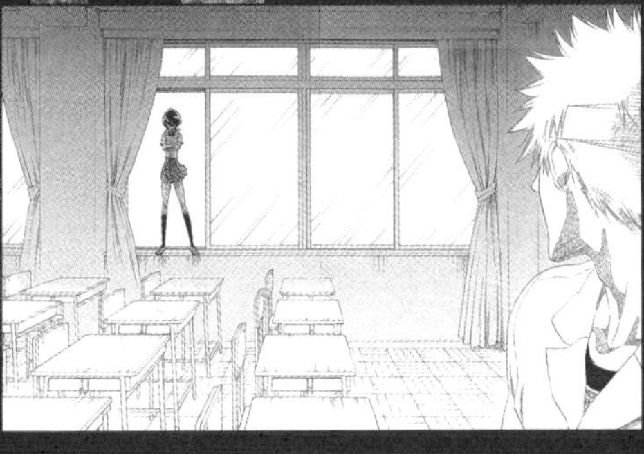

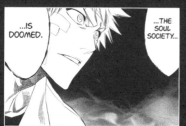

...IF AIZEN HAS TEN OR MORE OF THESE VASTO LORDES...
...UNDER HIS COMMAND...

...THE SOUL SOCIETY...
...IS DOOMED.

Aizen's plot disrupts both the world of the living and the Soul Society. The dark forces that appear in the world of the living all have their own agendas and begin to turn the wheels of fate.

ULQUIORRA...
YAMMY...
WELCOME BACK.

Invasion

NOW...
...TELL THE 20 BROTHERS...
...WHAT YOU HAVE LEARNED.

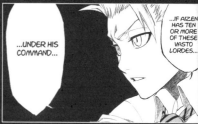

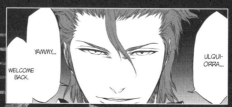

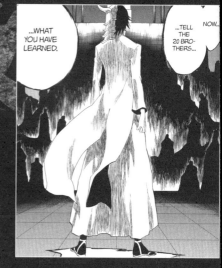

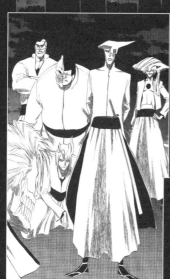

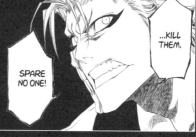

...KILL THEM.
SPARE NO ONE!

TO BE CONTINUED...

BLEACH FUN! FUN!! FUN!!!

Phone Crazy on Stage

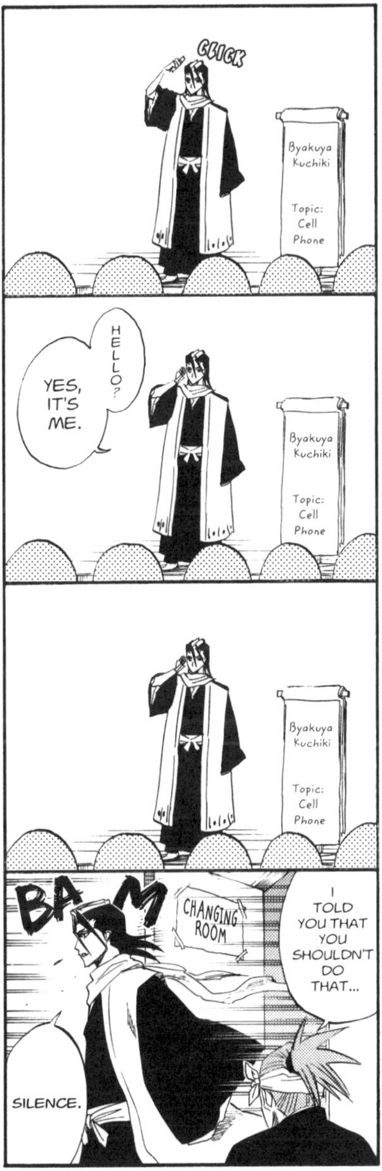
CLICK
Byakuya Kuchiki
Topic: Cell Phone
HELLO?
YES, IT'S ME.
Byakuya Kuchiki
Topic: Cell Phone
Byakuya Kuchiki
Topic: Cell Phone
BAM
CHANGING ROOM
I TOLD YOU THAT YOU SHOULDN'T DO THAT...
SILENCE.

EXTRA ISSUE GAG SPECIAL 2005

When You Are The Punchline

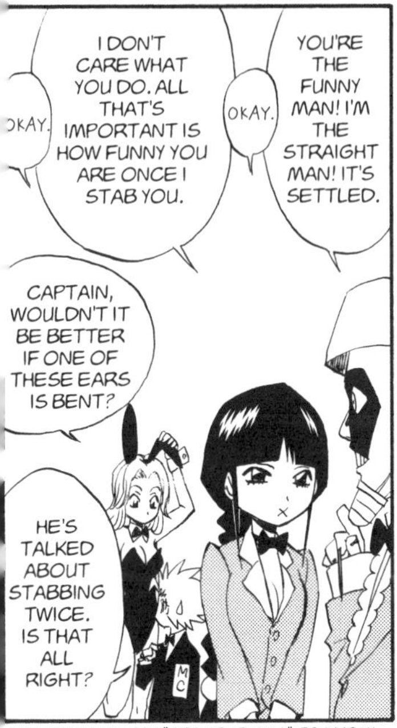
YOU'RE THE FUNNY MAN! I'M THE STRAIGHT MAN! IT'S SETTLED.
OKAY.
I DON'T CARE WHAT YOU DO. ALL THAT'S IMPORTANT IS HOW FUNNY YOU ARE ONCE I STAB YOU.
OKAY.
CAPTAIN, WOULDN'T IT BE BETTER IF ONE OF THESE EARS IS BENT?
HE'S TALKED ABOUT STABBING TWICE. IS THAT ALL RIGHT?
MC

THE JAPANESE FOR "STRAIGHT MAN," TSUKKOMI, ALSO MEANS "TO STAB."

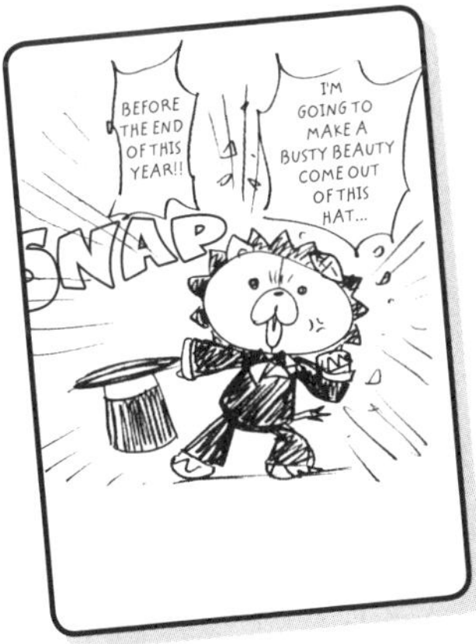
BEFORE THE END OF THIS YEAR!!
I'M GOING TO MAKE A BUSTY BEAUTY COME OUT OF THIS HAT...
SNAP

BONUS TRACK

ボーナストラック

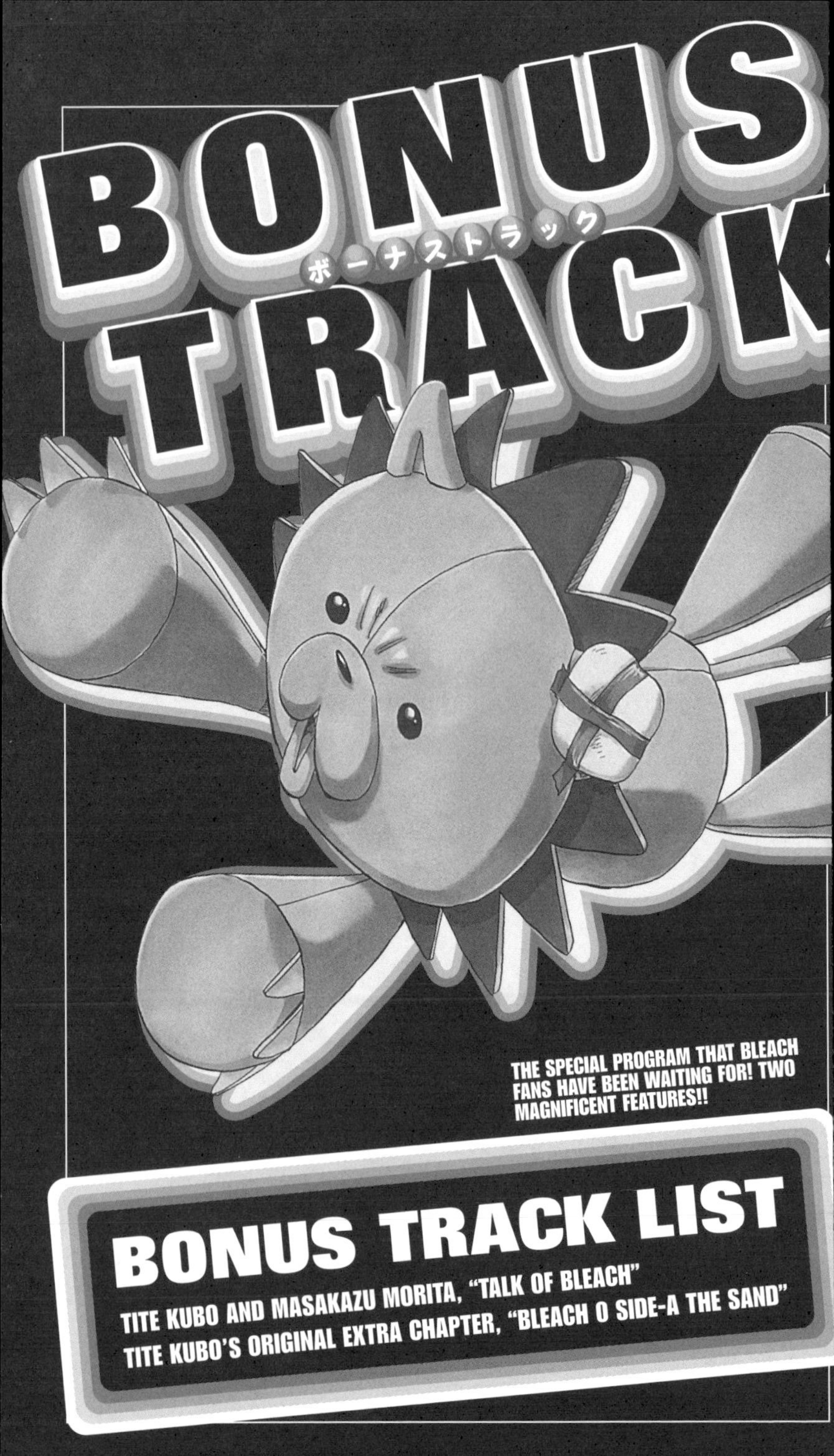

THE SPECIAL PROGRAM THAT BLEACH FANS HAVE BEEN WAITING FOR! TWO MAGNIFICENT FEATURES!!

BONUS TRACK LIST

TITE KUBO AND MASAKAZU MORITA, "TALK OF BLEACH"

TITE KUBO'S ORIGINAL EXTRA CHAPTER, "BLEACH 0 SIDE-A THE SAND"

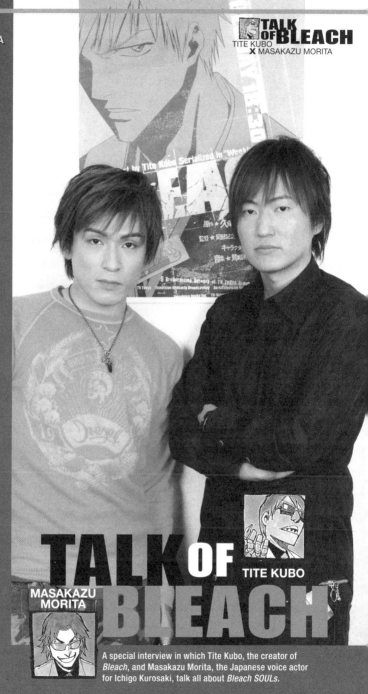

**TALK
OF BLEACH**
TITE KUBO
X MASAKAZU MORITA

久呆帯人 × 森丑戎一

TALK OF BLEACH

MASAKAZU MORITA

TITE KUBO

A special interview in which Tite Kubo, the creator of *Bleach*, and Masakazu Morita, the Japanese voice actor for Ichigo Kurosaki, talk all about *Bleach SOULs*.

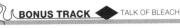

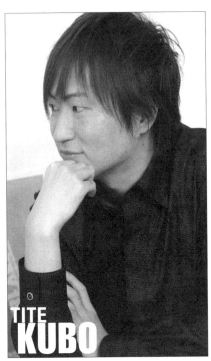

TITE
KUBO

MORITA: When Kubo told me about that, I frantically looked for the scenes he mentioned.
KUBO: It's the scene when everyone's returning to the world of the living, and Ichigo says, "Are they messing with us?!"[2]

WHAT HE WANTS TO DRAW

KUBO: Earlier, Morita said that stories are born through human interaction.[3] I thought that was amazing. I think drawing is not about drawing points and planes, but about depicting moods. Words aren't just lines, either. So whenever I

KUBO AND MORITA'S FIRST ENCOU
AND THEIR IMPRESSIONS

INTERVIEWER: *When was the first time y each other?*
KUBO: When we did our first dubbing,[1] I voice of Kon. I think that was the first ti met.
MORITA: I was going to work at another j day, so I had to leave early. We just passe other and didn't really get a chance to ta

INTERVIEWER: *What were your first impres each other?*
MORITA: He seemed shy.
KUBO: He seemed cheerful and full of er have a hard time getting along with en people, but Morita was very friendly. thankful that I worked with him. We chance to talk, we really got along.

ABOUT THE *BLEACH* TV ANIME

INTERVIEWER: *Kubo, have you watch anime?*
KUBO: Of course I have. I tape the shows they go on.

INTERVIEWER: *What's your impression of th*
KUBO: When I do the manga, I do thing by myself. But the anime is a co tion of various people's interpretations story. I watch it and think, "So that's w happened."(*laugh*)

INTERVIEWER: *Does Ichigo talk like Morita head?*
KUBO: Sometimes. (*laugh*) I told Morita that in an e-mail.

---

2 THE SCENE WHEN EVERYONE RETURNS TO THE WORLD OF THE LIVING.
It's what Ichigo says as he runs through the dangerous Dangai.

I THOUGHT THIS WAS THE OFFICIAL SENKAI-MON!!
WE'D EACH NEED A HELL BUTTERFLY TO TAKE THE SAFE ROUTE!!
SHOULDN'T THIS BE A NICE, SAFE ROUTE? WE WENT THROUGH THE OFFICIAL GATE!
ARE THEY MESS-ING WITH US?!
AND ONLY SOUL REAPERS CAN HANDLE HELL BUTTER-FLIES!!

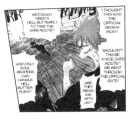

1 THE FIRST DUBBING
For the first *Bleach* anime that was shown at Jump Festa Anime Tour 2004. Kubo tried his hand at voice acting for the first time. He voiced Kon. But how was his acting?!

draw or write, I do it in a way that breathes life into the paper. For example, there's the background. The background is drawn to tell you where the characters are, but I don't think that's very important. I don't want to draw backgrounds in frames where characters come in. In *Bleach*, when a new character comes in, there are times when the background is blank.[4] This is because I want the character to create the mood just by standing there. I think a world is created by the interaction of the characters, so I try to draw my characters under that premise.

MORITA: When I read the original work, there are times when the mood is tense or relaxed. There are drawings that convey those moods. Even as an actor, whenever I read the original, I can hear the sounds. I think it is very important to be able to speak it exactly as it is without contamination.

> **"I think drawing is about depicting moods."**

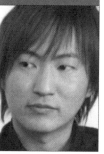

QUESTION AND ANSWER SESSION WITH KUBO AND MORITA

INTERVIEWER: *How do you each spend your days off?*

KUBO: I don't have any days off.

MORITA: What he said.

KUBO: On the days that I'm free, I do other things, like coloring. I don't even remember what I did during my last vacation. That's because I don't have any vacations. I only have a little time to cut my hair. Just enough to go out. When I get back home, I sit back down to work.

INTERVIEWER: *If you could do anything, what would you like to do?*

KUBO: I don't know how to answer such an abrupt question. I have a hard time thinking of things I want to do, so I usually plan things out two years in advance. What's with that, huh?

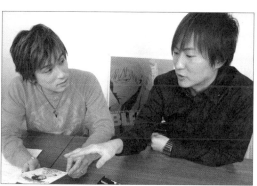

4 WHITE BACKGROUND
The picture of Aizen that shows that he's alive. As Kubo says, the background is white and there is nothing drawn behind the character.

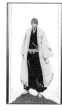

3 WHAT MORITA SAID
The conversation appears in the VIBEs. anime profiles. It refers to the anime version.

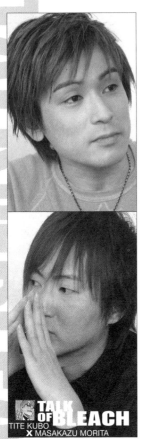

TALK
OF BLEACH
TITE KUBO
X MASAKAZU MORITA

INTERVIEWER: *Kubo, have you ever wanted to write a diffe*
series?

KUBO: I try not to think about that. If there's something I w
to draw, my mind tends to wander to that. If I think abo
too much, I can't concentrate on anything else. I shrug it
by drawing the characters that appear in my head. I can d
side stories for *Bleach*, but if I draw side stories for someth
else, I'll neglect *Bleach*. I think that's a little difficult to do
I haven't.

INTERVIEWER: *Is there anything that you would like to do in*
future?

MORITA: Regarding work, I'd try acting. I used to work on
stage. I'd like to do stage and film, but that's far off in the fut
Right now, I just don't have the time.

KUBO: Design work. I'd like to do clothing design.[5,6] But I wc
have to train a lot in order to do that... I don't know if I'd
want to do it several years from now, but I want to design clo
and furniture.

ABOUT THE VERSES THAT APPEAR
THROUGHOUT *BLEACH*

INTERVIEWER: *The title of the Aizen story*[7] *is terrific.*

KUBO: Thank you.

MORITA: The verse in the serialized comic is also terrific.

INTERVIEWER: *How long do you take to write verses?*

KUBO: I've been writing them down. I write them down as I th
of them and look for the ones that match the stories.

MORITA: You have an idea book?

KUBO: I do, I do. I've already written down fifty verses. I w
them describing characters or what characters are thinking
something that I've written doesn't match the image I've
I work on it until it does. It would be quite difficult if I di
write them down.

6 THE SOUTHERN
BELLE
Ichigo asks Uryû
to repair Kon
and he goes out
of control! The
fancy Southern
Belle is born!

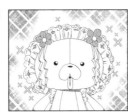

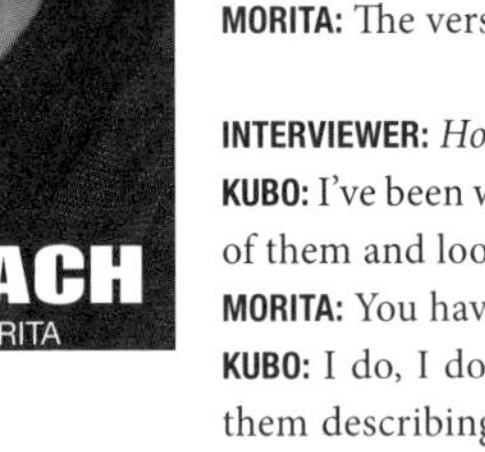

5 ANOTHER TALENT
The T-shirt that
Ichigo is wearing was
designed by Kubo.
It's currently on sale
at the Jump Shop.

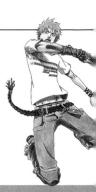

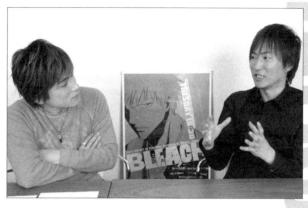

INTERVIEWER: *Are you doing that now?*

KUBO: Yes. I have to think of verses for this character book. I was only recently told that they wanted to put the same verses in the same chapters of the character book and the anime book, so I'm struggling.[8]

PLEASANT MOMENTS

INTERVIEWER: *Do you have pleasant moments when you're working?*

KUBO: It's pleasant when the scenes I've drawn come out the way I've imagined them. I have to do 19 pages a week, so I usually have to cut down my scenes. They almost never come out perfectly. Sometimes I'm happy just to be finished.

INTERVIEWER: *Sometimes the manga feels like a movie. Like the scenes in which Aizen has died and Momo attacks Ichimaru.*

KUBO: That was a pleasant part to draw.[9] I felt I really compressed it into the form of a manga. I'm really glad you like it. I appreciate it.

MORITA: Sometimes you read over those parts without realizing it. When I look at it afterwards, there are times when I'm surprised at how he used his frames. I'm amazed at how detailed they are.

KUBO: There are a lot of stories I'd like to draw. If only I had the time. Something about Kenpachi, for example. I think in time I'll use it in the story.

INTERVIEWER: *I've been wondering who Yachiru is.*

KUBO: I plan to draw it. It's still a secret.

---

8 STRUGGLING WITH VERSES
The verses on the cover and illustrations of this book are all gems created by Kubo after much agonizing thought.

9 PLEASANT PART
See volume 12, chapter 101 of the manga.

7 THE AIZEN STORY
Sôsuke Aizen's body is pinned to a wall... The title of this chapter is "Flower on the Precipice."

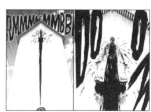

MORITA: There are also the Four Great Aristocratic Families. What are aristocrats?

INTERVIEWER: *The Kuchiki family, the Shihôin family...and the Shiba family?*
KUBO: The Shiba family isn't one of them. When the Shiba family was one of them, they were called the Five Great Aristocratic Families. I have a lot of other ideas. But I won't draw them unless I need to... I want to draw them at the best time.
MORITA: I'm looking forward to that. (*laugh*)

A WORD TO THE FANS

KUBO: I read all of my fan letters. Your reactions inspire me. I really want your letters. (*laugh*)

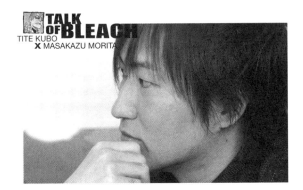

TALK OF BLEACH
TITE KUBO
X MASAKAZU MORITA

TITE KUBO'S Working Laboratory

A functional work desk that has subtle interior design. *Bleach* was born here.

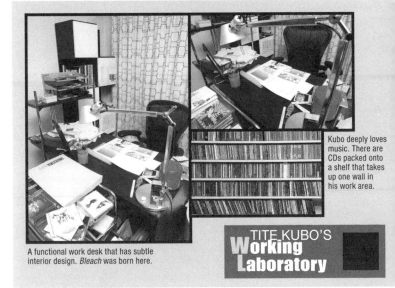

Kubo deeply loves music. There are CDs packed onto a shelf that takes up one wall in his work area.

Photography/Atsushi Wada Reporter•Writer/Tetsuya Hoshi (Brain Navi)

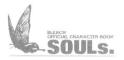

BLEACH
OFFICIAL CHARACTER BOOK
SOULs.

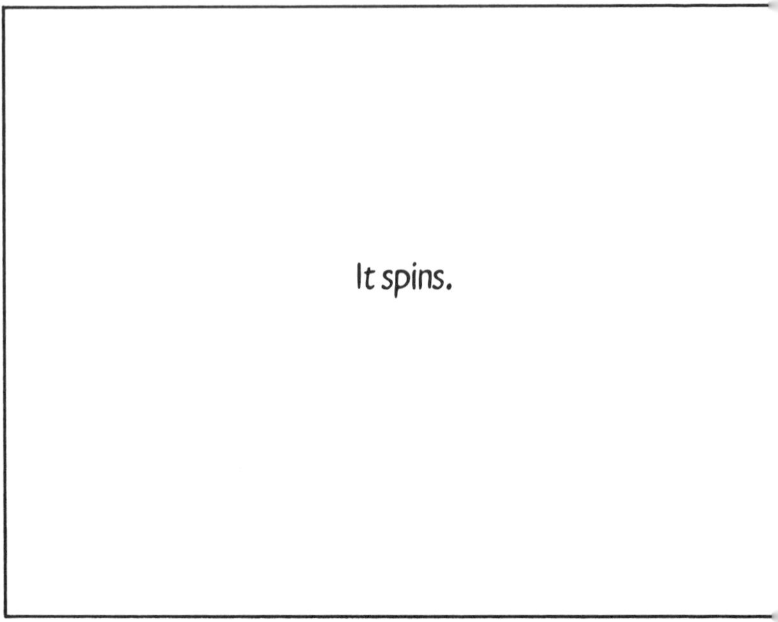
It spins.

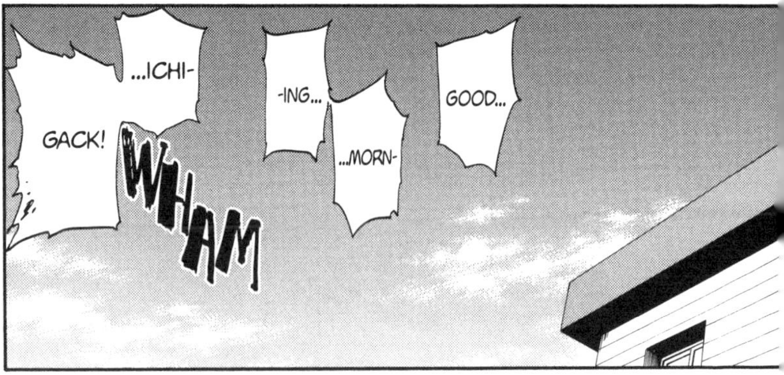
GOOD...
...MORN-
-ING...
...ICHI-
WHAM
GACK!

BLEACH *0* *side-A*

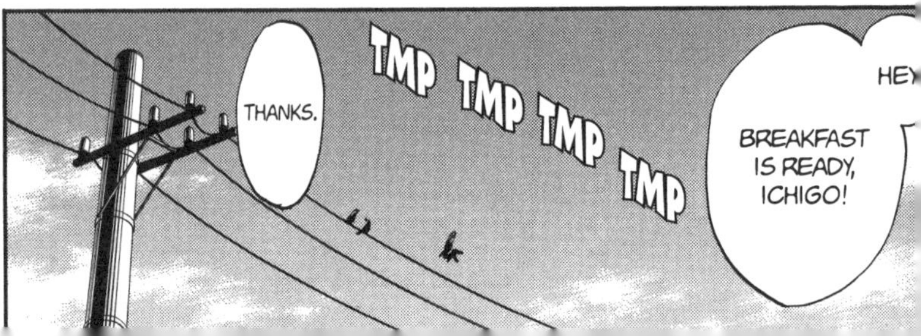
HE
BREAKFAST IS READY, ICHIGO!
TMP TMP TMP TMP
THANKS.

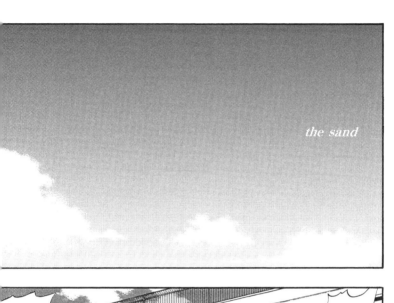

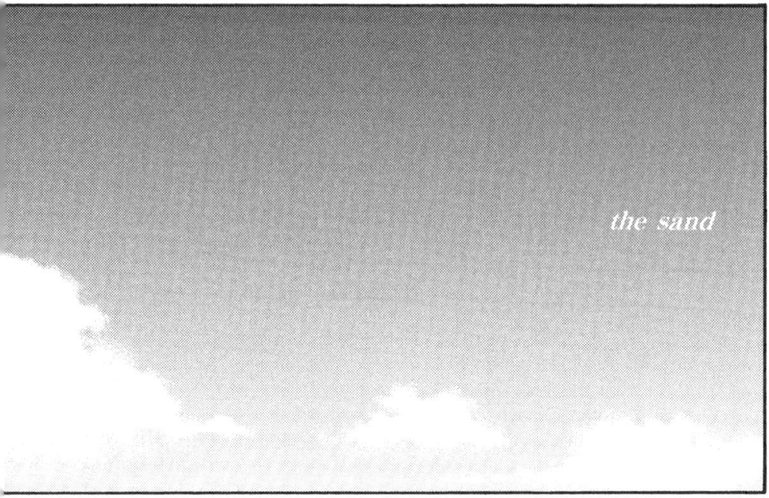
the sand

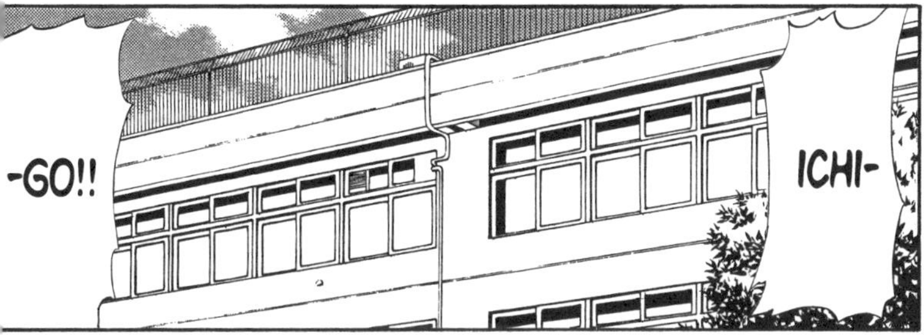
ICHI-
-GO!!

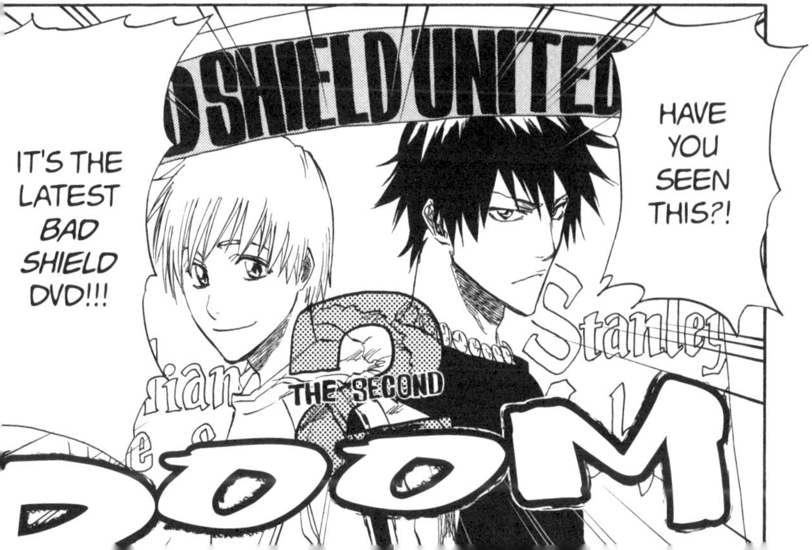
SHIELD
HAVE YOU SEEN THIS?!
IT'S THE LATEST BAD SHIELD DVD!!!
Stanley
THE SECOND
DOOM

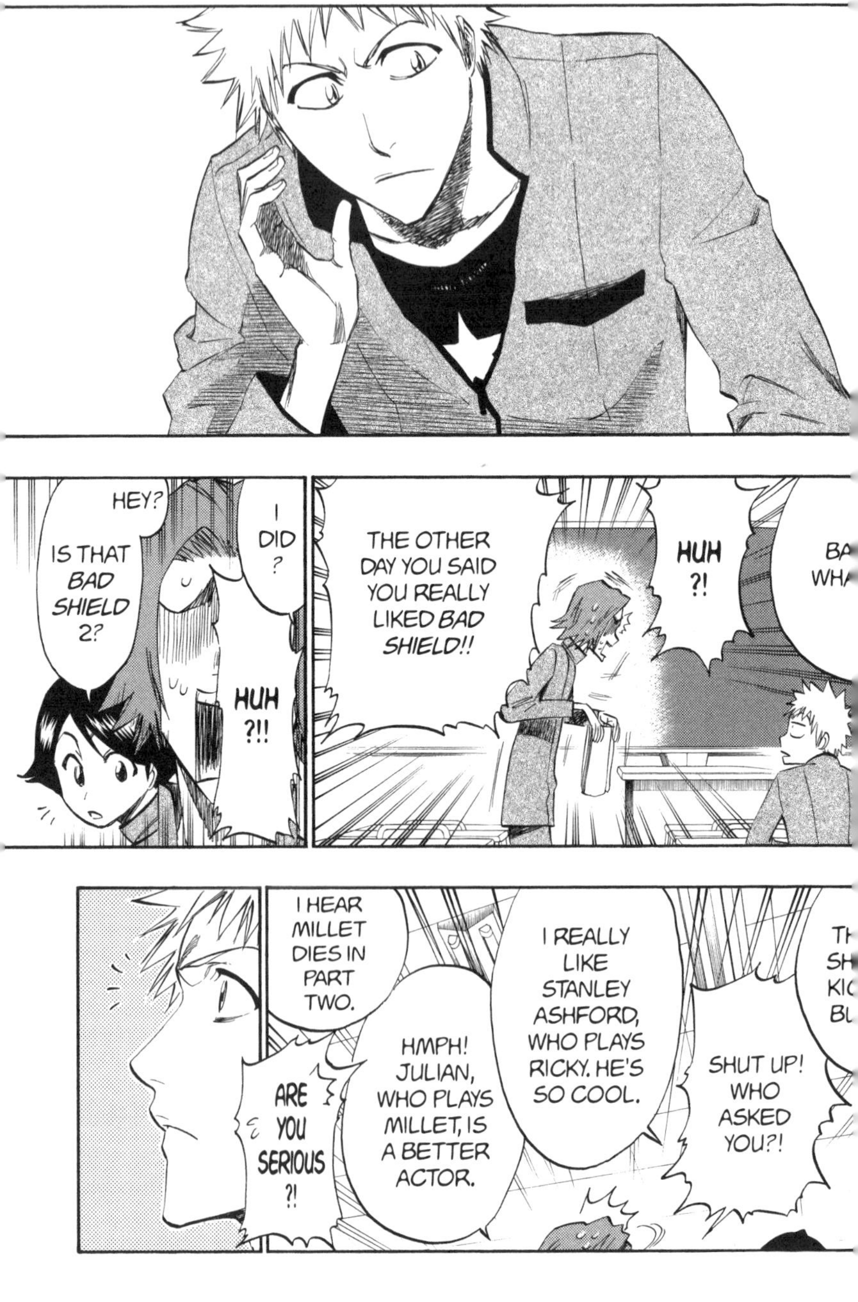
HUH ?!
THE OTHER DAY YOU SAID YOU REALLY LIKED BAD SHIELD!!
I DID ?
HEY? IS THAT BAD SHIELD 2?
HUH ?!!
I REALLY LIKE STANLEY ASHFORD, WHO PLAYS RICKY. HE'S SO COOL.
SHUT UP! WHO ASKED YOU?!
I HEAR MILLET DIES IN PART TWO.
HMPH! JULIAN, WHO PLAYS MILLET, IS A BETTER ACTOR.
ARE YOU SERIOUS ?!

The world changes.

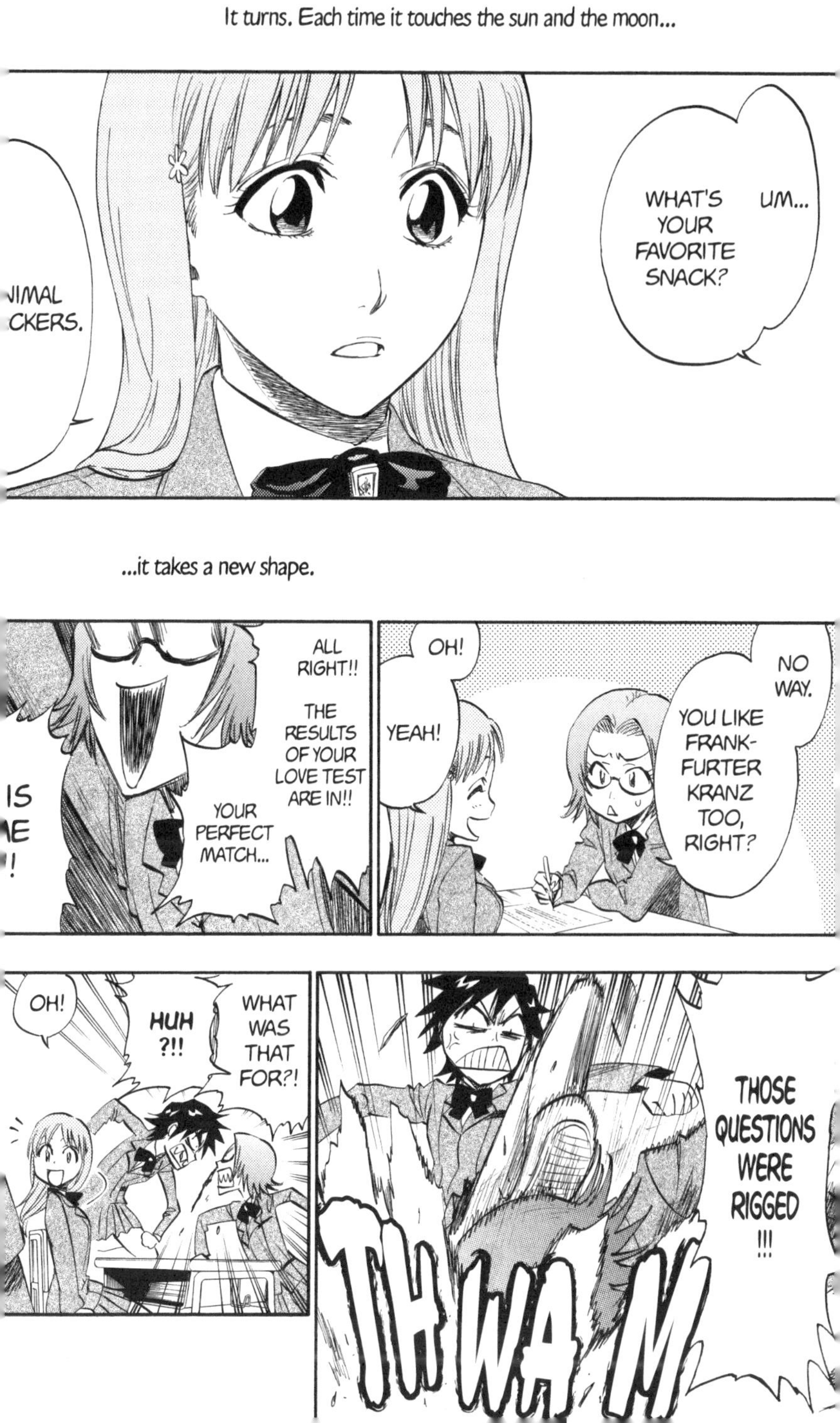
It turns. Each time it touches the sun and the moon...
UM...
WHAT'S YOUR FAVORITE SNACK?
IMAL CKERS.
...it takes a new shape.
NO WAY.
YOU LIKE FRANK-FURTER KRANZ TOO, RIGHT?
OH!
YEAH!
ALL RIGHT!!
THE RESULTS OF YOUR LOVE TEST ARE IN!!
YOUR PERFECT MATCH...
THOSE QUESTIONS WERE RIGGED!!!
THWAM
WHAT WAS THAT FOR?!
HUH?!!
OH!

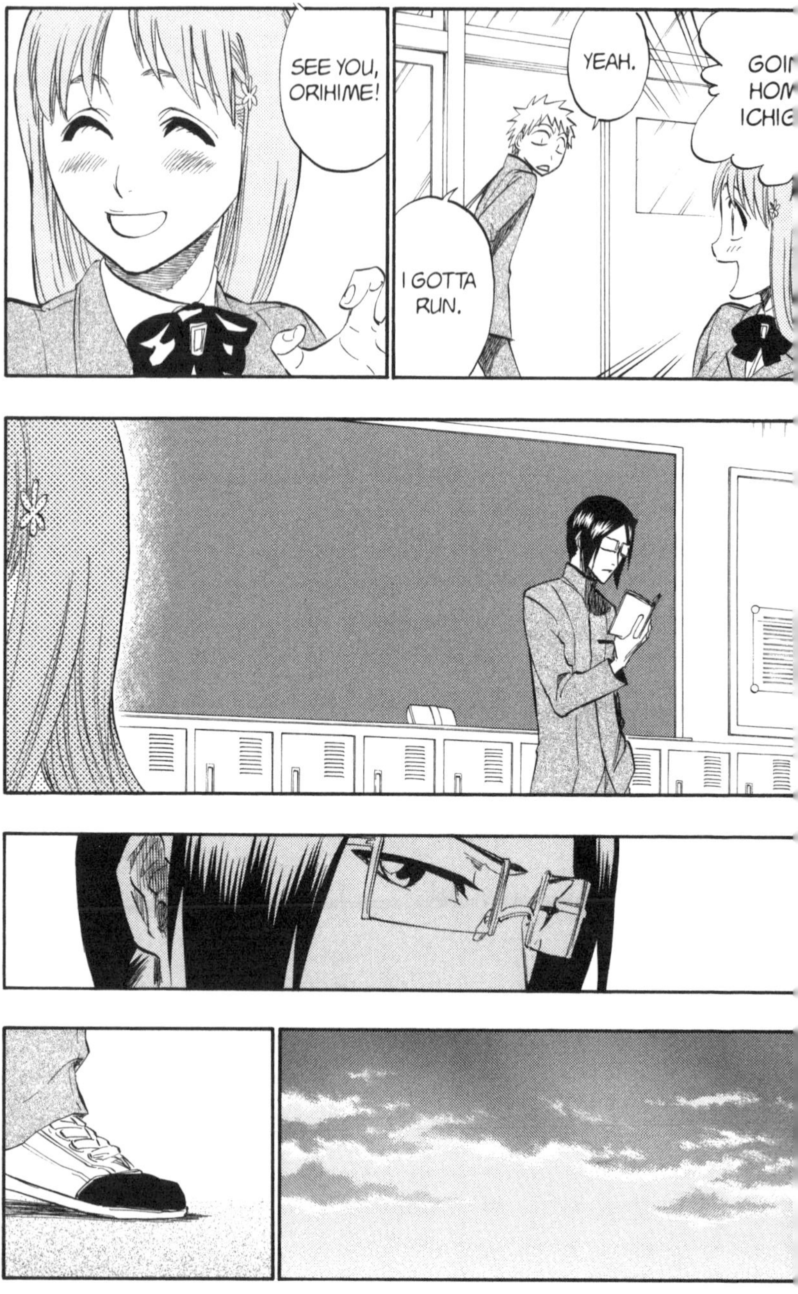
GOIN HOM ICHIG
YEAH.
I GOTTA RUN.
SEE YOU, ORIHIME!

The one thing that does not change...

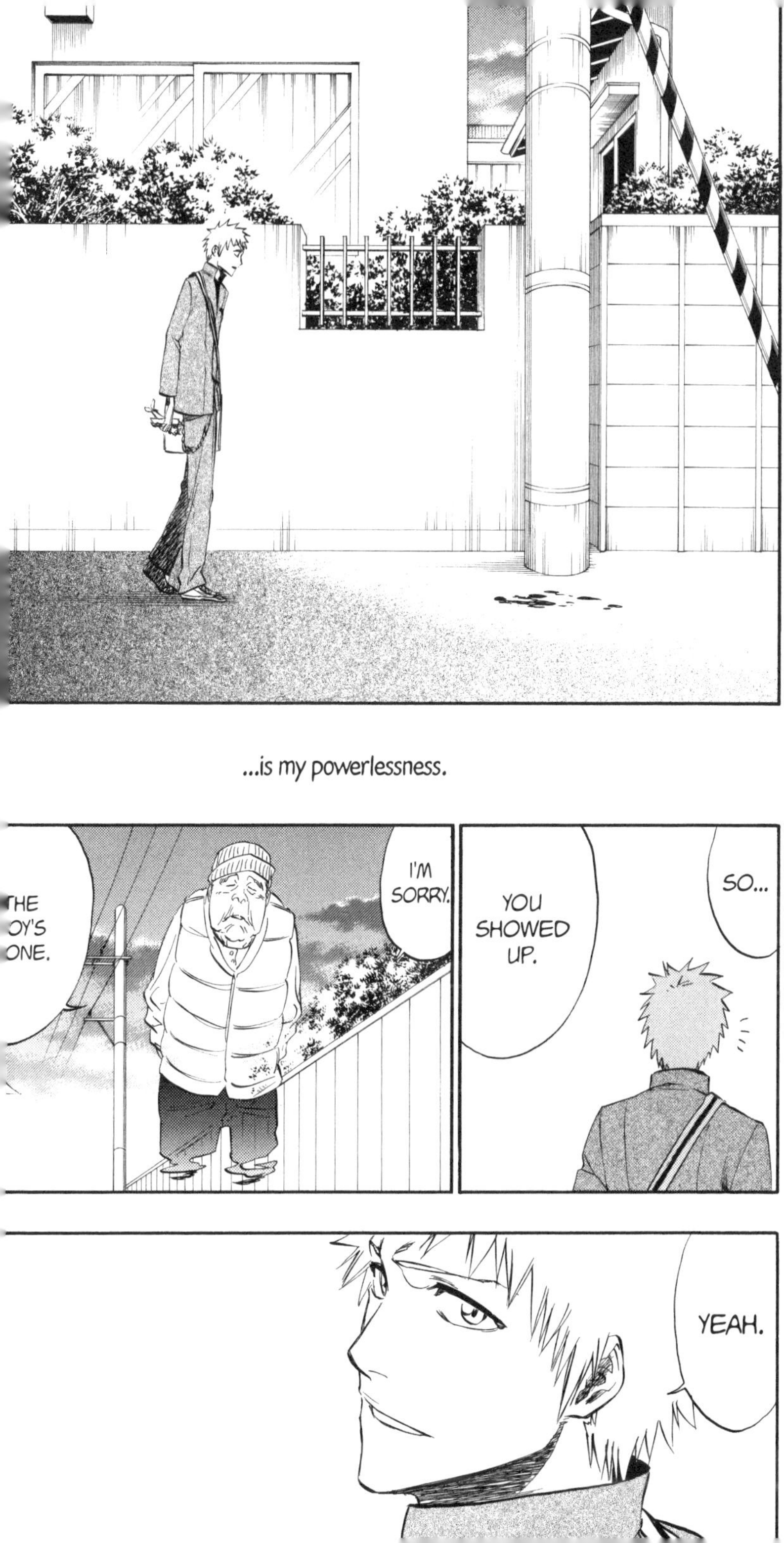
...is my powerlessness.
SO...
YOU SHOWED UP.
I'M SORRY.
THE OY'S ONE.
YEAH.

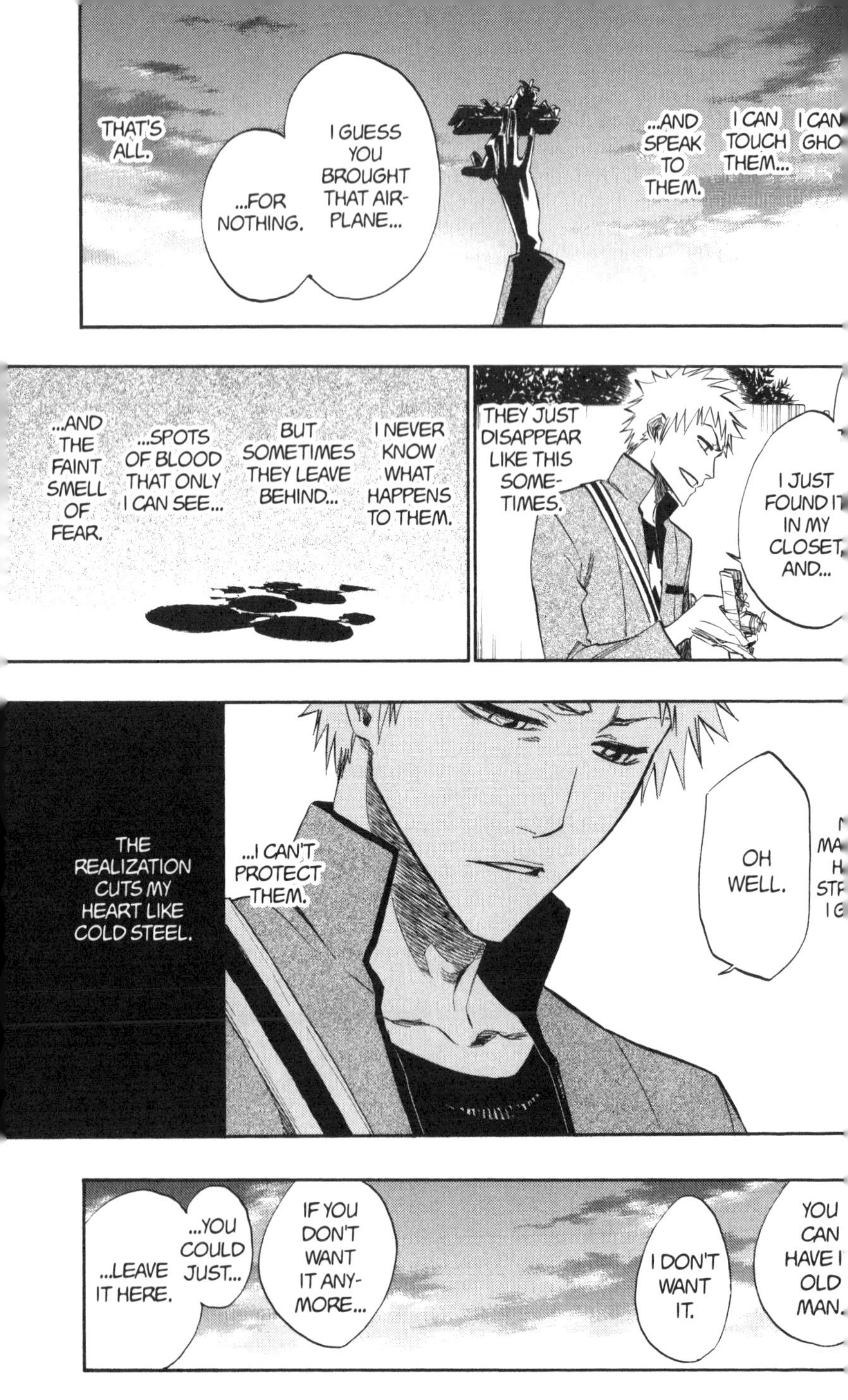
I CAN
I CAN TOUCH THEM...
...AND SPEAK TO THEM.
I GUESS YOU BROUGHT THAT AIRPLANE...
...FOR NOTHING.
THAT'S ALL.
I JUST FOUND IT IN MY CLOSET, AND...
THEY JUST DISAPPEAR LIKE THIS SOMETIMES.
I NEVER KNOW WHAT HAPPENS TO THEM.
BUT SOMETIMES THEY LEAVE BEHIND...
...SPOTS OF BLOOD THAT ONLY I CAN SEE...
...AND THE FAINT SMELL OF FEAR.
OH WELL.
...I CAN'T PROTECT THEM.
THE REALIZATION CUTS MY HEART LIKE COLD STEEL.
YOU CAN HAVE I OLD MAN.
I DON'T WANT IT.
IF YOU DON'T WANT IT ANYMORE...
...YOU COULD JUST...
...LEAVE IT HERE.

It's turning.

If fate is a millstone...

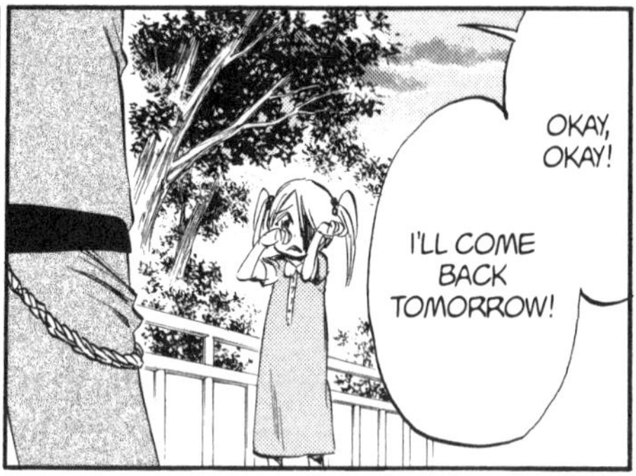
OKAY, OKAY!
I'LL COME BACK TOMORROW!

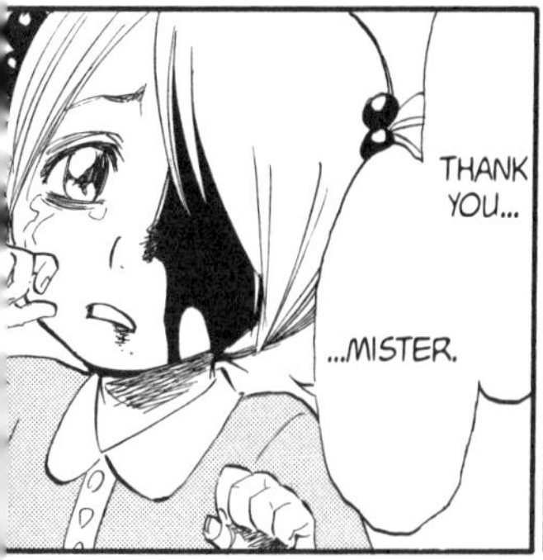
THANK YOU...
...MISTER.

...then we are the grist.

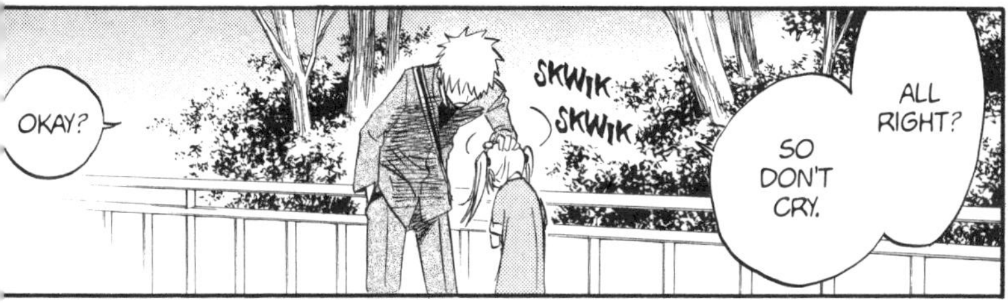
ALL RIGHT?
SO DON'T CRY.
SKWIK SKWIK
OKAY?

There is nothing we can do.

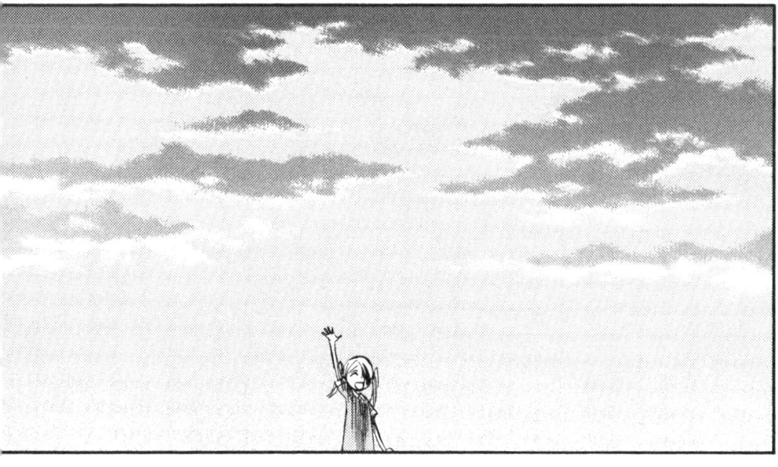

So I wish for strength.

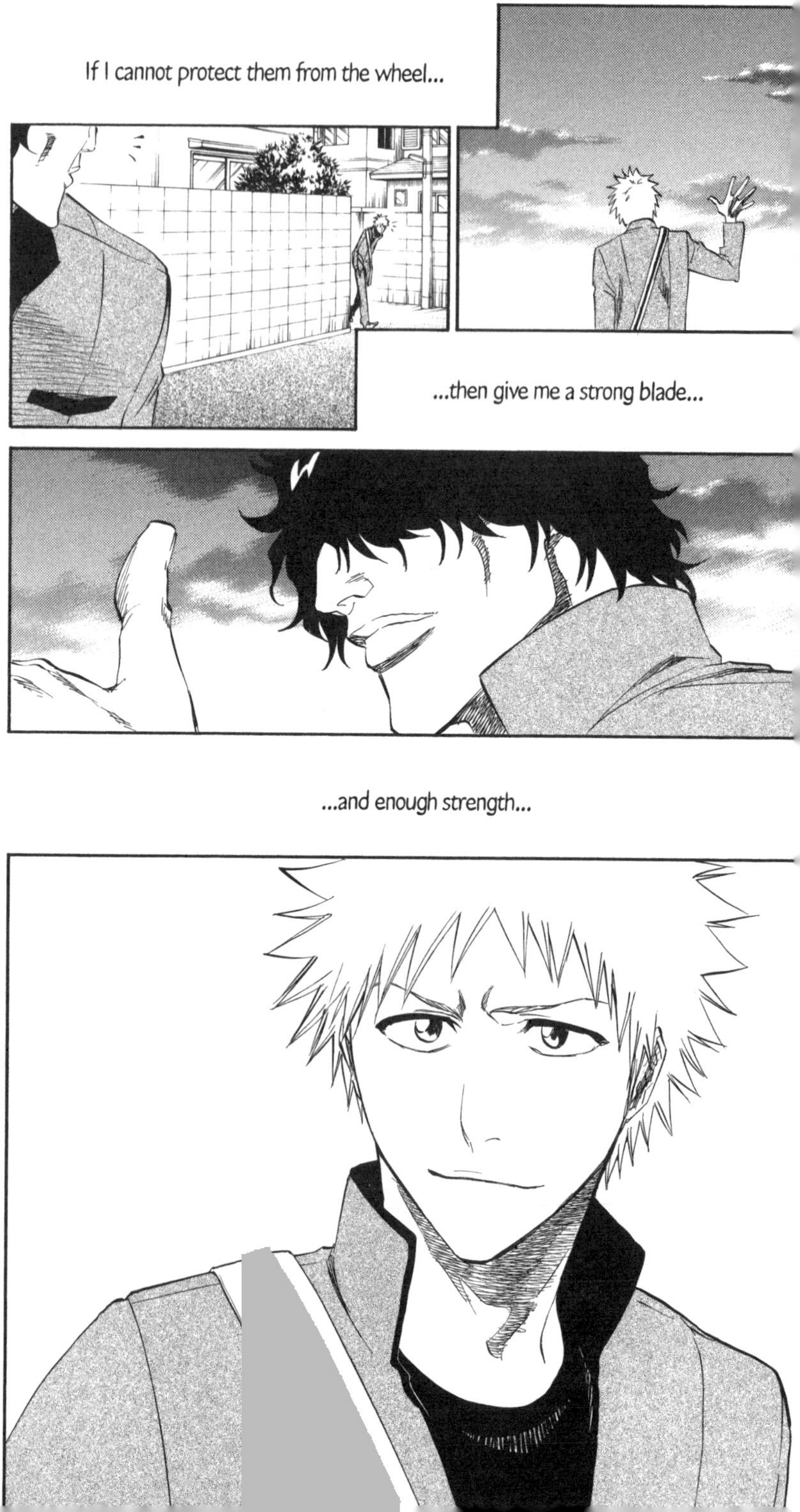
If I cannot protect them from the wheel...
...then give me a strong blade...
...and enough strength...

...TO
SHATTER
FATE.

Explanation of BLEACH Terms

Let's study! BLEACH Terms Explained

THE CODE OF YUZU: Yuzu takes care of all of the Kurosaki family's household chores and decided on these rules. They contain harsh laws as, "You must brush your teeth within ten minutes after a meal, or you won't get your next meal."

CROSSING THE RUBICON: The Rubicon is a river that begins in the Apennines in central Italy and flows into the Adriatic Sea. In 49 BC, Julius Caesar decided to go to war with the Triumvir Pompey. He said "The die is cast," and breaking Senate orders, crossed the Rubicon. Uryû said something similar when he confronted Ichigo. His line was meant to evoke Caesar and Pompey's confrontation.

DAD'S GREAT WHISTLE: Ichigo's father, Isshin, uses this whistle to gather his family.

DAIREISHOKAIRO: The Great Archive. Contains all the knowledge and history of the Soul Society.

DANGAI: The Precipice World. The area between the world of the living and the Soul Society. It is filled with kôryû, restrictive energy currents that paralyze konpaku in order to keep out Hollows and other foreign invaders.

DON KANONJI FAN CLUB: Ichigo was forced to join the club and was assigned the title "Number One Disciple."

EISHÔHAKI: A technique that releases kidô without a spirit chant. While this decreases the time needed to release the kidô, it also drastically weakens the spell.

ENRAKU: Orihime's teddy bear. He's named after the leader of the general emcee on *Shoten*.

FOUR-EYED SEWING MACHINE: Another name for Uryû Ishida, first-year president of the craft club.

ASANO, TADANOBU: Keigo discove these mysterious words on a popsic stick as he was eating a popsicle t kill time.

BIKINI BUSTERS: The magazine that wa offered to Kon by elementary scho students who wanted him to he them in a soccer game. It is unknown wh elementary school students would have th sort of magazine. You can imagine what it like from its title.

BOSTAV: The name that Yuzu gives to Kon th stuffed animal.

erk

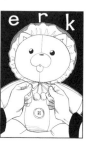

CENTRAL EXECUTION GROUNDS: A wid area in the Seireitei where criminal executions are carried out. Th Sôkyoku is located here.

CERO: The destructive beam that Meno Grandes release from their mouths. Sou Reapers know it as a Doom Blast.

CHAPPY: The most popular Soul Candy charac ter. Other designs include a duck and a dog.

MOST POPULAR "CHAPPY"
2ND MOST POPULAR "YUKI"
3RD MOST POPULAR "PUPPLES"

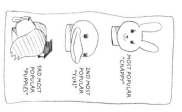

-ZAI: The flesh healing drug that Mayuri suchi uses. When taken, lost body parts stored and reconstructed.

KARAKURA SOUTH ELEMENTARY SCHOOL: The elementary school where Yuzu and Karin go.

IKAN: The hair ornaments Byakuya iki wears. Only aristocrats are allowed ar them.

SHINKI: A memory substitution device on humans who have seen Soul Reapers llows. Also called kiokuchikan.

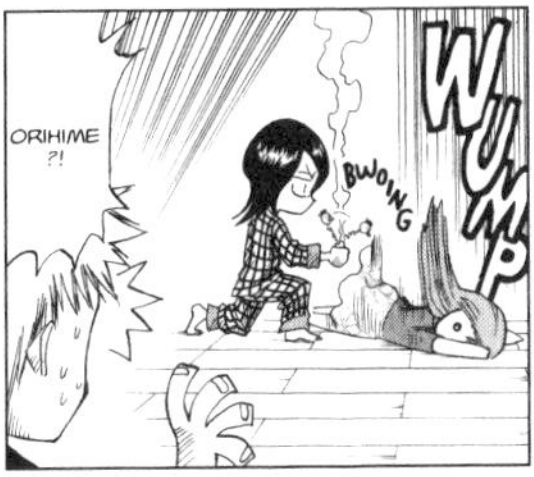
WUMP
BWOING
ORIHIME ?!

The material that makes up the things in orld of the living.

SU: The cleaner that patrols the Precipice d. It is a high-density restrictive current liminates intruders.

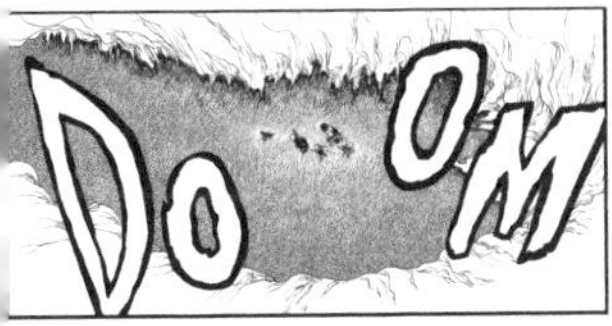
DO OM

AKI FAMILY TOMBSTONE DOMINO TOURNAMENT: really blasphemous event that the sakis hold whenever they visit their rela- graves. The priest goes into a rage when ds them playing it.

ON: Mirror Gate. An high level force field leflects attacks from the outside.

G

GIGAI: The temporary bodies that Soul Reapers use in the world of the living. They were created by the Department of Research and Development.

GREAT KÛKAKU ARMS: Kûkaku's residence is decorated with these flag-holding art objects.

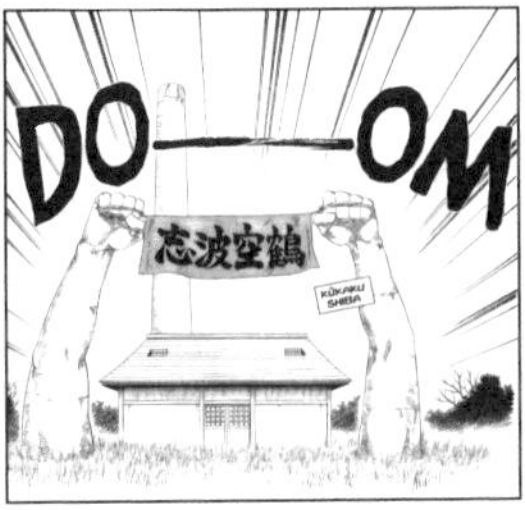
DO——OM
志波空鶴

H

HANKI SÔSAI: Anti-kidô Offset. A fighting technique that combats an opponent's kidô by hitting it with a kidô of the same quality and quantity spinning in the opposite direction.

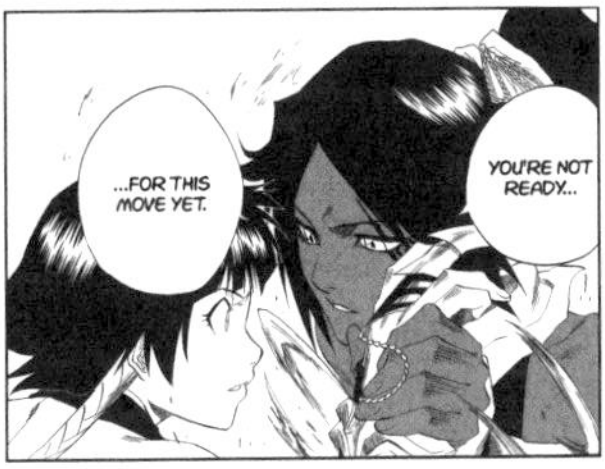
YOU'RE NOT READY...
...FOR THIS MOVE YET.

HAT-AND-CLOGS: What Ichigo calls Urahara.

HEADBAND OF JUSTICE: The headband that Ichigo wore when he trained in Urahara Shôten's basement to regain his Soul Reaper energy.

HELL BUTTERFLIES: The butterflies that Soul Reapers use to lead them to the world of the living. They are also used as messengers in the Soul Society.

HIREN KYAKU: An advanced Quincy moving technique. It allows for high speed movements by riding on the flow of reishi created below the user's feet.

ÔUNABARA, GENGORÔ: An instructor at the Soul Reaper Academy. He taught Renji's, Hinamori's, and Izuru's class.

PAPA GOAT-FACE: Karin's name for her dad.

PERPETUAL RELEASE TYPE: Zanpaku-tô that are always in shikai form because of the strength of their wielder's spiritual energy.

PIG STRADDLER: What Ichigo calls Ganju when Ganju barges into the room without warning.

RANSÔ TENGA: The ultimate Quincy combat technique. When Quincies can't move, they create strings of reishi and attach them to their bodies. They force their bodies to move like puppets.

REIRAKU: Spirit ribbon. A visible aura that looks like a sash. Soul Reapers have crimson reiraku.

REISHI: Spirit particles. The main component material of souls. All the things in the Soul Society are made of reishi.

REISHI HENKAN-KI: Spirit particle conversion machine. A device to convert kishi into reishi. Used when Ichigo and his friends go to the Soul Society.

RUKONGAI: It is the place outside of the Seireitei where most souls live.

RYOKA: Souls that have come to the Soul Society illegally. They are believed to be harbingers of ill fortune.

SEKKI-SEKI: Lethal presence rock. A rare mineral in Soul Society that blocks all spiritual energy. It also emits waves that break down spiritual energy.

KÛMON: Sky Ridges. The distortion in that appears when a Menos Grande a in the world of the living.

LUCKY DANCE: The dance that I Madarame dances when he feels

MAGICAL GIRL MEGALON: A magic series, that while targeted at youn has a core following among otak

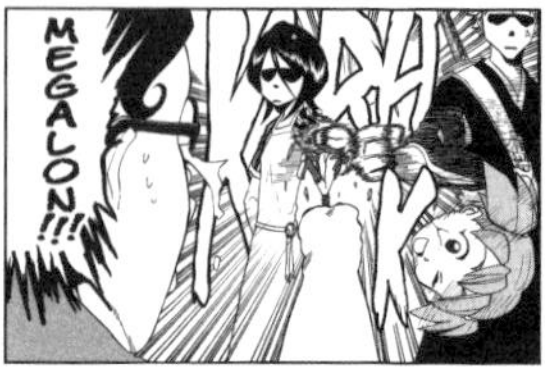
MEGALON!!!

MAKIMAKI: The nickname Yachiru gives M Aramaki.

MASHIBA MIDDLE SCHOOL: The middle s that Ichigo and Chad attended. "Cha Kurosaki of Machiba Middle Schoo famous in the delinquent world.

MIDORIKO TONO: Yuzu and Karin's class She is an unfortunate girl who is alwa pushed around. She has a crush on Asano.

NEGACIÓN: The beam of ligh Menos Grande use to save thei rades. Things outside the ligh things inside it are unable to interac each other. The light creates a complete lated void.

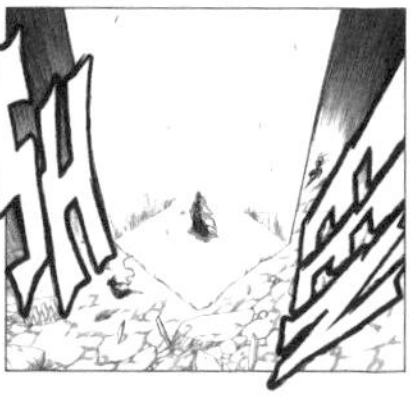

ORIHIME VISION: Reveals how O views the world and her daydream often involves romanticizing Ic

UGENDÔ QUARTERS: Thirteenth Company Captain Ukitake's room. Ukitake often takes treatment here for his poor ealth.

RYÛ'S FITTING ROOM A changing room that)rihime prepared for Uryû so that he can change nto a shihakushô. Its entrance (just a curtain) as pieces of masking tape that say, "Spacious!", Comfy!", and "Embarrassment Free!"

HERE YOU GO!
GO AHEAD, URYÛ!!
URYÛ'S FITTING ROOM
SPACIOUS!!
COMFY!!

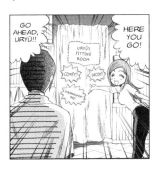

YAKKA: Orihime's soccer-baseball combo game. It is fundamentally one-on-one, so the defending side is at an xtreme disadvantage.

AOCHO: A greengrocery in Karakura Town. randpa Ken owns the store.

UMISAWA CHILDREN'S PARK: The Karakura Town ark where the Hollow Hexapodus appeared. his is where Ichigo decided to help Rukia vith her Soul Reaper work.

ZANKENSOKI: Basic Soul Reaper fighting techniques. "Zan" refers to sword fighting techniques. "Ken" refers to narmed fighting techniques. "So" refers to noving techniques like Shunpo. "Ki" refers o kidô.

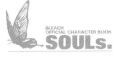

SHAKONMAKU: Soul Shield Membrane. The dome-shaped reishi barrier that surrounds the Seireitei.

SHINTEN: A kind of tranquilizer carried by the Fourth Company. One drop on the skin will knock out a person of low spiritual energy.

SHOTEN: A comedy storytelling variety show on Sunday nights. Orihime watches it every week. It is known for being most exciting when the performers heckle each other. *Shoten* is the second-longest running TV show in Japan.

SOMAFIXER: Internal soul fixing medicine. A drug that strengthens the bond between a gigai and a soul.

SOUL PAGER: The terminal that Soul Reapers in the world of the living use to receive orders and information from the Soul Society. It looks exactly like a cellular phone.

SPEARHEAD: A Soul Society project to inject fighting spirits into dead animals, and to use the reanimated corpses as advance guards against Hollows.

SPECIAL WAR TIME ORDER: The special order given throughout the Seireitei when the Ryoka invaded. It allows the top officers of the Thirteen Court Guard Companies, including Assistant Captains, to carry their zanpakutô at all times, and to release them during battle.

SPIRIT MOVEMENT: The movement or wavering of spirt energy.

SPIRIT WEAPON: The weapon that Quincies create by gathering the reishi in the air.

SPONTANEOUS TRIPS TO SPIRITUAL HOT SPOTS: The occult show hosted by the charismatic Spirit Medium, Don Kanonji. It has an audience rating of over 25 percent. It's called *Spiritual Hot Spots* for short.

TENTÔKEN: The tool that Yoruichi gave Ichigo. It is shaped like a cloak. Those who wear it can fly.

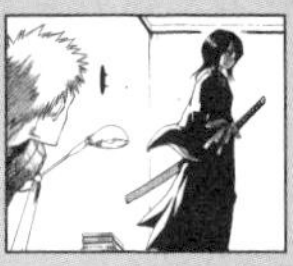

Rukia Kuchiki, the girl in black who suddenly appears before Ichigo's eyes.

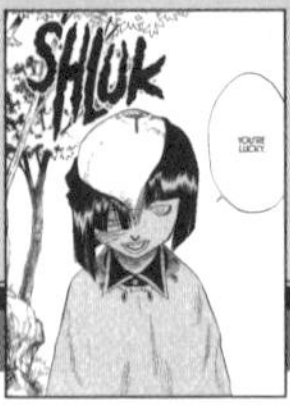

SHLUK

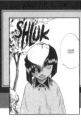

The evil spirit that killed Ichigo's mother Masaki. The Hollow appears before Ichigo six years later… It is a fateful reunion.

6/17 16 YEARS AGO

6/17

WORLD OF THE LIVING

- Ichigo Kurosaki is born.
- Masaki Kurosaki dies when a Hollow attacks her. (P.51)
- Extra Chapter "Bleach 0" (P.247)
- Ichigo meets Rukia and becomes a substitute Soul Reaper. (P.35)
- The battle against Acidwire. (P.39)
- The battle against Shrieker. (P.44)
- Meeting with Kon, the mod soul. (P.48)
- The battle against Grand Fisher. (P.52)
- Reunion with an old enemy.
- *Spiritual Hot Spots* is filmed in Karakura Town. (P.63)
- Battle with Uryû, the Quincy. (P.66)
- Chad and Orihime's energies awaken. (P.68, 70)

KISUKE URAHARA INVENTS THE HÔGYOKU.

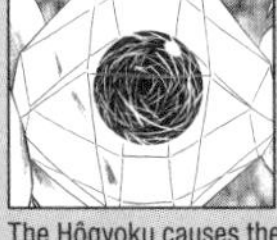

The Hôgyoku causes the disturbance in the Soul Society. It was discovered long ago.

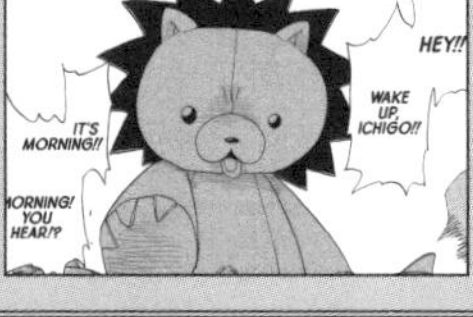

HEY!!
WAKE UP, ICHIGO!!
IT'S MORNING!!
ORNING! YOU HEAR?!

Bleach's beloved mascot character is born.

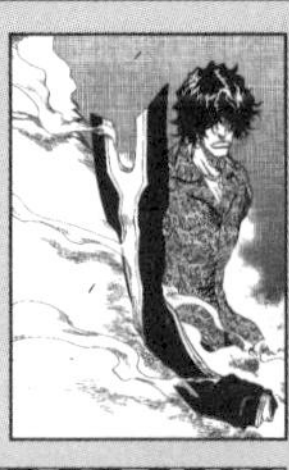

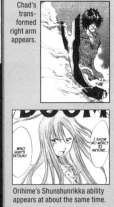

Chad's transformed right arm appears.

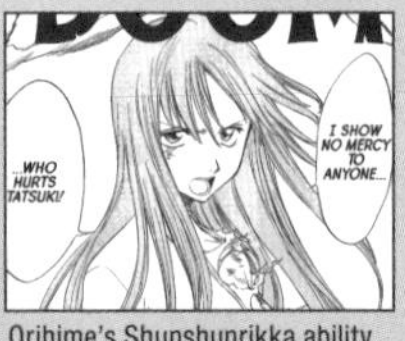

I SHOW NO MERCY TO ANYONE...
...WHO HURTS TATSUKI!

Orihime's Shunshunrikka ability appears at about the same time.

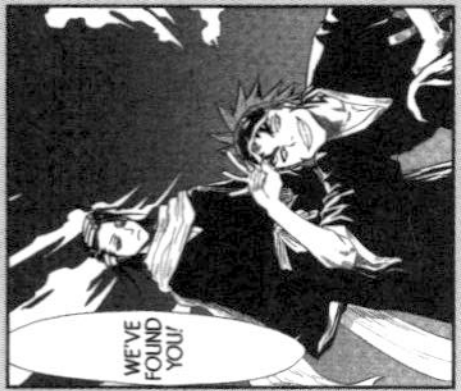
WE'VE FOUND YOU!
The Soul Society's best trackers go after Rukia.

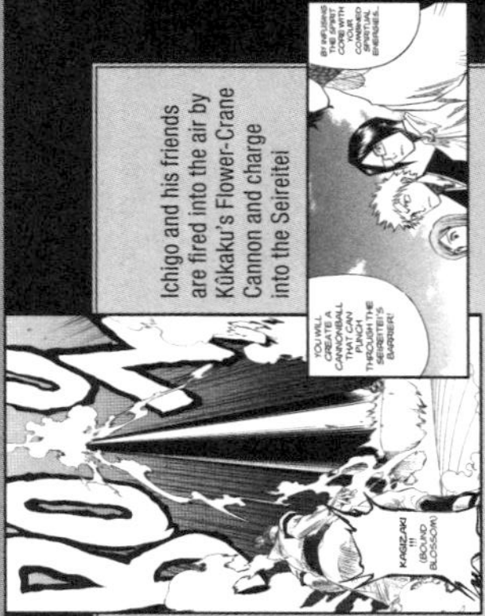
BY INFUSING THE SPIRIT CORE WITH YOUR COMBINED SPIRITUAL ENERGIES...
YOU WILL CREATE A CANNONBALL THAT CAN PUNCH THROUGH THE SEIREITEI'S BARRIER!
KAGIZAKI!!! (BOUND BLOSSOM)
Ichigo and his friends are fired into the air by Kûkaku's Flower-Crane Cannon and charge into the Seireitei

8/7

- Byakuya Kuchiki and Renji Abarai appear in the word of the living (P.76)
- Rukia is taken back to Soul Society. (P.79)
- Training with Urahara. (P.82)
  *The Hollow mask appears.
- Passing through the Senkaimon and going to the Soul Society. (P.91)

THE SOUL SOCIETY

- The members of the world of the living go to the Soul Society.
- The battle against Jidanbô. Meeting with Gin Ichimaru. (P.102-105)
- Using the Flower-Crane Cannon to get into the Soul Society. (P.114)
- The battle against Ikkaku & Yumichika. (P.116, 117)
- Meeting with Hanatarô Yamada. (P.119)
- Orihime and Uryû versus Jirôbô Ikkanzaka. (P.118)
- The battle against Renji.
  *The Hollow mask appears. (P.122)

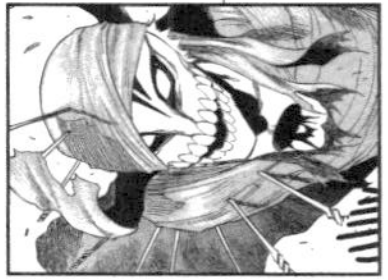

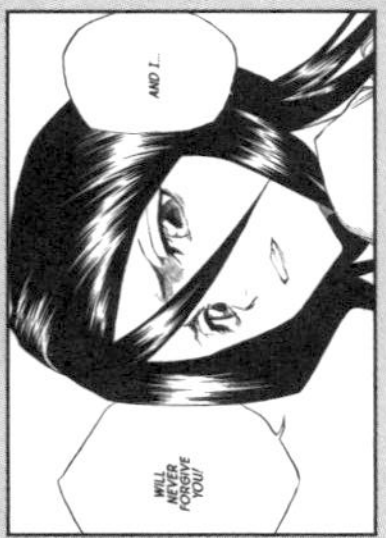
AND I...
WILL NEVER FORGIVE YOU!
Ichigo is defeated by Byakuya. Rukia decides to return to the Soul Society in order to save Ichigo.

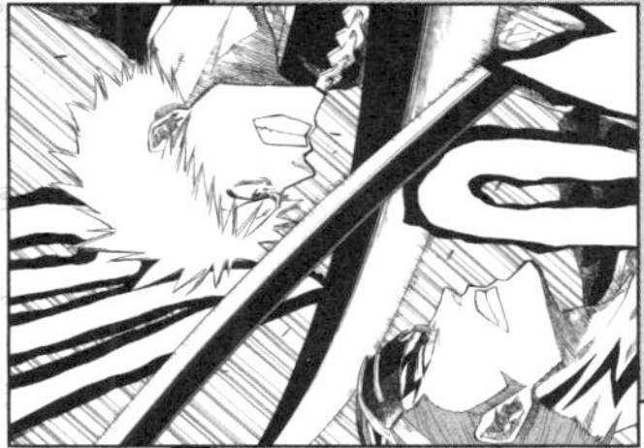
Ichigo and Renji cross swords to settle their dispute in the world of the living.

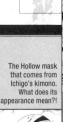

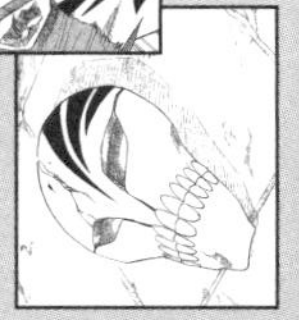
The Hollow mask that comes from Ichigo's kimono. What does its appearance mean?!

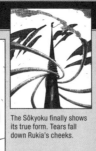

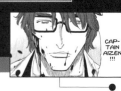

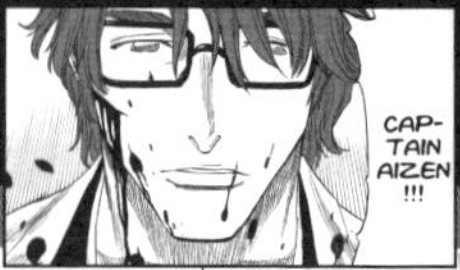
CAP-
TAIN
AIZEN
!!!

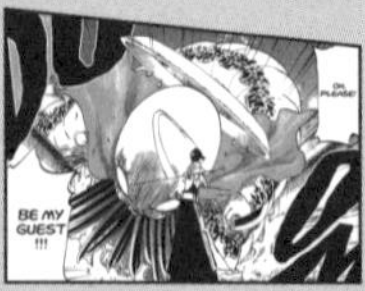
BE MY
GUEST
!!!

Kurotsuchi's bankai, Konjiki Ashisogi Jizô, shows its form and attacks Uryû!!

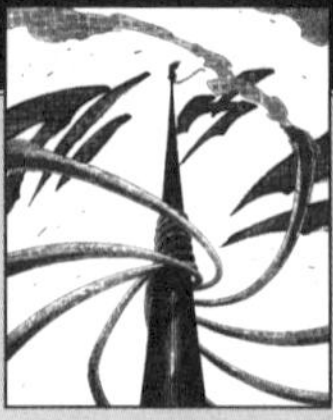

The Sôkyoku finally shows its true form. Tears fall down Rukia's cheeks.

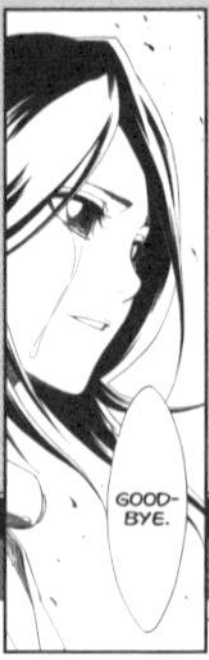
GOOD-
BYE.

EXECUTION DAY

- Aizen murdered. Momo goes wild. (P.131, 132)
- Chad versus Kyôraku. (P.136)
- The battle against Zaraki. (P.140)
  *The Hollow mask appears.
- The skirmish in front of the Senzaikyû Shishinrô. (P.148)
- Uryû versus Kurotsuchi. (P.156)
- Ichigo begins his bankai training. (P.160)
- Hitsugaya versus Ichimaru. (P.165)
- Renji versus Byakuya. (P.182)
- Zaraki versus Kaname & Komamura. (P.179)
- Sôkyoku released. (P.189)
- Ukitake & Kyôraku versus Yamamoto. (P.200)
- Yoruichi versus Soi Fon. (P.196)
- The battle against Byakuya. (P.204)
- Ichigo's bankai defeats Byakuya. (P.206-214)

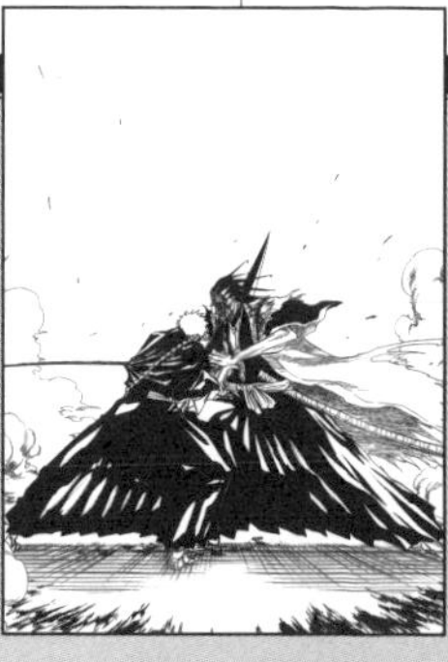

Ichigo's long battle with Kenpachi Zaraki, the Sword Demon, comes to an end. The mask appears again.

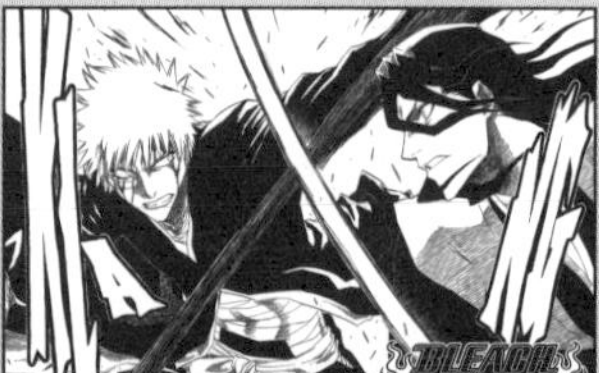
BLEACH

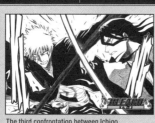

The third confrontation between Ichigo and Byakuya... Ichigo Kurosaki dominates the fierce battle with his black blade!!

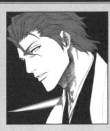

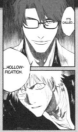

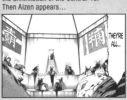

The Soul Society is greatly disturbed by the annihilation of the Central 46! Then Aizen appears...

THEY'RE ALL...

Aizen takes off his mask and reveals his true nature!!

IT'S CALLED...
...HOLLOW-FICATION.

- Hitsugaya discovers that the Central 46 has been annihilated. (P.218)
- Izuru versus Rangiku. (P.219)
- Aizen's corruption is brought to light. (P.220)
- Momo and Hitsugaya fall victim to Aizen's sinister blade. (P.220, 221)
- Unohana senses Aizen's plot. (P.222)
- Ichigo & Renji versus Aizen. (P.223)

The truth is revealed.

- The decisive battle on the Sôkyoku hill. (P.226)
- Rukia apologizes to Kûkaku and Ganju. (P.228)
- The members of the world of the living return there. (P.229)

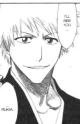

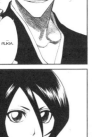

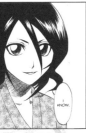

I'LL SEE YOU ...
... RUKIA.
I KNOW.

Ichigo and Rukia finally settle their feelings and head towards a new tomorrow...

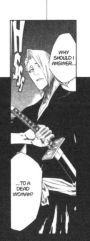

WHY SHOULD I ANSWER...
...TO A DEAD WOMAN?

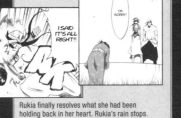

I'M SORRY!
I SAID IT'S ALL RIGHT!!
OH!

Rukia finally resolves what she had been holding back in her heart. Rukia's rain stops.

Translation Volumes 1~20

English & etc » Japanese — **Title Translation into Japanese** — Supervisor TITE KUBO

No.	Title	Japanese Title
	Vol 1 DEATH & STRAWBERRY // The Soul Reaper and Ichigo	"死神" と "一護"
1.	*Death & Strawberry // The Soul Reaper and Ichigo*	"死神" と "一護"
2.	*Starter // Begin*	始動
3.	*Headhittin' // Off with His Head!*	頭を斬れ!
4.	*WHY DO YOU EAT IT? // Why Do You Eat That?*	なぜあなたはそれを喰べるの?
5.	*Binda-blinda (※1) // The One who Binds, the One who Blinds*	縛るもの、瞳を閉ざすもの
6.	*microcrack // A Small Crack*	小さな亀裂
7.	*The Pink Cheeked Parakeet // The Pink-cheeked Parakeet*	ピンクの頬をしたインコ
	Vol 2 GOODBYE PARAKEET, GOODNITE MY SISTA	さようならインコ、おやすみ妹
8.	*Chase Chad Around // Go After Chad*	チャドを追いかけろ
9.	*Monster and a Transfer [Struck Down] // ——————*	怪物と転入生 [打ち倒す]
10.	*Monster and a Transfer pt.2 [The Deathberry] //* *The Monster and the Transfer Student [Soul Reaper Ichigo]*	怪物と転入生 その2 [死神一護]
11.	*Back. [Leachbomb or Mom] // Give Her Back! [Leech Bombs or Your Mother]*	返せ! [ヒル爆弾か母親か]
12.	*The Gate of The End // The Gates of Hell*	"地獄の門"
13.	*BAD STANDARD // Shoddy Goods*	粗悪品
14.	*School Daze!!! (※2) // The School Goes into a Huge Panic!!!*	学園大パニック!!!
15.	*Jumpin' Jack, Jolted // The Large Riot of He Who Jumped Out*	飛び出すアイツの大騒動
16.	*Wasted but Wanted // The One who Is Unneeded Is the One Who is Needed*	不用な者、求めたもの
	Vol 3 memories in the rain // Memories of Rain	雨の記憶
17.	*6/17 // June 17*	6月17日
18.	*6/17 op. 2 Can't Smile Don't Blame //* *He can't smile. Don't blame him*	6月17日 作品2 "笑えない彼、責める勿れ"
19.	*6/17 op.3 memories in the rain // Memories of Rain*	6月17日 作品3 "雨の記憶"
20.	*6/17 op.4 face again // Reunion*	6月17日 作品4 "再会"
21.	*6/17 op.5 Fighting Boy // A Fighting Boy*	6月17日 作品5 "戦う少年"
22.	*6/17 op.6 BATTLE ON THE GRAVEYARD // Showdown in the Graveyard*	6月17日 作品6 "墓地での決闘"
23.	*6/17 op.7 Sharp Will, Dull Blade //* *His Will is Sharp. His Blade is Dull*	6月17日 作品7 "意思は鋭し、刃は鈍し"
24.	*6/17 op.8 All One Way Sympathies // One-way Sympathy*	6月17日 作品8 "一方的な共感"

※1 "A" has been added to the ends of the words "bind" and "blind" to give them a
   feminine sound. Orihime was the one who bound and blinded Sora.
※2 "Days" has been tweaked to "Daze".

No.	Title	Japanese Title
25.	*6/17 op.9 A Fighting Boy (The Cigarette Blues Mix) // Fighting Boy 2 [Cigar Blues]*	６月１７日　作品９戦う少年２ ［煙草のブルーズ］
Vol 4 QUINCY ARCHER HATES YOU // The Bow-slinging Quincy Hates You		弓撃つ滅却師、キミを憎む
26.	*Paradise is Nowhere (※3) // There Is No Paradise*	楽園なんてどこにもない
27.	*Spirits Are Always WITH US // Spirits Are Always with Us… Sometimes*	霊はいつも一緒にいる…わけない
28.	*Symptom of Synesthesia // Signs of Sympathy*	共鳴の兆し
29.	*Stop that Stupid!! // Stop that Idiot!!*	あのバカを止めろ!
30.	*Second Contact [it was outside the scope of our understanding] // Second Contact [It was Beyond our Understanding]*	第２次接触 ｛それは我々の理解を超えて｝
31.	*HEROES CAN SAVE YOU (※4) // Champion of Justice*	正義のミカタ
32.	*Hero is Always With Me? (※5) // Do Heroes Really Exist?*	ヒーローってホントにいるの？
33.	*ROCKIN' FUTURE 7 // Seven People's Wavering Futures*	揺れ動く７人の未来
34.	*Quincy Archer Hates You // The Bow-slinging Quincy Hates You*	弓撃つ滅却師、キミを憎む
Vol 5 RIGHT ARM OF THE GIANT// The Giant's Right Arm		巨人の右腕
35.	*Can You Be My Enemy? (※6) // I Guess We Have to Duel*	勝負しかないか
36.	*They Died for Vengeance // We died for our vengeance*	我ら、報復の為に死に至りて
37.	*Crossing the Rubicon // Cross the Rubicon*	ルビコンを渡れ
38.	*BENT // Distortion*	歪曲
39.	*Rightarm of the Giant // The Right Arm of the Giant*	巨人の右腕
40.	*Grow? // Growth?*	…成長？
41.	*Princess & Dragon // The Princess and the Dragon*	姫君と竜
42.	*Princess & Dragon PART. 2 The Majestic // The Princess and the Dragon Part 2 Majestic*	姫君と竜　その２　"威風堂々"
43.	*Princess & Dragon PART. 3 Six Flowers // The Princess and the Dragon Part 3 Six Flowers*	姫君と竜　その３　"六輪の花"
Vol 6 THE DEATH TRILOGY OVERTURE // Three Soul Reapers' Overture		３人の死神の序曲
44.	*Awaken [to the Threat] // Awakening [Dragged Out]*	覚醒　［引きずり出された］
45.	*Point of Purpose // Goal Point*	目標地点
46.	*Karneades (※7)~Back to Back // Carneades~Back to Back*	カルネアデス～背中合わせ
47.	*Back to Back~Tearing Sky // Back to Back~Tearing the Sky*	背中合わせ～引き裂かれる空
48.	*———————— // Menos Grande*	メノスグランデ
49.	*unchained // The Released*	解き放たれしもの

※3 It can be read as "~is Now Here" on the cover art. ※4 Direct Translation: "Heroes can save you." ヒーローは君を護ことができる *Hiro wa Kimi o Mamorukoto ga Dekiru.* ※5 The sentence is grammatically incorrect to give the feel of a child asking its parent that question. ※6 Direct Translation: "Will You Be My Enemy?" 君は僕の敵になれるか *Kimi wa Boku no Teki ni Nareruka.* ※7 The situation posed by the ancient Greek philosopher, Karneades. You are in the ocean and holding onto a piece of driftwood that can support only one person. In front of you is a drowning man. It asks whether it is all right to sacrifice another's life to save your own.

No.	Title	Japanese Title
50.	Quincy Archer Hates You Part 2 [Blind But Bleed Mix] // The Bow-slinging Quincy Hates You [Bleeding in the Darkness]	弓撃つ滅却師、キミを憎む [暗闇の中で血を流す]
51.	DEATH 3 // Three Soul Reapers	3人の死神
52.	Needless Emotions // Unnecessary Emotions	必要のない感情
Vol 7 THE BROKEN CODA // An Interrupted Conclusion		途切れた結末
53.	Nice to meet you, I will beat you (※8) // I'm the man who's going to defeat you. Pleased to meet you!!	テメーを倒す男だ、よろしく!!
54.	The Nameless Boy // Child Who Doesn't Know His Name	名も訊けぬ子供
55.	SHUT // The End	終焉
56.	broken coda // An Interrupted Conclusion	途切れた結末
57.	Unfinished July Rain // Never Ending July Rain	降り止まぬ七月の雨
58.	blank // Blank	空白
59.	Lesson 1:One Strike+Jailed at Home // Lesson 1: Single-game Match! + Jailed at Home	レッスン1： 1発勝負!＋郷里での投獄
60.	Lesson 1-2: DOWN!! // Lesson 1-2: Plummet!!	レッスン1－2：落下!!
61.	Lesson 2: Shattered shaft // Lesson: The Pit of Despair	レッスン：絶望の縦穴
Vol 8 THE BLADE AND ME // The Blade I Acquired		手にした我が刃
62.	Lesson 2-2: Bad Endin' In The Shaft // Lesson 2-2 Bad Ending in the Shaft	レッスン2－2 縦穴の中でバッド・エンド
63.	Lesson 2-3: Innercircle Breakdown // Lesson 2-3 Collapse of His Inner World	レッスン2－3 内なる世界の崩壊
64.	BACK IN BLACK // Return to Darkness	暗黒回帰
65.	Collisions // Collision	衝突
66.	THE BLADE AND ME // The Blade I Acquired	手にした我が刃
67.	End of Lessons // End of Lessons	レッスン終了
68.	The Last Summer Vacation // The Final Summer Vacation	最後の夏休み
69.	25:00 gathering // Gather at 25:00	集合、25：00
70.	Where Hollows Fear to Tread // A Dangerous Area That Even Hollows Fear	"虚"も怖れる危険地帯
Vol 9 FOURTEEN DAYS FOR CONSPIRACY // Fourteen Days Until Rukia's Execution		ルキア処刑までの14日間
71.	INTRUDERZ // Intruders	侵入者たち
72.	The Superchunk // Hero	豪傑
73.	Drizzly Axes (※9) // Showering Axes	降り注ぐ斧
74.	Armlost, Armlost // My Axe, My Arm…	オラの斧、オラの腕…
75.	Crimson Rain // Blood Rain	血雨

※8 Direct Translation: "Pleased to Meet You. I Will Defeat You." はじめまして。俺はお前を打ち倒す
※9 "Drizzly" also means "misty rain" or "fine rain."

No.	Title	Japanese Title
76.	*Boarrider Comin' // The Boar-rider Comes!*	猪ライダー来襲!
77.	*————————// My Name is Ganju*	俺様の名はガンジュ
78.	*meeT iT aT basemenT // Encounter in the Basement*	地下室で出会う
79.	*FOURTEEN DAYS FOR CONSPIRACY // Fourteen Days Until Rukia's Execution*	ルキア処刑までの14日間
Vol10	*TATTOO ON THE SKY // Marching from the Sky*	空からの進軍
80.	*The Shooting Star Project // The Shooting Star Project*	流星計画
81.	*Twelve Tone Rendezvous (※10) // The Captains Assemble*	12隊長集結
82.	*Conflictable Composition (※11) // The Belligerent Captains' Meeting*	紛糾する隊首会
83.	*COME WITH ME // Come With Me*	一緒にこいよ
84.	*The Shooting Star Project 2 [Tattoo On The Sky] // The Shooting Star Project Part 2 [Marching From the Sky]*	流星計画 その２［空からの進軍］
85.	*INTRUDERZ 2 [Breakthrough the roof mix] // Intruders Part 2 [Break Through the Barrier]*	侵入者たち その２［障壁をぶち破れ!］
86.	*Making Good Relations, OK? // Let's Be Friends!*	仲良くやろうぜ!
87.	*Dancing With Spears // Dance with Hôzukimaru!*	鬼灯丸と踊れ!
88.	*SO UNLUCKY WE ARE // The Unlucky*	ツイてねえヤツら
88.5.	*KARAKURA SUPER HEROES // Karakura Super Heroes*	カラクラ　スーパーヒーローズ
Vol11	*A STAR AND A STRAY DOG // The Star and the Stray Dog*	星と野良犬
89.	*Masterly! And Farewell! // Wonderful! And Farewell!*	お見事! そしてさようなら!
90.	*See You Under a Firework // Lets Meet Under the Fireworks*	花火の下で会おう
91.	*KING OF FREISCHUTZ // The Strongest Projectile User*	最強の飛び道具使い
92.	*Masterly! And Farewell! [Reprise] // Wonderful! And Farewell! [Reprise]*	お見事! そしてさようなら［反復］
93.	*Steer For the Star // The Path to Senzaikyu*	懺罪宮への道
94.	*Gaol Named Remorse // The Prison of Guilt*	"自責"の牢獄
95.	*CRUSH // Clash*	激突
96.	*BLOODRED CONFLICT // A Red-stained Struggle*	赤に染まる闘争
97.	*Talk About Your Fear (※12) // The Fear Reflected in His Sword*	剣に映る"恐怖"
98.	*A Star and a Stray Dog // The Star and the Stray Dog*	星と野良犬
Vol12	*FLOWER ON THE PRECIPICE // The Flower on the Rock Face*	岩壁の花
99.	*Dead Black War Cloud // An All-out Soul Reaper War*	死神全面戦争
100.	*Flower on the Precipice // Like a Flower on the Rock Face*	それは岩壁の花に似て
101.	*Split Under The Red Stalk // The Clash Under the Crimson Flower Stem*	紅い花茎の下での衝突
102.	*Nobody Beats (※13) // The Invincible Man*	無敵の男

※10 The twelve captains are likened to the twelve tones on keyboard instruments. ※11 Direct Translation: "Opposed Composition." 対立に適した構図 */ Composition also means "musical composition." It is a metaphor for how Aizen pitted all the captains against each other. ※12 Direct Translation: "Let's talk about your fears."* 貴方の恐怖について語り合いましょう.

No.	Title	Japanese Title
103.	Dominion // "Control"	"支配"
104.	The Undead // The Imperishable Monster	不死の怪物
105.	Spring, Spring, Meets The Tiger (※14) // Shunsui and Chad	春水とチャド
106.	Cause For Confront // The Reason He Risks His Life	命をかける理由
107.	Heat In Trust // Burning Trust	アツい信頼
0.8.	a wonderful error // A Wonderful Error	素敵な間違い
Vol13 THE UNDEAD // The Imperishable Monster		**不死の怪物**
108.	Time For Scare // Time Of Terror	恐怖の時間
109.	Like a Tiger Trying not to Crush the Flowers // Like a Tiger That Won't Step on Flowers	花を踏まぬ虎のように
110.	Dark Side of Universe // The Dark Side of the World	世界の黒の部分
111.	Black & White // Black and White	黒と白
112.	The Undead 2 [Rise&Craze] // The Imperishable Monster 2 [Revival and Excitement]	不死の怪物 2 ［復活と熱狂］
113.	The Undead 3 [Closing Frantical] // The Imperishable Monster 3 [The End of the Crazy Party]	不死の怪物 3 ［狂宴の終焉］
114.	Everything Relating to the Crumbling World // Everything About This Crumbling World	崩れゆく世界のすべてについて
115.	Remnant // Resemblance	面影
Vol14 WHITE TOWER ROCKS // The Swaying White Tower		**揺れる"白い塔"**
116.	White Tower Rocks // The Swaying White Tower	揺れる"白い塔"
117.	Remnant 2 [Deny the Shadow] // Resemblance 2 [The Denied Shadow]	面影 2 ［否定された影］
118.	The Supernal Tag // God's Game of Tag	神の鬼事
119.	Secret of the Moon // Zangetsu's True Energy and Secret	斬月の真の力と秘密
120.	Shake Hands With Grenades // Shaking Hands with Bombs	爆弾と握手する
121.	In Sane We Trust (※15) // An Insane Captain	兇気の隊長
122.	Don't Lose Your Grip On // Grab Him and Don't Let Go	掴んで離すな
123.	Pledge My Pride To // On My Pride as a Quincy	滅却師の誇りに懸けて
Vol15 BEGINNING OF THE DEATH OF TOMORROW // The End of Tomorrow's Beginning		**滅びゆく明日の始まり**
124.	Crying Little People // The Crying Boy	涙を流す少年
125.	Insanely & Genius // Madness and Genius	狂気と天才
126.	The Last of a Void War // The End of a Pointless Battle	無意味な戦いの結末
127.	Beginning of the Death of Tomorrow // The End of Tomorrow's Beginning	滅びゆく明日の始まり
128.	The Great Joint Struggle Union // The Great Battle Alliance	偉大な共闘連合

※13 Direct Translation: No One Can Defeat Him 誰も打ち倒せない.
※14 Direct Translation: Spring Springs Out and Meets the Tiger. 春、ひょいっと飛び出して虎と出会う
Spring is the first character of Shunsui and Tiger is the second character of Yasutora. ※15 Direct Translation: In Sanity We Trust. 我々は正気を信じる / If you connect the words to form "Insanity," it reads, "Insanity We Trust."

No.	Title	Japanese Title
129.	Suspicion [for Assassination] // Suspected of Assassination	暗殺容疑
130.	Suspicion2 [of Tears] // One Tear Drop	一粒の涙
-17.	Prelude for the Straying Stars // A Prelude for Straying Stars	逸れゆく星々の為の前奏曲
Vol16	NIGHT OF WIJNRUIT (※16) // Night of the Rue Flower	ヘンルーダの花の夜
131.	The True Will (※17) // A Final Wish	最後の願い
132.	Creeping Limit // The Approaching Deadline	迫る期限
133.	memories in the rain2 the nocturne // Memories of Rain 2 Nocturne	雨の記憶２ "夜想曲"
134.	memories in the rain2 op.2 Longing for Sanctuary // Memories of Rain 2 Work 2 In Need of a Sanctuary	雨の記憶２ 作品２ "聖域を求めて"
135.	memories in the rain2 op.3 Affected By the Night (※18) // Memories of Rain 2 Work 3 Violated by the Night	雨の記憶２ 作品３ "夜に侵される"
136.	memories in the rain2 op.4 "night of the wijnruit" (※19) // Memories of Rain 2 Work 4 "A Night of Regret"	雨の記憶２ 作品４ "後悔の夜"
137.	Surrounding Clutch // Surrounded by Zangetsu	取り囲む斬月たち
138.	Individual Thoughts // Their Own Thoughts	それぞれの想い
139.	Drowsy, Bloody, Crazy // Drowsy, Bloody and Crazy	眠そう、血まみれ、イカれてる
Vol17	ROSA RUBICUNDIOR, LILO CANDIDIOR // Redder than Roses, Whiter than Lilies	薔薇より紅く、百合より白く
140.	Bite at the Moon // Snap at the Moon	月に咬みつけ
141.	Kneel to the Baboon King // Kneel Down to the Baboon King	狒狒王に跪け
142.	———————— // Announce the One Who Captures the Moon	月を捉うものへ告ぐ
143.	Blazing Souls // The Blazing Souls	燃え上がる魂たち
144.	Rosa Rubicundior, Lilo Candidior // Redder than Roses, Whiter than Lilies	薔薇より紅く、百合より白く
145.	Shaken // Shaken	動揺
146.	Demon Loves the Dark // Demons Love the Dark	魔物は暗黒を好む
147.	Countdown to The End: 3 [Blind Light, Deaf Beat] // ————————	終焉までのカウントダウン３ [盲目の光、無音の鼓動]
148.	Countdown to The End: 2 [Lady Lennon~Frankenstein] // Countdown to The End 2 [The Woman Who Wishes for Peace. Non-human Giant.]	終焉までのカウントダウン２ [平和を願う女性、人ではない巨躯]
149.	Countdown to The End: 1 [Only Mercifully] // Countdown to The End 1 [The Very Least Mercy]	終焉までのカウントダウン１ [せめてもの慈悲]
Vol18	THE DEATHBERRY RETURNS // Soul Reaper Ichigo Returns	死神一護、再び
150.	Countdown to The End: 0 // ————————	終焉までのカウントダウン０
151.	Deathberry Returns // Soul Reaper Ichigo Returns	死神一護、再び
152.	The Speed Phantom // The Instant Speed Illusion	瞬速の幻影

※16 Dutch for rue. ※17 Will also means "testament." ※18 Night is also a symbol of death, destruction and despair.
※19 The rue flower symbolizes regret

No.	Title	Japanese Title
153.	*Empty Dialogue // No Need For Discussion*	問答無用
154.	*The God of Flash // The Flash God*	瞬神
155.	*Redoundable deeds/Redoubtable babies // Ungrateful Student, Outstanding Child*	忘恩の生徒、飛びぬけた子供
156.	*Welcome to Purgatory // Welcome to Purgatory*	ようこそ煉獄へ
157.	*Cat And Hornet // The Cat and The Hornet*	猫と雀蜂
158.	*Sky Leopardess // The Flying Female Leopard*	空を翔る雌豹
Vol19 THE BLACK MOON RISING // The Rising Black Moon		昇りゆく黒き月
159.	*LONG WAY TO SAY GOODBYE // A Long Way until Farewell*	さようならまでの長い距離
160.	*Battle On The Guillotine Hill // The Battle on the Sôkyoku Hill*	双極の丘での戦い
161.	*Scratch the Sky // Stab the Heavens*	天を衝く
162.	*Black Moon Rising // The Rising Black Moon*	昇りゆく黒き月
163.	*THE Speed Phantom 2 [Denial by Pride, Contradiction by Energy] // The Instant Speed Illusion 2 [Denial by Pride, Refutation by Energy]*	瞬速の幻影 2 ［誇りによる否定、力による反駁］
164.	*That Who Change the World // Those Who Changed the World*	世界を変えた人
165.	*Dark Side of Universe 2 // The Dark Side of the World Part 2*	世界の黒の部分　その 2
166.	*Black & White2 // Black and White Part 2*	黒と白　その 2
167.	*The Burial Chamber // Center 46 Buried*	葬られし四十六室
168.	*Behind Me, Behind You // Be Careful of What's Behind You*	後ろに気をつけろ
Vol20 end of hypnosis // The End of the Dream		夢の終わり
-12.5.	*Blooming Under a Cold Moon // Bloom in Winter Months*	寒月に咲く
169.	*end of hypnosis // The End of the Dream*	夢の終わり
170.	*end of hypnosis 2 [the Galvanizer] // Part 2 [The Mask of Lies]*	夢の終わり　その 2 ［偽りの仮面］
171.	*end of hypnosis 3 [the Blue Fog] // Part 3 [The Indigo Fog]*	夢の終わり　その 3 ［藍色の霧］
172.	*end of hypnosis 4 [Prisoners in Paradise] // Part 4 [Prisoners of Paradise]*	夢の終わり その 4 ［楽園の囚人］
173.	*end of hypnosis 5 [Standing to Defend You] // Part 5 [Standing to Defend You]*	夢の終わり その 5 ［オマエを護るために立つ］
174.	*end of hypnosis 6 [The United Front] // Part 6 [The United Front]*	夢の終わり　その 6 ［共同戦線］
175.	*end of hypnosis 7 [Truth Under My Strings] // Part 7 [The Truth under My Strings]*	夢の終わり その 7 ［我が糸の下の真実］
176.	*end of hypnosis 8 [the Transfixion] // Part 8 [Shot to Death]*	夢の終わり　その 8 ［射殺す］
177.	*end of hypnosis 9 [Completely Encompass] // Part 9 [Completely Surrounded]*	夢の終わり その 9 ［完全包囲］
178.	*end of hypnosis10 [No One Stand On the Sky] // Part 10 [The Empty Seat of Heaven]*	夢の終わり その 10 ［天の空座］

Character Index
Gathering All Stars

KIYONE KOTETSU 70
虎徹清音
P. 111, 150

 IKKAKU MADARAME 71
斑目一角
P. 116

 YUMICHIKA AYASEGAWA 72
綾瀬川弓親
P. 117

 JIRŌBŌ IKKANZAKA 73
一貫坂攀楼坊
P. 118

 HANATARŌ YAMADA 74
山田花太郎
P. 119

 YASOCHIKA IEMURA 75
伊江村八十千和
P. 119

 HARUNOBU OGIDŌ 76
荻堂春信
P. 119

 TATSUFUSA ENJŌJI 77
円乗寺辰房
P. 135

 KAIEN SHIBA 78
志波海燕
P. 170, 173

 PARASITIC HOLLOW 79
寄生型虚
P. 172

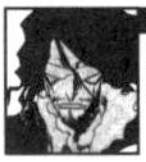

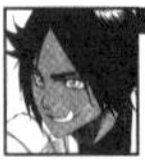

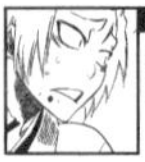

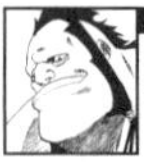

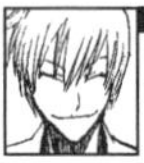

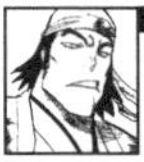

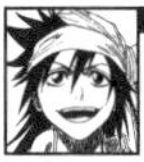

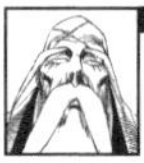

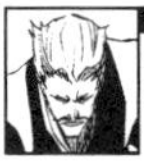

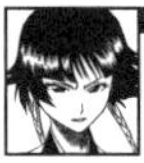

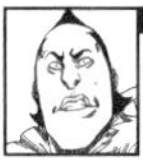

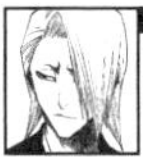

AND OTHERS

 MOMO HINAMORI 55
雛森桃
P. 111, 131

 SAJIN KOMAMURA 56
狛村左陣
P. 110, 180

 TETSUZAEMON IBA 57
射場鉄左衛門
P. 110, 178, 181

 SHUNSUI KYŌRAKU 58
京楽春水
P. 110, 136, 203

 NANAO ISE 59
伊勢七緒
P. 110, 139

 KANAME TŌSEN 60
東仙要
P. 110, 159, 179

 SHŪHEI HISAGI 61
檜佐木修兵
P. 110, 181

 TŌSHIRŌ HITSUGAYA 62
日番谷冬獅郎
P. 110, 133, 165, 220

 RANGIKU MATSUMOTO 63
松本乱菊
P. 110, 219

 KENPACHI ZARAKI 64
更木剣八
P. 111, 140

 YACHIRU KUSAJISHI 65
草鹿やちる
P. 111, 144

 MAYURI KUROTSUCHI 66
涅マユリ
P. 111, 158

 NEMU KUROTSUCHI 67
涅ネム
P. 111, 158

 JŪSHIRŌ UKITAKE 68
浮竹十四郎
P. 111, 150, 202

 SENTARO KOTSUBAKI 69
小椿仙太郎
P. 111, 150

 THE MAN IN BLACK/ZANGETSU 40
黒衣の男/斬月
P. 84, 160

 YORUICHI/YORUICHI SHIHŌIN 41
夜一/四楓院夜一
P. 89, 151, 198

 RIN TSUBOKURA 42
壺村リン
P. 100

 JIDANBŌ 43
兄丹坊
P. 102

 GIN ICHIMARU 44
市丸ギン
P. 104, 111, 166

 GANJU SHIBA 45
志波岩鷲
P. 106, 148

 KŪKAKU SHIBA 46
志波空鶴
P. 108

 GENRYUSAI SHIGEKUNI 47
山本元柳斎重國
P. 110, 200

 CHOJIRO SASAKIBE 48
雀部長次郎
P. 110

 SOI FON 49
砕蜂
P. 110, 196

 MARECHIYO OMAEDA 50
大前田希千代
P. 110

 IZURU KIRA 51
吉良イヅル
P. 111, 132

 RETSU UNOHANA 52
卯ノ花烈
P. 111, 193

 ISANE KOTETSU 53
虎徹勇音
P. 111, 192

 SŌSUKE AIZEN 54
藍染惣右介
P. 111, 130, 221

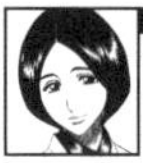

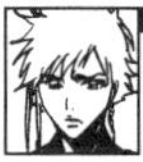

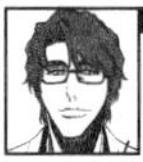

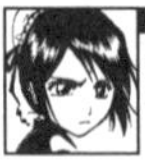

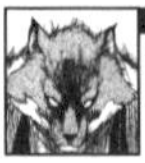

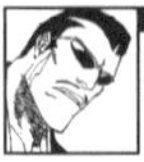

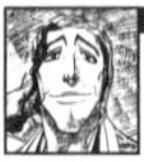

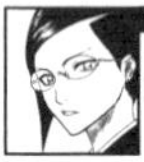

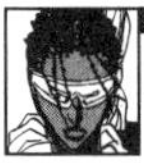

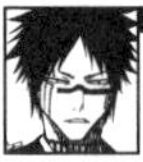

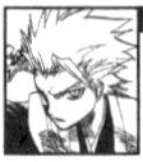

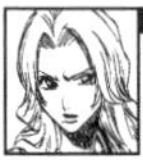

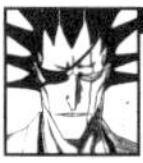

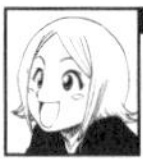

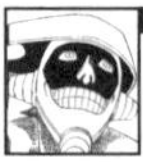

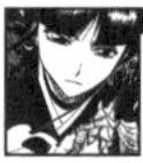

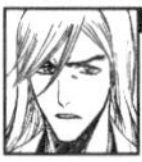

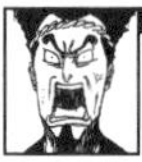

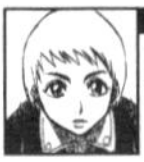

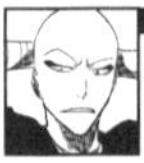

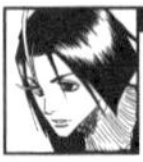

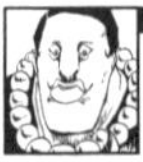

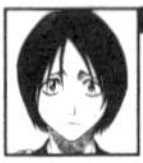

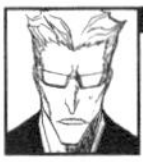

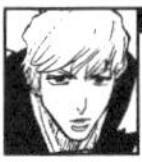

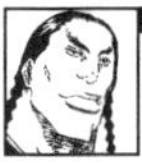

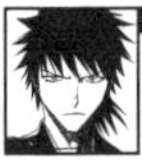

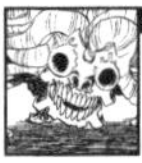

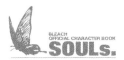

BLEACH Short Story Edition

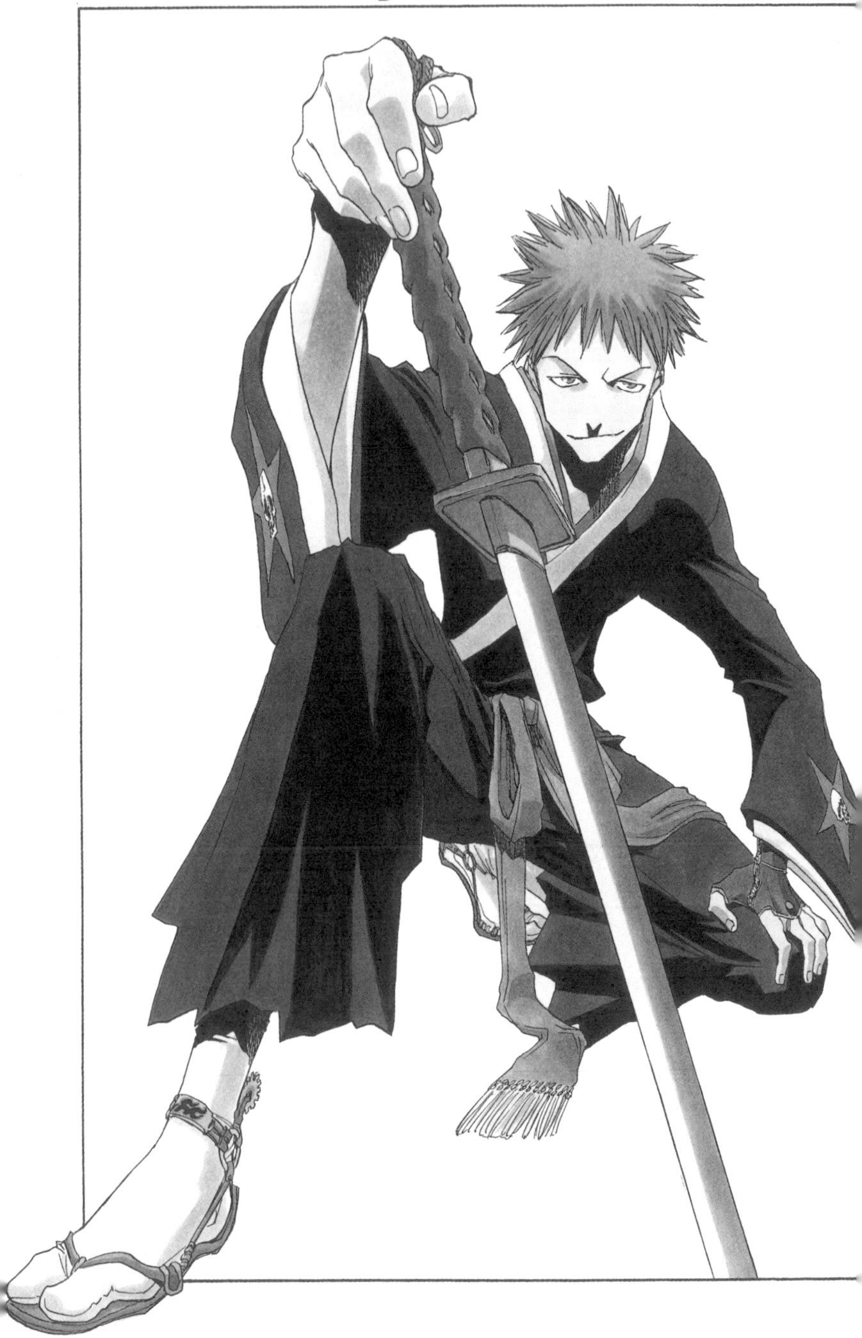

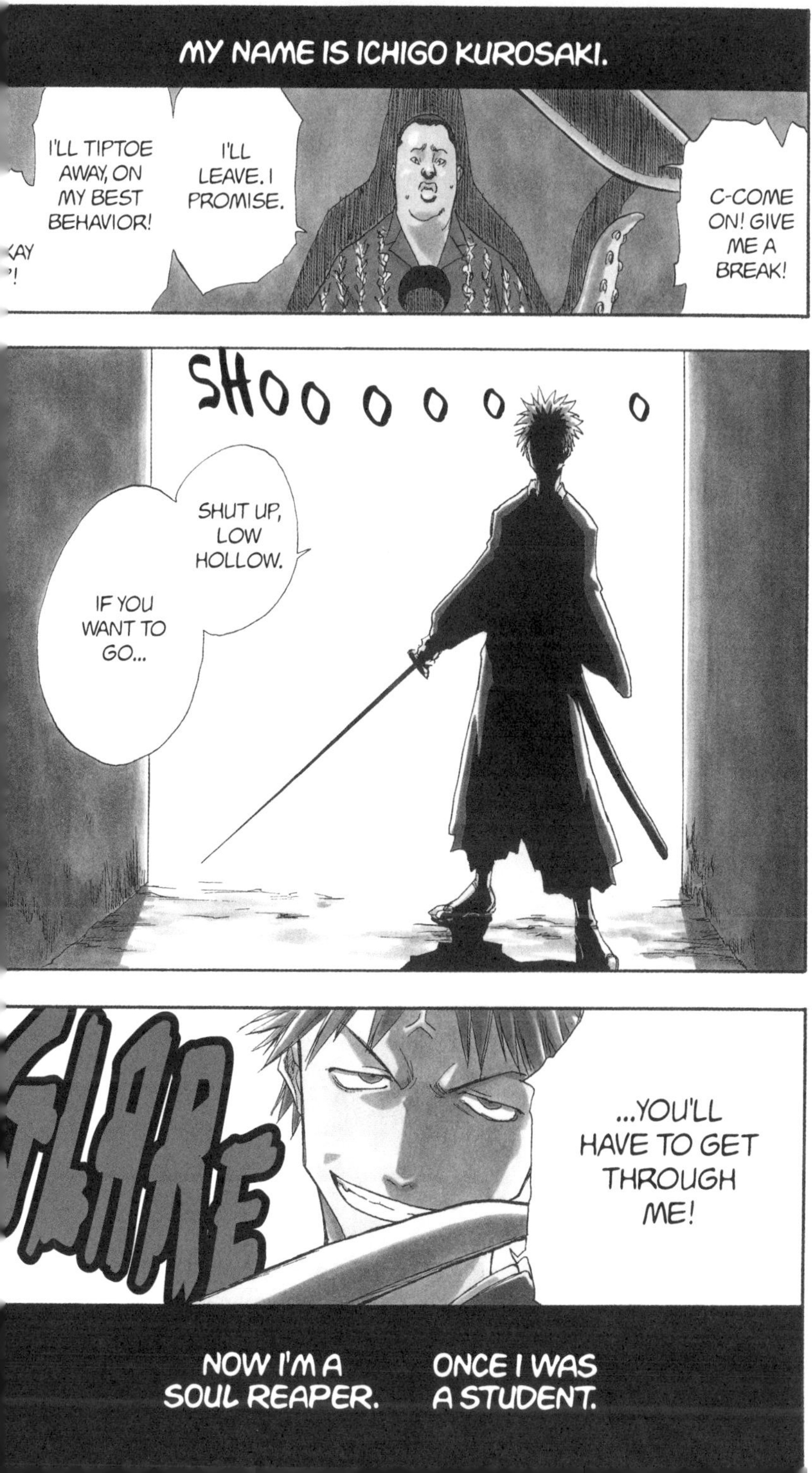
MY NAME IS ICHIGO KUROSAKI.
C-COME ON! GIVE ME A BREAK!
I'LL LEAVE. I PROMISE.
I'LL TIPTOE AWAY, ON MY BEST BEHAVIOR!
SHOOOOOOO
SHUT UP, LOW HOLLOW.
IF YOU WANT TO GO...
...YOU'LL HAVE TO GET THROUGH ME!
GLARE
ONCE I WAS A STUDENT.
NOW I'M A SOUL REAPER.

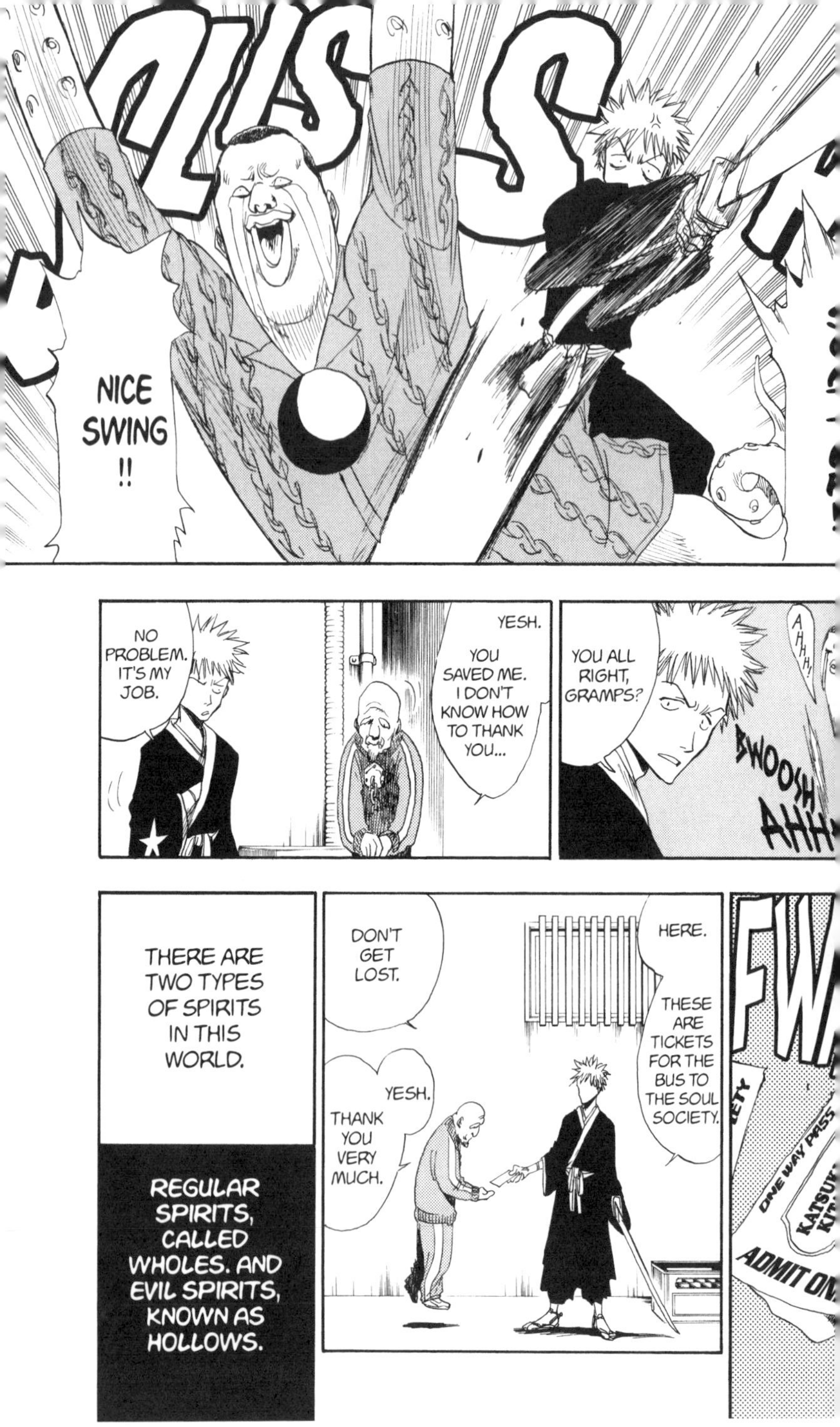
NICE SWING!!
AHHH!
BWOOSH
YOU ALL RIGHT, GRAMPS?
YESH.
YOU SAVED ME. I DON'T KNOW HOW TO THANK YOU...
NO PROBLEM. IT'S MY JOB.
ONE WAY PASS
HERE.
THESE ARE TICKETS FOR THE BUS TO THE SOUL SOCIETY.
DON'T GET LOST.
YESH.
THANK YOU VERY MUCH.
THERE ARE TWO TYPES OF SPIRITS IN THIS WORLD.
REGULAR SPIRITS, CALLED WHOLES. AND EVIL SPIRITS, KNOWN AS HOLLOWS.

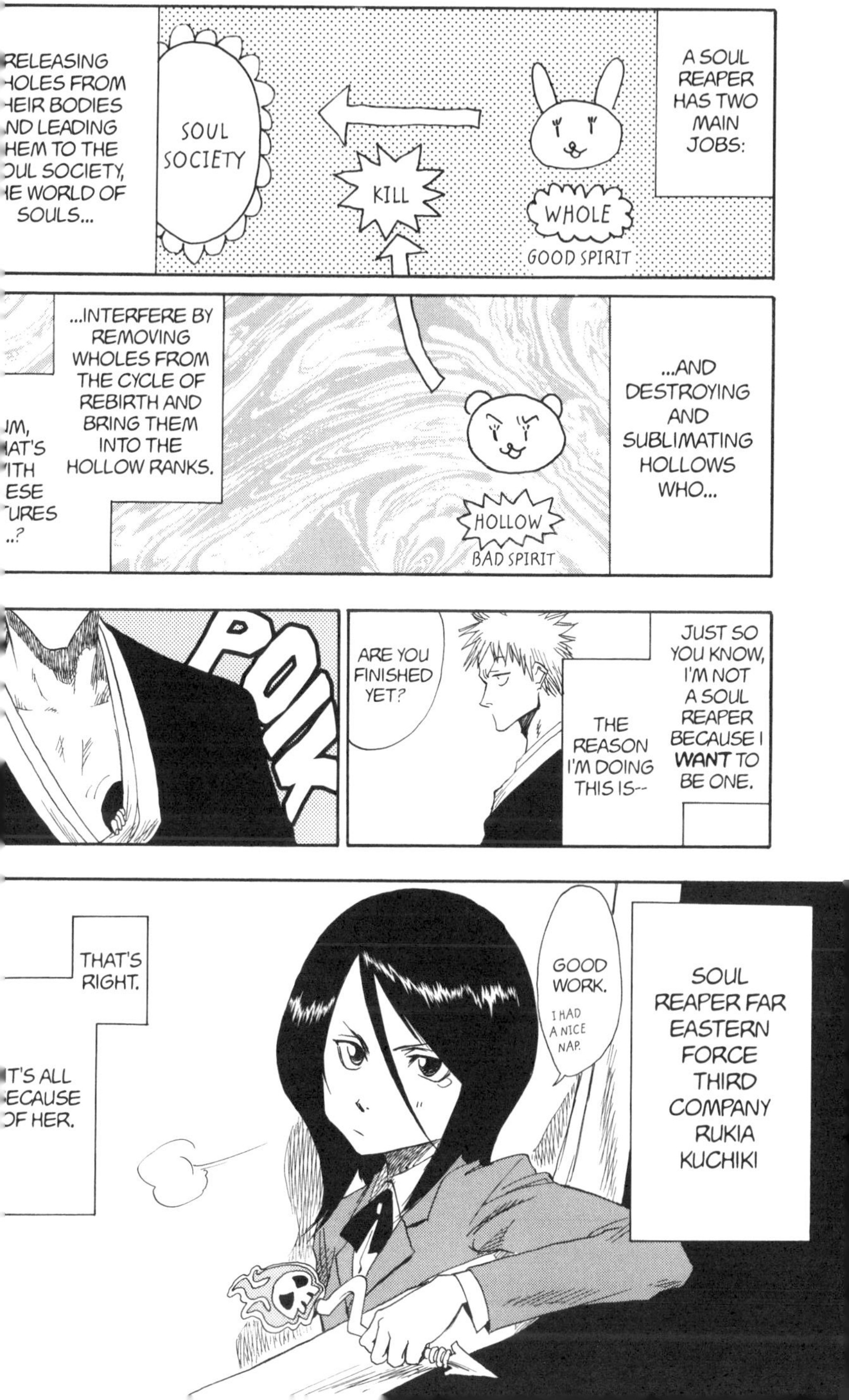
A SOUL REAPER HAS TWO MAIN JOBS:
WHOLE
GOOD SPIRIT
KILL
SOUL SOCIETY
RELEASING HOLES FROM HEIR BODIES ND LEADING HEM TO THE OUL SOCIETY, HE WORLD OF SOULS...
...AND DESTROYING AND SUBLIMATING HOLLOWS WHO...
HOLLOW
BAD SPIRIT
...INTERFERE BY REMOVING WHOLES FROM THE CYCLE OF REBIRTH AND BRING THEM INTO THE HOLLOW RANKS.
JUST SO YOU KNOW, I'M NOT A SOUL REAPER BECAUSE I **WANT** TO BE ONE.
THE REASON I'M DOING THIS IS--
ARE YOU FINISHED YET?
POK
SOUL REAPER FAR EASTERN FORCE THIRD COMPANY RUKIA KUCHIKI
GOOD WORK.
I HAD A NICE NAP.
THAT'S RIGHT.
T'S ALL ECAUSE OF HER.

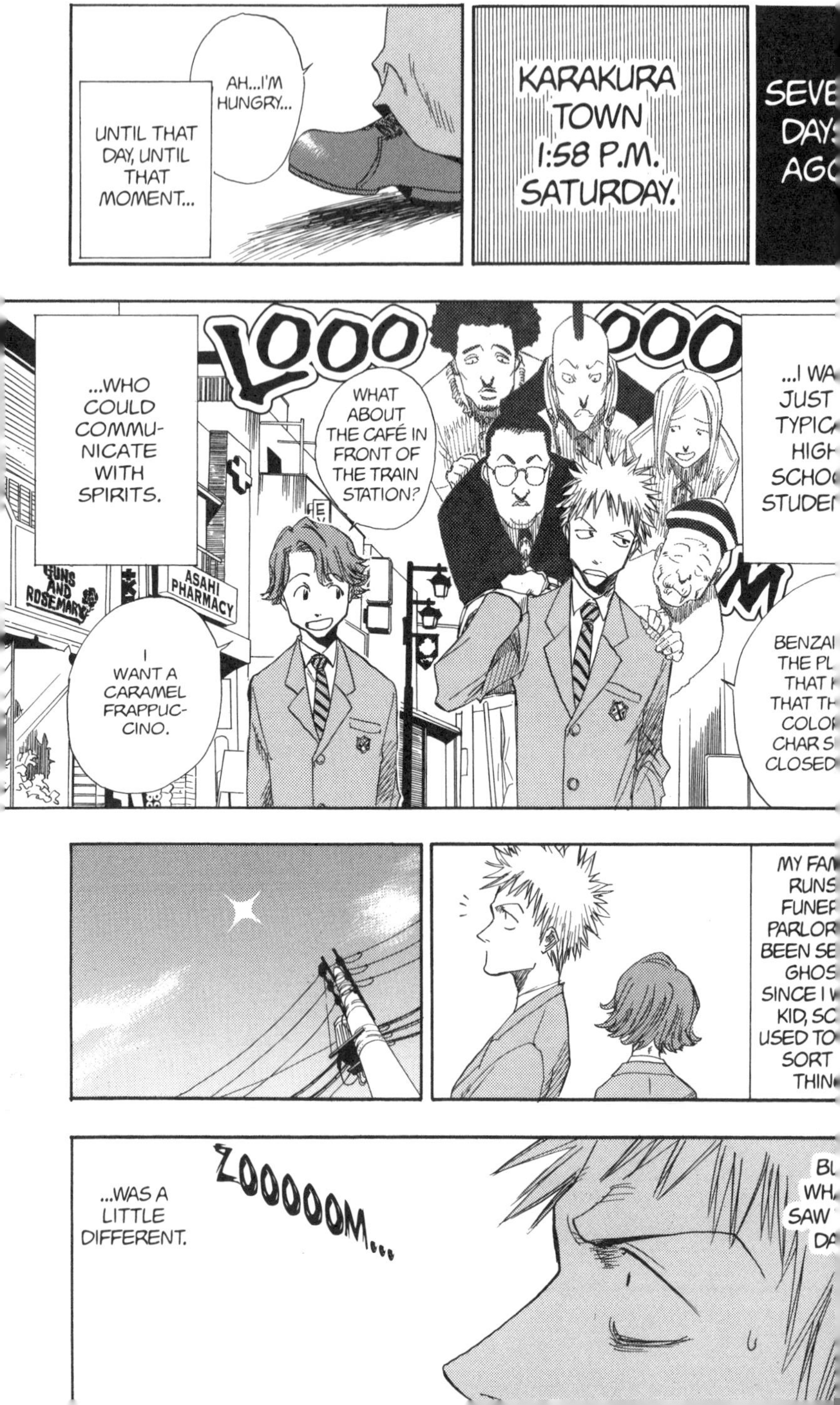
SEVE DAYS AGO
KARAKURA TOWN 1:58 P.M. SATURDAY.
AH...I'M HUNGRY...
UNTIL THAT DAY, UNTIL THAT MOMENT...
...I WA JUST TYPIC HIGH SCHO STUDE
LOOO OOO
WHAT ABOUT THE CAFÉ IN FRONT OF THE TRAIN STATION?
...WHO COULD COMMUNICATE WITH SPIRITS.
BENZAI THE PL THAT THAT TH COLO CHAR S CLOSED
ASAHI PHARMACY
GUNS AND ROSEMARY
I WANT A CARAMEL FRAPPUCCINO.
MY FAM RUNS FUNER PARLOR BEEN SE GHOS SINCE I W KID, SC USED TO SORT THIN
BU WHA SAW DA
ZOOOOOM...
...WAS A LITTLE DIFFERENT.

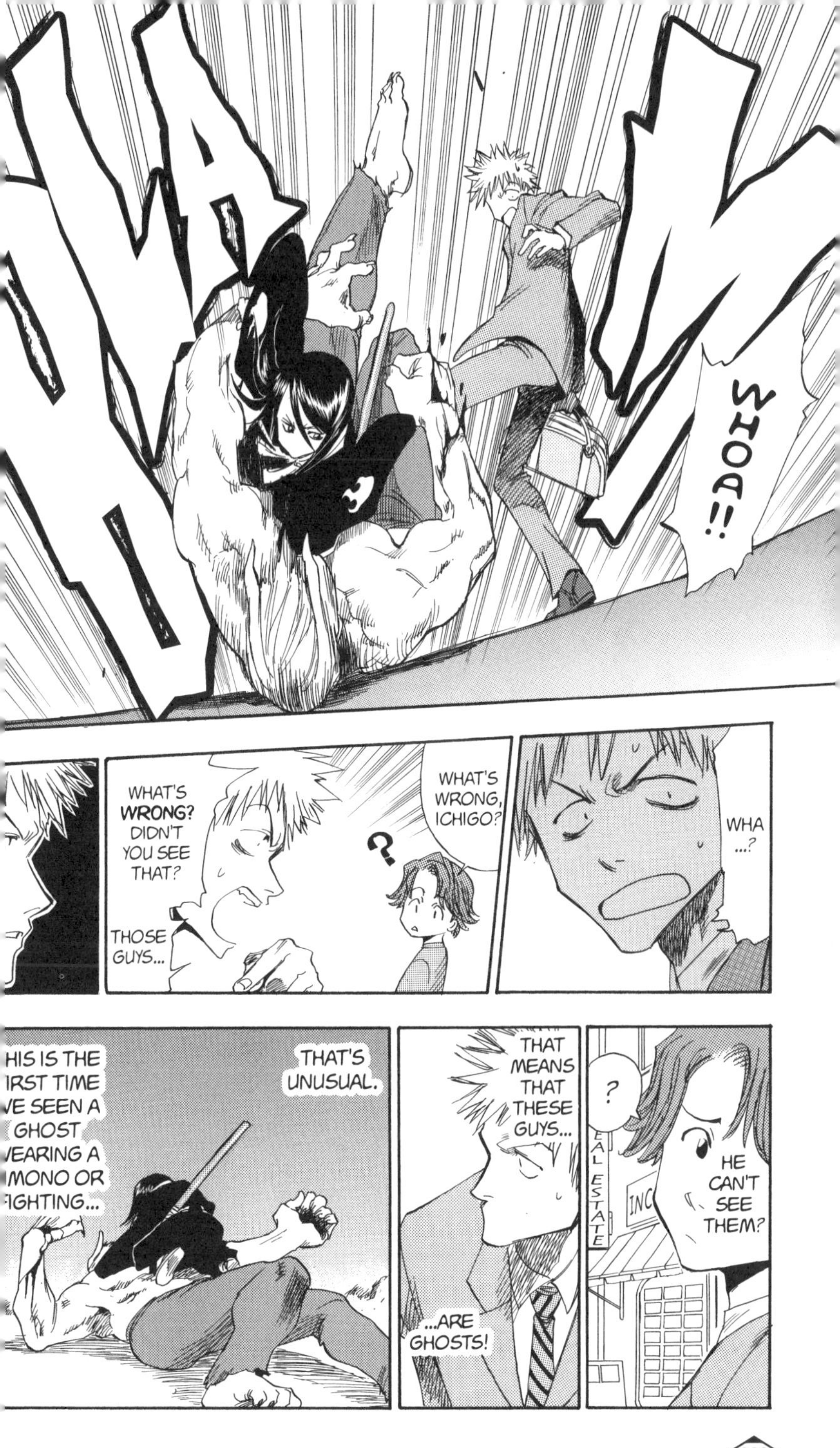
WHOA!!
WHA ...?
WHAT'S WRONG, ICHIGO?
?
WHAT'S WRONG? DIDN'T YOU SEE THAT?
THOSE GUYS...
?
HE CAN'T SEE THEM?
EAL ESTATE
INC
THAT MEANS THAT THESE GUYS...
...ARE GHOSTS!
THAT'S UNUSUAL.
HIS IS THE IRST TIME VE SEEN A GHOST VEARING A IMONO OR FIGHTING...

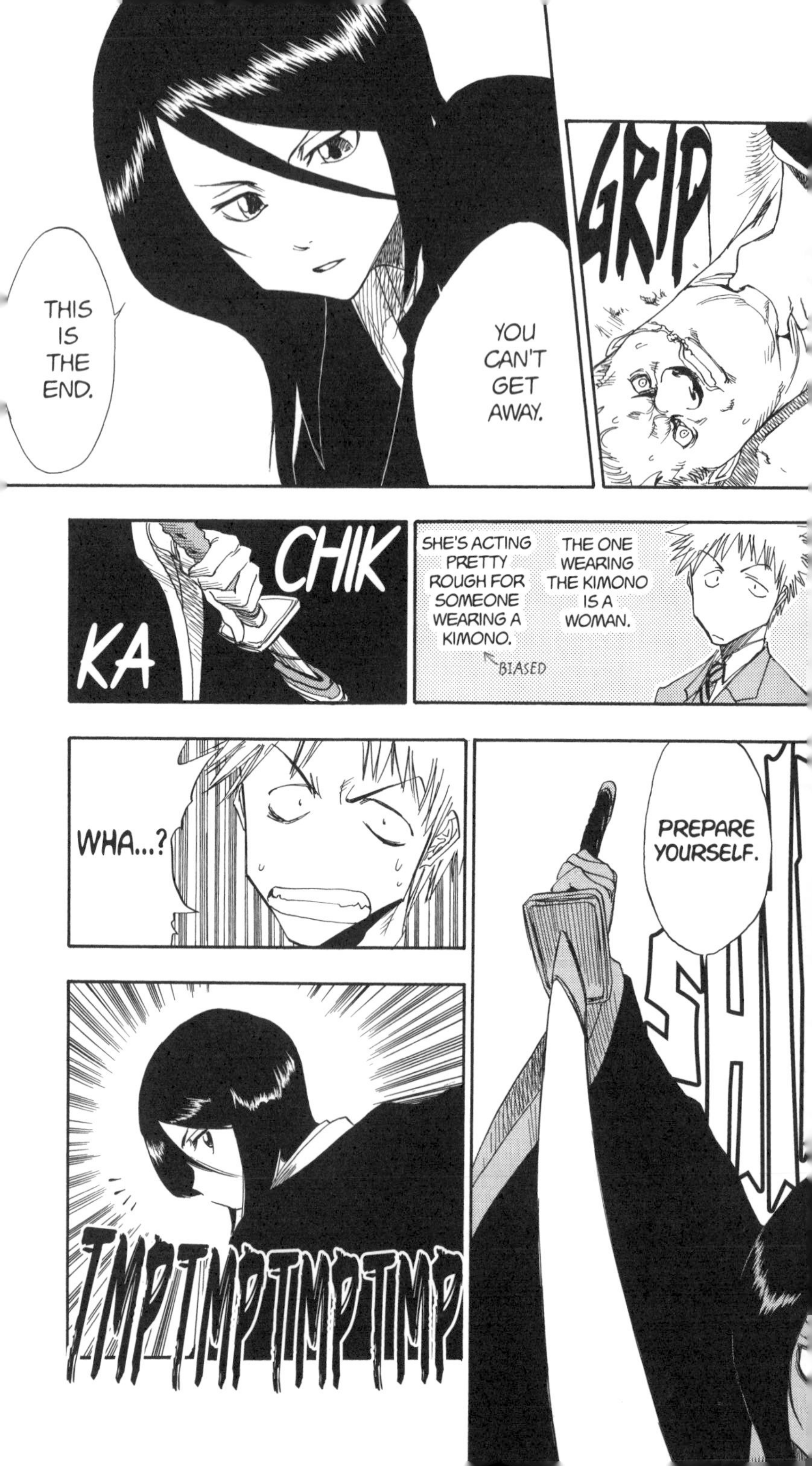
GRIP
YOU CAN'T GET AWAY.
THIS IS THE END.
THE ONE WEARING THE KIMONO IS A WOMAN.
SHE'S ACTING PRETTY ROUGH FOR SOMEONE WEARING A KIMONO.
BIASED
CHIK
KA
PREPARE YOURSELF.
WHA...?
TMP TMP TMP TMP

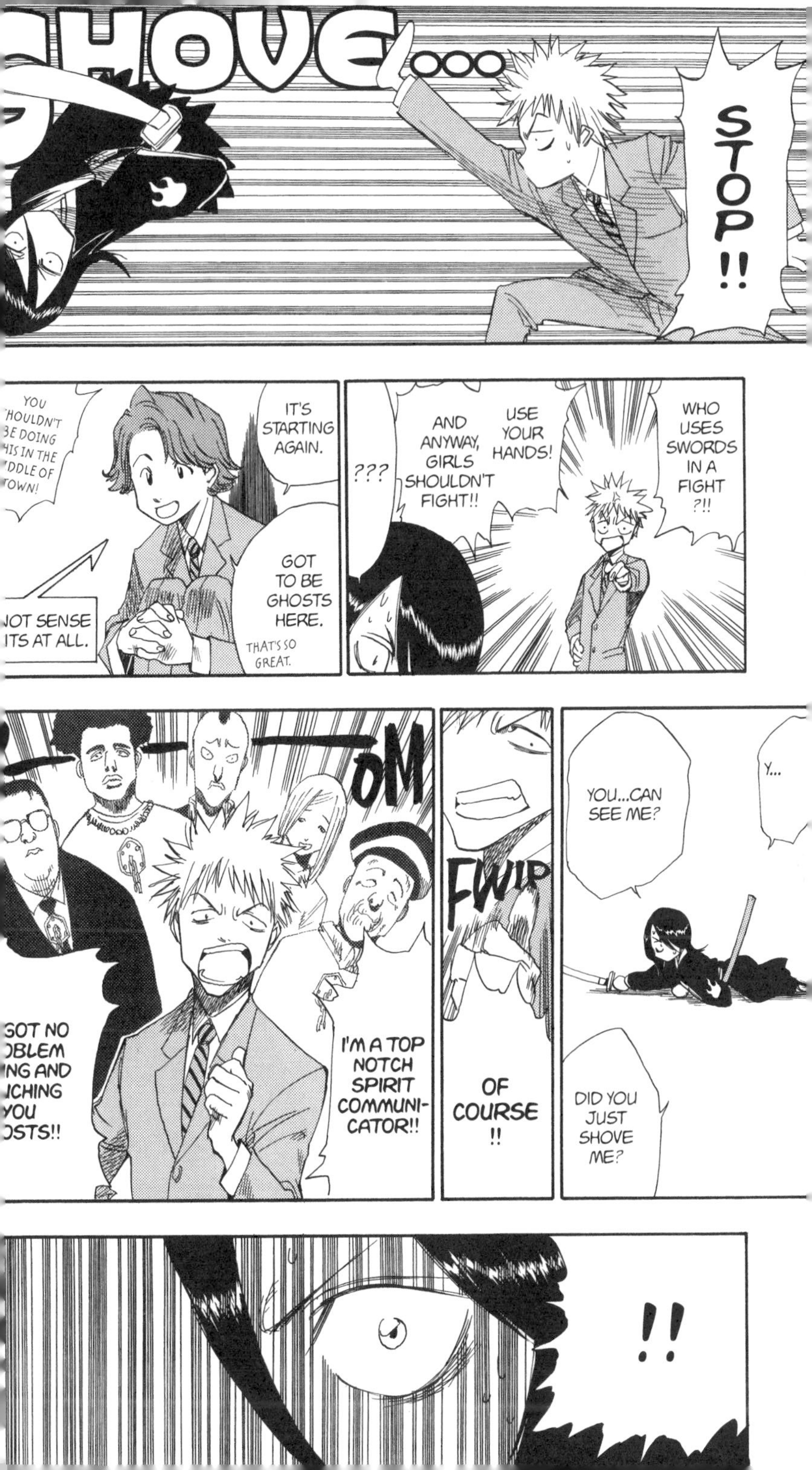
STOP!!
SHOVE...
WHO USES SWORDS IN A FIGHT?!!
USE YOUR HANDS!
AND ANYWAY, GIRLS SHOULDN'T FIGHT!!
???
IT'S STARTING AGAIN.
YOU HOULDN'T BE DOING HIS IN THE IDDLE OF TOWN!
GOT TO BE GHOSTS HERE.
THAT'S SO GREAT.
NOT SENSE ITS AT ALL.
Y...
YOU...CAN SEE ME?
DID YOU JUST SHOVE ME?
FWIP
OF COURSE!!
OM
I'M A TOP NOTCH SPIRIT COMMUNICATOR!!
GOT NO OBLEM NG AND ICHING YOU OSTS!!
!!

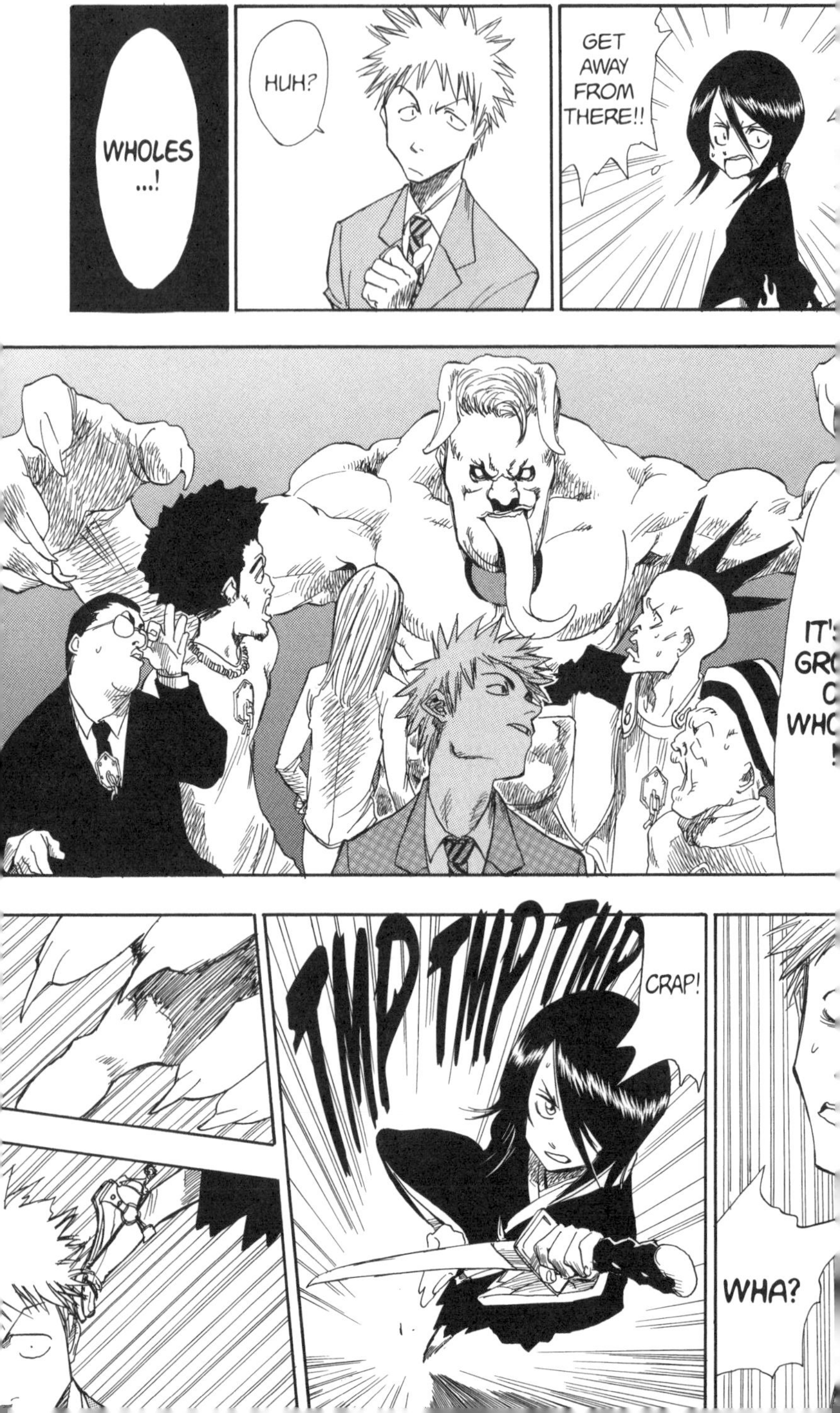
GET AWAY FROM THERE!!
HUH?
WHOLES ...!
IT'S GR
WHA?
THP THP THP
CRAP!

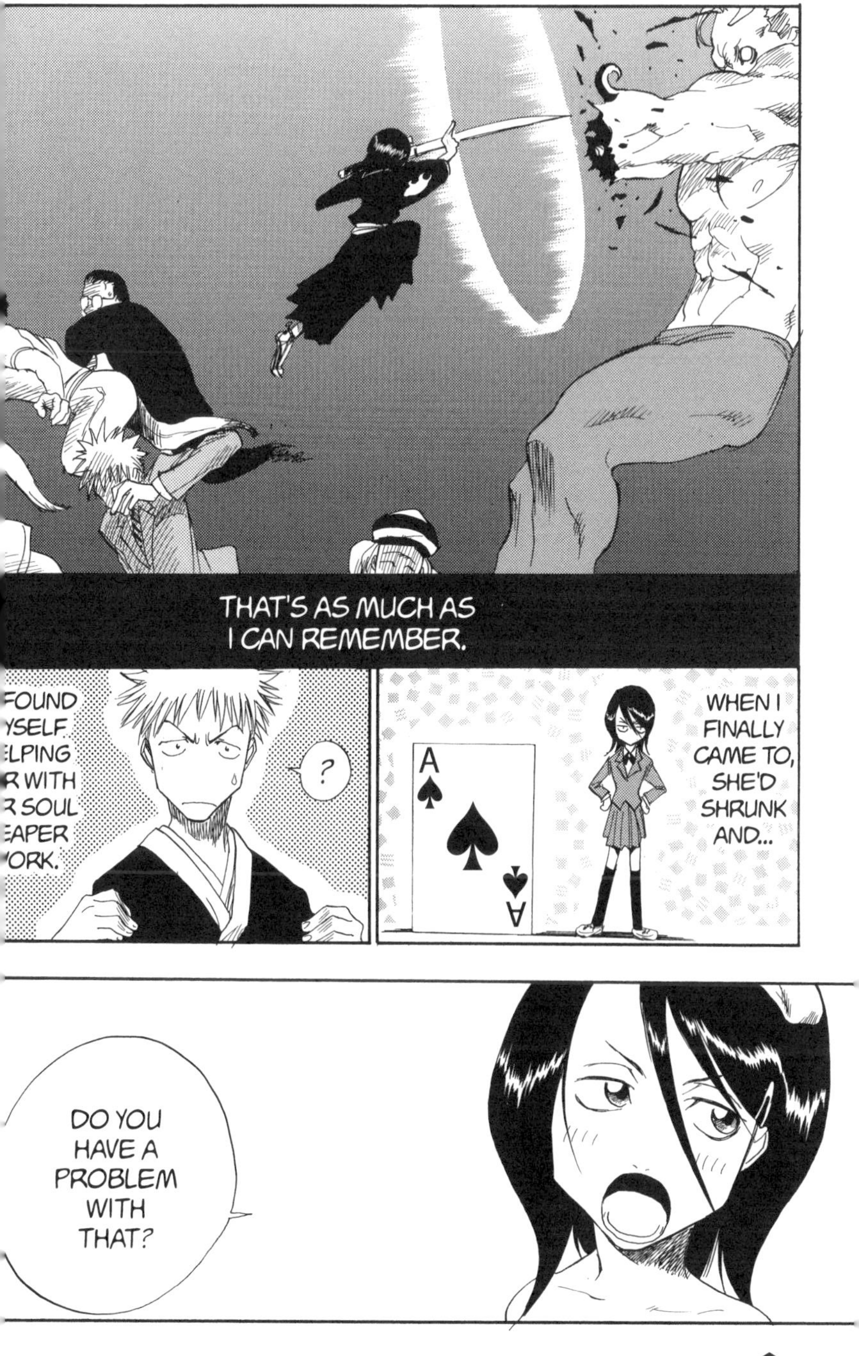
THAT'S AS MUCH AS I CAN REMEMBER.
WHEN I FINALLY CAME TO, SHE'D SHRUNK AND...
A
A
FOUND YSELF ELPING R WITH R SOUL EAPER ORK.
?
DO YOU HAVE A PROBLEM WITH THAT?

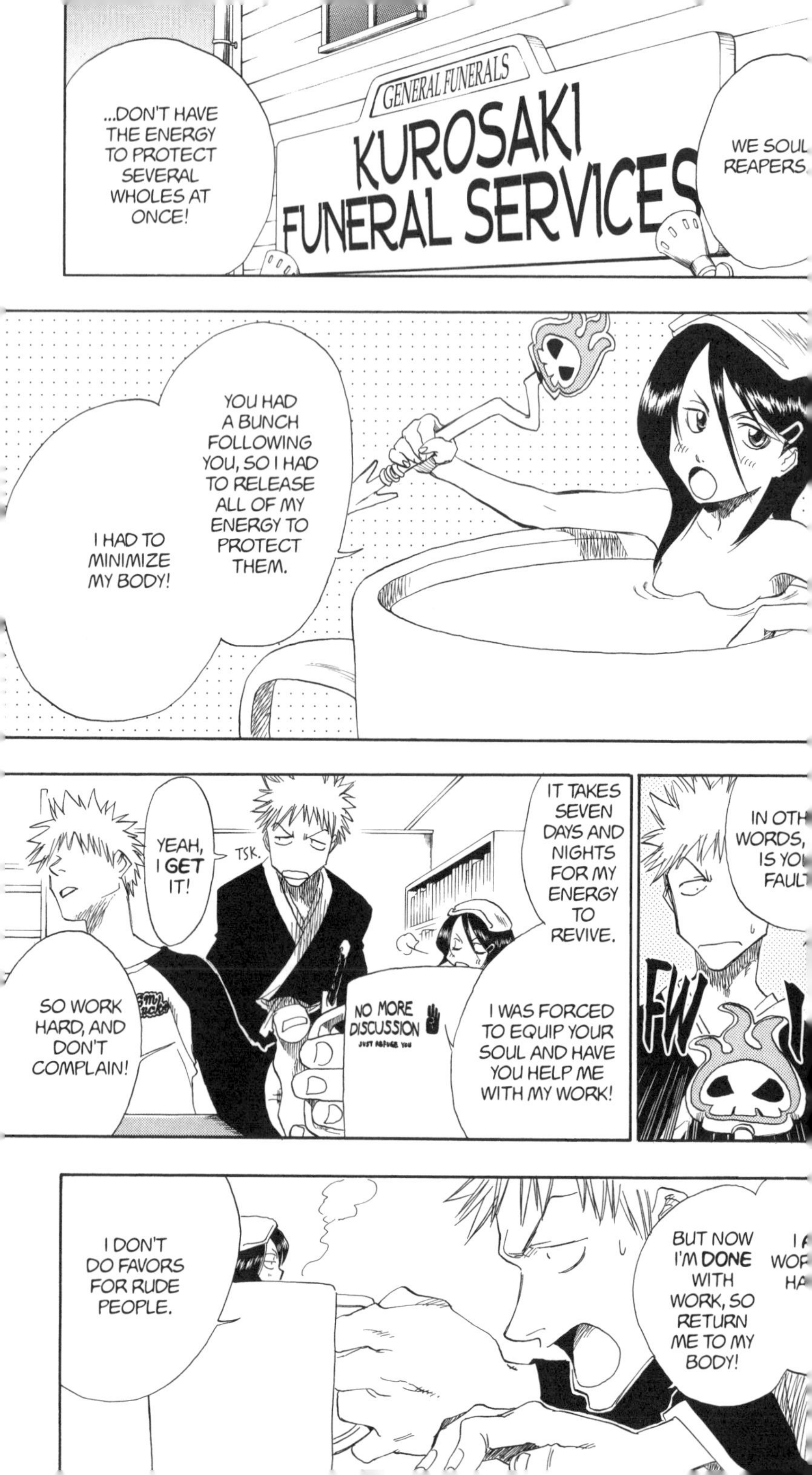
WE SOUL REAPERS.
GENERAL FUNERALS
KUROSAKI FUNERAL SERVICES
...DON'T HAVE THE ENERGY TO PROTECT SEVERAL WHOLES AT ONCE!
YOU HAD A BUNCH FOLLOWING YOU, SO I HAD TO RELEASE ALL OF MY ENERGY TO PROTECT THEM.
I HAD TO MINIMIZE MY BODY!
IN OTH WORDS, IS YO FAUL
FW
IT TAKES SEVEN DAYS AND NIGHTS FOR MY ENERGY TO REVIVE.
I WAS FORCED TO EQUIP YOUR SOUL AND HAVE YOU HELP ME WITH MY WORK!
NO MORE DISCUSSION
JUST REFUSE YOU
SO WORK HARD, AND DON'T COMPLAIN!
YEAH, I **GET** IT!
TSK.
BUT NOW I'M **DONE** WITH WORK, SO RETURN ME TO MY BODY!
I DON'T DO FAVORS FOR RUDE PEOPLE.

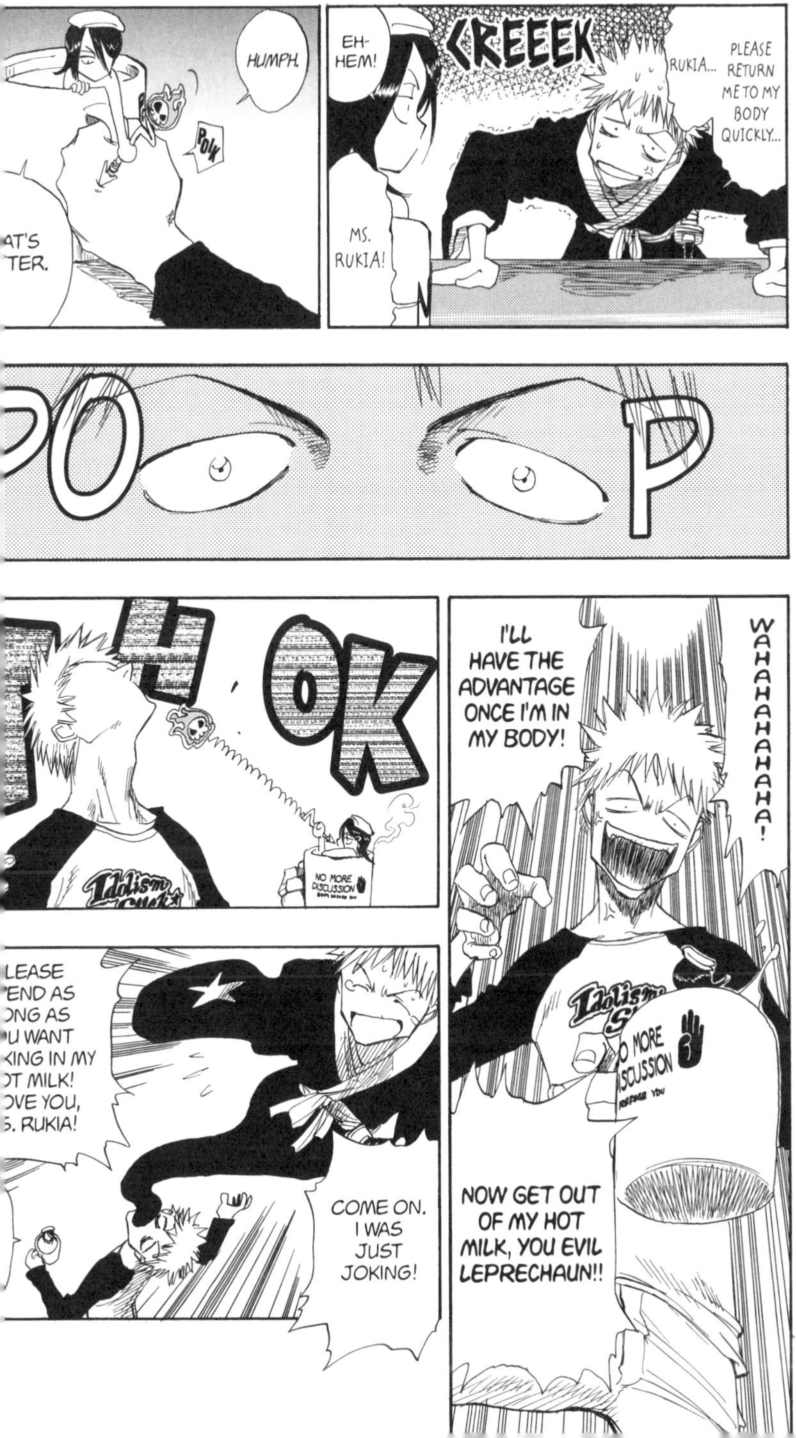
CREEEK
RUKIA...
PLEASE RETURN ME TO MY BODY QUICKLY...
EH-HEM!
MS. RUKIA!
HUMPH.
POK
AT'S TER.
PO
P
WAHAHAHAHAHA!
I'LL HAVE THE ADVANTAGE ONCE I'M IN MY BODY!
NO MORE DISCUSSION
NOW GET OUT OF MY HOT MILK, YOU EVIL LEPRECHAUN!!
H
OK
NO MORE DISCUSSION
LEASE 'END AS ONG AS U WANT KING IN MY OT MILK! OVE YOU, S. RUKIA!
COME ON. I WAS JUST JOKING!

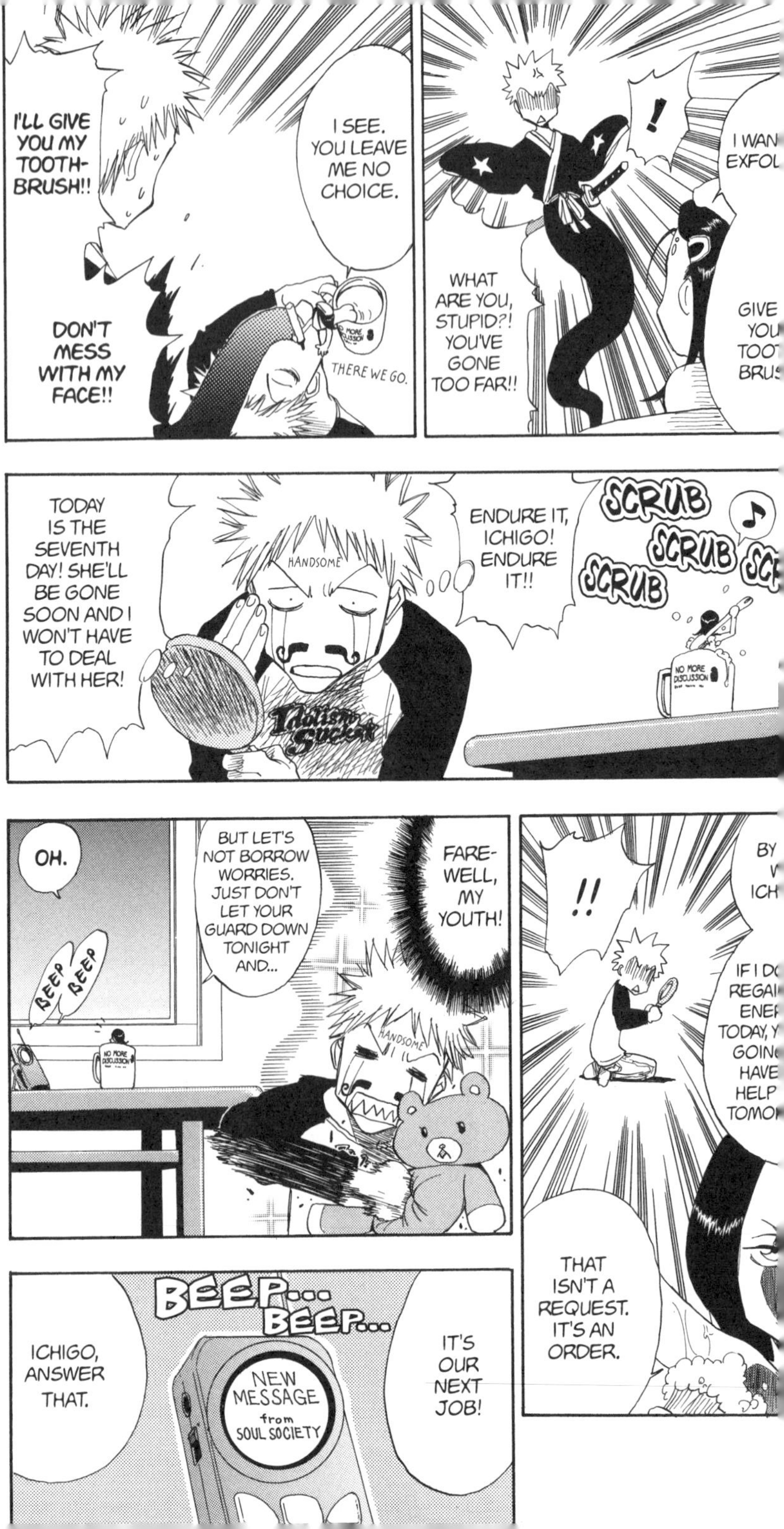
I WAN
EXFOL
!
GIVE YOU TOOT BRUS
WHAT ARE YOU, STUPID?! YOU'VE GONE TOO FAR!!
I SEE. YOU LEAVE ME NO CHOICE.
I'LL GIVE YOU MY TOOTH-BRUSH!!
NO MORE DISCUSSION
THERE WE GO.
DON'T MESS WITH MY FACE!!
SCRUB
SCR
SCRUB
SCRUB
♪
NO MORE DISCUSSION
ENDURE IT, ICHIGO! ENDURE IT!!
HANDSOME
TODAY IS THE SEVENTH DAY! SHE'LL BE GONE SOON AND I WON'T HAVE TO DEAL WITH HER!
BY
W
ICH
!!
IF I DO
REGAI
ENEF
TODAY, Y
GOIN
HAVE
HELP
TOMO
THAT ISN'T A REQUEST. IT'S AN ORDER.
FARE-WELL, MY YOUTH!
HANDSOME
BUT LET'S NOT BORROW WORRIES. JUST DON'T LET YOUR GUARD DOWN TONIGHT AND...
OH.
BEEP BEEP
NO MORE DISCUSSION
IT'S OUR NEXT JOB!
BEEP... BEEP...
NEW MESSAGE from SOUL SOCIETY
ICHIGO, ANSWER THAT.

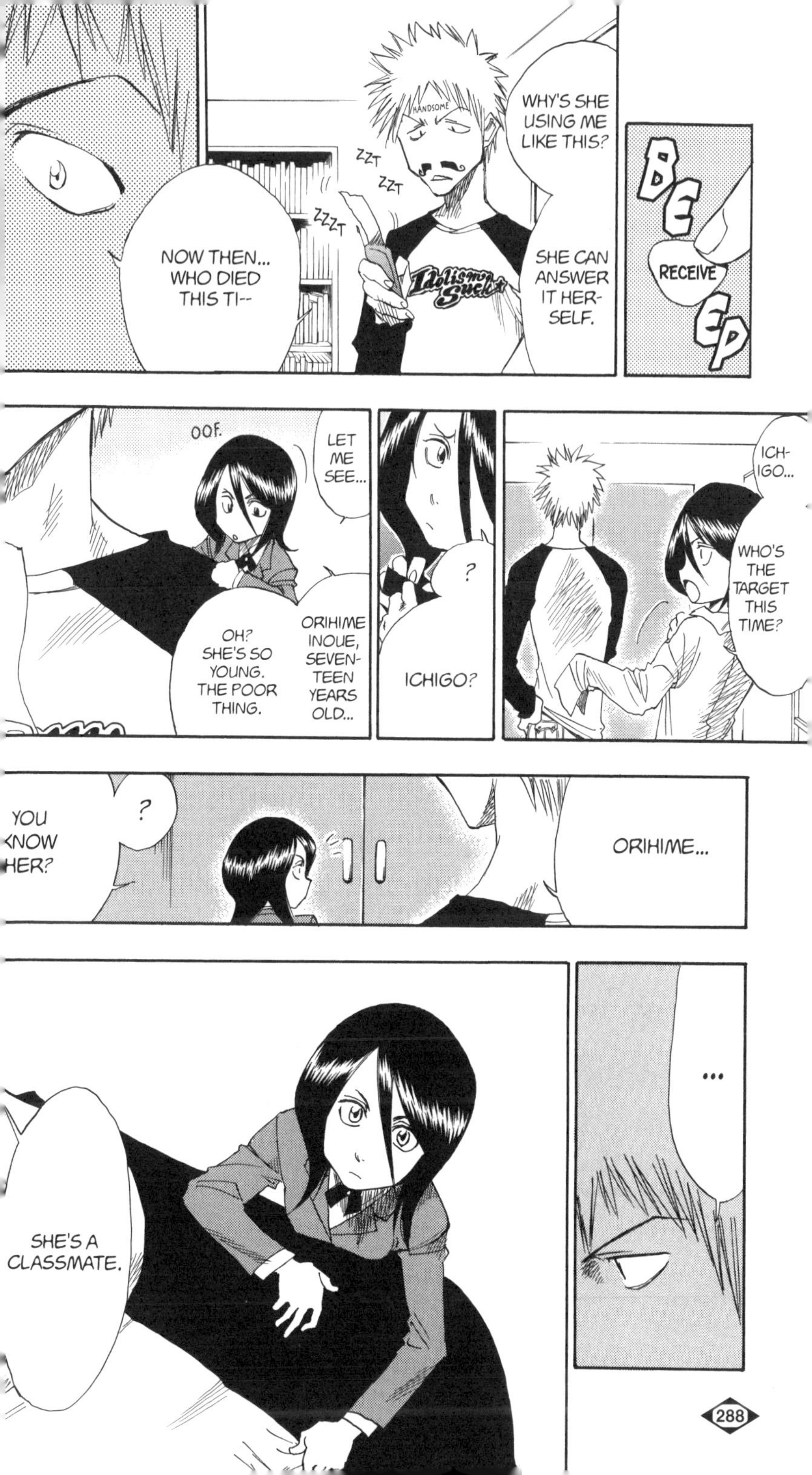
BEEP
RECEIVE
WHY'S SHE USING ME LIKE THIS?
HANDSOME
ZZT
ZZT
ZZZZT
SHE CAN ANSWER IT HER-SELF.
NOW THEN... WHO DIED THIS TI--
ICH-IGO...
WHO'S THE TARGET THIS TIME?
?
ICHIGO?
LET ME SEE...
OOF.
ORIHIME INOUE, SEVEN-TEEN YEARS OLD...
OH? SHE'S SO YOUNG. THE POOR THING.
ORIHIME...
?
YOU KNOW HER?
...
SHE'S A CLASSMATE.

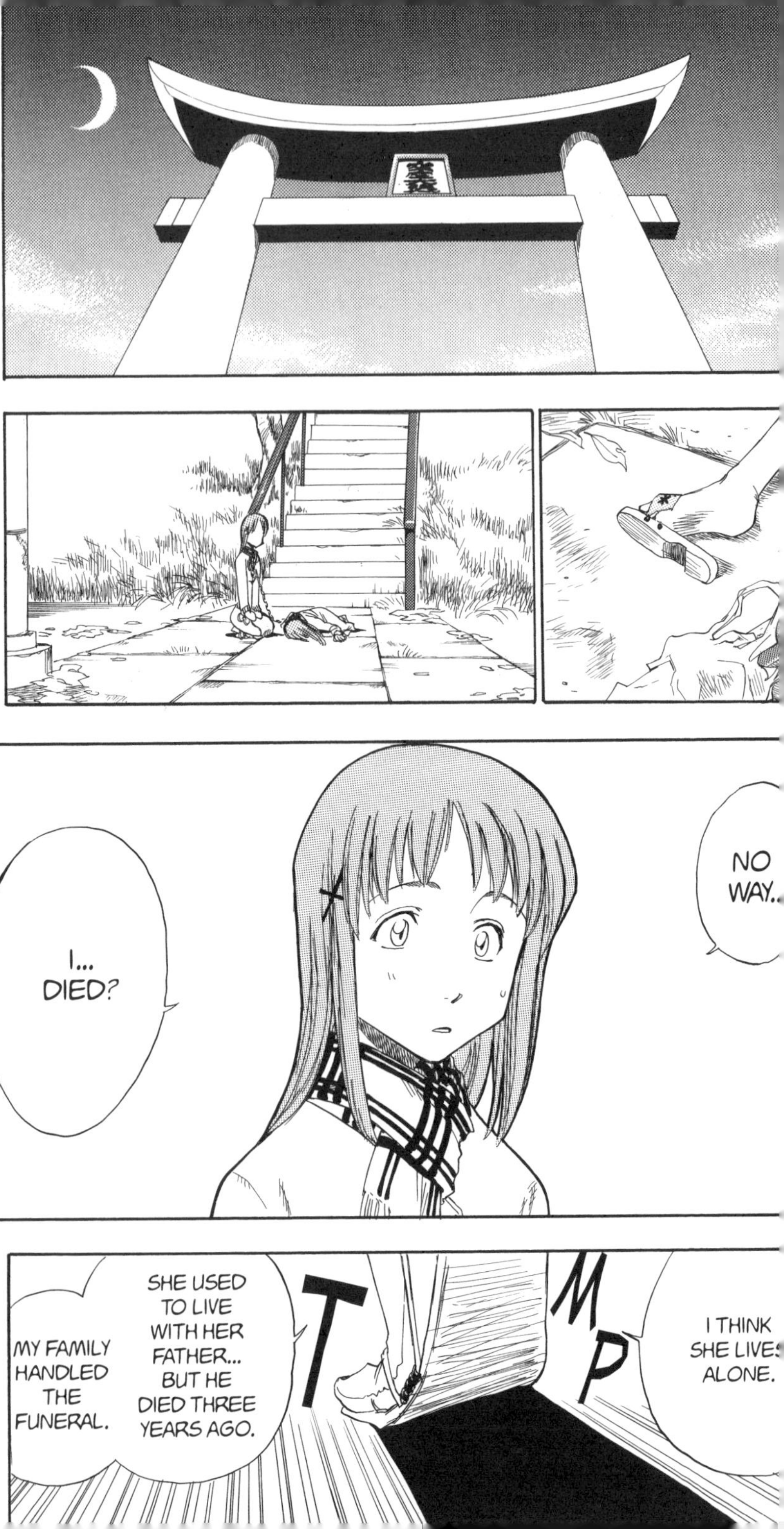
NO WAY...
I... DIED?
I THINK SHE LIVES ALONE.
TMP
SHE USED TO LIVE WITH HER FATHER... BUT HE DIED THREE YEARS AGO.
MY FAMILY HANDLED THE FUNERAL.

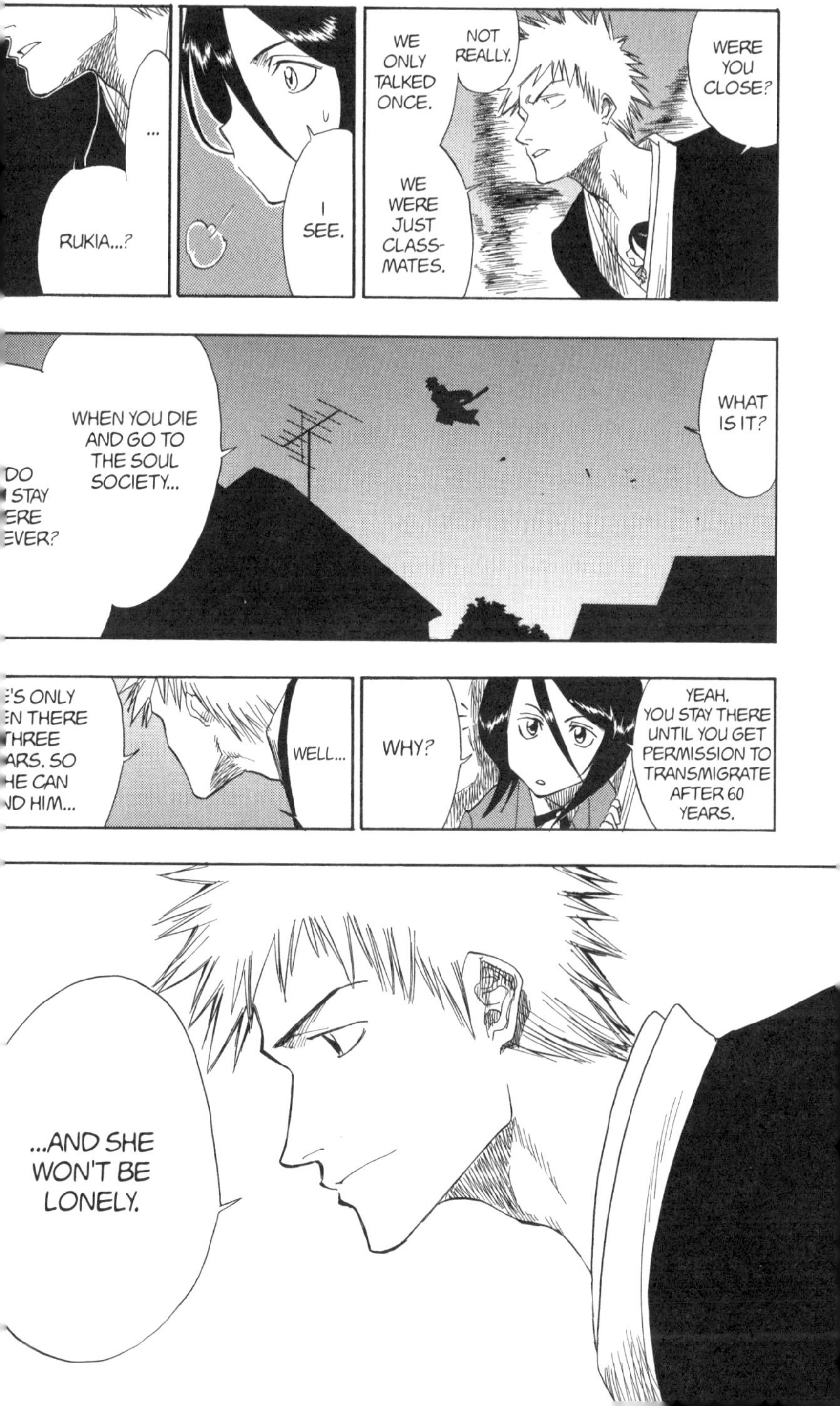
WERE YOU CLOSE?
NOT REALLY.
WE ONLY TALKED ONCE.
WE WERE JUST CLASSMATES.
I SEE.
...
RUKIA...?
WHAT IS IT?
WHEN YOU DIE AND GO TO THE SOUL SOCIETY...
DO STAY ERE EVER?
YEAH. YOU STAY THERE UNTIL YOU GET PERMISSION TO TRANSMIGRATE AFTER 60 YEARS.
WHY?
WELL...
'S ONLY EN THERE THREE ARS. SO HE CAN ND HIM...
...AND SHE WON'T BE LONELY.

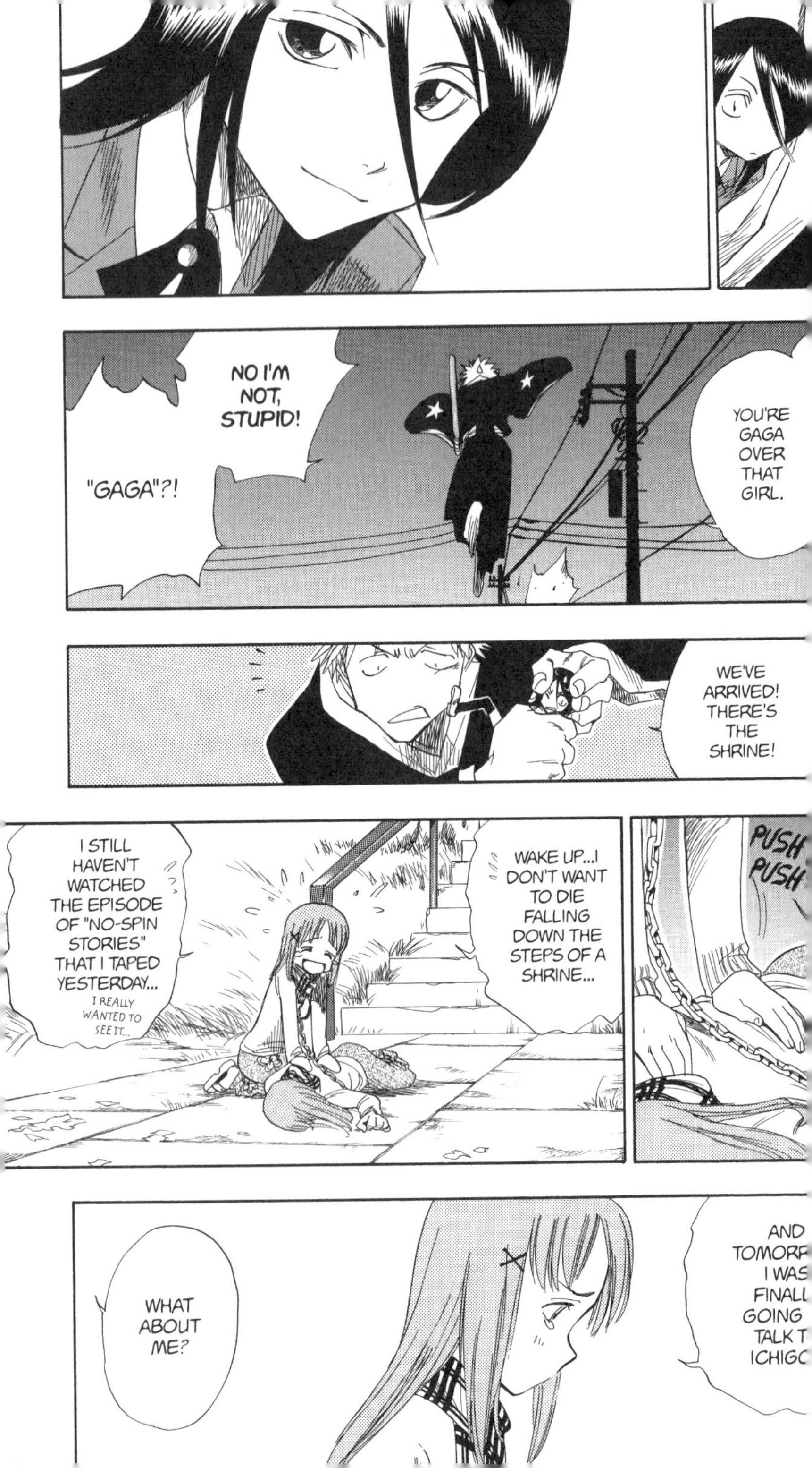
YOU'RE GAGA OVER THAT GIRL.
NO I'M NOT, STUPID!
"GAGA"?!
WE'VE ARRIVED! THERE'S THE SHRINE!
PUSH PUSH
WAKE UP...I DON'T WANT TO DIE FALLING DOWN THE STEPS OF A SHRINE...
I STILL HAVEN'T WATCHED THE EPISODE OF "NO-SPIN STORIES" THAT I TAPED YESTERDAY...
I REALLY WANTED TO SEE IT...
AND TOMORR I WAS FINALL GOING TALK T ICHIGO
WHAT ABOUT ME?

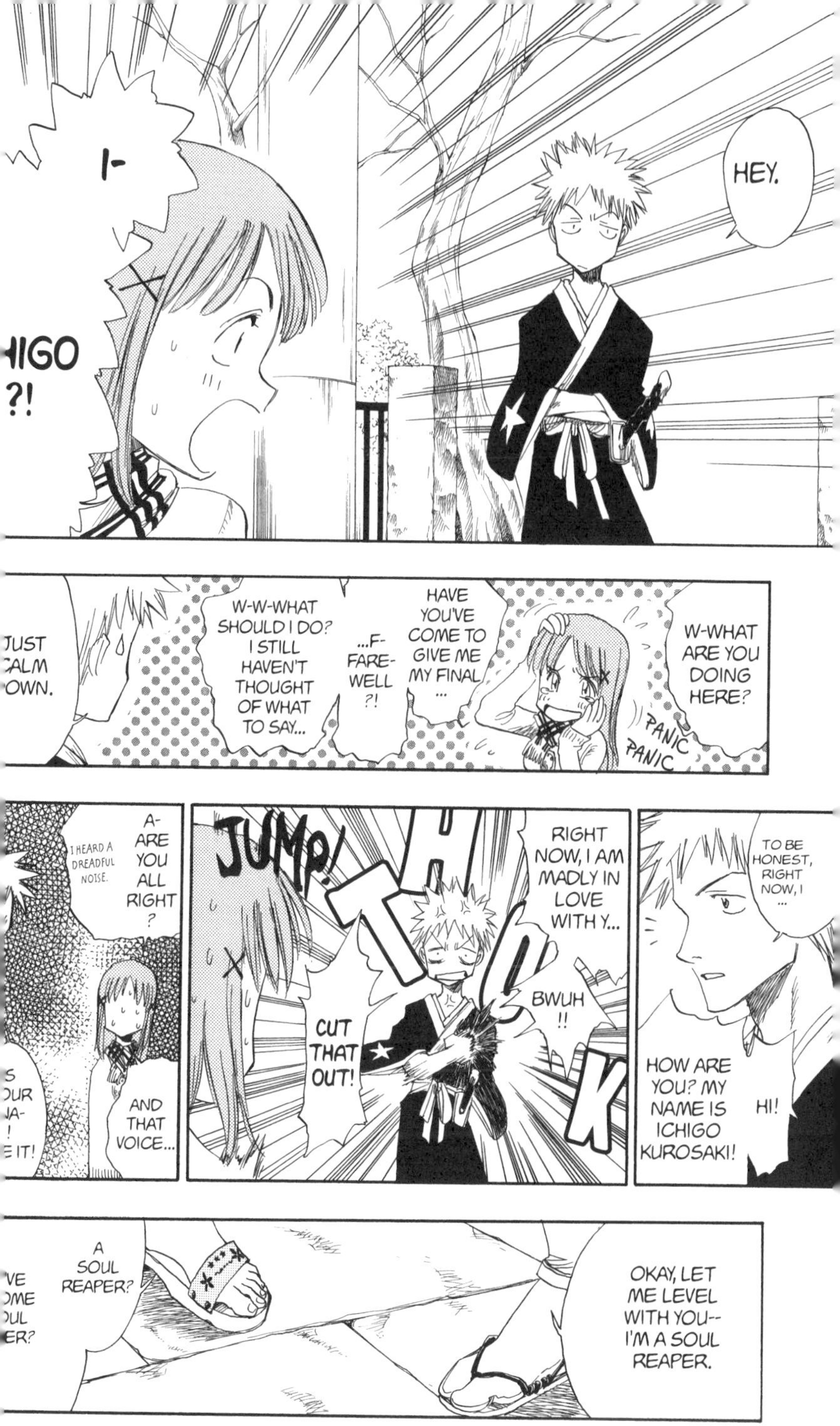
HEY.
I-
HIGO ?!
W-WHAT ARE YOU DOING HERE?
PANIC PANIC
HAVE YOU'VE COME TO GIVE ME MY FINAL ...
...F- FAREWELL ?!
W-W-WHAT SHOULD I DO? I STILL HAVEN'T THOUGHT OF WHAT TO SAY...
JUST CALM OWN.
TO BE HONEST, RIGHT NOW, I ...
HI!
HOW ARE YOU? MY NAME IS ICHIGO KUROSAKI!
RIGHT NOW, I AM MADLY IN LOVE WITH Y...
BWUH !!
JUMP!
CUT THAT OUT!
A- ARE YOU ALL RIGHT ?
I HEARD A DREADFUL NOISE.
AND THAT VOICE...
OKAY, LET ME LEVEL WITH YOU-- I'M A SOUL REAPER.
A SOUL REAPER?

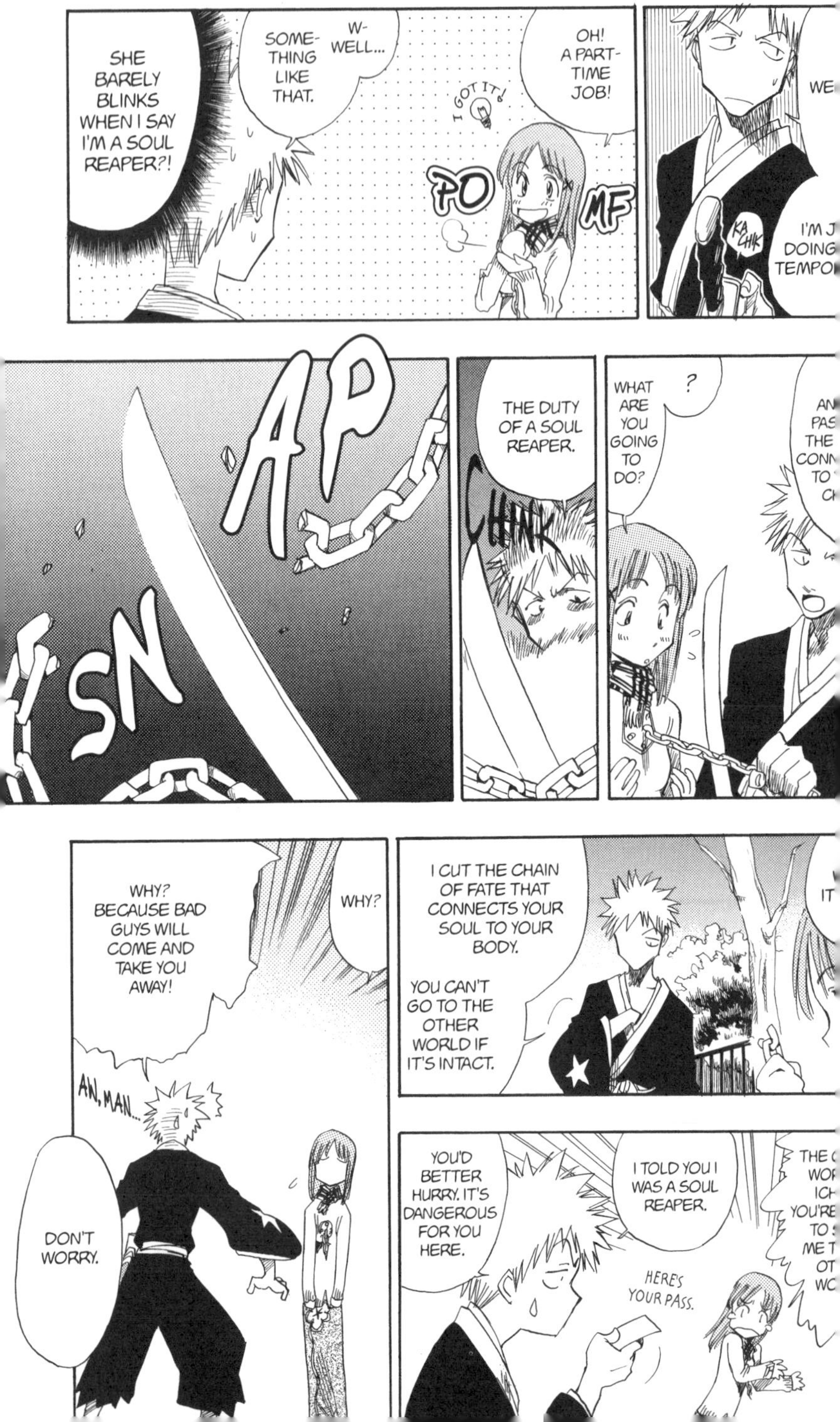
WE
KA CHIK
I'M J
DOING
TEMPO
OH! A PART-TIME JOB!
I GOT IT!
POMF
W-WELL...
SOMETHING LIKE THAT.
SHE BARELY BLINKS WHEN I SAY I'M A SOUL REAPER?!
AN
PAS
THE
CONN
TO
CH
?
WHAT ARE YOU GOING TO DO?
THE DUTY OF A SOUL REAPER.
CHINK
SNAP
IT
I CUT THE CHAIN OF FATE THAT CONNECTS YOUR SOUL TO YOUR BODY.
YOU CAN'T GO TO THE OTHER WORLD IF IT'S INTACT.
THE
WO
ICH
YOU'RE
TO
ME
OT
WO
I TOLD YOU I WAS A SOUL REAPER.
YOU'D BETTER HURRY. IT'S DANGEROUS FOR YOU HERE.
HERE'S YOUR PASS.
WHY?
WHY? BECAUSE BAD GUYS WILL COME AND TAKE YOU AWAY!
AW, MAN...
DON'T WORRY.

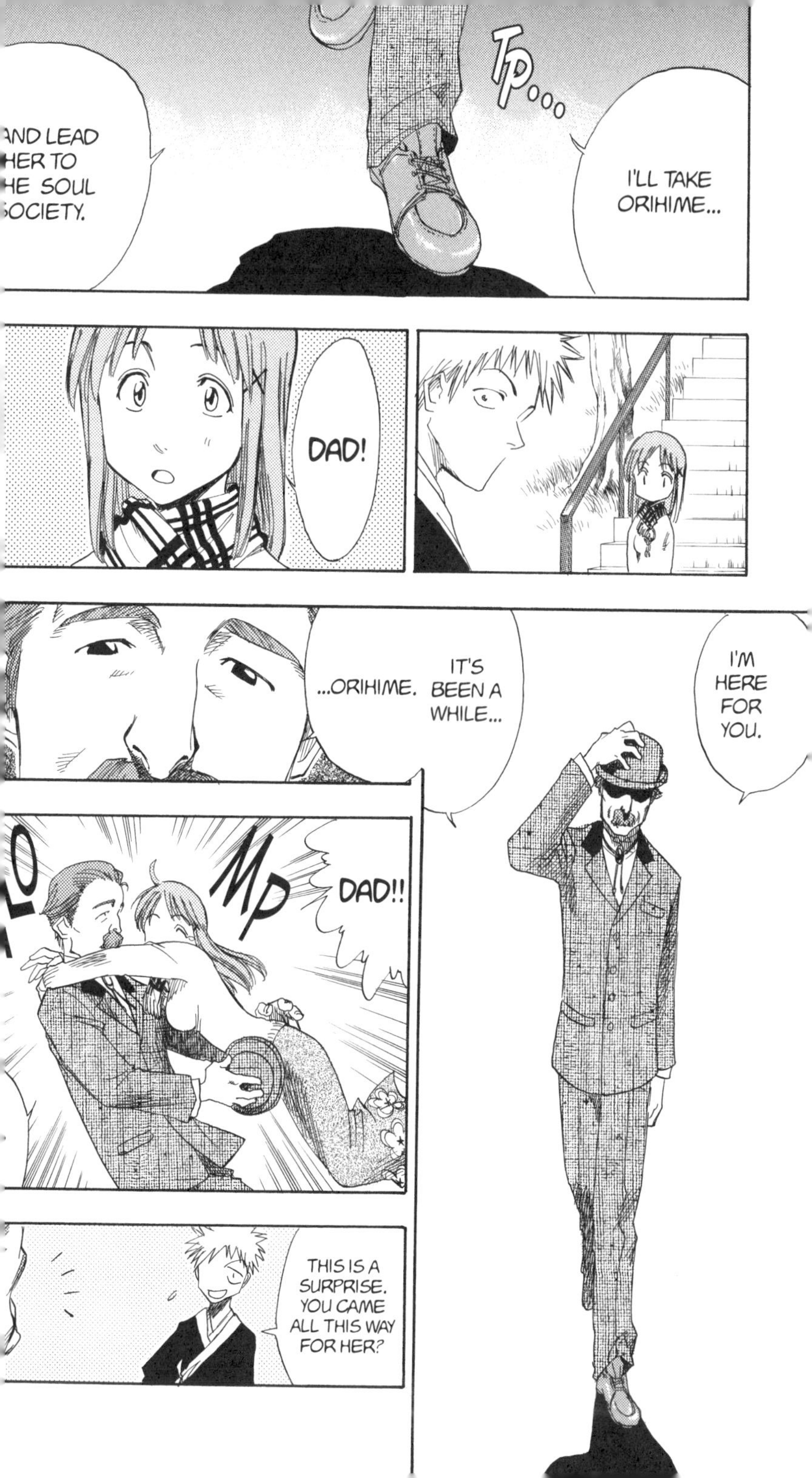
I'LL TAKE ORIHIME...
TPOOO
ND LEAD HER TO HE SOUL OCIETY.
DAD!
I'M HERE FOR YOU.
...ORIHIME. IT'S BEEN A WHILE...
MP
DAD!!
LO
THIS IS A SURPRISE. YOU CAME ALL THIS WAY FOR HER?

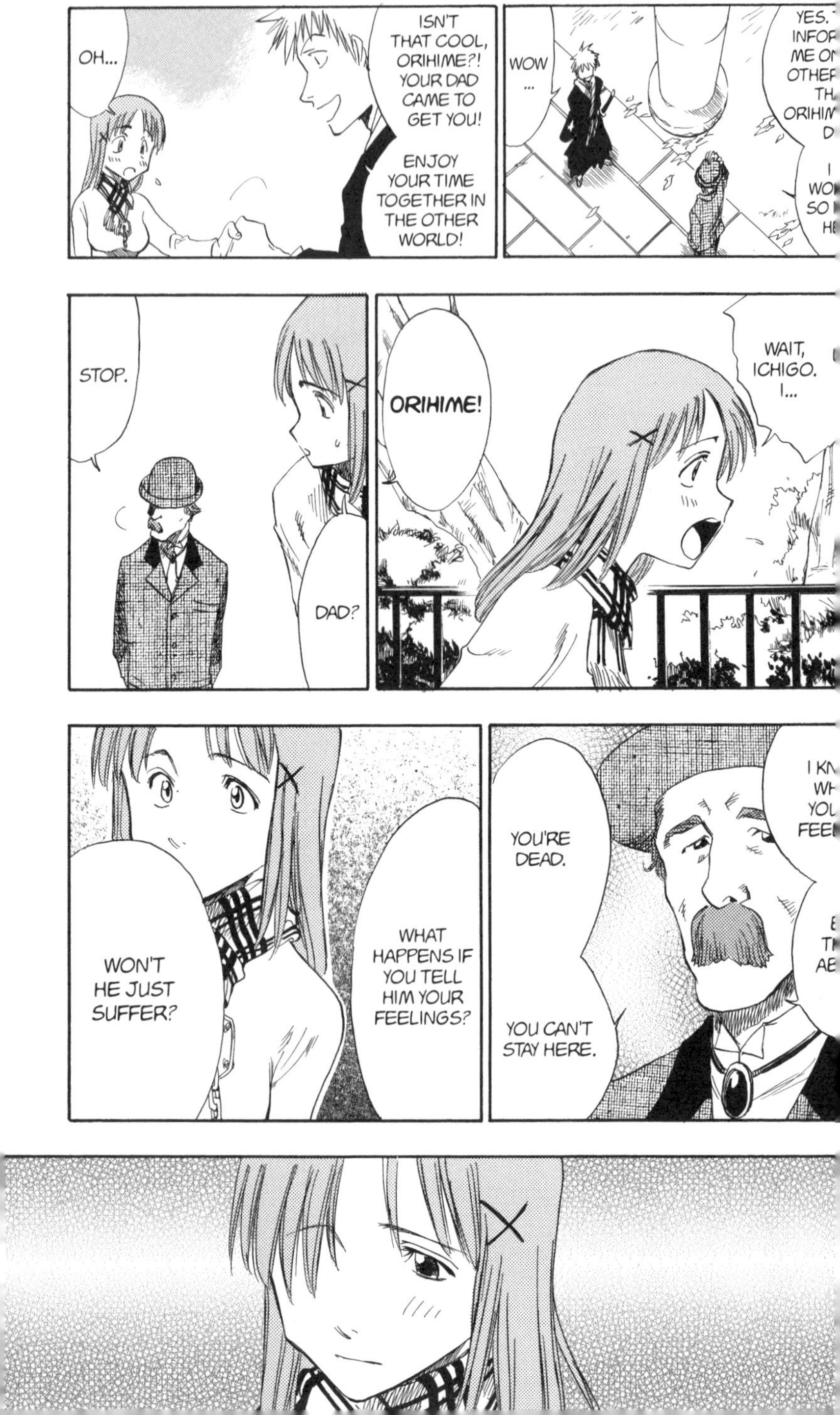
WOW...
ISN'T THAT COOL, ORIHIME?! YOUR DAD CAME TO GET YOU!
ENJOY YOUR TIME TOGETHER IN THE OTHER WORLD!
OH...
WAIT, ICHIGO. I...
ORIHIME!
STOP.
DAD?
YOU'RE DEAD.
YOU CAN'T STAY HERE.
WHAT HAPPENS IF YOU TELL HIM YOUR FEELINGS?
WON'T HE JUST SUFFER?

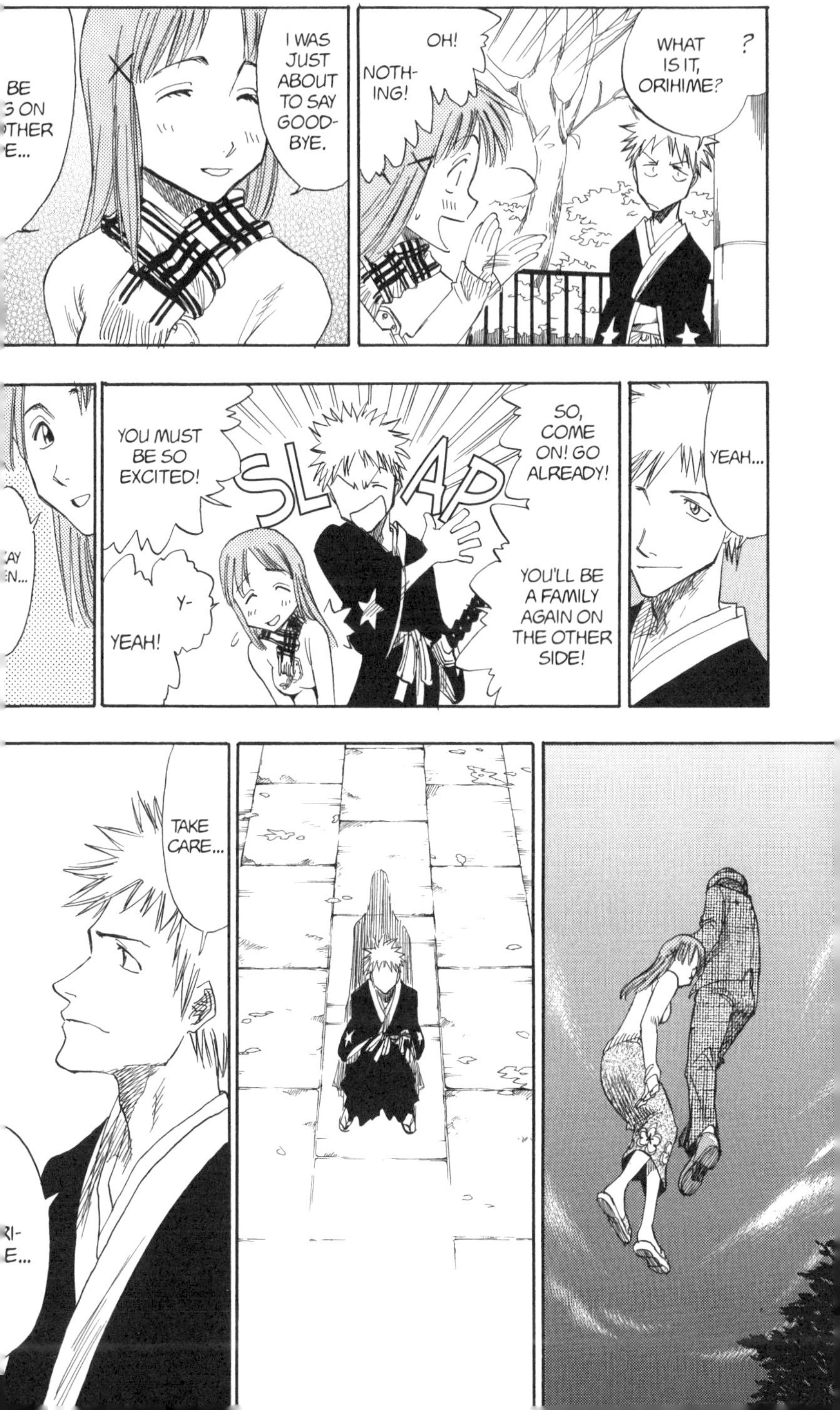
WHAT IS IT, ORIHIME?
?
OH!
NOTHING!
I WAS JUST ABOUT TO SAY GOOD-BYE.
YEAH...
SO, COME ON! GO ALREADY!
SLAP
YOU MUST BE SO EXCITED!
YOU'LL BE A FAMILY AGAIN ON THE OTHER SIDE!
Y-
YEAH!
TAKE CARE...

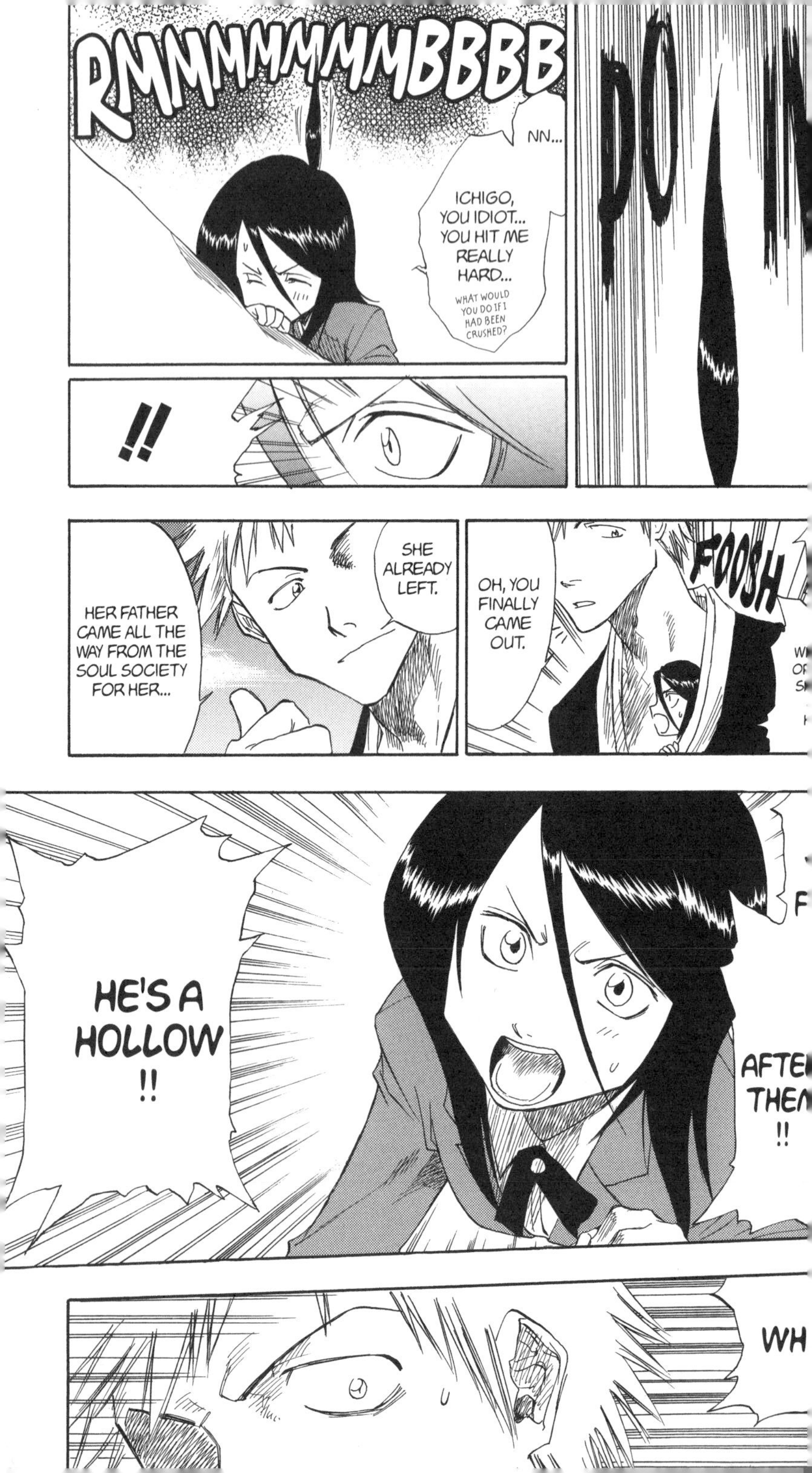
RMMMMMMMBBBB
NN...
ICHIGO, YOU IDIOT... YOU HIT ME REALLY HARD...
WHAT WOULD YOU DO IF I HAD BEEN CRUSHED?
!!
FOOSH
OH, YOU FINALLY CAME OUT.
SHE ALREADY LEFT.
HER FATHER CAME ALL THE WAY FROM THE SOUL SOCIETY FOR HER...
HE'S A HOLLOW !!

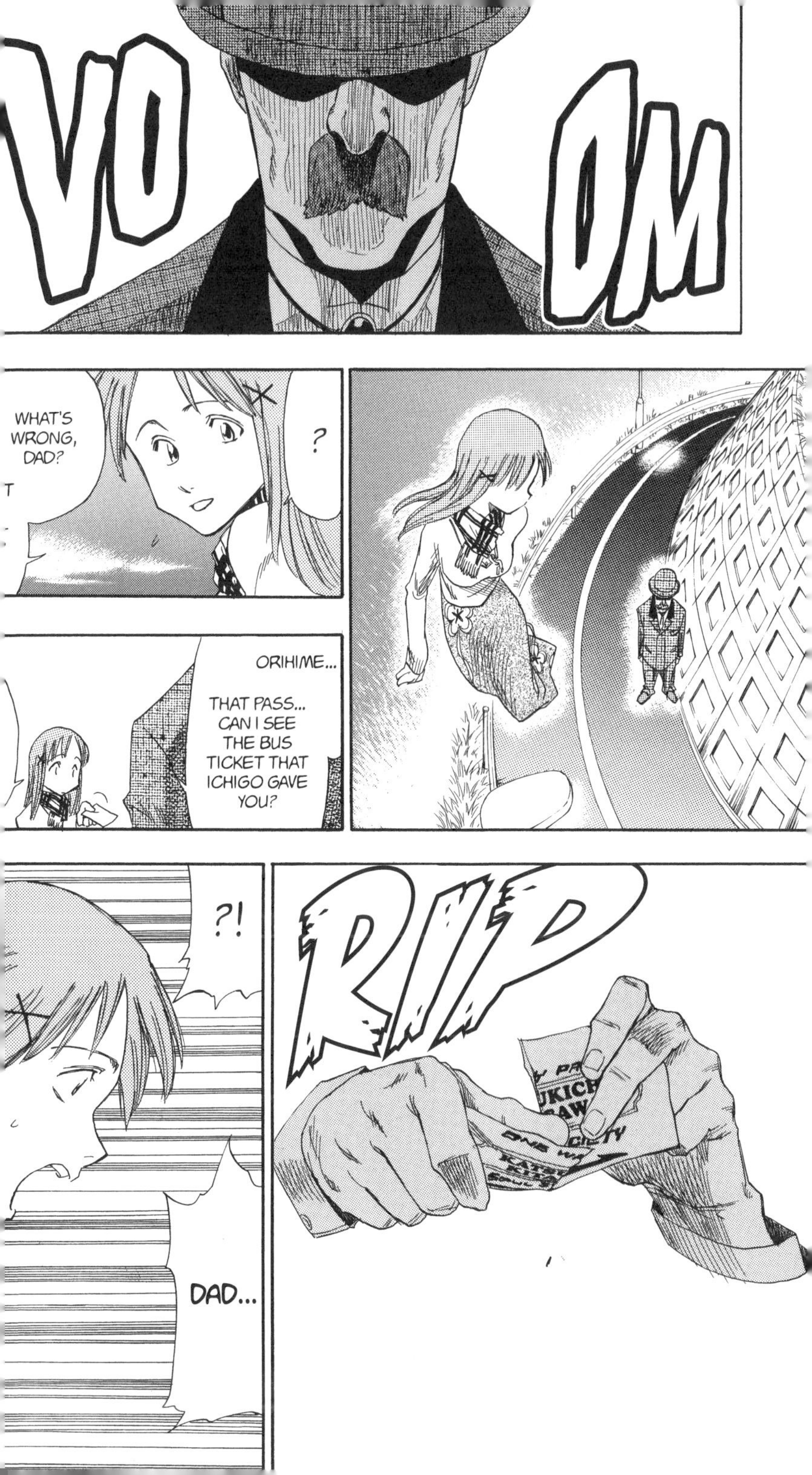
VOOM
?
WHAT'S WRONG, DAD?
ORIHIME...
THAT PASS... CAN I SEE THE BUS TICKET THAT ICHIGO GAVE YOU?
RIP
?!
DAD...

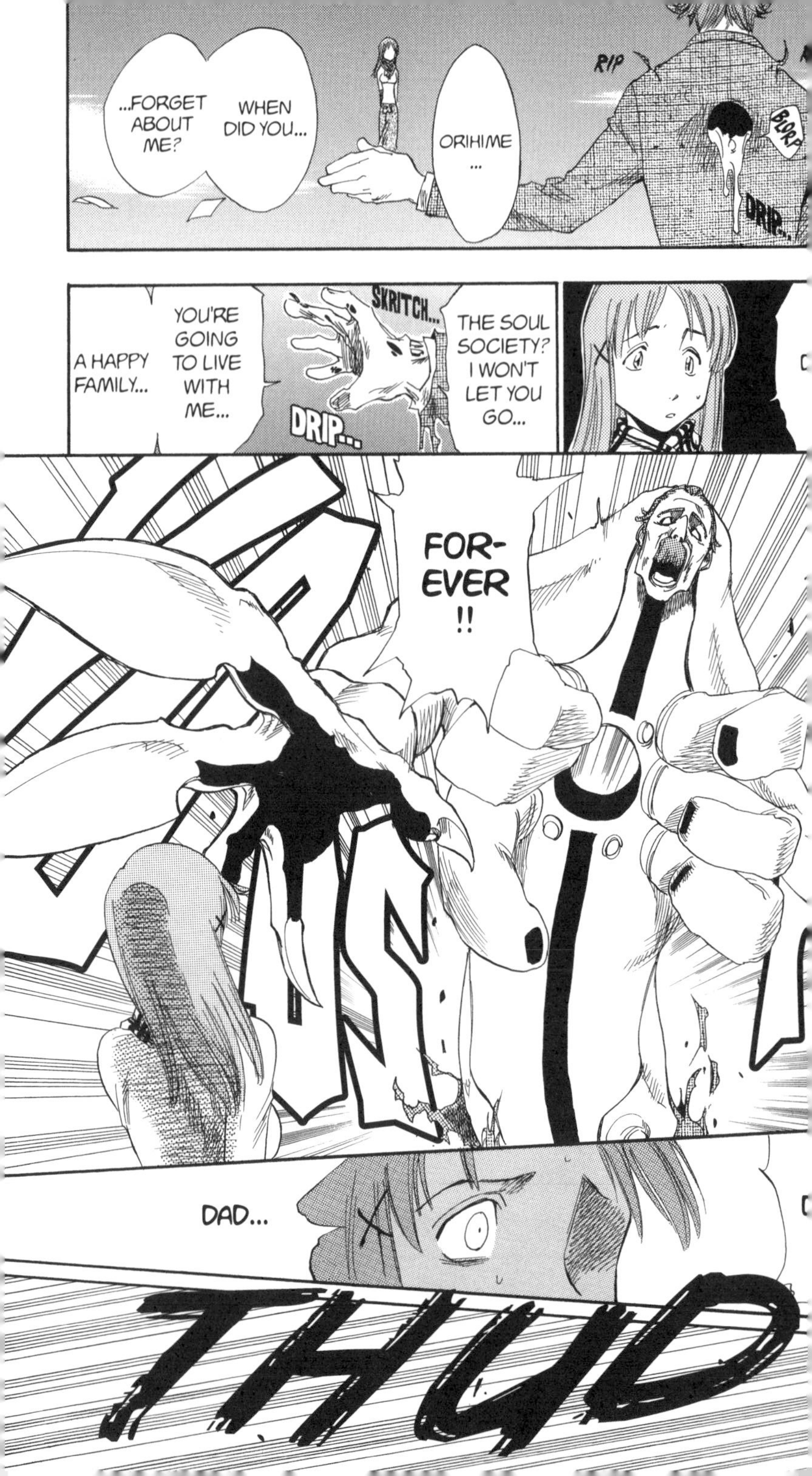
RIP
BLORP
DRIP...
ORIHIME...
WHEN DID YOU...
...FORGET ABOUT ME?
THE SOUL SOCIETY? I WON'T LET YOU GO...
SKRITCH...
DRIP...
YOU'RE GOING TO LIVE WITH ME...
A HAPPY FAMILY...
FOR-EVER!!
DAD...
THUD

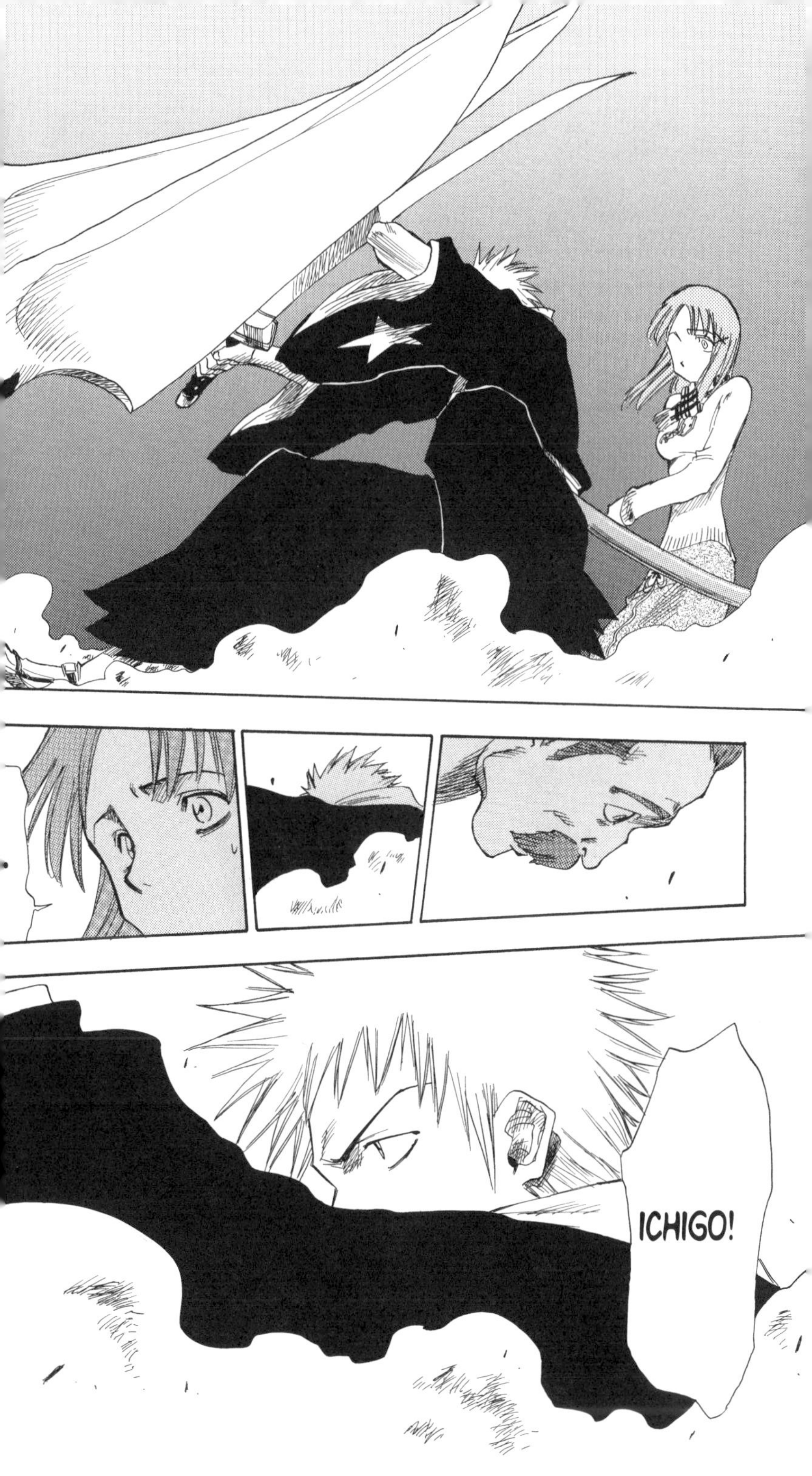
ICHIGO!

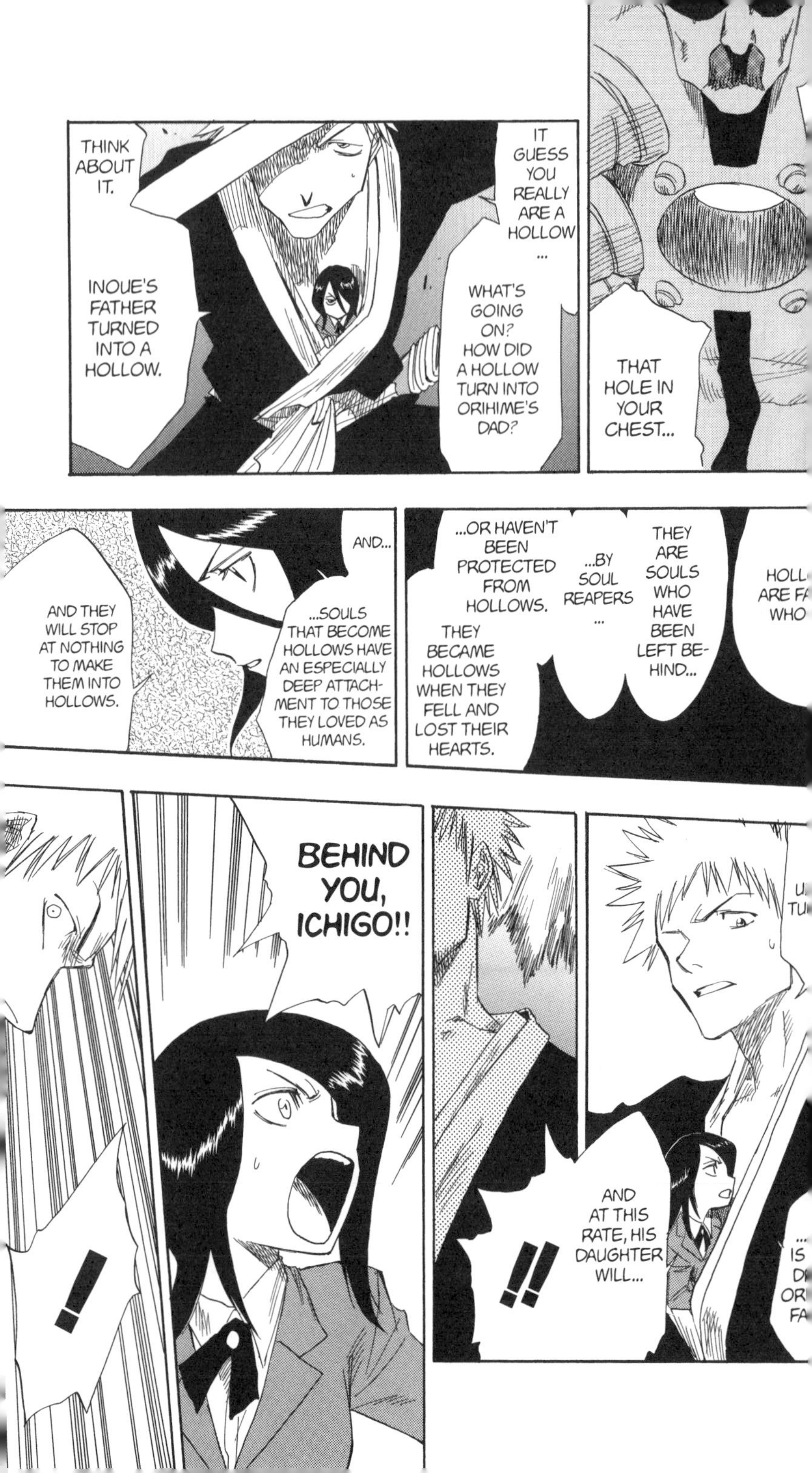
THAT HOLE IN YOUR CHEST...
IT GUESS YOU REALLY ARE A HOLLOW ...
WHAT'S GOING ON? HOW DID A HOLLOW TURN INTO ORIHIME'S DAD?
THINK ABOUT IT.
INOUE'S FATHER TURNED INTO A HOLLOW.
THEY ARE SOULS WHO HAVE BEEN LEFT BE-HIND...
...BY SOUL REAPERS ...
...OR HAVEN'T BEEN PROTECTED FROM HOLLOWS.
THEY BECAME HOLLOWS WHEN THEY FELL AND LOST THEIR HEARTS.
AND...
...SOULS THAT BECOME HOLLOWS HAVE AN ESPECIALLY DEEP ATTACHMENT TO THOSE THEY LOVED AS HUMANS.
AND THEY WILL STOP AT NOTHING TO MAKE THEM INTO HOLLOWS.
AND AT THIS RATE, HIS DAUGHTER WILL...
!!
BEHIND YOU, ICHIGO!!
!

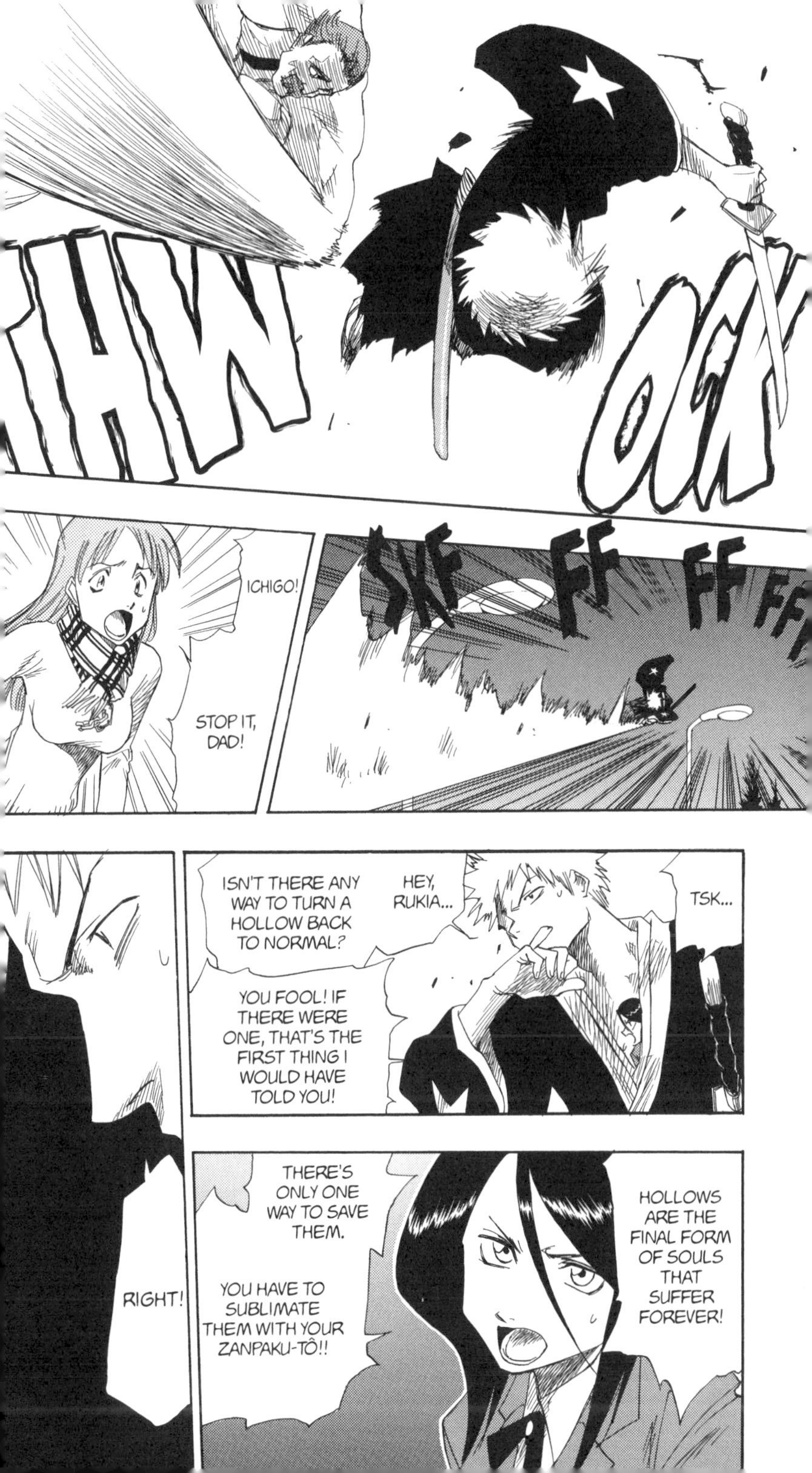
THWOCK
SHF FF FF FF
ICHIGO!
STOP IT, DAD!
TSK...
HEY, RUKIA...
ISN'T THERE ANY WAY TO TURN A HOLLOW BACK TO NORMAL?
YOU FOOL! IF THERE WERE ONE, THAT'S THE FIRST THING I WOULD HAVE TOLD YOU!
HOLLOWS ARE THE FINAL FORM OF SOULS THAT SUFFER FOREVER!
THERE'S ONLY ONE WAY TO SAVE THEM.
YOU HAVE TO SUBLIMATE THEM WITH YOUR ZANPAKU-TÔ!!
RIGHT!

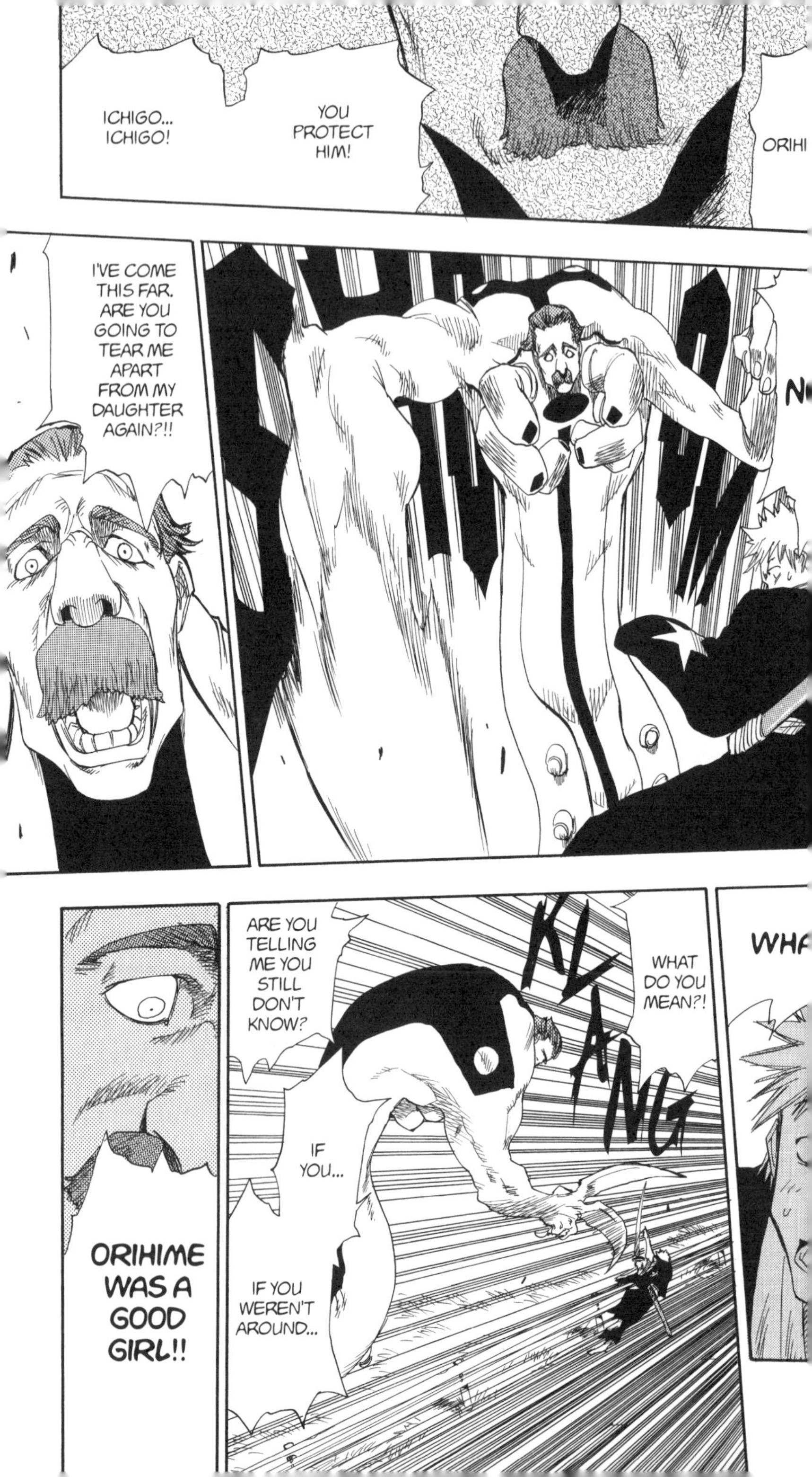
ORIHI
YOU PROTECT HIM!
ICHIGO... ICHIGO!
I'VE COME THIS FAR. ARE YOU GOING TO TEAR ME APART FROM MY DAUGHTER AGAIN?!!
WHA
WHAT DO YOU MEAN?!
KLANG
ARE YOU TELLING ME YOU STILL DON'T KNOW?
IF YOU...
IF YOU WEREN'T AROUND...
ORIHIME WAS A GOOD GIRL!!

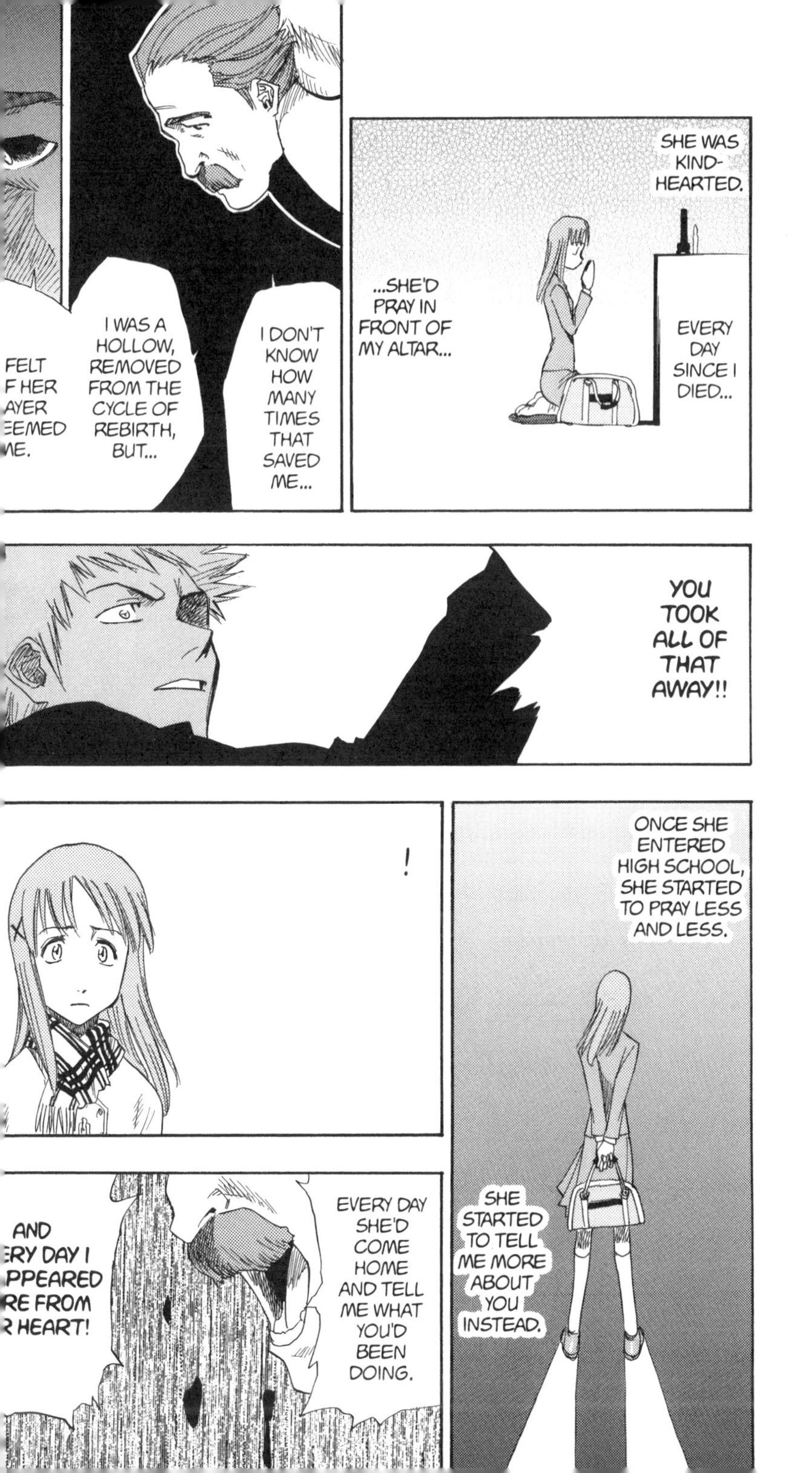

SHE WAS KIND-HEARTED.
EVERY DAY SINCE I DIED...
...SHE'D PRAY IN FRONT OF MY ALTAR...
I DON'T KNOW HOW MANY TIMES THAT SAVED ME...
I WAS A HOLLOW, REMOVED FROM THE CYCLE OF REBIRTH, BUT...
FELT F HER AYER EEMED ME.
YOU TOOK ALL OF THAT AWAY!!
ONCE SHE ENTERED HIGH SCHOOL, SHE STARTED TO PRAY LESS AND LESS.
SHE STARTED TO TELL ME MORE ABOUT YOU INSTEAD.
!
EVERY DAY SHE'D COME HOME AND TELL ME WHAT YOU'D BEEN DOING.
AND ERY DAY I PPEARED RE FROM R HEART!

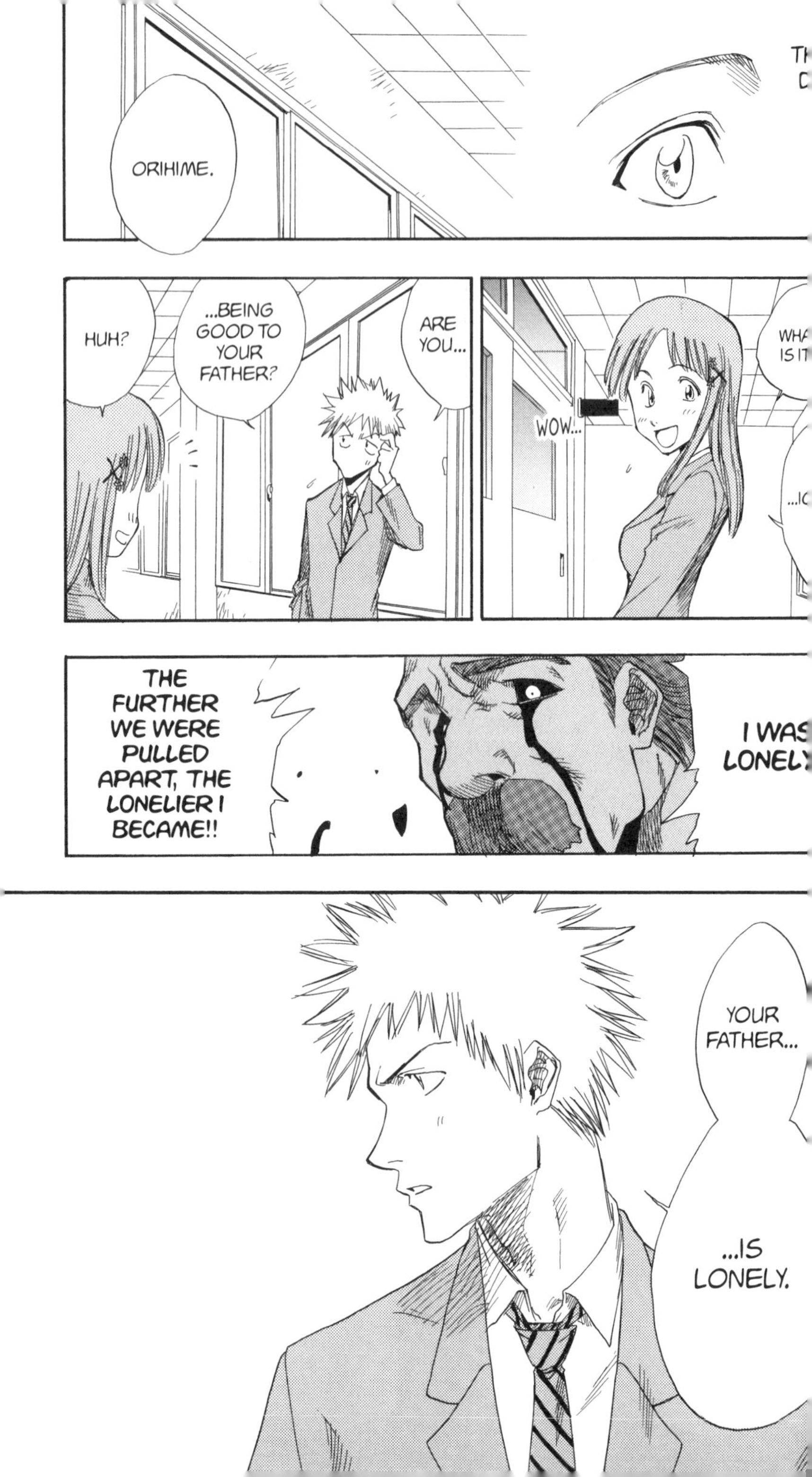
ORIHIME.
WOW...
ARE YOU...
...BEING GOOD TO YOUR FATHER?
HUH?
THE FURTHER WE WERE PULLED APART, THE LONELIER I BECAME!!
YOUR FATHER...
...IS LONELY.

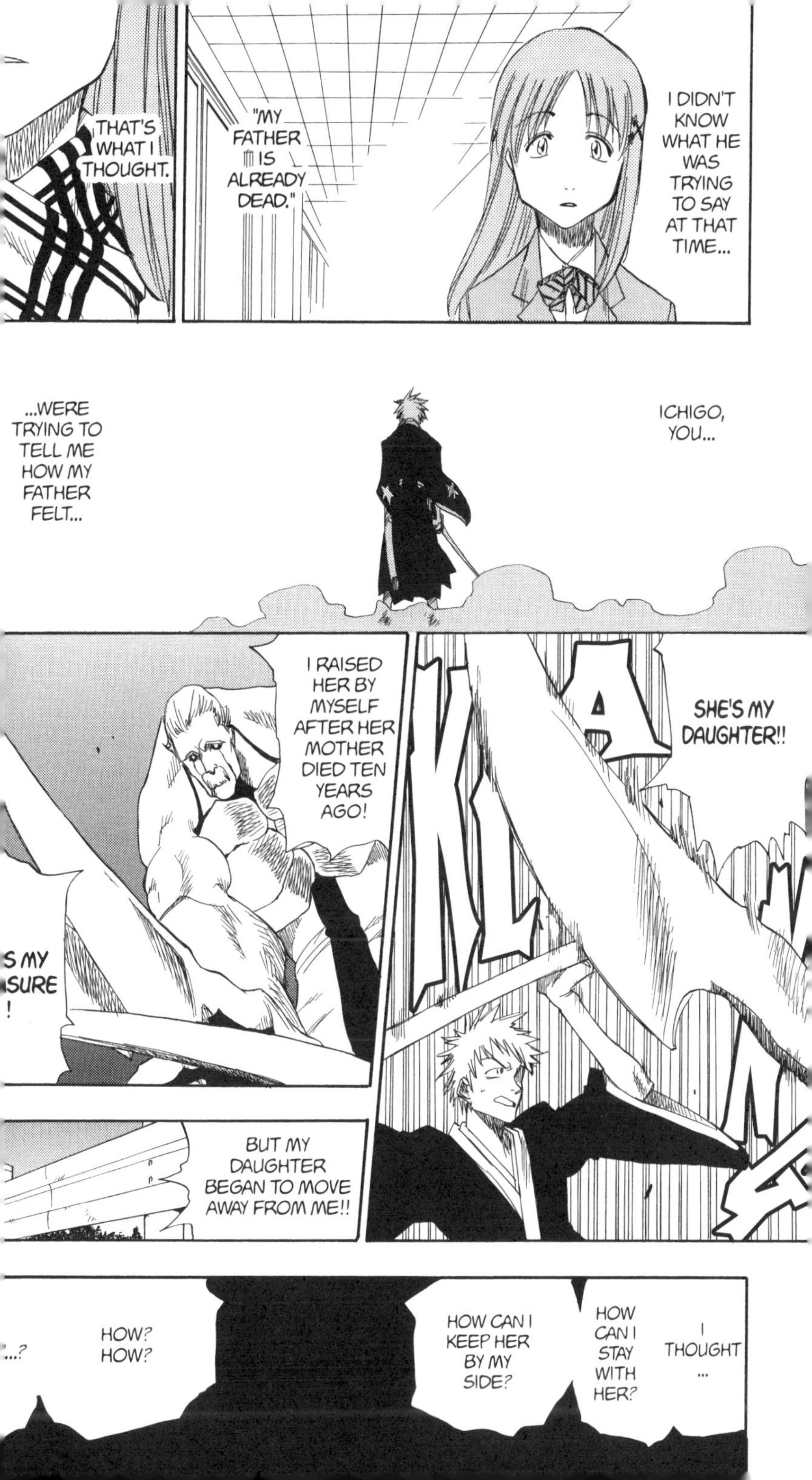
I DIDN'T KNOW WHAT HE WAS TRYING TO SAY AT THAT TIME...
"MY FATHER IS ALREADY DEAD."
THAT'S WHAT I THOUGHT.
ICHIGO, YOU...
...WERE TRYING TO TELL ME HOW MY FATHER FELT...
SHE'S MY DAUGHTER!!
I RAISED HER BY MYSELF AFTER HER MOTHER DIED TEN YEARS AGO!
BUT MY DAUGHTER BEGAN TO MOVE AWAY FROM ME!!
I THOUGHT...
HOW CAN I STAY WITH HER?
HOW CAN I KEEP HER BY MY SIDE?
HOW? HOW?
...?

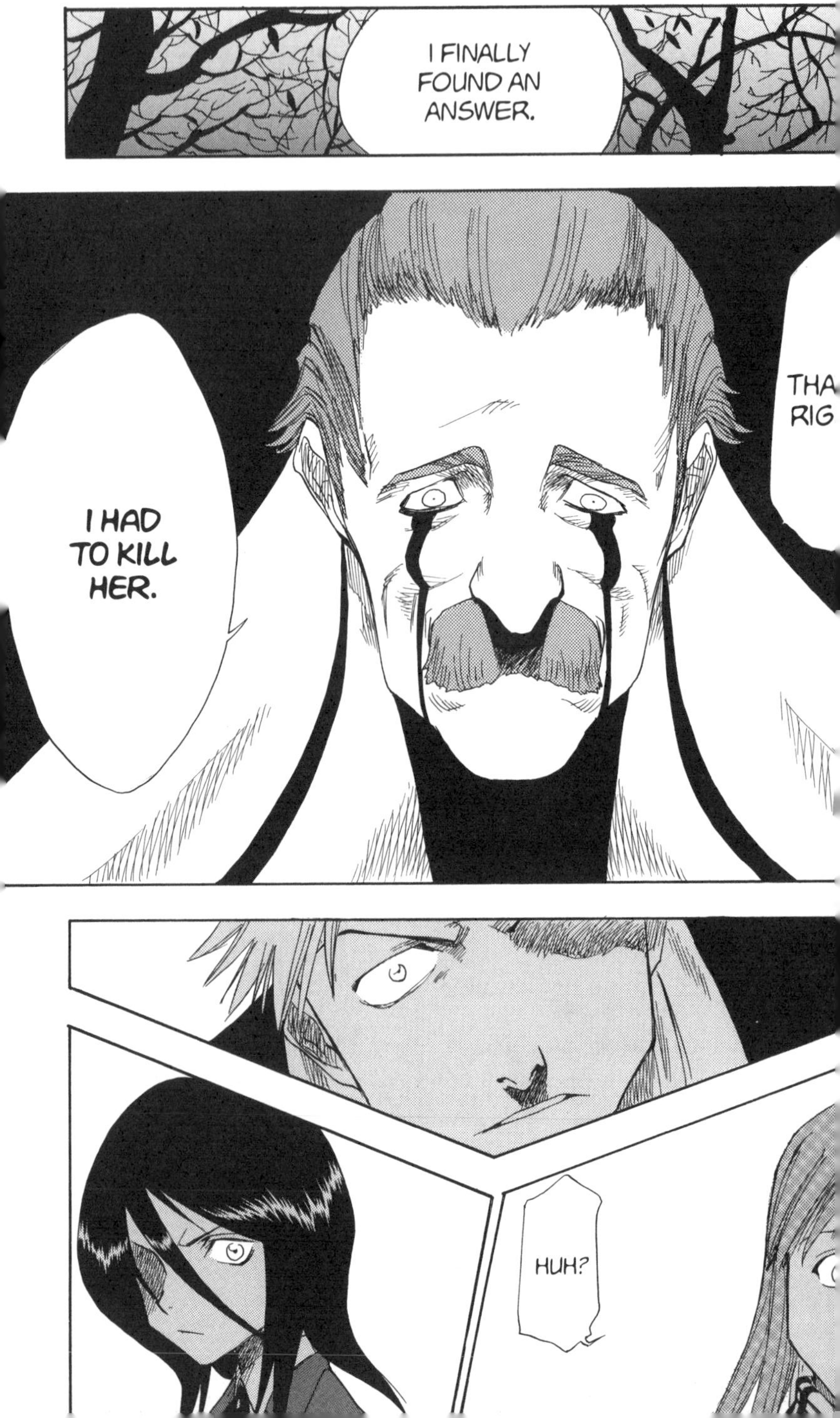
I FINALLY FOUND AN ANSWER.
THA
RIG
I HAD TO KILL HER.
HUH?

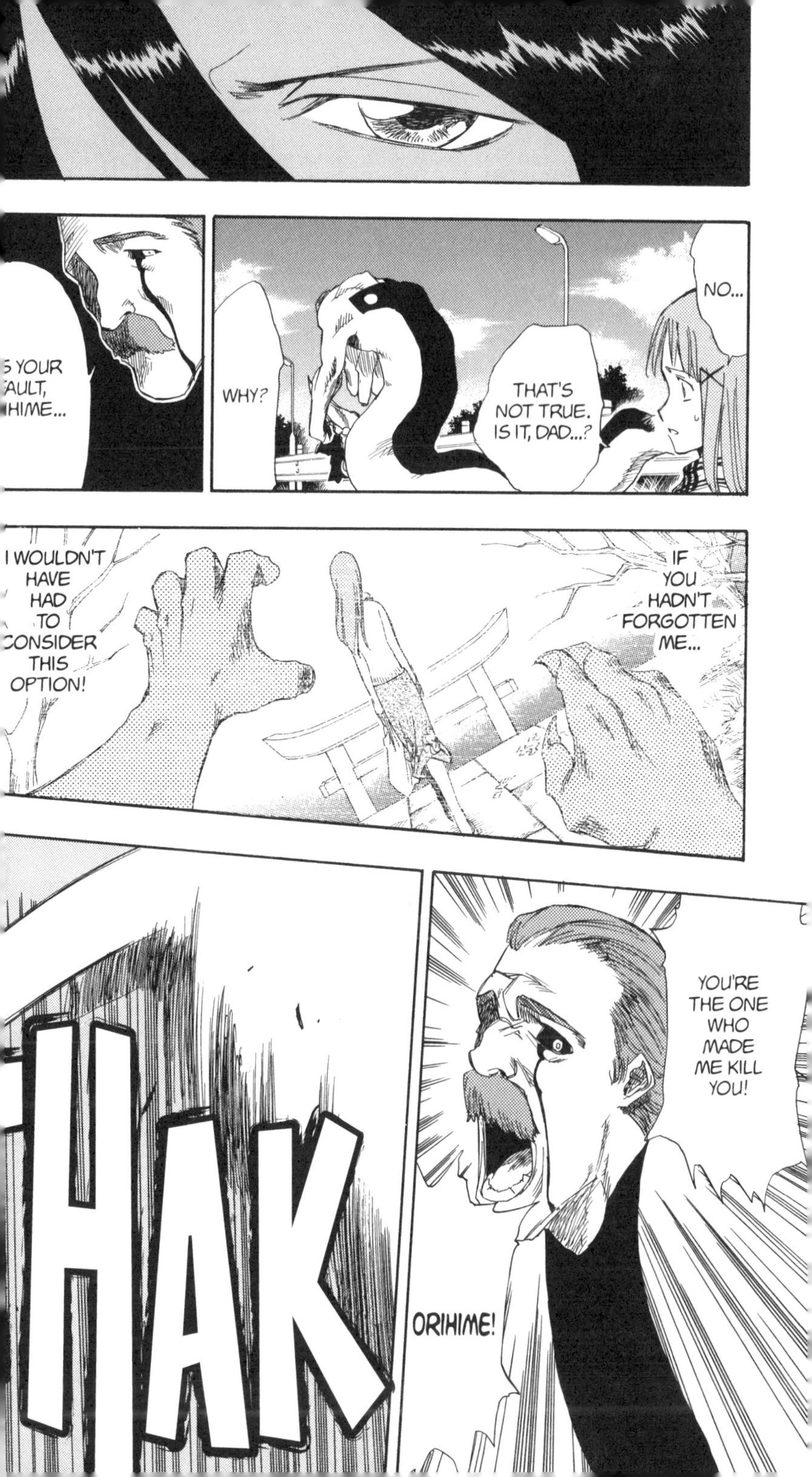

NO...
THAT'S NOT TRUE. IS IT, DAD...?
WHY?
S YOUR AULT, HIME...
IF YOU HADN'T FORGOTTEN ME...
I WOULDN'T HAVE HAD TO CONSIDER THIS OPTION!
YOU'RE THE ONE WHO MADE ME KILL YOU!
ORIHIME!
THAK

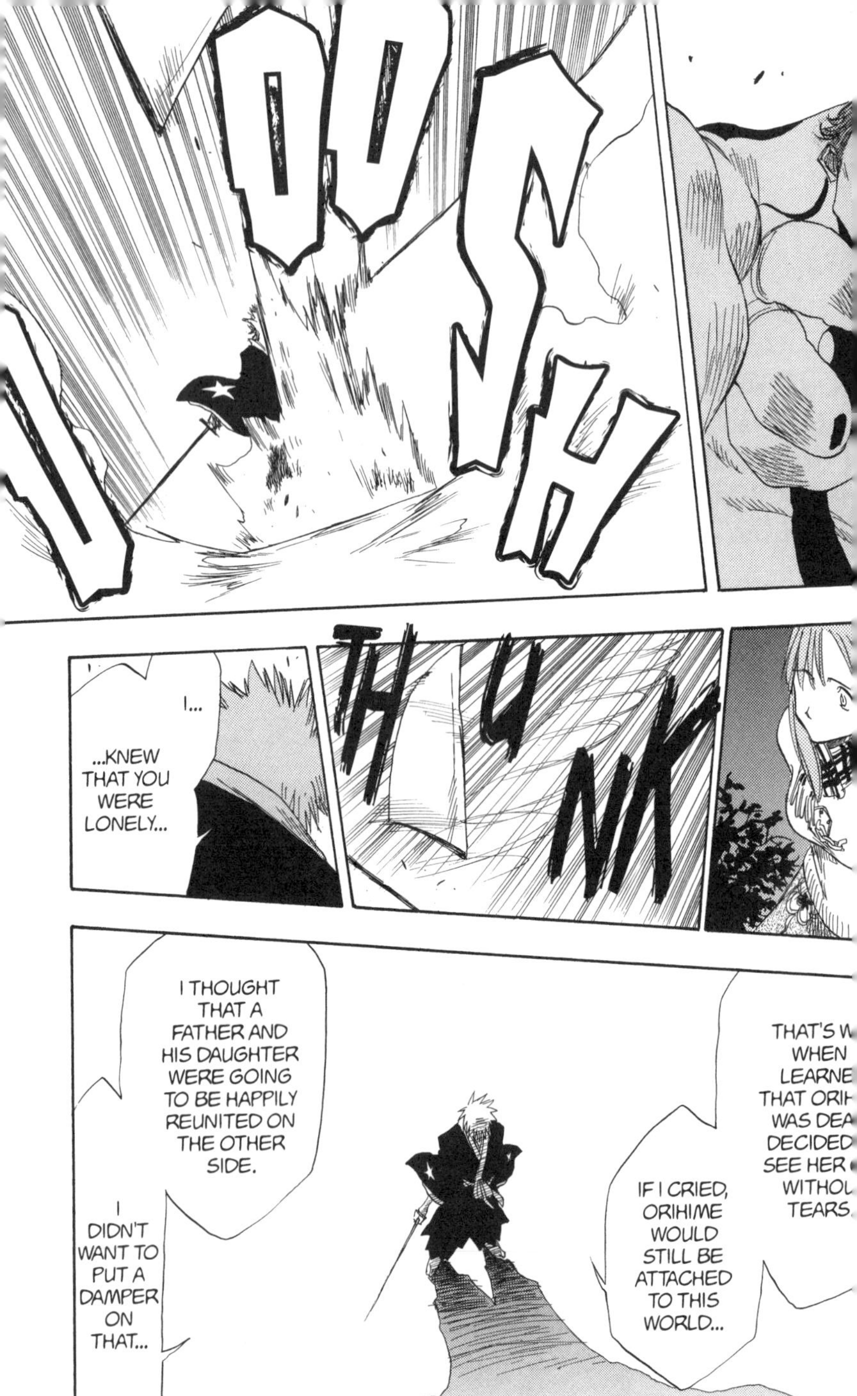
THUNK
I...
...KNEW THAT YOU WERE LONELY...
THAT'S W WHEN LEARNE THAT ORIH WAS DEA DECIDED SEE HER WITHOU TEARS.
IF I CRIED, ORIHIME WOULD STILL BE ATTACHED TO THIS WORLD...
I THOUGHT THAT A FATHER AND HIS DAUGHTER WERE GOING TO BE HAPPILY REUNITED ON THE OTHER SIDE.
I DIDN'T WANT TO PUT A DAMPER ON THAT...

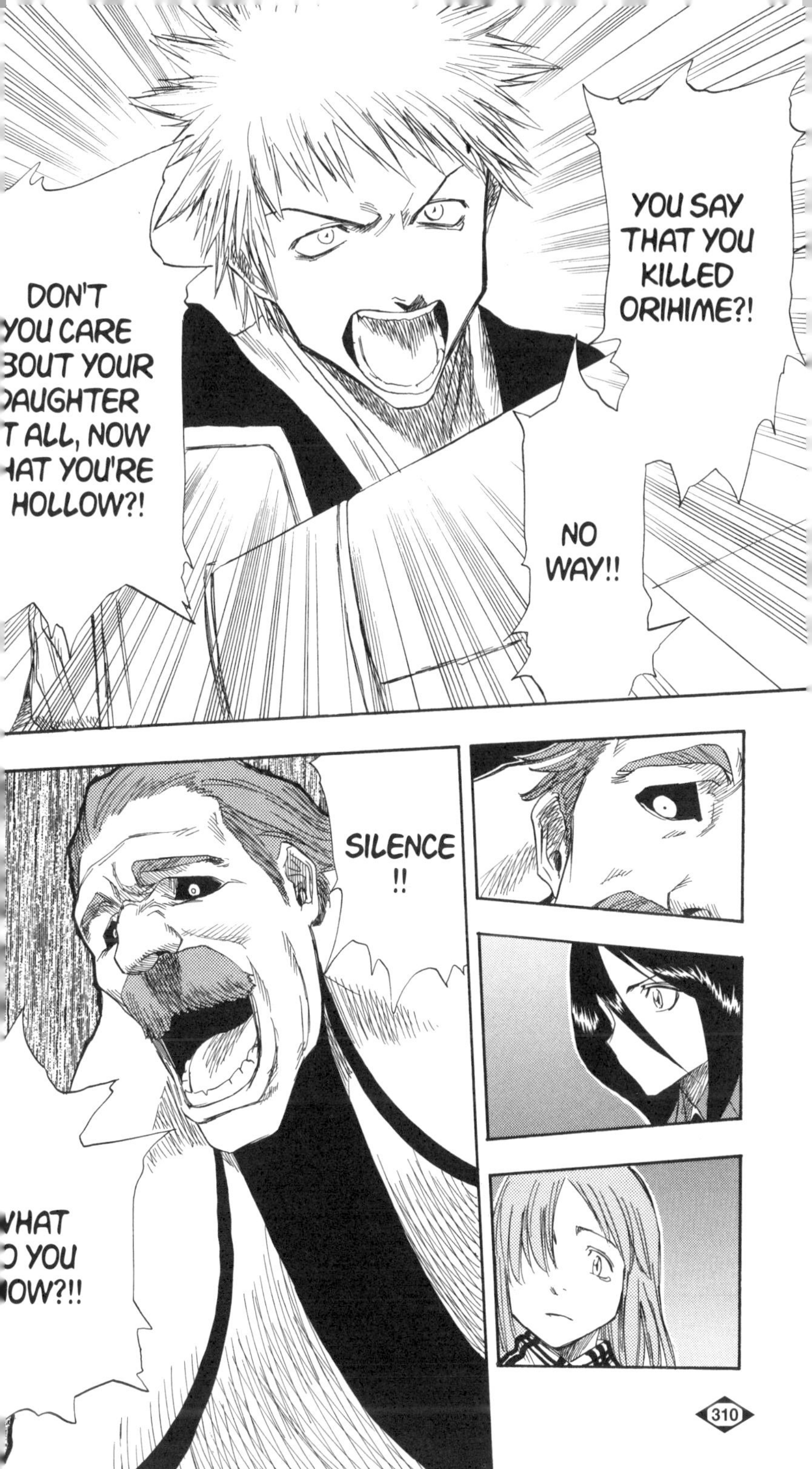
YOU SAY THAT YOU KILLED ORIHIME?!
NO WAY!!
DON'T YOU CARE BOUT YOUR AUGHTER T ALL, NOW HAT YOU'RE HOLLOW?!
SILENCE !!
HAT YOU OW?!!

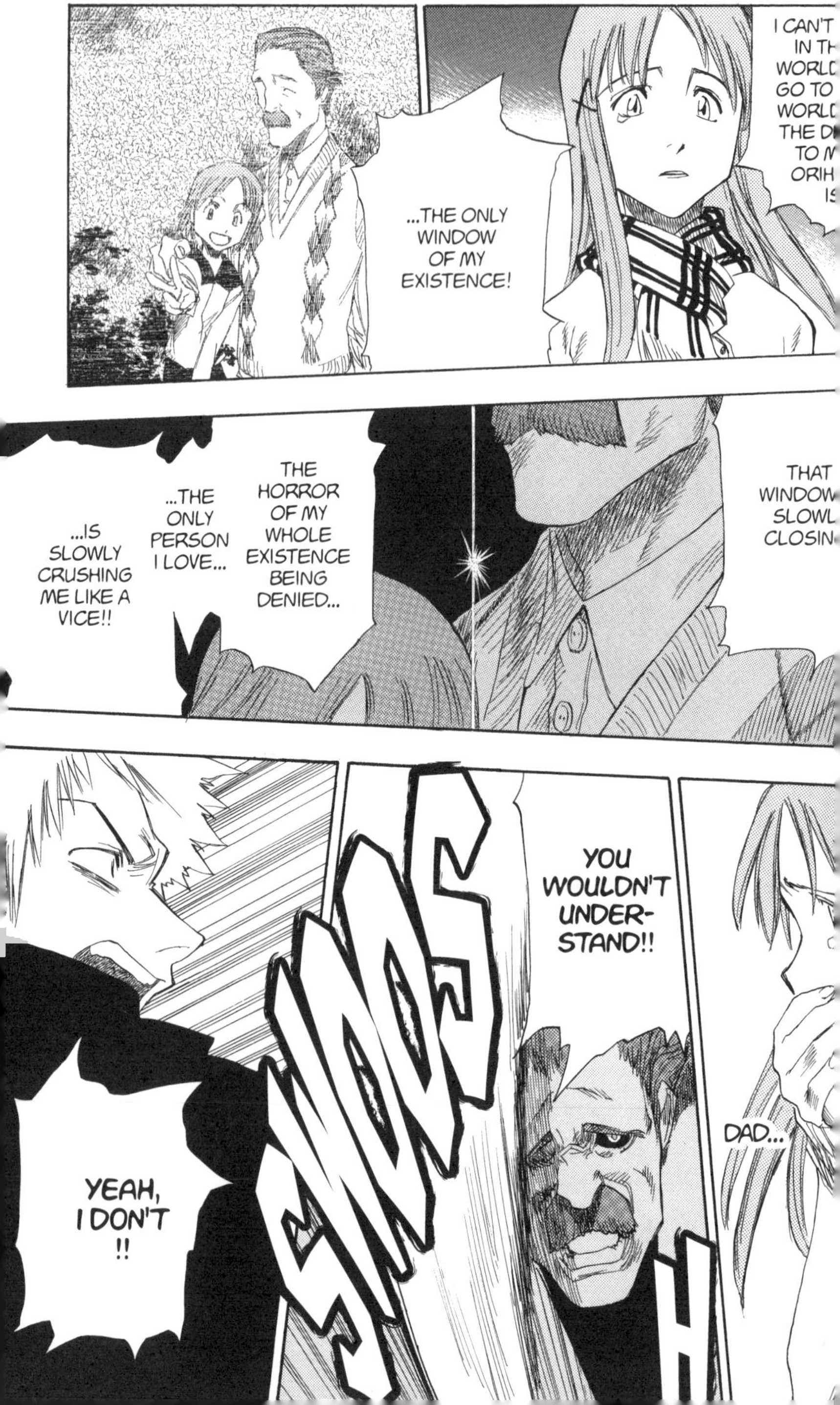
I CAN'T IN TH WORLD GO TO WORLD THE D TO M ORIH IS
...THE ONLY WINDOW OF MY EXISTENCE!
THAT WINDOW SLOWL CLOSIN
THE HORROR OF MY WHOLE EXISTENCE BEING DENIED...
...THE ONLY PERSON I LOVE...
...IS SLOWLY CRUSHING ME LIKE A VICE!!
DAD...
YOU WOULDN'T UNDER-STAND!!
SWOOSH
YEAH, I DON'T !!

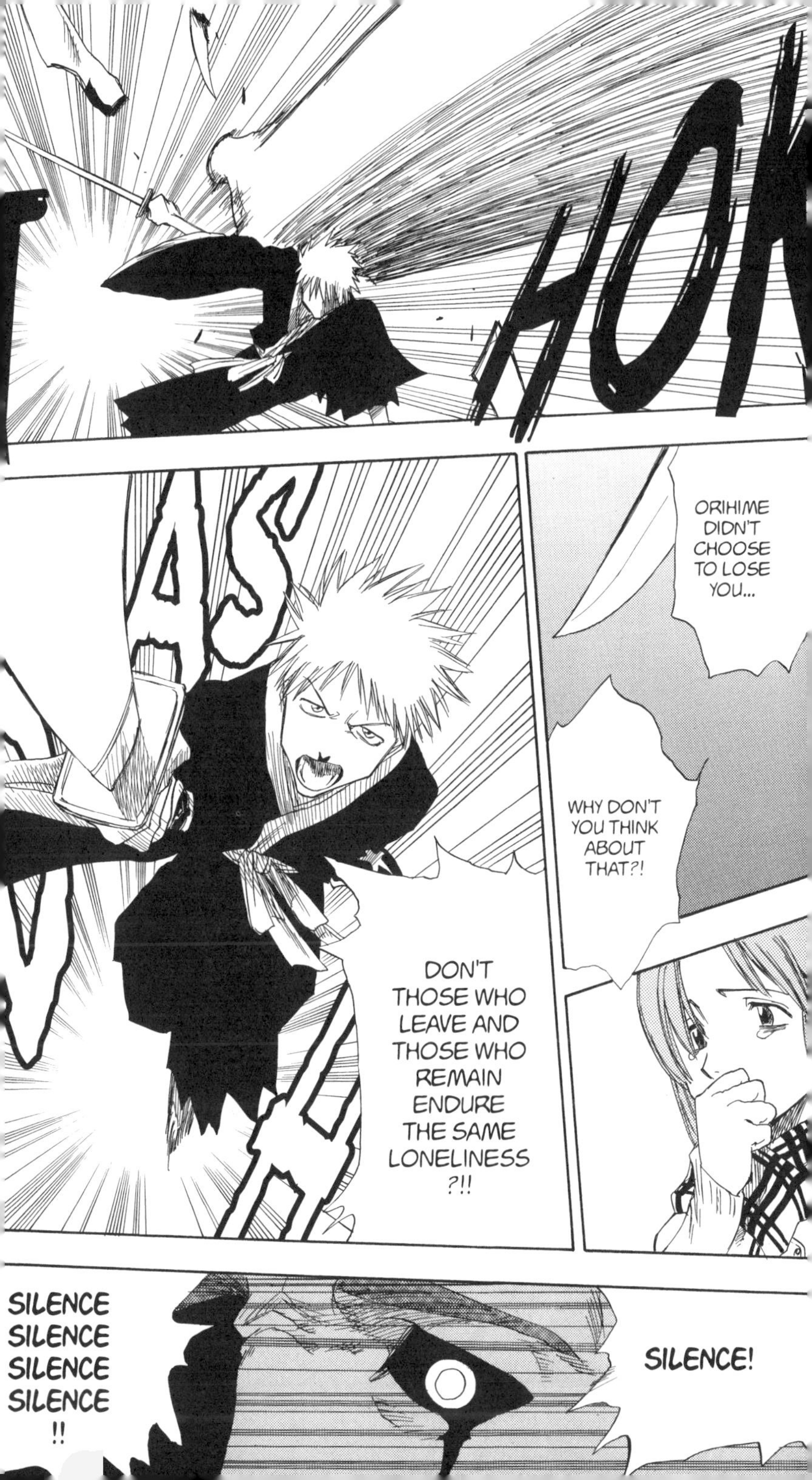
ORIHIME DIDN'T CHOOSE TO LOSE YOU...
WHY DON'T YOU THINK ABOUT THAT?!
DON'T THOSE WHO LEAVE AND THOSE WHO REMAIN ENDURE THE SAME LONELINESS ?!!
SILENCE!
SILENCE SILENCE SILENCE SILENCE !!

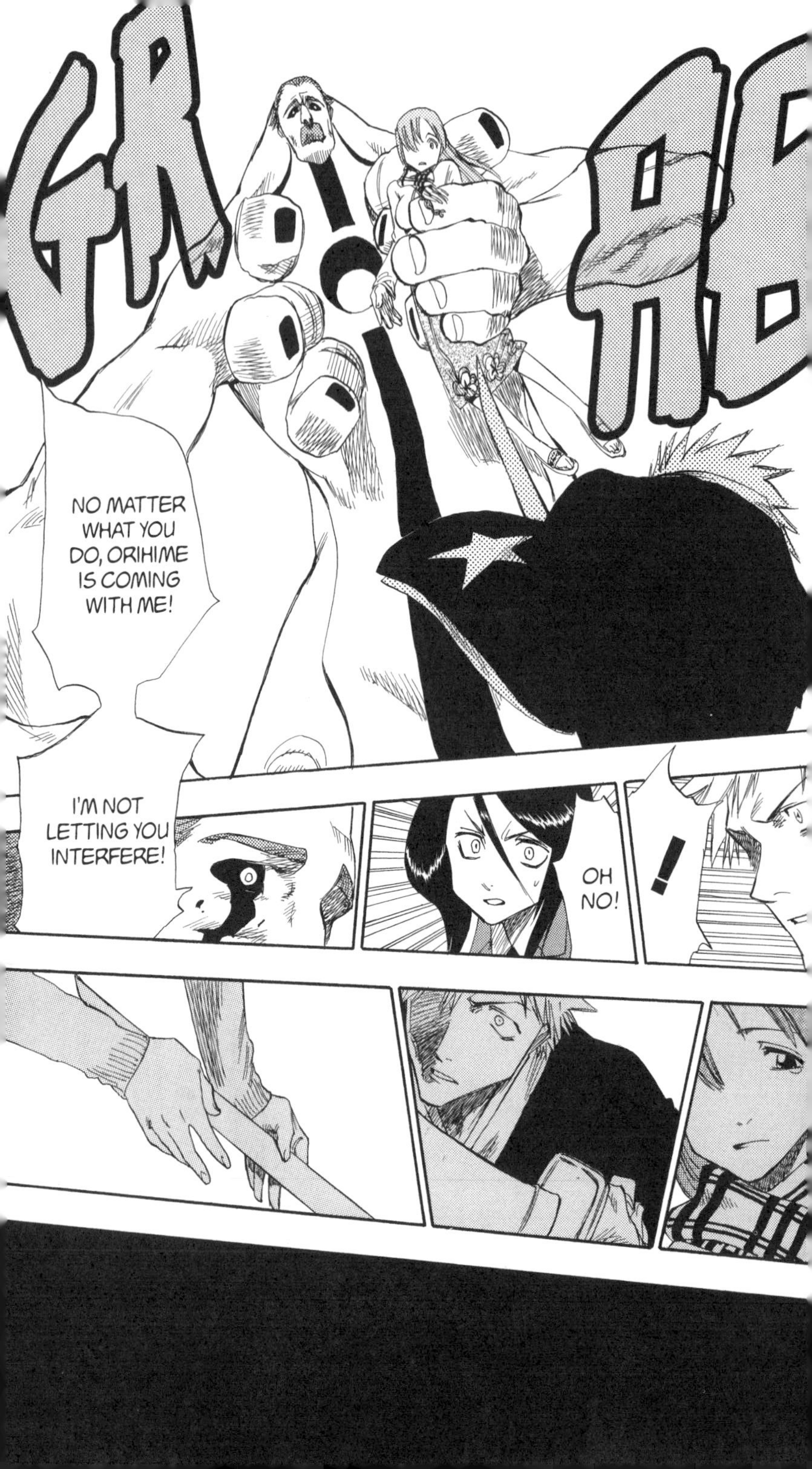
GRAB!
NO MATTER WHAT YOU DO, ORIHIME IS COMING WITH ME!
!
OH NO!
I'M NOT LETTING YOU INTERFERE!

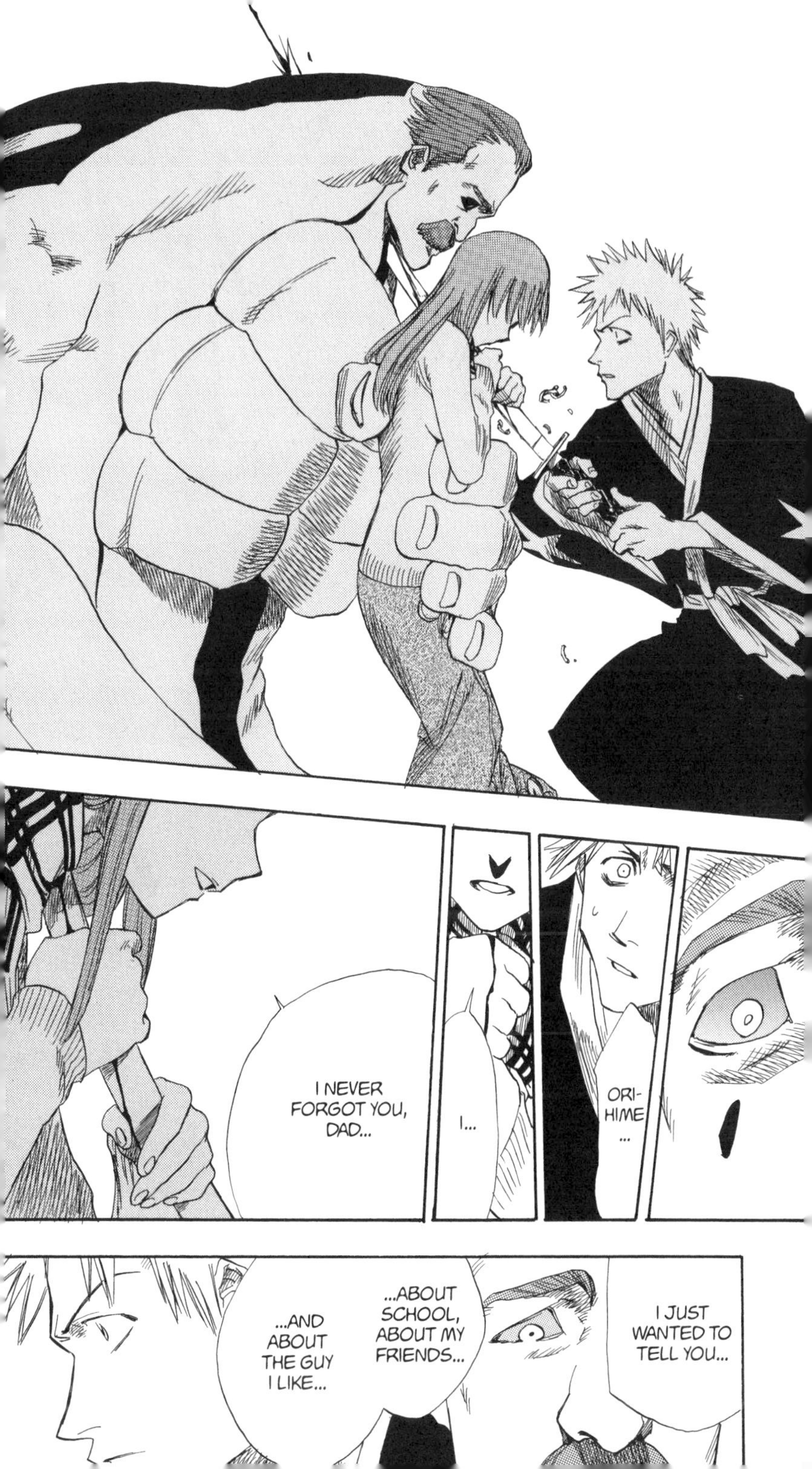
ORI-HIME...
I...
I NEVER FORGOT YOU, DAD...
I JUST WANTED TO TELL YOU...
...ABOUT SCHOOL, ABOUT MY FRIENDS...
...AND ABOUT THE GUY I LIKE...

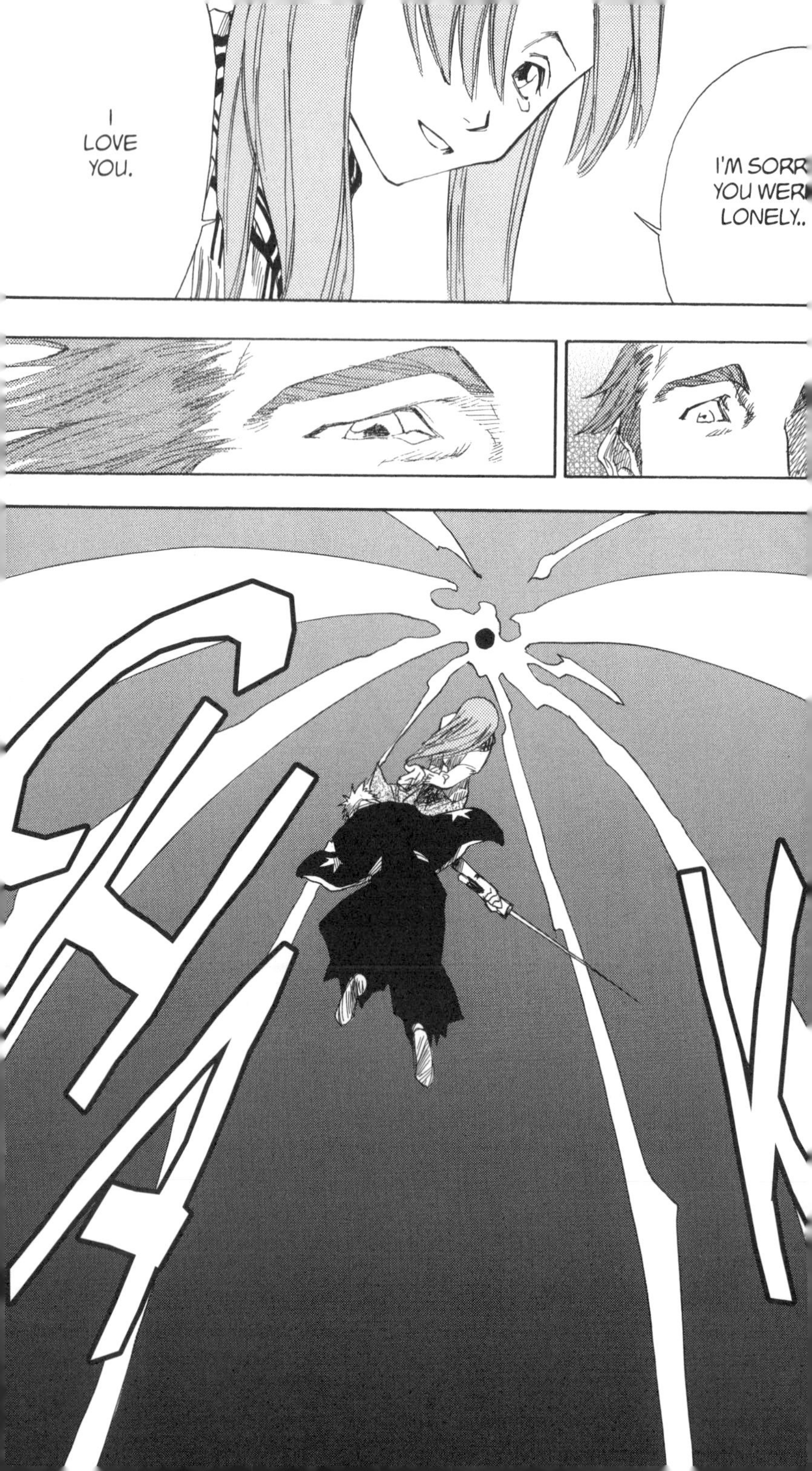
I'M SORR
YOU WER
LONELY..
I LOVE YOU.

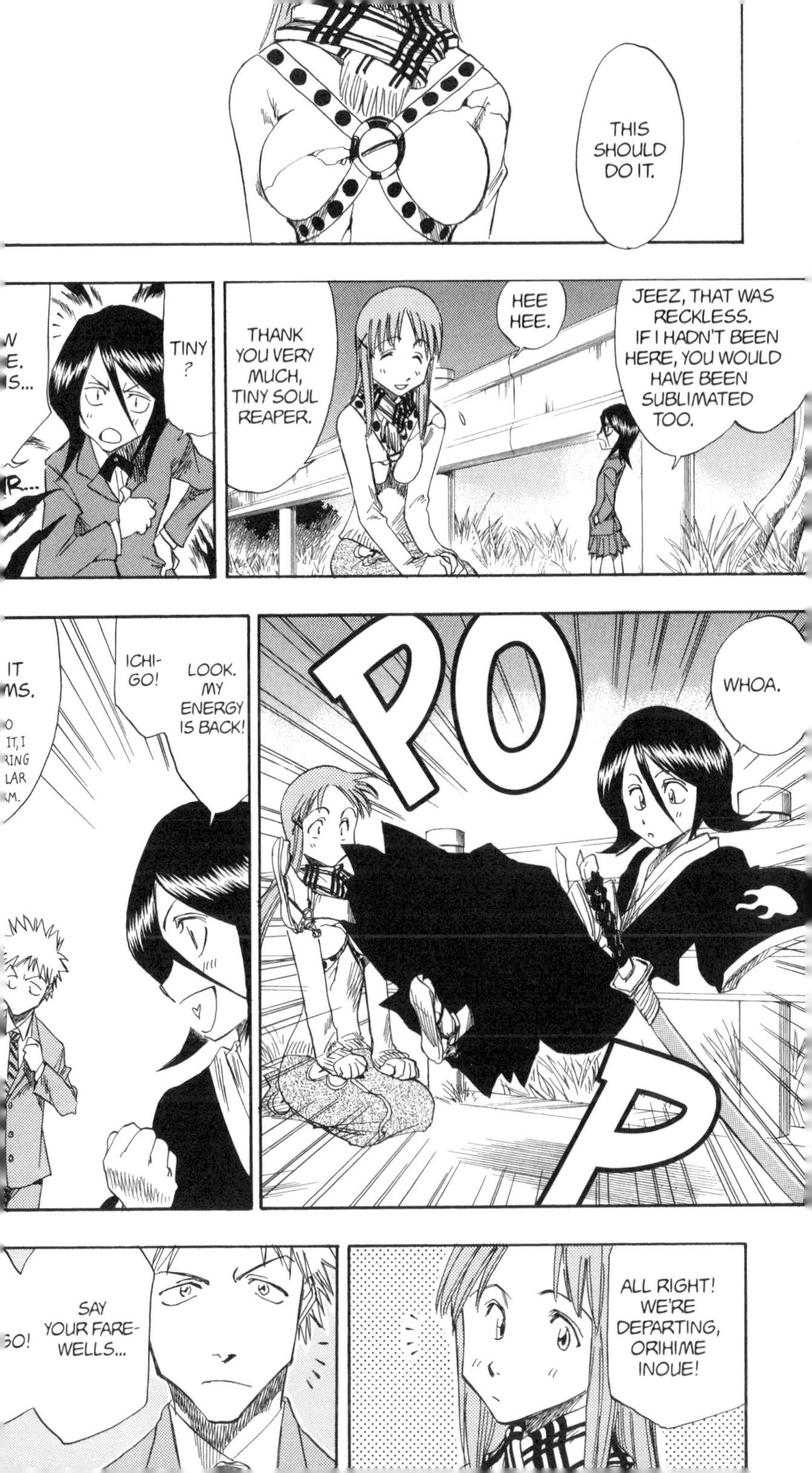
THIS SHOULD DO IT.
JEEZ, THAT WAS RECKLESS. IF I HADN'T BEEN HERE, YOU WOULD HAVE BEEN SUBLIMATED TOO.
HEE HEE.
THANK YOU VERY MUCH, TINY SOUL REAPER.
TINY?
WHOA.
POP
LOOK. MY ENERGY IS BACK!
ICHI-GO!
ALL RIGHT! WE'RE DEPARTING, ORIHIME INOUE!
SAY YOUR FARE-WELLS...

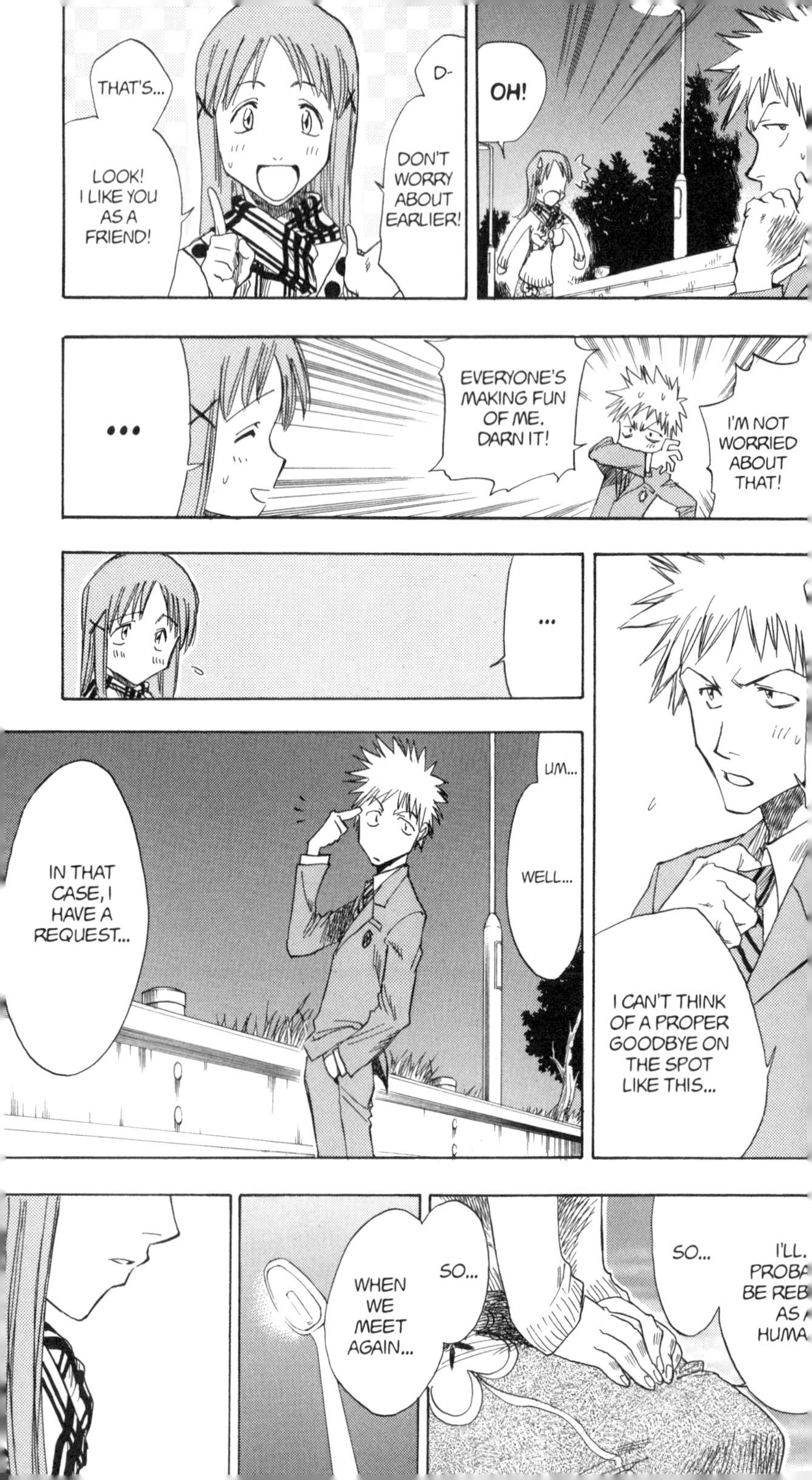
OH!
D-
DON'T WORRY ABOUT EARLIER!
THAT'S...
LOOK! I LIKE YOU AS A FRIEND!
I'M NOT WORRIED ABOUT THAT!
EVERYONE'S MAKING FUN OF ME. DARN IT!
...
I CAN'T THINK OF A PROPER GOODBYE ON THE SPOT LIKE THIS...
...
UM...
WELL...
IN THAT CASE, I HAVE A REQUEST...
I'LL. PROBA BE REB AS A HUMA
SO...
SO...
WHEN WE MEET AGAIN...

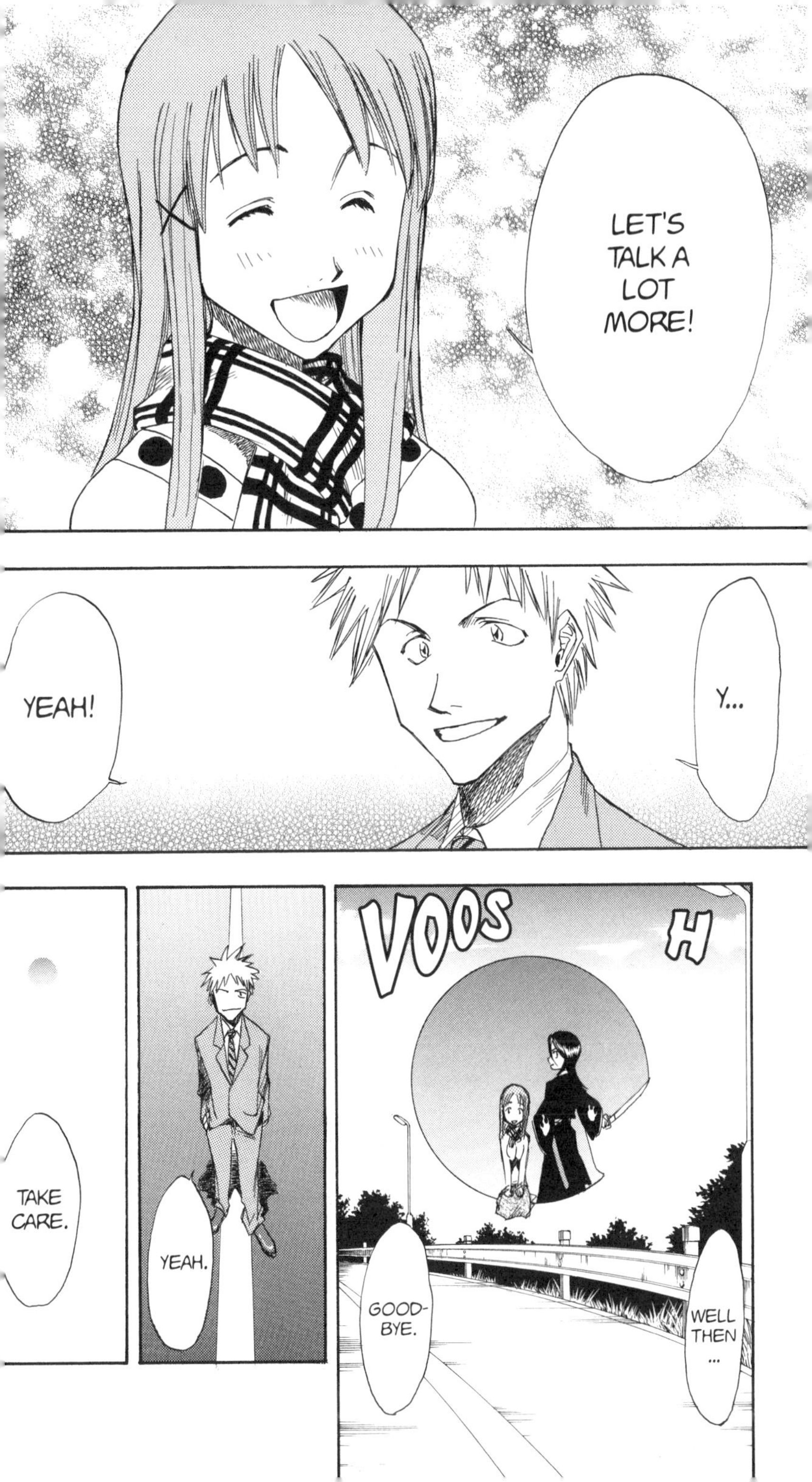

LET'S TALK A LOT MORE!
Y...
YEAH!
VOOSH
WELL THEN ...
GOOD-BYE.
YEAH.
TAKE CARE.

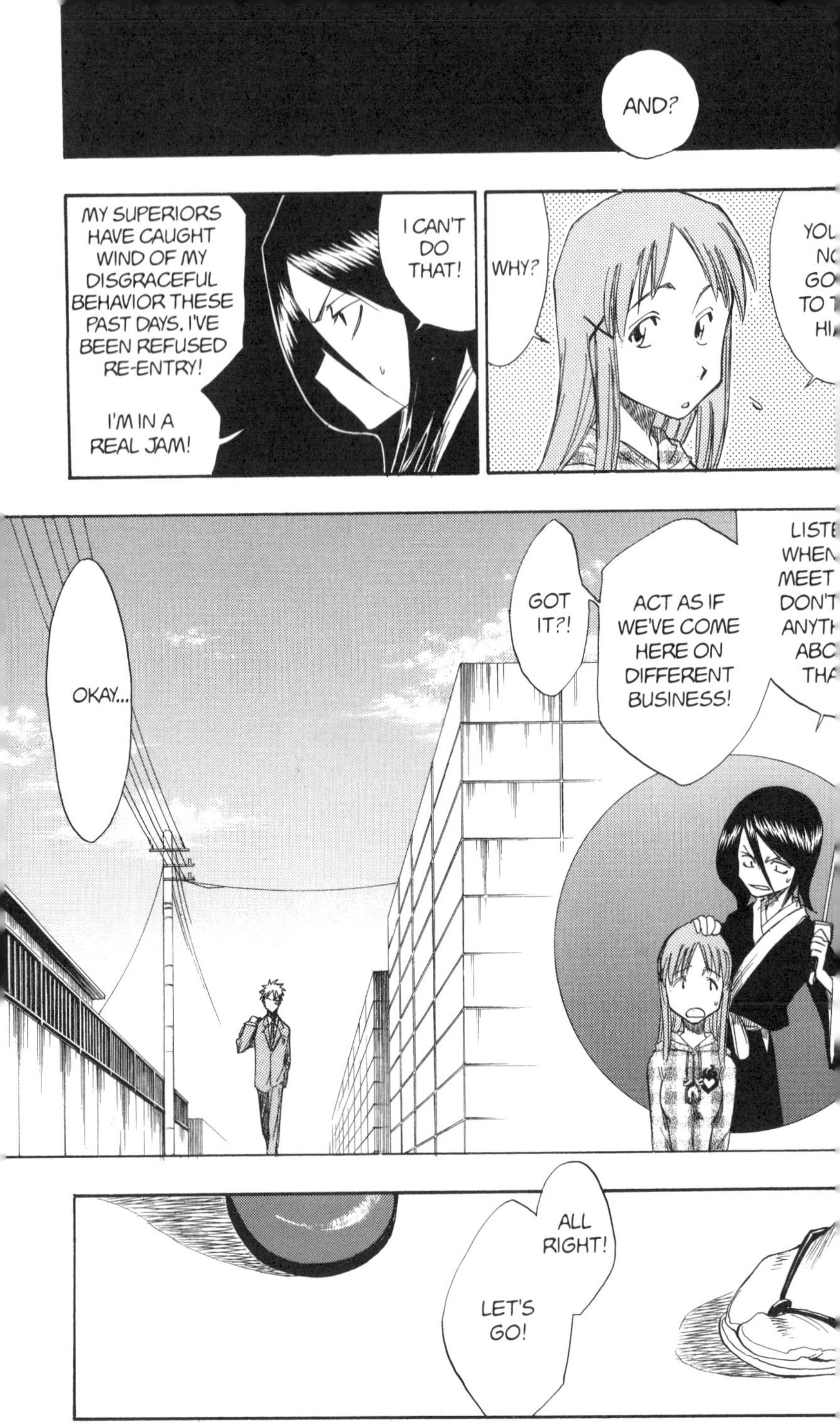
AND?
WHY?
I CAN'T DO THAT!
MY SUPERIORS HAVE CAUGHT WIND OF MY DISGRACEFUL BEHAVIOR THESE PAST DAYS. I'VE BEEN REFUSED RE-ENTRY!
I'M IN A REAL JAM!
ACT AS IF WE'VE COME HERE ON DIFFERENT BUSINESS!
GOT IT?!
OKAY...
ALL RIGHT!
LET'S GO!

end

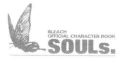

BLEACH
OFFICIAL CHARACTER BOOK
SOULs.

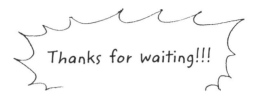

Thanks for waiting!!!

My readers have been telling me to put out a character book for a long time. It's come at last.

Furthermore, it's going on sale at the same time as the animation book (in Japan). A first for Jump. I've drawn the covers for both of them, written the English text for both of them, written the verses for both of them, drawn the short stories for both of them, checked them and checked them... Anyway, I did a lot of stuff. I didn't do it alone. My boss, the designers, and the writers all did a lot. They did the character profiles and the details on the Soul Society and the Rukongai, and wrote some things that I wanted to write.

This book is for everyone. Read it until you collapse. I'm going to read it so often that people will ask me why, since I'm the creator. Please try to read it as much as I will.

Laters!

2006 01 10 X

POSTSCRIPT

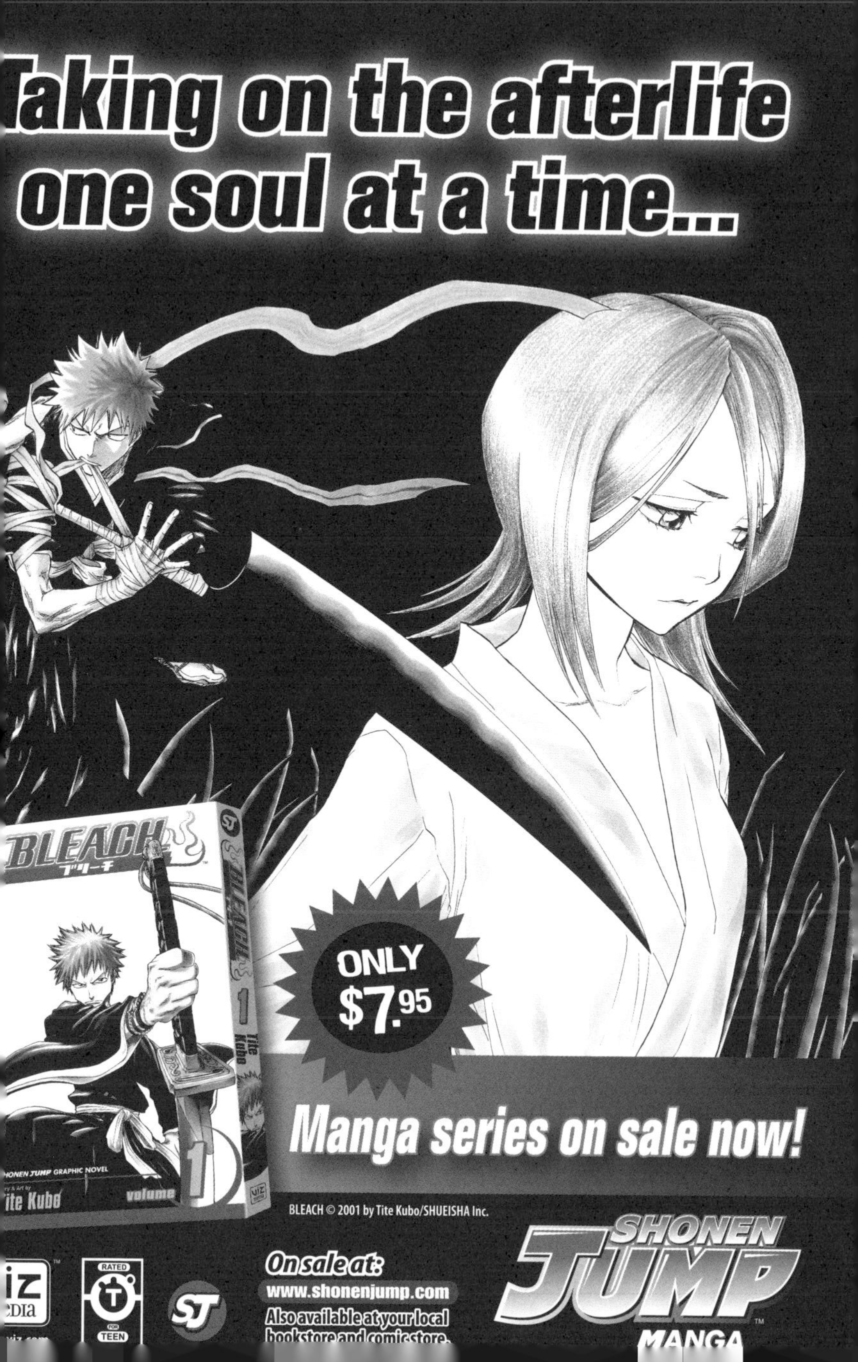

Taking on the afterlife
one soul at a time...
BLEACH
ブリーチ
SHONEN JUMP GRAPHIC NOVEL
Tite Kubo
volume 1
ONLY
$7.95
Manga series on sale now!
BLEACH © 2001 by Tite Kubo/SHUEISHA Inc.
On sale at:
www.shonenjump.com
Also available at your local
bookstore and comicstore.
RATED
T
FOR
TEEN
SJ
SHONEN
JUMP
MANGA

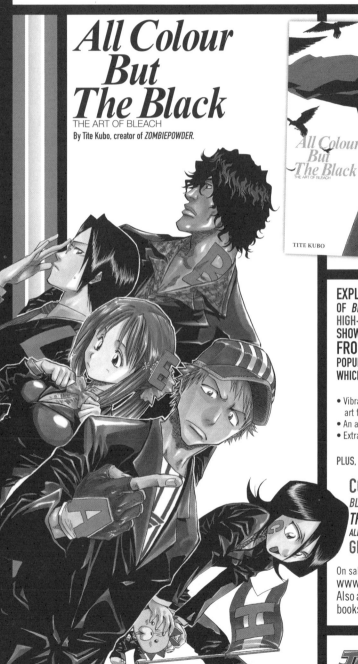
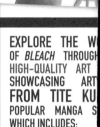

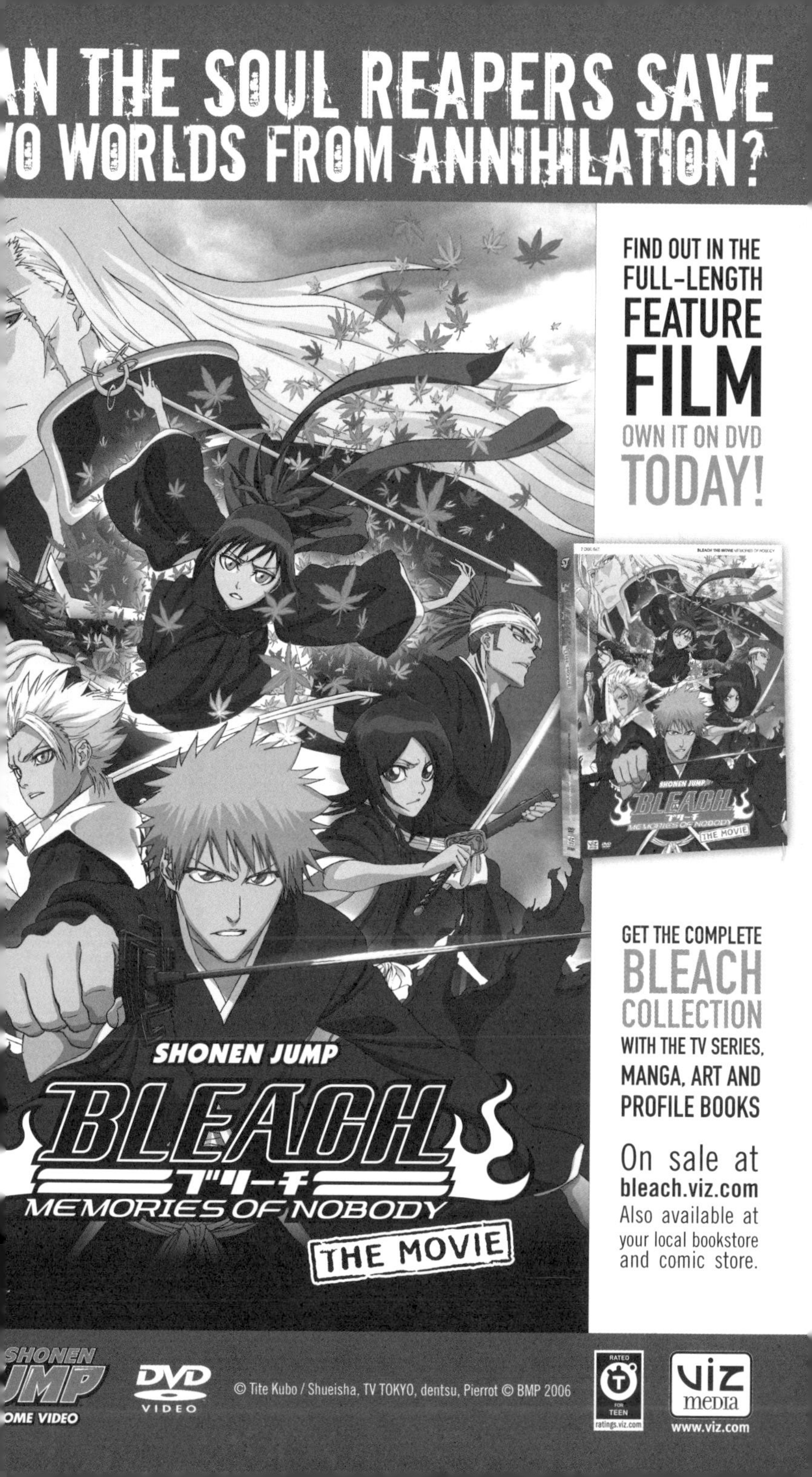
AN THE SOUL REAPERS SAVE
O WORLDS FROM ANNIHILATION?
FIND OUT IN THE FULL-LENGTH FEATURE FILM
OWN IT ON DVD TODAY!
GET THE COMPLETE BLEACH COLLECTION WITH THE TV SERIES, MANGA, ART AND PROFILE BOOKS
On sale at bleach.viz.com
Also available at your local bookstore and comic store.
SHONEN JUMP
BLEACH
ブリーチ
MEMORIES OF NOBODY
THE MOVIE
SHONEN JUMP
OME VIDEO
DVD VIDEO
© Tite Kubo / Shueisha, TV TOKYO, dentsu, Pierrot © BMP 2006
RATED T FOR TEEN
ratings.viz.com
VIZ media
www.viz.com

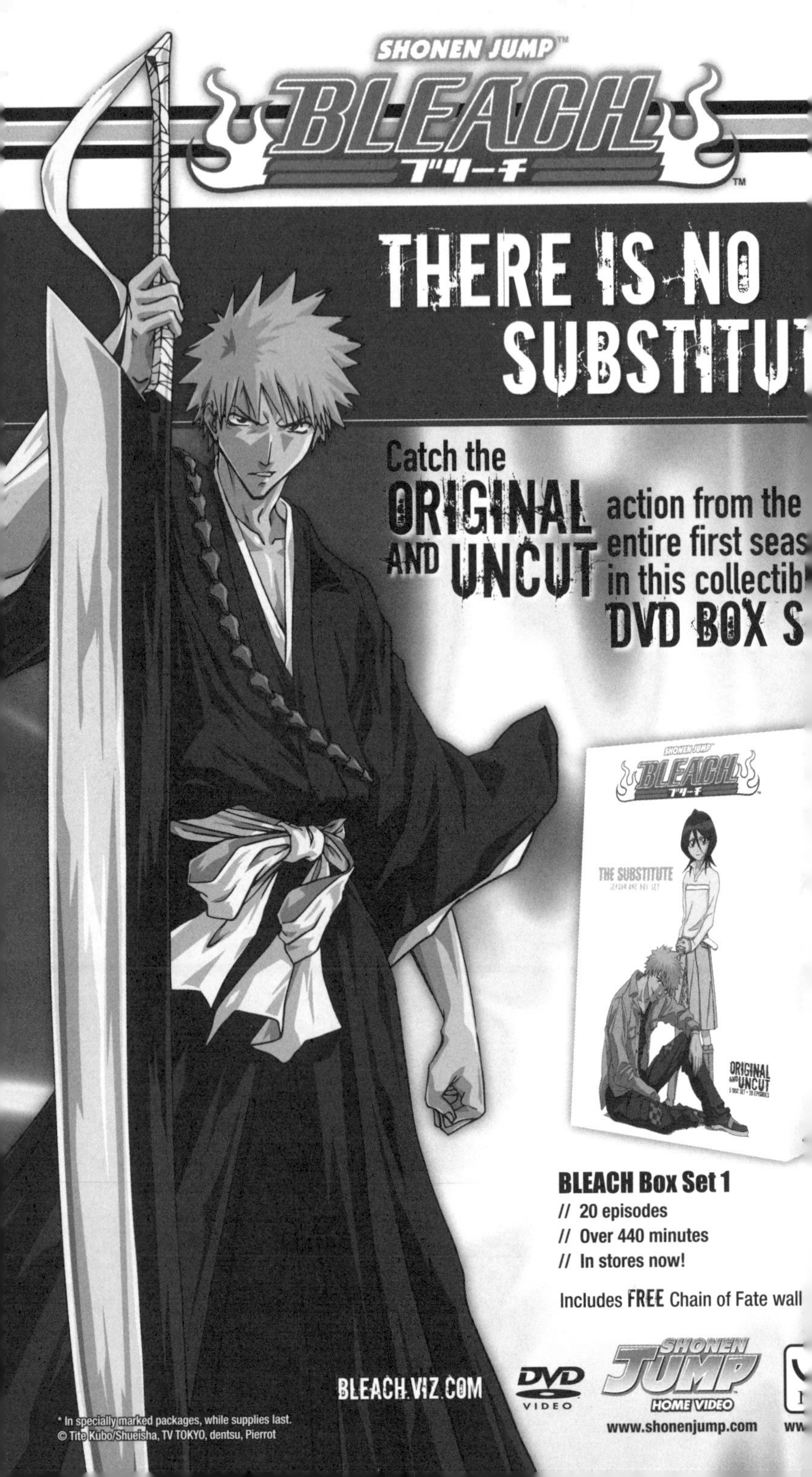
SHONEN JUMP™
BLEACH
ブリーチ
™
THERE IS NO
SUBSTITUT
Catch the
ORIGINAL AND UNCUT
action from the
entire first seas
in this collectib
DVD BOX S
SHONEN JUMP
BLEACH
ブリーチ
THE SUBSTITUTE
ORIGINAL AND UNCUT
BLEACH Box Set 1
// 20 episodes
// Over 440 minutes
// In stores now!
Includes FREE Chain of Fate wall
BLEACH.VIZ.COM
DVD VIDEO
SHONEN JUMP
HOME VIDEO
www.shonenjump.com
* In specially marked packages, while supplies last.
© Tite Kubo/Shueisha, TV TOKYO, dentsu, Pierrot

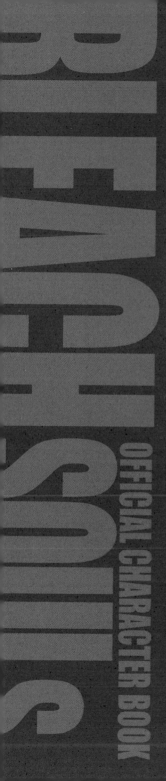

BLEACH SOULs OFFICIAL CHARACTER BOOK

BLEACH SOULs.
The Official Character Book
SJ PROFILES

...ark McMurray
...urtney Utt
GRAPHIC DESIGN **Gerry Serrano**
EDITORS **Pancha Diaz, Kit Fox**

EDITOR IN CHIEF, BOOKS **Alvin Lu**
EDITOR IN CHIEF, MAGAZINES **Marc Weidenbaum**
VP, PUBLISHING LICENSING **Rika Inouye**
VP, SALES AND PRODUCT MARKETING **Gonzalo Ferreyra**
VP, CREATIVE **Linda Espinosa**
PUBLISHER **Hyoe Narita**

Printed in China

Published by VIZ Media, LLC
P.O. Box 77010
San Francisco, CA 94107

SJ Profiles
10 9 8 7 6 5 4 3 2 1
First printing, October 2008

www.viz.com